A GEOGRAPHICAL ACCOUNT OF COUNTRIES ROUND THE BAY OF BENGAL

1669 TO 1679

A GEOGRAPHICAL ACCOUNT OF COUNTRIES ROUND THE BAY OF BENGAL

1669 TO 1679

THOMAS BOWREY

EDITED BY

R. C. TEMPLE

GYAN

Published by

GYAN

Gyan Publishing House
5, Ansari Road
Daryaganj, New Delhi-110002
Phone: 011-47034999, 9811692060
E-mail: books@gyanbooks.com

Distribution Network
gyanbooks.com
India, USA, Canada, UK, Australia, France

ISBN : 978-81-212-3431-3 (PB)
First Published, 1905

2nd Impression 2020

Printed at: Gyan Press, Delhi.

A Geographical Account of Countries Round The Bay of Bengal
1669 to 1679
Author: Thomas Bowrey

A GEOGRAPHICAL ACCOUNT

OF

COUNTRIES ROUND THE BAY OF BENGAL,

1669 TO 1679

BY

THOMAS BOWREY

EDITED BY

LT.-COL. SIR RICHARD CARNAC TEMPLE, BART., C.I.E.

CAMBRIDGE:
PRINTED FOR THE HAKLUYT SOCIETY.
MDCCCCV.

CONTENTS.

	PAGE
Preface	xi
Introduction:	
I. History, Contents and Value of the MS.	xv
II. Authorship of the MS.	xviii
III. Life of the Author	xxiv
IV. Other Works by the Author	xlviii
Asia	1
Of Choromandel	2
Golcondah	107
The Coast of Gingalee	120
Orixa	128
Bengala	131
Pattana	221
Janselone	235
Queda	259
Achin	285
Bibliography	327
Index	333

LIST OF ILLUSTRATIONS.

PLATE			
I.	The Pagod called Tressletore . . .	*To face p.*	8
II.	Dancinge Women at the great Pagod Jno. Gernaet	"	14
III.	Fig. 1. The figure of one of their Diabolical Chariots		
	Fig. 2. Fackeers	"	22
IV.	Fig. 1. Fackeers		
	Fig. 2. Gentues	"	32
V.	Mango, Arbor Triste, Palmito, Palmero Trees	"	49
VI.	Danceinge Snakes	"	60
VII.	Fig. 1. The Widow burneth alive		
	Fig. 2. A Roundel		
	Fig. 3. A Palanchino	"	86
VIII.	Fig. 1. A Massoola. A Cattamaran		
	Fig. 2. Hoocars		
	Fig. 3. The Manner of fixing their geere	"	104
IX.	A most Sumptuous Tombe	"	113
X.	Fig. 1. The Antilope		
	Fig. 2. A great Giant called Jansa Bainsa	"	119
XI.	Fig. 1. A barbarous Penalty		
	Fig. 2. The figure of an Elephant		
	Fig. 3. The Tyger	"	219
XII.	Fig. 1. Bears and a wild Hogge		
	Fig. 2. Jackalls		
	Fig. 3. The Rhinocerot	"	222
XIII.	Fig. 1. An Olocko		
	Fig. 2. A Budgaroo		
	Fig. 3. A Purgoo		
	Fig. 4. The Muske Deere		
	Fig. 5. A Boora	"	228

PLATE			
XIV.	Fig. 1.	Plantan and Samcau Trees	
	Fig. 2.	Bamboos	*To face p.* 250
XV.	Fig. 1.	A Patella	
	Fig. 2.	Pepper	
	Fig. 3.	Long Pepper	„ 277
XVI.	Fig. 1.	Pine Apples	
	Fig. 2.	Strange Fishes in Queda	
	Fig. 3.	The Alligator	„ 285
XVII.	Fig. 1.	Betelee. Areca Tree	
	Fig. 2.	A State Elephant	„ 308
XVIII.	Fig. 1.	Men of Warre Prows	
	Fig. 2.	The Buffalo	
	Fig. 3.	An Achin Cripple	„ 314
XIX.	Fig. 1.	An Achin House	
	Fig. 2.	A Mangastine Tree	
		A Durian Tree	„ 322

Chart of the River Hugli, Bengal, drawn by Thomas Bowrey.
(*In pocket in back cover of volume.*)

PREFACE.

IN preparing this MS. for the Hakluyt Society, I have had it copied exactly as it stands, retaining the original spelling and the use of capital letters. But the contractions have been written out in full and the letters u v i j and ff (for capital F) have been adapted to the present accepted usage. Also, where necessary for the sense, modern punctuation has been employed. The marginal notes have been omitted because they were, in nearly every case, merely repetitions of the text. The illustrations are reductions from exact photographs of the originals.

I make no apology for the voluminous notes appended to the text, as in a work designed to be of assistance to students it is in my judgment of value to show how far the statements of a writer, who was an independent trader in the East, are substantiated by the official records of the East India Company, and to exhibit the views and knowledge of residents about the East in the last quarter of the seventeenth century, and also to give every assistance practicable in acquiring information as to the men and manners of that period. The majority of the notes consist of contemporary quotations from unpublished documents at the India Office and British Museum, and extracts from existing printed works have been excluded except where the remarks of contemporary writers serve to elucidate the text. Anglo-Indianisms not given or only slightly treated in Yule's *Hobson-Jobson* have been traced, wherever possible, to their original source and have, I believe, in every instance, been explained and correctly translated into modern parlance. No other published record, at present known to me, covers the period 1669—1679, and this MS. therefore fills a gap in the early history of the doings of the English in Bengal, Madras and the Malay Archipelago.

In the preparation of this MS. for publication my thanks are in the first place due to Miss Lavinia Mary Anstey, without whose untiring perseverance, capacity for solid work of a nature uninteresting in itself, and accuracy and energy in research and in the copying of documents, cheerfully undertaken and spread over a period of five years, this edition would have been impossible.

My thanks are also due to Mr Eliot Howard for the loan of the MS. and for help in connection with the search for the identity of the author. To the authorities at the India Office for their courtesy in placing all contemporary information at my disposal, and when I consider that upwards of 150 MS. volumes alone have been examined during the editing of this work, I cannot but feel that the labours of those who have had to fetch and carry the ponderous tomes have been by no means inconsiderable. But in this most courteous of the Government Offices, there has been no grumbling at my voracious requirements! To Mr William Foster, Assistant Registrar, to whom I am specially indebted and whose intimate knowledge of the Records in his charge has materially helped me throughout the work. To Professor J. F. Blumhardt for the elucidation of many Hindustani titles and words. To Mr F. W. Thomas, M.A., Librarian at the India Office, and to Mr W. Irvine, lately of the Bengal Civil Service, for similar assistance. To Syed Hossain Bilgrami for two notes in the Golconda Section. To Mr Donald Ferguson for help with Malay words. To the Rev. E. Louis C. Clapton, M.A., Rector of Lee, Blackheath, for a gratuitous search among the parish registers in connection with the author of the MS. To Dr James A. H. Murray for assistance with Old English words. To Mr G. S. Forbes, M.A., of the Madras Civil Service, for furnishing copies of Bowrey's letters from the Madras Records.

I must further express my sense of the excellence of the printing and press reading of the Cambridge University Press, and my gratitude to Messrs J. and C. F. Clay for the labour saved in consequence in the matter of reading proofs.

A full Bibliography and Index are appended to this work.

R. C. TEMPLE.

THE NASH,
WORCESTER.
Dec. 27th, 1904.

INTRODUCTION.

I. HISTORY, CONTENTS AND VALUE OF THE MS.

PROFESSOR E. B. TYLOR, F.R.S., first drew my attention to the existence of this remarkably interesting MS., and subsequently its owner, Mr Eliot Howard, of Ardmore, Buckhurst Hill, Essex, to whom it came by inheritance, courteously allowed me to copy it. It was known to Yule, to Anderson, and to Murray, who have each a brief quotation from it[1]. The MS. is clearly and carefully written in the handwriting of the period and has been exceptionally well preserved, so that there is no doubt as to the reading of any part of it. The writer, who was a sailor, further illustrated his MS. profusely with pen and ink drawings, such as are common for the period. But crude as many of them are, his representations of ships and boats are not only valuable for the details they give, but also for their accuracy. The whole of the drawings have been exactly represented in the plates attached to the text, on a reduced scale, from photographs taken by my son, Lieut. R. D. Temple, 60th Rifles. The title of the MS. is, after the fashion of the time, unconscionably long and comprehensive, and purports to deal with many more subjects than is actually the case[2]. The contents, however, fall very far short of the author's intention, for he is full on the subject of the East Coast of India, but scrappy in his relation of the Coast of

[1] See *Diary of Wm. Hedges*, vol. iii. p. 183; *English Intercourse with Siam*, p. 266; *Oxford English Dictionary*, *s.v.* Cheroot.

[2] See page 1 of this vol.

Burma, the Malay Peninsula and Sumatra, perhaps owing to the loss of notes, and beyond these points his account practically does not extend.

As a matter of fact the accounts in the MS. are of the following places:—

I. Choromandel Coast, pp. 2 to 107[1].
  (1) Fort St Georg's [Madras], pp. 2—5.
  (2) The Pag[oda] of Jno. Gernaet' [Jagannath, Juggernaut], pp. 12—14, and several other places.
  (3) Careyro [Karēdu], N. of Madras, p. 36.
  (4) St Thomas, his Mount, pp. 44—50.
  (5) Pettipolee and Pullicat, pp. 51—60.
  (6) Metchlipatam and Guddorah [Masulipatam and Gūdūr], pp. 60—64, 71 f.
  (7) Narsapore, Madapollum and Pollicull, pp. 98—107.

II. Golcondah [Kingdom], pp. 107—119.

III. The Coast of Gingalee [Golconda], pp. 120—128.

IV. Orixa [Orissa, a fragment], pp. 128—131.

V. Bengala, pp. 131—234.
  (1) Dacca, pp. 149—151.
  (2) Cattack, p. 151 f.
  (3) Ganges and Hugly Rivers, pp. 165 f., 209—212.
  (4) Hugly [town], pp. 167—170.
  (5) Cossumbazar, pp. 213—215.
  (6) Pattana [Patna], pp. 221—232.

VI. Arackan, p. 234 *n.* [heading only].

VII. Pegu, p. 234 *n.* [heading only].

VIII. Tanassaree, p. 234 *n.* [heading only][2].

IX. Janselone [Junkceylon], pp. 235—258.

X. Queda, pp. 259—285.

XI. Achin, pp. 285—326.

---

[1] All these figures refer to the pages in the text.

[2] pp. 103 to 130 of the MS. left blank for these places.

The MS. breaks off abruptly in the middle of a sentence, but this circumstance is not to be explained by the author's death as he stayed nineteen years in India and the East altogether, and this "Account" purports to relate to the first ten years only; also it is not mentioned in his Will, which bequeaths, *inter alia*, a "Manuscript book in a Green Cover" to the East India Company. The probable explanation is that the "Account" of the years 1669—1679 was commenced in 1680, and afterwards abandoned in favour of his larger MSS. bequeathed to the East India and South Sea Companies, and his Malay Dictionary published in 1701, a work that was some twelve years on the stocks, or that the latter part of the MS. was lost before it was bound up.

Though, of course, the observations in the MS. fall far short of such as would be looked for in a traveller of the present day, yet there is no doubt that the author was a well-educated man for his time, an acute observer of all that went on around him, and deeply interested in the natives of the country. Many of his observations therefore are of exceeding interest to the student of things Indian and of Anglo-Indian history, being indeed in these directions of unusual value. Among his observations the following may be instanced. He shows clearly that the word "Gentile" meant a Gentoo, and that a Gentoo was a low-caste Hindu; his definitions of *rājpūt* and *rājā* are most accurate; so are his name for, and his account and knowledge of, the Chulias; his description and careful drawings of native boats are among the best of the kind for this period; he offers the earliest quoted instance of "bunko" and "cheroot" for a cigar; he carefully explains that the so-called Golconda Mines were in reality many miles distant from Golconda; his notices of "Currant Coynes" and of the Cowry are among the most valuable of their kind; he is very clear as to the limits of the Gingerlee Coast, a district only vaguely described in other contemporary accounts; his remarks on the Hugli, and his carefully-drawn chart of that river exhibit his practical knowledge of the configuration of its shores and banks, and of all its dangers; his frequent notices of *sati*, coming from an eye-witness, are important as evidences of the custom; his "Janselone" section is a unique contribution to the history of an island about which there is hardly any record in the 17th century; lastly, his references to many notable Anglo-Indians of his day are of additional interest as showing these men in their ordinary daily life, rather than in their official character as they appear in the Company's records, especially as he writes without the ill-feeling and petty spitefulness, common in his day and among the community with which he worked and associated.

II. AUTHORSHIP OF THE MS.

The author has hidden his identity under initials, and it needed a search occupying two years before the connection between T. B. and Thomas Bowrey could be proved. From the internal evidence of the MS. itself the following information was gathered. The author was by occupation a sailing-master[1]; he was in the East, at least from 1669 to 1679[2]; he began his career there at Fort St George, Madras[3]; he was well acquainted with the writings of Bernier and with Mogul history down to his own time[4]; he personally knew Ambrose Salisbury, chief at Pettipolee [Peddapalle] from 1662—1675[5]; and was employed by the notable William Jearsey on one, at least, of his many private trading vessels[6]; he was also acquainted with James Horner[7], Alexander Ogilvy[8] and Samuel Ware[9], all of whom are mentioned in the contemporary Records; and in Bengal he came in contact with Walter Clavell[10], Matthias Vincent[11], and "Chim Cham[12]," the Company's broker. These facts would have been a certain guide to the identity of an Englishman in

[1] See p. 172.
[2] See sub-title, p. 1.
[3] See p. 2.
[4] See pp. 135—145.
[5] See p. 57.
[6] See p. 250 f.
[7] See p. 263.
[8] See p. 264.
[9] See p. 262.
[10] See p. 158.
[11] See p. 164.
[12] See p. 154.

India in the 17th century, had the individual in question been a servant of the East India Company. He was, however, an independent trader, and hence the difficulty in tracing him.

That T. B. was by occupation a sailing-master is abundantly shown throughout the MS. From the fact that he was piloting the *Sancta Cruz* down the Hugli when he met Streynsham Master in 1676[1], I was at first strongly inclined to believe that he was Thomas Bateman, one of the first batch of apprentice-pilots sent out by the Company on a seven years' indenture to learn the navigation of the Hugli and Ganges, in order that the Company's ships might be brought up to Hijili and thus avoid the delay of transferring their cargoes into small boats at Balasor. Bateman's indentures would have expired in 1676, and it seemed reasonable to conjecture that he had left the Company's service and was acting as an independent pilot to "country" ships. Accordingly, I made an exhaustive search of the MS. records at the India Office relating to Bengal, and more especially to Hugli in 1669—1679. After many disappointments, I at last found a mention of Thomas Bateman in August, 1675, when he took the Company's sloop *Dilligence* up to Hugli. In September, on the return voyage from Hugli to Balasor, he encountered a violent storm, in which his ship was only saved "after a very great hazard," and he himself perished either at the time, or as the result of exposure[2]. Thus, after nearly two years, the identity of T. B. was still wrapped in mystery!

The next idea was that the initials might, after all, be J. B., and that the author was John Bugden, an independent trader, commanding his own vessel, and brother of the Company's servant, Edmund Bugden. As a man in a better position than an apprentice-pilot, I considered it more likely that he would have the education which the author of this MS. evidently possessed. Then, too, he was associated with Clement Jordan, who was T. B.'s

[1] See pp. 175—178.

[2] *Factory Records*, Hugli, No. 4.

purser in 1676[1]. Further, Yule in his reference to the MS. in *Hedges' Diary*[2] gives the initials as J. B. This clue seemed to promise well, and I followed it vigorously, until the owner of the MS. made it evident that the scent would lead nowhere. Mr Howard referred to the text, and examined the initials with great care, and expressed his confident opinion that the T. in question *was* a T. and *not* a J. He, however, spared no pains to assist me in the search and gave me every information possible about the MS. He stated that it came to him through his ancestor Peter Briggins, a Quaker, who, beyond holding East India Stock, appeared to have no connection with India. Neither was Peter Briggins a sailor, nor had any of the males of the family a Christian name beginning with T.

Later, Mr Howard supplied me with a clue, which eventually turned out to be the right one. He informed me that there was an idea that the MS. might have been a gift from a certain "Captain Bowry" (Christian name unknown), whose name is mentioned in the diaries of Peter Briggins. Mr Howard sent me a copy of the "Eliot Papers" containing extracts from these diaries, and afterwards entrusted me with the diaries themselves. A search through these volumes showed that Peter Briggins and "Captain Bowry" were acquainted, and that they met constantly from 1706 till 1713, when the Captain died, and that subsequently Peter Briggins rendered many services to the widow.

My next discovery was the will of Captain Bowrey[3]. This gave the name *Thomas Bowrey*, and contained the information that the testator had spent many years in India, and was the author of Maps and "Journalls," both of Africa and the "South Seas." There seemed ground, therefore, for identifying Thomas Bowrey with T. B. The difficulty was that there were no means for fixing the dates of Bowrey's residence in India, and the

[1] See p. 178. [2] See *Diary of William Hedges*, vol. iii. p. 183.
[3] Wills at Somerset House, *Luds*, fol. 53.

title of the MS. had naturally led to the assumption that the period of the author's residence in the East was limited to the ten years 1669—1679.

A further search among the India Office Records produced several references to Captain Thomas Bowrey, commander of a "country ship," who made numerous voyages from Madras between 1682 and 1688, when he sailed for England. I was still, however, without any proof that Bowrey was in India at the time occupied by the MS.

The next link in the chain of evidence was the discovery at the British Museum of a set of Charts of the islands of the Indian Archipelago, the River Hugli and the Persian Gulf by Thomas Bowrey[1]. The earliest of the charts was drawn in 1681, but the lettering and signatures bore a striking resemblance to the writing in the MS., and thus supplied further confirmatory evidence of the identity of T. B. with Thomas Bowrey.

Next followed an important discovery. In the General Catalogue of the British Museum Library, I found a printed work by Thomas Bowrey entitled "A Dictionary of English and Malayo[2]." This Dictionary, published in 1701, contains a preface in which the author says that he spent *nineteen years* in India and returned on the *Bengall Merchant* in 1688. He must, therefore, have arrived in India in 1669, and we know from his own MS. that T. B.'s residence at Fort St George dated from that year[3]. This practically settles the question, as it is hardly likely that *two* independent traders, each having the same initials, should have arrived in India at such a date as 1669, have visited the same places, and have recorded and illustrated their impressions there without being distinguished in the contemporary records. If two such persons did exist, it is extremely unlikely that one should have been mentioned in the records and not the other. Again, we know that

---

[1] *Sloane*, 5222, 6—17.

[2] British Museum Library, *Press mark*, 68. c. 12.

[3] See pp. 1 and 2 of this vol.

the MS. descended to Mr Howard through Peter Briggins, who, while keeping minute record of his daily life, alludes to no seafaring acquaintance except Captain Bowrey.

The identity of T. B. and Thomas Bowrey is also further confirmed by certain remarks in the Dialogues at the end of the Dictionary above mentioned, which strongly resemble those in the MS. Among these I select the following :—

MS.	Dialogues.
Janselone . . . affordeth nothinge Save Some Elephants and tinne . . . and tinne they have in abundance.	Junsalon . . . its Merchandize is only Tin, of which it yields about Four Hundred Bahar Yearly.
There [Achin] they measure by the bamboo.	Bamboo . . . the name of a concave measure, used at Atchee on Sumatra.
Quedah . . . The Neighbouringe Kings vizt. Pattany and Johore.	Kings of the Malayo country are those of Quedah, Johor, Patanee and many more.
The Citty Achin is . . . populous . . . famous . . . for . . . the great Traffick and Commerce from most parts of India, China, and South Seas . . . Many Ships and Vessels doe att all Seasons of the year arrive in this Port from Severall places, namely Suratt, Malabar Coast . . . Fort St. Georg's, Metchlipatam, Bengala, Pegu, Syam, China, Java Major and Borneo, with infinite Numbers of Prows from the Malay Shore . . .	Achee is a large City, and populous . . . the Port is never without Ships of English, Danes, Portugals, Moors, Chuleas, Chinesses and others and many Praws, which usually go into the River, all these come in their proper Seasons with the several sorts of Goods of Surat, the Coast, Bangala, China, and many other places.
Wee make all our pitch and Tarre with Dammar and Oyl . . . One third dammar and Oyle, well boyled togeather, make very good tarre.	Damar . . . is the Gum of a tree in India which being boil'd with Oil, makes Pitch or Tar.

MS.	Dialogues.
Achin is now and hath a Considerable time been Governed by a Queen, ever Since the time that the discreet and Pious Kinge James of happy memorie Swayed the Sceptre of great Brittaine, France and Ireland.	The City and Kingdom [of Achin] has for above an Hundred years been governed by Queens and Twelve Lords.

The last extract, in which the mistake as to the length of time Achin was governed by queens is repeated, would have proved the identity beyond cavil, had not the same error been made by other contemporary writers, such as Fryer, Dampier and Hamilton.

On the whole there is practically no ground for doubting that "T. B." represents "Thomas Bowrey." At the same time it would have been satisfactory if external evidence were forthcoming as to Bowrey's movements prior to 1682. Unfortunately, this is not the case, though I have made a careful search of the 1669—1679 Records at the India Office. The reasons why Bowrey's name does not appear before 1682 may be that, for the first few years after his arrival in India, he probably held a subordinate post as mate or pilot, and, until he was in a position to trade on his own account, he would have had very little contact with the Company's servants at the various factories.

In his Will Thomas Bowrey left his widow free to keep any of his "Maps and Journalls" (except those specially bequeathed to the East India and South Sea Companies), for her own use. The natural assumption is that, in gratitude to Peter Briggins for the many services he rendered her, after her husband's death, she gave him the MS., reproduced in this volume, together with a Chinese Cabinet now belonging to Lady Fry, a descendant.

III. LIFE OF THE AUTHOR.

circ. 1650—1713.

Of Thomas Bowrey's parentage nothing certain is known, but it seems reasonable to conjecture that he was related to John Bowrey, Thomas Bowrey, and Joseph Bowrey, who all served in the Royal Navy in the latter half of the 17th century. In 1652 John Bowrey was granted compensation for wounds received on board the *Unity* in the squadron under Sir George Ayscue[1]. In 1653 he commanded the fireship *Hunter*, which was sunk in an engagement with the Dutch. In the same year he went on a trading voyage to Leghorn[1]. In 1656 Captain John Bowrey was commanding the *Eaglet* Ketch and the *Drake*. In 1657 he commanded the *Death*, and in January, 1659, he is mentioned as acting as convoy with a fleet of eight ships[1]. In 1660 he was again commanding the *Drake* and was accused of taking goods on board and conveying them away unlawfully. He cleared himself from this charge. Two years later, in 1662, Captain John Bowrey was recommended to Pepys by Lord Inchiquin as having acquitted himself "extraordinary well in the two voyages with horses[1]." In February, 1667, "Mr. Bowry [? John] the former master [of the *Antelope*] was discharged, being uncapable to perform the Voyage to Gottenburg." In March, 1673, there is the note, "Trinity House. Certificate of the competency of John Bowrey of Wapping as Master." On the 4th November, 1673, the effects of "Johannes Bowry lately of H. M. S. *Swiftsure*" were administered by his widow Juditha[2], but whether this man is the John Bowrey of 1662 there is no evidence to show.

Captain Thomas Bowrey, who may have been "T. B.'s" father, was recommended by Captain Potter of the *Constant*

---

[1] *Calendar of State Papers, Domestic Series*, for the years 1652—1673; *vide* Index, *s.v.* Bowrey.

[2] *Administration Book*, 1673, at Somerset House.

Warwick as his Lieutenant in January, 1653, and is stated to have "behaved with much courage and discretion." In 1654 he commanded the *Roe* Ketch, in 1655 the *Warwick*, and in 1657 again the *Roe* Ketch. While in command of this last ship, in 1659, Bowrey engaged with a Spanish pirate, and chased an Ostend man-of-war. The last reference to him is in 1669, when he wrote to the Navy Commissioners reporting his arrival at Gravesend with the goods of two Spanish Ambassadors on board[1]. On the 25th January, 1666, the goods of a Thomas Bowrey of Stepney were administered by his widow, Elizabeth Bowrey[2]. The fact that this Thomas Bowrey resided at Stepney and that T. B. eventually settled down in that parish, added to the similarity of their Christian names, is ground for assuming their near relationship, though there is no proof of the connection nor even of the identity of Thomas Bowrey of Stepney with Captain Thomas Bowrey of the *Roe* Ketch.

The only other Bowrey that I have found associated with the sea at this period is "Joseph Bowrye of H. M. S. *Le Royall James*," who died in 1672 and whose goods were administered on the 25th June by his widow, Margareta Bowrye[2].

If our author came of the same family as these naval men, he would naturally have been bred up with a knowledge of the sea. Why he should have chosen to seek his fortune in India is not apparent. The name of Bowrey does not occur in any of the early Bengal or Madras records, so it is not likely that he followed a family tradition. In the Bombay records we find in a letter from Surat to Bombay on the 1st Nov. 1669[3], "To carry on the work of your fortification...Mr. Robert Barbor may be employed...and for his assistance you may appoint Captain Bowry who wee understand hath some knowledge

[1] *Calendar of State Papers, Domestic Series*, for the years 1653—1660; *vide* Index, *s.v.* Bowrey.

[2] *Administration Books*, 1670 and 1672, at Somerset House.

[3] *O.C.* No. 3361.

in the art." In January, 1670, a Matthias Bowrey was living in Bombay and was summoned on a jury[1]. He was probably the same Matthias Bowrey who was entertained as a soldier in January, 1669, to serve the Company at Bombay[2], but there is no evidence to show that he was related to the author of the MS.

To pass from surmise to fact. Thomas Bowrey tells us in the Preface to his *Dictionary of English and Malayo*, that he spent nineteen years in India and left that country in 1688. He must, therefore, have reached Fort St George (where he says he landed)[3] in 1669. If he went directly from England, he probably sailed in either the *Loyall Merchant*, *Rainbow*, *Unicorne*, or *Madras Merchant*, all of which started for the "Coast and Bay" in 1668. The Log of the *Unicorne* is extant[4], but contains no mention of Bowrey. It is therefore uncertain whether he formed one of the crew of the ship on which he sailed or whether he went as a passenger. If he voyaged as a "free merchant" he must have eluded the vigilance of the Company's agents, who had strict injunctions to prevent the commanders of ships from taking out persons unlicensed by the Court. And there is no entry of any license being granted to T. B. in 1668. Of his movements from the time of his landing till 1672 we have no record. In that year he went to Masulipatam and Pettipollee[5]. In 1674 he was living at Balasor[6]. In 1675 he was at Junkceylon[7] in command of one of William Jearsey's ships. In 1676 he took the *Sancta Cruz* from Hugli to Fort St George[8]. In 1677 he was again at Junkceylon, and was a witness of the insurrection in that island. During the ten years comprised in his "Account," he went to Persia[9], but, unfortunately, he does not give the exact

[1] *Factory Records*, Surat, vol. iii. p. 36.

[2] *Marine Records*, Miscellaneous, No. 13.

[3] p. 2 of this vol.

[4] In the MS. Dept. at the British Museum, *Harleian*, No. 4252.

[5] p. 57 of this vol.

[6] p. 152 of this vol.

[7] p. 250 of this vol.

[8] p. 172 of this vol.

[9] p. 216 of this vol.

date. The next mention of Bowrey is in 1681, when he drew his chart of Ceylon. At this time he was probably at Fort St George. In 1682 he was at Madapollam where he drew his chart of the coast of Tenasserim. In July, 1683, "Mr. Bouree with his sloop" sailed for Madapollam[1], and on the 4th December of the same year "a sloop from Madapollam Thomas Bowrey Master arrived here [Fort St. George][2]." In 1684 Thomas Bowrey went to Batavia on a vessel belonging to Mr James Wheeler of Madapollam. He returned to Fort St George in August of the same year. The Council there was desirous of buying the "Burneo Pepper" brought by Bowrey "if Procurable at a reasonable price." They offered 20 pagodas per candy, but Bowrey would take nothing less than "the supposed prices in Bengall," viz. 23 pagodas per candy. He set sail for Bengal on the *Borneo Merchant*, but lost his passage, and after putting in at Vizagapatam, returned to Fort St George on the 13th September. He was then ready to sell his pepper at a lower price, but now the Council would only offer him 17 pagodas per candy. We are not told whether he agreed to sell at such a reduced rate. On the 26th December is the note "Ship *Burneo Merchant* arrived here [Fort St George] out of Ennore River where she put in to Secure her selfe from the Monsoone[2]." Almost immediately after, Bowrey again left Madras for Madapollam, where he arrived on the *Borneo Merchant* on the 7th January, 1685. On the 9th he asked the Madapollam Council if they were inclined to dispose of the Company's Sloop *Conimeer*, and offered them 40 pagodas for it[3]. His offer was accepted, and the Madapollam Council wrote to Fort St George justifying their action as follows, "The Sloope *Connimeer* haveing Layd in this Factory a Considerable time in a Creaze rotten condition, wee thought fitt to dispose of to Mr. Bowrey." On the 10th February an attestation was

---

1 *Madras Press List.*

2 *Factory Records*, Fort St George, No. 3.

3 *ib.* Madapollam, No. 1.

signed, setting forth that, in consideration of "40 Pagodas new and Gurrant money to us in hand Paid by Mr. Thomas Bowrey of Madraspatam Mariner" the *Conimeer* Sloop, burthen 20 Tons "or thereabouts now being a Shoar" at Madapollam, with all her accessories be handed over to Thomas Bowrey[1]. After this purchase, Bowrey went to Achin and thence to Balasor, where he arrived on the 28th July. After a six weeks' stay, he set out for Fort St George on the 11th September, 1685[2]. His arrival is noted in December. It was in 1685 also that he drew his chart of the Persian Gulf.

In 1686, Bowrey, still in command of the *Borneo Merchant*, went to Cuddalore and Porto Novo. On the 15th January, after he had started on his voyage, a complaint was lodged against him at Fort St George by Captain Heath. It runs as follows:—"Capt. William Heath Commander of the *Defence* having complained to the President and Council that Mr. Thomas Bowrey master of the *Borneo Merchant* had carried away three of his ship's company viz. William Cannan Joseph Hon and Alexander Cobden and desiring them to write to Mr. Davis &ca. att Coodaloor to secure them, and send them hither, they agreed to advise thereof immediately, that Mr. Bowrey be secured in their Factory till the ship be searched, and if found to be returned speedily with trusty Peons to guard them, if not, to take a Bond of said Mr. Bowrey in the penalty of a Thousand pounds Ster. payable to the Right Honble. Company in case itt shall be proved that he hath them[3]." The three men arrived at Fort St George and were restored to Captain Heath on the 21st of January[4]. After leaving Porto Novo, Bowrey went to Borneo, and returned to Fort St George on the 11th September. On the 25th the ship sailed again for Porto Novo under the command of Thomas Flemming,

---

[1] *Factory Records*, Madapollam, No. 3.

[2] *ib.* Balasor, No. 1.

[3] *Madras Public Consultations*, vol. x. p. 227 (at Madras).

[4] *Madras Press List.*

went thence to Junkceylon, and returned to Fort St George on the 23rd January, 1687. Bowrey remained at Fort St George, for, on the 30th September, we find, "There having been Severall treaties with Mr. Bowrey and Mr. Massen about their Pepper, and the lowest they can be brought to being Pagodas 16 per Candy, Itt is order'd to be taken of them[1]." On the 30th November is the entry, "This morning Thomas Bowrey who went Pilot of the Boat that Señor Axell Ivell late Govr. of Trincombar took his passage in for Trincombar, arrived here from thence[1]." During his stay at Fort St George in 1686, Bowrey drew his chart of Amoy Bay.

In 1687 Captain Bowrey arranged for his return to England, but he subsequently altered his plans. On the 10th January "Mr. Thomas Bowrey having desired leave to go for England upon the *Shrewsbury* Itt is order'd that the Secretary do give the Commander an order to receive him and his necessarys he paying for his passage[2]." The *Shrewsbury* sailed on the 2nd Feb., but Bowrey was not among the passengers. His name figures in February in a list of "Freemen inhabitants of Fort St George," and on the 11th of the month he went to Porto Novo with the *Borneo Merchant*. The year 1687 was an unfortunate one for our author, and he must many times have regretted that he had not adhered to his first intention and sailed to England on the *Shrewsbury*. On the 18th May the Council at Fort St George received a letter from Mr Davis, the Company's servant at Cuddalore, enclosing two letters from Captain Thomas Bowrey, all dated the 14th May, detailing the sufferings of Bowrey at the hands of the "Avaldar" of Porto Novo[3]. These letters do not exist in the India Office Records, but by the kindness of Mr G. S. Forbes, M.A., of the Indian Civil Service, who had them copied for me (together with the letter quoted on p. xxviii.), I am able to reproduce them here.

---

[1] *Factory Records*, Fort St George, No. 4. [2] *ibid.*

[3] *Letters to Fort St George*, vol. iv. pp. 193—196 (at Madras).

"CUDDALORE the 14th *May* 1687.

To

The Honble. WM. GYFFORD Esqr.

President and Govr. &ca Councill in Fort St. George.

HONBLE. &ca &ca,

I here inclosed remitt you two letters which we received from Mr. Bowry at [?] this night (which will not permitt us to Enlarge thereon) to which desire you will please to be referred; haveing [written] before to him and the Subidar about it haveing had Intelligence of the bussiness from our Chiefe Dubash[1] at Porto Novo before to Mr. Bowry that as hee own'd the Right Honble. Companys Protection; so he ought to have applyed himself to us (as their Representatives) in all matters depending between him and any of the natives and not to have writ himself as hee has done in inflicting anything of punishment on them as [*portion damaged*] the import of his letters; and notwithstanding hee hath been so irregular in his proceedings we will do what lay in our power to Rescue him without incommoding the Right Honble. Companys affaires provided he will give Bond of pagodas 10,000 to indemnifie them; otherwise he must compose the difference himself, thus farr wee think ourselves obliged to maintain the honour of our nation and the priveleidge of our Countrey as to suffer none to bee clapt in Prison and Irons without being satisfied the reason; but to prevent such ill Presidents for the future; therefore desire your order how to proceed herein, till which shall offer nothing of hostillitys; tho' indeed tis so great an affront as sufficient to animate the spirits of any man to seek their satisfaction.

What wee have wrote to the Subidar about it is that wee admire his incivillity in tollerating so gross abuses to bee offered to us for which wee expect satisfaceon and that hee wold acquaint us the reason of his barbarous imprisonment of our people in that manner; and release him; otherwise hee might expect to hear further from us; wee

---

[1] Interpreter. See note on p. 37.

being competent Judges to punish the offences of our owne people according to merrit, being free Merchants, and no wayes to bee governed by their Laws, but only Oblig'd to pay the Customes of our Trade; which was a sufficient obligacon to them to treat us with more civillity; being almost courted everywhere; where wee might have much greater priviledges confer'd on us and bee free [?] imposed upon us here, which if not mittigated would oblige us (in him) to consider thereof....

Honble. &ca &ca

Your most humble and obedient Servants

(Sd.) JOHN DAVIS
RALPH INGRAM
CHR: WILSON."

"PORTO NOVO, *May* 14*th*, 1687.

To

Mr. JOHN DAVIS &ca Councill.

HONBLE. SIRS,

I Haveing given 400 Pagodas about two months since to Amad Marcar [Ahmad Maraikkar] to buy cloth for me and 4 dayes since I went to demand my cloth who denied it and say'd hee stopt my money on account of the last voyage my Ship made who by Contract was to go to Atcheen or Quedah; but the ship falling in with Junckseloan and being in want of wood and water they touched there; and when they were there the Master in two days had gott what he wanted and would have proceed[ed] the voyage to Quedah but Amad Marcars [Ahmad Maraikkar] Servant intreated him to stay there of which I can produce severall witnesses but the Ship staying there and his goods comeing to a bad market; hee demands the loss of mee which caused our falling out and one of his Servants talking and telling severall Impudent Lyes I Stroke him being in the Companys Factory on which Amood Marcar [Ahmad Maraikkar] went to the avaldar and haveing feed him with 50 Pagodas I was sent for I being in the Factory denied to go to him till he promised I should returne Immediately;

who contrary to his word has Kept me this Three dayes with a pair of Irons on my Leggs and putts mee in his peons Cookroom for a Prison and my servants and also Chillimbrum [Chilambaram] desired [? denied] to come to mee hee now demanding unjustly 1300 Pagodas for 100 slaves which Amad Marcar has told him went on my Ship without custome paying; which they say I must pay; or else produce the owner of the Slaves; who is Meer Cung Marcar [Mir Jang (?) Maraikkar] who they all Know very well and that hee now lives at Chiali out of their Reach but they say if I cannot produce him I must pay the money which Justice I referr you to Judge of, this is the Chiefe thing they demand now; Saying it is the diwans and must bee paid first, but when that is paid, they say there is other accounts to make with mee for Amood Marcars loss on his goods and Meer Cungs loss on his Slaves; although I have cleared what Meer Cung by Law in Trincumbar [?] haveing recovered 600 Pagodas of him all which they say I must pay they Intending to ruine mee, they haveing mee now in their hands I therefore desire and entreat you would please to order Some person down here and give mee your assistance to clear mee out of their hands, which unless somebody comes will not bee done by Letters; although the Subidar is willing to release mee and has ordered the Avaldar not to lett mee bee kept in Irons; yett contrary to his order I am and I fear I shall bee still unless assisted by your[self or] one of the Councills comeing here with the Chiefe dubash for the Avaldar I am [*portion damaged*] inveterate against mee for Chillimbrum speaking for mee; and Amad Marcar tells them I am a run away; and no [one] will Protect mee; that they may do what they please with mee without fear and ther[efore] as you are my Countrey men and I hope friends and also by my Protection which I have granted from the Honble. Company I hope and humbly desire your speedy assistance I have not been permitted pen and paper else should have wrote sooner I being treated at the rate of a Murtherer they sent Peons on board my Ship yesterday to unhang her Rudder but my mate would not permitt them which is all at present being not in a Condition of Presenting my Service to you but remaine

Sirs Your Most humble Servant that would bee;
but at present weighed down with Irons
THOMAS BOWRY.

I would enlarge but my Keepers comeing in I cannot. I hear Amad Marcar has got leave of the Avaldar to go on board my Ship to day with his people to unhang their rudder; hee saying hee intends to have the Ship. Since your Letter came last night to the Subidar to release mee I have been used worse than before."

"PORTO NOVO, the 14th *May* 1687.

Mr. DAVIS,

HONOURED SIR,

Since my letter which I wrot this morning I understand that this night came a letter to the Subidar and Avaldar from Nulla Buckoor Marcar [Nalla Bakr (?) Maraikkar] who is at Trimlevass [Tirumalvāsal ?] who advices them that they have done very ill in Imprisoning mee; and that by your assistance it may bring a great deal of trouble on them and also advices them that I am not in fault; the Slaves which went on my ship not being mine and therefore no reason I should pay the Custome and severall other arguments hee uses to them to clear mee but the Avaldar haveing taken a fee hee prosecuts the Chulea[1] Amad Marcars revenge on mee to the [*portion damaged*] Except they would murther mee I understand these things from one of the Avaldar's Servants who is always near him I haveing bribed him to acquaint mee with Passages; but I hope in God I shall have a time to have my satisfacson for Amad Marcar for his makeing mee wear Irons &ca.

Sir,

Your Most humble Servant in Affliction
THOMAS BOWRY."

[1] Madras Muhammadan. See note on p. 256.

The Council at Fort St George did not trouble much about the misfortunes of a "free merchant," and left the settlement of the affair to the Company's servants at Cuddalore. On the 27th May Mr Davis and Council wrote again.

"CUDDALORE, the 27th *May* 1687.

To

The Honble. WILLIAM GYFFORD Esqr. &ca.

HONBLE. SIR &ca.

Wee have received yours of the 21st Currant.... Mr. Bowrys bussiness is Referr'd by him and the diwan to us and wee have obliged Mr. Bowry to deliver us his Bond for pagodas 10,000 to Indemnifie the Right Honble. Companys Affaires from all demands that Shall bee lawfully made against him which believe will not bee [many]; hee haveing given Sufficient Testimony to clear himself as noted in [*portion damaged*] (to which Referr) which Shall bee Remitted you Therefore think it but Reasonable that Satisfaceon bee required of the Diwan for the abuse offer'd us; in the Imprisoning Mr. Bowrey in that barberous man[ner and] unlawfully for if this bee passed by, they will upon all occations abuse the Right Honble. Companys Servants in the like manner, So that wee Shall live in no Security but in fear of the diwan to the Right Honble. Companys prejudice; therefore desire you will please to order (which you have not in your last) Mr. Mansfen haveing acquainted you Mr. Bowrys Release how wee shall proceed in any bussiness of the like nature for the future; to waite your orders for it then may endanger our lives by their barberous usage and to take satisfacson for it afterwards would bee but a poor redress to the Sufferers; for tho Mr. Bowry was to blame in Striking Amad Mercawns Servant with whom the difference was as all others would bee that should do the like to any of the diwans people being Obliged to appeale to those that have the Authority of writing them and not to do it themselves which shall by noe means tollerate for prevention of disturbance, yet not so much considering the provocation given him as to be so rigorously dealt with by the diwans people which is by noe means to bee allow'd for the reason aforesaid but they bee obliged to appeal to us for Satisfaceon for any Injuries done by our people and not to wright themselves upon paine of answering the abuse; wee have been Something the larger on this Subject considering how much it Imports us which hope you will please to excuse....

Honble. Sir &ca.

Your Most humble Servants

JOHN DAVIS
RALPH INGRAM
CHR. WILSON."

In the letter "of the 21st Currant" referred to in the above, the Council at Fort St George had thus expressed their opinion with regard to Captain Bowrey's conduct in the affair at Porto Novo[1], "Mr. Bowry was very much too blame to strike any Merchant especially in the Factory and sure enough he ought to have made his applications to you upon any difference with the natives and not to have done him selfe Justice and were it not indeed for the honour of our nation and that the Subador might hereafter presume to do the same to any of the Right Honble. Companys own immediate Servants you might justly have left him to have sought his own remidy but upon the aforesaid consideration you did well to endeavour his rescue and but that we hear from Mr. Mastin [? Mansfen] that he is allready released wee should have given you further order and direction about itt, however when he comes hither wee shall call him to account for his irreguler actions, in the mean time wee would not have you omitt to take such a bond from him as you mention to indemnifie the Right Honble. Company from any demands of the Government upon his account."

[1] *Factory Records*, Fort St George, No. 20.

Captain Bowrey must have been released from confinement about the 20th May, 1687, for he reached Fort St George on the *Borneo Merchant* on the 25th of the month, and on the 2nd of June he sailed again for Achin, which place he reached without further impediment[1].

On the 4th June, 1687, the Council at Fort St George in a letter to Cuddalore again referred to the Bowrey affair[2]. "As to Mr. Bowrys case wee must needs say the abuse was not only to him but to the Right Honble. Company and therefore had wee power and were it convenient for us in respect of our concernes wee should right our Selvės in the same manner and fetch the Governour himself and put him in Irons as hee did Mr. Bowry without cause or att least before he had made his complaint of himselfe or his people receiving any wrong from said Mr. Bowry but as the case stands wee must only make our complaint to the Cheife Sobadar or to the King himselfe (if hee the Sobadar will not doe wright)...wee shall consider what to doe afterwards if wee have not Satisfaction."

From this letter it appears as if Bowrey, on his return, had enlisted the sympathy of the Council, and that if he had been "called to account" he had managed to make out a good case for himself. However, with Bowrey's departure for Achin, the Council's sympathy on his behalf quickly cooled down, and whether he ever obtained substantial satisfaction for his imprisonment is doubtful. On the 30th July, the Council at Fort St George wrote to Cuddalore, "Mr. Bowreys action against Amord Mercawne is withdrawne from our Court, appearing more of heat then matter and the attacht goods discharged[3]." The servants at Cuddalore were, however, anxious to uphold their dignity with the native governor, and the affair was still in abeyance in August, 1687. As the "attacht goods" were "discharged," Bowrey appears only to have suffered personal inconvenience and not financial loss.

---

[1] *Factory Records*, Fort St George, No. 4. [2] *ibid.*
[3] *ibid.* No. 30.

When he left Achin, Captain Bowrey went to Bengal. This was his third recorded visit to that province[1]. On the 23rd August, 1687, Captain Nicholson of the *Beaufort* wrote to Job Charnock, the Company's Agent, "This day the *Borneo Merchant* Captain Bowrey anchored of this place, he came from Acheen, he put in here [Hijili] to see if we had any advices to send to the Fort, which is all his business, I advised him to come up and acquaint your worship[2]." On the 26th August Job Charnock and Council at Bengal wrote to President Gyfford at Fort St George giving an account of the taking of the Ketch *Good Hope*, which had been "Ordered down into the Bay with 2 months provisions to ly there as a guard ship." The taking of the vessel "came but to our knowledge within these 2 days, by Captain Bowry who brought along with him the Master of the said Ketch from Acheen, his name is Samuell Heron Brother to Captain George Heron, both of them Pilots in the Right Honble. Companys service." This unfortunate man had arrived in Balasor Road on the 1st May. "On the 2nd May was overpowered by a gang of the crew who kept him in irons for 6 weeks when they put him in a Prow on the Coast of Sumatra with 5 daies provision... In 15 he arrived at Acheen where he mett with this [Captain Bowrey's] conveyance[3]." The letter containing this account was entrusted to Captain Bowrey, who reached Fort St George on the 23rd September, 1687[4].

This was Bowrey's last voyage on the *Borneo Merchant*. On the 4th October the vessel, together with the Company's ship the *Loyall Adventure*, was lost in a storm at Fort St George. The *Borneo Merchant* was driven ashore and "bilged into shatters[5]." No lives appear to have been lost. It was at this time, after his return from Bengal, that Bowrey drew his chart of the Hugli, which is reproduced in this volume[6]. His chart of Formosa was also drawn in the same year.

---

1 See pp. 152 and 172 of this vol.

2 *Factory Records*, Hugli, No. 11.

3 *Factory Records*, Fort St George, No. 30.

4 *ibid.* No. 21.

5 *O.C.* 13th October, 1687.

6 See p. 172.

We have now reached the final stages of our author's life in India. The *Borneo Merchant* was replaced by the *Frances*, on which, in spite of his former unpleasant experience, Bowrey sailed to Porto Novo early in 1688. On the 4th March he was back again at Fort St George[1]. On the 10th of the month he sailed for Achin, and there Dampier found him living in his own house. The following is the great traveller's account of his relations with Bowrey:—"When I was a little recover'd...I made a shift to go abroad; and having been kindly invited to Captain Bowry's House there [in Achin], my first visit was to him, who had a Ship in the Road, but lived ashore. This Gentleman was extraordinary kind to us all, particularly to me, and importuned me to go his Boatswain to Persia; whither he was bound, with a design to sell his Ship there; as I was told, tho not by himself. From thence he intended to pass with the Caravan to Aleppo, and so home for England. His business requir'd him to stay some time longer at Achin; I judge, to sell some commodities, that he had not yet disposed of. Yet he chose rather to leave the disposal of them to some Merchant there; and make a short trip to the Nicobar Islands in the mean time, and on his return to take in his effects, and so proceed towards Persia. This was a sudden resolution of Captain Bowry's, presently after the arrival of a small Frigot from Siam, with an Ambassador from the King of Siam, to the Queen of Achin. The Ambassador was a Frenchman by nation. The Vessel that he came in was but small, yet very well mann'd, and fitted for a fight. Therefore it was generally supposed here, that Captain Bowry was afraid to lye in Achin Road, because the Siamers were now at Wars with the English, and he was not able to defend his Ship, if he should be attackt by them.

"But whatever made him think of going to the Nicobar Islands, he provided to sail; and took me, Mr. Hall, and Ambrose with him: tho all of us so sick and weak that

---

[1] *Factory Records*, Fort St George, No. 5.

we could do him no service. It was some time about the beginning of June when we sailed out of Achin Road; but we met with the Wind at N.W. with turbulent weather, which forced us back again in 2 days time. Yet he gave us each 12 Mess[1] a piece, a Gold Coyn, each of which is about the value of 15 pence English. So he gave over that design: and some English Ships coming into Achin Road, he was not afraid of the Siamers who lay there.

"After this, he again invited me to his House at Achin, and treated me always with Wine and good Cheer, and still importuned me to go with him to Persia: but I being very weak, and fearing the Westerly Winds would create a great deal of trouble, did not give him a positive answer: especially because I thought I might get a better Voyage in the English Ships newly arrived, or some others now expected here. It was this Captain Bowry who sent the Letter from Borneo directed to the Chief of the English Factory at Mindanao...[2]." The letter here referred to was written by Captain Bowrey when he was at Borneo in 1687, and seen by Dampier at Mindanao in the Philippine Islands. He says[3], "Some of our men...bought a Canoa, and designed to go in her to Borneo: for not long before a Mindanao Vessel came from thence, and brought a Letter directed to the Chief of the English Factory at Mindanao. This Letter the General would have Captain Swan have opened, but he thought it might come from some of the East India Merchants, whose Affairs he would not intermeddle with, and therefore did not open it. I since met with Captain Bowry at Achin, and telling him this story, he said that he sent that Letter, supposing that the English were settled there at Mindanao, and by this Letter we also thought that there was an English Factory at Borneo: so here was a mistake on both sides."

In spite of his expressed intention to go to Persia, Bowrey ultimately changed his mind, and, as in the previous year, on leaving Achin, went to Bengal. At the end

---

[1] See note on p. 115 of this vol.

[2] Dampier, *Voyages*, vol. i. p. 503 f.

[3] *ibid.* p. 370.

of September he returned once more to Fort St George on the *Frances*, bringing the "Bengall and Bencolen Generalls[1]." He also brought news of the massacre of the English at Mergui, the detention of his own and other English ships, and his subsequent escape. These matters are referred to in a letter from the Council at Fort St George to the English Ambassador, Sir William Norris, under date 29th September, 1688[2], "This instant arrived here Captain Thomas Bowery from Atchein via Bengall who acquainted us he left Mr. John Hill and severall there upon the *Pearle* frigatt we sent in September last on the Merge Expedition who were ever Since detained there and att Siam but by what accident or Strataguem he got free we cannot learne having noe letter from them only Mr. Bowery tells us he heard Mr. Hodges with near 100 more English men detained prisoners att Siam and Severely treated..."

In this last voyage Bowrey had probably realized most of his property. At any rate, his stay at Fort St George was very short. On the 20th October, 1688, he sailed for England on the *Bengall Merchant* under the command of Captain William Pearse[3]. The voyage was a long one, and Bowrey employed his time in collecting the materials for his *Dictionary of English and Malayo*, published in 1701[4].

The next reference to Captain Bowrey is in the Home Records on the 29th November, 1689, when the Court of Directors ordered £100 to be paid to "Captain Thomas Bowrey in part of a farther sum due to him from the Company," and again on the 24th March, 1690, "It being represented to the Court that two Cannisters of Tea belonging to Captain Bowry were put up at the Companys Sale and did not go off, It is ordered that the Said Commodities be delivered him he paying the Companys Duties according to the rate they were put up at." On the 31st March there is another entry ordering the account of raw

[1] *Factory Records*, Fort St George, No. 5. [2] *ibid.* No. 21.
[3] *ibid.* No. 5. [4] See the Preface to the Dictionary.

silk brought home on the *Rochester* for Captain Thomas Bowry to be stated[1].

Our author had now time and means to settle down in comfort in his native land. In the Marriage Licences issued by the Vicar General of the Archbishop of Canterbury[2], we find, "September 14th 1691. Thomas Bowrey of Greenwich, Kent, Merchant, Bachelor, about 31 and Mary Gardiner, of the same, Spinster, about 20, with her father's consent; at St. Mary Magdalen, Old Fish Street, London, or [ ]." Were it not for the "about," the age of the bridegroom would constitute a serious difficulty, for, even allowing that Bowrey was only seventeen when he sailed for India in 1668, he would have been forty-one at the time of his marriage. The marriage did *not* take place at St Mary Magdalen, Old Fish Street, but in the Parish Church of Lee, Blackheath, on the 17th September, 1691[3].

Whether Thomas Bowrey went to sea again after his marriage is uncertain. If he made no more voyages, his knowledge of the Coast of Africa, embodied in the "MS Book in a Green Cover," bequeathed to the East India Company, must have been acquired during his journeys to and from India. At the same time it seems highly probable that his "Manuscript book of draughts and discriptions of the Coasts of America," bequeathed to the South Sea Company, was the product of personal observation, and if the *Dictionary of the Hudson's Bay Language* (bound up with one copy of the *Dictionary of English and Malayo*) were really the work of Bowrey, then he must also have voyaged to North America. From the date of his marriage until the early part of 1699 I can find no mention of him (except in 1694, 1695 and 1696 as a holder of East India Stock[4]), so that whether he was voyaging abroad or trading at home must be left to conjecture.

---

[1] *Court Book*, No. 35.

[2] *Harleian Society's Publications*, vol. xxxi.

[3] The marriage is entered in the Registers of Lee Church, Blackheath, and I am indebted to the Rev. E. Louis C. Clapton for a copy of the entry.

[4] *Home Series*, Miscellaneous, No. 2.

In February, 1699, the Court of Directors debated the wisdom of a Settlement in the "South Seas," *i.e.* the East Indian Islands, and "Captain Rossey and Captain Bowrey who had been in those parts were called in and discoursed at large about their knowledge of what may probably be done by a settlement there." The two Captains "delivered in a Proposall" concerning the Settlement, which the Court at first seemed inclined to adopt, but eventually adjourned "the furthur debate thereof," and there is no later reference to the matter[1].

At this time Bowrey must have been fully occupied with his *Dictionary of English and Malayo*, a work on which he expended infinite pains, and which was produced in 1701; after its publication, there is again a gap of five years in the author's life. In 1706 Bowrey turns up again as an acquaintance of Peter Briggins[2], through whom the 1669—1679 MS. came to its present owner. On the 22nd October, 1706, there is an entry in the diary of Peter Briggins[3] of the receipt of a half-year's rent from Captain Bowrey. All through 1707 and 1708 there are frequent notes of meetings between the two men, *e.g.* "Went to the Garter Coffe hous to meet Capt. Bowry...Met Capt. Bowry and Sold Share A Old India bond for 210 premio... Went to Change to look for Rickits and Capt. Bowry... Received of Capt. Bowry ½ years Rent." The fact that Peter Briggins was a holder of East India Stock may have led to his acquaintance with Thomas Bowrey, or, more probably, the house occupied by the Bowreys in Wellclose (or Marine) Square, Stepney, was owned by Peter Briggins.

Although his roving days were over, Captain Bowrey still took an active interest in the East India trade. On the 28th July, 1708, we find in the *Court Book*[4] the following entry, "Sir Thos. Cooke, Sir Gilbert Heathcote, Mr. Shepheard, Mr. Moore or any two of them to discourse with Capt. Bowry touching some Proposalls he offers to

---

[1] *Court Book*, No. 37 A.

[2] See *Eliot Papers*.

[3] These diaries are in the possession of Mr Eliot Howard, the owner of the MS.

[4] No. 43.

communicate concerning the East India Trade and make report." There is no record as to whether these "Proposalls" were adopted. That Bowrey's interest in the shipping trade of his country suffered no diminution as time went on is proved by the fact that in 1711 he delivered to the Lord High Treasurer a "Proposall for taking Baldivia in the South Seas" and a "Proposall for Settlement in the way to the South Seas[1]." These "Proposalls" were dated from Marine Square, Stepney, the 10th and 11th September, 1711. In the first Bowrey described the coasts of Chili and Peru, their climate, productions, harbours, etc. In support of his suggestion he urged, "Baldivia produces the most gold of any Place on the South Seas and it being a cold country may be probably brought to Vend large quantities of our Woollen Manufactures to the Natives more than Peru which is a moderate or rather hot Climate." In support of the second "Proposall" Bowrey declared that it was absolutely necessary to secure some harbour between "Rio de Plata and the Straits of Magellan for the Refreshment of our men &c." On the 28th February, 1712, Captain Thomas Bowrey again wrote from Marine Square[2] urging the Committee of Directors of the South Sea Company that the time was appropriate for a voyage to the South Seas, and again emphasizing the need of finding a port for refreshment. His insistent eagerness about the matter lends weight to the supposition that he had himself voyaged to the coasts of America and had felt the want of the "port for refreshment" that he advocated. There is no record of any answer to Bowrey's "Proposalls" nor of any further correspondence between him and the South Sea Company. Possibly he was disgusted with the want of appreciation of his efforts towards the promotion of trade.

At this time Bowrey was still paying rent regularly to Peter Briggins and meeting him socially, but after the 15th October, 1712, there is no reference to Captain Bowrey in the Diary of Peter Briggins until the 5th March, 1713,

---

[1] British Museum, *Add. MS.* 28.140, ff. 31—33. [2] *ibid.*

when the following entry occurs, "In the Morning at Captain Bowrys...in the Evening at the Insuerance office about Capt. Bowrys Affaire." On the 11th March is a similar entry. The Captain was most likely unable to execute any business personally, and consequently left the "insuerance" to his friend. On the day of Peter Briggins' last visit, the 11th March, Thomas Bowrey signed his will. Three days later he was buried in the same Church in which he had been married twenty-one and a half years before[1]. His will[2] was proved on the 16th of the month by his widow Mary Bowrey. Legal formalities were managed with more expedition in the 18th than in the 20th century!

In his will Thomas Bowrey describes himself as of Wellclose Square, Stepney. He leaves his wife Mary Bowrey sole executrix. The most important portions of the document are the following:—"I give and bequeath unto the United East India Company my Manuscript Book in a Green Cover containing a description of the Coast of Africa Etcetera supposing that if they print the same (all except the Scheme for a settlement[3] and part of the Preface) it will be of use to their Shipping and Servants in India Item I give and Bequeath to the South Sea Company my Manuscript Book of draughts and discriptions of the Coasts of America Item I give and bequeath unto my Cousin Thomas Studds the summe of Fifty pounds of lawfull money of Great Britain and also all my wearing apparell Sword Books (Except such as my Executrix aforesaid shall keep for her own use) Journalls and Maps and also Five pounds for mourning and a Twenty Shilling ring...Item I give and bequeath unto the poor seamen of the Hamlett of Wapping Stepney in the County of Middlesex the summe of Ten pounds of lawfull money of Great Britain to be given and distributed by my Executrix aforesaid as she shall think most charitable and with a

---

[1] Parish Registers of St Margaret's Church, Lee, Blackheath.

[2] Wills, Somerset House, *Luds*, fol. 53.

[3] This may be the "Settlement" referred to on p. xlii

particular regard to such as have been at East India Item I give and bequeath unto poor seamen of the Parish of Saint John Wapping in the County of Middlesex the summe of Ten pounds of lawfull money of Great Britain to be given and distributed by my Executrix aforenamed as she shall think most charitable and with a particular regard to such as have been at East India and therein to devise with my good Freind Mr John Russell the present minister of the said Parish to whom I give and bequeath a Twenty Shilling ring."

During the first six months after Captain Bowrey's death, the widow received much material assistance in her business affairs from Peter Briggins, and (as remarked above) it seems only reasonable to conjecture that the MS. which forms the present work was given to him as an acknowledgment of his many services. At the time of his death Captain Bowrey either owned or rented the "King's Head Inn in Southwark." Briggins arranged "about insuering the Same for Widow Bowry," and in his will, dated 14th July, 1714[1], he says he has lately bought the "Ground Rent of the King's Head Inn, Borrough," in which the widow Bowrey had a leasehold interest. This inn was owned by a descendant of Peter Briggins till within a few years ago.

Mary Bowrey, "widow of Captain Bowrey from Wellclose, near Wapping," was buried with her husband on the 25th May, 1715[2]. Her will is dated 28th April, 1715, and was proved by her mother, Frances Gardiner, on the 4th June[3]. She described herself as of "Marine Square in the parish of Stepney, alias Stebunheath," so it seems as if Marine Square and Wellclose Square were synonymous. She desired to be "decently buried in the Vault wherein my dearly beloved husband Captain Bowrey is laid in the Church yard of the Parish Church in the County of Kent And my Will is that my Executrix hereafter named doe

[1] Wills at Somerset House, *Luds*, fol. 53.

[2] Parish Registers of St Margaret's Church, Lee, Blackheath.

[3] Wills at Somerset House.

bury me in the same devout private manner as my said late husband was buryed and that She doe in some convenient time after my death Expend the Summe of £200 in a Monument to be Erected in remembrance of me and to be placed on or near the vault And I give unto my good Friend Mrs Hannah Lockard the summe of five pounds and a gold ring of the value of twenty shillings to Supervise the erecting of the said monument She having promised me so to doe."

Unfortunately, time has obliterated the inscription on the monument and it is impossible to distinguish it from many others in the same Churchyard, all in an equal state of decay. Mary Bowrey left to her mother Frances Gardiner "The Inn in the Burrough of Southwarke commonly called or knowne by the name or Signe of the Old King Harrys head" for the term left to run; she also left to her mother her farm in Chapton Magna, Essex, yearly value £32. There were various other legacies amounting to nearly £1000. Her charitable bequests were as follows:—She left £100 "in charity amongst poor decayed Seamen or Seamens widows...a particular regard to be had to such Seamen as have used the East India trade or Navigation or their widows, my said dearly beloved Husband having gott or improved his Fortune in the world by that Trade." She desired that her Stock in the South Sea Company, her houses in Goodman's Fields and the rest of her property should be sold, and the money placed out at Interest (after the payment of her debts and legacies) for her mother's benefit; but after the death of her mother Frances Gardiner, Captain Hugh Raymond and John Hungerford of Lincoln's Inn were to be trustees for the property. "My will and mind is that my said Trustees...do with all convenient speed after the death of my said Mother with such part of the said residue of my present estate as shall be requisite for that purpose, purchase the Inheritance of a convenient piece of Ground in some place between Stepney Church and Bow in the County of Middlesex and build such a number of Almshouses thereon as they shall Estimate and

Judge the said residue of my personal Estate to them devised for that purpose will be sufficient to build and endow with a convenient Maintenance for the poor people to be placed therein......And I do hereby direct and Order that the poor persons Men or Women to be placed in the said Almshouses be such as have been bred up to the Sea and past their labour and that the women be such likewise as are past their Labour and be the Widows of Seamen. And my Will and Mind is That my said Trustees and the Survivor of them doe cause such writeing or Inscription to be made upon the said Alms Houses as may perpetuate the Memory of my said dear Husband and me." After the death of the trustees the recipients of the charity were to be nominated by the Minister and Churchwardens of the parish of Stepney. The trustees were to receive £40 each for their trouble. Frances Gardiner was made Executrix and the two trustees were to be representatives of Mary Bowrey after her mother's death. Mr Hungerford was requested to assist Mrs Gardiner "and to continue the same friendly regard for her which he did always Show to me and my said Husband."

Captain Hugh Raymond, one of the trustees, commanded the *Duchess* 1702—1705 on a voyage to and from Calcutta, and again 1705—1708 on a voyage to and from Fort St George. From 1709—1712 he was in command of the *Bouverie*, also on a voyage to Fort St George. After that date he appears to have settled down at home. He was in London in October, 1714.

John Hungerford was the Company's legal adviser, and was elected to be their "Standing Counsell" in 1713.

Frances Gardiner died in 1728 and there was a second administration of Mary Bowrey's estate in July of that year. But the trustees were evidently in no hurry to carry out the terms of the will, and the parish of Stepney was compelled to institute a Chancery Suit in order to enforce the establishment of the Charity. A decree was obtained in 1740. Four years later the trustees purchased a piece of ground on the south side of the (then Bow, now) London Road, and built eight almshouses, one for each hamlet, and a committee room in the centre, over which was a "neat tablet[1]" with the following inscription:—

"These Almshouses were built A.D. 1744 Under the will of Mrs Mary Bowrey The relict of Captain Thomas Bowrey for poor Seamen and their Widows of Ratcliff, Poplar, Bethnal Green, Mile End Old Town, Mile End New Town, St. George, St. Anne, Christ Church."

Dunstan, writing of the Bowrey Charity in 1862, says, "Of late years the occupation has been confined to seamen's widows each of whom receives the small pittance of 14/- a (calendar) month and one ton of coals a year[2]."

In 1878 the site of the almshouses was sold for £2700, and the money was invested in Three Per Cent. Annuities, which produce £167. 18*s.* 4*d.* per annum. The income is administered by the Rector of Stepney and the church-wardens of the other parishes mentioned in the inscription, and is applied for the benefit of eight widows, of the average age of 69, who each receive £21. 12*s.* per annum and £2 per annum for coals[3].

IV. OTHER WORKS BY THE AUTHOR OF THE 1669—1679 MS.

That Thomas Bowrey was the author of two "Manuscript Books" besides the one contained in this volume, as well as other "Maps and Journalls" we know from the fact that they are specified in his will. Of these, no trace can be found with the exception of twelve charts, now in the MS. Department of the British Museum[4].

These charts are (with the exception of No. 8, reproduced in this volume opposite page 172) of no great value,

---

[1] See Lysons' *Environs of London*, 1795, vol. iii. p. 486 f.

[2] See Dunstan's *History of the Parish of Bromley St Leonard's*, 1862.

[3] See pamphlet entitled *Endowed Charities* (County of London), Parish of Limehouse, St Anne, 1895, pp. 3, 4, 17.

[4] *Sloane*, 5222, Nos. 6—17.

but they are of interest as showing the many places visited by T. B. during his sojourn in India. The similarity of the writing to that of the 1669—1679 MS. also serves as an additional proof of the identity of T. B. with Thomas Bowrey. Nos. 7, 9, 10, 11 and 12 are unsigned, but the writing is the same as in the seven that are signed by Thomas Bowrey. The five unsigned charts are:—

No. 7. "Phillipines and Formosa."

No. 9. "Mindanao." There is no record to show when Bowrey visited these Islands, but, if he ever went there, it must have been just before his return to England, for, in 1687, as already stated[1], he wrote from Borneo to Mindanao under the impression that there was an English factory in the latter place.

No. 10. "A chart of the Straits of Sincapura," drawn on a scale of 8 inches to a degree. 1 ft. 10 in. by 1 ft. 4 in. This chart is coloured. It shows "Sincapura" and the Straits of "Sincapura," "the Peick of Johr and The Point of Johr," between which "Here is good masts easy to come by." On an island in the Straits of "Sincapura" is the remark, "on this Island is Cock and Hens wild and Deer." On another point we read, "Here is roebucks."

No. 11. "A chart of the south coast of the western leg of the island of Selebes, with the west coast of the island Zeyllyer (Salayer) drawn about 1680," on a scale of 11 inches to a degree. 16 ft. 7 in. by 1 ft. 5 in. This chart is also coloured and gilt. The date, 1680, if correct, is the earliest mention of Bowrey in India.

No. 12. "Chart of the coast of Australia and Van Diemen's Land with the islands south of the line": the track of Abel Tasman's voyage in 1642 is marked out. 2 ft. 8 in. by 1 ft. 9 in. The remark, "These Islands was taken out of the Journall of William Shoutens," seems to indicate that this chart is a copy.

The earliest of the signed charts is No. 17. It is "A chart of the island of Zeyloan, with the opposite coast of the Carnatic." 3 ft. by 2 ft. 4 in. It contains "The

---

[1] See p. xxxix.

Island Zeyloan" and "The Bay of Totecoryn, Made by me Thos. Bowrey. Anno Dom: 1681."

The next in order of date is No. 13, "A chart of the coast of Tenasserim from 9° 30′ to 14° 30′ north, with the Andaman and Nicobar Isles, drawn by Thomas Bowrey, in Madapollam, Dec. 1, 1682." 2 ft. 10 in. by 2 ft. 4 in. Bowrey must have become well acquainted with this coast during his voyages to Junkceylon, Kedah and Achin in 1675, 1676 and 1677, as described in the MS.

No. 15 is "A chart of the Persian Gulf made by Thomas Bowrey in 1685"; drawn on a scale of 6 inches to a degree. 2 ft. 4 in. by 1 ft. 8 in. We have no record as to whether Bowrey visited Persia in 1685, but we know from the MS.[1] that he went there between 1669 and 1679.

No. 14 is a copy. It is "A chart of Amoy Bay, on the coast of China, between 23° 50′ and 24° 30′ north, with the isle of Amoy, and part of the isle of Quenoy; drawn by Thos. Bowrey in Fort St. George, 1686; copied from a chart made by J. N., in Dec. 1676." 2 ft. 7 in. by 1 ft. 8 in. There is a remark about the soundings which concludes:—"Aboard the *Advice* Pinke December the 20th 1676: By J: N:" This J. N. was Captain John Nicholson, commander of one of the Company's ships. In March, 1676, he was sent from Bantam to Batavia with the *Advice* Pink. In April he was ordered to sail for Tywan and Amoy, and he received his dispatch on the 24th May, 1676[2]. His stay at the Chinese port was probably of some duration, and it was at this time that he drew the chart from which Bowrey made his copy.

No. 16 is "A large chart of the Island of Formosa with the Pescadores, and part of the opposite coast of China, drawn by Thomas Bowrey, 1687." 2 ft. 6 in. by 2 ft. 6 in. Whether this is a copy or drawn from personal observation there is no evidence to show.

No. 8, "A chart of the river of Hugly, drawn by Thomas Bowrey in Fort St. George, 1687" (2 ft. 6 in. by 1 ft. 8 in.), is by far the most valuable in this collection.

---

[1] See p. 216.

[2] *Factory Records*, Java, No. 6.

There are many interesting points in it. These have, however, been ably dealt with by Yule in *Hedges' Diary*[1], where nearly all the names marked in Bowrey's map are given with their history and correct spelling. Six names only of those found in Bowrey's chart are omitted by Yule. These are, on the right bank, Salt river, Norricoel, Hanchparra, Lords Trees and Tody Trees; and, on the left bank, Bowl Punch Tree.

The last chart in the series is No. 6, "A chart of the north coast of Java, shewing the situations of Batavia and Bantam; drawn by Thomas Bowrey, in 1700." 2 ft. 6 in. by 1 ft. 4 in. This must have been drawn in England after Bowrey's return, and was probably reproduced from sketches made while in India.

Thomas Bowrey's only published work is his Dictionary of English and Malayo. There are two copies[2] of the work in the Library at the British Museum, one copy from the George III. Library, and the other, a duplicate, marked "date of acquirement 1798." The book is entitled "A Dictionary English and Malay, Malayo and English. To which is added some short Grammar Rules and Directions for the better Observation of the Propriety and Elegancy of this Language. And Also Several Miscellanies, Dialogues, and Letters, in English and Malayo for the learners better understanding the Expressions of the Malayo Tongue. Together with A Table of Time, computing the Years and Moons of the Hegira to the Years and Months of the English Stile, which Table will serve in the Malayo Country, all the South-Sea-Islands, India, Turkey, Arabia, Morocco, and generally in all Mahometan Countries. To which is annex'd, The Malay Alphabet, with a Specimen of the Character. By THOMAS BOWREY."

In the preface Thomas Bowrey says, "I am to tell you, that by nineteen years continuance in East-India wholly spent in Navigation and Trading in most places of those

---

[1] Vol. iii. pp. 117—220.
[2] *Press marks*, 68.c.12 and 12907.dd.13.

Countries, and much of that time in the Malayo Countries, Sumatra, Borneo, Bantam, Batavia, and other parts of Java, by my Conversation and Trading with the Inhabitants of which places, I did Furnish my self with so much of the Malayo Language as did enable me to negociate my Affairs, and Converse with those people without the assistance of a prevaricating interpreter, as they commonly are.

"In the year one thousand six hundred and eighty eight, I embarked at Fort St. George, as a passenger on the *Bangala Merchant*, bound for England, which proving a long Voyage, and I being out of Imployment, did at my leisure time set down all that came into my Memory of the Malayo Language, which together with some helps that I have attained since, has furnished me with so much of that Language, as I think may be of great use to Trade and Conversation in the Malayo Country, or any of the South-Sea-Islands, in which Countries so great a part of the Trade of India is negociated and capable of being much Improved, especially to this Nation, who I hope will not be unmindful of so Valuable a part of that Trade; but as we may by convenient Settlements in those Southern Seas share with the Dutch, the Profits thereof; and I finding so very few English Men that have attained any tollerable Knowledge in the Malayo Tongue, so absolutely necessary to Trade in those Southern Seas, and that there is no Book of this kind published in English, to help the attaining that Language; These Considerations, I say, has imboldened me to Publish the insuing Dictionary, which I am sensible has many imperfections, I having had very little help to assist me, and not having had the opportunity of Conversation with any Malayo, since I begun this Work, nor in several years before.........I do not question but any ingenious Reader, upon perusing the following work, and considering that there was no Book of this kind extant in English to assist me, together with the little other help I had in it, but will in some measure be sensible of the great Labour I had in reducing the Malayo words into an Alphabetical order, in Spelling the said words with proper

Letters according to the English Pronunciation and in applying the most apt Sentences, the better to give the Reader the true meaning of many words. And this Laborious Task I have undertaken, not out of any Prospect of Gain that I could ever expect by the Sale of the Book, for that it will be bought by few, besides those who are designed to those Countries where the Malayo Language is spoken, and by the Old and New East India Companies, both which have been pleased to incourage the printing of it, but it was done out of a sincere desire to serve my Country, by giving my Country-Men all the helps my attainment in the Language has made me capable of, which, altho I am sensible is attended with many Imperfections, yet will I doubt not, be a great Assistance to the Learners of this so easie, Diffusive, and (as it may be made) Profitable Language to England in general, and to those Persons in Particular who shall Trade to, or Travel the Malayo Countries. And that it may have those Effects is the Hearty Desires of Thomas Bowrey."

At the end of one of the copies of the Dictionary[1] is inserted a Pamphlet of seven pages entitled "A Dictionary of the Hudson's Bay Indian Language." No author is given, but the Catalogue has [T. B.], I do not know on what authority. At the end of the other volume[2] is inserted a Leaflet containing the "Chinese Compass of 24 points, The Names of the Solar half-months, Ordinary Numbers (Learned and Vulgar), and the Private Numeral Notes used only by the China Merchants." At the back of this leaflet is a note in MS. signed by Michael Burghess, stating that he received £2 from Captain Bowrey per Mr Hyde[3] for engraving the plate.

After the Preface is "A Map of the Countrys wherein the Malayo Language is spoken." In this are marked "Old Queda, New Queda, Patany, P. Ladda, Banga

---

[1] British Museum Library, *Press Mark*, 12907.dd.13.

[2] *Press Mark*, 68.c.12.

[3] For Hyde's connection with the Dictionary, see p. lv f.

[? Bangaree], Perach, Landa in Borneo [? Landock of MS.], Jambe, Andrageree, Priaman."

The work must have been of great value two centuries ago, when the Malay language was very little known, and it is therefore remarkable that Bowrey received no acknowledgment of his services from either the Old or the New East India Company. At any rate no record of their acceptance or appreciation of the work is extant.

The many references that have been made, both from the Dictionary and the Dialogues, in the foot-notes to this volume fully illustrate its usefulness, especially in connection with 17th century records of East India.

Many of the remarks too are couched in almost the same words as those in the 1669—1679 MS. and are hence additional evidence as to the identity of the author[1].

In 1800 the first part of Bowrey's book was reprinted under the title of "A Grammar of the Malay Tongue as spoken in the Peninsula of Malacca, the islands of Sumatra, Java, Borneo, Pulo Pinang, &c., &c. Compiled from Bowrey's Dictionary, and other authentic documents, manuscript and printed[2]." In the "Advertisement," which is unsigned, the editor says, "In the compilation of the following Grammar and Dictionary, great part of which is printed off, the work of Mr. Thomas Bowrey, (which has now become exceeding scarce) has been the grand foundation. Bowrey's Dictionary was published without the Malay character, which defect has been remedied in the present undertaking[3]."

In 1801 James Howison, a member of the Asiatic Society, published a Dictionary and Grammar of the Malay Tongue. In the "Advertisement" he remarks, "Untill now the only assistance to be obtained by the Malay scholar was through the medium of Bowrey's Grammar, printed a century ago, a work of great industry and merit, that distant period considered, and to which

---

[1] See p. xxii f.

[2] British Museum Library, *Press Mark*, 67 . d . 9.

[3] For Marsden's opinion of this addition, see under the comments on his *Malay Grammar* of 1812.

in the present volume we acknowledge our many obligations. Its great scarcity, independent of the errors and defects consequent to its being the first attempt to form an English and Asiatic Grammar, we believe, ever made, renders the present work not less necessary." In a footnote Howison further remarks, "No account can be traced of Mr Bowrey or his book in the present Remembrancer's Office, so as to do him the credit due to his memory, or foresight, which the publisher is desirous of doing, who, though engaged in an extensive business ever since May 1752, never could see more than three copies, notwithstanding his frequent enquiries."

Howison might have gone further and admitted that his "many obligations" to Bowrey included wholesale copying from the Dictionary of English and Malayo. On p. 31 f. of Howison's book the "Weights and Measures" of Acheen are given in Bowrey's exact words, and this is only one of many instances that might be cited.

William Marsden, F.R.S., who published "A Grammar of the Malayan Language" in 1812, was apparently the first scholar to produce such a work in English. His remarks on Bowrey's Dictionary are rather severe; but these are mild compared with the scathing criticism he bestows on the Dictionary published under Howison's name. Of Bowrey's work Marsden says[1], "This, although the work of an illiterate person, possesses considerable merit, and derived, as is evident, no advantage whatever from the preceding publications, of the existence of which the author was probably ignorant. His extensive knowledge of the language of the people whose ports he frequented as a trader, he laudably rendered permanent and useful to his countrymen by committing to paper all the words with which his memory furnished him, but he appears to have been entirely ignorant of the written language, as even the short specimen of words in the original character, printed at the end of his book, he acknowledges to have been prepared for him at Oxford by that learned and indefatigable orientalist, Thomas

[1] *Introduction*, pp. xl—xlii.

Hyde[1]. Owing to his want of sufficiency in this and some other respects, he has unavoidably fallen into numerous errors, and the sentences he has employed to exemplify the words, being of his own composition, and not quotations, are for the most part incorrect or vulgar, and uncouth in their phraseology." Marsden quotes from Bowrey's preface, and says that he had in his possession a copy of Bowrey's Dictionary "full of manuscript corrections made at an early period" by Henry Smith, and containing a memorandum in the same writing which runs as follows: "My Dictionary which the foregoing should have bin onely the Coppy off, is so strangely perverted thro' Ignorance of the genuine Elegancy and Meaning of the Wordes in this language, that it would have puzled a learned Malayer to have pickt out the meaning of the short sentences, for they are very concise in their discourse useing noe circumlocutions or tautalogie." This remark savours strongly of Bowrey's style, and how Henry Smith came to have anything to do with the Dictionary is inexplicable. Marsden says that nothing further respecting him ever came to his knowledge.

Howison's Dictionary, according to Marsden, was not Howison's, but the work of some unknown editor or editors (*i.e.* a copy of the reprint of Bowrey's Dict. in 1800), who attempted to improve Bowrey's Dictionary by adding the Malayan character to the words as they stood in Roman orthography. These editors "composed them of such Persian characters as best suited their idea of the sounds, and consequently when right, it is only by chance." Marsden adds that he believes Howison was not "a principal in the transaction," although the work was published in his name.

It says much for Bowrey's Dictionary that, though the work of an "illiterate" man, it should have been still a living force more than a century after its compilation.

[1] See the last 10 pp. of Bowrey's *Dictionary of English and Malayo* which are introduced with the remark, "Here follows a Specimen of the Malayo Character, which I have obtained from the Reverend Dr Hyde Hebrew and Arabick Professor in the University of Oxford."

ASIA,

Wherein is contained the scituation, comerse, cus[toms], &c., Of many Provinces, Isles, &c., in India, Persi[a], Arabia, and the South Seas, Experienced by me T.B., in the forementioned Indie[s], Vizt., from Anno MDCLXIX. to MDCLXXIX.

CONSIDERINGE the many Advantages which our Creator hath been pleased to bestow Upon this part of the knowne World from the despite beginninge of the Creation, with the famous and flourishinge present Condition of most Monarchies and Kingdoms herein Contained, with many more remarkable Observations, I am induced to take Some pains; and, Since I have begun the insertinge of Some Particulars, the Vaster and Stronger my desire is to particularize many things of the present State, Religion, Commerce, laws, &c., of Some Eminent places in India, Persia, Arabia[1], and the South Seas, Vizt., of Sumatra, Java Major, and Borneo[2], which, although it swel not to any great Volume, yet I hope it may tend to the Satisfaction and good of Others as well as to my Selfe, neither shall I touch or meddle

---

[1] The writer has not carried out his intention with regard to Persia and Arabia. These descriptions may have been included among the "Journalls" which he bequeathed to his cousin, Thomas Studds. *Vide* Introduction.

[2] There is no account of "Java Major" and Borneo in this MS.

with little more then befits my Owne Experience, Observinge little else but what are the most remarkable passages that have presented themselves within the Compasse of my Small Travaile[1].

The Maine Continent of Asia is of noe Small Extent, as most men may Very well and Easily Imagine; but, for Satisfaction to those who are ignorant in the division of the Earth, one of the most Easie things in Geographie, I have here inserted it as followeth.

It doth Containe in Longitude, vizt., East and West, 125 degrees, or 7500 English miles, and in Lattitude, vizt., North and South, 72 degrees, or 4320 English miles. It comprehendeth many Vast and plentifull Islands of riches and what else necessarie for mankinde, many Small ones alsoe, the Major part of which be not inhabited, &c.

OF CHOROMANDEL.

The begininge of my residence, or first Part of my Arrival (in India Orientalis) was att Fort St. Georg's[2], an English Garrison Upon the Coast of Choromandel[3]. This Coast begineth at Negapatam[4], formerly a place Subject to the Kinge of Portugal, but some years Since

---

[1] The author's "Small Travaile" covered a period of 19 years. For its extent, *vide* the account of his life in the Introduction.

[2] *i.e.* the town and fort of Madras. Madras is still in official documents "Fort St George."

[3] See *Hobson-Jobson*, *s.v.* Coromandel.

[4] Negapatam (Snake-town) was one of the earliest settlements of the Portuguese on the Coromandel Coast. It was taken by the Dutch in 1660. According to *Delestre* (p. 164 f.), the town, in 1672, was half-ruined by the wars between the Dutch and Portuguese, and the fortifications were weak; the "fine warehouses" of the Dutch were, apparently, the most distinctive feature of the place at that period.

taken from them by the Dutch, who now possesse it with great force and Splendor.

It Extendeth it Selfe to point Goodaware[1], on the South Side of the bay Corango[2], which, by Computation, is in length 400 English miles, Containinge many great and Eminent places of traffick and commerce, of which as followeth. But first of Fort St. Georg's.

This Fort and towne[3], which is very Considerable, is scituated very neare the Sea, indifferent well populated by the English, and wholy Governed by them, very well fortified and Surrounded with very potent and Stronge Bulwarks, Points, and Battaries, within which many Portugals[4] are admitted to dwell[5], beinge Subject to our English Goverment, many of which are very Eminent Merchants,

---

[1] *i.e.* Godavari. See *Hobson-Jobson, s.v.* Godavery. For various modes of spelling the name, see also *Ind. Ant.* vol. xxx. p. 351 f. and 392.

[2] *i.e.* Coringa. See *Hobson-Jobson, s.v.* Coringa. On the 12th Nov. 1668, the Agent and Council at Fort St George in a letter to the Court remark, "These two Ships [the *Rainbow* and the *Loyal Merchant*] in going from hence were deceived by the Currents and over shot their port of Metchlepatan as far as Carango." *O. C.* No. 3238.

[3] See *Fryer*, p. 37 f. for a good contemporary description of Fort St George. See also *Schouten*, vol. i. p. 488 f. for the showy display (from the Dutchman's point of view) customary with the English captains when visiting the fort.

[4] By Portugals was meant Portuguese half-breeds and also Roman-Catholic converts, often pure natives of the country. *N. and E.* p. 38, for 1st Nov. 1680, has a valuable quotation: "It is resolved to Entertain about 100 Topasses or Black Portuguez, the better to guard the washers."

[5] The following passage confirms the author's statement: "The Portuguezes and Musteza's [half-breeds] were Invyted hither by the severall Agents from our first setling here. And some came with our people from Armagon and [were] encouraged, and severall had money Lent them to build Upon the open sand Under the protection of the Gunns which by degrees has been walled in, they doeing the duty of trayn'd Bands in watching and warding in tymes of trouble Upon the Out-Works. They have never paid any Rent or Acknowledgment nor taken out any Leases." Reply to Major Puckle, the Company's Supervisor, who asked (at a Consultation at Fort St George, on the 29th Feb. 1676) why so many "Portuguez" were permitted to dwell n the English town. *O. C.* No. 4178.

and are admitted a free trade payinge Custome, vizt. 4 per Cent to the English in and out for theire goods; many of them alsoe beare arms in the Honourable English East India Company's Service as private Centinels, but not Otherways, none of them beinge raised to any place of Office; and although theire Sallary be Smal, yet they live very well of it, beinge paid monthly as all the English Soldiery are, and provisions with cloths well befittinge Suche a Climate very Cheape and good. This Fort lyeth in Lattitude North 13^{d}–10″, and is not at any time very cold or on the Contrary Very hott, haveinge the full benefit of all Sea breezes of wind; but in these following Months, May and June, although there be for the most part fresh Gales, yet it is something Sulphurous, which may most of all be alledged to the wind it Selfe, more then to the heat of the Sun.

It blowinge then for the most part at West and West N. West, beinge hot and dry land winds. The Coldest Season of the yeare is September, October, and November, yet not much colder then the middle of Summer is in England, but affor[d]eth raine in great abundance. But, in fine, it is a very healthy and moderate climate, much Exceedinge many places both in India and the South Seas, and consisteth of as great traffick both by Sea and land as any one place or more Upon all this Coast. It is without all dispute a beneficiall place to the Honourable English India Company, and with all the Residence of theire Honourable Agent and Governour[1] of all their Affaires Upon this Coast and the Coast of Gingalee[2], the Kingdoms

[1] George Foxcroft, who had been reinstated after his three years' captivity at the hands of Sir Edward Winter, was Agent at Fort St George when T. B. arrived in India, in 1669. Foxcroft was succeeded by Sir William Langhorne in 1672.

[2] "You are not certain of the Investments that may bee made about Neglawanch as also towards Gingerlee." Letter from Salisbury

alsoe of Orixa[1], Bengala[2], and Pattana[3], the said Governour and his Councell here resideinge, for the Honour of our English Nation keepinge and maintaineinge the place in great Splendour, Civil and good Goverment, Entertaineinge nobly all Foraign Embassadors, and provideinge great quantities of Muzlinge[4] Callicoes[5] &c. to be yearly transported to England.

Yet notwithstanding Such vast quantities are yearely Sent hence for England, great Stores are transported and Vended into most places of note in India, Persia, Arabia, China, and the South Seas, more Expecialy to Moneela[6] one of the Molucca[7] Isles, belongeinge to the Kinge of Spaine, but are Sent thither in the name and Under the Colours of The Portugals borne and bred in India[8], noe others beinge admitted a free trade thither, and Especialy the English, haveinge the Same prohibition as to trade to the Spanish Garrisons in Mexico, and Peruana[9], in America.

---

at Pettipolle to the Chief at Masulipatam, 2nd Sept. 1675. *Factory Records*, Masulipatam, No. 10.

"He [Mr Mainwaring] sent his Peons to force all the Boatmen to goe away with their Boats for Gingerlee [to fetch Paddy]." Callor Vissina's complaint against Mr Mainwaring, 23rd May, 1678. *Ibid.* The exact extent of this coast is explained later on.

[1] See *Hobson-Jobson*, *s. v.* Orissa. The above is the direct Portuguese form of the word.

[2] See *Hobson-Jobson*, *s.v.* Bengal. The contemporary spelling is usually Bengall, Bengalla.

[3] *i.e.* Patna.

[4] Later on it will be seen that by muslin was meant a very fine calico. See also *Hobson-Jobson*, *s.v.* Muslin.

[5] The above, and the references later on, show that in "calico" were included muslin, longcloth and chintz: in fact, it was a generic term for cotton cloth.

[6] *i.e.* Manila.

[7] The earliest example, so far as I am aware, of the modern spelling of the word.

[8] See note on p. 3.

[9] *i.e.* Peru.

The Native inhabitans are for the most part Gentiles, (commonly called Gentues[1]) and Mallabars[2], many of which live within the Outermost walls of this place called Fort St. Georg's[3]. I have heard it reported, and can well give credit thereto, that there are noe lesse then fourty thousand of them, vizt. men, Women, and Children that live under St. Georg's flagge and pay customes for all Sorts of goods they buy and Sell with in the Compasse or Command of our Guns.

They are a Sort of harmlesse Idolatrous people; they Worship many Gods of Sundry Shapes, and metles, as Gold, Silver, brasse, Coppar, Iron &c., many alsoe of Stone, clay, or the like, but theire Chiefe God of all is in forme of a man Somethinge deformed, and is Set up in theire great Pagods[4], or temples, and is very circumspectly and with great adoration attended and prayed Unto at all hours both of day and night, with many Others Set up in theire Pagod Courts and small Stone buildings thereunto adjoyneinge, beinge of most hideous Shapes, as Satyrs, Cows, bears[5], Rhinocerots, Elephants, &c., with many Smooth and well polished marble Stones, Sett upon an End of 3 or four foot high, on all which they powre Oyle, and adorne with flowers, worshipinge them with Strange and admirable reverence.

---

[1] This and the references later on are valuable as showing that Gentile meant a Gentoo, and Gentoo a low-caste Hindu. *N. and E.* p. 38 for 20th Nov. 1680, has "the Mutineers threaten to kill the Gentue Oxmen if they bring goods or provisions into the Town."

[2] Later references will show that the term Malabar was applied to the inhabitants of both the East and West Coasts of Southern India. In the passage above, the author is using the words Gentue and Mallabar in their secondary sense. He means that the natives are low-caste speakers of Telugu (Gentue) and Tamil (Mallabar).

[3] For a description of the "Heathen Town" of Madras, see *Fryer*, p. 39.

[4] See *Hobson-Jobson*, *s.v.* Pagoda. For the use of the word in the sense of "idol," see later on.

[5] ? boars.

Many, yea most of theire Pagods, are very Stately buildings of Stone of curious workman Ship of the Same, representinge all Sorts of musick and dances to theire Gods, and are Surrounded with cloysters of marble, flat roofed with large and Exeedinge fine marble, Supported with Pillars of the Same, flagged below alsoe with marble, with walks to the great gate of the Pagod, as alsoe to the great Pond or tanke[1], where they frequently wash themselves all over before they assume to Enter the Pagod. The Entrance, vizt. the Great gate of Some of these Pagods, I have often Observed, are most rare and Admirable worke, vizt. a man on horsebacke cut out in one Entire piece Set upon each Side one full as bigge or bigger then any naturall ones, all of marble[2], and, which is more rare, I have Seen within Some of these great Pagods, a large Cart and 2 horses, with all theire appurtenances, cut out of an entire Stone, as bigge as most dungcarts and horses; and these they often bow to in representation of theire God Jno. Gernaet[3], beinge as he is Upon Some festivals, carried about in a large triumphant Chariot, most rarely carved, painted, and gilded, and drawne by men of which in Order[4]. Here followeth the figure

---

[1] For the history of this word, see *Hobson-Jobson*, *s.v.* Tank.

[2] Thevenot, who journeyed from Surat to Golconda in 1666, notes :—" In most places Inhabited, there are Pagods, and every now and then, we met with Waggons full of Gentiles, who were coming to perform their Devotions in them. The first Pagod (I saw) was by the side of a great War [Banyan-tree, see *Thevenot*, p. 25]; and before the Door of it, there was an Ox of Stone, which a Gentile (who spake Persian) told me was the figure of the Ox, which served to carry their God Ram. We found besides, many other Pagods like to that, but we saw others, which consisted of one single Stone about six Foot high, on which the Figure of a Man is cut in relief." *Thevenot*, part iii. p. 73. Compare also *Tavernier*, vol. i. part ii. pp. 173–178 for a description of various Pagods.

[3] This is the most interesting variant I have come across of this much-corrupted name. The word is Jagan-nāth, by metathesis such as is common in India, Janganāth ; hence, of course, John Gernaet.

[4] See the account on p. 17.

of the Pagod called Tressletore[1], 5 and ½ miles to the Northward of Fort St. Georg's; but they have Pagods farre Exceedinge this.

Of all the false Gods these idolatrous people Worship (save John Gernaet)[2], a Cow is held in greatest reverence[3], both naturally liveinge, and artificialy made with hands, those of the latter Sort beinge kept within theire Pagods. But, for the true Worship thereof (as they doe realy confide), most, or all indeed that are men of Estates, doe diligently keep one or more in theire dwellinge houses, thereby to have them dayly and hourely for theire families to make Supplication to; and Upon theire festivals, they adorn the Cow very Splendidly with ribbons and bells, gold, Silver, precious jewels, &c., in which State the Cow is led through the Streets and round the Pagods, with a Vast multitude of men, women, and Children attendinge, Some of which devout persons doe dance, and pray aloude with great zeale, as that pious Kinge David did before the Arke of God.

As I said before, they doe in generall adore this Creature above all Others, in soe much that theire Nuptials,

---

[1] This is the Thiāgar Rāja Temple at Trivettore (Tiruvottiyūr). It is N.N.E. of Madras, ¾ m. inland. It is an old Saiva temple with a large annual festival in February. It is known under various forms, of which Trivatore, in Wheeler's *Madras in the Olden Time*, is as near as may be expected to the correct form. See *Mad. Man. Admn.* vol. iii. *s. v.* Tir. "Trevitore a towne within fewe miles of this place [Fort St George]." Fort St George "Generall" to the Court, 23 Jan. 1669, *O. C.* No. 3247, p. 3. Compare Fryer's description of what he calls the Triblitore Pagoda:—"At Triblitore, four Miles North of Maderas, is a Pagod transcending both in respect of Building and Antiquity; there being Characters, the Expounders of the Gentu Language or Holy Writ understand not: To this Mother-Pagod, at certain Seasons of the Year, long Pilgrimages are set on foot, at what time there is an innumerable Concourse, whereat some of the Visitants count it meritorious to be trod to death under a weighty Chariot of Iron made for the carriage of their Deities; and with themselves lay their Wives and Children to undergo the same Self-martyrdom." *Fryer*, p. 44 f.

[2] This spelling is consistently followed throughout the MS.

[3] For a penance inflicted for allowing a cow to die uncleansed, see *Tavernier*, vol. i. part ii. p. 181 f.

Plate I

p. 8.

"THE PAGOD CALLED TRESSLETORE."

theire way of dealeings, there Oath beinge taken upon Extraordinary businesse, cannot be performed without Cow to Sweare by, which is the greatest Oath they can imagine; nay, not one person of all this Sect called Gentues[1], dares to Sell a bull, Cow, or Calfe to any religion but theire owne, and they themselves are not permitted to kill or Eat any of them; it is soe Severely forbidden by theire Brachmans[2], and as diligently Observed by all of them both rich and poore. Alsoe they are Strictly forbidden to Eat or drinke Or dwell under the Same roofe with any Save of theire Owne Cast[3].

In soe much that if any one, that is not of theire Cast, doe accidentaly or willingly touch any Vessel of theirs, out of which they Eat or drinke, or pot or pan, whether it be Earthen ware or China or Coppar &c., they throw it away from them in great disdaine, and will not be perswaded to receive it againe or to be put within theire doors.

They are generally a very Subtile and Cunninge Sort of men[4], Especially in the way of merchandizeing, also Very ingenuos in workinge Cotton Cloth or Silks, pantados[5],

---

[1] See note on p. 6.

[2] The writer has followed the usual spelling of the time. See *Hobson-Jobson*, *s. v.* Brahmin.

[3] This, and the references later on, give the whole idea of "caste" as understood in the 17th century. See also *Hobson-Jobson*, *s. v.* Caste.

[4] The "Gentues" had a reputation for surgery. On the 20th February, 1663, the Court of Directors wrote to Fort St George, "We pray you to purchase a Couple of Gentue Barbers such as are most expert amongst them in letting of Blood, and send them on some of our Shipps for St. Hellena." *Letter Book*, No. 3, p. 229.

[5] *i.e.* Chintz. *Fryer*, p. 12, speaks of "Pintado Birds, those feathered Harbingers of the Cape...remarkable for their painted Spots of black and white." Compare also the following passage in a letter from the Court of Directors to Masulipatam, dated 7th Dec. 1669, "Our Agent &c[a]. from Bantam writes...that in all the Cargo of Cloth, which came in the Madras, there was not One peece of Pintadoe, or any other Paintings which Mr. Jearsey knew well, were the most required goods for that place." *Letter Book*, No. 4, p. 301. See also several references later on.

Striped cloth of Gold or Silver, of very curious Workemanship, a Very Sober people never touchinge any manner of Stronge drinke, in fine they want nothinge but couradge, But indeed now they have lesse occasion for Soldiery then they had but a few Generations past, beinge then Sole Lords and masters of all the Coast of Choromandell, Orixa, and Bengala[1].

All Very Stronge and rich Kingdoms, but never had the inhabitants been trained Up to any warlike Exercises, not havinge foreseen any dangers or casualties that might befall them, but I suppose wholy depended Upon the Sorceries of theire Brachmans, the which if soe did in a great measure deceive them for these mighty Kingdoms were in a Short Space wholy Subdued[2] by the Moors[3] and brought Tributary to the Great Mogol[4], all of them now in generall wholy Submittinge to the Mahometan yoke, and Very much Oppressed[5], few of them arriveinge to that height as to beare any place of Office Save Collectors of the Emperours revenues[6]; they are indeed

---

[1] The Hindu Power in Southern India was destroyed at the battle of Talikote in 1564.

[2] The author underrates the fighting abilities of the Southern Hindus, who, for a century and a half, held the Muhammadan power at bay, and whose valour at the battle of Talikote is unquestioned. However, as the Hindus with whom the writer came in contact, had been a subject race for many decades, his inference is not unnatural.

[3] Muhammadans. A term specially applied to Indian Muhammadans. See *Hobson-Jobson*, *s. v.* Moor.

[4] The "Great Mogol" was the Emperor Aurangzēb. About the year 1675 he reimposed the detested *jazia* or capitation-tax upon Hindus, an act which excited much discontent. In his time also, an import duty of five per cent. was levied on Hindu goods, while Muhammadans only paid two and a half per cent.

[5] This "oppression" took place in the reign of Aurangzēb. Under the wise rule of Akbar, the Hindus had been treated with the greatest moderation. Jahāngīr continued the policy of his father, and Shāh Jahān employed Hindus to command his armies. Thus, for nearly a century before the accession of "the Great Mogol," there had been but little antagonism between Hindus and Muhammadans.

[6] Under Akbar, Hindus were employed impartially with members of other races and creeds in the offices of state and in the army, and,

allowed theire old Idolatrous way of Worship all Hindostan Over, save neare the Mosquees[1] or Tombs of the Mahometans, but for that priviledge they pay very deare, which lades the Emperours treasury in great measure, Summs of Gold and Silver, Diamonds and other jewels of an inesteemable Value[2].

They are Very precise in theire idolatrous ways of devotion, in soe much that if they very circumspectly looke not to Every particular of their laws, they may come to bee accompted the vilest of men, and loose their religion which they call Cast[3]; and, if soe, that party is not admitted to Enter the doore of the Pagod or any Other Gentues dwellinge house, noe not where his nearest relations dwell, neither will he be admitted to Eat or drinke with any of them, if soe they all loose theire Cast that doe accompanie him in any Such actions, soe that this very party is a most Scandalous person, and accompted but a Hololcore[4] untill he hath regained his cast, which is but one way to be procured, Vizt:

---

in the two succeeding reigns, their position remained unchanged. Aurangzēb, however, with his hatred of infidels, excluded all the more capable Hindus from office.

1 See *Hobson-Jobson*, *s.v.* Mosque, *i.e.* *Masjid*.

2 Akbar had tolerated the observance of the Hindu religion, and had remitted the tax on Hindu temples and places of pilgrimage. In 1669, Aurangzēb issued orders for the destruction of infidel schools and temples. It does not appear that this order was carried out literally. Indeed, it would hardly have been possible to have done so. A few signal examples were made, and then permission to exercise the rites of their religion was probably compounded for by the Hindus, as the writer describes. "T.B.'s" statement is supported by Alex. Hamilton, who says, *East Indies*, vol. i. p. 386, "The Prince exacts a tax of half a Crown per Head on every Pilgrim that comes to the Pagod [Jagannāth] to worship which generally amounts to 75000 L. per Annum." See *Aurangzēb*, by Stanley Lane-Poole, ch. vi–viii., in Rulers of India Series.

3 See note on p. 9.

4 A very low-caste man, a "sweeper," scavenger. See *Hobson-Jobson*, *s.v.* Halalcore. Compare also the following extracts:—"Among the particular Castes, there is one that goes by the name of Alecors,

The Party soe misdemeaneinge him selfe, whether he be rich or poore, (Except he intends to live in perpetuall ignominie) must take his travaile to the great Pagod Jno. Gernaet[1], the remotest part of the

whose employment is only to clean Houses ;...it being one of the greatest scorns you can put upon an Indian, to call him Alacor.... These Alacors having no other business but only to make clean the Houses, eat the scraps of all other Castes ; and so without scruple feed upon anything." *Tavernier*, vol. i. part ii. p. 162.

"We are very glad by the timely care you tooke about the Hollolcore boy that was Shott the 27th ult. in your factory that he is on the mending hand." Letter from Hugli to Littleton at Kasimbazar, 15th Feb. 1679. *Factory Records*, Hugli, No. 5.

[1] Compare the following descriptions of the Pagoda of Jagannāth, the name of which has been variously rendered as Jakernot, Juggernaut, Guggernat, Jaggerynat, Jaggernat, &c.

"We had a view of a great and celebrated Pagoda, which looks quite white, and which is called Jagernate, or Jaguernate, situated on high ground rising from the centre of a large wood...so that it is visible from a long distance. We were told that the Gentues had a particular reverence for it, and that those of Coromandel, Orixa, Golconda, and Bengala went on pilgrimage thither, there being many of them to whom the Bramins only gave absolution from their sins on condition of their going to visit the Pagoda of Jaguernate." *Schouten*, ii. p. 58 f.

"Wee sailed in sight of the black Pagoda and the white Pagoda, the latter is that place called Jaggerenaut to which the Hindoues from all parts of India come on pilgrimage." *Diary of Streynsham Master*, p. 292, under date 13th Dec. 1676.

"If it [the robbery] was done nigh Jagranaught complain to the Rajah of that countrey." *Factory Records*, Hugli, No. 5.

"At 12 this noon [31st Jan. 1681] the white pegodo (alias Jagrenett)...bore North dist. per Judgment 17′ at this bearing and dist. Jagrenett maks in 3 pegodas, the S. most the highest, the midle one somewhat lower, the N. most the lowest, the tops of each being blunt and very white ; on each side are buildings and seemeth to be within a large compoun, and small trees on each side which are not disernable at a great distance." *Marine Records*, Log of the *President*, 1679–1682, No. lxxv.

"The four most celebrated Pagods, are Jagrenate, Banarous, Matura, and Tripeti. Jagrenate is one of the mouths of Ganges, whereupon is built the great Pagod, where the Arch Bramin, or chief Priest among the Idolaters keeps his residence. The great Idol that stands upon the Altar in the innermost part of the Pagod, has two Diamonds for his Eyes, and another that hangs about his neck, the least of those Diamonds weighing about forty Carats. About his Arms he wears Bracelets sometimes of Pearls, and sometimes of Rubies ; and this magnificent Idol is called Resora. The revenues of this Pagod are sufficient to feed fifteen or twenty thousand Pilgrims every day ; which is a number often seen there, that Pagod being the greatest place of devotion in all India. But you must take notice, that no Goldsmith is suffer'd to enter this Pagod, because that one of them being lock'd in

Golcondah[1] Kingdome North Eastwards from Fort St. Georgs, neare 1000 English miles. When he cometh there, makes his case knowne to Some of the Brachmans, of which there are 1000 or 1200 very Splendidly here maintained, where he must give as large gratuities to this great Pagod as his abilitie can well afford, and sure it is that cunninge delusions are not here wantinge to Screw him Up to the highest pin he can reach, the which accomplished, he is admitted to Sit downe and Eat with the Chiefest of the bewitchinge Bráchmans, if his liberalitie Extended to a very Competent Value; if not, he may demand the priviledge to Eat with the meaner Sort, Upon which he receiveth theire blessinge with great reverence, and hath by these means regained his Cast[2], and now may returne home with as great joy and Triumph, as he was cast out with Shame and dishonour both to himselfe and relations.

In this Vast Pagod (as I said before) there are noe lesse then 1000 or 1200 Brachmans maintained. The Brachmans are theire Priests, but I am Sure, and without all controversie, very Diabolicall Ones. Many hundreds

---

all night long, stole a Diamond out of one of the Idols eyes. As he was about to go out, when the Pagod was open'd in the morning, he dy'd at the door; their God, as they affirm, revenging his own sacriledg. That which renders this Pagod, which is a large building the most considerable in all India, is, because it is situated upon the Ganges; the Idolaters believing that the waters of that River have a particular quality to cleanse them from their sins. That which makes it so rich (for it maintains above twenty thousand Cows) is the vast Alms that are continually bestow'd by so incredible a number as comes from all parts. Which Alms are not so much as at the discretion of the Donor, [as] at the Will of the chief Priest, who before he gives them leave to shave and wash in the Ganges, taxes them according to their quality, of which he has information." *Tavernier*, vol. i. part ii. p. 173f.

Compare also the account in Alex. Hamilton's *East Indies*, vol. i. pp. 381–386.

[1] For the writer's description of the "Kingdome of Golcondah" see later on.

[2] See note on p. 9.

of Women are here maintained to dance on theire festivals and days of Sacrifice and Offerings, with all Varieties of musick that Asia affordeth, to play before theire Gods, vizt. pipes, drums, trumpets, with Varieties of Stringed instruments, with multitudes of Voices very delicate to heare and behold were it acted in a better Sence, and not onely soe in this theire Cathedral Pagod, but in all Others, as many as theire Abilities will Extend to the maintainance of, and for their activities of body are much admired by all Spectators. They are for the most part very Streight handsome featured and a well limbed people. These Dancinge Women have a priviledge above all Others in these Easterne parts, which causeth such multitudes to Endeavour to attaine to Such Employs, where they may Enjoy Earthly pleasure Enough, without any Scandall to themselves or relations. They are wholy at theire own choice whether they will marry or noe, or live Subject to any one man, and have the liberty to be made use of by whom they please; therefore I think Seldom or never that they leave this life to retire to theire homes and leade a Chast life, or to marry, whereby theire pleasure is very Uncertaine, not onely through the means of a jealous Husband, but for that Diabolicall Custome of this Sect in Generall, that by theire longe practised Evil ways, cause the Wifes to be burnt to ashes in the fire at the Death of the Husbands, as I will further relate before I End my discourse of this Coast of Choromandell[1].

But first I will describe Some of theire activities of body, danceinge before the front of the Pagod as I my Selfe have often Seene with admiration much rarer then Ever I beheld amongst us Europians, or indeed any Other people in Asia.

Theire irreligious Religion is wholy Composed of

---

[1] Later on the writer is very full in his descriptions of *satī*.

Plate II

p. 14.

"DANCINGE WOMEN AT THE GREAT PAGOD JNO. GERNAET."

nothinge Save Idolatry, intermixed neither with Judaisme nor Mahometisme, but quite averse from them both, (Saveinge in their burnt offerings and Sacrifices) more Especially from Christianitie. The[y] neither circumcise, nor baptise, but yet doe believe there is a God in heaven[1], that Created male and female, and made the Earth, the Seas, and all that therein moveth, and all the reason they give for worshipinge the Devil is, they hold that God Ordained the Devil to Governe this World and to torment all mankind, and that God himselfe resteth in the heavens, wherefore Upon Earth they worship Gods of much deformitie, as partly to please the Devil whom they say is of no lesse deformitie, and the Other reason is, they say that theire prayers are to God to Deliver them from such Satyricall Creatures[2].

They Often wash themselves in Ponds or Rivolets, vizt. two or 3 times, or more, Every day, but never faile of once. They burne many lamps in theire Pagods, and pray with a Very quick and lowde Voice to those molten Gods, often prostrating themselves and kissinge the Earth with great reverence.

In that great and Sumptuous Diabolicall Pagod, there Standeth theire greatest God Jno. Gernaet[3], whence the

---

[1] Compare the description of the Jentives in *Mandelslo*, p. 61. "These are a sort of very ignorant people, who refer themselves, as to matter of Religion, to their Bramans. They believe, that in the beginning there was but one God...They believe the Immortality and Transmigration of Souls, upon which perswasion they abhor the effusion of bloud. Accordingly there are not to be found any Robbers or Murtherers among them ; but on the other side, they are generally Lyars and Cheats, in which good qualities they exceed all the other Indians."

[2] "The Natives are Idolaters worshipping many Penates or Household Gods, yea, the Devil too for fear : Yet they acknowledge but one Supreme God ; and the various Representations or Shapes adored, are but so many different Attributes." *Fryer*, p. 34.

[3] "Now for the description of a particular Idol which stands upon the Altar in the Pagod of Jagrenate : It is cover'd from the Shoulders downward with a great Mantle that hangs down upon the Altar.

Pagod received that name alsoe. This Imadge is of massy Gold very richly wrought, and in the full Stature of a man, kept in a large dark roome of it Selfe, but by the lustre of his Eys which are two Diamonds[1] of Exceedinge Value, the place is by relation as light as though there were more then 2 Candles lighted. In another Stronge and close roome is placed an Artificiall Cow[2] of it's full Stature richly adorned, Especially with it's two Eys, which are reported to be the richest that Ever were Seen in the World, to which the Golcondah Kings have had longeinge desires, in soe much that Since the Conquests performed by the Moors they have attempted to take this Pagod and ransacke it of these faire Jewels, but I have heard many Credible Mahometans affirme that the Brachmans with theire Sorceries prevented them of doeinge the least injury to this Pagod or Towne surroundinge it, of which the Gentues doe Publickly boast of theire holy Temple of God.

Sundry Festivall times[3] they keep here with great Splendour, One amongst the rest continueth 7 or 8

This Mantle is of Tissue of Gold or Silver, according to the Solemnities. At first it had neither feet nor hands; but after one of their Prophets was taken up into Heaven, while they were lamenting what to do for another, God sent them an angel in the likeness of that Prophet, to the end they might continue their Veneration toward him. Now while this Angel was busie in making this Idol, the people grew so impatient, that they took him out of the Angels hands, and put him into the Pagod without hands or feet; but finding that the idol appear'd in that manner too deform'd, they made him hands and arms of those small Pearls which we call Ounce-Pearls. As for his feet, they are never seen, being hid under his Cloak. There is no part op'n but his hands and feet; the head and body being of Sandal-wood." *Tavernier*, vol. i. part ii. p. 174. Compare also the description of this god in Alex. Hamilton's *East Indies*, vol. i. pp. 383–386. He gives a different legend.

[1] See note on p. 12.

[2] "The Temple [of Jagannāth] is built in the Shape of a Canary Pipe set on End, about 40 or 50 Yards high, about the Middle is the Image of an Ox cut in one intire Stone, bigger than a live one. He looks towards the South-east, and his hinder Parts are fixt in the Wall." Alex. Hamilton's *East Indies*, vol. i. p. 382.

[3] For contemporary accounts of Hindu festivals see *Fryer*, p. 44, for one at Madras, and *Schouten*, vol. ii. p. 244 f., for one in Bengal.

days, to which Devilish feast resorteth many very rich Merchants and Brachmans, with many Others from the remotest Parts of Hindostan, in soe much that it is very rare if fewer then 150000 persons resort to one of the festivalls at the great Pagod[1], and noe few thousands to the Subordinate Pagods in the whole Empire. The maine Spectacle and purpose is to behold their graven God Jno. Gernaet, which at Such times is carried in a Chariot (richly adorned and of curious and costly Workmanship) round the Pagod and through the broadest Streets of the towne in great triumph and with great Solemnitie.

This Chariot is of Exceedinge great weight, beinge made of Very Solid wood, very rich, with much iron worke thereon and finely Engraven, with the Shapes of men and women dancinge, as alsoe many hideous Shapes of Satyrs, bulls, bears, Tigers, Elephants, Rhinocerots, &c., in soe much that it is soe Ponderous, that although it be fitted Upon 6 or 8 Good Axletrees, with good wheels on each Side; yet requireth more then an hundred Stronge men to draw it alonge Upon hard and Smooth ground (and this they accompt the Arke of God)[2].

They have Small ones alsoe, fitted onely with one or two axletrees, that 8 or 10 men can draw, and doe

---

[1] "Festivals are kept there for many days together, [at Jagannāth and Benares] and millions of People repair thither from the other Countreys of the Indies; they carry their Idols in triumph, and act all sorts of Superstitions; they are entertained by the Bramens, who are numerous there, and who therein find their Profit." *Thevenot*, part iii. p. 69.

[2] "He [Jagannāth] is never removed out of the Temple, but his Effigie is often carried abroad in Procession, mounted on a Coach four Stories high. It runs on eight or ten Wheels, and is capable to contain near 200 Persons. It is drawn thro' a large Street about 50 yards wide, and half a League long, by a Cable of 14 Inches Circumference, and, at convenient Distances, they fasten small Ropes to the Cable, two or three Fathoms long, so that upwards of 2000 People have Room enough to draw the Coach." Alex. Hamilton's *East Indies*, vol. i. p. 384.

frequently on the Ordinary feast days, theire ordinary Gods beinge placed therein.

In the Middle of that great Diabolicall Chariot, is placed theire great Patron Jno. Gernaet, have[ing] the foremost end Open, fairely to be beheld by many of the people, which in Generall they Endeavour to doe, but more then one halfe are prevented by the infinite multitude, in soe much that many of them are pressed downe by the crowde and Smothered, not much regardinge one another, but all in generall Showteinge their prayer [a]like to this Statue.

And which is both Stranger and more incredible, many of them come a great many miles to End their days here, Under the wheels of this ponderous but, accompted by them, holy Arke.

They Voluntarily and with great Couradge castinge themselves Under the wheels thereof, as it is drawne alonge, and are there crushed to death, the which is accompted by all of this Sect a most Noble, Heroick, and Zealous death.

A Very remarkable relation of a Very rich Gentue Merchant and of his devotion I shall here insert, it happeninge in time of my Stay in India Anno Dom: 1673[1].

This great Merchants Residence was Agra, the faire City of the Emperours Seat[2], which is many hundred miles from the Great Idolatrous temple. He, beinge very rich, had Vowed to bestow liberaly on the Pagod Jno. Gernaet,

---

1 A proof that the MS. was *not* written during the nineteen years that the writer spent in India.

2 The "Emperour" was Aurangzēb. He "divided his residence between Delhi and Agra....Agra had been the metropolis of Akbar, and usually of Jahāngīr; but its sultry climate interfered with the enjoyment of their luxurious successor, and the Court was accordingly removed, at least for a large part of the year, to New Delhi, the 'City of Shāh-Jahān.'" *Aurangzēb*, Rulers of India Series, p. 89.

I suppose in hopes thereby to merit Eternall happinesse, the former of which he performed to admiration as followeth,—

.Hee brought with him in this his travaile great Store of silver, Gold, jewels, &c., with a great number of men of his own Cast[1] to be Spectators to that years first[2]. His retinue were as followeth, (his riches let who will guesse) 500 Rashboot[3] Soldiers, Six Palanchinos[4], 6 State horses, 3 or 4 very large and Stately tents, 6000 naked Fackeers, 6000 more that wore there ragged and patched Coats of Several colours, 500 labouringe men to carry burthens, to wit the Palanchinos, tents, treasure, provisions, &c., with noe Small number of Others that journeyed with him, some to See fashions and Some to regaine theire Cast[1].

This Charitable Heathen Extended his bounty to the Poore in a Surpassinge measure, for, dureinge this his devout but Sumptuos Pilgrimadge, his custome was to give Unto the Poore 500 rupees Every morninge (with his owne hands) fearinge they might be wronged of it, the fame of which doubtlesse caused many poore people to draw near where he pitched his tents overnight. He very rarely Stayed more then one night in a place, neither did he travaile very fast, not Exceedinge 24 English miles per diem, Employinge Severall forerunners to provide Store of

---

[1] See note on p. 9.

[2] So in MS., but is probably an error for "feast."

[3] See *Hobson-Jobson*, *s.v.* Rajpoot. This and later references are valuable as showing that by *Rājpūt* the old British trader meant the squalid "military" retinue of the petty chiefs and dignitaries he came across in his work.

[4] See *Hobson-Jobson*, *s.v.* Palankeen. In his seven references to this word, the writer spells it five times as above, and twice with a final *e*. Compare *N. and E.*, p. 25, for 28th June, 1680. "In consequence of a duty of Dustoory or Baratta having been exacted without authority by the Governor's Pallenkeen Booys from all the coolies that carry Pallenkeens, it is resolved to let this right to receive the said Dustoor for one year for the sum of 20 Pagodas."

riće and butter &c. for his whole retinue; but often times sufficient thereof was provided for them by Some rich and devout men of his Own Cast, who took it as a great honour to themselves if he wold accept of it, by which they thought these gifts meritorious. When this his travaile was perfected that he arrived at theire holy Pagod, doubtlesse he was courteously received, where he neglected not to performe his Vow. I heard it very credibly reported that he gave 10 lack of rupees, Vizt. One hundred twenty five thousand pounds Sterlinge to the Pagod, with many faire and rich jewels, vizt. Diamonds, pearle, Saphir, Rubies, &c., of great Value. He alsoe caused many Vast Stone buildinge[s] (that had many years been falling to decay) to be repaired at his own proper cost and charges.

The which beinge accomplished, he returned to Agra, there to End his days amonge his Owne kindred. As for the before mentioned people called Fackeers[1], they are pilgrims but very Strange Ones, but are very much Encouraged to what they doe, the law haveinge noe power to touch them in any respect, save for Murther, and very rarely for that. They range all Asia over, and with great power, for, wherever they come, the inhabitants of the Countrey are forced, by their Antient Custome, (now not Easily to be broken) to give them rice, butter, tobacco, Oyle, or what else they demand (Except moneys), in soe much that many thousands of them doe range all the Mogol's territories over, alsoe the kingdoms of Vizepoore[2]

---

[1] Compare *Fryer*, p. 95, and *Tavernier*, vol. i. part ii. pp. 165–167, for a full description of the faquirs. See *Hobson-Jobson*, *s.v.* Fakeer. The writer uses it in the sense of a *Hindu* ascetic.

[2] *i.e.* Bījapūr (Beejapore). This kingdom then extended from Coast to Coast, and was the largest by far of the Deccan Dynasties. Compare Schouten's account in 1662—"...the kingdom of Visiapour, said to be 250 leagues long and 150 broad. Those who have written about it differ as to the dimensions of it. Some include in it a large part of Deccan and others place some towns of Visiapour under the jurisdiction of this latter kingdom. It is very likely that

and Golcondah with many Other Countries, but for the most part they doe frequent the Kingdome of Bengala, I suppose more for the plenty of provisions that Countrey affordeth then for Ought else, although theire pretences be for the Sake of that much adored River of Ganges, to which indeed many thousands resort, that are not Fackeers.

Many of these Fackeers goe after a most carelesse manner, as though they abhorred this life, vizt. quite naked, and daube theire bodies over with ashes, not combeinge theire haire nor shaveinge their faces, nor paireinge their nailes, but let them grow like Vultures claws, and indeed they may very well be accompted Vultures, in respect to the many injuries they doe the poor inhabitants in the Countrey, theire haire by that means doth grow very longe and tangle togeather like Unto as much Ocom[1]. Some, yea many there be, which onely weare the skin of a Leopard over their Sholders.

---

the frequent changes in these countries, caused by war, during which states are dismembered, invaded, or reunited, may have given rise to the discrepancies which occur among the writers. What is certain is, that it is bounded on the north by the kingdom of Delhi and the other provinces of the Mogul....Formerly, the king of Visiapour...could, so it was said, raise 100,000 cavalry, and infantry in proportion...but lately he has been so much under the yoke of the Mogul that he is now said to be looked upon only as one of his vassals....Visiapour,... the capital of the kingdom...is 70 leagues from Goa." *Schouten*, vol. i. p. 410.

"The Cawn of Chengy, Nasir Mahmud Cawn brother to the Regent of Visiapore, who has the Sea Coast from the borders of this country into Trangambar exclusively." Fort St George General Letter to the Directors, 20th Aug. 1674. *O. C.* No. 3992, p. 6. "The King of Visiapour has three good ports in his Dominions, Rejapour, Daboult, and Cra-paten...The King of Visiapour and the King of Golconda have been formerly tributary to the Great Mogul: but now they are absolute of themselves." *Tavernier*, vol. i. part ii. p. 72.

In 1639, when Mandelslo travelled in India, there was, according to him, a "Queen of *Visepour*." *Mandelslo*, p. 72.

See also *Bernier*, pp. 197 and 207 f., for an account of the weakness and strength of this part of the Deccan in the middle of the 17th century.

[1] *i.e.* oakum.

Some weare patched coats of divers colours, with Peacocks feathers, bobs of rags, and great Shells hangeinge about their necks and Sholders.

Some, nay Severall, that I have Seen doe weare a very broad round plate of beaten iron about their necks. I judge it may be 4½ or 5 foot over, haveinge theire necks through a round hole in the midst thereof, and thus fastened on by a Smith very strongly rivotted on, soe that the party cannot ly downe, soe as to Sleepe, neither feed himselfe, but must Sleep Sittinge, and be fed by Others. To Such Fackeers, moneys are given, Especially by them of his cast[1], towards a helpe of performance of his Vow made, and that he may be at Libertie. I have, for curiosities Sake, sometime Enquired into the reasons of such Sorts of harebrained penalties, which is thus—They Vow that their bodys shall Endure such penants, Vntill they (by the Charitie of Others) can procure soe much moneys as will build a Pagod of Such a price, but I Suppose many or most of them are frustrated of theire designes.

I have likewise Seen Severall Fackeers, who, in their infancie, have been hunge Up by the Arms with their fists grippen fast, (in imitation of a continual liftinge Up of hands to God Almightie) but by hangeinge up Some few years in this Posture, theire nerves have soe hardened that, dureinge life, they can never pull downe theire arms one inch, or Open theire hands beinge very much Stiffened, and clasped round with theire Nailes; they looke as on the Other side, I have described.

One Old Fackeer I very well remember, that tooke up his habitation Under the Shade of a great tamarin tree[2],

---

[1] See note on p. 9.

[2] See *Hobson-Jobson*, *s.v.* Tamarind. There is no quotation with the spelling as above.

Plate III

p. 18.

"THE FIGURE OF ONE OF THEIR DIABOLICAL CHARIOTS."

p. 22.

"FACKEERS."

in Hugly (in Bengala), and whether he was asleepe or awake, he continually kept noddinge his head and body, soe that as low as his Waste it kept as true a motion as if it had gone by Clockworke, and, by relation, he had Sate in this posture above 40 years; these and the like are accompted very devout men, and these that are soe devoted are, for the most part, Gentues[1].

As for those Seduceinge and bewitchinge Brachmans, they beare great Sway over the Gentues in Generall, causeinge all (or most of them) soe much to confide in theire Sorceries and faire Stories, as if they onely were the true Worshippers of a Deity, and noe Other Sect to live Eternally save theire Owne.

There is dayly great abundance of Provisions, Sweetmeats, &c., and under a colour given to theire Molten Gods they Worship, and is dayly consumed. Certainly none of us are soe ignorant but may, with noe great difficulty, give a neare guesse which way, and by what means these delicacies are made Use of, beinge assured that Stocks or Stones, of whatsoever Shapes, are Voide of life, therefore deficient in Eatinge or drinkinge, Soe that with all reason (indisputable), wee may be assured that these great preparations of food are devoured by those ravenous priests of Belial, Even the Same way and manner that the meat and drinke dayly allowed by Cyrus Kinge of Persia to their God Bel was. Apoc. 1 Chap. V. 13 of the History of Bel and the Dragon[2].

And they doe not onely deceive the ignorant Gentues of the best increase of the Land, but alsoe theire hansomest

---

[1] Here, and in the following paragraph, seemingly used in the general sense of "Hindu."

[2] The reference is a little misleading. The writer means—Apocrypha—History of Bel and the Dragon, chapter i. (there is but one chapter) verse 13. This verse runs:—"And they little regarded it: for under the table they had made a privy entrance, whereby they entred in continually, and consumed those things."

younge Girles of about 10, 11, 12 years of age of their Virginities, perswadeinge theire parents that they must, Upon Such a night, be Entertained in the Pagod, and that theire Patron Jno. Gernaet[1] will appeare to them and Embrace them, giveinge many holy admonitions to them, makeinge them Sensible of many tran[s]actions, which they must be very attentive too, not declareinge any thinge to man, Woman, or Child, Save to the Brachmans; and thus Seldome or never passeth away one night but one young Virgin or more are Soe robbed of their Virginities by Some of these insatiable Idolatrous Priests, who cause the innocent people to confide in all their base actions to be most just and good.

In soe much that I take this Sect to be the most Simple and dull headed of all Others, that are soe blindly ledd not to perceive Such Diabolical actions, the which I doe admire the more at, beinge they are a people as quick of Apprehention as any in the Universe, in all Other things. Those that are tradesmen are very ingenuous, and those that are accompted Merchants are Very accute, and the most Excellent Arithmeticians in the World[2]. They will resolve the most difficult questions therein with much brevitie. They write Upon the leaves of Palmero[3] trees, and with a Sharpe pointed Iron (for the penne), an antient

---

[1] See *ante*, pp. 12—17.

[2] "The Bannians...are altogether addicted to Trade; of whom some are Sheraffs or Bankers, others Broakers, employ'd between Merchant and Merchant for buying and selling. Those of this Caste are so subtil and nimble in Trade, that as I have said before, the Jews may be their Prentices. They accustom their Children betimes to fly idleness. And instead of suffering them to lose their time in playing in the Streets, as we generally do, they teach them Arithmetick; which they are so perfect at, that without making use either of Pen or Ink, or Counters, but only of their memories, they will in a moment cast up the most difficult account that can be imagin'd." *Tavernier*, vol. i. part ii. p. 161.

[3] The fan-palm. See later on for other uses of the "Palmero." See also *Hobson-Jobson*, *s.v.* Palmyra.

(yea I suppose of the greatest antiquitie) custome, whence I doe Suppose wee had that Usual word a leafe of paper. Theire Secretaries are called Conecopola's[1]. Their languadge is farre more difficult to learne then most Other Langu[ad]ges [in] these Easterne parts; I take it to be the hardest Save the Chineeses, which consists of little else but monosillables.

The Gentues[2] accompt themselves a very antient people, as realy they are, and that which they often boast of is, they alter not theire Religion from the begininge. They are indeed the Antient Gentiles, and, as I imagine, of the Seed of those who revolted from Moses, forgettinge God to Worship a Molten Calfe.

Their Languadge is certainly altered Since those days, for I have Seen in many of theire Pagods on the greatest Marble Stones thereof, Especially in the Pagod of Armagon[3]. Severall lines Engraven in the marble, which they doe

---

[1] This is the Tamil *kanakkapillai* still used by Europeans as conicopoly, meaning a clerk or writer, properly an accountant. "Agreed...to allow One per Cent. Dustoory for the wages of the Companys Dubasses, Cancoplys, and Bramminys." Fort St George Consultations, 5th July, 1680. *Factory Records*, Fort St George, No. 2. "The Governour accompanyed with the Councell...attended by six files of Soldyers...the Cancoplys of the Towne and of the grounds went the circuit of Madrass ground, which was described by the Cancoply of the grounds, and lyes soe intermixed with others (as is customary in these Countrys) that 'tis impossible to be knowne to any others, therefore every village has a Cancoply and a Parryar who are imployed in this office which goes from Father to Son for ever." *N. and E.* p. 34 for 21st Sept. 1680.

[2] Hindus of the lower orders.

[3] Pringle, *Consultations* for 1683, has the following note on Armagon, vol. ii. p. 140, "Armagon (Ārumukam), the site of an old English factory to the north of Madras, founded in February, 1626, and abandoned in favour of the settlement at Fort St George in 1641. In *N. and E.* vol. ii. (p. 27), there is a description of the factory house by Streynsham Master:—'the walls two Storeys high of one part of it, and a round Bulwart built single by itself.' In Surat letter to the court 29th December, 1640—I. O. Records, *O. C.* No. 1764—it was called an 'old ruinous building.' Armagon was hastily abandoned at the last, Andrew Cogan on the *Eagle* bringing away whatever belonged to the factors (*ibid.*), even before the foundations of Fort St George were laid. Armagon is said to have received its name after

acknowledge none in this Generation (or many before) can read, and as yet they have a large Chronologie kept in most Pagods, that differ little from the Characters now Extant in their owne languadge, which Chronologie makes the World's Age to Exceed our accompt more then one thousand years, accomptinge each yeare to contain 13 Moons.

They Owne Adam to be the first man created, Eva the first of women, Cain, Abel, &c., but nothing of Noah's flood. Now, how those Vast differences happened of ours and theirs is past my apprehension.

But, in fine, they are a most Subtle people, very worldly given, and many of them Very rich in this World, and yet miserable poore in respect of theire liveing, and little good Use they make of theire riches, for they in generall live meanly both in cloths, diet, and all Other things. Theire dwellinge houses are very rarely better then a low thatched barne in Europe, containing but 2 or 3 very small darke lodgeinge rooms; and Some, that are worth many thousands of pounds Sterlinge, doe dwell in Such Silly holes, the inner walls of which and floore too, onely Smoothed Over with Cow dunge, not at all Commodious, or becomeinge better then the Cows they soe circumspectly reverence.

---

one Ārumukam Mudaliār, who gave the English some assistance in 1625; derivations of the kind, even when supported by family documents are, however, to be suspected, and in the present case there is no trustworthy evidence. Streynsham Master observed in his official diary that 'the true name' of the place was 'Duraspatam' (*N. and E.*, vol. ii. p. 27)."

"There are several Places along the Coast to the Northward, which in former Times had Commerce abroad, but are now neglected and unfrequented. Armagon is one." Alex. Hamilton's *East Indies*, vol. i. p. 369. See *Ind. Ant.* vol. xxx. p. 346 f. for various forms of the word.

Armegam, otherwise Monapollem, exists at the present day. It is a small port in the Nellore district notable for a lighthouse which warns vessels off the Armegam shoal, 6 miles off shore. The still water inside the shoal is called Blackwood's Harbour. See *Madras Man. Admn.*, *s.v.* Armegam and Doogarauzpatam.

There is Another Sort of these Idolaters, who are accompted to be of a higher Cast, (then the Gentues be). These are called Banjans[1], an idolatrous people as the former, and farre more zealous in their way; they are as much dispersed all Asia over, as the Jews in Europe and Africa; their ways of Worship differ little or nothinge from the Gentues[2]. They weare the Same Sort of habit, and are of the Same Complexion, their laws onely differinge in Some points of their irreligious religion, and theire Languadge farre more different. These are not admitted to kill or Eeat any Sort of fish or flesh, or any thinge whatever that ever had or like to have life in it, which although it Seemeth a Strange Sort of Penaltie to us, yet is more Severely Observed by all (as well the rich as the poore) of this Sect.

The Gentues may kill or Eat any thinge Save the Bull, Cow, or Calfe.

The Banjan dare not offer any Violence to any animal

---

[1] There is a delicious account in *Fryer*, p. 82, of "two sorts of Vermin, the Fleas and Banyans."—"to this place [Swally] belong two sorts of Vermin, the Fleas and Banyans; the one harbouring in the Sand, fasten upon you as you pass; where 'tis some Pastime to see what Shift the Banyan makes, being bit by them, he dare not kill them, for fear of unhousing a Soul, according to their Notion of Transmigration; but giving them a severe Pinch will put them to shift for themselves in a Nest of Cotton-Wool. The other Vermin are the Banyans themselves, that hang like Horse-leeches, till they have suck'd both *Sanguinem and Succum* (I mean Mony) from you: As soon as you have set your foot on shore, they crowd in their Service, interposing between you and all Civil Respect, as if you had no other Business but to be gull'd; so that unless you have some to make your way through them, they will interrupt your going, and never leave till they have drawn out something for their Advantage." Compare also *Tavernier's* description of the Bannians, vol. i. part ii. p. 161 f. "The third Caste is that of the Bannians....They never eat any thing that has life; nay they would rather dye, than kill the smallest Animal or Vermin that crawls, being in that point above all things the most zealous Observers of the Law. They never fight, nor go to War; neither will they eat or drink in the House of a Raspoute, because they kill the Victuals they eat, all but Cows, which they never touch."

[2] See note on p. 23.

whatever, not soe much as a rat, a Snake, a toade, a lowse, but will rather purchase their redemption by good words, or moneys, if they see them apprehended Either by a Christian or Mahometan, (for these following reasons).

They hold the Pithgorean Philosophie, believeinge the immortalitie of Souls, and that when the body is deprived of life, the Soule passeth out of that into another.

They are of an Opinion that the Souls of those who have lived well in this World, without either fraude or Guile, and have been Charitable, Especially to the poore of his own Sect &c., doe infallibly Enter into the harmlesest and tame creatures, as Chickens, pidgeons, turtle doves, lambs, or the like[1].

Many of them are men very well accowtred with worldly riches, and most Zealous in theire way, soe that in Charity they doe much resemble the jews, relieveinge and Encouradgeinge all of their own Cast, if any whit ingenuous. They feed for the most part upon that which is very good, as Rice, peas, bread, butter, Sweetmeats, potatos, yamms[2],

---

[1] Compare *Tavernier*, vol. i. part ii. p. 167. "'Tis an Article of the Idolaters Faith, that the Souls of Men departing out of the body, are presented to God, who according to the lives which they lead, orders them another body to inhabit. So that one and the same person is born several times into the World. And that as for the Souls of wicked and vicious persons, God disposes them into the bodies of contemptable Beasts, such as Asses, Dogs, Cats, and the like; to do Penance for their crimes in those infamous Prisons. But they believe that those Souls that enter into Cows are happy; presuming that there is a divinity in these creatures. For if a man dye with a Cows-tail in his hand, they say it is enough to render him happy in the other World. The Idolaters believing thus the transmigration of the Souls of men into the bodies of other creatures, they abhor to kill any creature whatever, for fear they should be guilty of the death of some of their kindred or friends doing Penance in those bodies. If the Men in their life-time are famous for their vertuous deeds, they hold that their Souls pass into the bodies of some Potent Raja's: where they enjoy the pleasures of this life in those bodies, as the reward of those good works which they did."

[2] *Fryer*, p. 104, has "Yawms." See *Hobson-Jobson*, *s.v.* Yam.

Salatinge[1] &c.; they eat noe Eggs, nor Cheese, the former by reason they will not prevent increase of liveinge Creatures, the latter, by reason it cannot be made without Useinge Some Small part that did appertaine to a liveinge creature, commonly called the Runnett.

Neither of these Casts[2] drinke any manner of Liquor Save water and milke, or Congye[3], which is noe more then fresh Water boyled with a little rice in it, but they doe allow theire Wifes to drinke wine or distilled waters, dureinge the time of theire beinge with childe, but at noe Other times, and then but Very Sparingely, and of Liquor not Over Stronge.

They allow but of one Wife, an Excellent Principle in or amonge Such Heathens, were it not corrupted with Other large Liberties of Conscience, for they may notwithstandinge take to themselves soe many concubines as they are able and willinge to maintaine.

Theire Ceremony of Marriadge is after a most absurde Simple manner, (as followeth). The Parents of the younge Couple beinge agreed, (for that must be the first instrument, the younge ones beinge of soe few and tender years, that they be not capable of Understandinge what marriadge meaneth) the Brachman joyneth theire hands to a liveinge Cows taile, before many Spectators, which done, after some mutteringe Speeches Used, (not very tedious) they are let goe againe. This is done by some River or pond of water, a multitude of men, Women, and Children accompanyinge them. They are carried

---

[1] Salading, *i.e.* vegetables for salads.

[2] See note on p. 9.

[3] A generic term for invalid diet; also a substitute for starch in stiffening cloth. "Their sick do nourish themselves only with boiled Rice, which they do make extreamly liquid: the Portuguese of the Indies do call it Cange." *De La Loubère*, p. 63. "The washers engage to wash, whiten, conjee, beat and well cure according to custom all callicoes and cloth at the rates following." *N. and E.*, p. 18, 13th April, 1680. See also *Hobson-Jobson*, *s.v.* Congee.

home in a Palanchino[1], where the Brachman repeats some ribble rabble Stuffe over with a lowde Voice, to this Effect, that they may have length of days, great Successe, and that theire Seed may multiplie, be benefactors to the Pagods, &c., which ceremony Ended, they all Sit downe crosse legged upon Carpets, or Matts, or cringeinge upon their heels, and make merry with Betelee Areca[2], tobacco, or the like, accordinge as theire abilitie can afford.

Att Night, about the 7th or 8th houre, and from that to the 12th, the Bridegroom and bride are carried in a Palanchino through all the principle Streets of the towne, attended with many Lamps and Torches, danceinge women, with all Sorts of the Countrey musick, as pipes, drums, trumpets, Voices, and the Streets thronged with Spectators. Such Ceremonie as this is performed to the meanest marriadges, but the richer Sort they have it soe for many nights, with fine Shews and rope dancings, tricks of activitie of bodie, with a traine proportionable, many flaggs and Pendans flying, with great feastings many days and nights followinge to great Admiration[3].

Noe man is admitted to marry, Unlesse he can purchase moneys to the Value of 20 or 25 pagods[4], a Coine very Current here, which moneys the Male must bestowe upon

---

[1] See note on p. 19. Compare also *Fryer*, p. 34, on "Their hanging Coaches, and those that carry them."

[2] The modern *pān* [pawn], which consists of the leaf of the betel creeper, dried areca-nut, lime, etc. Compare *Streynsham Master's Diary* for Sept. 25th, 1676, p. 65. "I Incouraged him [Anuntram] to speak the trueth and not to feare any, and then gave him beetle which is a token of kindness and favour." Compare also *Schouten*, i. p. 293, and *Fryer*, p. 40. "The Marchants were sent away with Beetle and Rose water well contented." Consultation at Fort St George, 5th July, 1680. *Factory Records*, Fort St George, No. 2. See *Hobson-Jobson*, *s.v.* Betel and Areca. The various references to "Betelee Areca" in this MS. are valuable for the history of betel and the betel-nut, which are two separate things.

[3] Compare *Tavernier*, vol. i. part ii. p. 181, for a description of marriage ceremonies in Surat.

[4] See *Hobson-Jobson*, *s.v.* Pagoda. See later on for other mentions of the coin and its value.

the Parents of her he purposeth to be his Wife, to gaine their consent. This must be done although they give him nothinge with her, or if they are able and willinge to give her it againe tenne or 20 fold, yet this acknowledgement must first be made.

They are not admitted to marry one Occupation with another[1]. A merchant must marry a Merchant's Daughter, a Weaver a Weaver's Daughter, a Taylor with a Taylor's Daughter, a Gold Smith with a Gold Smiths Daughter, and soe of the rest. Every man must Consequently traine theire Sons up to the Occupation he is of himselfe, and not assume any Other.

The Rich Merchants make Sure to marry theire children before they come to 8 years of age.

And the Poorer Sort faile not much in the Same, not at all Save in the Male, who must be Capable of Some Occupation or an Apprentice to it at least wise. They are generally married at the age of 15 or 16 years, but the females doe rarely Exceed 8 years before they are married, but not admitted to Use Carnal Copulation untill She bee 11 years Old, and then thought ripe Enough.

Many of these women in Asia, Especially in the Southern Parts thereof, doe conceive at Eleven years of age. I have known many bringe forth at 12 or Under, to us Seeminge Strange, but not to them; but againe, on the Other hand, as they are Soon ripe, they are Soon Withered, for a Woman of 30 years of age Shall Seem

---

1 "The rest of the Natives that are not reckon'd in the number of these Castes, are called Pauzecour. These are such as employ themselves in Handicraft Trades; among which there is no other distinction, but according to the Trades which they follow from Father to Son. So that a Taylor cannot prefer his Son, but only in his own Calling, though he be never so rich; nor marry either a Son or Daughter, but to one of his own Craft. By the same rule, when a Taylor dies, all those of his own Trade accompany the corps to the place where it is burnt: and the same practise is observ'd in all other Trades." *Tavernier*, vol. i. part ii. p. 162.

as though she [were] 50 or upwards, and Seldome any of them beare Children after they see 25 or 26 years.

Theire Garments are Very thinne, Suitable Enough in that respect for the Climate they live in, but not at all fashionable. They are a Slender, Straight Limed, well favoured people, of a tawny complexion, black haired. Their Children for the most part goe Starke naked to 6 or 7 years of age. Theire Garment[s] are then as here described.

They often wash themselves over with water, and daube all theire bodies with Oyle, more Especially the haire, and are for the most part dayly marked in the forehead with a Stroke or two of red or white lead, or both, Exactly between the Eye brows, which marke is put on by a Brachman (Otherways of noe Esteeme). They say it is a Sure badge or token of good luck that day[1], and with these and many the like fopperies they are apparently deluded and cheated out of a great deale of moneys.

I was oftentimes very desirous to discourse with some of the Learndedst of theire Brachmans, which I never was denied, after I had learned Some of theire languadge and gesture of body. One I very well remember in the towne of Ballasore (in Bengala). About the 11th houre in the night, I was converseinge with Sundry of them, neare the English Broker's house[2] (a very Zealous Gentue), and after Some discourse with them, the Moone, which but a Short Space Shone very gloriously, was now

---

1 "The Bramin marks the forhead of all...with a kind of Vermillion." *Tavernier*, vol. i. part ii. p. 166.

2 The only mention I have found of the English broker at Balasor is in the following passage, contained in a deposition by Shem Bridges against William Blake, dated in Balasor 7 June, 1669, *O. C.* No. 3288, "Mamood Izzuff whilst Governour of Ballasore intended to prejudice the English in...falling on Narrandasse [Nārāyan Dās] the English house broker." The broker at Kasimbazar was Anantram, who gave evidence at the enquiry into the death of Raghū the Poddār, in which Matthias Vincent was implicated.

Plate IV

"FACKEERS."

p. 22.

"GENTUES."

p. 32.

Eclipsed[1], at first Sight whereof they all rose Up in great hast, mutteringe many words in theire form of prayer, with theire hands Elevated towards the Heavens, and went with all Expedition into a great tanke of water which was very nigh. Many Brachmans came in, and with them Sundry persons more, I dare Say above 100 in number, some Sprinklinge themselves with water or Mudde, Some prayinge, bowinge theire faces close to the water, Others prostrateinge themselvs at the brinke of the water, many women hasteninge with Small lamps lighted, Store of Sweet flowers I judge for theire Offerings. I Stayed there to See Such sort of transactions, at the least 2 hours. The Brachmans kept a Chattaringe with a lowde Voice, and soe fast that I cold scarce Understand them one word. The moone appearinge in its former beauty, and theire (as it were) passion mitigated, I asked some of them (my intimate acquaintance) what they meant to acquire by Such Strange fancies and Notions they Used at that time, or what was the[i]re Opinion of an Eclipse of Sun or Moone.

Theire answer was, that they prayed to Jove, that he

---

[1] *Tavernier*, vol. i. part ii. p. 179, thus describes the eclipse of July, 1666. "The second of July 1666, about one a Clock in the afternoon, at Patna in Bengala, there was an Eclipse of the Sun, at which time it was a prodigious thing to see the multitudes of people, men, women, and children, that ran to the river Ganges, to wash themselves. But it behoves them to begin to wash three days before the Eclipse, all which time they labour day and night in providing all sorts of Rice Milk, meats, and Sweetmeats, to throw to the Fish and Crocodiles, as soon as the Bramins give the word. Whatever Eclipse it be whether of the Sun or Moon, the Idolaters as soon as it appears, break all their Earthen Pots and Dishes in the house, which makes a hideous noise altogether.... And as soon as the victuals are thrown into the River, the people are to go in and wash and rub themselves till the Eclipse be over. So that in regard the waters were at that time very high, for more than three Leagues above and below the City, and all the breadth of the River, there was nothing to be seen but the heads of the people."

Bernier, who saw this same eclipse from Delhi, also gives a good description. See pp. 301 f. Compare also *Fryer*, p. 109, and *Schouten*, vol. ii. p. 286, for other accounts.

wold remove the Venemous Serpent that did bite the Moone, and put her to Such an intollerable paine, that She lost the glory of her wonted light[1]. I presumed to ask Some of the Brachmans, that are Such great Magicians, whether they were soe well Versed in Astronomie, as to give accompt when the next Eclipse of Sun, or Moone shold happen. They answered noe, not any cold tell that, but God that dwelleth soe neare them By which I found theire ignorance, and told them many things to that purpose, which they tooke Slender Notice of. I asked them if theire God Jno. Gernaet[2] had any knowledge of Such things. Theire answer was Very Sharpe, and to the Effect that he knoweth all Secrets.

The Banjans and Gentues, as well male as female, doe in generall Suffer the Nailes of theire hands and feet to grow of a great length, more like to birds claws then otherways, which amongst them is Esteemed as a great Ornament, alsoe weare in theire noses a ringe or pendant of Gold or Silver. The males alsoe generally weare one 2 or 3 large rings in each Eare, and the females have very

[1] Compare *Bernier*, p. 303 f. "I shall now mention the wise and convincing reasons assigned for the festival of the eclipse, and for the rites with which it is attended. We have, say they, our four Beths [Vedas]; that is, our four books of law, sacred and divine writings given unto us by God himself, through the medium of Brahma. These books teach that a certain Deuta [godling], an incarnate divinity, extremely malignant and mischievous, very dark, very black, very impure, and very filthy (these are all their own expressions) takes possession of the Sun, which it blackens to the colour of ink, infects and obscures; that the Sun, which is also a Deuta, but of the most beneficent and perfect kind, is thrown into a state of the greatest uneasiness, and suffers a most cruel agony while in the power of and infected by this wicked and black being; that an endeavour to rescue the Sun from so miserable a condition becomes the duty of every person; that this important object can be obtained only by the means of prayers, ablutions, and alms; that those actions have an extraordinary merit during the festival of the eclipse, the alms then bestowed being a hundred times more valuable than alms given at any other time; and who is he, they ask, that would refuse to make a profit of cent per cent?"

[2] See note on p. 7.

large holes cut in the eare, wherein they weare very large rings like to small hoops, not as pendants, but hoops Surrounded with the Skin of the Eare. When they are younge (yea in theire infancie), they have Small Ones made of palmero[1] leafe thrust in, and soe, as they encrease in age, larger and larger, Untill they many of them come to have them 2 or 3 inches broad in each Eare, and if larger, Esteemed soe much the more beautifull. The Mallabars[2] Use the Same customes, and differ in many points of theire Idolatrous Sect, and as much alsoe in Complexion, for they are for the most part of a Very black colour, not Unlike in that to the Ethiopians, but much comlier, haveinge very longe haire, and well favoured both in face and body.

They are for the most part very poore in Comparison of the Other, not beinge in abilitie to weare soe many rich Jewels, but neverthelesse they imitate as nigh as theire abilities will allow. The Wealthiest Sort have Sheckels[3] of Silver upon theire Arms, neare soe high as the Elbow, from the wrist upwards, Others of brasse, or Coppar, and Some have them of greene glasse, with great brasse rings Upon theire tows.

When any man of the Banjan or Gentue Sect give up the Ghost, Either by Sicknesse, or any accident Soever, they bury not theire dead carcases, but they carry them into the field that imitates the buryinge places, and there burne them to ashes[4], the which custome of theirs a more cruel Tragedy accompanieth, of which as followeth.

---

[1] See note on p. 24.

[2] See note on p. 6.

[3] Shackles.

[4] Compare *Bernier*, p. 315. "Most of the Gentiles burn their dead; but some partially broil the bodies with stubble, near the side of a river, and then precipitate them into the water from a high and steep bank."

The Husband beinge dead, and his body prepared for the fire, his Wifes and concubines prepare themselvs for the fire alsoe[1], beinge very Sumptuously adorned with very fine linnen, after theire best mode, beset with many Jewels, (accordinge to theire abilitie) accompanied by the Hellish Brachmans, who discourse with them very Zealously or at least wise pretendinge it, highly commendinge the fidelitie of those Vertuous women, that remaine soe constant in accompanyinge theire deceased Husband or Master, and cease not to Singe Over the joys they will attaine to in the Elizium. Their Friends and neare Relations strive to accompany them to the fire, doteingly praiseinge their fidelitie. I had heard of many Upon this Coast e're I had Sight of One, but in my journey, Anno Domini 1672, from Fort St. Georg's toward Metchlipatam[2], overland, I happened to Stopp at a towne called Careero[3]. When I had dined, and made preparations to pack up our bag and

---

[1] See later on for other accounts of *satī*. Compare *Fryer*, p. 33; *Tavernier*, vol. i. part ii. pp. 169–172; and *Bernier*, pp. 307–314, on the same subject.

[2] Masulipatam.

[3] "Careda which is in the midway betweene this and Metchlepatam." Letter from Agent Langhorne at Fort St George, dated 10th Sept. 1673. *Factory Records*, Miscellaneous, No. 3, p. 138.

"Leaving Ramapatam and passing through Careda (Karedu) which is a seaport and the best towne on the road hitherto." Streynsham Master's Memoriall, quoted in *N. and E.* for 18th March, 1679, p. 28.

"Bundalela Shawhe Governour of Carera and thereabouts having sent us word possitivly, that he will entertaine the Interlopers, in case we will not make a Settlement in his Government,...itt is agreed that as soon as with c[on]veniency, we Settle a Factory att Carera, and that the said Governour be acquainted therewith." Consultation at Fort St George, 6th August, 1683, Pringle, *Consultations*, vol. ii. p. 72.

"Carrera has the Benfit of a large River that reaches a great Way into the Country." Alex. Hamilton, *East Indies*, vol. i. p. 369.

"Caraid (Karedu, Telugu). From *kari*, Tel. black and *vidu*, Tel. town. Village, Port; Nellore district ;...Hardly any trade now. Noted for Betel gardens. Ancient temples....Noted for dyeing cloths. Large tank. Festival of Shiva in February." *Madras Man. Admn.*, vol. iii. *s.v.* Car. See also *Ind. Ant.*, vol. xxx. p. 349 f.

bagadge in readinesse to proceed further, my Dubashee[1], whose name was Narsa[2], asked me if I wold Stay to See a handsome younge Widdow burned, by reason her husband was dead and to be burnt that afternoone, whereupon I Stayed out of Curiosities Sake to See the truth of Such an action that I had often heard of, and, about the third houre in the afternoone, I saw a multitude of men, women, and Children comeinge out of the towne. I went to them on hor[s]eback, thereby to get the better Spectacle of this barbarous action. About ½ a mile from the towne, on a greene plaine, was a great fire prepared, that burned very light, about which they thronged. I alsoe rode close up to it, where I cold discerne the body of a man on a light fire, neare to which lay much combustible matter piled round, hollow in the middle, which they Soon Set fire too, and then most of the crowde did Separate themselves, standinge round it at 2 or 3 yards distance. I rode close up to the younge woman, who was Seemingly Extraordinary chearefull. I asked her the reason why she was soe deluded by the Brachmans, who overheareinge me Seemed to be angry, but She, e're they had time to Speake, Smiled and Said it was the happiest houre that Ever She Saw. She Spake something quick, which shewed great desperateness in her, and without all controversie these Satyrical Priests give them something to intoxicate

---

[1] An interpreter and mercantile broker. See *Hobson-Jobson*, *s.v.* Dubash. *N. and E.* p. 20, for 25th May, 1680, has—"bringing letters...that Verona the Dubass was dead." And p. 27, for 5th July, 1680, "the wages of the Company's Dubasses." And p. 43, for 28th Dec. 1680, "Resolved to Tasheriff the seven Chief Merchants and the Chief Dubass upon New Years Day." In his preface to his *Dictionary of English and Malayo*, T. B. says that he learned the "Malayo Language" in order that he might "Converse with those people without the assistance of a Prevaricating Interpreter, as they commonly are."

[2] Narsa was responsible, no doubt, for the mispronunciation Janganāth (for Jagannāth), which produced "Jno. Gernaet." In 1680 the Dutch had a Dubash called Narsa, at Golconda.

them, by which they are Exited to this Valour and Eagernesse of workinge theire owne destruction.

This Silly Creature, with a most chearefull Smileinge countenance, lift up her hands, and accordinge to the countrey complements, Salam'd[1] to all her friends, Especially to the Brachmans, and lookeinge Earnestly upon me, gave me some white and yellow flowrs she tooke from her haire of her head that was beautifully adorned after the Gentue fashion, and with Strange nimblenesse Sprange into the fire.

Whereupon, to make the Ceremonie Seeme more pleasant, they at that instant tuned up Severall Sorts of musicke, vizt. pipes, drums, trumpets, accompanied with Shouting in Such a measure, that not one Screach of the woman in torment cold be heard. Many of the bystanders keep throwinge on much more combustible things, to wit, dry faggots, Oyle, butter, dried palmero[2] leaves, or the like.

The richer Sort, more Especially those in Office, as Naiques[3] (for soe the Hindoo Governours are Entitled), when one of them dye, they, as they kept many Concubines, have many burnt at theire decease, as for Example:—

A Naique that lived neare Mylapore[4], vizt. St. Thomae,

---

[1] Saluted. See *Hobson-Jobson*, *s.v.* Salaam. This is a very early instance of the use of "Salaam" as a verb.

[2] See note on p. 24.

[3] See *Hobson-Jobson*, *s.v.* Naik, in its sense of nobleman. Compare *Thevenot*, part iii. p. 105, "There are many Naiques to the South of St. Thomas, who are Sovereigns: The naique of Madura is one; he of Tangiour is at present a Vassal to the King of Viziapour. Naique properly signifies a Captain; heretofore they were Governours of Places, and Officers of the King; but having Revelled [? rebelled], they made themselves Sovereigns."

[4] Now a part of Madras itself. Compare *Mandelslo*, p. 93, "The Town of Meliapour, then the Metropolis of the Kingdom." "There are several Towns on this Coast, some of which are good,...Meliapour or St. Thomas, which lyes in the heighth of thirteen degrees and a half, and which the Moors (with the assistance of the Dutch) took back from the Portuguese in the year One thousand six hundred sixty two." *Thevenot*, part iii. p. 105. For note on St. Thomé, see p. 45.

died the Same yeare I arrived in East India[1], and for his celebration of the Funerall, which was very fiery, 27 women that were his Wifes and Concubines were burned. Oh! horrid destruction! Who can Otherways imagine but the Devil to be the author of Such base inventions?

Such Cruelties are most in Use in the parts of India where the Countrey is Governed by the Gentue Naiques, or Radja's[2], as some term themselves, which signifieth Vice Kinge; and, on the Contrary, where the Governours are Mahometans, not one halfe soe much in that respect can be acted, the women, Especially those that are handsome, beinge disswaded from the fact, and counselled, immediately at the death of theire Husbands, to forsake theire Friends and Brachmans, and repaire to them, where they shall be very Courteously Entertained; but they dare not rescue any by force and Violence, by reason the Idolaters doe annually purchase theire freedome of theire heathenish laws, and Diabolicall customes, with noe Small Summs of moneys[3], and condescendinge Obedience to the Mogol and his Omrahs[4].

---

[1] I have been unable to identify this individual.

[2] This and later references are valuable as showing that in the 17th Century the true position of a Raja was understood by the merchants and traders of the time: a point that is missed by Yule. See *Hobson-Jobson*, *s.v.* Raja. "Among those not paying tribute may be numbered more than a hundred Rajas, or Gentile sovereigns of considerable strength, dispersed over the whole empire, some near and some at a distance from Agra and Delhi." *Bernier*, p. 208, who missed the point that the Raja is a subordinate ruler or governor.

[3] The writer is probably alluding to a special administration of the hated *jazia* or poll-tax. See note on p. 10.

[4] See *Hobson-Jobson*, *s.v.* Omrah. It is the plural *umarā* of *amīr* (ameer), and signifies a high official, a court grandee. Compare *Thevenot*, part iii. p. 102, on the "Omras or Omros of Golconda." "The Omras are the great Lords of the Kingdom, who are (for the most part) Persians, or the Sons of Persians; they are all rich, for they not only have great Pay yearly of the King for their Offices, but they make extream advantage also by the Soldiers, scarcely paying one half of the number they are obliged to entertain; besides that, they have gratifications from the King, of Lands and Villages, whereof he allows them the Use, where they commit extraordinary exactions by the Bramens, who are their Farmers."

Some of the women they burne at the fiery flames of theire deceased Husbands are not very willing thereto, notwithstandinge all the wicked devices practised by those wretches; yet, when they have once condescended, they practice that Villainie Upon them with Strange Severitie, though the party repent her Selfe of that folly, and be Unwillinge to destroye her Selfe for many reasons, as the leaveinge theire poore Children behind them to be dealt with they know not how, which is a maine and principall reason all tender Mothers ought to have, but these Devilish Brachmans will not consider these things, or looke upon theire dolefull lamentations as any thinge worthy of commiseration, but will by force and Violence destroy them. One I saw very Unaturaly handled by the Brachmans and theire associates, for, repentinge of Such an intended act, they laid Violent hands on her and threw her into the fire, which was not throughly inflamed, and there pressed the poore Creature downe with a long powle Untill she was consumed.

I have knowne One who was rescued from the hands of those Heathenish Devils, (at the Very instant she was to be consumed by fire); it was done by a parcell of English Seamen, without any resistance of the parties concerned, Onely did very much Stomach them, that had not beene Soe Served before, and cold find noe remedie for it. She was a younge fresh complexioned Girle not exceedinge tenne years of age. Some few hours after her conveyance to an English house, she began to be much in her sences, but admired how she came thither, and, upon information of the whole Story, She was very penitent and Sorry that She shold condescend to such Evil councel of her Friends and the Brachmans, and, in a few days, beinge better instructed, She was Baptized, and lived with the English in our Factory of Metchlipatam [1].

[1] Masulipatam. One reason for her conversion was that she could not possibly go back to her people.

The Mallabars, as I said before, doth much vary both in Customes of Idolatry, Languadge, and what else, but are indeed rather a more ignorant Sort of people then these be, and are of many Sectaries amongst themselves, Every individual trade haveinge different molten Gods to Worship. Besides, they are a more dull headed people, few of them ingenuous in any art whatever, vizt. the Mallabars that reside Upon this Coast, but those Naturall Mallabars that inhabit Upon the Mallabar Coast (commonly called the Coast of India) are a very briske, ingenuous folke, but too bloody minded to all Nations whatever they can Overpowre, but these are for the [most part] Very laborious men, but of noe gentile[1] Occupations, neither are they admitted into the Society of the Banjans or Gentues, Either in theire houses or Pagods. There are another Sort of inhabitants about this Coast that are the Offscum of all the rest; they are called Parjars[2]; they are of noe Cast whatever, deficient in the knowledge of any Religion whatever, worshipinge nothinge, but live and dye quite after the manner of beasts and noe better, neither do they abstaine from any thinge that is fit for a man to eat or drinke, yet they keep a good decorum in some things of theire owne heads. They have every man one woman, and do labour hard for the maintenance of her and her Children; they dwell in Small Cottages apart, not intermixed with any Other of the inhabitants; many of them nowadays are yearly converted to the Christian faith by the Portugal Priests[3] and Jesuites. As I said

---

[1] *i.e.* Hindu.

[2] See *Hobson-Jobson*, *s.v.* Pariah. *N. and E.* p. 34, for 21st Sept. 1680, has "Every village has a Cancoply [clerk] and a Paryar [Servant] who are imployed in this office which goes from Father to Son." "The Parreas are the vilest caste of all." *Schouten*, vol. ii. p. 23. "Buy me...a Slave boy...Let him not be of a Parryar, but a good Cast." *O. C.* No. 4583.

[3] The Court of Directors in England had a very poor opinion of the "Portugall Priests." In a letter to Fort St. George, dated 7th

before, they are all of them laborious, as bricklayers, Masons, Smiths, fishermen, or the like; those are called Moquaes[1]. The boats they doe lade and Unlade Ships or Vessels with are built very Sleight, haveinge noe timbers in them, Save thafts[2] to hold their Sides togeather. Theire planke are very broad and thinne, Sowed togeather with Cayre[3], beinge flatt bottomed and every way much deformed, as on the Other Side demonstrated[4].

They are Soe Sleightly built for conveniencies sake, and realy are most proper for this Coast; for, all along the Shore, the Sea runneth high and breaketh, to which they doe buckle and alsoe to the ground when they Strike.

December, 1669 (*Letter Book*, No. 4, p. 289), they wrote, "In our former Instructions, Wee advised you cheifely to encorage the Protestant religion, and to indulge those that discented therefrom, Since which wee understand that your over much familiarity with the Portugall and French Padrees becomes a great snare to our Factors and Servants, for that they are a very great meanes to lead them into all manner of debauchery, and disorder, which wee desire you for the future, to take care to prevent."

[1] See *Hobson-Jobson*, *s.v.* Mucoa. See also Pringle, *Consultations*, vol. iii. note (90), p. 187. *Schouten*, in his description of the different castes in Ceylon, vol. ii. p. 23, has "The Carreas and the Mockuas are fishermen." At a Consultation held at Fort St George on the 10th Jan. 1678, great complaints were made against the "Macquaus." They had desired an increase of pay so that they might have no temptation to steal, and, as many had left Fort St. George for Pulicat, where the Dutch gave them higher wages, their pay was raised to "fower fanams per Mosullas lading of 6 bales." With this increase they appeared to be satisfied, but, "in the Night they run all away, carrying their Oars with them." The Council was compelled to send after the "Macquaus," and offer them 5 fanams, which they accepted. *Factory Records*, Fort St George, No. 1. *N. and E.* p. 2, for 29th January, 1679, has, "'tis of absolute necessity to build the curtain next the Muckwa or Fishers' Town from St. Thomas' Point by the sea side to the Round Point by the river side." The word Moquae is from Tam. *mukkuvar*, plu. of *mukkuvan*, a caste of fishermen, or a member of the caste.

[2] Thwarts. Smyth, *Sailors' Word Book*, p. 678, has "Thaughts, properly Athwarts; see Thwarts."

[3] See *Hobson-Jobson*, *s.v.* Coir. It is used above, and elsewhere in this MS., in the sense of rope made from cocoanut husk. "The cable being new made of Maldiva Cair never started a stran." *Diary of Streynsham Master*, 10th Sept. 1676, p. 58. See *Ind. Ant.* vol. xxx. p. 390, for various forms of the word.

[4] See Plate VIII. facing p. 44.

They are called Massoolas[1], and are for little Use Save carryinge of light goods (as bailes of Callicoes or Silkes, not exceedinge 6 or 8 at one time).

When any great Ordinance, Anchors, butts of water or the like ponderous ladeinge is carried off or on, they Seize 4, 5, or 6 large pieces of boyant timber togeather, and this they call a Cattamaran[2], Upon which they can lade 3 or 4 tunns weight. When they goe on fishinge, they are ready with very Small Ones of the like kind, that will carry but 4, 3, 2, or one man onely, and upon these Sad things, they will boldly adventure [out] of sight of the Shore, but indeed they Swimme (in generall) as naturaly as Spanyall dogs. I have often Seen them one leage or more off Shore, when the Westerly winds have blowne very hard, which is right off, soe that they cold by noe means paddle any nearer in, and they have made Sleight of it, onely let fall theire line with a Stone fast thereto,

---

[1] See *Hobson-Jobson*, *s.v.* Mussoola. "This operation [lading the vessel] was accomplished by means of little boats, called Porcas and Mossels, which are round and long, hollow, high, made of rough planks, without keel, the planks being simply sown together. They are rubbed with a coating of hair and tar, and can be easily inclined in any direction. The passenger sits in the stern. They pitch and roll continually, and often broach to, being on the water almost like buckets or basins when empty." *Schouten*, vol. i. p. 303. "Having encreased the Mosullas from 7 to 13 and now to 17 we could as soon fill twice their number." Fort St. George "Generall" to the Court, dated 12th Jan. 1675. *O. C.*, No. 4044, p. 15. *N. and E.* p. 3, for 9th Feb. 1680, has "Muckwars or Mussulamen." "Mussoolas; large flat bottom'd, ill-shap'd Boats, not nail'd as ours, but sow'd together with Coyr-twine, whence they are so pliable, that the Planks never start with the most violent Shocks." Lockyer, *Trade in India*, p. 11.

[2] See *Hobson-Jobson*, *s.v.* Catamaran. "Catamarous are nothing more than three or four little planks or beams joined together and fastened securely like a raft. There were some [on the Coromandel Coast] which were covered with a mat, and could carry a little sail made of the bark of trees, with which they sailed very quickly. But when they wanted to row, the fisherman, or the owner sat partly in the water rowing with his feet, and also with an oar which had flat ends, so that he got along very quickly." *Schouten*, vol. i. p. 297. Compare also Lockyer, *Trade in India*, p. 10 f. "Catamaran, *kattumaram*, Tamil. Raft, consisting of three logs of very buoyant timber." *Mad. Man. Admn.* vol. iii. p. 137.

and let the Cattaraman ride by it, (for such are theire Anchors) and they Swimme on Shore both against wind and Sea.

One of these Mallabars, (an inhabitant of Enore[1]) about 11 English miles Northward of Fort St. Georg's, a fellow I knew very well, chanced to be out on fishinge when Extremitie of weather tooke him, and soe Violently, that he lost Sight of the Shore, and was soe farre out that he cold not ride at anchor, but was constrained to leave her, and betake himselfe to Swimminge, but lost his way both to Shore and findinge his Cattamaran againe, and in that helplesse condition this poore fellow lay, keepinge himselfe above water with all the Ease he cold, but e're he got the Shore, it was almost 4 days and 4 nights, and at length by meere accident, more then his owne Endeavours, he was thrown upon the Shore about ¼ of [a] mile from the barre in the night time, by the helpe of a Stronge tide of flood and an Easterne rowleinge Sea, after he had been 90 hours at least Upon the Water.

Hee was taken up by Some of his neighbour fishermen, who perceiveinge Some life to be in him, Used all means theire Genius wold afford them to recover more, which they did in a Short time. I knew the person Very well, and have Seen him Some years Since.

Their Massoolas and largest Sort of Cattamarans are built in the followinge forme. [Plate VIII.]

Six miles to the Southwards of Fort St. Georges standeth Severall mountains pretty high, the One of which is called St. Thomas's Mount, Where the Apostle St. Thomas is Said to preach Salvation to this Nation, Strongly confirmed by most Roman Catholicks, both Europeans and

---

[1] "Ennore, *Ennūr*, Tam. Village just north of Cuttiwaukum backwater...from Madras N. 12 miles...Ennore beacon is a trig. station." *Mad. Man. Admn.* vol. iii. p. 291. *N. and E.* p. 17 for 10th May, 1680, has "The Agent, &c., went to take the air at Enoor."

the Native Christians, who doe in generall reverence this Mountaine, from the bottom to the top of which there are Excellent Stone Staires for the better ascendinge it, whereon there is a Papist Church, and a reverend Fryar or two maintained, whose benefice is none of the Smallest, by the often concourse of people that resort thither, both for pleasantnesse of aire and Satisfaction of takeinge a View of the Saints tombe which is in the Chappel[1].

---

[1] "S. Thomas, formerly called Meliapour, where, according to tradition the Apostle S. Thomas was martyred, is 8 leagues from Sadrispatnam, towards the north, and at a little less distance from Paliacatte. The Portuguese had formerly a flourishing trade there and had made a fine town of it; but the Maures [Moors] took it from them some years ago. A quantity of painted Coromandel cloths, handkerchiefs, stuffs, white cotton cloths were procurable here....The water of the place is so suitable for these manufactures, that a number of good workmen, painters and weavers are always to be found there..." *Schouten*, vol. i. p. 488. See also p. 467 for the legend of the removal of the tree from the harbour by St Thomas.

"The Mores,...having made themselves masters of the town [of St Thomé], rebuilt the fortifications and the walls, which are very good, well built and cemented. They are 12 ft. wide and 28 ft. high, and are constructed of a very strong and smooth stone on which cannon has little effect. The houses are underground, protected from the ravages of time and war, and are not so high as the walls, with the exception of three churches, those of Notre-Dame, the Jesuits, and the Hostel-Dieu...." *Delestre*, p. 173 f.

Fryer, p. 43, writes as follows, "Of St. Thomas. It is a City that formerly for Riches, Pride, and Luxury, was second to none in India; but since, by the mutability of Fortune, it has abated much of its adored Excellencies. The Sea on one side greets its Marble Walls, on the other a Chain of Hills intercepts the Violence of the inflaming Heat; one of which, called St. Thomas his Mount, is famous for his Sepulture, (in Honour of whom a Chappel is dedicated, the Head Priest of which was once the Metropolitan Bishop of India)...Within the Walls seven Churches answer to as many Gates; the Rubbish of whose stupendious Heaps do justify the truth of what is predicated in relation to its pristine State. The Builders of it were the Portugals. The Confounders the Moors, who surprized them wallowing in their Wealth and Wantonness. The present Competitors [in 1673] are the French,...the Moors, and thirdly, the Hollanders."

"Chyna Vincatadry having a House and Garden at St Thomas Mount...which he now offer[s] to the Honble. Company for the use of their Servants, 'tis therefore hereby agreed that the said House be accepted...it being a very Commodious pleasant place for sickly People to Recover their healths at...." Pringle, *Consultations*, 15th Jan. 1685, vol. iv. p. 14. Compare also Alex. Hamilton's *East Indies*, vol. i. p. 356 f.

Att the foot of this mountaine, for some miles in Circuit, I have knowne delicate Groves and Gardens[1], fountains very pleasant to the Eye, (and healthy for the body), the Groves consistinge of Mangoe and Palmero[2], Palmito[3], and Coco nut trees, which are now quite demolished by the forces and Order of the Golcondah Kinge, meerly to doe what diskindnesse they cold to theire Enemies the French, who in the yeare 1672 tooke the Citty St. Thomae from the Moor's forces[4].

---

[1] See Alex. Hamilton's *East Indies*, vol. i. p. 357.

[2] Palmyra. See note on p. 24.

[3] Wild date tree. In the text, the *palmito* is the date-palm in contradistinction to the *palmyra* or toddy-palm.

[4] The contemporary accounts of the taking of St Thomé by the French are various and interesting. Those by *Delestre* and *Fryer*, with Mr Lawrence Sawcer's bitter remarks on Agent Langhorne's policy, are worth quoting. The Frenchman is naturally very full on the subject. "Monsieur de la Haye having somewhat refreshed himself on the coast of Coromandel, continued his journey to St. Thomé, which the Mores [Moors] had occupied for eleven years after having driven out the Portuguese by famine. He anchored before the walls of this town...he sent to request the Governor to furnish him with provisions in return for money; but the More having replied that he had not enough for his own garrison, Monsieur de la Haye sent back the same officers to assure him that he would not go out of the roadstead without having some; and that if they were refused him for money, he would certainly have them by force....The Moorish Governor treated it [the demand] with contempt. This being reported to the General of the French fleet, he had the Council Flag hoisted in order to assemble all the Captains and Officers, who immediately came on board his ship. He unfolded his design to them, showed them that it was easy to surprise this town, which the Dutch had ineffectually and ignominiously besieged for ten years, and pointed out to them what glory they would procure from this expedition. He described the means which he thought ought to be adopted; and, having taken the opinion of the whole assembly, it was resolved that the Master Gunner and his Assistants should that very night place in a long-boat three small pieces of cannon, of three to four pound balls each, with three hundred bullets, and carriages and cartridges in proportion; that they should silently land before dawn, and direct their artillery against the large town-gate, where they would be supported by three hundred men armed with sabres, axes and pistols. Half of these men would divide to scale the walls with rope ladders, which they would bring for that purpose. All this was executed with admirable order; for, hardly had the dawn begun to appear, when the gunners fired three pieces of artillery, at which the Mores, who were not expecting this morning serenade, were so astonished, that they rushed in a crowd towards the town-gate, where they believed

the peril to be the greatest, for they disregarded the heavy fire that the ships' artillery was pouring on the town and its walls. But while they were abandoning the latter, Capt. de Rebré climbed up with five hundred men, whom he commanded, and, sword in hand, made himself master of the walls. He did not give time to the Mores who opposed him to recover themselves, but commanding his soldiers to make a great noise and to shout "kill, kill," he routed them and put it out of their power to rally. Then, taking off his shirt, he divided it into two parts. He fastened one piece to the end of the short pike of a More whom he had killed, and fixed it on the wall nearest the sea to cause the artillery to cease firing. The other he fixed on the landward side to proclaim that he was master of the town, into which the French entered shouting, "Long live the King of France," "Long live the King!" and ended by putting to flight the Mores who carried arms. The inhabitants asked permission to withdraw and to go away with their families. This request Monsieur de la Haye most humanely granted them. Having gone through the town, he gave orders for fortifying it, and for putting it in a position to resist the attacks which he anticipated from the Mores....After this glorious expedition, the brave General de la Haye did not rest satisfied with having chased the Mores four leagues from the town. He made a sortie at the head of 400 men in order to drive them still further away and to hinder them from entrenching themselves so near to St. Thomé, because he rightly anticipated that they would not delay besieging it. Indeed, on the 22nd of Sept. of that year, 1672, they advanced with an army composed of 16000 foot and 4000 horse...six months went by without any considerable action on either side, but Monsieur de la Haye, growing impatient at the length of the siege, made a sortie on the 1st March, 1673, and attacked the enemy at midnight with 600 men. He got possession of their large battery, in which was that great piece of artillery which held 108 lbs. of shot. This he spiked, and afterwards blew it up....General de la Haye made another sortie on the 8th of the same month, and again routed them [the Mores]....There was much firing on both sides, and the action was obstinately contested....From this time forth, the Mores did not attack the French so often; they even wished to live at peace with them; but the Dutch excited them to continue the war, and lent them assistance for that purpose." *Delestre*, pp. 170–173, 177–180, 182.

Fryer's account supplements that of the Frenchman. "[The French] with Ten Sail came before St. Thomas, demanding Victuals of the Moors; but they denying, they brought their Ships to bear upon the Fort, and landing some small Pieces they stormed it, driving the Moors to the search of new dwellings. After they had taken it, they broke up their weather-beaten Vessels, and brought ashore their Ordnance, keeping their Trenches within, and mounting it with the Sea without; they still maintain it maugre all the great Armies the King of Gulconda has sent against it. Till now the 18th Month of its Siege, and the fourth year of their leaving France, the Dutch of Batavia, in revenge of the Inroads the French have made on their Countrey at home, undertaking to waylay them, that no Sustenance might be brought to them by Sea, came against it with 20 Sail, 15 Men of War, great Ships, some of 72 Brass Guns apiece, well mann'd. For all that, the Viceroy, who had been gone out with four Sail, but returning alone, got betwixt them and the Fort with his single Ship in the Night: The Device this: He left his Light upon a Catamaran, so

The Mangoe[1] is a very faire and pleasant fruite; the Palmero[2] tree affordeth that rare liquor formerly termed

---

that they thought him at an Anchor without them, when the next Morn he play'd upon them from under the Fort; This Exploit, and the bruit of our Approach, made them withdraw to the Southward for fresh Recruits of Men and Ammunition. Which gave the French encouragement to sally out upon the Moors (they before being beaten from their Works near the City, had decamped Seven Miles off St. Thomas), and with an handfull of Men pillaged and set fire to their Tents, foraging the Countrey round about, returning loaden with Spoils." *Fryer*, p. 42.

"You may please to take notice that the French were incouradged to take St. Thomay by Sir Wm. [Langhorne] or else they had Never adventured upon it, hee wrott to the vice Roy that the Moores had but 4 Gunns in the Fort and very few men, and as Soone as they heard this, they presently began to fire at the Fort and Since the French possest themselves of St. Thoma Letters have past every day between the Vice Roy and Sir Wm. His first was to Congratulate him in his Victory wherein hee did express a great deale of joy, told him he was his very humble Servant and that in any thinge he was ready to Serve him, whereupon he presently made use of him, Sending Some of his Commanders to him for Cables for his Shipps and all Sort of Cordage, which he Caused our Comanders to Spare him, and what else they had occasion for. He invited the French Comanders to dine with him, where, for their better welcome, fired all the Gunns round the Fort, expressing himselfe how joyfull hee was of Soe good Neighboures. When the king of Gulcondah had Sent an army to besiege and take that place againe, Sir Wm. gave the French the Liberty of this towne to buy up all Sorts of provisions which not only doubled or trebled the price of Provisions but disgust[ed] the Moores. They have sent to him above 20 times to forbid him to send Provisions to the French, But he takes no notice of it, only getts Verena to tell them that he doth not Send them any Supplyes....And yet for all this Sir Wm. hath Continued to Send boates and Masullaes every night Since with provisions which doth very much incense the King against this place, and thus he Not only hazards the Loss of the trade but all the presant treasure that is here, not making any Account of our Lives at all. And all this to assist Such a people that if once they Come to be Setled will Not only prevent your Trade, but will take your Fort too if they can. They begin to Say already that the Fort St. George is too neare them...." Mr Lawrence Sawcer, his information from Fort St George to the Company.. No date, circ. 1673. *Factory Records*, Miscellaneous, No. 3, p. 112 f.

[1] See *Hobson-Jobson*, *s.v.* Mango. Compare *Bernier*, p. 249, "Ambas, or Mangues, are in season during two months in summer, and are plentiful and cheap; but those grown at Dehli are indifferent. The best come from Bengale, Golkonda, and Goa, and these are indeed excellent. I do not know any sweetmeat more agreeable." See also *Fryer*, p. 182.

[2] See note on p. 24.

Plate V

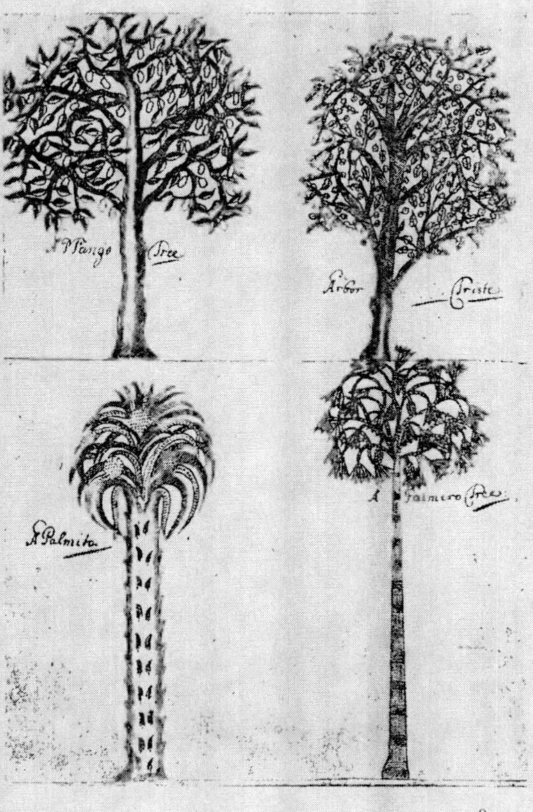

pp. 48, 49.

"MANGO, ARBOR TRISTE, PALMITO, PALMERO TREES."

Palme-Wine, now vulgarly called Toddy[1]. The Palmito[2] is noe more then a rough Sort of wood Especially the Rhine of noe great Use; they beare Some bunches of fruite, very lucious, but noe way pleasant, beinge noe better then wild dates; they afford liquor alsoe that drop from the top of it, vizt. from the younge branches, and is called date Toddy, not soe good as the Other, more lucious, but Soon Eager.

Upon the top of Mount St. Thomas, groweth naturaly a Very remarkable tree, larger then most mulberrie trees be, which is called Arbor triste[3], vizt. the Sorrowfull tree, and not improperly so called. It Seemeth not to flowrish all the day longe, but from Sun Settinge to Sun riseinge it is Exceedinge full of white blossoms, both fragrant and beautifull, but noe Sooner is but broad day light, but all the blossoms fall to the ground and Suddenly wither; and the Very leaves Shut themselves, and Seeme to be in a very languishinge posture, and furthermore, the next

---

1 See *Hobson-Jobson*, *s.v.* Toddy. Compare *Mandelslo*, p. 17, "In this village (Bodick [near Surat]) we found some Terry, which is a Liquor drawn out of the Palm-trees, and drunk of it in Cups made of the leaves of the same Tree. To get out the Juyce, they go up to the top of the Tree, where they make an incision in the bark, and fasten under it an earthen pot, which they leave there all night; in which time it is fill'd with a certain sweet Liquor very pleasant to the taste. They get out some also in the day time, but that corrupts immediately, and is good only for Vinegar, which is all the use they make of it." "Terri, a liquor extracted from palm-trees" *Schouten*, vol. i. p. 406. Toddy (*tārī*) is an intoxicant made from several palm-trees, but chiefly from the *tār* or palmyra tree.

2 See note on p. 46.

3 See *Hobson-Jobson*, *s.v.* Arbol Triste. "The Arbre Triste...resembles the Lime-tree, and it is tall and beautiful. By day it is covered with branches and leaves with closed buds, which, about nine o'clock in the evening, expand, and exhibit white scented flowers, so that the tree appears quite white, and emits such an agreeable odour, that scent and sight are equally charmed. These flowers remain thus all night long, and when day begins to dawn, the buds shut up again, and nothing is seen of them but the outside green." *Schouten*, vol. i. p. 476. "St. Thomas his Mount is famous for...a Tree called *Arbor Tristis*, which withers in the Day, and blossoms in the Night." *Fryer*, p. 43.

Eveninge it appears as flourishinge as before, and thus not Once but every day and night throughout the yeare.

I have Seen many of the like Sort in Other places of India and Persia; but, however, the Portugal Patrees[1], whose dependence is meerly upon telling faire tales to Strangers that come here, will, and have ready to tell you very Strange Constructions upon Such rarities and reliques of the blessed Apostlė, which the Proselytes of India, Especially this Coast, doe much confide in; and they take it as a great favour to be called Christians of St. Thomas[2].

Our Fort (and towne) of St. Georg's hath been often Molested by Some of the Inland Native Forces, raised in very considerable Numbers by some of the disaffected Governours. I have knowne an army of Some thousands both horse and foot, come down and pitch theire tents

---

[1] Portuguese Padres. See *Hobson-Jobson*, *s.v.* Padre, a Christian priest. See also note on p. 41. *N. and E.* p. 13, for 19th March 1680, has "would now be buryed by the French Padrys." And *N. and E.* p. 37, for 28th Oct., shows that the still existing difference between international courtesies, as understood by the English and Continental nations, is an old story:—"It is observed that, whereas at the Dedication of a New Church by the French Padrys and Portuguez in 1675 guns had been fired from the Fort in honour thereof, neither Padry nor Portuguey appeared at the Dedication of our Church nor so much as gave the Governor a visit afterwards to give him joy of it."

[2] In the seventeenth century the martyrdom of St Thomas was made responsible for elephantiasis, nowadays held to be a mosquito-borne infectious disease due to the presence of malignant microbes. It is still common in Madras. "About this Mount [St. Thomas] live a Cast of People, one of whose Legs are as big as an Elephant's; which gives occasion for the divulging it to be a Judgment on them, as the Generation of the Assassins and Murderers of the Blessed Apostle St. Thomas, one of whom I saw at Fort St. George." *Fryer*, p. 43. "The Malabars who are Christians, relate many remarkable traditions about the Apostle St. Thomas, and say that he preached the Gospel in those countries....There are a great number of Malabars, men and women alike, who from their youth, and as others say, from their birth, are subject to swellings in their legs. The enlargement generally begins under the knee, and ends at the foot, or close to it....The Christians of St. Thomas say that this malady has been sent to them as a punishment for the martyrdom of the Saint, and that all who are so afflicted, are descended from his persecutors." *Schouten*, vol. i. pp. 466, 468 f.

within 2 miles of the Walls[1], where they have put a Stopp Upon all Sorts of provisions, and most Chiefely the East India Company's goods, that were to be Sent that Monsoone[2] for England, threateninge what Strange Feats they wold play, if in Case our Agent and Governour Sent them not Soe much moneys, 10 or 20 thousand Pagodes[3], (each Value 9s.), but they are Generally mistaken in the Summ, and be Satisfied with a farre Smaller present, and sometimes with none at all. Nothinge of Such transactions is ordered by the Golcondah Kinge, in whose Countrey this place is, but these are Flyinge Armies hatchinge Rebellion.

Some twenty or twenty two miles to the Northward of Fort St. Georg's, the Dut[c]h have a towne and Garrison called Pullicatt[4], which is nigh hard if not

[1] In 1670, Fort St George "was besieged by a local Naick or Hindoo district officer, but on application to his superior the Nawab of the Carnatic the siege was raised." In 1674, on the refusal of Sir Wm. Langhorne to expel Peter Deltor and 3 other Frenchmen, who were staying at Fort St George, and whose dismissal had been demanded by both Dutch and Mussulmans, a Muhammadan army laid siege to Fort St.George. The Frenchmen were eventually sent to Bījapūr, and peace was restored. See *Mad. Man. Admn.* vol. i. pp. (163) and (165). In a Letter from the Agent and Council at Fort St George, dated 19th July, 1670 (*Factory Records*, Misc. No. 3, p. 83) they write, "Of the late Seige laid to this Towne by Mirzah which Continued near a whole Month, but wee can give you noe Cause that he would ever assigne to bee the Reason, it began with the Alvedore [hawāldār] of St. Thomae and by his Instigation was followed and Continued Soe long by Chene Pella Mirzah." See also *N. and E.* for 31st May, 1674, p. 30.

[2] That is, the North-East Monsoon or winter season.

[3] In his "Currant Coynes of this Kingdome," in the "Golcondah" section, the writer assigns a different value to the pagoda, viz. New Pagod (of Fort St. George) 8*s*., Old Pagod (of Golconda) 12*s*. The text contains a curious comment on Native notions as to the value of English money at this period and on English methods of financial dealings with them.

[4] The following is Schouten's description of Pulicat as he saw it in 1662. "Paliacatte is the principal factory of the Dutch on this [Coromandel] coast. They have a fort here called Gueldres. It is situated in 13½ N. Latitude, in a sandy plain which is barren because its foundation is brackish. Ships anchor at about half a league from the land, in 8 or 9 fathoms on a sandy clayey bottom; but it needs a thorough knowledge of the sandbanks and the inequalities of depth

to get a vessel into safe anchorage. The fort of Gueldres is a fairly good one and capable of resisting the attacks of the Maures [Moors]. It is within a cannon shot of the water. It has four very strong bastions, built of stone as are the walls, all well furnished with cannon. The moat which surrounds it is considerable, but is generally dry. As the foundation is of shifting sand, it has sometimes happened that the currents, which in the rainy season are veritable rapid torrents, have shaken the fort. The Governor resides there, and it is he who is the superintendent of the whole Dutch trade on this coast....In the rainy monsoon it often happens that the low ground behind the fort is covered with water, but the inundation does not last long. The water quickly flows into the sea, and it is only the little rivers which always remain swollen, and in which, on account of the sand which accumulates and blocks them, deep channels are formed. The Maures and the Gentues tow their flat boats over these in order to secure them from the violence of the sea until the favorable monsoon arrives. The town is open. The houses are somewhat low and confined. Those inhabited by Maures and Gentives are situated on the South of the fort of Gueldres. There are other villages around which are also under the jurisdiction of the Dutch. About 6 or 7 leagues inland there is a high mountain. The water which flows from it in the rainy season helps considerably to inundate the lowlands which surround it." *Schouten*, vol. i. p. 489 f. When Hamilton visited Pulicat about thirty years later, the place had greatly declined in importance,—"Policat is the next Place of Note to the City and Colony of Fort St. George, and, as I observed before, is a Town belonging to the Dutch. It is strengthned with two Forts, one contains a few Dutch Soldiers for a Garrison, the other is commanded by an Officer belonging to the Mogul. The Country affords the same Commodities that Fort St. George doth; and the People are employed mostly in knitting Cotton Stockings, which they export for the Use of all the European Factories in India." Alex. Hamilton's *East Indies*, vol. i. p. 369.

"Senr. Coleer" succeeded "Governour Pavillion" at "Pullicat" in 1676. *Vide Diary of Streynsham Master*, 17th Aug. 1676, p. 42 f. Thevenot, who visited Pulicat in 1667, apparently found it as flourishing as when described by the Dutch traveller. "Poliacate is to the North of St. Thomas, and the Factory (which the Dutch have established there) is one of the best they have in the Indies, by reason of the Cotton-cloaths, of which they have great Ware-houses full there. At Poliacate they refine the Salt-Petre which they bring from Bengala, and make the Gun-powder, with which they furnish their other Factories;" *Thevenot*, part iii. p. 105.

"Poolicat (*paliyāghāt*, Hind.; *pazhavērkkādu*, Tam. pulicat)... (*pazha vēl kādu*, old acacja forest)...from Madras N. 24 miles. On Coromandel coast at southern extremity of an island in the inlet between the sea and lake of the same name....Off the coast are the Poolicat shoals. The Dutch erected a factory here in 1609. This was their earliest settlement in southern India. They built a fort and called it Geldria...Fort, factory and dependencies taken from the Dutch 2nd July 1781. Finally surrendered to Great Britain in 1825.... There is an old Dutch cemetery. Poolicat lake...is under the influence of the tide. The water is constantly changed, yet brackish." *Mad. Man. Admn.* vol. iii. p. 671, *s.v.* Pazha. See also *Ind. Ant.* vol. xxx. p. 355 f. for various forms of the word Pulicat. By *zh* the compilers of the *Mad. Man. Admn.* meant a peculiar cerebral form of *l*.

altogeather as bigge as our Fort, but our outworks doe much Exceede theirs, but againe theirs is a more safe and Commodious place for ladeinge and dischargeinge Goods, haveinge a Very good River that cometh close to the towne Side, but the barre is not very good, noe better then for boats of 20, 30, or 40 tunns, all this Coast indeed wantinge nothinge but Some good harbours for Shippinge.

Armagon, Some 20 miles Northward of Pullicat, was Once the Residence of an English Governour and his Councell, but was many years agoe broke off, the English Company findinge that Fort St. Georges cold well Supply them with the Commodities of this Coast[1].

Soe that the Next English Factorie wee have is Pettipolee[2], a Very pleasant and healthy place, and very

---

1 "In 1625 the English obtained a piece of ground at Armaghaum, about forty miles to the north of Pulicat, and made it a subordinate station to Masulipatam...three years afterwards they were all compelled to retire from Masulipatam to Armaghaum in consequence of the oppression of the Native Governor. Subsequently some of them returned to Masulipatam, but still the oppressions and embarrassments went on...Accordingly Mr. Francis Day, member of the Council at Masulipatam, was dispatched to examine the country in the neighbourhood of the Portuguese settlement at St. Thomé. Mr. Day met with unexpected success....The Naick of the district promoted his views to the utmost, and procured for him a grant of land, with permission to build a fort, from the Rajah of Chandragheri...The territory granted extended five miles along the shore and one inland. Thus was formed the first establishment in Madraspatnam in 1639..." Wheeler's *Madras in the Olden Time*, p. 19 f. See also note on p. 25.

2 Pettipolee (Peddapalle), later on known as Nizampatam, was one of the first places on the Coromandel Coast at which the English made a settlement. The *Globe* anchored here in 1612, and the merchants in Captain Anthony Hippon's ship met with a good reception and were allowed to trade. According to the *Mad. Man. Admn.* (vol. iii. p. 593) a factory was established at Pettipoly in 1621; dissolved, 1653; resettled, 1697. It was however existing in 1663, for on the 16th Dec. of that year the Court wrote to Fort St George (*Letter Book*, No. 3, p. 336) directing that due respect should be shown to Mr Nicholas Buckridg, should he decide to visit the Factories of "Mesulapatam, Verashroon and Pettipoly." In the Commission to Buckridg of the same date (p. 349) he was ordered to "Consult with our Agent &c. about deserting Pettipoly Factory." In Jan. 1665, the Agent &c. at Fort St George wrote to the Court explaining their reasons for wishing to retain a settlement at

Pettipolee (*Factory Records*, Misc. No. 3, para. 24, p. 11), "Pettypolee is noe otherwayes made use off then for the provision of Salt peter, which if we doe not encourage, the Dutch will quickly snatch it from us, they having after many years absence renewed their Factory in that place." In 1672, as "T.B." tells us, the factory was in full existence with Ambrose Salisbury as chief; but two years later, in a "Generall" from Fort St George to the Court, dated 20th Nov. 1674, (*O.C.* No. 4044, p. 12) it is stated, "The Factories of Verasheroon and Pettipolee are both laid down and of no further charge, Metchlepatam is the place for business." On the 5th May, 1678, John Tivill reported of the Factory at Pettipolee that it was so decayed as not to be worth repairing. Yet the Company's servants at Fort St George seemed loth to abandon the place as a trading centre. They valued it as "a great Place for Sault and Large in compass...lying commodiously for the Investment of the fine Cloth, Ramalls and Allejaes yearly procured in these Parts, besides a quantity of Salt Peter upon occasion" (Fort St George to Masulipatam, 3rd June, 1678, *Factory Records*, Masulipatam, No. 10). No chief was appointed at Pettipolee after Salisbury's death, in 1676; and, in Dec. 1678, the Council at Fort St George decided to leave the question of continuing a settlement there to "the Honble. Company" (*Factory Records*, Masulipatam, No. 10, p. 103). On the 20th March, 1679, Streynsham Master visited Pettipolee, and thus describes it, (*Memoriall of Streynsham Master* quoted by Mackenzie in his *Manual of the Kistna District*, p. 130)—"About midnight we sett out of Yentapollam a Gentue league and halfe from which lyes Baupautla which we went through, and tis a league and a half further to Pettepollee, about two miles short of Pettepollee we ferryd over a branch of the River Kishna that runs into the sea near Pettepollee which was very muddy and troublesome for our Horses, our Pallankeens and men were ferryd over by gun boates, at the other side of this River Mr. Hatton met us with Mr. Wynne, Mr. Colborne and Mr. Scattergood, about 10 o'clock we arrived at the Factory house at Pettepolee which is a very sorry rotten ruinous timber building much of it being fallen, and that which stands being ready to follow ye same fate, in the afternoon we walked about the Town and visited the old Factory, which hath been a large building, but all of Timber and much of it fallen down, the flagg stafe a very high one still standing and the principal lodgings, it stands between the English house and the River, by the River side, there is a new choultry railed in and a key of Timber made into the River, built and prepared in December last for the King of Gulcondah's reception, but he did not come to this town, the same place is now used for the Custom House, the River is deep and severall vessells of 50: to 80: or 100 tons were in it and haled ashore on the towne side by it, the other side of ye River is muddy and there is an Island about two mile over between the River and the Sea, upon which Island is a large tope of Trees which is called the English Garden, and 'tis owned to belong to the English, the town is much decayed many houses being empty ruined and forsaken, the proper name of the Town which we call Pettepolee is Nyshampatnam, being soe called by all the Country people....The Saysummitt-Tahadar and the Catwall of the Town came to visit the Agent...they very much importuned that a Factory might be settled here againe promising all friendly assistance to our business, to which was answered...the Agent would take it into consideration. [March, 1679.]" After years of indecision, definite orders were received from Court, dated Oct. 1686 and Jan. 1687, and

well populated by the Gentues, of whom many are very Wealthy. It lyeth to the Southward of Point Due[1], in a Sandy bay called Pettipolee bay. The English and Dutch have each of them a Factory in the towne, but very few Factors reside here, not above 2 or 3 who provide goods accordinge to Order from the Governour of Fort St. Georg's or Chiefe of Metchlipatam.

Very Considerable quantities of these followinge Commodities are here wrought and Sold to Foraign Merchants vizt. Longecloth, Murrees, Salampores, Lungees[2], Painted

---

repeated in Jan. 1688, commanding the abandoning of Pettipolee as a factory. The order was carried out, and in 1687 all the factories subordinate to Fort St George were withdrawn. The further history of Pettipolee is as follows. In 1697 it was resettled, was in existence in 1702; in 1753 ceded to the French having been abandoned by the English in the interval; in 1759 ceded back to the British, and confirmed to them in 1765.

[1] "In the morning [23rd March, 1679] we went downe to the River about 2 miles from Collepelle where was two great Metchlepatam Boates, and two Sangaries or Gun boates which sett us over upon the island of Dio." *Streynsham Master's Memoriall*, in Mackenzie, *Kistna District*, p. 131. "Fire-wood from the Islands of Diu, a low Point of Land that lies near Matchulipatam." Alex. Hamilton, *East Indies*, vol. i. p. 368. Point Divy, at the mouth of the Kistna river, is on the Western side of the Bay of Masulipatam.

[2] "Long-cloth. The usual name in India for (white) cotton shirtings, or Lancashire calico; but first applied to the Indian cloth of like kind exported to England,...Or it is just possible that it may have been a corruption or misapprehension of *lungī*." *Hobson-Jobson*, p. 518 a. "Take into your considerations what Callicoes you are able to acquire either at the Fort St. George, Mesulapatam, Verasheroone or else where in Long Cloath Sallampores Moorees or Parcallaes." 14th Dec. 1655, *Letter Book*, No. 1. "Sallampores Longcloths and Morees [from Masulipatam] are exceeding badd." 10th Nov. 1661, *Letter Book*, No. 3, p. 67. "Wee desire that all our Long Cloth may hold out 38 and 40 Yards in Length, and our Sallampores 18 and 20 Yards and none under if possible." 16th Dec. 1663, *Letter Book*, No. 3, p. 346.

"Moory (*mūri*, Tel.) Blue cloth; principally manufactured in Nellore district." *Mad. Man. Admn.* "Ordinary Long Cloth Strong and Substantiall and close Struck, Brown Long Cloth thick and full lengths and breadths, Ordinary Long Cloth without any Stiffening, Fine Long Cloth, blew Long Cloth cut in halves dyed out of the browne, Ordinary Sallampores white Substantiall thick Cloth, fine Sallampores, Ordinary Moores full ell wide, fine Moores, superfine Moores" in list of goods to be provided at Fort St George, 13th Dec. 1672, *Letter Book*, No. 5, p. 23. "Procure...tenn Bales of redd Maurees fit for that [the Bantam]

Callicos of divers Sorts, Salt peeter, Iron, Steele, which is brought downe from the high land Over this place which is called Montapolee[1].

Great Abundance of White salt is made in the Vallies of Pettipolee, with very little industry, onely fencinge in the lowest of Soile which is soe brackish that the Sun doth cause the water which lyeth there not ab[o]ve one foot deep to harden into a perfect good and cleare Salt. It is afterwards laid in great heaps, and vended all the Kingdome over. Noe Merchant is admitted to deale in this Commoditie, beinge the Kings Commoditie as is bees Wax alsoe[2].

Markett." 28th July, 1675, *Factory Records*, Masulipatam, No. 10. "Course Morees...not vendible here." Letter from Court, 15th Dec. 1676, *Letter Book*, No 5.

Salampores, chintz. "Wee approve of your accepting more of the fine Sallampores and Bettelees then wee ordered." Letter to Fort St George, dated 12th Dec. 1677, *Letter Book*, No. 5, p. 497. Salampore "(from *sale*, Tel., weaver and *pura*, San., town, weaver's town) a kind of cotton cloth formerly manufactured at Nellore." *Mad. Man. Admn.* vol. iii. p. 799, *s.v.* Sauley.

Lungees, scarves or loin-cloths. In Burma it is now a woman's petticoat, as well as a man's dress. In the Army it means a turban: "50 Blue Lungis a/c Rs. 2–4–0 each: Rs. 112–8–0"—in a bill of the Port Blair Military Police for 30th Sept. 1900. See *Hobson-Jobson*, *s.v.* Loonghee, and *Mad. Man. Admn. s.v.* Lag.

1 "When you leave Maabar and go about 1000 miles in a Northerly direction you come to the kingdom of Muftili;" *Marco Polo*, ii. p. 295, identified by Yule as Mōtupalle (p. 297).

"On the coast is Mōtupalle, now an insignificant fishing village, but identified as the port where Marco Polo landed in A.D. 1290. It was much used as a landing place for stores for the French troops at Guntūr a hundred years ago." Mackenzie, *Kistna District*, p. 206.

"Large ships lie about a mile from the shore, with Mootapilly pagoda bearing N.W. by N." Milburn, *Oriental Commerce*, vol. ii. p. 85.

"From Montepoly to Petapoly the course is E.N.E. 6½ leagues." Dunn's *Directory*, p. 147.

"Mootapilly or Motupalli, in lat. 15° 42′ N., lon. 80° 17′ E. and about 8 leagues to the N.N.E. of Gondegam, is a small village half a mile inland, not discernible from a ship; but with the assistance of a glass, a small pagoda is perceptible. There are about twenty detached palmyra-trees to the northward of the landing-place, and about a mile to the southward, a thick grove of trees with a clump on its southern part higher than the rest." Horsburgh, *India Directory*, ed. 1855, vol. i. p. 596.

2 Compare the *Diary of Streynsham Master*, p. 57, under date

I have heard it by Severall Eminent persons affirmed that this very Commoditie Salt draweth into the King's Exchequer two millions of Old Pagodos[1] yearly.

This place alsoe hath the benefit of a pleasant River, such another as Pullicat hath, the barre but indifferent, which is a vaste hinderance to this part of the Countrey that doth afford, and is replenished with Such quantities of the beforementioned goods, which are proper for Sale all India and the South Seas Over as well as to be transported into Europe by the Christians.

Anno Domini 1672 I stroke downe to Pettipolee in a Journey I tooke Overland From St. Georg's to Metchlipatam, where I visited and paid my respects to Mr. Ambrose Salsbury[2], at his new house he built in a pleasant

8th Sept. 1676, on his journey from Balasor to Hugli. "This day wee...sailed up the river Ganges, on the east side of which most part of the great quantity of beeswax is made, which is the Kings comodity, and none suffered to deale therein but for his account and Swarmes of Bees flew over our Vessell, alsoe we passed by great numbers of salt pitts, and places to boile salt, which is alsoe appropriated to the King or great Mogull, and none suffered to be made but for his account."

[1] See later on where the value of an "Old Pagodo" is given as 12*s*.

[2] From the MS. Records at the India Office (*Court Books*, *Factory Records*, *Letter Books*, &c.) a fairly connected account of this interesting personage has been obtained. Ambrose Salisbury (the name is variously given as Salsbury, Saulsbury, Sallisbury and Salisbury) was appointed by the Court as Second in the Factory at Pettipollee, at a salary of £20 per annum, in Feb. 1658. He sailed in the *Persian Merchant*, was wrecked off the Maldives, and did not reach Fort St George until June, 1659. In Oct. 1662 he became "Chief" at Pettipolee, where he remained till his death, in Dec. 1675. Sir Edward Winter, the turbulent Governor of Fort St George, accused Salisbury of embezzling the Company's money, and wrote to the Court that he had discharged him. The dismissal, however, did not take effect. Others there were besides the Governor who had no opinion of Salisbury. In April, 1668, an unsigned letter from Fort St George to the Directors contains the remark—"Truly your Factory at Pettipolee is rather a charge than a benefitt to you (being managed by a very debauch't Idle fellow one Salisbury) not furnishing from thence a piece of Cloth towards your returnes this yeare...they are all greate abusers of the Company in words and deedes especially Salisbury at Pettipolee—that miscreant." In 1669 Mr Richard Smithson complained of irregularities in Salisbury's books and of his extravagant expenses. But before these complaints reached England, the Court had written to Fort St George (in Dec.

part of the towne, he beinge Chiefe of the Affaires of the Honourable English East India Companie here. He treated me and my people very Gentilely, and wold not Suffer me to depart that night. I condescended to Stay all night and take my leave Early in the Morneinge, but he was as loth to part with me then; I Staid to take a View of the towne and after dinner set forward.

All Sorts of Provisions are here to be had in very great Plenty, and at very Reasonable rates, vizt. Cows, Buffaloes, hoggs, all Sorts of Poultry, Severall Sorts of wild fowle, Many Excellent Sorts of Sea and River Fish,

---

1669) ordering the Agent to send immediately for Mr Ambrose Salisbury, "whome wee have discharged our Service, being represented to be a person of very prophane Spiritts, scandalous in his behaviour and notoriously wicked." Meanwhile, Salisbury's friends had exerted themselves in his defence, and the result of their letter to Court in 1670, remarking "Wee have neither had any Sattisfaction, either by particular information or by Common Report that Mr. Robert Fleetwood or Mr. Ambrose Salisbury are persons of Such profane Spirrits Scandalous lives, or notoriously wicked as they are represented to you, unless their Zeale for Conformity and against nonconformity are made the ground of that accusation," was an order for the re-instatement of Salisbury. "We doe also order that Mr. Ambrose Salisbury be againe admitted into our Service and that he receive such incoragement as his abiilityes and faithfulness in our Service shall merritt." For the next few years Salisbury remained in favour, his chief trouble being with "pittifull Merchants the Salt Peeter Men." In 1675, however, he was again in ill odour with the Council at Fort St George and was accused of being implicated with Richard Mohun in unlawful private trade. Salisbury retorted that too much was expected of him in the way of investment, and that he had expended money in repairs to the factory and journeys to Masulipatam, "there being noe person in the Honble. Companys servis but hath allowance only my selfe." His letters to Fort St George and Masulipatam became petulant and querulous. Mr William Puckle, the Company's Supervisor, who was at Masulipatam in Sept. 1675, wrote, "Here is also a letter from Mr. Salusbury a most pitifull Impertinent piece of morrallitie, that doth dayly follow us with letters that we understand not, and therefore lesse concern to answer them." The now unpopular Chief at Pettipolee was in failing health, and declared himself unable to take the journey to Masulipatam to vindicate his conduct. He repaired to the adjoining settlement at Madapollam, the usual sanatorium, and died there, in Mr Mohun's house, on or about the 31st Dec. 1675. He left many debts and but little personal property. Nevertheless, five years were occupied in the settlement of his affairs, which were administered by his mother, Susannah Salisbury, in England.

but most Especially Venison, as Deere, hares, Wild hoggs, or that most Nimble Annimall the Antilope.

All these Varieties before mentioned are brought to the Christian Factories, Namely the English and Dutch, and Sold by Some Mahometans that live about and in this towne, Rice, butter, Oyle, Fruit, &c., are Sold by the Gentues, and as Cheape here as in any place upon this Coast. Theire Weights and Measures be the Same with those of Metchlipatam, of which in Order, as alsoe the Coines the Same, that are Currant there.

The Antilope is a very comely Annimall, very Slick and Smooth, of a browne Colour, neater in Shape then any Deere, very Slender leggs, the body bespotted with round or Ovall Spots of white in many places, as some deere be, but the horns of this Creature differ quite from those of any Other, beinge in length from two foot to 3½, pointinge backwards, of Colour very black, And wreathinge as though they were Artificially turned. The figure of whose head and neck is as followeth[1]. [Plate X.]

Dureinge my Short abode in this towne, (reports beinge Spread amonge the Inhabitants that an English man a Stranger travailinge the Countrey was here) they brought to the Factory gate Severall twiggen baskets, bore Upon mens Sholders. Theire request was to let their Snakes dance for me and my people to behold, in hopes of Something of a gratuitie, Such things beinge the livelyhood of many in these countreys. For Curiosities Sake

---

[1] Compare *Fryer*, p. 45—"In the way hither are store of Antilopes, not to be taken but by a Decoy made of Green Boughs, wherein a Man hides himself, and walking with this Bush upon his Back, gains so near on them, while grazing or browzing rather on Shrubs or Bushes, as to hit one with an Arrow, when it may be run down with Dogs, the rest of the Herd shunning it: They are of a delicater shape and make than a Deer, their horns not jagged, but turned as an Unicorn's; nor spread into Branches, but straight, and long, and tapering, rooted on the *Os frontis*, springing up on both sides."

wee bad them Use theire owne pleasure, with which they opened the baskets Singly, 4 or 5 in number. Out of each came very hideous and large Snakes, 3 or 4 men attendinge with Stringed Musical instruments, whereof one, beinge the Chiefe over the rest, took his Stringed Instrument and played to the Serpents, which to my thinkinge, made Straight at him as though they wold have destroyed him; but the Musicianer, or rather Magician, soon corrected them Onely with Some Verbal punishment, and, like a Secound Orpheus, Sat downe upon the bare ground and played, at which musick these great and Venemous Serpents danced much after the Same tunes, to my astonishment, without doeinge the least hurt to theire keepers, who all Sat very neare them, and when wee Seemed to be Satisfied with the Sight thereof, they put them into the baskets againe[1]. They have a very deformed broad head, and are accompted the most poysonous of all Others, for where they Stinge or bite any liveinge creature, it is sudden death.

In soe much that I have been credibly informed that the Emperors and Kings of Asia have often put to death many of their criminal Subjects with these Sorts of Snakes, nay, of the Very Same that are thus carried about the Countreys for Shews. But these, theire keepers have soe enchanted them, that they have taken away theire power of harmeinge them. To me it Seemed most Strange, as beinge the first of my beholdinge any Such Sorceries, but Since have Seen many more Incredible.

Metchlipatam, Soe called from the Hindostan ore Moors

---

[1] Compare *Fryer*, p. 34 f. "Reptiles, Snakes, Serpents, and Amphisbena and other kinds; all which they pretend to charm, carrying them up and down in baskets to get Money of the People, as well as Strangers; when they strike up on a Reed run through a Cocoa-Shell, which makes a noise something like our Bag-Pipes, and the subtle Creatures will listen to the Musick, and observe a Motion correspondent to the Tune; a Generation of Vipers that well deserve to be stiled so, knowing when the Charmer charms wisely."

Plate VI

"DANCEINGE SNAKES."

p. 60.

Languadge, word Metchli signifieinge fish, and patam or Patanam a towne[1], first given to it by reason of the Abundance of fish caught here for the Supply of many countrey[2] Cities and inland towns, for the which it Still doth retaine the Said name, but of late years much increased by Merchandize, soe that the fishinge trade is Very inconsiderable, and not at all followed, more then by the poore Mallabars or Gentues, whoe doe as yet in great plenty Supply this place and all the Ships that frequent the Roade.

It is now without all dispute the most Eminent place of trade Upon the Choromandel Coast, Very populous and hath a Commodious Scituation, which causeth many Christians to resort and Settle here. The English and Dutch have each of them a Stately Factory in the heart of the towne[3], haveinge Obtained Very large priviledge

---

[1] The word Metchli is for Hindostani *machhlī*. This old and persistent derivation is not now accepted. See *Hobson-Jobson*, *s.v.* Masulipatam. The name of this place has, in Indo-European history, been one of the most widely corrupted of all. See *Ind. Ant.*, vol. xxx. pp. 354 and 397 f., for many variations.

[2] See *Hobson-Jobson*, *s.v.* Country. It means "Indian" as opposed to "European." *N. and E.* p. 38, for 21st Nov. 1680, has "some Country ships being cast away." Compare also *O. C.* No. 4581, 24th Feb. 1679, "Wee doe not...aprove of spareing Pilotts to navigate the Countrey ships."

[3] Compare Schouten's description of Masulipatam—"Masulipatam is a celebrated town situated in 16½ degrees North Latitude. It is under the rule of the King of Golconda or the Maures [Moors], as well as Petapouli and other places which are near it. The English, the Dutch and the Danes have had factories there for a long time. It is built on the sea shore, on a gulf, and further watered by a shallow river during the dry season...There are a quantity of crocodiles, and abundance of fish. Vessels are compelled to anchor, at least half a league from the shore, because of the banks of clay at the depth of 3 or 4 fathoms....The town is fairly large. The buildings are very close together. It is flourishing on account of the trade carried on there. The greater part of the inhabitants are Maures. There are also rich Persians and a large number of Gentives, who are in less esteem. Vessels of both Christians and Maures constantly frequent its harbour. Many foreign merchants from the countries of Aracan, Pegu, Bengal, Malaca, Surat and Persia are to be seen there." *Schouten*, vol. i. p. 491.

Of the Dutch Factory at Masulipatam, Streynsham Master wrote, under date 8th Jan. 1677, "Their Factory is very large, and they have bought and are still a buying in the houses adjacent to them, which they levill the better to preserve themselves from fire, and it is thought

from the Golcondah Kinge, more Especially the English, payinge not above one halfe the Customes the Other doth, but each Factory weareth the Colours of theire owne Nation.

This towne is famous alsoe for a bridge that was built at the Charge of one [of] the Kings of Golcondah, who in his Progresse, found the way out of the Countrey into the towne, for a great Space surroundinge it, very difficult through the deep mudde and water, which was no little hinderance to the Merchants, as well as to poore people for the bringeinge in of goods and Provisions &c., which bridge reacheth from the great gate of Metchlipatam over

---

to make their Factory defensible, they had ten or twelve souldiers a gaurd at the doors who fired three volleyes and some Chambers or ordinance at our goeing and comeing." *Diary of Streynsham Master*, p. 306.

For the early history of Masulipatam, after the *Globe* anchored there in 1611, see Mackenzie, *Kistna District*, pp. 88–99. In 1669 (*Letter Book*, No. 4) the Court gave permission to enlarge the Company's house at Masulipatam, at a cost not exceeding 2000 rs., but the building was to be delayed until a renewal of the *farmān* was obtained. In 1687 the factory was temporarily withdrawn. Three years later it was re-established. Hamilton visited the place in its period of decay—"Matchulipatam lies in the Way along the Sea-coast....In the latter part of the last Century this Town was one of the most flourishing in all India, and the English Company found it to be the most profitable Factory that they had. They had a large Factory built of Teak Timber; but now there are no English there, tho' the Dutch continue their Factory still, and keep about a Dozen of Hollanders there to carry on the Chint Trade...The Town is but small, built on a little Island, and is much stronger by Nature than Art." Alex. Hamilton, *East Indies*, vol. i. p. 370. Tavernier's description is somewhat different,—"Maslipatam is a great City, the houses whereof are only of Wood, built at a distance from one another. The place it self, which stands by the Sea, is famous for nothing but the Road for Ships which belongs to it, which is the best in the Gulf of Bengala." *Tavernier*, vol. i. part ii. p. 70. Thevenot's account also varies from the others,—"Though the Town [Masulipatam] be but small, yet it is well Peopled; the Streets are narrow, and it is intollerably hot there from March till July. The Houses are all separated one from another, and the Water is brackish, because of the tides that come up to it; there is great Trading there in Chites, because, besides those that are made there, a great many are brought from St. Thomas, which are much finer, and of better Colours than those of the other parts of the Indies." *Thevenot*, part iii. p. 104 f. For a good contemporary account of "Mechlapatam" compare *Fryer*, p. 26 f. Masulipatam was taken by the French in 1750, retaken in 1759, and confirmed to the English in 1765.

to Guddorah[1], which is one English mile in length and of a Considerable breadth, and is called by the Name of Guddorah bridge.

Both these towns have very Stately dwellinge houses in them of brick and Stone[2], but the Streets are very narrow Especially those of Metchlipatam.

Theire houses are very Spacious to behold at Some Small distance, but the houses beinge of 4, 5, or 6 Stories high, and the Streets Soe narrow is at Some Seasons of the yeare Very inconvenient beinge Excessive hot, neither are they well Contrived, but indeed they are wholy after the Mahometan Custome, a large Fabrick containing many Small rooms very ill furnished, and few or noe lights to the Streetward, or any way whereby they may behold any people that pass by, which is Ordered soe meerely

---

[1] Practically part of the town of Masulipatam. The place appears as Gundore in 1670, and Fryer has the same spelling :—"Mahomed Beague to be welcomed at Gundore 1 Gentu League out of towne." 27th July, 1670, *Factory Records*, Masulipatam, No. 1. "Sir William Langham...is Superintendent over all the Factories on the Coast of Coromandel,...Viz....Gundore" *Fryer*, p. 38. Streynsham Master refers to two bridges at Masulipatam in 1677,—"The Towne of Metchlepatam stands about halfe a mile from the sea a small Creick with a barr to it going up to it, and every spring tide the water over flowes round about the towne soe that there is noe goeing out but upon two wooden bridges, and when it raines there is a noisome smell in the Towne." *Diary of Streynsham Master*, under date 11th Jan. 1677. In his second journey, Streynsham Master again refers to the place, "Aga Telloll the Governor of Metchlepatam having been toward Narsapore and those places under his Government returned to Goodera last night....This evening we went to the English garden which is about two miles out of town over the long bridge, the water overflowing round the Towne now at spring tides. 2nd April, 1679." *Memoriall of Streynsham Master* quoted by Mackenzie, *Kistna District*, p. 137. The two bridges, mentioned in 1677, are described by Fryer as follows: "On the North-East a Wooden Bridge, half a Mile long, leading to the Bar Town ; on the North-West one, a Mile Long, tending to the English Garden, and up the Country. Each of which have a Gate-house, and a strong Watch at the beginning, next the Town : Both these are laid over a Sandy Marsh, where Droves of People are always thronging." *Fryer*, p. 27. The writer is evidently referring to the bridge on the North-West. Streynsham Master (*Memoriall*, 7th April, 1679, p. 141 of *Kistna District*) says that both bridges were "made by Meir Abdulla Baker lately dead."

[2] All the other contemporary accounts of Masulipatam describe the houses as being built of wood. See above note 3 to p. 61.

out of a Jealosie they harbour of theire Women, and are therefore Strangely Confined, Seldome or never after growne Up to 10 or 11 years of age that they are Soe happy soe much as to get the Sight of Any man Save theire Master.

Those of any Considerable Estates keep Eunuchs to attend (or rather guard) theire Wifes and Concubines, and Some Women Servants, or little boys and girles to attend and doe what Necessary for them, they of themselves not admitted to doe any thinge of houshold businesse or to Exercise themselves in any affaire whatsoever, save to honour and respect theire Master, or nurse theire owne Children.

The French had a Factory in this place not many years agoe[1], but Since those troubles of St. Thomae[2],

[1] The French Factory at Masulipatam was founded in 1669. "Last night came to this Towne 6 French Men from Golchondah, they at present lodge in the house where Mr. Jearsey formerly lived. This Day they viewed the House that was the Danes Factory, but rejected it as not having sufficient accommodation, (it was new built this yeare by the Owner, and is much better then it was when Mr. Sambrooke was here.) They have since treated about a stately House built but 2 years since by the Shabander. They have not as yet given or received any visit. Only the Second called at Goodrah to acquaint this Governour of their being come." Letter from Mr Smithson at Masulipatam to Fort St George, 28th Aug. 1669. *O. C.*, No. 3330. The French took the "stately house" and also "3 other houses which lye between that and the River" at 30 Pagodas a month. *O. C.*, No. 3337. In 1670 John Vickers at Hugli wrote to Richd. Edwards at Kasimbazar, *O. C.*, No. 3414, "The French at Masulipatam are together by the ears, the Chief and Second fighting a duel in the garden." In 1674, after the retaking of St. Thomé, the French left Masulipatam,—"The French at Metchlepatam upon a difference with the Moores have deserted it, taken a small sloope and come hither, [Balasor] the Chiefe slaine the day before." *Factory Records*, Hugli, No. 4, May 14th, 1674. Mackenzie, *Kistna District*, p. 99, *f. n.*, says, "There is no mention in these old records of the French factory, [but see above] except that in May, 1674, the Dutch picked a quarrel with the Government at Fort St. George for giving asylum to 'Monsieur Peter Deltor, second for affairs of the Royal Company of France at Mechipatam.' In 1693 a small square was built for the French factory, which is still known as Frenchpettah, and having been restored to France after the peace of 1814, still remains (1882) French territory. It is a space of some 71 acres and includes two bungalows, a chapel and some other buildings."

[2] The writer is here speaking as a contemporary witness. See p. 46 and note.

A Citty 3 English miles Southward of Fort St. Georg's, they, beinge Ambitious of honour and Conquest in these Easterne parts of the World, tooke that Citty from a Small handfull of Moors, the Citty beinge weakely guarded not Suspectinge any warre[1].

Monsieur Delahay the French Viceroy (as they called him) arrived in India with a fine Squadron of the French King's Men of warre[2], Upon a designe of purchaseinge great trafficke in East India by Compulsion, but was shrewdly Mistaken in the End. They tooke St. Thomae with much Ease, and kept it but 3 years and with much trouble, and losse of his whole Squadron and above 3000 men, beinge destitute of all Succour both from home and from any part of India, but continually beseiged and perplexed by the Golcondah forces by land, and the Dutch by Sea[3], in soe much that the Ships the Dutch tooke not from them, they were forced to hall them On Shore as neare the Walls of the Citty as they cold and theire pull them in pieces for the Sake of theire Stores.

Soe that in fine, they were forced to Surrender up

---

[1] See note on p. 46.

[2] Compare *Fryer*, p. 41, "Lewis the XIVth...put in a Stock with his Merchant Adventurers, fitting out a Fleet of Twenty Sail of lusty Ships, to settle a Trade in India, committing them to the Charge and Conduct of a Viceroy; who coming late about the Cape, touched at St Lawrence, where they did but little besides burying their Viceroy, and dispatching four Ships into Europe. In the stead of the Viceroy deceased, the now reigning succeeded. From thence they sailed to Surat...With fourteen Sail of Ships they roved on the Coasts of Malabar, and at last came to the Island Ceilon...From whence they passed along the Coast of Coromandel, and with Ten Sail came before St. Thomas...now [1673] they are 600 strong in the Fort and Ships, all stout Fellows, every Soldier fit to be a Commander." According to Delestre, when the French fleet anchored in Surat Road, in October, 1671, it was composed of eight ships of war under Monsieur de la Haye. The fleet sailed from Surat on the 9th Jan. 1672. *Delestre*, pp. 34 and 59.

[3] "The Dutch and Moores Lyinge still before St. Thoma with 3 shipps of the former still in the roade, who expect other 3." Letter from Fort St George to the Court, 22nd Nov. 1673, *Factory Records*, Misc. No. 3.

the place, but yet Upon very Honourable terms, vizt. They marched out with bagge and baggadge, theire owne Colours flyinge, trumpets Soundinge, Straight from the Shore, On board of 2 men of warre of Considerable force, which the Dutch contracted to give them, well fitted with what Necessarie for theire returne to France, as alsoe a passaport for theire Safe Conduct. All this the Dutch (although Conquerours) did to be ridde of Such troublesome Neighbours[1].

---

[1] Compare the account of the evacuation of St Thomé by the French, given in the "Generall" from Fort St George to the Court, dated 13th and 16th Sept. and 1st Oct. 1674, "Monsr. De la Hay embarqued just now and resolves to sett sayle within few houres. The Dutch pretend to send three shipps along with them so far as Ceyloan there to deliver unto him about 100 French prisoners which will make him up somewhat above 600 men, besides about 60 others bound for Surrat with Monsr. Baron, from Ceyloan they pretend that other shipps of theirs shall see him cleare of the Maldives in order to his proceedinge directly for Europe according to capittulations made the 26 of last month [Aug. 1674]. The Dutch have possession of St. Thoma for the present, but beside their own flag sett up to seaward, they have also sett up that of the King of Gulconda to Landward, to whom it is not unlikely but they may soone after resigne the place, to be dismantled according to their agreement with him. The French had leave to carry off everything that was their own except the Artillery, whereof 2 brass pieces were allowed them, they were meerly famished out of the place, having not above 5 daies provisions left when they capittulated....Since the above heere has happened nothing of novelty only that the Dutch have admitted about 1000 of the Kings people into St. Thoma so have the more hopes to see that place surrendred and razed as has been all this while pretended, which shall not want our furtherance. We sent Mr. Jacob Smith and Mr. Oneal with a present of Europe refreshments of Beer, Wine, Olives, and a Parmezan Cheese to Monsr. De La Hay then ready to sett sayle as he did soone after which he accepted very kindly, the Dutch not attending him with any of their shipps as was given out....The Dutch quitted St. Thoma to the Mores, and departed the 27th and 28th past, Govr. Paviloen for Paliacatt, and the shipps for the Southward; by which day they must yearely be cleared off from the whole Coast, on paine of their being responsible for all accidents, who detaine them; we hope the Mores will raze it for their own quiet sake; if the French or Portugueses do not fool them into delayes. Monsr. Baron is still here, on pretence of passage for Surrat, but more likely some such designe; whose stay, though not at all desirable, we know not how to help it as yet." *O. C.* No. 4002. In a "Generall" from Bombay to the Court, dated 23rd Jan. 1675, the Council wrote, "The French since the losse of St. Thoma, hang their heads downe all India over. If they would take their leave civilly of Surat also, wee would wish them a good

And never Since the beginings of these warrs upon this Coast[1], have the French had any thinge to doe in Metchlipatam. Onely in May, Anno 1672, the Viceroy in Person came downe hither with 2 men of warre, all that he had then left, and a Small Sloope of 6 gunns. The One was called the Grand Brittania, the Other the Grand Flemingoe[2], Ships of 65 and 70 Coppar piece of Ordinance each, the Brittania manned with 500 Chosen men, the Other 300. His designe was to burne the towne of Metchlipatam, and compell the Moors to a peace, but was mistaken in that alsoe, although the Coast was Cleare of all Dutch Ships, which was caused by want of able Pilots, more then any thinge Else. Otherways he had come Suddenly upon them to their terrour, but was drove 50 mile to Leeward of the place, and there Sent 4 or 5 men On Shore for Spies to Narsapore, who were very Suddenly Surprized in the English Factory, where the Moors cut off theire heads Upon the doore thrashold, notwithstandinge all the Entreaties and faire words wee cold give them. I was there a Spectator to that bloody Fact, and begged their heads and bodies off the Governour, and tooke care for their buriall[3].

Voyage, for their stay there is equally injurious to themselves as to their neighbors." *O. C.* No. 4072.

From the above it will be seen that the French did not return to Europe according to the treaty with the Dutch. They eventually established themselves firmly at Pondicherry under Monsr. Martin. Compare the following curious phonetic spelling of St Thomé in a letter from John Billingsby, the Company's servant at Balasor, to Richard Edwards, under date 27th March, 1673, "the Moores have taken Santamay from the french soe that they are all fled." *O. C.* No. 3771.

[1] Dutch versus English 1665 to 1674; Dutch versus English and French as local allies 1670 to 1674.

[2] *i.e.* the *Great Breton* and the *Great Fleming*; the writer probably got the names through a Portuguese interpreter.

[3] I have been unable to find any confirmation of this story in the contemporary records, though, as the writer speaks as an eye-witness, there is no reason to doubt his accuracy.

This was Soon noysed abroad, and great forces Sent[1] into the towne of Metchlipatam, and a Stronge Wooden Fort erected within the narrow of the River's mouth, and what Ships lay in the Roade Unladen of all theire fine goods, haveinge a Considerable time to performe all this, beinge a Week's worke for the Viceroy to turne up to the Roade. Soe that when he arrived, he durst not attempt any thinge Save burneinge of 5 Moors Ships and carried away One Small Ship laden with Rice and Butter and Oyle. Thence he Returned for St. Thomae, but e're he got there, the Dutch had got Start of him, and lay in the Roade with 14 Saile of men of warre of Considerable force, which put him to a hard Straite how to get in, but did in the night and Ran his Ship on Shore[2]. The Flemingoe and Sloop were taken by the Dutch[3].

---

[1] *i.e.* by the Moors.

[2] It is amusing and instructive to quote the Frenchman's view of this action, "Monsieur de la Haye, having taken all necessary precautions for the preservation of the town of St. Thomé, embarked on the 10th of April in the *Great Breton*, which was furnished with 48 pieces of good cast iron artillery and an excellent crew. Another vessel called the *Fleming* had orders to follow him. She was armed in like manner with 40 pieces of cannon and was manned by 150 men, both soldiers and sailors. He sailed in the direction of Masulipatam, where, as I have already said, the French Company has a factory. There he met with some Mores' [Moors'] vessels anchored in the river. He burned some and carried off the others, and, after having victualled his own ships, and provided for those he had left at St. Thomé, he set sail for that town. But a great tempest arose, which lasted a whole day and blew with such fury that it rent some of the sails of the *Breton*, without however injuring her masts. The *Fleming*, who was not such a good sailer, lost her course. This did not hinder Monsieur de la Haye from continuing his own way, and the weather having moderated, he sighted 18 Dutch vessels not more than 3 leagues off. This encounter, which would have alarmed anyone but himself, did not even make him turn aside, but, having encouraged his crew to do their best, and having had some 'harac' (which is a beverage nearly as strong as brandy) served out to his soldiers in order to rouse their strength and courage, he commanded them to take up arms at the first signal, and ordered the gunners to have their firebrands in readiness. Then he sailed before the wind straight to the Dutch squadron. General Riclof, who had perceived the *Great Breton*, had already prepared to give chase. Believing her capture to be a certainty, he

had had his ships boat fitted up in order to receive Monsieur de la Haye. On seeing the latter approach, he had the boat lowered to fetch him, thinking that he was about to give himself up, and that he did not dare to risk a fight against so many vessels. But his astonishment was unparalleled when he saw this brave General de la Haye with a single ship pass like a flash of lightning through the midst of all his own, some of which he injured by the discharge of his two port and starboard batteries. The whole Dutch squadron followed him for thrice twenty-four hours, and often came near him, but were unable to board his vessel. He defended himself until he had neither a grain of powder nor a bullet left. Yet he economized his strength and his time so admirably that he reached St. Thomé without having sustained injury and with only the loss of three or four men. This action appeared so extraordinary that it was soon known all over India. People said, when they told us about it, that Monsieur Massiere, General of the East Indies for the States of Holland, had written to General Riclof in terms which implied that General de la Haye could not have escaped such an evident peril if there had not been some secret understanding between them, adding some threats which were as offensive as the reproach was unjust. However, the taking of the *Fleming* calmed the wrath of the Generalissimo Massiere." *Delestre*, pp. 182—185.

The burning of the "5 Moors Ships," mentioned above, is described in a note of "Occurrences in India in 1673," dated in Bombay 14th November, 1673, "The French at St. Thoma beat off the Golcondah Army and raised the seige,...after Mounsr. La Hay the Vice Roy, with two ships of warr, went to Metchlepatam where he burnt 5 or 6 Jounks and threatend the Towne, if that King would not come to a peace with them, haveing spent there some time in the month of June, hee returned to St. Thoma where unexpectedly he found Rickloff Van Goens with a Fleet of 19 men of warr before it, he stood for the Road but the winde chopt about, and haveing discharged some broad sides with the outermost ships, he stood off to sea and fell in with some port about 30 Leagues to the Southward, where he had not been long, but he espied a Fleet of ships bound from England which he took to be the Dutch Fleet persuing him, hee sett saile againe and put in for St. Thoma; where it was his good fortune that the Dutch were gone from the place, after they had discharged some broad sides against it, and he got safe into his Government...." *O. C.* No. 3794. It is a little difficult to reconcile these widely differing accounts of the French prowess.

[3] The taking of the *Fleming* is also described from two different points of view. The Frenchman says, "This vessel, which bad weather had separated from the *Great Breton*, had anchored at Sombresse [=Sombrero or Chowra Island in the Nicobars], where water had only been obtained by force, the savages of the country... attempting to board and take possession of the vessel...but were driven off by the fire directed on them by M. Machaut the commander. He resolved, while waiting for a favourable wind to sail to S. Thomé to get refreshments and water in Bellefort [Balasor] river, where he anchored and sent his boat ashore with part of the crew. The country people killed the Quarter Master and wounded several sailors. Meanwhile, three Dutch vessels going to Bengala laden with merchandize perceived this ship, which they would not have dared to attack if they had seen her boat on board; but presuming that it was on land with a

The French Chiefe resident in Metchlipatam was killed by the Moors[1]; what more of them there made their Escape by Sea.

---

part of the crew, they anchored within musket shot of the *Fleming*, in which there remained only 40 men. They attacked her the next day, and pressed her on all sides with so much advantage, that after 4 hours fighting Capt. Machaut, who had defended himself to the last extremity, finding himself almost alone...was obliged to surrender. The Dutch took this ship to Batavia...and imprisoned Capt. Machaut and his seven or eight remaining men." *Delestre*, p. 185 f.

Walter Clavell, the Company's chief representative in "the Bay" in a letter to the Court, dated at Balasor, 28th Dec. 1674, writes as follows: "The last yeare a Ship of the French Kings named the *Flemen*, Commander Macoshull [the Capt. Machaut of *Delestre*], Seperrated from the rest of the Squadron which the Vice Roy brought before Metchlepatam in her Intended return to St. Thoma being Seperrated from the rest by foule weather. After having been neer Anchor at the Nicobar Islands and not able to geet the Course of Cormendel came in Ballasore Roade, where Rode not long before She was Surprized by three Dutch Merchant men bound for Hugly, who took the Said Ship when most of the Chief people were a Shore in this Toun and yet had the Confidence to bring her up to Hugly before their one Factory, Severall Specious pretences was made that the Ship should be taken from the Dutch and Redelivred to the French; and the Dutch be fined for attempting acts of Hostillity in the Kings Port, to which purpose the Governour of Ballasore perswaded some of the French personally to Complaine at Decca; the Issue whereof was that the Dutch ware faine to by [the] Prize of the Moores, and the French Sent away with good words and a liberty to build Factories and have a trade in what part of Bengala they would. In Hugly they made a Small house neere the Dutch Factory from which the Dutch by their application and present to the Moores have routed them, and they thereupon pretendedly but really because they can borrow no more money have lately left Hugly and are Intended for the Coast in an open boate and taking a long farewell of Bengala whare they are in debted a bout Rupees 8000." *Factory Records*, Hugli, No. 4, p. 22 f.

[1] The only mention I have been able to find of this French Chief is in the passage from *Factory Records*, Hugli, No. 4, under date 14th May, 1674, quoted in note 1, p. 64: "The French at Metchlipatam upon a difference with the Moores have deserted it...the Chiefe slaine the day before." This individual appears to have returned to Masulipatam and met his fate some time in 1673, for, on the 15th of Jan. in that year, Agent Langhorne wrote from Fort St George to the Court, "The French Cheif is come away from Metchlipatam, leaving only 2 persons to look after their Factory." *O. C.* No. 3742. Monsieur Martin probably succeeded the murdered Chief, as, in a letter from Fort St George, dated 20th Aug. 1674, in connection with remarks on the expulsion of Monsr. Del Tor, the French Second at Masulipatam, reference is made to "Monsieur Martin the Chief of Metchlapatam." *O. C.* No. 3992, p. 4.

Metchlipatam Affordeth many very good and fine Commodities[1], vizt. all Sorts of fine Callicoes plaine and coloured[2], more Especially fine Palampores[3] for Quilts, divers Sorts of Chint[4] curiously flowred, which doth much represent flowred Sattin, of Curious lively Colours, as alsoe Chaires and tables of that admirable wood Ebony, Chests of drawers, Screetores[5] finely wrought inlaid with turtle Shell or ivory, for which a Very great trafficke is driven into most parts of India, Persia, Arabia, China, and the South Seas, as well as into England and Holland.

Our Factory here is but a Subordinate One to Fort St. Georg's, As that of the Dutch is to Pullicat.

It alsoe is a place very well populated, and for the

---

[1] Compare *Fryer*, p. 34, "Staple Commodities are Calicuts white and painted, Palempores, Carpets, Tea, Diamonds of both Rocks the Old and New; Escretores and other Knick-Knacks for Ladies, because far-fetch'd and dear-bought."

[2] See note on p. 5.

[3] See *Hobson-Jobson*, *s.v.* Palampore. It is curious that though both Fryer and T. B. mention Palempores (Chintz bed-covers) as one of the staple commodities of Masulipatam, this class of goods is not named in the contemporary MS. records as being produced there. The Piece-goods in constant demand from Masulipatam were Longcloth fine and ordinary, Sallampores fine and ordinary, Percullaes, Dungarees, Allejahs, Oringall Betelees, Morees, Isarees and Ginghams. However, it seems probable that the "16 Pallampose at 3 rups. per peece," enumerated in Wm. Callaway's "Outcry" (entered at the end of the *Diary of Streynsham Master*, p. 361), were purchased at Masulipatam, since Callaway left that place with Master in 1676, and was drowned in the Hugli a few weeks later. Also in a letter from Fort St George, 4th May, 1680, *Factory Records*, Fort St George, No. 28, under "What goods desir'd at Bantam," there is the item, "3 or 4 Cor [corge=score] of Pallampores."

[4] See *Hobson-Jobson*, *s.v.* Chintz. Compare *Thevenot*, part iii. p. 105, "there is great trading [at Masulipatam] in Chites." The form chints or chintz is the plural of chint. Compare *Fryer*, Index, p. iv. "Chint, a sort of Callico painted."

[5] *i.e.* Escritoires or writing-cases. "Carpetts Scrittores and Such like Left with your dear Consort," Letter from Agent Langhorne to Mrs Fleetwood at Masulipatam, 21st Nov. 1676, *Factory Records*, Fort St George, No. 18. "I had sent the Screetore sooner but could not gett Madapollam Cooleys," Letter from Mr Wm. How at Masulipatam to Mrs Mainwaring, 22nd April, 1679, *O. C.* No. 4600. See also *Ind. Ant.* vol. xxix. p. 116.

most part Very rich men, Especially of the Moors, Persians, and Gentues, many Villages not obe: [? above] 2, 3, or 4 miles off very well inhabited by ingenuous tradesmen Especially Weavers and Chint Makers.

Many Ships and Vessel[s] resort here to lade the beforementioned Commodities, haveinge a reasonable good harbour and the Conveniencie of the River that runneth up to the towne Side, which is not above one English mile above the barre[1]. They doe lade and Unlade with good Stronge boats of 10, 12, or 15 tuns in burden, and with noe great difficultie.

Severall of the Inhabitants are great Merchant adventurers, and transport Vast Stocks in the goods aforesaid, both in theire owne Ships as alsoe Upon fraught in English Ships or Vessels[2].

---

[1] Sir Edward Winter, in a letter to Mr Proby of the 5th Dec. 1670, speaks of "The Roade of Remilldey or Metchlepatam." *Factory Records*, Fort St George, No. 16.

[2] Among the miscellaneous papers at the end of the *Diary of Streynsham Master*, there is, pp. 337—339, an "Account of the Trade of Metchlepatam," by Christopher Hatton, dated 9th Jan. 1676-7. He says, "I shall Confine my discourse concerning the Traffick used in this mart of Metchlepatam within the Limitts of my owne Experience haveing now neare overpassed 20 yeares in these parts. Arriveing first in the yeare 1657, at which time I found this place in a very flourishing condition, 20 sayle of ships of good burden belonging to the Native Inhabitans here constantly imployed on Voyages to Aracan, Pegu, Tenassery, Juncceloan, Queda, Mallaca, Johore, Atcheen, Moca, Persia and the Maldiva Islands, and to all these parts the goods and Merchandize were of the production of the parts here Circumjacent, as all sorts of Callicoes, Cotton Yarne, Paintings of divers sorts, Iron, Steel, and all sorts of Graine and all Commodityes again imported where hence dispersed in the Dominions of the Mogull, Visapore, and Golcondah, and in this state it continued for many yeares, untill the Netherlandish Company settled their Factory at Golcondah, where keeping stores of all sorts of commodityes they furnished those merchants that usually came downe every yeare to this place and thereby first occasioned a decay of trade here. The next and fatallest prejudice this place received arose from the corruption of Government at Golcondah...which...have now reduced this place and indeed all the Countrey to this low Condition it now appears in...at my first arrivall into these parts The Towne was soe well stored with able merchants that many ships Ladeings of Divers sorts of Callicoes might and were procurable in the space of two or three dayes...."

The Kinge of Golcondah hath Severall Ships, that trade yearely to Arackan, Tanassaree[1], and Ceylone to purchase Elephants for him and his Nobilitie. They bringe in Some of his Ships from 14 to 26 of these Vast Creatures. They must of Necessitie be of Very Considerable burthens and built exceedinge Stronge.

Each of these huge Annimals must have at the least 70 plantan trees laid in for his provender to the time of his transportation, and, at Some Seasons of the yeare 100, when they Expect a more tedious passadge at Sea. They never let them drinke any water at Sea, a Plantan tree beinge a Very liquorish thinge Naturally, and will not dry up much in lesse then 2 months, and many times they doe not Exceed 15 or 16 days, but at Some time of the Monzoone[2] I have knowne them be at Sea one month, and yet landed all theire Elephants with Safety.

The means Usuall in gettinge these Overgrown beasts On board Ship are Severall[3], accordinge to what con-

---

[1] *i.e.* Tenasserim.

[2] "Wee should have dispatched them [the ships] much sooner had not the Monzoon hapned contrary this yeare to what it hath in other yeares," Letter from Clavell at Balasor to Langhorne at Fort St George, 17th Dec. 1672, *Factory Records*, Hugli, No. 4. "Wee must also write to the Coast and desire that they order two or three of the Metchlepatam boates in the Monzoones who may goe ashore and carry off your goods," Balasor "Generall" to the Court, 31st Dec. 1672, *Factory Records*, Hugli, No. 4.

[3] Compare Schouten's description of embarking elephants at Ceylon: "It is a great deal of trouble to get them on board: the rafts and the boats must be covered with grass and branches of palm-trees, or else the elephants could not be induced to pass along the rafts or bridges. When they have been conducted close to the ship, their eyes are covered, and large bands are passed under the belly embracing the whole body; to these, pulleys are hooked. Then the elephants are hoisted by means of the capstan, and are placed in the bottom of the hold." *Schouten*, vol. ii. p. 34. On the 12th April, 1661, the Council at Fort St George acknowledged a letter from "Acheen," from Mr Henry Garey per the *Anne*, "now called the *Hope*." They commended the "great paynes" taken to get a cargo of elephants, and remarked that the *Anne* was the first ship to do so, the other commanders having refused to lade elephants because they could not "cutt downe the sides of their ships as the Moors Juncks doe." *Factory Records*, Fort St George, No. 14, p. 55.

veniencie the Port they lade at doth afford. In Arackan and Tanassaree, the Rivers are very large and Navigable for the biggest Ships in India or Elsewhere, Soe that they float up to the Side of the Citty or towne, and have as it were a bridge made of timber and Planke Set from the Shore to the Ship Side, and those Ships Sides of her Upper Worke is to be taken Up Soe low as the deck, from which Entrance are placed 2 or 3 Stronge Planke loose, upon which when the Elephant is brought by his keepers, they fall downwards gradually, upon which the Elephants slides downe into the Ships hold, where Some Elephant keepers are ready to receive them and place them in Order, vizt. a Stronge Spulshore[1] on each Side the neck, soe that he cannot goe further forward or Further aft; but if he is a Very tame One he hath his Liberty in the hold, onely his leggs Seized a foot asunder with rattans[2].

Sometimes for want of takeinge good care over them, doubtlesse they receive dammadge both to the Ship and Endanger their lives, as for Example.

A great Ship of 5 or 600 tunns in burthen that belonged to a great Merchant, an Eminent man in Bengala, whose name was Narsam Cawn[3], In her

---

[1] I have been unable to identify this word with any certainty. No similar spelling occurs in the dictionaries. T. B. may have been using a word derived from O.E. *spelc*, *spilc*=splint, splinter. This occurs as subs. spelch, and, in the *Century Dict.*, as a verb, a by-form of *spelk*, whence, possibly the subs. spelcher, rendered by T. B. phonetically, as spulshore. But, against this suggestion, there is the difficulty that *spelc*, in all its forms, refers to slender splinters of wood, and consequently does not fit in with the evident meaning of spulshore. Therefore, if spelcher be accepted as the equivalent, it must also be inferred that it had a special local or nautical significance, and was applied to a beam rather than a splint. I am indebted to Dr James A. H. Murray for kind assistance in compiling this note.

[2] See *Hobson-Jobson*, *s.v.* Rattan.

[3] Probably the merchant meant is the one to whom there are frequent allusions in *Factory Records*, Hugli, No. 4, as "Naseb Cawne," "Naseeb Chaan," "Nassib Caune" (Nasīb Khān); he is described as

Voyadge homeward from Ceylone, One of theire Elephants not well Secured, did, with all the force he cold possibly, run his tooth through the Ship Side in such a measure that they cold not keep her free 2 hours longer, and were forced to betake themselvs to their great boat, and haveinge faire Weather and not beinge above 30 leags off Shore, they all Saved theire lives. I knew the Master of her very well, one Petro Loveyro, an antient Portuguees[1].

When they discharge Elephants, they hoyse them over with good Runners and tackles with the help of a good Cabstant[2] or two, and Ship them On Shore if the Ship is neare; if not, they Send them On Shore in great flatt bottomed boats built for that purpose, Such as they in Point de Gala[3] or Queda doe bringe them on board

---

one of the "considerable merchants" at Hugli. In 1678 there is the following note as to this merchant, "A ship belonging to Nasib Kaun Shaubander of Ballasor, having lost her voyage to Maldiva, Sett Saile again for Bengale." By "Narsam Cawn" the writer, however, may have meant Nāzim Khān.

[1] The references to this "antient Portuguees" that have come to light among the India Office records are the following found in *Factory Records*, Hugli, No. 1, and in the *O. C.* collection, Nos. 4331, 4342, and 4343. "I have procured you an experienced Pilott Pedro De Lavera." Letter from Shem Bridges at Balasor to Capt. Charles Wilde, 13th Oct. 1663. "If the Coreas and boards I wrote for be not ready to come by the *St. George*, send her up with the Iron and any freight that is ready which possibly you may have from Pedro O Lavera, who Mr. Vincent tells mee is arrived....Pray give my recadoes [greeting] to Pedro O Lavera,...Pray aske him [Pedro O Lavera] for a small basket marked E. R. and another small parcell he brought from John Meeke. The basket please to send per first sea convayhance and the parcell (being two petrified crabs) send by the bearer, chargeing him to have a care of breakeing them in the way....I understand from Mr. Bugden that Pedro O Liveira is going to the Maldivas, and that he carried an adventure of Mr. Clavells with him the last Voyage." Letters from Vincent and Reade at Hugli to Edwards at Balasor, 29th Jan., 6th and 7th Feb. 1678.

[2] *i.e.* capstan.

[3] A very valuable form of the name. Compare *Hobson-Jobson*, *s.v.* Galle, Point De; there is no quotation with this spelling. "The next day [11th April, 1662] we anchored in the bay of Pointe de Galles." *Schouten*, vol. ii. p. 4. "The Flemings have nested themselves in the Portugals Castles at Columbo, Point de Gaul, and elsewhere"; *Fryer*,

On. If they live 3 days after they land, the fraught is due, from 500 to 800 Rupees accordinge as he is in Stature and bulke. They are the most Sensible Annimal in the Universe in many respects, and not onely for what action they are trained Up to, but the Affection they beare one another after beinge Civilized; for if one chance to dye, as I have sometime Seen On Ship board, they must be sure to hide him quite from the Sight of the rest, which is done by covering a Saile round him Untill they cut him up into quarters and hoyse the dead carcasse Up, otherways it wold Endanger the lives of Some if not all the rest, and another Strange thinge is they will never runne wild after once tamed, nor will they ingender to Captivate theire Younge.

Most Eminent Men that inhabit Metchlipatam and Guddorah[1] are Mahometans, vizt. Moors and Persians, a Sort of most Insolent men, Entitleinge themselves Mussleman[2], vizt. true believers, although very Eroniously, and not onely in that but in theire carriadge and behaivour, haveinge got a predominancy over the Weake Spirited Gentues and Mallabars[3], Some of which are Merchants

---

p. 23. "Colombo, which was at first built by the Portugueze, about the Year 1638, but, by their Pride and Insolence, had made the King of Candia (who was at first Sovereign of the whole Island) their Enemy. The Dutch taking that Opportunity, made a League with the King offensive and defensive, and first attacked and carried Galle or Ponto de Galle in Anno 1658, which is a Fort and Harbour on the South-west Point of the Island, about 20 Leagues from Colombo." Alex. Hamilton, *East Indies*, vol. i. p. 337.

[1] See note on p. 63. Compare the following in "A Narrative of the Inundation at Metchlepatam" in 1679, *O. C.* No. 4663, "Goodra (the usual residence of the Governour) carried clear away and some drowned."

[2] See *Hobson-Jobson*, *s.v.* Mussulman. Compare *Mandelslo*, p. 63, "They [the Mahumetans] are called Mansulmans or Mussulmans. They...believe that there is no salvation out of their Communion, treating as Hereticks and Infidels, not only the Christians, but also all such as profess any other Religion then theirs." See also *Ind. Ant.* vol. xxii. p. 112.

[3] See notes on p. 6.

here, but more of them Laborious and Industrious handicraftsmen vizt. Carpenters, Smiths, Barbers[1], Shroffs[2], vizt. Changers of money, and multas alias.

That Stronge East India Liquor called Arack[3] is made and Sold in great abundance by the Gentues here, but not by the Mahometans, beinge averse from the law of their Patron Mahomet, as alsoe the drinkinge of any Stronge drinke, which in Publick is pretty well Observed, but they find means to besott themselves Enough with Bangha and Gangah, and, Some of them, with any manner of Stronge drinke they can have in Private.

Arack[3] is a liquor distilled Severall ways, as Some out

---

[1] See note on p. 9.

[2] See *Hobson-Jobson*, *s.v.* Shroff. Compare *Tavernier*, vol. i. part ii. p. 161, "the Bannians...of whom some are Sheraffs or Bankers, others Broakers, employ'd between Merchant and Merchant for buying and selling." *N. and E.*, p. 31, for 5th Aug. 1680, has: "Report of the weight of 2 chests of gold and 2 Bags of Ryalls of 8/8 delivered to the Sharoffs for alloy." Compare also Lockyer, *Trade in India*, p. 28, "A considerable Quantity [of Bullion] is seldom bought or sold, but the Shroffs, who are of the Chitty Cast, and in general Brokers to this Business, examine and weigh it impartially betwixt both Parties; having a small Allowance for their Care."

[3] See *Hobson-Jobson*, *s.v.* Arrack. *N. and E.* for 30th Dec. 1680, p. 43, has, "for the good service performed by the Soldyers and Peons ...it is thought fit to gratify them...a hhdd. Arrack to the garrison." Compare Lockyer, *Trade in India*, p. 266 f.: "Goa...Its chief Produce is Arack, which is made in such great Quantities, that all India is supply'd with it, as far as the Straits of Malacca. There are several Sorts, as Single, Double, and Treble distill'd: the Double distill'd, which is commonly sent abroad, is but a weak Spirit in Comparison with Batavia Arack; yet it has a Flavour so peculiar to itself, that it is justly preferr'd to it, and all other Aracks in India. We bought it for 13½ Rupees per Hogshead, Cask and all; Treble distill'd old Arack was worth 18 Rupees. A Goa Hogshead contains 50 Gallons more or less. Arack seems to be an Indian Word for Strong-Waters of all sorts; for they call our Spirits and Brandy, English Arack. What we understand by that Name is distill'd from the Liquor, that runs from the Coconut-tree without any other mixture....Batavia Arack is drawn in Copper Stills; but, I am told, at Goa their Works are altogether of Earth, which makes their Arack so mild and pleasant. I have met with Colombo and Quilone Arack with a Cinamon Flavour, as hot and fiery as the Spirits we usually burn in Lamps." See also *Ind. Ant.* vol. xxx. p. 391, and Crawfurd, *Dict. of the Indian Islands*, *s.v.* Arrack.

of the graine called Rice, another Sort from the Jagaree[1] or Very course Sugar, with Some drugs, another Sort there is that [is] distilled from Neep toddy and that is commonly called Nipa de Goa[2], but the weakest of these is much Stronger then any Wine of the Grape.

Bangha[3], theire Soe admirable herbe, groweth in many places of this Coast as alsoe in Bengala; but Gangah[4] is brought from the Island Sumatra, and is oftentimes Sold here at Very high rates. It is a thinge that resembleth hemp Seed and groweth after the Same mannar, but the Other is of a larger leafe and grosse Seed. Gangah beinge of a more pleasant Operation, much addictinge to Venery, is Sold at five times the price the Other is. They Study

---

[1] See *Hobson-Jobson*, *s.v.* Jaggery. *Fryer*, p. 99, has "Jaggaree or Mulasso's made into Past," and Index, p. vi, "Jaggaree, Melossees, or course Sugar." In *Mad. Man. Admn.* vol. iii. *s.v.* Arrack, among descriptions of various kinds, we find, "What is called in Southern India puttay arrack or pariah liquor or country liquor is distilled from a fermented solution of jaggery, the course sugar obtained from the juice of the date, cocoanut, palmyra and other palms, or from the sugar-cane."

[2] See *Hobson-Jobson*, *s.v.* Nipa. It is the thatching-palm of the estuaries East of the Hugli River, and the liquor distilled from it. It is now known as the Dhani (Dhunnie) palm. Compare *Fryer*, p. 157, "At Nerule is made the best Arach or Nepa de Goa, with which the English on this Coast make that enervating Liquor called Paunch [punch, Hind. *pãnch*] (which is Indostan for Five) from Five Ingredients."

[3] *i.e.* Bhang, Indian hemp. See *Hobson-Jobson*, *s.v.* Bang, and the quotations given from *Fryer*, p. 91; Lockyer, *Trade in India*, p. 61, and Alex. Hamilton, *East Indies*, vol. i. p. 131.

[4] See *Hobson-Jobson*, *s.v.* Gunja. Also Crawfurd, *Dict. of the Indian Islands*, *s.v.* Hemp, who says it was introduced by the Telugus into the Archipelago for the use of Indian settlers. The writer seems to look on "bangha" and "gangah" as products of two different plants, but as a matter of fact they are different preparations of the same plant, Cannabis Indica (or sativa). See *Ind. Ant.* vol. xxiii. pp. 260—262 for valuable historical notes taken from Dr Grierson's evidence before the Hemp-drugs Commission, 1893–4. He says that the earliest mention of *gãnjã* is about 1300 A.D. See also Watts, *Dict. of Economic Products of India*, *s.v.* Cannabis, for an exhaustive article on the subject. From this we learn that the narcotic is derived from "the young tops and unfertilised female flowers, *gãnjã* (or *gãnja*), and the older leaves and fruit-vessels, *bhãng*."

many ways to Use it, but not One of them that faileth to intoxicate them to admiration.

Sometimes they mix it with theire tobacco and Smoak it, a very Speedy way to be besotted; at Othersometimes they chaw it, but the most pleasant way of takeinge it is as followeth:—Pound or grinde a handfull of the Seed and leafe togeather, which mixt with one Pint of fresh Water, and let it Soake neare one quarter of an houre or more, then Strained through a piece of Calicoe[1] or what else is fine, and drinke off the liquor, and in lesse then ½ an houre it's Operation will Shew it Selfe for the Space of 4 or 5 hours.

And it Operates accordinge to the thoughts or fancy of the Partie that drinketh thereof, in Such manner that if he be merry at that instant, he Shall Continue Soe with Exceedinge great laughter for the before mentioned Space of time, rather overmerry then Otherways, laughinge heartilie at Every thinge they discerne; and, on the Contrary, if it is taken in a fearefull or Melancholy posture, he Shall keep great lamentation and Seem to be in great anguish of Spirit, takeinge away all manly gestures or thoughts from him[2]. I have often Seen these

---

[1] See note on p. 5.

[2] Compare *Dampier*, vol. ii. p. 126, "They have here [in Achin] a sort of Herb or Plant called Ganga or Bang. I never saw any but once, and that was at some distance from me. It appeared to me like Hemp, and I thought it had been Hemp, till I was told to the contrary. It is reported of this Plant, that if it is infused in any Liquor, it will stupify the brains of any person that drinks thereof; but it operates diversly, according to the constitution of the person. Some it makes sleepy, some merry, putting them into a Laughing fit, and others it makes mad: but after 2 or 3 hours they come to themselves again. I never saw the effects of it on any person, but have heard much discourse of it. What other use this Plant may serve for I know not: but I know it is much esteemed here, and in other places too whither it is transported." Crawfurd, *Dict. of the Indian Islands*, p. 148, quotes the above description, and says, "The earliest account of hemp as a product of the Archipelago is by the observant Dampier, who saw it at Achin, in 1688." T. B.'s account is, however, at least nine years earlier, and, at the time of Dampier's visit, he was a resident in Achin. See Introduction.

humors Experienced in Bengala. One for instance:—Eight or tenne of us (Englishmen) to trye practice, wee wold needs drinke Every man his pint of Bangha, which wee purchased in the Bazar for the Value of 6d. English. I ordered my man to bringe alonge with him one of the Fackeers[1] (who frequently drinke of this liquor), promiseinge him his dose of the Same to come and Compound the rest for us, which he Cordially and freely accepted of, and it was as welcome to him as a Crowne in moneys. Wee dranke Each man his proportion, and Sent the Fackeere out of dores, and made fast all dores and Windows, that none of us might runne out into the Street, or any person come in to behold any of our humors thereby to laugh at us.

The Fackeere Sat without the Street dore, callinge us all Kings and brave fellows, fancyinge himselfe to be at the Gates of the Pallace at Agra, Singeinge to that purpose in the Hindostan Languadge[2].

It Soon tooke it's Operation Upon most of us, but

---

[1] See note on p. 20.

[2] Hindōstanī. See *Hobson-Jobson*, *s.v.* Hindostanee. The Directors in England endeavoured to promote the study of Hindōstanī among their servants in India. On the 18th December, 1671, they wrote to Fort St George, *Letter Book*, No. 4, p. 495, "Wee are sorry to heare that wee have not any One of our Servants that can speake the language, Wee now purposely send you over some young men, which wee would have instructed therein, as also to write it, that wee may not depend on accidentall persons, And for the encouragement of those that shall atteyne thereto, so as to transact businesse with the Nātives, wee order you to pay each of them 20*l.* as a gratuety, and that a Schoole Master bee allowed for teaching them, Wee are informed that John Thomas hath made some progress herein, wee would have you encourage him to proceed to perfection." On the 20th Nov. 1674, in a "Generall" from Fort St George to the Court, *O. C.*, No. 4044, p. 8, is the remark, "We have paid the pagodas 50 or lb 20 to John Thomas, according to your order of 18 December 1671 finding him very well introduced in the Gentue language." On the 12th December, 1677, the Court wrote again to Fort St George on the subject, *Letter Book*, No. 5, p. 502, "Wee did some yeers since propose an encouragement of £20 a peece to any of our Writers that should attain to a perfection in the Gentue or Indostan language, but as yet have heard but of one proficient therein, wee doe require you to reminde them hereof in all your Agency...."

merrily, Save upon two of our Number, who I Suppose feared it might doe them harme not beinge accustomed thereto. One of them Sat himselfe downe Upon the floore, and wept bitterly all the Afternoone; the Other terrified with feare did runne his head into a great Mortavan Jarre[1], and continued in that Posture 4 hours or more; 4 or 5 of the number lay upon the Carpets (that were Spread in the roome) highly Complementinge each Other in high termes, each man fancyinge himselfe noe lesse then an Emperour. One was quarralsome and fought with one of the wooden Pillars of the Porch, untill he had left himselfe little Skin upon the knuckles of his fingers. My Selfe and one more Sat sweatinge for the Space of 3 hours in Exceedinge Measure.

Taste it hath not any, in my judgement lesse then faire water, yet it is of Such a bewitchinge Sottish nature, that whoever Use it but one month or two cannot forsake it without much difficultie.

The Governour of Metchlipatam[2] is a Moore put into

---

[1] Pegu Jar. See *Hobson-Jobson*, *s.v.* Martaban. "Mr. White hath not taken the Mortevan of Butter with him." Letter from Wm. How at Masulipatam to Mrs Mainwaring, 22nd April, 1679; *O. C.*, No. 4600. For an article on Pegu Jars, see *Ind. Ant.* vol. xxii. p. 364 f. *Tavernier*, vol. i. part ii. p. 180 has, "They take a great Earthen pot, well glaz'd within, which they call Martavane."

[2] The Governor at the time of which T. B. writes was "Aga Gilloll" [Agha Jalāl], of whose oppressions there are frequent and bitter complaints in the letters from Masulipatam, 1673—1677 (*Factory Records*, Masulipatam, No. 6). On the 2nd January, 1677, Streynsham Master, who stayed at Masulipatam on his return journey to Fort St George, received a visit from the Governor; "Agga Geloll the Governour of the Towne with the Shabundar and others came to the Factory to see me, he was very civill in his expressions, and noe pretence would serve to excuse receiving an entertainment at his house he was soe earnest in his invitation." *Diary of Streynsham Master*, p. 297. At a Consultation at Fort St George on the 4th Aug. 1677, mention is made of "a demand of Aga Gilloll Governour of Metchlepatam for about pagodas 550 owing to him from the deceased Robert Fleetwood." *Factory Records*, Fort St George, No. 1. In 1679, Streynsham Master made a second tour of inspection of the Company's factories on the "Coast and Bay," and again exchanged visits with the Governor of Masulipatam. In the *Memoriall of Streynsham Master*, quoted by Mackenzie, *Kistna District*, pp. 137 and 139, the name is given [by

that Office by the Kinge of Golcondah, Sole Lord and Kinge of all this Coast Saveinge to the Southward of Porto Novo[1], which appertaineth to the Vizepore Kinge[2].

? a misreading of the MS. text] as Aga Telloll, "April 2nd. Aga Telloll the Governor of Metchlepatam having been toward Narsapore and those places under his Government returned to Goodera last night, whereof having notice this day the Agent sent to complement him, and to acquaint him of his being to these parts to inspect the Company's business, to which message he returned a complementall answer, and that he should take a day to visitt the Agent, and to invite him to an entertainment at his house....4th April. Aga Telol the Governour came to Towne this morning by 8 o'clock directly to the English Factory to visit the Agent with a traine of Persians &c., he stayed about an hour...it was thought best to returne the visitt this evening... and his treate was very civill after a plentifull supper being closed with a present of a Horse...." The next day "Aga Telol" was presented with 250 pagodas privately, "he being a person rising in favour at Court."

[1] Of this place Alex. Hamilton, *East Indies*, vol. i. p. 350, has the following description, "The next Place of Commerce [to Negapatam] is Porto Novo, so called by the Portugueze, when the Sea-coasts of India belonged to them; but when Aurengzeb subdued Golcondah, and the Portugueze Affairs declined, the Mogul set a Fouzdaar in it, and gave it the Name of Mahomet Bander. The Europeans generally call it by its first Name, and the Natives by the last. The Country is fertil, healthful and pleasant, and produceth good Cotton Cloth of several Qualities and Denominations, which they sell at Home, or export to Pegu, Tanasereen, Quedah, Johore, and Atcheen on Sumatra." *Fryer*, p. 175, speaking of the Sea-ports of the King of Visiapour, mentions six, and adds, "the rest are Possessed by the Malabar Raja's round to Porto Novo, which only is properly the King's." See *Hobson-Jobson*, *s.v.* Porto Novo. *N. and E.* for 20th March, 1680, p. 13, has "Intelligence received from Porto Novo that the Dutch have leave to settle a Factory there," and on the 6th Jan. 1681, p. 44, "Accordingly it is resolved to apply to the Soobidar of Sevagee's Country of Chengy for a Cowle to settle Factories at Cooraboor and Coonemerro and also at Porto Novo, if desired, the Company's Merchants engaging to deliver cloth there at the same rates as here." In a "Generall" from Fort St George, dated 15th April, 1669, *O. C.* No. 3171, there is a remark which shows that a settlement at Porto Novo had been discussed many years before 1680: "It hath been severall times proposed to us to send some persons to Portanova to make provision of Cloth for England Wee finde that it is a place where Quantityes of Cloth may be provided at easy rates, but being soe farr distant it is not convenient to bring it thence by Land the charge of bringing them soe farr, and the severall Junckans [transit duties] in the way hither swell the charge too much, besides the length and difficulty of the way and the Seasons that must be taken to pass the Rivers: but to these proposalls as yet wee have given noe other answer, but that for this yeare wee have disposed of all our monyes and goods, but may take it into consideration hereafter...."

[2] This is a neat bit of historical, political and geographical evidence. See map for 1625–40 at the end of Gribble's *History of the Deccan*.

This Governours place is very considerable, his honour great as a Viceroy, his revenues Very large, his attendance Very Stately, accordinge to the Custome of this Countrey.

His Retinue of Attendants and Menial Servants are in great number; he keeps Severall Palanchinoes[1], State horses, and Roundels[2], pipes, drums, and trumpets, many Pikemen, 2 or 300 Punes[3] and Resbutes[5].

Punes[3] are noe Other then waiteinge men, waiteinge on their Masters, wherever they goe, and in time of any journey, they runne by his Palanchino[1] or Elephant as foot boys[3], which is here accompted a Princely piece of honour. I have knowne Some persons that have not had any Goverment conferred Upon them keep above 300 in constant Sallary, which is Ordinarily 2 rupees every Moone[4].

Resbutes[5] are of another Cast. They are accompted a

---

[1] See note on p. 19.

[2] Umbrellas.

[3] Peons. See *Hobson-Jobson*, *s.v.* Peon. "My last to you was per Mr. March together with the small fardle per one of the Punes." Letter to Mr Vickers at Casimbazar, 17th Sept. 1670. *O. C.*, No. 3478. The "boy" in "foot-boys" is probably also an Anglo-Indianism: see *Hobson-Jobson*, *s.v.* Boy.

[4] A valuable reference to the old Indian custom of payment by the month, still obtaining for every kind of servant, from highest to lowest, official, commercial, and private. See *ante*, p. 4.

[5] Rājpūts. See note on p. 19. In Lord's *Discoverie of the Sect of the Banians*, 1630, pp. 76, 77, 82, we have, "The Second Cast or Tribe being the Cutteryes...were the Ancient Kings and Rulers of India... called by the name of Raiahs which signifieth a King...having many resolute Souldiers...called Rashpootes, which implyeth as much as the Sonnes of Kings." Compare *Tavernier*, vol. i. part ii. p. 161, "The second Caste is that of the Raspoutes or Ketris, that is to say, Warriors and warlike people....All the Raja's are of this Caste...all of this second Caste are not Warriours; for they are the Raspoutes only that go to War, and are all Horsemen. But for the Ketris, they are degenerated from their Ancestors, and of Soldiers are become Merchants." *Fryer*, p. 27, has, "Next in esteem [after the Brahmins] were the Rashwaws, Rashpoots, or Souldiers." *Thevenot*, part iii. p. 63, says "The second is the Tribe of the Catry or Raspoutes, who make profession of Arms." "The Mazar or certificate about the Rajapootes Sonn have not yet received." 6th Jan. 1680, *Factory Records*, Hugli, No. 5. Compare also *De la Loubère*, p. 97, "The foreign Guard [of the King of Siam] consists...

most Valiant people that live by the Sword, and Ought, when upon any occasion they are forced to draw theire great backswords for defence of theire Lord and Master, never to put them up againe Unrevenged of their Enemies, but Utterly to destroy them. But these are but Scare-crows to the poore ignorant natives, for I have Seen them take themselves to their heels, and make a Runninge fight, when a Small number of Frenchmen, not Exceedinge one dozen, drove about 200 of them before them, and as it was Upon theire owne Dunghill, vizt. within this Towne. And a more memorable fight Sir Edward Winter had with above 300 of them horse and foot Upon Guddorah[1] bridge, when he and his Trumpeter cleared the way and drove Severall of them Over the bridge to the great Astonishment of all the Natives and Fame of that Worthy Knight[2].

---

lastly in two Companies of Twenty five Men each, Pagans of the true India, habited like the Moors, which are called Rašbouts, or Raggibouts, who boast themselves to be of the Royal blood, and whose Courage is very famous, though it be only the effect of Opium."

[1] See note on p. 63.

[2] This is a characteristic story of the fiery Sir Edward Winter, who was appointed Governor of Fort St George in 1661. He arrived in India in 1662, and held the office by right for three years, and by usurpation for an additional three. In 1665, Winter was superseded from home by George Foxcroft. Instead of resigning, he imprisoned his successor and governed on his own account in Foxcroft's place. In 1668 Winter was compelled to release Foxcroft, who assumed office; but Sir Edward's outrageous conduct was practically condoned. With regard to the skirmish above mentioned, it may have taken place in 1663, for on the 2nd January, Sir Edward wrote to Sir Thomas Chamberlin, Deputy Governor in London, *O.C.* No. 2964, "I have bin in much trouble to compose a difference with the Moores, created by them, who at my being at Mesulapatam one evening fell upon us, and kild one of our English Servants and wounded mee in severall places, and hurt others, without any reason knowne to us." Sir Edward was not likely to avoid retaliating when the chance occurred, but I can find no actual account in the records of the time of the fight on "Guddorah" bridge. I am, however, indebted to Mr W. Foster, for drawing my attention to the monument erected to Sir Edward Winter in the Parish Church of Battersea. A Latin inscription is followed by eulogistic lines, seven of which run as follows:

"Nor less in Martiall Honour was his name,
Witness his actions of Immortal Fame:

Roundels[1] Are in these Warm Climats very Necessarie, to keep the ⊙[2] from Scorchinge a man; they may alsoe and are Serviceable to keep the raine off. Most men of accompt maintaine one, 2, or 3 roundelliers[3], whose office is onely to attend theire Masters Motion. They are Very light but of Exceedinge Stiffnesse, beinge for the most part made of Rhinocerots hide, very decently painted and Guilded with what flowrs they best admire. On the inside exactly in the midst thereof is fixed a Smooth handle (made of wood) by which the Roundeliere[3] doth carry it, holdinge it up, with one hand, a foot or more above his Master's head, directinge the Centre thereof as Opposite to the ⊙[2] as possibly he may. Sumbareros or Catysols[4] are here very Usefull and necessarie for the Same purpose, which are carried 3 or 4 foot or more above a mans head,

---

Alone, unarm'd a Tygre He opprest,
And crusht to death the Monster of a Beast.
Thrice twenty mounted Moors he overthrew
Singly on foot, some wounded, some he slew;
Dispers'd the rest: what more cou'd Sampson do?"

A quaint representation of these two exploits is engraven on the monument. In all probability the overthrow of the "mounted Moors" and the skirmish related by T.B. are identical.

[1] A state umbrella and a constant source of bickering in the old Anglo-Indian days. *N. and E.* p. 40, for 16th Feb. 1676, has "Whereas each hath his peon and some more with their Rondells, that none be permitted but as at the Fort;" and p. 15 for 1680, "To Verona's adopted son was given the name of Muddoo Verona and a Rundell to be carried over him in respect to the memory of Verona;" and p. 72 for 8th January, 1680, "Six men for dutys, Rundell, and Kittesale." See *Hobson-Jobson*, *s.v.* Roundel.

[2] Sailors' mark in old logs for "the sun."

[3] Roundel-boy, umbrella-carrier. Compare the following reference in a letter from Madapollam to Masulipatam, 19th July, 1679, *O.C.* No. 4633, "The bearer is my rundelleere who you may send on board."

[4] An umbrella, especially the Chinese variety of paper with a bamboo handle. See *Ind. Ant.* vol. xxx. p. 347. Compare the following in a letter from John Haines at Hugli to Job Charnock, 21st Sept. 1687, *Factory Records*, Hugli, No. 11, "The kittysol will take about 2½ yds. scarlet." See *Hobson-Jobson*, *s.v.* Kittysol, and also *s.v.* Sombrero. In the old writers, sombrero was always an umbrella and never a hat.

and Shade a great matter, beinge rather more Convenient then the Other but not soe fashionable or Honourable, by reason any man whatever that will goe to the Charge of it, which is noe great Matter, may have one or more Catysols to attend him, but not a Roundell Unlesse he be in a Credible Office, and then noe more then one Unlesse he be a Governour or One of the Councell. The Same Custome the English hold good amongst their own people, whereby they may be distinguished by the Natives[1].

A Palanchino is of the forme above described[2], beinge

---

[1] The whole paragraph is a valuable contribution to the history of the words roundell, sombrero, and kittysol (as it is usually spelt), all meaning umbrellas of sorts. The use of umbrellas, especially of roundells, formed the subject of sumptuary regulations on the part of the Company for over a century. The allusion in the text is to a fulmination at Masulipatam during Streynsham Master's visit, 16th Aug. 1676 (*Diary of Streynsham Master*, p. 41)—"There being an ill custome in the Factory of writers haveing roundells carried over their heads which is not used or allowed by the Government of the Towne, but only to the Governour and three next principall officers and to two or three eminent merchants of ancient standing and by the Dútch only their Cheife, Second, and third who are of their Councell, and at Fort St. George is allowed only to the Councell and Chaplaine, It is therefore ordered that noe Person in this Factory shall have a roundell carried over them but such as are of Councell and the Chaplaine." The present editor recollects a certain Colonel of the older fashion in Madras in 1872–3 who regularly had a roundell carried by a roundell-boy after him wherever he went in Fort St George in the daytime. Compare *Fryer*, p. 30, who calls them Arundells.

[2] The illustration is of interest as showing that the author by palanchino meant, not the palankeen of to-day, but the glorified litter known as the munchieel (*manchāl*) in the Madras Presidency. See note on p. 19. Compare the description of "Palanquins" in *Thevenot*, part iii. p. 54—"Palanquin...is a kind of Couch with four feet, having on each side Ballisters four or five Inches high, and at the head and feet a back-stay like a Childs Cradle, which sometimes is open like Ballisters, and sometimes close and Solid. This machine hangs by a long Pole, which they call Pambou, by means of two frames nailed to the feet of the Couch, which are almost like to those that are put to the top of moving Doors, to fasten Hangings by; and these two frames which are the one at the head, and the other at the opposite end, have Rings through which great Ropes are put, that fasten and hang the Couch to the Pambou....If a Woman be in it, it is covered close over with red Searge, or with Velvet if she be a great Lady....Every one adorns his Palanquin according to his humour, some have them covered with plates of carved Silver, and others have them only painted with Flowers and other Curiosities, or beset round with guilt Balls...."

Plate VII

"THE WIDOW BURNETH ALIVE."

p. 40.

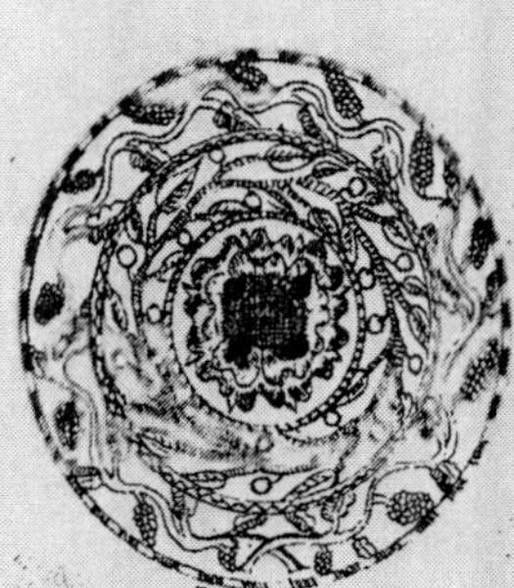

"A ROUNDEL."

p. 85.

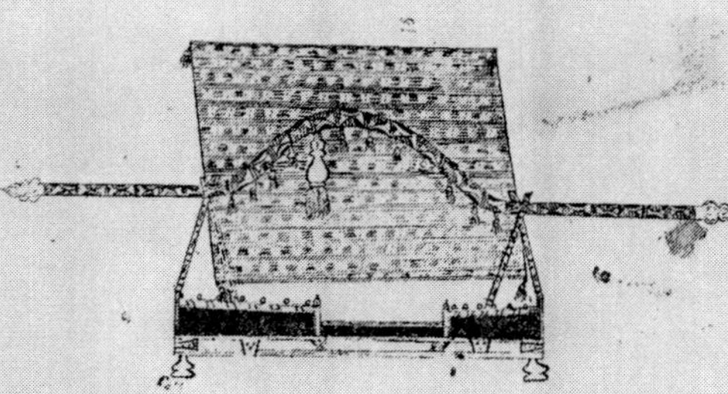

a longe Square Frame about 6 foot in length, and 3 or 3½ foot broad, very neatly inlaid with Ivory and Turtle Shell of Excellent Workman Ship plated with Silver, (as the Owner's pleasure is to bestow Cost thereon) with a large Bamboo, of about 15 or 16 foot longe, crooked in the middle for the conveniencie of sittinge Upright, or may ly downe and Sleep in it, with a Scarlet or broadcloth coveringe (called a Pingaree)[1] Stretched out Square. This is carried by 4 men at once (as in the figure). Upon a journey they goe 8 for the relieveinge one another; they are called Gualas[2], and will carry one 40 miles per diem with noe great difficulty.

They are of a Cast by themselvs, worshipinge Stocks and Stones, and differ in many respects from the rest of the Idolaters, and live amongst themselves.

---

[1] The author seems to mean the Hindōstanī word *pinjarī*, a bier, small cage, small frame-work.

[2] The Gowāla (cow-keeper) caste were employed as "bearers" in Bengal, and the author is probably confusing the "Guallas" of the northern province with the Kāval of Madras. Compare the following extracts from contemporary Bengal records: "We shall, as soon as you advise you are ready, send Gwalies and Cahars to meete you at Kendoa." Balasor, 4th July, 1674; *Factory Records*, Hugli, No. 4. "You may have it [the wine] carried overland...by the Gualloes." Balasor, 29th May, 1678; *O.C.* No. 4433. "This morning a Gualla came from the Town and informed us &c." Balasor, 17th Dec. 1687; *Factory Records*, Balasor, No. 1. "This comes by the Gualla's whom your worship sent up upon my boat to fetch the pumpelmouces from Cossimbuzar." Hugli, 11th Sept. 1687; *Factory Records*, Hugli, No. 11. These "Guallas" however, seem to have been porters and messengers rather than palankeen-bearers. The bearer-caste is the Kahār, and there are many references to them in the Bengal records, *e.g.* "Wee find not that Cahars for a Palenkin were ever kept in Hugly when any under the Second were there however wee ordered you to keep four cahars in constant pay." Hugli, 10th Feb. 1673; *Factory Records*, Hugli, No. 4. "We allow you 8 Caharrs for the Pallenkeene and no more." Hugli, 28th Sept. 1677; *Factory Records*, Hugli, No. 4. Of "Guallas" Risley, *Tribes and Castes of Bengal*, vol. ii. p. 284, remarks, "Goalas are very strong in Orissa, and a large proportion of the Uriyas employed as personal servants by Europeans belong to that caste." The Tamil word Kāval is a guard, palankeen-bearer, body servant; but the usual European term is "boy" from the Boyi (Telugu) Caste, primarily fishermen, with common or secondary occupations as bearers of letters and palankeen and domestic servants. On the whole, it seems probable that the author was thinking of the Bengal palankeen-bearer when he wrote "Guala."

The Moors have, within a Very few years, put many grievous Affronts both Upon the English and Dutch, which formerly they durst not attempt the meanest of them, Soe that without all dispute wee have occasioned Such things by our low Spiritednesse, and Selfe interest, mindinge that more then any future benefit or Nationall good, as I my Selfe can instance in many respects, but rather leave it to theire Own Considerations to Seeke theire remedies. For one thinge I dare be bold to assert, that our Chiefe nor his Councill did Ever make their agrievances known to the Kinge of Golcondah, when English men have been most bloodily murthered in the Open Streets[1].

Anno Domini 1675/6 The Kinge[2] came on Progresse to Metchlipatam with a Very great Retinue. He adventured his Person On board 2 English Ships (that lay in the Roade) which, if I mistake not, is more then his Ministers ever did, but the [?by] Some wise men in his dominions it was accompted a great piece of lightnesse in him[3].

---

[1] The high-handed and spirited policy of Sir Edward Winter was not encouraged by the Court nor maintained by his successors, Foxcroft and Langhorne. The records during the time of these two Governors are full of complaints of oppression by the "Moors" and constant stoppages of trade, but, in almost every instance, recourse was had to bribery rather than force.

[2] This was Abū'l-Hassan Shāh, the lāst of the Qutb Shāhī Dynasty of Golconda, 1672—1683. See Gribble, *History of the Deccan*, vol. i. pp. 285, 299—309.

[3] In the MS. records preserved at the India Office (*Factory Records*, Masulipatam, Nos. 6 and 10, Miscellaneous, No. 3a; *Letter Book*, No. 6; *Diary of Streynsham Master*) full particulars of the King's visit to Masulipatam are given. From these I have extracted the following details: On the 19th Dec. 1675, Mr Mainwaring informed Mr Puckle, "Just now our Govr. Sarsamut Shabandand &ca officers of the towne who are together at the Nababs house advised mee that the King would be here in a very Short time and therefore would have us prepare our Selves to meet him with a present, this affaire being of great concerne to our Honourable Imployers I desire you all immediately upon receipt hereof to repaire hither to Consult the needfull and bring with you 100 peons with what else you think needfull that soe wee may appeare with as much Splendour as our Neibours the Dutch who are making all the preparations possible...if any of you have any thing by you that you may judge may be acceptable to the King please to bring it with you, allso as many Settes of boyes as

you judge may be sufficient for us all in this towne being already taken up." On the 21st Dec. orders were sent to the Company's servants at Masulipatam "to prepare themselves to meet the King at Rezwar two days Journey from hence with a present." On the 22nd the "Chief &c of Metchlepatam" wrote to Maddapollam, "Wee are strongly allarmed with the Kings approach which putts the whole towne into a Hurry for his reception and you can but be Sensible what we Labour under Seeing the Dutch make large provissions to meet him and to present him." Again, on the 29th Dec., "Wee understand that the King arrived at Cundapella last night and intends to come to Madapollam and from thence to Cummum," and, in a letter to Fort St George of the same date, "he [the King] is Reported to March with So Numerous a traine that he devours all the Country up where he comes. Wee expect every hour to be summoned to goe to meet him." On the 1st Jan. 1676, news was sent to Madapollam that "Here is a report that the King is gone to Rogermundrum, and from thence intends to come to Metchlepatam." A letter to Fort St George dated 19th Jan. gives a full account of the royal visit—"Wee advised you [on the 15th Jan.] that in a day or two wee would dispatch the other two remaining Ships, but the King coming to town the 17th, commanded us to stop these two Ships, [the *Loyall Subject* and the *Unity*] untill he should have gone aboard them, yesterday he went aboard a Dutch Ship, which they had detained and fitted for his reception, amongst other their Galantry they had the impudence to put ours and the French Kings Flag under theirs in the mizen topp, and thereby to render us low and contemptable in the Kings eyes, whereat wee were all highly concerned, and thereupon wee repaired on board our Ships, and ordered the Commanders to Salute his majesty with their Gunns, and from thence went with the trumpets to waite on his majesty on his owne Shipp the *Indulgence* where wee acquainted him with the indignity offer'd to our King, who thereupon ordered it to be taken downe (which was immediately performed) and afterward upon our invitation was pleased to come on board the *Loyall Subject* (notwithstanding the Dutch endeavoured all they could to oppose it) where he continued two houres and did express much Satisfaction, ordering us to fire Severall Gunns for his delight which he would not permitt on board the Dutch Shipp, and at his departure declared that he would this morning visit them againe early and commanded us to be ready to attend him, whereupon we last night sent our order to both the Commanders for the fitting their Shipps in a better Equipage for his reception and this morning we were early at the Banksall to attend his majesties motion, but being by some other pastimes diverted he came not to the Barr where wee waited for him till the Ebb was so far spent that it was too late for him to pass the Barr, and thereupon returned againe to towne whether wee attended him with a noyse of trumpets and makeing inquiry of the Serkell concerning his Majesties further purpose of goeing on board our Ships, wee received answer that his majesty would now desist from it, whereupon wee resolved and do now accordingly give them dispatch, which before his majesties purpose was knowne wee thought it not safe to doe for the avoiding all occasion of offence." The Agent and Council left their Factory for the accommodation of the King during his visit, having first taken the precaution to remove the Company's treasure "to their garden for safety during their absence." The entertainment of the King amounted to "Pagodas 6149 : 04,

The Ships were the Loyall Subject, Captain Goodlad[1]

A great sum but unavoidable and a good Phirmaund obteyned." The following are the details of the present:

	Pags.	fan.
His Majesty	2552	20
To Maddana the second person	1110	04
To the Cirkell chancellor	1251	08
To the Governour of Metchlepatam	300	24
Scarlett us'd 17 yards	42	16
Broad cloth us'd 7 pces 14½ yds	138	16
Lead to the Cirkell 10 mds. 2½ seer	5	1
Dungarees us'd 4½ pces	1	5
Longcloth us'd 16 pces	18	—
Twine ½ maund		3
Ropes 2 maund		10
8 Pottles of Canary and Brandy	8	00
Charges Extraordinary for peons Boyes Cooleys Provisions &ca	625	25
To the Sarsamutt	25	00
To the Shabander	20	00
To the Banksall people	6	00
To the Governours Bramina and Servants	40	00
To the Gate people	2	00
To the Cattwalls people	2	00
Pagodas	6149	04

The insolence of the Dutch was not allowed to pass unnoticed. It was reported to the Court, and, in October, 1676, the Directors wrote as follows to the "Honble. Directors of the Netherlands East India Co.—Wee cannot but acquaint you with what advice wee received from Metchlepatam by our last shipping Vizt. That on the 18th January 1675/6 when the King of Gulcondah was in the Road of Metchlepatam goeing on board severall ships That a Ship of yours did put our Flagg under their own in the fore and Mizen Top, which had occasioned a Broyl, had not the king immediately commanded the takeing of it down; One of our Commanders sent on board to know the name of the ship and Captain, but they denied to tell them." No notice appears to have been taken of this remonstrance, nor had the earlier protests of the Company's servants in India received any attention if we may judge from an entry in the *Diary of Streynsham Master* under date 17th August, 1676—"The Skipper of the ship who affronted the English in the business of the Flag the last yeare was now in the same ship in the Road [of Masulipatam] and a report went that he was turned out for that fact but the English looked upon it as a juggle."

[1] The Goodlads were a notable family of sea captains in the 17th century. They all appear to have been related to William Goodlad, Master of Trinity House, who died on the 23rd Jan. 1640, and is buried in Leigh Church, Essex. There were five Goodlads, captains in the Company's service, between 1667 and 1687, and two at least among the number had most adventurous careers. The one referred to in the text is Captain William Goodlad. He commanded the *Greyhound* from about 1669 till 1671, when, on his return from a voyage to

Commander, and the Unity, Captain Cruffe[1] Commander.

Bantam, he succeeded Captain Arnold Browne as commander of the *Loyall Subject*, in which ship he made four voyages. In 1671, William Goodlad sailed the *Loyall Subject*, burthen 450 tons, owners Messrs. Squire, Breton, and others, to Fort St George. While there, in 1672, he was present at a Consultation held to discuss the advisability of strengthening the fortifications after the taking of St Thomé by the French. He concurred in the advice given to raise the wall 5·ft. from "St. Thoma poynt to the Salt petre Godowns." From Fort St George William Goodlad went to Balasor, returning to England in May, 1673. In Dec. 1674 he again went to Fort St George with the *Loyall Subject*, burthen 470 tons. She arrived on the 9th July, and at the end of the month was sent to Masulipatam "with her sickly crew of men...whereof 21 buried." Matthew Mainwaring, the Agent at Masulipatam, was ordered to provide the *Loyall Subject* with more English, "or at least Lascars." It was in this voyage that the celebrated Samuel White came out as mate, and while at Masulipatam, during the time our author mentions, stole away "Mistress Povey that was sent for to Madras to marry young Mr. Jearsey" and married her there himself. On the 6th Aug. 1675 William Goodlad was ordered to take his ship to "the Bay," but was delayed for some days owing to a "violent sicknesse." He returned to Masulipatam at the end of the year and was to have been despatched to Fort St George early in January, but the King's visit, as described by T. B., kept him at Masulipatam till the end of January. On the 24th of the month he wrote the following letter to the Agent at the Fort: "On board the *Loyall Subject*, 24th January, 1675/6. Right Honble. Sir, The 22d Instant we sailed from out of Metchlepatam roade, the 18th and 20th the King of Gulcondah with all his nobles was aboard our Ship with our Commissioners to waite upon him, we fired at least two hundred and fiftie, or sixtie Peices of Ordnance, was forced to run out all our lower Gunns, and pull downe our Bulke head of the Partition in the great Cabine, which put us to a great charge and trouble, our powder spent in the two daies comes to neare eight hundered pounds for which I have the Commissioners order to your honour to supplie, The King was extreemly pleased with our shipp, and very familiar, at his going ashore tooke Capt. Cruft and my Selfe with him, And visited us, which was no small griefe to the Dutch, which putt our English Anctent under their colours, But was forced to take them downe to their disgrace, I shall wait upon your Honour with all convenient speed...." In October, 1676, Capt. William Goodlad set out from England to Bantam, whence he returned in Dec. 1677. In Dec. 1678 he went on his last voyage, also to Bantam. The ship's burthen was then 650 tons. While at Bantam the *Loyall Subject* sprang a leak, and during their enforced detention the Captain and crew suffered from the effects of the climate. They reached England in a sickly condition in 1680, and the Captain died almost immediately after landing. (The information here given has been extracted chiefly from *Court Books*, *Letter Books*, *Factory Records*, Masulipatam, Hugli, Java, and Fort St George.)

[1] Captain William Cruft, Croft, Cruffe, or Cruff commanded the *Unity* for about ten years, from 1669 to 1679, and, during that time, made four voyages to India. He twice fell under the displeasure of the Court, once for the non-observance of religious duties on board

He staid here Severall days, and went On board a Dutch Flyboate[1] alsoe, they then haveinge noe Other in the Roade.

---

his ship, and once for lukewarmness in an engagement with the Dutch on his return voyage in 1674. He was dismissed the Honble. Company's service on each occasion, but on "promising reformation, acknowledging his offence and begging pardon" he was reinstated. With regard to the first dismissal we read, "The Capt. Acknowledgeth his Error and saith there was noe publique prayers on board his shipp but yett he permitted not any vice as Swearing Drunkenesse or other disorders in any persons of the shipps Company." The *Unity* was owned by Mr Lethioulier; her burthen in 1672 was 325 tons, and she carried 26 guns and 78 men. Captain Cruft brought out the great traveller, Fryer, in 1672 (vide *Fryer*, p. 11). It was during her third voyage (1674—1676) that the King of Golcondah went on board the *Unity* at Masulipatam. Her fourth voyage occupied 2½ years; for she went to St Helena, Fort St George, Bantam, Syam, Bangkok, back to Bantam, thence to Persia, and reached the Downs in March, 1679. After this date there is no further mention of the ship or her captain. In 1673, when Captain "Cruff" was at Masulipatam, seven of his men deserted "with his skife." They were seized and sent back, but pleaded in self-defence, that "they had very severe usage from their Captain in abridging them of Victualls." The following extracts from two accounts of the engagement with the Dutch in 1674 show a want of energy on Capt. Cruft's part during the action: "Captain Cruft bore away out of the fleet to Leeward...Captain Cruft at the latter end of the day came something nearer then he was, but Lay to Leeward of me, fired some Gunns at the enemy, but could not doe them any damage being at soe great a distance from the Enemy, what his defects were, which made him bare away I know not, little to be seene in his masts, sailes, hull or rigging...." *Narrative of the late Ingagement with the Dutch*, August, 1674, by William Basse. "As for the *Massenburd*, *East India Merchant* and the *Unity* they were nearrer the observation of the Admirall [than the '*Ceaser*'] who Cane best give account of the service they did, Butt to my best disserninge as also to others they did noe greate mischeife to the Enemie, And as little service to their owne partie Lyeing for the most part to Leward of theire devision, soe your honnours May Judge how they Answred your Commandes and performed their dutie...." Account of the engagement by — Earving, purser's mate of the ship *Sampson*. If these accounts are correct it does not appear that Capt. Cruft cut a very creditable figure in this action with the Dutch. (The particulars here given have been taken from the same sources as those given above for Capt. Goodlad, with the addition of the *O. C.* Collection, and Anderson's *Siam*.)

[1] Fly-boat, a fast-sailing vessel used chiefly in the sixteenth and seventeenth centuries for rapid transport of goods, etc., especially in the coasting trade. Murray, *Oxford Eng. Dict.* Compare the *Diary of Streynsham Master*, under date 6th Sept. 1676, p. 57, "This morning wee overtooke a Dutch Fly boate and a Sloope attending her, which sailed out of Ballasore roade the 30th Instant." Compare also the following from *Factory Records*, Hugli, No. 1, under date 18th July, 1677, "A great Dutch flyboate Arrived from Battavia and touched at Metchlepatam."

His Majesty tooke great delight and Affection to the English, and granted them as much priviledge by a new Chartar[1] as cold in reason be requested.

---

[1] On the 25th of February, 1676, Mr Mainwaring wrote from Masulipatam, "The King hath given us a new phyrmaund in which the words (*Salam Salamband*) are totally left out, which was the occasion of the Governours frequent abuseing us, as likewise Severall other expressions which did limitt us, and Severall needfull additions inserted, and the Charge of transportation by oxen one third abated as per the Copy of the phyrmaund which wee send you herewith...so that now wee hope to live much freer from the Governours &c abuses then here of late." In a letter from the Court to Fort St George, dated 15th Dec. 1676, there is a paragraph headed "The King of Gulcondah's being at Metchlepatam not improved." It runs as follows: "Wee expected a large accompt from you of our affairs at Metchlepatam and in particular of the King of Gulcondah's being there but have received none, and you refer us for it to the Commanders or to a Relation to be given us by the Commanders, Wee desire you to reflect a little upon the Civillity thereof in turning us to our Commanders to be informed of our own affairs and doe fear that none or very little improvement was made of that happy opportunity, and are not to expect such another, what better Accompt you or the Commanders can give us hereof, wee hope the next letters will let us know, for we are not at all satisfied with the indiscreet management of so good an Occasion." These severe remarks were a little premature, for, by the next shipping, the Directors received copies of the *farmān* obtained from the King. Three copies are still in existence at the India Office, two of which are identical; the third appears to be the work of a different translator. The version here given is the one found in the Appendix to the *Diary of Streynsham Master*, pp. 344—346: "Copy of a Phirmaund granted by the King of Golcondah to the English at Metchlepatam January 1675/6. By the Grace of God Sultan Abdula Hossein—The Royall Phyrmaund or Command of our Majesty that shines like the Sunn; wee have thought fitt and convenient and doe hereby require and command all our Ministers of State, Governours, Sub Governours and Juncanners [customs officers] as well for the time being as to come, of Metchlepatam, Pettepolle, Nassapore, Madapollam, Coranga, Wattara, Canara, Vizagapatam, Bimlepatam and throughout all our Dominions and Kingdom of Golcondah to know and take notice That our well-beloved friends of the English nation and Mr. Mainwaring the English Companyes Chiefe have binn in our Royall presence and have found grace and favour from us. We will and Command that whatsoever Quantityes and Qualityes of goods and Merchandize, Gold, and Silver, they bring in by Sea to Metchlepatam, That it be free from all manner of customes and impositions what soever, and that they have free liberty to export the same or send or dispose of it in any part of our Dominions according as it stands with their owne Conveniency, rice, Paddy, and all other merchandize which they bring from abroad either by land or Sea for their own use or to sell, and all other sort of goods whatsoever they buy or sell to be free from all manner of customes and Impositions at the Bancksall the scall gate and all other places for receipt of custome belonging to our Royall

There is Liberty of Conscience allowed to all persons [to] be of what Religion they please, to inhabit here payinge the Kinge his Duties, but must beware withall thay [?that] they upbraide not, nor affront the Mahometans; and, though one of them be a meere Villain, yet in Courts of Justice hee Shall be heard and believed before any Other, and indeed they doe Often Oppresse the Gentues, as the Turks doe the Jews in Turkia or Barbary.

It is needlesse to Speake at large as to the Religion of Mahomet, most men haveinge the full accompt thereof from Turkia, a neighbouringe Countrey to Christendome. These followinge the Very laws of that Saracen law giver, and have many Native Turks amongst them.

Onely this of the better Sort of them I must needs relate, (as I have found by Experience) they are lovers of Justice, and doe Issue it out soe farre as they dare, or may with Safety Escape the fury of the raskaly Sort. They Punish Adultery with death, abhorre drunkenesse and Blasphemy, eat noe Swines flesh. They weare longe Garments, very thinne, generally of fine Linnen; they Uncover not the head in anyway of Courtship. They have many Wifes and Concubines for prevention of Adultery, And, although they hold an irreligious Religion, yet

---

Majesty according and agreeable to this our new Phyrmaund and Command and the Liberty wee have herein granted, The servants, Broakers, Merchants and all depending and imployed by the English nation and Company Workmen Tradesmen and Mechanicks that they be not molested or hindered, and wee give them liberty to imprison and confine their Debitours or those upon whome they have any demands in their Factory without any Protection from our Governour and officers till they have recovered full satisfaction, and all our Governours and other officers are hereby required to assist the English Nation and Company in all their business and Negotiations, and if they send any goods or Merchandize to Golcondah to pay but 4 pagodas new per Candy for the oxe hire The English nation and Company being much in our esteem and favour. This being our new Phyrmaund and command wee will and require a punctuall observance upon pain of our high displeasure. In the moneth of January 1675/6 by and with the advice of Madu Banjee our great Minister of state and Councellour."

it consists of great reverence to God and theire Prophet. They Congregate the people to their Mosquees[1] 4 times a day by Voice of man, and on Fryday (theire Sabbath) 5 times, not Sufferinge any thinge to be pictured or Engraven in them, to avoide Idolatry.

They allow of God the Father, but Utterly deny the Trinitie. They reverence the 3 professors of Religion, Moses for the Jews, Christ for the Christians, and Mahomet for themselves. They are Very liberall to the poore, and bury theire dead very decently.

The Alcoron[2], which contains the Scope of theire irreligious Religion, is written in Arabique Rhime, after a most hodge podge manner, noe way consistinge of due proportion of numbers, nor is it admitted to be written or read in any Other Languadge, but in it's Original tonge, Arabicke, and in the Persian languadge for its antiquities sake, which is now become the Court languadge in the Courts of the greatest Emperours and Kings of Asia.

This booke is held by them in noe Small Veneration. They terme it the booke of Glory, and director to Paradise, never offeringe to touch it before they wash their hands and arms up to the Elbow, and theire feet and legs to the knee. In time of prayer they turne theire faces toward the Sun, first Spreadinge their Upper garments, or a Carpet or Matt Upon the ground, then lookeinge every way 2 or 3 times. When they come to the Salutation

---

[1] See note on p. 11. Compare the following from a Consultation at Fort St George on the 28th March, 1680, on the death of the great merchant Cassa Verona (Kāçu Vīranna), *Factory Records*, Fort St George, No. 2, p. 38, "In the Morning about 3 a Clock Cassa Verona Dyed...And as his body was carrying out of towne to be burned by the gentues some Moors, Fackeers and others put a stop to it, saying he ought to be buryed as a Moor for he was a Mussleman and built a Musseet in the town to be buryed in."

[2] *i.e.* The (Al)Koran. Compare *Fryer*, p. 94, "At Funerals, the Mullahs or Priests, make Orations or Sermons after a Lesson read out of the Alcoran."

of Mahomet, they fall upon their knees, mutteringe many Sentences for ½ an houre or more, bowinge their foreheads often to the Earth with great fervencie, thus Sometimes Standinge Upright, then againe prostrateinge themselves, they Stroke downe their faces and beards, with looks of devout gravitie, &c.

They hold a fast, as they call it, for one month in the yeare, abstaininge from all Sorts of food in the day time, but, to make amends, they feast all night. It beginneth on the New Moone in the Month of October, and continueth the Whole Moone. They doe call it the Ramazan[1], and is Observed annually in Celebration of the Alcoron, affirmeinge that at this time of the yeare it was delivered by God Almightie to theire Prophet Mahomet.

They Seldome or Never accustome themselves to Walkinge for recreations Sake, as wee Europians doe, but if they hold any Conversation it must be Sittinge, and not Upon Chairs, Stools, or benches, but Upon Carpets or Matts Spread Upon the ground, and on them they Sit crosse legged with much facilitie, Often Smoakinge their Hoocars[2] as they call [them] of tobacco,

---

[1] See *Hobson-Jobson*, *s.v.* Ramdam. Anglo-Indians, however, usually call it Ramzān, as the author did no doubt. As this fast moves all round the year, the text alludes to the time of year it occupied when the author observed it. Compare *Fryer*, p. 107, who saw it in November, "But that which affects them all, is at the end of their Ramazan or Lent, which is always the first New Moon in November; which as it is observed with the greatest Strictness, not swallowing their Spittle all the Day of its Continuance, so it is celebrated when it concludes, with the highest Expression of Joy and Solemnity." Compare also the following from a Consultation at Fort St George on the 26th (? 29th) March, 1680, *Factory Records*, Fort St George, No. 2, p. 122, "The King is intended to take his progress into these parts, after this Ramasan Moone is over."

[2] See *Hobson-Jobson*, *s.v.* Hooka, where the earliest quotation is, however, 1768. Compare the following in a letter from Allen Catchpole at Janavad to Richard Edwards at Balasor, 28th Aug. 1676, *O. C.* No. 4222, "I have per this Cossit [messenger] sent Mr. Sayon such a hooker as he desired." In a list of the things to be presented to the Fouzdar [*faujdār*] of Hugli, 3rd April, 1682, *Factory Records*, Hugli, No. 3, there is, "one Aftowel and Chillumchee [ewer and basin], one Hoocka one pigdan [spittoon]...."

drinke[ing] much Coffee and often chawinge Betelee Areca[1], which they call Paune[2].

Hoocars: commonly called hubble-bubble[3].

The Poore Sort of Inhabitants, vizt. the Gentues, Mallabars, &c. Smoke theire tobacco After a Very meane, but I Judge Original manner, Onely the leafe rowled up, and light one end, and holdinge the Other betweene their lips, and Smoke untill it is soe farre Consumed as to warme theire lips, and then heave the End away; this is called a bunko[4], and by the Portugals a Cheroota[5].

Theire food in Generall consists of very little more then very coarse rice and Water, and Sometimes a little dryed fish to relish it.

Theire habit is noe more then a Small Clout just to cover theire privities, wherewith they Seemingly live very contentedly, much better then many that pamper up themselves with plenty of Varieties, and have plenty of Children, and in generall as chearefull in poverty as any mortals can

---

[1] See note on p. 30. Compare *Dampier*, vol. i. p. 318 f., and *Schouten*, vol. i. p. 292 f.

[2] See note on p. 30.

[3] See *Hobson-Jobson*, *s.v.* Hubble-bubble. Compare *Fryer*, p. 31, "The Moors are very grave and haughty in their demeanor, not vouchsafing to return an Answer by a Slave, but by a Deubash, who is the Interpreter. Their chiefest Delight and Pride is to be seen smoking Tobacco cross-legg'd in a great Chair at their doors, out of a long Brass Pipe adapted to a large Crystal Hubble-bubble, fixed in a Brass Frame, their Menial Servants surrounding them." Compare also the following from *Factory Records*, Hugli, No. 1, under date 19th July, 1678, "They [the factors at Dacca] writ for 6 large Maldiva Atcheene Coconutts and nuts for hubble-bubbles for the Prince."

[4] See *Hobson-Jobson*, *s.v.* Buncus. The above is the earliest quoted instance of the word, and is given in Murray, *Oxford English Dict.*, *s.v.* Cheroot. In his *Malay Dict.* T. B. gives Booncoos, a Fardle, a parcel. *Fryer*, p. 52, under the "Wares" of the Malabar coast, has. "Bunco, *i.e.* Tobacco, and Hubble-bubble Canes, the Product of this Coast."

[5] See *Hobson-Jobson*, *s.v.* Cheroot. Like bunko, the above is the earliest known quotation of the word.

be that enjoy the riches and fatt of the Land; they dance and Singe very frequently, Even as men Secured from all Cares and fears that doe accompanie the Wealth of the Universe.

Narsapore[1] is the lowest[2] towne of any Upon this Coast.

---

[1] Morris, *Godavery District*, gives the following information about Narsapur: "Nursapore (Narsapuram) is situated in latitude 16° 26′ N., and in longitude 81° 41′ 49″ E., on the western bank of the Vasishta or the most southern branch of the Godavery. It is about six miles from the sea. Its northern suburb is Madapollam....The trade of the town has steadily declined since the abolition of the Company's factory in 1827, and the abandonment of the Company's 'investments.' The sites of the old buildings have been carried away by successive encroachments of the river, which makes a very considerable bend opposite the town (p. 39). In January, 1611, Captain Hippon was despatched by the Directors of the East India Company in the ship 'Globe' to open a trade with the people on the Coromandel coast. A Dutchman, named Peter Williamson Floris, who was in the English Company's employ, accompanied him in the capacity of factor, with authority to conduct all commercial transactions....Floris has left an interesting account of these voyages....'On the 18th [Feb. 1613] Mr. Floris went to Narsapur Peta, and the 19th the ship was brought into the River, drawing 9¾ feet, and having 10½, contrary to the Reports of some who wished no good to the English....In August, there happened in Narsapur Peta, and thereabouts, a greater Overflowing than had been seen in twenty-nine Years. The whole Salt Hills, Towns, and Rice were drove away, and many thousand Men and Cattle were drowned; the Water rising three Yards above the Highway.'...From the above extract it will be observed that Nursapore, where, if the obstruction of the bar across the entrance of the river could be overcome, there is an excellent harbour for ships of the largest size, was well known more than two centuries ago for its docks for the building and repair of large vessels. Being situated on the bank of the Godavery it has always been exposed to inundations during the high freshes of the river (pp. 177—179)." In 1679 Streynsham Master visited Narsapur. In his *Memoriall*, quoted by Mackenzie, *Kistna District*, pp. 141 f., under date 9th and 16th April, 1679, there is the following description of the place: "The townes of Madapollam and Narsapore joyne together, the Dutch house for their Iron worke in Narsapore being a little above muskett shott from the English Factory in Madapollam, Narsapore lyes below Madapollam downe the River, and that place is under the Governour of Metchlepatam and has the command of all the River for the Customes as far as Corango, but Madapollam, Mellick, Mahmudpet and Naurasporam, tho they all joyne near together to Narsapore, yet they have every one distinct Havaldars for the gathering the ground rent independent from Narsapore or Metchlepatam at present....We went to view the Dutch house and compound at Narsapore which is a very large piece of ground divided into two large inclosed quadrangles, in one of which is as many forges as 300 smiths may worke in them, the compound

It lieth Some 40 or 45 miles below[3] Metchlipatam, haveinge the benefit of an Excellent River, which addeth much to the benefit of the place, and is called Narsapore river[4]. It runneth close to the towne Side, which is nearest foure English miles above the barre or Entrance thereof, and the River Navigable Severall miles above the towne. There be many Other Villages neare it, Some one, 2, 3, 4 or 5 miles distance, but this is the Chiefe[5], and is the Seat of the Governour, who alsoe is a Mahometan, as most men of Office in the Kingdome are. He goeth in pretty large State, but not like to him of Metchlipatam[6], this part of the Countrey affordinge the Kinge noe great Revenues; the best it affordeth is it aboundeth well in timber, and conveniencies for the buildinge and repairinge Ships[7].

---

reaches downe to the River side upon the sandy banke of which lyes many vessells which are imployed in that great Rice trade of Gingerlee." Compare also Alex. Hamilton, *East Indies*, vol. i. p. 371, who, however, evidently included Madapollam in his remarks upon Narsapur: "Next to Matchulipatam is Narsipore, where the English had a Factory for long Cloth, for the Use of their Factory of Matchulipatam, when they manufactured Chintz there. It also affords good Teak Timber for building, and has a fine deep River, but a dangerous Bar, which makes it little frequented."

[2] *i.e.* most Northerly.

[3] *i.e.* to the North.

[4] "If goodes may be brought from Mesulapatam, at the returne of the Monsoone, and that the ship may ride in security at the Fort, then let her remayne there, But if this may not bee done with security, wee conceive it might bee safe to send her into Nassapore River if there shall be water enough for her over the Barr." Letter from the Court to Fort St George, 28th Dec. 1666, *Letter Book*, No. 4. From the *Diary of Streynsham Master*, under date 17th Aug. 1676, p. 43, we learn that the Dutch were "building a new Factory upon Nasapore River between Madapollam and the Rivers mouth."

[5] See *ante* p. 98, extract from Streynsham Master's *Memoriall*, where four villages are named.

[6] According to Streynsham Master, Narsapur was under Masulipatam. In his *Memoriall*, quoted by Mackenzie, *Kistna District*, under date 2nd April, 1679, we read, "Aga Telloll [Jālal] the Governor of Metchlepatam having been toward Narsapore and those places under his Government returned to Goodera last night." See also the extract from the *Memoriall* on the 9th and 16th April quoted above, note 1, p. 98.

[7] In a "Generall" from Balasor, dated 16th Dec. 1670, the Factors

The English East India Company have a Very good Factory called Madapollum[1], from the name of the

at the Bay wrote to the Court (*Factory Records*, Misc. No. 3) that they had ordered a ship to be built at "Massapore" in place of the "Madrass Pinnace"; they added, "Wee should ourselves have built another but that neither Timber nor workmen are soe good as at Massapore."

[1] Like so many notices in this MS., these remarks on Madapollam are valuable as showing that the place was a flourishing ship-building and manufacturing station, as well as a health resort, when T. B. visited it. See *Hobson-Jobson*, *s.v.* Madapollam. From the *Letter Books*, *Factory Records*, *O. C.* Collection, *Coast and Bay Abstracts*, *Madras Press List*, and *Mad. Man. Admn.*, the following interesting particulars about the place have been gleaned. As early as 1662 an attempt was made to found a factory at Madapollam (Mādhavayapālem), but it was not till some years later that it was in full swing as a "subordinate" to Fort St George. In Feb. 1662, the Court ordered that a house belonging to Sir Edward Winter at Madapollam should be retained for the Company. The letter expressed the wish that it "may be soe commodious and fitting for our use and benefitt, that thereby wee may bee eased of continuing a factory at Verasheroone." Nicholas Buckridge, who was ordered to report on Madapollam, thought the house unsuitable—"Madapollam House I Vizitted at the same time [in 1664] and finde it was builded by Sir Edward Winter for his Particular occasions on a peece of ground formerly graunted for your Use by the King of Gulcondah, on the river side for a Wharfe or Bunder convenient for building, or repairing Shiping, and as now it is repaired at your cost it is A plesant place, but I cannot Imagine it were necessary or that you will allow soe costly A [? building] maintained at soe great A Charge, only for the delight and convenience of your Servants, nor can I beleive that Sir Edward Winter would have consented to it had it not been his owne and much out of repaire, when he put it to your Account." The business done at Madapollam did not satisfy the Directors and, in July, 1669, Foxcroft received orders that no factory was to be settled there. In Sept. he gave it as his opinion, in which he was supported by Jearsey, that it would be unwise to discontinue the Madapollam Factory. In Dec. 1669, the Court wrote—"Madapollam hath cost us a great deale of Mony and is a place of little use to us, wee would therefore have you by your next, to advise us how wee may best improve or dispose thereof." In compliance with this order, Mohun, who succeeded Jearsey as Chief at Masulipatam, enquired into "the state of Madapollam Factory." On the 14th July, 1670, Mohun wrote to Fort St George, "Madapollam wee are informed is a Factory necessary to be continued, and will yearly afford you greater and greater quantityes of Callicoes if Supplyed with Monies and that this Factory doth much depend upon it for Investments, being cheaper bought there then here [Masulipatam] by 20 per Cent or more, all the Country neare it being Weavers...." In spite of this encouraging report, the Company continued averse to retaining Madapollam except at a small expense. In Dec. 1671, the Court wrote to Fort St George that though "our House at Madapollam...

Villadge adjoyninge to it. It is accompted a most healthy and pleasant place and not a whit Undeservedly, haveinge the benefit of Such a pleasant River that cometh up even to one of [the] Gates thereof, with very pleasant Gardens almost Surroundinge it, noe way hindered of all benefit of Sea breezes, for which reasons our English Chiefe (and most Eminent Factors of Metchlipatam) repaire hither and Stay 2 or 3 months, dureinge the time of the heats, vizt. April, May and June.

---

is a very handsome and usefull place,...yet doubt not but a Lesse expensive place, either there or at Verasheroone may doe as well, Wee therefore desire that you...endeavour to sell our said Howse at Madapollam upon the best termes you can for our most advantage." This order was evidently disregarded. Fryer, writing in 1673, speaks of Madapollam as a sanatorium for the factors at Masulipatam and remarks that the English had a "wholesome Seat there." The healthiness of Madapollam was the reason of its popularity with the factors on the Coromandel Coast. In a "Generall" from Masulipatam dated 25th Aug. 1673, we find that Madapollam House was repaired and enlarged and made "fitt to receive the whole Factory," and that Madapollam was "in a much more healthy ayre than Metchlepatam." The Court, however, was still unsatisfied. In March, 1674, they wrote that "The 4 Factoryes of Mesulapatam, Madapollam, Verasheroone and Pettipolee are not worth the charge" and desired information as to which of the four was best to be retained. On the 9th Oct. Major Puckle, who had been sent on a visit of inspection to all the "subordinates," wrote, "I have seen the Factorie of Madapollam, and also Verasharoon, and doe find they are both of use, and good investments may be made in them." At this time Robert Fleetwood was "Chiefe" at Madapollam. He was succeeded by Christopher Hatton in Sept. 1676, who, in his turn, was followed by John Field and Samuel Wales. In April, 1679, Streynsham Master spent several days at Madapollam, and transacted much important business there, *vide* his *Memoriall* as quoted by Mackenzie, *Kistna District*, pp. 141—147. In 1686 and 1687 there was much correspondence about the dissolution of the "Subordinate Factoryes." In January, 1688, the Court wrote ordering them all to be withdrawn except Madapollam, it "alone being sufficient for our business on that Coast, and it is not so far from Pettipollee but that the black Merchants there may carry their Cloth to Madapollam." However, in the same year, this factory too was withdrawn. It was resettled in 1698. In 1705 the Agent and Council wrote from Fort St George that they intended "to pull down the old factory at Madapollam," but in 1708 two Factory Houses, old and new, were in existence. Madapollam was captured by the French in 1757, ceded to the English in 1759, and confirmed to them in 1765. The place gave its name to a fine kind of white piece-goods manufactured there.

Many English Merchants and Others have yearely Ships and Vessels built here, beinge the onely Commodious Port on this or the next Coast adjoyneinge thereto, vizt. Gingalee[1].

Here is the best and well growne timber in Sufficient plenty; the best Iron upon the Coast is for the most part Vended here and att reasonable rates, with the Workmanship alsoe[2]; any Sort of Ironworke is here ingenuously performed by the Natives, as Speeks[3], bolts, Anchors, &c.

Very Expert Master builders there are Severall here who have most of their dependancie Upon the English, and indeed learnt theire art and trade from some of them, by diligently Observeinge the ingenuitie of Some that built Ships and Sloops here for the English East India Company and theire Agents, Soe that they build very well and give good reasons for what they doe, and lanch with as much discretion as I have Seen in any part of the world, which I will by and by relate; but I must not forgett theire falseheartednesse to our English builders, to whom doth Issue forth most horrid enviteracie from these Gentues that have learned of them what doth in a Measure Suffice. They Poyson all Ship Carpenters that are Employed by any, Either Moore, Dutch, nay, of the English, Especially, that Undertake the buildinge of any Ship, as for instance I have knowne 2 or 3 very ingenuous Master builders, (English Men) that have Staid behind the Ships they were to returne to theire Native Countrey in, on purpose to build Ships for theire Employers, the English Chiefs, and notwith Standinge they very circumspectly Shunned conversation, or what else, with these Gentue Workmen, yet before they cold finish one bottom, they

---

[1] This MS. will, later on, throw much light on this obscure word.

[2] For a mention of the Dutch iron factory in this district, see note on p. 105.

[3] ? Spikes.

have by one Stratgem or Other been Sent to theire longe homes[1].

As I said before, there lanchinge and hallinge Up the Ships is after a most Excellent manner, for which they are highly to be Commended.

I have Seen a Ship, (belongeinge to the Kinge of Golcondah) a Ship of great burthen, built for the trade to Mocho in the Red Sea[2], and after 2 Voyadges thither, She was halled Upon the Westerne Side of this River a little above the towne, to the intent they might Sheath and repaire her. She cold not be lesse (in my judgement) then 1000 tunns in burthen, and they halled her up by Strength of men with good purchase as follows:—They prepared 2 very Substantial timbers, of 20 foot longe each, and 20 or 24 inches in thicknesse, upon which they Erected a Cradle fittinge for the bildge of her, the 2 main timbers beinge placed at that distance that the Cradle beinge put Under her, the foremost was 8 or 10 foot abaft the Scarfe of her Stemme, the Other as much before the heele of her Sternepost, with girdlines from the said cradle to her ports or Scopeboards[3]; to the dogs were fitted good straps and fourefold tackles, the falls of 15 or 16 inch Coyre Cable[4], the which are brought to too (*sic*)

[1] The author evidently speaks with conviction. He had ample opportunity of knowing what went on at Madapollam, for he paid several visits to, and spent a considerable time at, that place. He was there in 1682 when he drew his map of "Tanasarim," again in 1683, and in 1685 when he bought the "Conimeer Sloop" of the Company. *Vide* Introduction.

[2] T.B. is careful not to confuse Mocha in Arabia with Moca in Sumatra (commonly called Moco Moco). Trade was carried on with both places. English and Dutch factories were established at Mocha early in the 17th century, and, from that time, a constant interchange of commerce went on with the Indian ports.

[3] *i.e.* scuppers.

[4] See note on p. 42. Compare *Fryer*, p. 121, "Cair Yarn made of the Cocoe for Cordage." Compare also *Dampier*, vol. i. p. 294 f., "The husk of the Shell [of the Coco-nut] is of great use to make Cables; for the dry husk is full of small strings and threads, which

very substantiall Crabbs, placed a little above the height they purpose to have the Ship to, and heave first at one end then at the Other 5 or 6 foot at a time, and Soe on Untill She is high Enough, the Doggs runinge Upon good rowlers, as in manner followinge—

A: One of the doggs, vizt. the aftermost.
B: The Square pins (or fids).
C: The Rowlers.
D: The Ships Keele.
E: The Cradle.
F: The bedds and quoynes to Support the Cradle.
G: The Ships bildge.
H: The Ends of the yards or Powles from End to End.
I: Girdlines from the Cradle Upwards.
K: Great Strapps sweepinge round the dogs.
L: The Great blocks. M: The Tackle falls.
N: The Crabbe. O: The Barrs.

The Cables, Strapps, &c. are made of Cayre, vizt. the Rhine of Coco nuts very fine Spun, the best Sort of which is brought from the Maldiva Isles[1]. They are as Stronge

---

being beaten, become soft, and the other substance which was mixt among it falls away like Saw-dust, leaving only the strings. These are afterwards spun into long yarns, and twisted up into balls for convenience; and many of these Rope-yarns joyned together make good Cables. This Manufactory is chiefly used at the Maldive Islands, and the threads sent in balls into all places that trade thither, purposely for to make Cables. I made a Cable at Achin with some of it. These are called Coire Cables: they will last very well."

[1] See *Hobson-Jobson*, *s.v.* Maldives. The principal trade of these islands was in cowries, of which they exported a large quantity to Bengal. Compare Alex. Hamilton, *East Indies*, vol. i. p. 346, "the Maldiva Islands...their only Product is Cocoa-nut...of that Tree they build vessels of 20 or 30 Tuns, Their Hulls, Masts,...Cables...are all from this useful tree." See also Pringle, *Consultations* for 1684, p. 174, note 46. The following extract from a letter, dated Hugli, 15th Feb. 1675, to Edward Reade at Balasor, is interesting in this connection, "Inquier a bout the Maldiva Char it being 14 mds. this weight at its going hence and Should hould more with you unless there was any part of it used for the Sloope Ganges." *Factory Records*, Hugli, No. 4.

Plate VIII

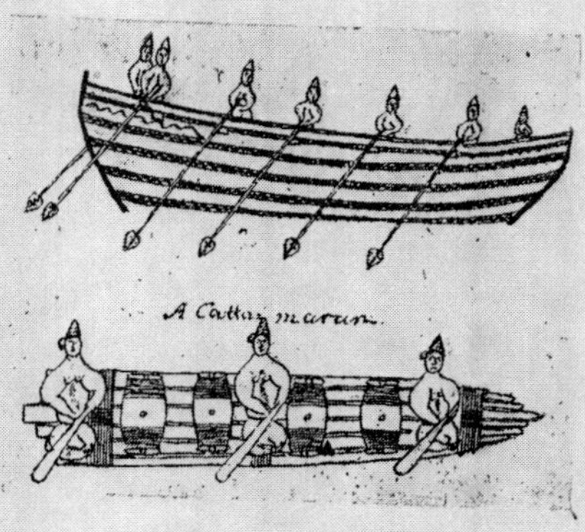

"A MASSOOLA. A CATTAMARAN." p. 44.

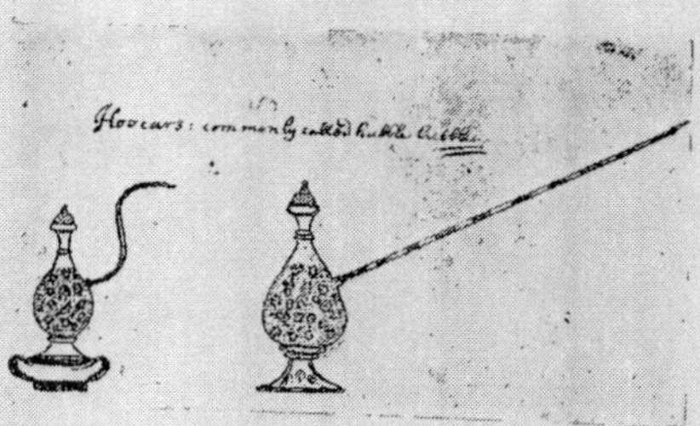

"HOOCARS." p. 97.

"THE MANNER OF FIXING THEIR GEERE." p. 104.

as any hempen Cables whatever, and much more durable in these hott climates, with this provisor, that if they chance to be wet with fresh water, either by raine or rideinge in a fresh River, they doe not let them drye before they wett them well in Salt water, which doth much preserve them, and the Other as much rott them. All the reason I can give for it is, that the Cayre of the Maldiva grows Upon a very brackish Soyle.

They have an Excellent way of makeinge Shrowds, Stays, or any Other Rigginge for Ships. They, for the most part, make them of good twine, which is heare as Cheape as course hemp Unspun is in England, and when laid with Europe[1] tarre prove most Serviceable.

The Dutch have a Factorie 4 English miles above ours, and is called Pollicull[2], after the name of a Villadge thereunto adjoyneinge, where they are soe ingenuous to keep Severall ropemakers, (men of theire owne Nation) at

---

[1] See *Hobson-Jobson*, *s.v.* Europe for European. Compare Wilson, *Early Annals*, vol. i. p. 394, "the books kept for the Account Silk of Europe dye shall be so kept no longer." *N. and E.* p. 6 for 23rd Feb. 1680, has "Ballast for our Europe ships."

[2] "Pālakollu (Palkole)...5 miles north of Narsapūr town...was the first settlement of the Dutch on this part of the coast. They opened a factory here in 1652, and for a long time it was their head-quarters. In the churchyard, Dutch inscriptions as old as 1662 are still legible. The Dutch founded indigo factories, ironworks, and extensive weaving industries, and planted large orange and shaddock gardens." Hunter, *Imperial Gazetteer of India*, *s.v.* Palakollu. Streynsham Master mentions "Pollicull" in 1676 and again in 1679. Under date 17th Aug. 1676, he remarks, "They [the Dutch] rent a Towne of the King of Golcondah called Pollicull where they make store of ordinary cloth, and have another Factory at Naglewanch." *Diary of Streynsham Master*, p. 43. On the 14th April, 1679, "The Agent &c. went to visit the Dutch at Pollicull this evening which is about 7 miles inland from Madapollam. There the Dutch have a Factory of a large compound, where they dye much Blew Cloth, having about 300 Jars set in the ground for that worke, also they make many their best paintings there, the Towne being first rented by them at 2,000 old Pagodas per annum is now given them free by the king...." *Memoriall of Streynsham Master*, quoted by Mackenzie, *Kistna District*, p. 143. By the treaty of Versailles in 1783, Palakollu fell to the English, but the Dutch paid a small quit-rent for the place up to 1804. In 1818 it was formally restored to them, but was again ceded to Britain in 1824.

worke all the yeare rounde, as alsoe Severall black Smiths, makeinge all Sorts of Iron worke, (necessarie for Ships) whereby they doe Supply most of theire fleets with Such Necessaries.

This part of the Countrey affordeth plenty of divers Sorts of Callicoes[1] and Paintings[2], Lungees[3], Pallampores[4], &c., but are for the most part carried to Metchlipatam, and vended there, that beinge a great market place, and indeed, the Great Bazar[5] of these parts for above 100 miles in Circuit.

The Inhabitants of this part of [the] Countrey are, for the most part, Gentues, Save in Narsapore there are many Moors, beinge the Retinue of the Governour.

---

[1] See note on p. 5.

[2] *i.e.* prints, printed calicoes. See note on p. 9. Compare the following contemporary extracts: "Wee have sent to our Factors at Guinea a Small fardle of fine Paintings made in your parts." Letter from the Court to Fort St George, Aug. 1661, *Letter Book*, No. 2. "Encorage...the making of all Sorts of Callicoes and Paintings." Letter from the Court to Fort St George, 26th Oct. 1668, *Letter Book*, No. 4. "Mr. Hopkings...is now Second of Pettipolee where all such things as gownes and Chinses are painted." Letter from Masulipatam to Balasor, 16th March, 1670, *O.C.* No. 3413. "If wee should keepe her [the *European*] there [at Masulipatam] till Paintings be ready, she might endanger the loss of her passage." Letter from Fort St George to the Court, 14th July, 1671, *O.C.* No. 3575. "The people of the place [Edelumburoo] are cheifly painters, they told me there was not fewer of them than 200 familyes in that Towne, that they understood all sorts of painting, but that their cheife employment at present was upon course goods." Extract from Elihu Yale's *Memoriall*, Dec. 1681, *O.C.* No. 4776. "I have with all dilligence encouraged the painting trade and have been at some Charge to doe itt, without any manner of partiallity I think wee farr out doe Metchlepatam and hope by next Ship to send you a thousand pieces Such as never were seen in the world, if I can but Keep these Cursed fellows from mixing the Southern Chay [red madder] with the Northern, the latter being the best and costs much more." Pitt in a letter dated 11th Feb. 1700, in *Hedges' Diary*, vol. iii. p. 62 f. See also Pringle, *Consultations* for 1683, p. 139, note 65.

[3] See note on p. 55.

[4] See note on p. 71. "Yours...I Received...with a Pallampore, which is very fitt for my use...the Pagoda you paid for said Pallampore." Letter from Fort St George, 11th Sept. 1678, *O. C.* No. 4491.

[5] Compare *Fryer*, p. 27, "For places of resort [at Masulipatam] there are three Buzzars, or market-places, crowded both with people and Commodities."

Noe Commodities this countrey affordeth are any ways prohibited to be Sold to men of any Nation, the Seller thereof Payinge the Kings Duties, which is about 4 per Cent. Onely tobacco that hath its growth in any part of this Kingdome is not admitted to be Sold to any Save to the Commissioners that have farmed it from the Kinge for more then 100 miles round the towne of Metchlipatam, and what Merchants or Others doe buy of them by wholesale may then with freedome goe to any Bazar and there Vend in Publique[1].

They are Soe Severe in it, that in most places of note in the Countrey they keep waiters to Search any travailer, and if they find more tobacco then what they judge convenient for his journey, they Seize upon it, and perhaps he Escapes not Unpunished.

The Natives in Generall Smoke much tobacco, in soe much t[h]at children of 3 or 4 years of age frequently take it, and it is made as frequent amongst them as meat and drinke.

Now before I leave this Coast, I shall Speake Somethinge of the Metropolitan Citty.

GOLCONDAH.

These beforementioned places, (with many more I have not discoursed of) are Scituate Upon the Coast of Choro-

[1] I can find no contemporary confirmation that tobacco was a government monopoly in this district. In Fort St George, at any rate, in Lockyer's time, the tobacco farm was in the hands of the Company. *Vide* Lockyer, *Trade in India*, p. 12. However, the following extract in a letter from the "Braminy" at Golconda to Fort St George, dated 21st June, 1680 (*Factory Records*, Fort St George, No. 28), seems to support T.B.'s statement, "Futty Cawn hath of late wrote from thence [Fort St George] to his Excellency the Sharlaskar [Governor of the Golconda Coast] that Chinnapatnam [Madras town] is not now as formerly but is mightily encreased, and that the English have even farmed Beetle and Tobacco, and that they were encreasing the Fort."

mandell, and neare to the Indian Sea. The Kingdome of Golcondah doth Extend it Selfe Some hundreds of miles to the North Eastward[1], even to the black Pagod[2] Some 20 miles below[3] the Pagod Jno. Gernaet[4], but many of the Gentues and Brachmans hold lands there, and call themselves Radjas[5], accomptinge Some miles thereabout to be Subject to noe Mahometan Kinge whatever[6]; but, let it be how it will, the Golcondah Kinge reapeth much moneys thence, both by Customes and Other Acknowledgements.

The Faire and Beautifull Citty Golcondah is an inland one and the Metropolitan of the Kingdome, the Residence of the Kinge and Queen, and many Lords, and of most of the forces of the Whole Kingdome. It is a Citty of very Small Antiquitie[7], for the most part built within these

---

[1] Compare *Thevenot*, part iii. p. 93, "The most powerful of the Kings of Decan, next to Viziapour, is the King of Golconda. His Kingdom borders on the East side, upon the Sea of Bengala; to the North, upon the Mountains of the Countrey of Orixa; to the South, upon many Countries of Bisnagar, or Ancient Narsingue, which belongs to the King of Viziapour; and to the West, upon the Empire of the Great Mogul, by the province of Balagate, where the Village of Calvar is, which is the last place of Mogolistan on that side."

[2] Sailors' name for the temple at Kanārak, dating from about 1250 A.D. See quotation from the *Diary of Streynsham Master*, in note on p. 12. See also *Ind. Ant.* vol. xxx. p. 348, for this well-known mark on the Orissa Coast.

[3] Above (*i e.* to the North), as we should say nowadays.

[4] See note on p. 12.

[5] See note on p. 39. T. B. in his *Malay Dict.* has "Raja, a King."

[6] Compare *Thevenot*, part iii. p. 94, "The boundaries of Mogulistan and Golconda are planted about a League and a half from Calvar: They are Trees which the[y] call Mahoua [*mahwā*]; these mark the outmost Land of the Mogul, and immediately after, on this side of a Rivulet, there are Cadjours [*khajūr*], or wild [date] Palm-trees, planted only in that place, to denote the beginning of the Kingdom of Golconda, wherein the insolence of collectors is far more insupportable than in the confines of Mogolistan; for the duties not being exacted there, in the Name of the King, but in the Name of private Lords, to whom the villages have been given, the Collectors make Travellers pay what they please."

[7] Compare *Thevenot*, part iii. pp. 94 and 98, "The Capital city of this Kingdom [Golconda] is called Bagnagar, the Persians call it Aider-abad...The Castle where the King commonly keeps his Court,

100 years past[1], begun when the Ancestors of the familie of this present Kinge revolted from the Mogoll[2] and conquered this Kingdome, then called by the name of Bisnagar[3], that beinge the Metropolitan and Seat of a Viceroy; but, Upon the Conquest hereof, they did, as the Mahometan Custome hath been of Antient times, in a manner demolish the Old one and Erect a New one giveinge another Name thereto.

So that now the Whole is called the Kingdome of Golcondah, but what they tooke from the Emperour, and what Soon after they tooke from the Hindoos, or Idolaters, and what by their Couradge, and more Especially the great Masse of riches these lands Enjoyed, which caused the Christian Nations to Settle and trade here, it is become a Very Glorious and Potent Kingdome, or rather Empire,

---

is two Leagues from Bagnagar; it is called Golconda, and the Kingdom bears the same name. Cotup-Sha the first, gave it that name, because after his Usurpation seeking out for a place where he might build a strong Castle, the place where the Castle stands was named to him by a Shepheard, who guided him through a Wood to the Hill where the Palace is at present; and the place appearing very proper for his designe, he built the Castle there, and called it Golconda, from the word Golcar, which in the Telenghi Language signifies a Shepheard: all the Fields about Golconda were then but a Forest, which were cleared by little and little, and the Wood burnt. This place is to the west of Bagnagar; the plain that leads to it, as one goes out of the Suburbs, affords a most lovely sight, to which the prospect of the Hill that rises like a Sugar-loaf in the middle of the Castle, which has the Kings palace all round upon the sides of it, contributes much by its natural situation." The above "derivation" for Golconda is quite fanciful as most old Indian derivations are. It is quite possible that the writer is mixing up Bhāgnagar, now Haidarabad, which was the town, and Golconda, which was the fort. Aurangzēb, "the Great Mogull," was Viceroy for his father Shāh Jahān in the Deccan from 1635 to 1642, and again from 1652 to 1656.

[1] Historically the Qutb Shāhī Dynasty rose out of the dismemberment of the Bāhmanī Dynasty of Kulbarga in 1489 and took the royal style at Golconda in 1512. But the king, who chiefly made the territory and helped to destroy Vijayanagar, was Ibrāhīm Qutb Shāh, 1549—1581, that no doubt being the reference in the text. See *Tavernier*, vol. i. part ii. pp. 65—69 for a history of the rise of "Abdoul-Coutou-Sha."

[2] *i.e.* Akbar, 1556—1605.

[3] Vijayanagar.

of above 2000 English miles in Circuit, very well populated and replenished with all things Necessarie[1] Save Some Sorts of Mineralls, haveinge none but of Iron, deficient in those of Silver or Gold, but yet Enjoyeth that which purchaseth it from all or most parts of the Universe, (namely Diamonds, of which in Order).

There be many Stronge holds in this Kingdome, but most places of Eminencie and force, but the Souldiery as well as the Governours are Mahometans.

The fort[2] of this Metropolitan is an admirable One, noe lesse then 5 English miles in Circuit, the walls of Vast height and Substance proportionable thereunto, gunned all round, which addeth much to the Excellencie of this Cittie, which is alsoe blessed with many more conveniencies that adde much to the Strength hereof, the Soile most wholesom and fertile, aboundinge with all Sorts of graine and in great Measure, the temperancie of the Aire, and famous for the River Kishna[3], that Spreadeth it Selfe into many branches runninge Up neare this Citty[4] which is above 200 miles, and issueth out Upon Point Due[5], the Entrance of the Roade of Metchlipatam. All

---

[1] Compare *Tavernier*, vol. i. part ii. p. 63, "The whole Kingdom of Golconda, take it in general, is a good Country, abounding in Corn, Rice, Cattel, Sheep, Poultry, and other necessaries for human life. In regard there are great store of Lakes in it, there is also great store of Fish."

[2] Compare *Thevenot*, part iii. p. 98, "This Fort is of a large compass, and may be called a Town; The Walls of it are built of Stones three Foot in length, and as much in breadth, and are surrounded with deep Ditches, divided into Tanquies, which are full of fair and good Water. But after all, it hath no works of Fortification but five round Towers, which (as well as the Walls of the place) have a great many Cannon mounted upon them for their defence."

[3] Kistna.

[4] Golconda was not however on the Kistna, but on the Musi, a tributary of the Kistna.

[5] Well known to mariners of old as the Southern point of the Kistna estuary. See note on p. 55.

which conveniences cause great resort of Merchants[1] and other both Natives and Forraigners.

Many Europeans, Especially of our English Nation, are here become inhabitants, Entertained in the King's Service[2], and are for the most part in One Office or Other, accordinge to their deserts, as Gunners, Gunners Mates, Armorers, and Some Troopers[2], and have very considerable Sallary, which hath Encouraged many English Soldiers of Fort St. Georg's to flee theire Colours, and hasten thither, but nowadays are but Ordinarilie respected or Entertained, by theire debauched and Unchristian like behaviours, in Soe much that they are now become Odious that repaire thither for Succor, and that come Upon Such frivolous accompts, without Either good repute or habit.

This Kingdome amongst the many Merchandizes it affordeth, as all Sorts of Callicoes[3], Saltpeeter, paintings[4], Carpets of all Sorts, raw and wrought Silkes &c., hath the Enjoyment of the most plenty of rich Diamonds in the Universe. About 100 miles from Golcondah[5] the Earth

---

[1] James Horner, the "free merchant" mentioned by T. B. in the "Queda" section, resided at Golconda from 1679—1681. Compare *Thevenot*, part iii., p. 97, "There are...at Bagnagar...many Rich Merchants, Bankers and Jewellers...Besides the Indian Merchants... there are many Persians and Armenians...There are many Franks also in the Kingdome, but most of them are Portuguese, who have fled thither for Crimes they have committed: However the English and Dutch have lately setled there...." From this extract, it seems, as stated above, p. 108, note, that T. B. confused the town of Bhāgnagar with the fort of Golconda.

[2] The reference is to Mīr Jumla's Artillery. See *Bernier*, p. 17.

[3] See note on p. 5.

[4] See note on p. 106.

[5] The author again shows his accurate personal knowledge of what he describes, and does not fall into the common error of locating the mines at Golconda itself. Mackenzie, *Kistna District*, p. 244 f. combats this error—"The diamond mines in the Kistna District were under the control of the Kings of Golconda for the whole of that period [circa 1500—1686]...Golconda is a common enough name in the Telugu country,...but the Golconda which gave a title to the Qutb Shāh dynasty is a hill fortress near Haidarabad. There are no diamonds in that locality, and when poets wrote of Golconda's

doth most abound therewith, where any Merchant adventurer may purchas a piece of land of halfe an Aker, a whole Aker or more, but at deare rates, as it Sometimes fall out. The Merchant giveinge 8, 10, 20 thousand Pagodes[1] for a Small Spot of land, hath the liberty to digge soe deep as he pleaseth[2], and wash out the Earth Searchinge for what hidden treasure he may happilie find, but severely inspected by the King's Officers, soe that if he meet with a rough Diamond that weyeth above 70 or 72 Conderines[3], the Exact weight of one Royal of 8[4], it must be for the King's owne Use, he payinge or causeinge to be paid soe much moneys for it, (but little more then one halfe the just worth) the rest of Smaller weight and magnitude are att the Adventurers owne disposall, and thus Sometimes they reape Vast Estates in Short time. and Some loose them.

Amongst the famous buildings of Golcondah may well be in the number the Mosquees[5] and Tombs of the deceased Kings and Queens, Especially that of the last queen Mother that deceased, whose Bones, after 7 years interred were taken Up and Sent to Mecha, there againe

---

gems and Golconda's mines they were not aware that Golconda was only the residence of the king, where were displayed the diamonds collected in the outlying tracts of his dominions." Compare also *Tavernier*, vol. i. part ii. pp. 134—138, who gives the earliest reliable account of these mines.

[1] See note on p. 51.

[2] Compare *Tavernier*, vol. i. part ii. p. 135, "They [the Merchants] pay two per cent. to the King for all that they buy: besides that, he has also a duty from the Merchants for leave to dig....And from the day that they begin to work, to the day that they end, the Merchants pay to the King two Pagods a day; and four when they employ an hunder'd men."

[3] See *Hobson-Jobson*, *s.v.* Candareen. This quotation is useful for the history of the word. See *Ind. Ant.* vol. xxvi. p. 315 f., vol. xxvii. pp. ii ff., 91 f.

[4] *i.e.* a dollar.

[5] Masjids. See note on p. 11.

Plate IX

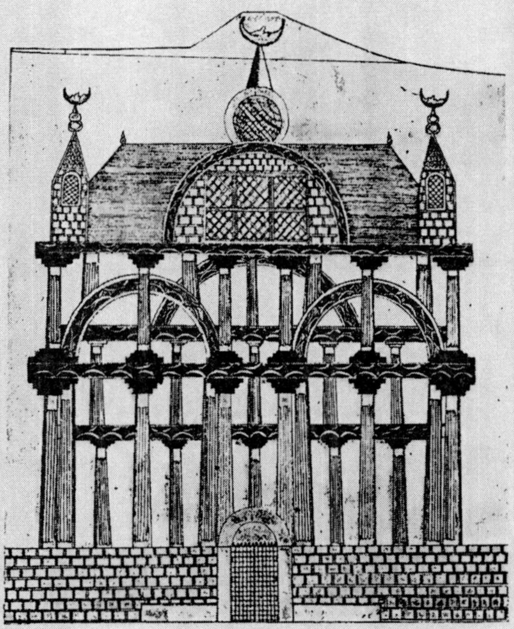

"A MOST SUMPTUOUS TOMBE."

p. 113.

interred in the Land of their Ungodlie Patron[1], the tombe of her first buriall haveinge much added to the repaire thereof, done by this King's father, who deceased Soon after he had finished the Worke, Anno 1671[2]. Hee caused 3 Globes of Massy Gold to be placed on the topp of the Tombe with 3 large halfe Moons of the Same[3]. And caused the Said Tombe to be reverenced as a most Sacred Monument. And gave, and Confirmed many Strange Priviledges Upon it, (one for instance). If any Person have Comitted the most inhumane Crime of theft, Murther, or what else, that by theire Laws deserve a most horrid

---

[1] T. B. appears to have confused two of the daughters of Ibrahīm Quli Qutb Shah, 4th king of the Qutb Shāhī line. Haiyāt Bakhsh Begam was the mother of Abdullah Qutb Shah the 6th king, who died in 1672. She was buried at Golconda, but her body was *not* afterwards removed. Among the "King's Tombs" described in vol. ii. p. 519 of the *Nizam's Dominions* by Bilgrami and Wilmott, mention is made of that of "Haiyāt Baksh Begam, daughter of Ibrahīm Kuli Kutub Shah and the wife of Sultān Mahomed the 5th king, and mother of Sultān Abdulla Kutub Shah, 6th and last but one of the Kutub Shahi line. The date of her death as inscribed on the tomb is H. 1047 (A.D. 1617)." On p. 486 of the same vol. it is stated that the mother of Abdullah Qutb Shah, who died in 1672, pre-deceased her son by only 2 years and 4 months. As Ibrahīm Quli Qutb Shah died in 1580/1, the date of his daughter's death is more probably 1617. For information about the other daughter, evidently the one referred to by T. B., I am indebted to Syed Hossein Bilgrami, who says—"The only court lady whose body was exhumed after seven years and sent to Kerbela (not Mecca) for burial in holy ground was Khairāt-un-Nissā Begam, a daughter of Ibrahīm Qutb Shah. She was buried temporarily under a dome erected for this purpose in Khairātābād not far from a mosque built by herself, and the remains were removed to Kerbela seven years after. The empty mausoleum and mosque are standing to this day, but there are no inscriptions on either of them."

[2] Abdullah Qūtb Shāh, 1624/5—1672. T. B. is a year out in the date of his death.

[3] There is no doubt that the tomb described by T. B. is that of Abdullah Qūtb Shāh. Syed Hossein Bilgrami informs me that it is the only mausoleum in the district with three domes, and that Abdullah Qūtb Shāh is buried in it with his two Hindu queens, Pema Mathi and Tara Mathi. In the *Nizam's Dominions*, vol. ii. p. 520, the tomb is thus described, "Between the walled enclosure and the fort walls is the tomb of the sixth king, Sultan Abdulla Kutub Shah, who died in H. 1083 (A.D. 1672) after a reign of forty-eight years. This is one of the finest tombs here, being enriched with very fine carvings and minarets at each corner of the platform...."

death, if the Party before apprehended can make his Escape into the Tombe, he not only Saveth his life, but cannot for the future be taken out by Violence, but live theire very peaceably, and at the Kinge (*sic*) Charge[1].

Currant Coynes in this Kingdome[2].

Fort St. Georg's, vizt.

	lb	s	d
New Pagods[3] here coyned passe all the Kingdome over att the Rate of	00	08	00
Fanam[4] of gold at	00	00	03
Cash[5] made of Coppar 80 make one fanam	00	00	03
Royals[6] of 8 are worth	00	05	00
Rupees[7] are worth	00	02	03½
The Abassin[8] of Persia 7 to one Pagod or	00	08	00

[1] Compare *Thevenot*, part iii. p. 99 f. "The Sepulchres of the King who built Golconda, and of the five Princes who have Reigned after him are about two Musquet-shot from the Castle. They take up a great deal of ground because every one of them is in a large Garden. ...The Tombs of the six Kings are accompanied with those of their Relations, their Wives, and chief Eunuchs....All these Sepulchres are Sanctuaries, and how criminal soever a Man may be that can get into them, he is secure."

[2] This is one of the most valuable accounts of the confusing money of the time in existence. See article on Southern Indian weights in *Ind. Ant.* vol. xxvii. p. 57 f. This table compares fairly well with that of *Fryer*, p. 208 f. Compare the "Account of the Money of Asia" in *Tavernier*, vol. i. part ii. pp. 2—6.

[3] See note on p. 51. See also *Tavernier*, vol. i. part ii. p. 5, who gives illustrations of "the Money which the English coin in their Fort St. George, or else at Madrespatam, upon the Coast of Coromandel. They call them Pagods, as those of the Kings and Raja's of the Country are call'd. They are of the same weight, the same goodness, and pass for the same Value."

[4] A small gold and also silver coin in Southern India. This, and the three references which follow, are valuable for values. See *Hobson-Jobson*, *s.v.* Fanam.

[5] See *Hobson-Jobson*, *s.v.* Cash.

[6] Royal of eight, (Span. *real*), *i.e.* a piece of eight *reales*, or a dollar. *Fryer*, p. 210, gives the value of a Royal at Bussorah as "3½ Abbassees." Taking the value of the Abassi at about 1*s.* 4*d.*, this would agree with T. B.'s estimate.

[7] See *Hobson-Jobson*, *s.v.* Rupee. The quotation above, and those later on, are interesting as additional evidence that the form "rupee" had become fixed by the last quarter of the 17th century.

[8] The table here must be read with some care. What the writer

	lb	s	d
The Mase[1] of Achin 5 fanams 20 cash or	00	01	$03\frac{1}{4}$
Pullicatt			
The Pagod Valueth	00	08	06
24 fanams make one Pagod or	00	08	06
24 Coppar Cash make one fanam or	00	00	$04\frac{1}{4}$
Golcondah			
The Old Pagod[2] Valueth	00	12	00
The fānam	00	01	00
Porto Novo and Trincombar[3]			
The Pagod there Coyned Valueth but	00	06	00
Theire Fanam is worth	00	00	04
Metchlipatam			
The forementioned coynes passe as per Idem rates			
The Syam Ticull[4] Values one rupee $\frac{1}{4}$ or	00	03	07

means is that the abassin of Persia are 7 to the pagoda of 8*s.*, or 1*s.* $1\frac{5}{7}$*d.* each. In 1672 John Marshall, *Notes and Observations on East India*, says, "1 Abassee weighs $10\frac{3}{16}$ an. Sicca," and in 1679 we have the following in *Factory Records*, Hugli, No. 2, under date 25th June, "204 whole Abassees 336 halfe ditto making in all 237 [should be 372] abassees at $8\frac{3}{4}$ a. per abass." These values tally almost exactly with T.B.'s statement, taking the standard *anna* of the period to be worth about $1\frac{3}{8}$*d.* and the *sicca anna* at sòmething less. Sir Thos. Herbert rates the abassi at sixteen pence in 1677, *Travels*, p. 314. The coin took its name from Shāh Abās II.

[1] See *Hobson-Jobson*, *s.v.* Mace. See also *Ind. Ant.* vol. xxvii. p. 37 ff.

[2] See *Tavernier*, vol. i. part ii. p. 4, for a representation of "one of the ancient Pagods. They are as heavy as the new ones; and though they be no better Gold, yet some years since they went at 20 and 25 per Cent. more than the new ones; the reason is, for that the Bankers being all Idolaters, they are so superstitious as to believe, that if they melt down that Money, some Calamity will befall their Country; and they hold this for such a certain truth, That for fear the King of Golconda should melt it, they paid him for certain Years 20000 Pagods. But you must observe, that these old Pagods are nowhere currant but in the Kingdom of Golconda,...."

[3] Tranquebar.

[4] See *Hobson-Jobson*, *s.v.* Tical. See *Ind. Ant.* vol. xxvi. p. 253 ff. for an exhaustive treatment of this word, weight and coin. The statement in the text is an interesting proof, too, of the vigorous trade at

	lb	s	d
Coppar Cash Value each	00	00	01

Narsapore and Pettipolee.

The forementioned moneys passe Currant, but in Narsapore, and the Villadges 20 or 30 miles off, they have a Small Sort of moneys made of lead like Swan Shot, and are called Picans[1]; many hundreds of them passe for One Rupee.

Theire Weights, vizt.

The Usuall Weights of this Coast are the
Candil[2], the Maund[3], and the Veece[4].

A Candil Contains	500 pound weight Avordupois
Or twenty Maunds	
A Maund Contains 8 Veece	
⅛, or	025 Idem
A Veece Contains	003 Idem

Measures.

All Sorts of Graine is Sold by measure,
as alsoe Oyle, butter, or any liquid thinge.

The Para[5] contains	Markalls[6]
The Markall contains	

---

this time between Masulipatam and Mergui, then belonging to Siam. Compare *De la Loubère*, p. 94, "Anciently this service [due to the King of Siam] was esteemed at a Tical a month, because that one Tical is sufficient to maintain one Man."

[1] This word is not to be found in *Hobson-Jobson*.

[2] See *Hobson-Jobson*, *s.v.* Candy. For the value of this form of "Candy," see *Ind. Ant.* vol. xxvi. p. 245, *n.* 40 and p. 253, *n.* 42.

[3] See *Hobson-Jobson*, *s.v.* Maund. This reference and those in the Bengal Section are valuable for descriptions and weights of some of the old varieties of the maund.

[4] See *Hobson-Jobson*, *s.v.* Viss. See *Ind. Ant.* vol. xxvi. p. 327, and vol. xxvii. p. 58 ff. It is the well-known South Indian and Indo-Chinese weight about 3½ lbs.

[5] *N. and E.*, p. 23, for 3rd June, 1680, has a very valuable quotation, "Eight small measures make one Tomb [=Mercall], Five Tombs make one Parra, Eighty Parras make one Garce." It is a pity that the text has a blank just here. See *Ind. Ant.* vol. xxx. p. 408.

[6] See *Hobson-Jobson*, *s.v.* Mercall. It is tantalizing that the text

One thinge more I must needs Mention for the honour and Praise all travellers ought to give it, (beinge what is it's desert) I meane the Kingdome in General, through out which great care is taken both for the Safety wee Enjoy, and for relieve all travailers may have, which is first it is blessed with good and cleane Roades, and Upon Every common of above 4 or 5 miles in length, there is built a Small house or two where, if the travailer is thirsty, a thinge frequent in these warme climates, he may have milke or Congy[1], which is water boyled very well with Some rice in it, at the King's charge, and the people demand nothinge for it, but if any man will give them a penny or two, they have the wit to receive it very thankfully.

Moreover, att Every 12 miles End a house or two[2], (accordinge as the Roade is frequented) are built and kept in repaire (att the King's charges) for the conveniency of lodgings, for any comers or goers, the first come first Served, without any respect of Persons, which are fine conveniences for them, more Especially for that the Idolatrous people who inhabit most of the Countrey Villadges dare not admit of any of another Cast[3] to enter theire doors.

Then for the Safety thus, If the travailer hath goods or moneys, whereby he is Suspicious of beinge robbed,

---

should be incomplete here. The Mercall as a Madras measure of capacity varied a good deal. At the present day, in modern commercial parlance, 5 mercauls make 1 parrah in measuring grain, the parrah being about 2⅓ cubic ft. The mercaul is still also a liquid measure.

[1] See note on p. 29.

[2] *i.e. sarāī.* Compare *Schouten*, vol. ii. p. 248 f., "There are no inns in Bengal nor in hardly any of the provinces of India for the convenience of travellers. But in many spots are to be found tents, sheds, and stone buildings which were formerly erected by pious and charitable people, who by this means have perpetuated their memories, and a traveller may pass one or more nights in them. It is true that one is not very comfortable but in any case it is better than nothing. These buildings are called Sarais."

[3] See note on p. 9.

at Every Eminent towne (the residence of a Governour) he is Very ready to give his Chopp[1], which is Signet, by Vertue of which he goeth very Safely to the next Goverment, and there tendered with his Chopp and soe forward. It is a Seale put upon his wrist in black, which gives a durable impression, not at once Easily washed off, and if in case it soe happens that he is robbed, a thinge lesse common in this Kingdome then any Other, he hath, Upon Shewinge that Signet (in the Same Goverment) restitution made.

In the Latter End of February they have one remarkable day, which is Annualy Observed with great Mirth and Rejoyceinge. They Say it is the Very day and Month theire Forefather Slew a most terrible and deformed Giant, which if ever there was one accordinge to what they imitate, he was Certainly the most Devil like. They place him in a great Chaire made for the

---

[1] See *Hobson-Jobson*, *s.v.* Chop. T. B. in his *Malay Dict.* has Chap=a Printing Iron. Compare the following contemporary instances of the use of the word:—"Wee Received your 2 Chops for liberty of trade to Emoy which are very satisfactory, but wee desire to know whether it be necessary to have them yearly renewed, or if the same will serve." Bantam "Generall," 22nd Dec. 1675. *Factory Records*, Java, No. 6.

"The Virtue of the Chopp or passe for Amoy is that noe duties are payable there." Bantam "Generall," 5th June, 1676. *Ibid.*

"The favour the Young King was and still is pleased to doe him [the Agent] and this Factory [Bantam] in permitting noe one to come of (*sic*) his message without his ring or Chop, and whosoever hath brought it yett never failed to obtein his desires." Bantam "Generall," 26th June, 1678. *Ibid.*

"The Persian writeing before mentioned is drawne up here... and you are to get the Cogee [? *khwājājī*, chief merchant] to Chopp it." Letter from Fort St George to Masulipatam, 14th Feb. 1677/8. *Factory Records*, Masulipatam, No. 10.

"If the Vaqueel [*vakīl*, agent] occasions that you pay any thing more then what is usuall for the Writing Chauping &ca. Small usuall Charges he is severely to be Checked for it." Letter from Hugli to Dacca, 27th Dec. 1678. *Factory Records*, Hugli, No. 5.

"We are glad the Controversy about our ground is decided, it imports you now to gett such Authentique Papers Chauped by the Cozzee [*qāzī*, judge] as may Confirme what now passed in the future and stave off the like Claimes." Letter from Hugli to Balasor, 10th May, 1679. *Ibid.*

Plate X

"A GREAT GIANT CALLED JANSA BAINSA."

p. 119.

"THE ANTILOPE."

p. 59.

Same purpose, runninge Upon 4 Wheels, for the Easier drawinge of him through the towne. He is called Jansa Bainsah[1], made of pastboard, leather, &c. Stuffed with Straw and Other Combustible ingredients, covered with blew cloth, his head and face painted with Redd and White, Severall Resbutes[2] and Others danceinge Round him with great drawne Swords, after the manner of fenceinge, callinge Upon him by his Name, with many torches, flaggs, Pipes, and drums, and in this Posture, he is drawne throught the Principall Streets of the towne. They burne him to dust in The Open Street about the 12th houre in the night.

They Say he was a most terrible Giant, a great Destroyer of man and beast, and was at last destroyed by a Moore (of noe Small couradge), for which they Celebrate the day and night of his Destruction, a thinge their Ancestors Ordered, that their Posteritie may not bury in Oblivion Such a mighty Restauration of their Countrey from Such Destruction.

---

[1] One is tempted to refer "Jansa Bainsah" to our old friend Hobson-Jobson in yet another form, especially as Valentyn in the paragraph entitled "Het Feest van Hassan en Hossein," chap. iv. p. 107 of vol. v., says that the Dutch call the cry of Shah Hussain, "Jaksom Baksom." See *Hobson-Jobson*, *s.v.* Hobson-Jobson. However, Syed Hossein Bilgrami has given me the following explanation of T. B.'s statement: "It is said that the country about Tuljapur was at one time infested by a Rakshaso of the name of Mahesha Asura [whence Maheçāsura, Maisūr, Mysore], who came in the shape of a monstrous buffalo, ravaged the country far and wide and destroyed everything that lay on his way. The black Bhavani of Tuljapur, however, fought with and destroyed this monster, in commemoration of which event an effigy of the buffalo called Mahesha Bhainsa (corrupted into Ainsa Bhainsa) is made every year and carried about with every mark of indignity until it is deposited somewhere to be brought out again at the next anniversary. The ceremony is performed by the lower castes only in the Deccan, and they do *not* burn the effigy. Ainsa Bhainsa, in my opinion, has nothing to do with Hassan Hossain or the Moharrum."

[2] See notes on pp. 19 and 83.

THE COAST OF GINGALEE.

This Coast called Gingalee[1] is Certainly the most pleasant and Commodious Sea Coast that India affordeth, pleasant in many respects, beinge a most delicate Champion[2] Land, and one of the most fertile lands in the Universe, and Commodious for Navigation's Sake, enjoyinge many pleasant and good harbours, very well populated, and of a reasonable good Extent.

It beginneth at Point or Cape Goodawaree[3], the Entrance or South Side of the bay Corango[4], which Cape

---

1. Now Golconda. See *Hobson-Jobson*, *s.v.* Gingerly; the note is, however, inadequate. The text shows clearly that the term meant the Coast between the "Coromandel" and "Orissa" Coasts, *i.e.* between the Godāvarī estuary and Juggernaut Pagoda. It was more commonly known to mariners as the Golconda Coast. See Pringle, *Consultations* for 1682, p. 109f. note 41. Compare the following contemporary extracts: "This place [Balasor] finding a small vend [of cloth] by the Gentues throughout Orixa and part of Gingerley." Letter from Balasor to the Court, Jan. 1673, *Factory Records*, Hugli, No. 4. "The business toward Corango and the Coast of Ginglee did not goe on well neither." Letter from the "Braminy" at Golconda to Fort St George, 6th Jan. 1680, *Factory Records*, Fort St George, No. 28. "The Avaldar of Metchlepatam...would not permitt our people to send Boats to the Coast of Gingerlee." Letter from Ditto to Ditto, 14th Jan. 1680, *Ibid.* "The Sloop Dispatch was cast away very near Bengall out of the Gingerlee Nabobs government." Letter from Madapollam to Fort St George, 14th Dec. 1680, *Ibid.* "At this time of year there are not many boats to be had, being employed to Gingerlee for Paddy." Letter from Golconda to Fort St George, 14th Dec. 1680, *Ibid.* See also quotations in note on p. 4.

2. *i.e.* level, open, country. Compare the following: "We...travailed through a pleasant Champion Country, which brought us about 12 a clock to Utromeloor, a Garrison pagodoe in the Genau Kings time." Extract from Elihu Yale's *Memoriall*, Dec. 1681, *O. C.* No. 4776. "The middle Cluster [of the Nicobars] is fine champain Ground." Alex. Hamilton, *East Indies*, vol. ii. p. 69. Here the writer means to infer "fine open country," for none of the islands are level. "The Land for about 60 miles up in the Country [Tonquin] is still very low...with some gentle risings here and there, that make it a fine pleasant Champian; and the further side of this also is more level than the Champian Country it self...." *Dampier*, vol. ii. p. 19.

3. Godāvarī. See note on p. 3.

4. Kōrangi, nowadays in Anglo-Indian, Coringa. See note on p. 3. Morris, *Godavery District*, pp. 40 f., 167, gives the following de-

lyeth in Lattitude , and reacheth or Extendeth it Selfe Soe farre as to the Great Pagod Jno. Gernaet[1]. The Inland is very Mountainous, but 20, 30, and in Some places more English miles from the Ocean, very delicate good Land affordinge the greatest plenty of Graine, vizt. Wheat, Barley, Rice[2], Severall Sorts of gramme[3], with much more plenty of Cattle, as beefs, Sheepe, goats, &c. then any part (of Asia) besides affordeth.

They have annually 3 crops, each yeildinge great Encrease, and notwithstandinge the Sea Coast as also the Inland be Extraordinary populous, yett they transport above 10000 Gorse[4] of graine yearly, with great quantities

---

scription: "Coringa (Kōrangi) is situated nine miles south-west of Cocanada. It is situated in 16° 49′ N. lat., and 82° 19′ E. long. It used to be a place of very great importance, but it has very much fallen off during the present century. It was the only place between Calcutta and Trincomalee where large vessels used to be docked; but the river is now so shallow, and the approaches to it so difficult, that only small craft are now built or repaired there....Being situated on a low site near the coast, it has frequently been subjected to inundations of the sea, and to the effects of hurricanes and storms."

[1] Juggernaut. See note on p. 12.

[2] Compare the *Memoriall* of Streynsham Master as quoted by Mackenzie, *Kistna District*, p. 146, 16th April, 1679, "the Dutch... compound at Narsapore...reaches downe to the River Side upon the sandy banke of which lyes many Vessells which are imployed in that great Rice trade of Gingerlee."

[3] The earliest quotation in *Hobson-Jobson* for Gram=pulse, chick-pea is 1702. But there are many instances of the use of the word in the 17th century. Compare the following: "The Gram which wee desired seeing you could not doe it by the *Blackmoor*, wee must bee content to waight your better oppertunity." Letter from Fort St George to Masulipatam, 17th June, 1669, *Factory Records*, Fort St George, No. 16. "150 parrahs of wheat 10 Garse of Gram the Gunnys...wee likewise recommend as allready enordered." Letter from Fort St George to Masulipatam, 24th Aug. 1676, *Factory Records*, Masulipatam, No. 10. "The Gram is ready to be clapt on board as soone as the Boats are ready to saile." Letter from Madapollam to Masulipatam, 9th Dec. 1677. *Ibid.* "There is neighther Black Gram nor Red Gram yet procurable." Letter from Madapollam to Fort St George, 14th Feb. 1685, *Factory Records*, Madapollam, No. 3.

[4] A large grain measure in the Madras Presidency: anything up to 4 tons and more. In T. B.'s time it contained 80 parrahs. See quotation from *N. and E.* in note 5 on p. 116. Compare also *N. and E.* p. 40, for 2nd Dec. 1680, "Upon application from Lingapa for a garse of wheat upon payment, it is resolved to supply it gratis," and the

of butter and Lacca[1]. And great Store of Calicos[2] are made here, most Especially beteelis[3] (which wee call Muzlin[4]). For the better transportinge of the beforementioned commodities, Ships and Vessels in great Numbers resort hither att all times of the yeare, beinge a Very Secure Coast to harbour in,

---

following in a letter from the "Braminy" at Golconda to Fort St George, 25th Dec. 1680, *Factory Records*, Fort St George, No. 28, p. 277, "I had need of a Garce of Wheeat." In *Factory Records*, Masulipatam, No. 10, there are frequent requisitions from Fort St George to Masulipatam for "10 Garse of Gram." Lockyer, *Trade in India*, p. 9, has "Liquid and Dry Measure [in Fort St George] viz. one Measure is one Pint and a half. Eight Measures, one Mercall; and four hundred Mercalls are one Garse."

[1] See *Hobson-Jobson*, *s.v.* Lac. Wilson, *Early Annals*, vol. i. p. 379, quoting from "Kenns advices about Bengall in 1661" has, among "Commodities procurable at Patna," "Gumlack or Sticklack very dear, from 9 to 11 Rupees," and on p. 398, under "Exports from Bengal," "Lack worth 3 Tale per Bahar when plenty." In England, Pegu Sticklack was the kind always requisitioned by the Court, "100 Tunns" being the usual order. *Thevenot*, part iii. p. 106, remarks, "The Traffick of those parts [Bimlipatam and its neighbourhood] consists in Rice, fine Cloaths, Iron, Wax and Lacre, which is as good as at Pegu." In this connection, it may be noted that Crawfurd, *Dict. of the Indian Archipelago*, *s.v.* Lacca, says the term is used for a red-wood used in dyeing.

[2] See note on p. 5.

[3] See *Hobson-Jobson*, *s.v.* Betteela. This material (under the name of Organdy Muslin) was greatly in vogue in England during the first half of the 19th century for ladies' dresses. The clearest sort was used for bonnets and veilings. Compare the following references: "We shall be able to invest all our Stocke...in Long Cloth, Salempores, Morees, Percalls, Batilles, but as for the Ginghams, Alligese, Oringall Batillas,...it must needes rest upon you." Letter from Fort St George to Masulipatam, 17th June, 1669, *Factory Records*, Fort St George, No. 16, p. 130. "Wee have...15 Bales Oringall Beteelaes three quarters done, but cannot gett Packers to finish them." Letter from Masulipatam to Fort St George, 17th Jan. 1675, *Factory Records*, Masulipatam, No. 10.

"Wee finde quantities of Betteleez and other fine Callicoes sent home yeerly by our Factors and Servants to their Freinds, to our great prejudice....The Betteleez per the *Unity* No. 28 prove very bad and worse then usuall...in particular provide 5000 Oringall Betteleez and 8000 Allejaes at Metchlepatam." Letter from the Court to Fort St George, 15th December, 1676, *Letter Book*, No. 5, pp. 370, 373 f.

"Wee approve of your accepting more of the fine Sallampores and Bettelees then wee ordered." Letter from the Court to Fort St George, 12th December, 1677. *Ibid.* p. 497. See Pringle, *Consultations* for 1681, p. 71, note 103.

[4] See note on p. 5.

namely in Corango[1], Vizegapatam[2], Bimlipâtam[3], Wattara[4],

---

[1] See notes on pp. 3 and 120.

[2] Not in Hobson-Jobson, but should be as it turns up in all sorts of queer forms in the old books. See *Ind. Ant.* vol. xxx. pp. 357 and 400, where, among numerous forms the following are noted, "Inzipatam, Bizipatam, Wisagapatam, Vasingepatam." As to the derivation of the name, Carmichael, *Vizagapatam District*, pp. 21 and 164, says that the term Vizagapatam is properly Visakha-pattanam, the city of Visakha or Kartikeya, the Hindu Mars, to whom a pagoda was erected in the 14th century. He adds that, owing to the encroachments of the surf, this edifice has long since disappeared. On p. 164 he says, "A branch of the English East India Company appears to have settled at Vizagapatam about the middle of the seventeenth century. In A.D. 1689 in the reign of Aurangzeb, during the rupture between that monarch and the company, their warehouses here were seized, and all the English residents put to the sword." Clement Jordan, T. B.'s purser on the *Sancta Cruz*, held an official position in the factory at Vizagapatam from 1682—1684.

Pringle, *Consultations* for 1684, p. 170, suggests that Gingerlee and Vizagapatam are identical. In support of this theory, it is urged that a factory was established at Vizagapatam in 1668, which must have been abandoned some time before the earliest consultations extant, but had a factory existed in T. B.'s time, he would hardly have failed to mention it. It seems in fact to have been re-established a little later, from the following evidence. In Feb. 1682 the Court wrote to Fort St George that an interloper was designed for "Metchlepatam or Gyngerlee." It was left to the discretion of the Council at Fort St George whether or not to make part of their Investment at "Gyngerlee or thereabouts." The Company could not decide if it would be advisable to settle a factory at "Gyngerlee" subordinate to Fort St George (*Letter Book*, No. 6). On the 28th August of the same year the Court wrote, "Wee shall be very Glad to heare that in persuance of our former order you have found such incouragement to settle a Factory at Gingerlee as at Porto Nova..." (*Letter Book*, No. 7). On the 1st Aug. 1682 George Ramsden was appointed Chief at Gingerly and Clement du Jardin a factor there. On the 8th Sept. there is a note of Mr Ramsden's departure to Vizagapatam and his return to Masulipatam. From this time a regular official correspondence was interchanged between Vizagapatam and Fort St George, and on the 11th Oct. 1682 there is a note as to the building of a factory at Vizagapatam. As Ramsden was at the head of this factory, there seems no doubt but that the town at first known as Gingerlee was subsequently called by the native name of Vizagapatam. Alex. Hamilton, *East Indies*, vol. i. p. 372, described Vizagapatam as he saw it some years later, and says it produced the "best Dureas, or stript Muslins, in India."

[3] Of Bimliapatam *Schouten* says, vol. i. p. 493, "Bemilipatnam is barely four leagues from Visiagapatnam in 18° N. Latitude. A fairly good trade is carried on, owing to the fact that the Dutch have, for a long time, had a settlement there." Compare the *Diary of Streynsham Master*, under date 20th Aug. 1676, p. 44, "Wee Sailed by Bimliapatam where the Dutch have a Factory, and there was two Ships rideing." See *Ind. Ant.* vol. xxx. p. 348.

[4] In a protest of Callor Vessina against Mr Mainwaring, enclosed

Pondy[1], Manichapatam[2]. There be many Other faire towns alonge this Shore but noe more good harbours, Some Fortifications alsoe but all Under the Goverment of the Moors, Subject to the Golcondah Kinge, Of which Chicacol[3] is the

---

in a letter from Masulipâtam to Fort St George, 23rd May, 1678, *Factory Records*, Masulipatam, No. 10, p. 44, we find the following: "He [Mr Mainwaring] told them all [the boatmen] he must have their Boats to fectch (*sic*) Paddy from the Coast to Gingerlee, at a place called Wattarra." Compare Alex. Hamilton, *East Indies*, vol. i. p. 372, "Coasting along the Shore, there are several little Ports between Matchulipatam and Vizagapatam, besides Narsapore and Angerang, but Watraw is the most noted, for it produces Rice for Exportation, besides some long Cloth, but it is not frequented by Europeans."

Dunn, *East Indies Directory*, p. 150, says, "Point Godvarin and Vatare (Watare or Watsare) bear off each other north and south 10 leagues....Vatare is known by a mosque built on the top of a hill."

[1] Compare *Schouten*, vol. i. p. 58, "We passed by Visiagapatnam, Binnilipatnam, Connare, Sicocol, Pondy,...."

Compare also Alex. Hamilton, *East Indies*, vol. i. p. 378, "There are several other Places...on the Coast, that drive a small Trade in Corn. Pondee, Callingapatam and Sunapore are the most noted, but are not frequented by Europeans." See Pringle, *Consultations* for 1685, p. 166 and note. Of Pondy, Dunn, *East Indies Directory*, says, "From Caletaer to Pondy, the coast trenches N.E. easterly, distance 5½ leagues....Close in shore, before the river of Pondy are 10 or 12 rocks, and within land some high rugged mountains which thwart the river." See *Ind. Ant.* vol. xxx. p. 356.

[2] Manikpatam. Compare Dunn, *East Indies Directory*, p. 153, "From Karikpar to Manikpatnam or Manicapatnam, the bearing is N.E.b.E. ¾ E. distance 9 leagues....Off Manikpatnam a bank of sand projects 2 miles....Manikpatnam may be seen when the Mountain of Karapar bears W.S.W. 7 or 8 leagues. It is known by a little pagoda, encompassed with houses and other buildings, with some large trees."

[3] The name of this place appears in many forms. *Schouten*, vol. ii. p. 58, has "Sicocol." "Tell them [the Cossids] they must not goe in to Chickrecole by the Way for they will be stoped if they doe." Letter from Reade at Hugli to Edwards at Balasor, 3rd April, 1678, *O. C.* No. 4392. In *Madras Press List* for 11th Oct. 1682 we have "Copy of letter from the Chief &c. at Vizagapatam to the Governor and Council of Fort St George relative to George Ramsden's departure to Chickeracole to procure a cowle from the Seir Lascar." Under date 23rd May (Pringle, *Consultations* for 1683) there is the entry, "Recd. a Generall from Mr George Ramsden and Mr Charles Fleetwood at Checracoll dated the 5th Instant." On this Mr Pringle remarks, note 55, p. 137, "Checracoll (Srikākulam, pop. Chicacole). A town on the coast of the modern Ganjam district, situated about four miles from the sea on the Nagavali river, and at one time the head quarters of the *faujdār* of Golconda." Compare *Thevenot*, part iii. p. 106, "From Bimlipatam to Cicacola it is fifteen hours travelling by Land, and this is the last Town of the Kingdom of Golconda, on the side of Bengala." Alex. Hamilton, *East Indies*, vol. i. p. 371, says, "The Nabob or

most famous for large and stately buildings, the richest Merchants, the most populated, and Especially for that it is the residence of Sr. Larskare[1], the Kings deputy or Viceroy, Who bears as great Sway Over this Coast in Generall as the Kinge his Master doth in Golcondah. He liveth in great State and Splendor, and hath continually a great Retinue of Lifeguard men and Soldiery, being for the most part Moors and Persians. Hee keeps many Stately Elephants, and a huge number of Concubines, which are the 2 Chiefe pieces of State Esteemed On amonge the Inhabitants of Asia.

Having this Entire Sea Coast Under his Command, and power Soe great Over the Inhabitants hereof, he can in one day raise a Very Considerable army of at least 100 thousand fightinge men.

Vice-roy of Chormondel, who resides at Chickacul, and who superintends that Country for the Mogul...." Pitt in a letter to Fleetwood, Sept. 1699, *Hedges' Diary*, vol. iii. p. 47, writes, "Wee have taken care to manage the affair at Siccacul to the best advantage...." Dunn, *East Indies Directory*, p. 151, has, "From the point of Conar to Ticacoel or Chicacol, the coast trenches N.E. ¾ E. distance 34 miles.... Chicacol is by a river near which are 3 or 4 great trees, and some palm-trees."

[1] Sar-i-Lashkar, *Indice* Sarlashkar, the head of the forces. This Anglo-Indianism is not in *Hobson-Jobson*, except in a quotation for 1682 under Lascar. This particular official is constantly mentioned in the records of the period. Compare the following: "The Dutch in persuance of their demands upon the Seer Lascar of Gingerlee upon his refusall of coming to Agreement with them...." 29th April, 1678, *Factory Records*, Masulipatam, No. 2. "They told us that one who aforetime was King of Orixa was risen with a great army of 35,000 Horse upon your coast and country of Gingerlee, who had beseiged the Seer Lascar or Gratt [Grall, for General] of the King of Gulcondah in a Castle and had taken away 500 laest of Pady of the Dutch Companys." *Memoriall* of Streynsham Master, under date 10th April, 1679, quoted by Mackenzie, *Kistna District*, p. 142. "There came one Sheake Ahmud to Town with letters from...the Ser Laskar Nabob Mahmud Ibrahim." 25th May, 1680, *Factory Records*, Fort St George, No. 2. "The pagodas 1200...I paid the same day unto the Sharlaskar. ...The Sarlaskar having considered farther, told me...." Letters from the "Braminy" at Golconda to Fort St George, 21st March and 12th June, 1680, *Factory Records*, Fort St George, No. 28, pp. 74 and 103. "Copy of Mr. Jardin's Cattapa to the Sier Lascar, Sier Lascar's Cowle for Vizagapatam given to Mr. Jardin." 15th Oct. 1683. *Madras Press List.*

The Merchants, as alsoe most tradesmen, are of the Gentue Cast[1], and live for the most part in admirable Subjection to the Moors[2], payinge the King's taxes and duties to the Uttermost farthinge, besides many Oppressions of taxes the Governour and his Mahometan Councell lay heavily Upon them, and, which is more grievous, they are compelled to beare it with the largest Extent of Patience, by reason little or noe justice is to be acquired where the Mahometans are Lords Over them; for, if complaint be made to the high Court of Justice, the Mussleman[3], as they call themselves, Shall Certainly carry it (if he appeare in Person) Onely with this one Saying, Ka Mussleman jute bolta, Will a true believer lye[4]?

As for theire Idolatrous way of worship, they Enjoy it as fully as in any Other place in the Empire of the Grand Mogoll[5] (or territories of Golcondah), and without doubt pay largely for it. They have many delicate groves, tanks[6] of water, and large Fabricks of Stone called Pa-

---

[1] See note on p. 9. Pringle, *Consultations* for 1681, p. 64, note 17, says, "Gentoo—A corruption of the Portuguese gentio (heathen) as opposed to moros (the Moors or Mussulmans). It was suggested in Hobson-Jobson that the word might still linger at Madras in the limited sense of Telugu Hindus. This is the case, and it seems to be very extensively so used even now [1893]. With the singular tendency, however, of obsolescent words to pass from stage to stage of degradation, it is, at this date, applied to the talk of the lowest classes of Telugus, in especial to that of sweepers. Among Europeans it has fallen out of use."

[2] Muhammadans. See note on p. 10. Pringle, *Consultations* for 1681, p. 69, note 78, remarks that it "is much to be regretted that we have almost lost this useful word for Mussulmans of whatever race."

[3] Muhammadan. See note on p. 76. Compare the following in a letter from the "Braminy" at Golconda to Fort St George, 21st June, 1680, *Factory Records*, Fort St George, No. 28, p. 114, "Verona being a Moor man yet he was burnt, which [was] a great dishonour to the Mussulman's sect."

[4] This expression shows that the writer had really mastered colloquial Hindostani, for the expression would run correctly: Kyā? Musalmān jhūt bōltā? What? the Musalmān speak a lie?

[5] Aurangzēb. See note on p. 10.

[6] A sheet of water. See note on p. 7. See also *Thevenot*, part iii. p. 96, for a description of a "great square Reservatory or

gods[1], more large and of greater Antiquie (*sic*) then all the land of the Hindoos beside doth afford. And, what maketh this Countrey most famous, is the Scituation of theire most holy and Esteemable Pagod Jno. Gernaet[2], Soe much resorted to by both the rich and Poore from the Remotest parts of India and Persia.

Some of the richest Indian Merchants Inhabit upon this Coast; but many of them dare not be knowne to be soe, for feare of receiveinge injurie from the Mahometans, and for some reasons more, the Chiefe of which is, if any of them die, theire Estates in full falls to the Kinge, none of his Seed dareinge to claime any of it by right or title, onely lyeth at the mercie and benevolence of the Kinge or Emperour[3].

Theire habit is generally but meane, more like to Servants then Masters, theire houses very Ordinary low and for the most part thatched over, and are for the foregoeinge reasons forced, for the benefit of theire Posteritie, to bury the Major part of their treasure in the Earth.

But all Forraigners, more Especially the English and Dutch, have great freedome here, the Same wee have in Other parts of this King's Dominions, and live Very pleasantly Upon the fatt of the land, provisions Vizt. Cows, fowle, Sheep, goats, fish, and all Sorts of Venison beinge to be had in great abundance and incredibly Cheap

---

Tanquie" at Bhagnagár. Compare the *Memoriall* of Streynsham Master as quoted by Mackenzie, *Kistna District*, p. 150, under date 25th April, 1679, "We lodged in a mangoe garden by the tanke side, a pleasant green place."

[1] See note on p. 7.

[2] Jagannāth, Juggernaut. See note on p. 12. Compare the following in a letter from Hugli to Balasor, 16th May, 1678, *O. C.*, No. 4416—"Pray write to the Rajah of Jagrenaut to passe our Cossids."

[3] The dispute about the creed of Cassa Verona (Kāçi Vīranna) was most probably on account of his wealth. See note on p. 95.

and good. Theïre Cows are the largest and fattest I have Seen in India. They have Excellent good Pasture ground, the fields and trees always green, theire butter and rice and Oyle the best in India. Theire Oyle is for the most part made of Mustard Seede, and is Vendible all India and South Seas over.

In fine, it is a most delicate countrey for the Use of man, the Aire good and comfortable, and the land aboundinge with all Necessaries for the Sustainance of mankind.

ORIXA[1].

This Kindome is of noe great Extent, but is an indifferent pleasant Countrey, Subject to the Great Mogoll[2] for the most part but not altogeather, by reason of Severall Radjas[3] who (before the Mahometan Conquest of the Hindoos[4]) possessed this Kingdome, some of which are not as yet Subdued and brought Under the Moorish Yoke, but inhabit the Mountains and woods, and Some yea a Considerable part of the plaine land, more Especially neare to Point Palmeris[5] the Entrance into the Bay

---

[1] See note on p. 5. Compare *Schouten*, vol. ii. p. 142, "The 4th January, 1664...we came in sight of the low coasts of Orixa." *Thevenot*, part iii. p. 67, has "Oulesser" for "Ouresser" by a common mistake of *l* for *r* in Oriental words.

[2] Aurangzēb. See note on p. 10.

[3] See note on p. 39.

[4] See note on p. 10.

[5] Palmyras. See *Hobson-Jobson*, *s.v.* Palmyras. Compare the *Diary of Streynsham Master*, under date 22nd August, 1676, p. 44, "This night wee lay by, driveing in the Sea off point Palmeras from 27 to 34 fathome water, a fresh gale at Southwest." Compare also Yule, *Hedges' Diary*, vol. i. p. 30, "About 2 in the afternoon we doubled the point of Palmiras, and between 6 and 7 in the evening we came to an anchor in the Bay." Of Point Palmiras, Horsburgh, *India Directory*, ed. 1855, vol. i. p. 607, says, "Point Palmiras (called by the natives

of Bengala, where, for above 100 miles, the land is divided by Rivers and Rivolets into Islands, and thereby become Invincible.

Sea Ports this Kingdome affordeth onely one, and that none to be admired, affordinge not water Enough for a Ship of 200 tunns in burden to goe into the River, and to ride out is very Unnecessary and dangerous, by reason it is noe better then a very wild Open bay that Extendeth it selfe from Point Conjaguaree to Palmeris; the River is called Haraspoore[1]. Here are considerable quantities

Mypurra, from the contiguous sandy island of this name)...bears from the False Point about N.E. by N. distant 8 leagues....The land of Point Palmeris is low, and clothed with Palmyra-trees, having on each side of it, at a small distance the mouth of a river; that on the South side is navigable by boats or small vessels."

[1] Haraspore, Harssapore, Arsipore, &c. is first mentioned in 1633, when Bruton with seven other Englishmen (who had set out from Masulipatam with the design of settling a factory at "Bengalla") landed there. It was the earliest English factory in the Bay of Bengal, as is seen by the statement in Walter Clavell's "Accompt of the Trade of Ballasore" (*Diary of Streynsham Master*, p. 323) "Harrapore where our first Factory was settled." Yule, *Hedges' Diary*, vol. ii. p. 240 and vol. iii. p. 176, identifies the port with Hurrichpore Gurh on the coast of the Mahānadi Delta. Wilson, *Early Annals*, vol. i. p. 2, gives the following additional information: "On reaching Harṣapur or Hariçpur, the modern Hariçpur Gaṛ, at the mouth of the Pātuā, in Orissa they [Bruton and party] transferred themselves and their merchandise to small boats, and so ascended the river some eight miles, as far as Kōṣīdā." In a note on Patua, Wilson says, "This river is called R. Pāṭali above, and R. Pātuā below, Basanta-Pāṭali, and at its mouth R. Bōita-kuliyā, ship-haven, a name significant of the former importance of the now sand-barred harbour of Hariçpur." See *Hobson-Jobson*, *s.v.* Factory, where the place is given as Arzepore, and its existence as a factory is queried. Compare *Schouten*, vol. ii. pp. 59 and 142, "Afterwards we passed by the Pagoda of Connercon, the little Pagoda of Arcsepour, Casigere, and other places...on the 4th January, 1664...on approaching it [the low coast of Orixa] we fell down toward Arsapouro."

Compare also Alex. Hamilton, *East Indies*, vol. i. p. 388, "From the dominions of Jagarynat [Jagannāth] I came into those of Arsepore. The Town, where the Raja resided, is named after the Province, and there is a fine River that invites Strangers to frequent it for Cotton Cloth and Rice, that this Country affords in great Plenty." "Harrapore Sannoes [*sanahs*]" were a class of cotton goods in great repute in T. B.'s time. Compare the following in a letter from Hugli to Balasor, dated 13th August, 1678, *O. C.* No. 4480, "Make enquiry among the Merchants whether...Sannoes of Mohunpore, Harrapore, and Sura Sannos may not bee gotten cheaper." The author's "Point Conja-

of Callicoes[1] made and Sold to the English and Dutch, but are first brought over land to them to their Factories in Ballasore[2], in the bay of Bengala.

These inhabitants are called Ourias[3], and be a very poore Idolatrous people[4], poore in generall and very low Spirited, Save those Radjas and their armies who live by the Sword, and will not pay homadge to any Kinge or Emperour in the Universe.

Citties or townes of Note they have very few, Save

---

guaree" is perhaps False Point, which is so called by the English because it is so easily mistaken for the important Point Palmyras. However, Horsburgh, *India Directory*, ed. 1855, vol. i. p. 606 says, "Near this place [the mouth of the Gonga, called also Cuttack River] other small branches of the Gonga fall into the sea, forming low islets, and this elbow, or projecting part of the coast, called Cojung Point, has sometimes been mistaken for the False Point, as the shore from it takes a northerly direction 2½ or 3 miles, forming a small concavity in the land, nearly midway between the Black Pagoda and False Point, called Cojung Bay....In the former charts of this coast, a bay, 3 leagues deep and 5 leagues wide, was erroneously delineated in this part." In the 1809 edition of the same work, vol. i. p. 353, Cojung appears as Codgone, and there is the remark, "Codgone Bay, instead of being represented as a small concavity in the coast, about half way between the Black Pagoda and False Point, is placed close on the west side of this point in the charts, and delineated about 3 leagues deep, and 5 leagues wide; the land from the bottom of it being made to stretch in a S.E. and southerly direction about 3½ leagues to False Point, whereas in reality, there seems to be only a very small concavity on the west side of that Point, or rather an inlet to the river Gonga." By the statement "the river is called Haraspoore" the writer seems to refer to the continuous inland channels along the coast from the Devi mouths of the Mahānadi to the Maipārā and Dhamrā mouths of the Brāhmanī. In the neighbourhood of False Point I find, in a collection of old maps:—Arsepoor and Arsepore in 1720: Mirepour and Irsepour in 1705, 1710, 1720 and 1781. What the native name for False Point is I have been unable to ascertain. However, in a map of that neighbourhood in 1687, I find Segogora and Lonuary (=? Conjaguaree), which seem to explain that Barro's Cabo Segogora (1553), quoted in *Hobson-Jobson*, *s.v.* Palmyras, is still another corruption of the old native name for False Point, whatever that was.

[1] See note on p. 5.

[2] See quotation from Alex. Hamilton, *East Indies*, in note 1 on p. 129.

[3] Inhabitants of Orissa. See *Hobson-Jobson*, *s.v.* Ooriya.

[4] Compare *Thevenot*, part iii. p. 67, "The Province of Oulesser,... which the Idolaters name Jaganat, because of the famous Idol of the Pagod of Jaganat which is there, is inhabited by Gentiles no less fanatical in point of Religion than those of Halabas."

what are inhabited or Governed by the Moors, and it is a very troublesome Kingdome for travellers, the Kingdome not beinge Setled Under one Goverment[1], both parties make many pretences to injure the poor travailer, Except he goe with a Competent force or traine.

BENGALA[2].

It is one of the largest and most Potent Kingdoms of Hindostan[3], Containing in Circuit noe lesse then   English miles, blessed with many fine Rivers that Issue out into the Sea or Gulph of Bengala[4], vizt. between Point Palmeris[5] (the Entrance thereof) and the Arackan[6] Shore, the whole Extent of the bay beinge about 300 English miles Over, Some of which are navigable both for great and Small Ships, togeather with many Other conveniences, this Kingdome is now become most famous and Flourishinge[7].

---

[1] Compare *Thevenot*, part iii. p. 68, "The Country was kept in far better order under the Patan Kings, (I mean) before the Mahometans and Moguls were Masters of it, because then they had Uniformity in Religion. It has been found by experience that disorder came into it with Mahometanism; and that diversity of Religions hath there caused corruption in Manners."

[2] See *Hobson-Jobson*, *s.v.* Bengal. See also *Ind. Ant.* vol. xxx. p. 347 f.

[3] The earliest quotation in the restricted sense of the text given in *Hobson-Jobson*, *s.v.* Hindostan, is 1803.

[4] This quotation is valuable as showing exactly what was known in the 17th century as the "Bay of Bengal," the limits being so very much more restricted than is now the case.

[5] See note on p. 128.

[6] See *Hobson-Jobson*, *s.v.* Arakan.

[7] Compare *Schouten*, vol. ii. p. 153 f. "Bengale is a great and powerful country, which was formerly an independent kingdom. At present it is under the rule of the Mogol...It is situated in and beyond the twenty-first parallel of North Latitude. On the East it is bounded by the Kingdoms of Aracan and Ava; on the North by the provinces of Mevat, Patna and Narvat which are part of the same Empire; on the West by the mountains of Ratipore whose vast extent separates Bengale from Gusaratte, and by the countries of Indostan, Orixa, and Golconda; on the South by the gulf of Bengale. The Ganges traverses

First for the great River of Ganges[1] and the many large and faire arms thereof, Upon the banks of which are Seated many faire Villages, delicate Groves and Fruitefull lands, affordinge great plenty of sugars[2], Cottons[3], Lacca[4], honey, beeswax[5], butter[6], Oyles, Rice[7],

---

it in the centre from North to South, and it is there, so it is said, that Alexander the Great ended his conquests."

[1] This and the quotations later on in this section give the several uses of the word in the 17th century, *viz.*, for the Hugli River, any large mouth of the Ganges in the Gangetic Delta, the Ganges Proper.

[2] Compare *Tavernier*, vol. ii. p. 140, "Further, it [Bengale] also abounds in Sugar, so that it furnishes with it the Kingdoms of Golkonda and Karnates, where there grows but very little. Arabia also and Mesopotamia are thence provided with it, by the way of Moka and Bussora; and Persia it self, by Bander-Abassy."

[3] Compare *Tavernier*, vol. ii. p. 140 f., "As to the Commodities of great value, and which draw the Commerce of Strangers thither, [to Bengale] I know not, whether there be a Country in the World that affords more and greater variety: For, besides the Sugar...there is such store of Cottons and Silks, that it may be said that Bengale is as 'twere the general Magazine thereof, not only for Indostan or the Empire of the great Mogol, but also for all the circumjacent Kingdoms, and for Europe it self. I have sometimes stood amazed at the vast quantity of Cotton-Cloth of all sorts, fine and others, tinged and white, which the Hollanders alone draw from thence and transport into many places, especially into Japan and Europe, not to mention what the English, Portingal and Indian Merchants carry away from those parts."

[4] See note on p. 122. Compare *Tavernier*, vol. ii. p. 141, "'Tis Bengale, whence the good Lacca...do come."

[5] Compare the *Diary of Streynsham Master* under date 8th Sept. 1676, p. 57, "[We] sailed up the river Ganges, on the east side of which most part of the great quantity of beeswax is made, which is the King's comodity and none suffered to deale therein but for his account, and Swarmes of Bees flew over our Vessell."

[6] Compare *Tavernier*, vol. ii. p. 141, "Butter is to be had there in so great plenty, that though it be a gross Commodity, yet notwithstanding 'tis thence transported into divers places." See the "Janselone" section of the MS. where the writer says, "butter and Oyle from Gingalee or Bengala [to Junkceylon] turneth to a great accompt." By "butter" the old travellers must have meant *ghī*, *i.e.* butter clarified by boiling, and so preserved and made fit for transport.

[7] See the "Janselone" section, "Commodities brought hither [Achin]...From Bengala, Rice, wheat, Oyle, butter, Sugar, Sticklack...." Compare also *Tavernier*, vol. ii. p. 140, "It [Bengale] bears Rice in that abundance, that it not only furnishes its Neighbours, but many very remote parts. 'Tis carried up the River Ganges to Patna; and 'tis transported by Sea to Maslipatan, and to many other Ports of the Coast of Coromandel. Besides, 'tis sent away into forrain Kingdoms, and principally into Ceilan and the Maldives."

Gramme[1], with many Other beneficiall Commodities to Satisfie this and many Other Kingdoms[2].

Many both great and Small Ships, both English, Dutch, and Portugals doe annually resort to lade and transport Sundry Commodities hence, and great Commerce goeth on into most parts of accompt in India, Persia, Arabia, China and South Seas.

It is also the abode and Settlement of the Major part of those that professe and Embrace the Doctrine of our Saviour Jesus[3].

This Kingdome most plentifully doth abound with the before mentioned commodities, as alsoe Callicoes[4] of Sundry Sorts, Rammals[5], raw and wrought Silks[6], Opium

---

[1] See note on p. 121.

[2] Compare *Tavernier*, vol. ii. p. 140, "In a word, Bengale is a Country abounding in all things; and 'tis for this very reason that so many Portugueses, Mesticks, and other Christians are fled thither from those quarters, which the Dutch have taken from them." Compare also *Delestre*, p. 189 f., "The country, [Bengala] which is one of the most beautiful in the world, is extremely fertile; there are a number of woods and forests of orange and lemon trees....Sugar is very common there, as well as ginger and long pepper, which is preserved when it is green....The pasturage is excellent, and it produces such an abundance of milk, that an enormous quantity of butter and cheese is exported into all the adjacent and maritime towns, and even into the most distant countries, especially Batavia." See also *Schouten*, vol. ii. p. 154.

[3] Compare *Tavernier*, vol. ii. p. 140, "The Jesuits and Augustinians, that have great Churches there, wherein they exercise their Religion with all freedom, did assure me, that in Ogouli alone there were no less than eight or nine thousand Souls of Christians; and (which I will easily believe) that in the rest of that Kingdom (Bengale) there were above twenty five thousands."

[4] See note on p. 5. Compare Alex. Hamilton, *East Indies*, vol. i. p. 393, "Their Manufactories [in Bengal] are of Cotton in Sannis, Cassas, Demeties, mulmuls, Silk, and Silk and Cotton Romals, Gurrahs and Lungies."

[5] *Rūmāl*, kerchief. See *Hobson-Jobson*, *s.v.* Roomaul. Compare the following:—In the *Diary of Streynsham Master*, under date 31st Aug. 1676, p. 52, we have "The twelve thousand single peices of silke Romalls they offered to furnish at 3½ Rups. the single peece [in Balasor]." Again, in a letter from Hugli, 12th Sept. 1677, *Factory Records*, Hugli, No. 4, there is another spelling, "Rohamalls we have provided here"; and in *O. C.*, No. 4612, letter from Fort St George to Balasor, 23rd May, 1679, we have "the investment...I now desire may be half in Rummauls of an old cheap sort."

[6] Compare *Tavernier*, vol. ii. p. 141, "One would not imagin

(the best in India)[1], Muske in Codd and out of it[2], Long Pepper[3], and Severall Sorts of druggs, which causeth it to be soe admirable well populated and Effected by the best European travellers[4].

---

quantity [of Silks and Silk-Stuffs] that is hence [Bengal] transported every year; for this Country furnishes generally all this great Empire of Mogol as far as Lahor and Caboul, and most of the other forrain parts, whither Cotton-Cloth is carried....The Hollanders alone have sometimes seven hundred or eight hundred men of the Natives at work in their Factory of Kassem-Bazar; as the English and other Merchants have theirs in proportion." Compare also *Mandelslo*, p. 94, "They drive here [Bengal] a great trade in...Silks, which are esteem'd the best in all the Indies."

[1] See *Hobson-Jobson*, *s.v.* Opium. Compare *Tavernier*, vol. ii. p. 141, "'Tis Bengale, whence the good Lacca, Opium, Wax,...do come." Marshall, in his MS. *Notes and Observations of East India* has, p. 35, "Best Ophium comes from near Pattana, and that from Mungeer is not nigh so good." Among "Goods from Bengall proper for the Coast of Cormandell," *Add. MSS.* 34,123, quoted by Wilson, *Early Annals*, vol. i. p. 398, is "Anno 1684. Ophium Cost 80 Rs. per md.... Ophium, when no ships go from Bengall to Malacca, Sells well." Milburn, *Oriental Commerce*, vol. ii. p. 219, says, "The monopoly in the trade of opium, or the cultivation of the poppy, may be traced at least as far back as the commencement of the British influence in Bengal."

[2] See *Hobson-Jobson*, *s.v.* Musk. Marshall, *Notes and Observations*, has, p. 17, "From Neopall comes Muske which at Pattana is sold for 49 r. per Seere being 16 Pice to the Seere 40 of which pice make a great seere of about 31 oz." Wilson, *Early Annals*, vol. i. p. 378, quotes from *Add. MSS.* 34,123, "Patna. Commodities procurable....Musk—the greatest quantity is bought in the codd, some out, but that not considerable...the price usually from rupees 35 to 40 the Seer...Musk out of the Codd sold by the Tola from rupees 3 to 6 if high price, then its all in small hard Knobs round, if about 3 then dust without them." See also *Tavernier*, vol. i. part ii. p. 153. Compare the following from the "Chief and Mr Clavell's reply to the Auditor's Remonstrance," 29th July, 1670, *Factory Records*, Miscellaneous, No. 3, p. 72, "That the Sear of Muske holds out 30 oz. is a mistake: for the weight by which muske is sold differs from all other: it being but 16 pice weight to the Seare, where as the Seare for grosse goods is 40 pice weight; and this muske Seare weighs nearest 10½ oz. troy... it [muske] being to be bought att Pattana from October to February."

[3] Compare *Schouten*, vol. ii. p. 356, "Bengale, Malabar, and a few other countries of Asia produce long pepper which is used more for medicine than for ordinary food." Compare also *Tavernier*, vol. ii. p. 141, "'Tis Bengale, whence the good...Civet, long Pepper do come." Wilson, *Early Annals*, vol. i. p. 380, quotes from *Add. MSS.* 34,123, "Hugly...Long Pepper to be bought at said time [December], it grows about 16 course [*kōs*] thence, it may be had at 4 to 5 Rupees per maund, and in the shipping it is usually worth 9 to 10 Rupees, but much of it must not be bought because Bulkey, and will not vend."

[4] Compare *Tavernier*, vol. ii. p. 140 f. and the extracts given above.

Anno Domini 1653 *and Even to* 1660:
Vide Chron: of Hindostan and Monseur Bernier Historia de Mogol in Octavo:[1]

This Kingdome was Governed by an Absolute and lawfull Prince (by name) Sultan Sujah[2], One of the Sons of Chah Jehan[3], (then Emperour of Hindostan) but was from this Kingdome defeated as followeth:—

The Great Emperour of Hindostan had 4 Sons who were growne Up to man's Estate, and then did begin to Contend who Shold Succeed theire Father in the Throne of the Vast Empire (of Hindostan). Whereupon, theire Father, Chah Jehan, was not a little grieved, but, after Serious Considerations, concludes to Seperate them, by Settlinge them in good Goverments, to avoide all such Contentions, most Especially before his face, and thereby to remove the jealousie they had of Each Other findinge himselfe overcharged with all 4 of them, all beinge at age, all married, all pretendinge to the Crowne, Enemies to one another.

Hee Sent Sultan Sujah his Secound Son into Bengala, his third Son Aureng-Zebe[4] into Decan[5], and his youngest

---

[1] From this point to the account of Mīr Jumla's death the writer has followed the translation of *Bernier* which was published in London in 1671, and has made extracts therefrom more or less accurately. *Vide* Constable's edition of *Bernier*, p. xxvii. and pp. 14—115. For other early accounts of this revolution, compare *Schouten*, vol. i. pp. 194—238, and *Tavernier*, vol. ii. pp. 1—36.

[2] Shāh Shujā'.

[3] Shāh Jahān. The French spelling Chah betrays the origin of this Account.

[4] Aurangzēb.

[5] See *Hobson-Jobson*, *s.v.* Deccan. Compare *Thevenot*, part iii. p. 87, "Decan was heretofore a most powerful Kingdom, if one may believe the Indians; it consisted of all the Countries that are in that great Tongue of Land, which is betwixt the Gulfs of Cambaye and Bengala, all obeyed the same King; nay, and the Provinces of Balagate, Telenga and Baglana, which are towards the North, were comprehended within it, so that it may be said that at that time there was no King in the Indies more powerful than the King of Decan; but that Kingdom in process of time hath been often dismembered;

Son Morat Bakche[1] into Guzaratt[2]; and to the Eldest Dara he gave Cabul[3] and Multan[4].

The 3 first went away Seemingly contented, and acted there as Soveraigne Lords and Kings, and wholly retained to themselves the Revenues of the Said Kingdoms. But Dara Stirred not from his Father's Court, for as he was Eldest, soe he Expected the Crowne, which Soon after caused bloody Civil warrs in Hindostan. Yett Aurenge-Zebe, the Emperour's 3d. Son, haveinge the best Friends

---

and in the beginning of the last Age, (when the Portuguese made Conquests therein) it was divided into many Provinces,...and the Dominions of him (who was called King of Decan) reached no further than from the limits of the Kingdom of Cambaye or Guzerat, to the borders of the principality of Goa, which did not belong to him neither."

[1] Murād Bakhsh. The spelling Bakche again betrays the French origin of the statement.

[2] See *Hobson-Jobson, s.v.* Goozerat. Compare *Thevenot*, part iii. p. 6, "The Province of Guzerat, which was heretofore a Kingdom, fell into the Possession of the Great Mogul Ecbar, about the year 1565.... This is the pleasantest Province of Indostan, though it be not the largest. The Nardaba, Tapty, and many other Rivers that water it, render it very fertile, and the Fields of Guzerat look green in all the seasons of the Year, because of the Corn and Rice that cover them, and the various kinds of Trees, which continually bear Fruit. The most considerable part of Guzerat is towards the Sea, on which the Towns of Surrat and Cambaye stand, whose Ports are the best in all Mogulistan."

[3] See *Hobson-Jobson, s.v.* Cabul. The quotation is useful for the history of the word. Compare *Thevenot*, part iii. p. 57, "The Province of Caboul or Caboulistan is limited to the North by Tartary, from which it is separated by Mount Caucasus, which the Orientals call Caf-Dagai. Cachmire lies to the East of it: It hath to the West Zabulistan, and part of Candahar; and to the South the Countrey of Multan. Two of the Rivers that run into the Indus have their source in the Mountains thereof, from whence they water the Province, and for all that, render it nothing the more fruitful; for the Countrey being very cold, is not fertile, unless in those places that are sheltered by Mountains: Nevertheless it is very rich, because it hath a very great Trade with Tartary, the Countrey of the Usbecs, Persia, and the Indies."

[4] This passage is quoted almost direct from *Bernier*. See Constable's edition, p. 15. Compare *Thevenot*, part iii. p. 55, "Multan, which comprehends Bucor [Bukkur], has to the South the Province of Sinde, and to the North the Province of Caboul; as it hath Persia to the West, and the Province of Lahors to the East. It is watered with many Rivers that make it Fertile...the Province yields plenty of Cotton...Sugar, Opium, Brimstone, Galls, and Store of Camels."

att Court, namely of the Omrahs[1] and Emperours Councell, from whom he had immediate Notice of all transactions touchinge Soe weighty an Affaire, most Especially of Dara's proceedings, Soe that Dara noe Sooner had an Army in field, but Aurenge Zebe was in readinesse alsoe, and Upon his march towards Agra, the Metropolitan of the Empire[2], and which added more to his Strength he now Enjoys the Assistance of that great and Politick Warriour Emir Jemla[3], Sometime Generall of the Golcondah forces[4]. Dara meeteth him with a Very Potent army, and noe Sooner mett but a most bloody battle was fought, and Aurenge-Zebe proved the Conquerour. Dara fled, and was pursued soe close that he was Slaine some few days after[5]. Whereupon Aurenge-Zebe now marched into Agra, the Citty of his Father's Residence, Seizeth old Chah Jehan and imprisoneth him. Then, by advice of that Politician Emir Jemla, he dissemblingly Submits to his Brother Morat Backe, declareinge that he was the Onely Emperour both by gift of his Father and consent of the Lords and Commons throughout the whole Empire, and that what he had done was Onely to Establish him in the Throne, by which policie he Overcame him, and they joyned forces togeather. Soe that Now Aurenge-Zebe getts faire Opportunitie to cutt his Brother's head off, and made Use of itt as an advantage.

---

[1] See note on p. 39.

[2] Compare *Schouten*, vol. ii. p. 163, "Agra is the capital of this Empire. The fortress is situated in thirty-eight degrees North latitude, on the banks of the river Jemini, which flows into the Ganges. The surrounding country is very agreeable, and is adorned with trees that are always green. The town is very large, beautiful, and thickly populated with Maures, Persians, Idolaters." See also *Tavernier*, vol. i. part ii. pp. 48—50, and *Bernier*, p. 284 f.

[3] Mīr Jumla. In the MS. records (*O. C.* Collection) for 1659, he appears as "Merjumbelow, Meerejumbler, Jumbler"!

[4] See *Bernier*, pp. 16—20.

[5] *Bernier's* account (pp. 97—103) of Dārā's end is somewhat different, as is also *Schouten's*. They both describe the wanderings of the unfortunate Prince before he was taken prisoner.

Now hath he none to Conquer Save Sultan Sujah (the Prince of Bengala), who indeed was Enough for him to doe, the Sultan haveing a most invincible Army, and most of the best Military Commanders of Asia to assist him, himselfe alsoe beinge a very discreet and absolute Soldier, and Certainly had not failed to Overcome Aurenge-Zebe to have been absolute Conquerour of him and Emperour of Hindostan, had he not been falsely and treacherously betrayed, as followeth :—

One of Sultan Sujah's Persian Commanders of the horse, called Allah Verdikan[1], who doubtlesse was gained by gifts and large promises of honour to worke the plott, Upon the Very Pitch of the battle, Seeinge the whole Army of Aurenge-Zebe and Emír Jemla to be much disordered and in great Perill, hastened Upon a Persian horse toward the Sultan, and called aloud to him in these words:

Moh-barock-bad, Hazarót, Salamet,
El-hamd-ul-ellah[2]. vizt.

God Save your Majestie, you have Obtained the Victorie, why Stay you longer Upon your Elephant, in the name of God come downe, he hath made you the great Kinge of Hindostan[3].

Sultan Sujah (In the highest measure of Comfort to See his Enemies flee, and as it were Utterly rowted, cold not then Suspect any thinge of Victorie) confided in this perfidious man, and consideringe not or haveinge the least Suspicion of treason, lighted off his Elephant, which wrought his owne destruction with many Others of his loyall Subjects, his owne Army thereat beinge much dis-

---

[1] 'Alī Vardī Khān (Alahwirdī Khān, Ilahwirdī Khān).

[2] Quoted direct from *Bernier*. See Constable's edition, p. 53.

[3] T. B. refers the story to Shāh Shujā' in place of Dārā. See *Bernier*, p. 53, and p. 77, where he credits 'Alī Vardī Khān with employing a similar trick to procure the discomfiture of Shāh Shujā'.

comfitea, for they Suddenly missinge him, concluded he was Either taken or killed, at which instance of time Aurenge-Zebe's army Suddenly advanced, and put the Sultan's army to a great Confusion, and with much facilitie rowted them. Most of them, without resistance, left off and Fled, perceiveinge their Prince they fought for noe more in beinge, in Soe much that Sultan Sujah was (in a moment of time) from a great Conquerour, and the greatest of Emperours, Reduced to a Sudden change, brought to a Vaste Straight to flee for his life and libertie, with a Small retinue (not Exceedinge 500 persons). Hee fled to a Small Villadge Seated upon the banks of Ganges[1], and thence to Dacca[2] the Metropolitan of this Kingdome, where in a Small time he got recruite, but not Sufficient to keep him longe there, or of hopes to keep his countrey, for moneys and Other large promises from his adversaries had soe corrupted the most potent men in the Kingdome and Court, that it was now impossible for him to be Safe in his own Pallace, the Goverment of which, and the Goverment of the 3 kingdoms (namely, Orixa, Bengala, and Pattana[3]) was Established Upon Emir Jemla by Aurenge-Zebe (now absolute Emperour) for the terme of his life and of his Eldest Son, In Consideration of his great fidelitie and Conduct in these great Warrs.

Sultan Sujah (now in adversitie), destitute of Ships[4]. whereby to transport himselfe, his case beinge most desperate, not knowinge which way lyeth his Safety, he sendeth to the Kinge of Arackan[5], (a neighbouringe

---

[1] Monghyr. See *Bernier*, p. 80.

[2] See *Hobson-Jobson*, *s.v.* Dacca.

[3] *i.e.* Patna.

[4] See *Bernier*, p. 109.

[5] Compare Alex. Hamilton, *East Indies*, vol. ii. p. 27, "Arackan is the next maritim Country to the Southward of Bengal, and in former Times made some Figure in Trade. It was into this Country that the unfortunate Sultan Sujah came a Supplicant for Protection, when

Kingdome) craveinge his Assistance and Entertainment there, which was readily granted, and not more readily then accepted[1]. The Arackan Kinge Sends a parcell of Gylyars[2], vizt. Gallys, well fitted and manned with Arackaners[3] and Frangues[4], who came through the Rivers to

---

Emirjemal chased him out of Bengal. He carried his Wives and Children with him, and about Two hundred of his Retinue, who were resolved to follow his Fortune, and he carried six or eight Camels Load of Gold and Jewels which proved his Ruin, and in the End, the Ruin of the Kingdom of Arackan."

[1] Compare *Schouten*, vol. i. p. 219 f.

[2] See *Hobson-Jobson*, *s.v.* Gallevat. See also *Ind. Ant.*, vol. xxix. p. 408. The text is exceedingly interesting for the history of the word and proves its identity with the galley, and also with the Bengali form *jaliā*. Compare *Bernier*, pp. 109, 175, 179, 181, "Sultan Banque returned to Dake with a large number of galeasses (as they call the half galleys of this King)....They scoured the neighbouring seas in light galleys, called galleasses...These also are the identical freebooters who...repaired in their galleasses to Daka,...these unworthy Portuguese were one day seized with so strange a panic as to embark in forty or fifty galleasses and sail over to Bengale,...." Yule, *Hedges' Diary*, vol. ii. p. 184, quotes a letter from Richard Keigwin, under date 18th October, 1679, *O. C.* No. 4665, in which the following passage occurs, "the Enemy thinking we were as easily swallow'd as the other, came up our sterne, with 24 Grobs [see *Hobson-Jobson*, *s.v.* Grab], I know not how many Galwets...." Compare also the following: "At the returne of the Surviving lascars with some Arracan people and Gelliays Mr Everard was buried ashoare." Sloop Princess driven ashore on the Aracan coast 25th Dec. 1680. [I have unfortunately lost the location of this extract.] "The Governours Juliars mett with William Haggs who left the Ship *Degrave* some days agoe." Letter from *John Pitt* at Masulipatam to Capt. Young, 14th Aug. 1699, *O. C.* No. 6703. *Tavernier*, vol. ii. last section, p. 49, says, "I took one [of these barks] with four and twenty men....These Barks are little Galliots, which will undertake to carry you to your journey's end, and name your own day...I never made so pleasant a Voyage in my life, nor with less trouble. For in these Barks there is a Room where the Sun cannot come in, where you may repose in the day time, and sit in the cool Air on that side from whence the Breez comes." *Schouten* has also several mentions of the "Jelyasses" of Aracan. "Hardly had the sun risen when we descried the Jelyasses or oared-galleys of the King [of Aracan]." Vol. i. p. 166. "A little while after this storm,...twelve jeliasses of Aracan...anchored at Pipely." Vol. ii. p. 63. "Jeliasses are very long and narrow boats, apparently constructed principally with a view to swiftness. Indeed they cover long distances on the rivers. They carry no sails, but they have as many as thirty-eight or forty oars." Vol. ii. p. 66.

[3] The pirates of Aracan, of whom the writer speaks more fully later on.

[4] See *Hobson-Jobson*, *s.v.* Firinghee. *Fryer*, Index, has "Fringi,

Dacca, where they received the Sultan, his Wifes and Children, &c. necessaries, with about 200 of his Attendants, great Store of treasure, vizt. Gold and Silver Rupees, vast riches in Jewels, namely Diamonds, Rubies, and Pearle, which caused a kinder reception then he Expected, and Soon after Destruction, Fore one yeare was scarse Expired, but the Overthrow of the Prince (and most of his retinue) was brought to Effect.

I have heard it Related 2 ways[1], (as followeth), and I doe believe they were both put in Execution. The Kinge of this Countrey, now Seemingly the Protector of the distressed Prince Sujah, is an Idolater, and doth request the Sultan's Eldest daughter to wife[2]. The Sultan layeth the thinge plainely downe to him that it is against the laws of God and his Prophet Mahomet, he not beinge a Mussleman[3], ergo begged of him to desist such his desires; at which the Kinge was Sorely displeased, and cold not be pacified, but Sought the totall destruction of the Sultan and all that appertained to him, and to bringe this his malice to perfection, himselfe ordered one part of his owne pallace to be Set on fire in the night, and,

---

an European," and p. 113, "These [Diamonds cut with a mill] are sold most in the Country, they coming short of the Fringies in Fancy." Compare the *Memoriall* of Streynsham Master under date 19th March, 1679, quoted by Mackenzie, *Kistna District*, p. 130, "Between 3 and 4 in the morning we sett out and about 9 with easy travailing came to Yentapollam, in the way we passed over a place which have formerly been inhabited by Portuguese called Fringe Burane: some stones with inscriptions lay in the way." Compare also p. 206 of the same book, "Near the line of the old Madras road is the spot known as Feringhi or Frangula Dibba, the mound of the foreigners, where there was once a Portuguese settlement." See also Pringle, *Consultations* for 1684, p. 189, where, in a note on "Castez and Mustez" he quotes the following, "the Portuguese, whether of Europe or Brazil, are at Goa called indifferently Frangues or Fringuins or Reiñoes." *Tavernier*, vol. ii. p. 53, has, "there have always been in the Kingdom of Rakan or Moy, some Portugueses...and other Franguis, gather'd from all parts."

[1] Copied from *Bernier*, see p. 112 f.

[2] See *Bernier*, p. 110 f.

[3] See note on p. 76.

at the Uproar thereof, gave it out that Sultan Sujah and his Retinue had done the Fact, thereby to accomplish some great desine he had in Swayinge the Scepter of this Kingdome, which soe incensed the Guards and Soldiery of the Citty that next to squenchinge the fire they Endeavour to Squench theire thirst with the blood of the Sultan and those that appertained to him. The Sultan fled towards the Mountains, and his Small traine with him, but were soe Severely pursued that the Woody Mountains became theire Sepulchres.

Much flyinge News arrived att Agra and Delly[1], and most Eminent places in the Empire concerninge Sultan Sujah, that it was affirmed 2 or 3 years after his death that he was alive, and wold by the helpe of God and his Prophet, Seeke revenge off his Brother, Aurenge-Zebe.

But, Since it was truely made to appeare that he was soe basely Murthered in Arackan, Aurenge-Zebe, now the present Emperour, and once the Sultan's greatest Enemie, Seeketh revenge for that innocent blood, and will never, (as himself hath often Sworne) be at amitie with the Kinge or Kingdome of Arackan.

Emir Jemla hath now the Goverment of Bengala, Orixa, and Pattana, firmly by Phyrmand[2] Setled Upon him with an absolute Power and title of Nabob[3]. Hee

---

[1] See *Hobson-Jobson, s.v.* Delhi. It is a pity that Yule did not trace the rise of the wrong transposed *h* in the modern word "Delhi," as it does not represent any vernacular form and is not found, so far as I know, in any of the old 17th century writers. Compare *Thevenot,* part iii. p. 40, who gives the *h* of the Indo-Persian form Dehli in its right place, "The Province of Dehly bounds that of Agra to the North, and at present the Great Mogul Auran-zeb keeps his Court in the chief City of it, which is about fourty five Leagues distant from Agra. In Indostan it is called Gehan-abad, and elsewhere Dehly." The Hindi form is Dilli.

[2] *i.e. firmān.* See *Hobson-Jobson, s.v.* Firmaun. This and the quotations later on are valuable as showing the use of the word for Royal Letters-Patent or Charters.

[3] *Nawāb,* a Muhammadan Viceroy. See *Hobson-Jobson, s.v.* Nabob.

makes Dacca[1] the Metropolitan, beinge a fairer and Stronger Citty then Radja Mehal[2], the antient Metropolis, the Kingdoms wholy Submittinge to him, Save the Radjas of Orixa, Scarce worth his while to Send an army against, haveinge greater and more Noble designes in his head, and now he is noe Sooner Setled in this Kingdome, but begins a warre with the Radja of Acham[3], a Stronge and Potent Neighbouringe Prince. Makeinge Use of the best of time, his army beinge now well Seasoned to warre and Martiall Discipline, he makes hay while the Sun Shines, and with all speed marcheth into the Countrey, ransacks and Subdues all before him, fortifieth many stronge holds, and in a Small time brought the Kinge of that Countrey to such a Straite that he was forced to flee, and leave it to the mercy of this great Heroe[4], who next purposed to adventure both life and fortune against South

---

[1] Compare *Thevenot*, part iii. p. 68, "Daca, or Daac, is properly the capital City of Bengala; it lies upon the banck of the Ganges, and is very narrow, because it stretches out near a League and a half in length, along the side of that River. Most of the Houses are only built of canes, covered with Earth: The English and Dutch Houses are more solid, because they have spared no cost for the security of their Goods: The Augustines have a Monastery there also. The Tide comes up as far as Daca, so that the Galleys which are built there may easily Trade in the gulf of Bengala; and the Dutch make good use of theirs for their Commerce."

[2] Rājmahāl, once a place of great importance in Bengal. Compare *Tavernier*, vol. i. part ii. p. 54, "Rage-Mehale is a City upon the right hand of Ganges; and if you go by Land, you shall find the high-way, for a League or two, pav'd with Brick to the Town. Formerly the Governors of Bengala resided here; it being an excellent Country for hunting, besides that it was a place of great Trade. But now the River having taken another course, above a good half League from the City, as well for that reason, as to keep in awe the King of Aracan, and several Portuguese Banditti, who are retir'd to the mouths of Ganges, and made excursions even as far as Daca it self; both the Governour and the Merchants have remov'd themselves to Daca, which is at present a large City, and a Town of great Trade."

[3] Assam. The spelling Acham does not occur among the quotations given in *Hobson-Jobson*, *s.v.* Assam.

[4] The author says nothing of Mīr Jumla's enforced detention during the rainy season, nor of his costly retreat. See *Bernier*, p. 172 f.

Tartaria[1]; but Death, the Certaine call of all Mortals, now takes away the famous Emir Jemla[2], to the great griefe of all wise and Eminent Persons in these kingdoms, not a little dolefull to the poore, and the great losse these Kingdoms Sustained is Unmeasurable. They lost the best of Nabobs[3], the Kingdome of Acham[4], and, by consequence, many large priviledges.

The Europeans (Especially the English here resideinge) had great cause to Lament his death. He was an absolute lover and a most Indulgent Prince to all Ingenuous men, very charitable, and a real lover of the English Nation, all in generall (that Ever knew him) were Enamoured with his perfections, and a great many admired him in a great measure, Esteeminge him as the glorious mirror of all Princely Graces[5].

Aurenge-Zebe was Seemingly grieved to heare of his Death, although he not longe before repented himselfe that Emir Jembla had such an Invincible Power conferred Upon him, insomuch that, for Some years before, Aurenge-Zebe cold scarse heare of his name, or have the least cogitations of him, but wold Shake his head, haveinge noe power to retaine his griefe, or Ever thought of the

---

[1] The authority for this statement is to be found in *Bernier*, p. 171.

[2] The date of his death was the 31st March, 1663.

[3] See note on p. 142. For an account of the exact extent of power enjoyed by a *nawāb*, see Dow, *History of Hindostan*, vol. iii. p. lii.

[4] For a further account of the Assam campaign, see *Tavernier*, vol. i. part ii. p. 178, and vol. ii. p. 52 f. In vol. i. Mīr Jumla appears as Mirgimola.

[5] T. B. could hardly have obtained this impression of Mīr Jumla from the English themselves. The records of the time are full of complaints of the exactions of the Nabob. In 1659, he stopped the saltpetre boats on their way down from Patna, and hampered the trade of the English in every way, besides exacting an annual offering of three thousand rupees. See Wilson, *Early Annals*, vol. i. p. 34 f. However, Stewart, *History of Bengal*, p. 295, says, "His death was even regretted by the Europeans, who had formerly complained of his exactions."

flourishinge State of Emir Jemla, but looked Upon it as the dismall Coffin in which he himselfe was buried alive.

Beinge timorous that Emir Jemla's growinge greatnesse wold at length tend to his owne prejudice if he shold once aime at the Empire, which caused the Emperour at the news of his Death (although he Sighed) yet Uttered these words, "Now am I absolute Emperor of India"[1].

Emir Jemla's Son Succeeded not his Father (accordinge to Phyrmane); however, the Mogoll was Extraordinary kind to him in all Other respects, passinge the Custome of this Empire, more Especially after the death of his Father. He kept him at his owne Court, made him one of his Chiefest Omrahs[2] and associates, and freely gave him all his Fathers Estate and riches into his own possession, and to be wholly at his owne disposall[3].

Nabob Shah-hest-Kan[4] (Soon after the death of the Emir) had the goverment of these 3 Kingdoms tranferred Upon him[5] dureinge the Emperour's pleasure, who thought to himselfe that he had now put in one who wold in all respects be very Obedient, meerly out of beinge soe neare of blood and an antient man, vizt. his owne Uncle[6]. But he, findinge his Revenues to be very great, altogeather as much if not Exceedinge the Emperours revenues, that he Soone grew insolent, and denied any tribute to Aureng-

---

[1] See *Bernier*, p. 173, where, however, the remark is not attributed to the Emperor himself. See also *Tavernier*, vol. ii. p. 53, who tells the same story.

[2] *Umarā*, Ar. plu. of *amīr*, noble. See note on p. 39. Compare also *Fryer*, p. 195, on "Ombrahs."

[3] Here the writer again follows *Bernier*, p. 173.

[4] Shāyista Khān. Chah-hestkan is *Bernier's* spelling throughout. See pp. 174 ff.

[5] In 1664. See Hunter, *History of British India*, vol. ii. p. 238 f. According to *Bernier*, p. 174 (Constable's note) it was in 1666 that Shāyista Khān became Viceroy of Bengal. Stewart, however, gives 1664.

[6] His maternal uncle. Shāyista Khān was a son of the Vizier Asaf Khān, and brother of Shāh Jahān's favourite wife, Mumtāz Mahāl, the eponym of the Tāj at Agra.

Zebe, to whome it was due[1]. By sufficient testimonie, his revenue came to a lack vizt. 100000 rupees per diem, which is 12 thousand 500 pounds Sterlinge[2]. The first yeare I arrived in India[3], he Sent the Emperour 80 lacks of rupees, but the Ensueinge yeare, and soe forwards, he Seemed to be very Unwillinge to send him any, and retained the whole revenues to himselfe; soe that now all the tribute this great Cœsar cold get hence was a Short answer that the treasure was as safe in Dacca as in his owne Exchequer in Agra or Delly[4].

---

[1] The writer can now no longer follow *Bernier*, but writes from his own experience or from stories current in his time. There is no confirmation in either Elliot's or Stewart's history for the statement that Shāyista Khān failed to give the Emperor his due, at any rate during the early years of his rule in Bengal.

[2] *i.e.* placing the rupee at 2*s.* 6*d.* at the time of the author. On the 28th October, 1676, Streynsham Master wrote from Kasimbazar to the Court (*Diary of Streynsham Master*, p. 221), "This Person ['Shasta Chaun'] hath binn Nabob or Governour of Bengala 15 yeares, and hath got so great a treasure together as the like is seldome heard of now a dayes in the world, being computed by knowing Persons at 38 Curore of rupees, each Currore is a Million sterling at 2*s.* 6*d.* Rupee so his treasure is above 40 millions Sterling and his income dayly 2 Lack or 200000 Rupees which is above 20000 lb. Sterling of which his expence is above the one halfe, and yett he is every day more coveteous then other...."

[3] 1669.

[4] Here again the writer seems to be repeating the stories afloat soon after his arrival in India. Of the covetousness of Shāyista Khān, there were bitter complaints by the English during the whole of his rule. As early as 1665, the Factors at Hugli wrote (*Factory Records*, Miscellaneous, No. 3), "Dacca could take a large quantity of Europe goods if it were under another Nabob, the present being most covetous." Compare also another paragraph in the letter from Streynsham Master quoted above (*Diary of Streynsham Master*, p. 221), "he is every day more covetous then other, soe that to relate to you the many wayes that are continually invented by his Duan (one of the Craftiest men in the Kingdome) and his Governrs. to bring money in to his Coffers wold be as endless as admirable, both for their witt and Cruelty...." In the "Accompt of the Trade of Hugly" by Walter Clavell, among the papers forming the appendix to the *Diary of Streynsham Master*, pp. 317—322, there is the following detailed account of the exactions of Shāyista Khān: "But since the yeare 1663 or thereabouts, that Nabob Shasti Chaun the present Kings Uncle became Suba or Vice Roy of Bengall, and obtained Hugly as part of his Jaggere (or lands assigned him for his Person) his Servants being made soe far Governours as to receive all the rents, profitts,

For now this Shah-hest-Kan hath Entertained such false principles to accomodate his haughty humour, that he makes no question but it is his right not to obey any longer then till he cold get power to Command, and concluded that noe method was Unlawfull by which he cold make himselfe Supreme. Where upon Aurenge-Zebe weighed his Uncles most Unpleasinge actions with most serious consideration.

And, in the yeare 1678, the Emperour's Son beinge at age, a fitt and most palpable Opportunity for him to reduce this Goverment to a better State, he sends him into the Kingdome of Pattana, with proclamations forerunninge, proclaiminge him the true and lawfull Prince of Bengala &c., beinge well Satisfied that the Nobilite, more Especially the Commonalty, wold be very ready and joyfull to reverence him their lawfull Prince and Issue of their great Emperor.

Many of the Grandees of these 3 Kingdomes mett their Prince at Pattana, and the rest at Radja Mehal[1], who, by behaveinge himselfe courteously towards them, soon winne their hearts, soe that now by Joint consent they Send to Nabob Shah-hest-Kan to prepare himselfe for his Journey to Agra. Hee now beinge Sensible there is noe Safety for him, Unlesse he can procure the Emperour's favour, hasteneth with all Speed, Openeth his (laden) Exchequers of Gold and Silver, and was Soone in readinesse for his Journey, soe that he left Dacca before

---

Perquisites, fines, Customes &ca of the place, the Kings Governours hath little more than the name and for the most part sits Still whilst the Nabobs Officers oppress the people, monopolize most Commodityes even as low as grass for Beasts, canes, firewood, thatch &ca nor doe they want wayes to oppress those people of all sorts who trade, whether Natives or Strangers, since what ever they doe, when complained of to Dacca, is palliated under the name and Colour of the Nabobs interest...." See Hunter, *History of British India*, p. 238 f. who says that all infidels suffered alike under the rapacious rule of "Shaista Khan," the English neither more nor less than others.

[1] See note on p. 143.

the Prince came from Radja Mehall. His treasure was now growne to an Incredible height[1]. He laded 60 Patellas[2] with Silver, and, by credible report, tenne with Gold Moors[3], each Patella not carryinge lesse one with another (besides his lumber of travailinge Necessaries, vizt. Tents, Palanchinoes[4], Servants, Souldiery, &c.) then 25 or 30 tunns of Plate. And Now Shah-hest-Kan is gone in peace towards Agra, and noe question but may Easily make up his peace at Court, carryinge more riches with him to present the Emperor with then Ever his Forefathers or himselfe Enjoyed att once[5].

---

[1] See note on p. 146.

[2] Large flat-bottomed boats.

[3] Mohurs. See *Hobson-Jobson*, *s.v.* Mohur. Compare the following in a letter from Hugli to Balasor, 14th Oct. 1678, *O. C.* No. 4502, "One John Vander Vall...finding kind entertainment in the Factory [at Dacca] in the night opened a scrittore of Mr. Nedhams and stole out 25 or 26 gold Mohurs." See *Bernier*, p. 60 and Constable's note, also p. 476 f. *ibid.*

[4] See note on p. 19.

[5] From contemporary records, we get the following accounts, from the English point of view, of Shāyista Khān and his recall. In Oct. 1677, there is the first mention of "Shasty Cawhns" recall. According to rumour, he was summoned to "Dilly" to quiet a disorder caused by the "killing of a sonne of a great Rajahpoot." Later in the month a report was current that the "Nabob" by the "intercession of his old Begum" had obtained leave to remain "Subah of Bengall" at the cost of a present to the King of "3 Croer" of Rupees. In Nov. the factors at Hugli "had advice from the Dutch that Shausteh Caun Nabob of Bengall was turned out and that Feddei Caun was appointed to come in his place but we can give but little creditt to it as to all news of this nature." Four days later there is the record [*Factory Records*, Hugli, No. 1], "By advices this day from Decca are given to understand that Nabob Shausteh Caun is called away from the Government of Bengall and that another Nobleman named Aazzum Caun is deputed and sent by the Emperour in his place, this day write to Pattana concerning it ordered them to vissit this new Nabob in his way hither and to learne what they could about our Businesse of paying custome in those parts and to give us punctuall advice." Again, four days later, there is the entry, "This day received advices from Cassimbuzar treating of the great difficulty they found to gett our Masters peter boats cleered at Meirdadpoore where they have been detained ever since the 13th current by Nabob Shausteh Cauns people to carry up his luggage to Pattana." In Dec. 1677 "Auzum Cawne" formerly "Phuddy Cawne" the new Suba of Bengal arrived at Hugli. In Feb. 1678 "Shaste Cawne" arrived at "Pattana" and visited the Prince and "departed the next day for Dilly." In April the following

And Now the Prince is Entertained with great Solemnitie and Splendour att his Royal pallace in Dacca.

The Citty Dacca[1] is a Very large spacious one, but

---

report was current (*O. C.* No. 4394) "Nabob Shausteh Caun...is now in great disgrace at Dacca...how he will come off we cannot tell." On the 26th June the factors at Hugli wrote to Balasor (*O.C.* No. 4444) confirming "the Princes having the Government of Bengall bestowed upon him and of his entrance into Rajamaull, we have advices that he is proceeded thence to Dacca." In June, 1678, news reached Hugli "that the king had been to Vizit our old Nabob Shaster Caun where he presented him with incredable sums, whereupon he had given him Agra and Elohebaud for his Jaggeer or rents, and he is appointed to keepe neare the king but is not by reason of his great age made Vizier as formerly reported." [*Factory Records*, Hugli, No. 1.] From these extracts it will be seen that gossip was very busy as to the reason of the recall of the *nawāb*. From Stewart, *History of Bengal*, pp. 300—307, we get a clear account of Shāyista Khān's recall, of his two successors, and of his re-instatement in 1679/80. He says, "Shaista Khan governed Bengal, with great prudence and vigour, till the end of the year 1087 [1677]; when, at his own request, he was recalled to Court. On his arrival, he presented the Emperor with thirty lacs of rupees (nearly 350,000*l.*) in specie, some elephants, and a number of curiosities. He was most graciously received, and soon after appointed Governor of the province of Agra." See also Taylor, *Topography of Dacca*, p. 77. On the return of "Shasteh Caun" orders were given at Hugli for him "to be presented with 2 Persian Horses, less can't be given him as he will be absolute Governour having paid 30000000 rs. for it." *Factory Records*, Hugli, No. 2, under date 26th Jan. 1680. Shāyista Khān resigned the government of Bengal in 1689 and died at Agra in 1694, aged 93 lunar years.

[1] Compare the description of Dacca by *Tavernier*, vol. i. part ii. p. 55, "Daca is a great Town, that extends it self only in length; every one coveting to have an house by the Ganges-side. The length of this Town is above two leagues. And indeed from the last Brick-Bridge which I mention'd to Daca, there is but one continued row of Houses separated one from the other; inhabited for the most part by Carpenters that build Galleys and other small Vessels. These Houses are properly no more than paltry Huts built up with Bambouc's, and daub'd over with fat Earth. Those of Daca are not much better built: The Governours Palace is a place enclos'd with high Walls, in the midst whereof is a pitiful House, built only of Wood. He generally lodges in Tents, which he causes to be set up in a great Court of that Enclosure. The Hollanders finding that their Goods were not safe in the ordinary Houses of Daca, have built them a very fair House; and the English have another, which is reasonably handsom. The Church of the Austin-Friers is all of Brick, and is a very comely Pile." See *Thevenot's* description quoted on p. 143. Compare also Alex. Hamilton, *East Indies*, vol. ii. p. 23, "I...must visit Dacca, which lies under the Tropick of Cancer, on the broadest and eastermost Branch of Ganges. The City is the largest in Bengal, and it manufactures Cotton and Silk the best and cheapest. The Plenty and Cheapness of Provisions are incredible, and the Country is full of Inhabitants...."

standeth Upon low marshy Swampy ground, and the water thereof Very brackish, which is the onely inconvenience it hath, but it hath some very fine conveniencies that maketh amends, haveinge a fine and large River that runneth close by the walls thereof, navigable for Ships of 5 or 600 tunns in burthen, and the water of the River beinge an arme of the Ganges is Extraordinary good, but it is a great way to be fetched by Some of this Citty, for it is not lesse in Circuit then 40 English miles.

An admirable City for it's greatnesse, for it's magnificent buildings[1], and multitude of Inhabitants. A very great and Potent army is here in constant Sallary and readinesse, as alsoe many large, Stronge, and Stately Elephants, trained Up for a Warlike Service, which are kept continually neare to the Pallace.

Many Elephants, both for Warre and State, are here kept by Severall rich men, and therefore by consequence a Very great Soldiery, for noe man in the Kingdome is admitted to ride an Elephant in State, Unlesse he Continually keep 500 horse to be ready at the Princes Service.

The English and Dutch have each of them a Factorie in the Citty of Dacca[2]; yet theire investments are but

---

[1] Both Mīr Jumla and Shāyista Khān were great builders. Taylor, *Topography of Dacca*, p. 78, says, "A considerable number of public buildings as mosques, alms-houses &c. were raised by Shaista Khan, and judging from the prevalence of the style of building which is here [Dacca] called 'Shaista Khany,' a great portion of the large brick-built houses of the town appear to have been erected in his time." On p. 95 of the same book, we read, "The palace of the Lall Baug was commenced in 1678 by Sultan Mohammed Azim, the third son of the Emperor Aurengzebe, and was left by him in an unfinished state to Ameer Al Omrah Shaista Khan his successor in the government.... Shaista Khan appears never to have completed this structure...the little Kuttra...was erected by Shaista Khan in 1663, and is still the property of his descendants."

[2] The English Factory was started about the year 1666. In a letter to Hugli dated 24th Jan. 1668, the Court comment on information received in the previous year that "Decca is a place that will vend much Europe goods, and that the best Cossaes, Mullmuls &c. may there be procured." If the factors at Hugli were of opinion that the settling a Factory at Dacca would result in a large sale of broad

Small, on each Side beinge very Inconsiderable, and yet are of great consequence in Some Other and weightier concerns, for here they are neare the Prince and Court, Under whom all our Factories in Bengala and Pattana hold their Phirmane[1], soe that if wee receive any wronge or prejudice from a Governour, or Merchant, or Others of this Countrey, or any Other Under his precinct, wee are heare ready to demand Justice.

The Secound best Citty that is in this Kingdome[2] is called Cattack[3], a very decent and more comely Citty then

cloth, they had liberty given them "to send 2 or 3 fitt persons thither to reside." *Letter Book*, No. 4. From this it appears that the Dacca Factory did not receive official sanction until 1668. In 1670 it was in full swing with John Smith as chief. During the time comprised in T. B.'s "Account" there were two other chiefs, viz. Robert Elwes who died there in 1675, and Samuel Hervy who was assisted by Fytche Nedham. In the *Diary of Streynsham Master* under date 23rd Nov. 1676, p. 269 f., we find that "Mr Walter Clavell was desired to draw up Instructions to Mr Hervy and Mr Nedham for the management of the Honble. Company's business at Dacca....Mr Hervy representing to the Councell that the Companys house in Dacca is very streight and not capable to receive and secure the Honble. Companyes goods by reason of severall thatcht hovells within and round about the compound which are very dangerous in respect of fire which often happens in Dacca. The Councell did therefore order that brick buildings be forthwith erected to secure the Companys Goods not exceeding one thousand rupees for this yeare...." Taylor, *Topography of Dacca*, p. 97, says that the only portion of the English Factory now remaining is the outer wall, and that of the Dutch Factory no trace exists except the walled terrace on which it stood.

[1] See note on p. 142.

[2] Orixa, Pattana, and Bengala collectively formed the Muhammadan Kingdom or Province of Behar.

[3] See *Hobson-Jobson*, *s.v.* Cuttack. Compare the following from the *Diary of Streynsham Master*, 28th Aug. 1676, p. 45, "Mirza Wooly the Governour of this Towne [Balasor], and yesterday the Duan went hence to Cateck the Capitoll citty of Orixa to meet the new Governour of that Province one of Shatta Cawnes Sonnes." Alex. Hamilton, *East Indies*, vol. i. p. 390 f. thus describes Cuttack—"Cattack is still a large City, walled round, and a good many Cannon planted on its Walls, but neither the Wall nor Artillery are kept in good Order. The Town is not one Quarter Part inhabited; but the Ruins of many large Buildings shew sufficiently its ancient Grandeur, when Kings kept their Courts there. Its Figure is an Oblong for a League long, and a Mile broad. It is garrisoned with 5000 Foot, and 500 Horse. The English Company had once a fine Factory in Cattack. Most of its Walls were standing in Anno 1708 and a Garden that belonged to the Factory was then in good Repair..."

Dacca, but not one halfe soe large, but much more beautifull, although an Inland one, five days Journey from Ballasore, adorned with goode and Sumpteous buildings, broad Streets, surrounded with Excellent Ponds and Water Springs, delicate Groves of Mango[1], tamarin[1], Palmito[1], Palmero[1], and Coconutt trees all very much adorninge.

The Governour hereof hath a very large traine, a very Potent army, and liveth Prince like, and is the next in place to the Prince himselfe, and hath the title of Nabob.

Hee is put into place by the Prince of Bengala and his councell. Dureinge theire pleasure he continueth in it, but noe longer, which Seldome Exceedeth 3 or 4 years[2], for feare of his growinge overrich and Powerfull. The Revenues and Exactions of this Nabob beinge very incredible, (yet in one respect not[3]) consideringe the power he doth and may take over the richest of Gentues and Banjan Merchants, of which this Part of the Kingdom hath great Numbers.

I Remember, in the yeare 1674, when I lived in the towne of Ballasore, (the onely Sea Port in the Bay of Bengala), a new Nabob was Sent from Dacca to Settle in Cattack, the Old one beinge first sent for to avoide contention betweene them[4]. The new Nabob in his

---

[1] See notes on pp. 48, 22, 46 and 24.

[2] There were five *nawābs* in the ten years 1669—1679.

[3] The writer does not explain this reservation.

[4] The "new Nabob" was "Ruzzeed Chaan" [Rashīd Khān] who succeeded "Suph Secund Chaan" [Safshikan Khān] in 1674. From the *Factory Records* and *O. C.* Collection, we get the following particulars about the *nawābs* of Orixa at this period: In March, 1673, "Advises" were received at Hugli "from Cateck that Nabob Zoffy Chaan [Safī Khān] is come to Pattana in the place of Ibrahim Chaan" who was "jaggered" [granted an estate (*jāgīr*), pensioned]. A few months later "Softy Chaan Jaggeer'd and Saph Secund chaan to succeed him in his place." In Dec. 1674, Walter Clavell, chief at the Bay, wrote from Balasor, "To Cateck wee have lately a nother Nabob arrived of the Pattana Cast in place of Suph Secund Chaan who is caled to Court and there advanced to be droga. of the Topecanna which Answers to our Master of Ornance: he was called hence in hast

Journey tooke all Opportunities to get moneys, in soe much that he lett Slipp none whereby he might Enrich him selfe Either by legal or Illegal means. He came neare to Ballasore, Vizt. within one mile and ½ of it, where he sent for most rich Merchants of Gentues[1] and Banjans[2], commandinge theire Estates, or considerable portions of them, att his owne pleasure. His demands off Some were 10, 20, 30, 40, 50 thousand rupees, and of Some more, accordinge as they were of abilitie, (haveinge Subtle fellows near him that had first pryed into their Estates).

And for noe Other law or reason, but that he told them he wanted a great Summ of moneys to welcome him into the Place, and (in Short) that he wold have it by one means or Other. In soe much that the Merchants can now plead nothinge but Poverty, whereby to come off the Cheaper, and yet deare Enough too, as for Example—

One day I was close by his Tent in Company with an acquaintance of mine (a Dutch Doctor[3] then belonginge to

---

Personally to attend the King in his advance against the Pattans who had made great Incead [? inroad] into Indostan, this Alteration of Nabobs and Governours doth Continually Augment your Charges and yet Such is the Persimonious Nature as well of those who are Advanced as those that are removed if they do not proportion their expences to their Incommodities as the Prince (Shah) Sujah and after him Mierjumlah did: nor is it to be hoped that broad Cloath and other wolen goods will find any Saile in these parts unless Some young Nabob or a Son of the Kings come to succeed the Nabob of Decca." Of the "new Nabob" we have the following accounts: "Ruzzeed Caan is a man of so bad a temper that wee have no hopes of sending by Narragur [from Kasimbazar] without having greate trouble and charge in presents." "We have notice [in 1675] of not a worse Nabob come to Orissa then the present Ruzzard Chaan who robs the hole Country in and a bout Cateck." "Ruzzeed Chaan" probably assumed office in May or June, 1674, for in the *O. C.* Collection there is a document in Persian endorsed "Nabob Ruzzeed Chaans Phirwanna procured in Ballasore in June, 1674." In Nov. 1677 "Azzum Caun his Son is to be Nabob of Orixa." The "Nabob of Orixa" in Dec. 1678 was "Nouralla Caun" [Nūru'llah Khān].

[1] See note on p. 6.

[2] See note on p. 24.

[3] Perhaps De Graaf, the Dutch Surgeon who made six voyages to the East Indies between 1640 and 1687. See Orme, *Historical*

the Campe), att which Juncture of time a great Banjan Merchant called Chim Cham[1], great broker to the English

Fragments, vol. ii. pp. xiv. and xlvii. f., and *Voyages de Nicolas de Graaf aux Indes Orientales*, from which several extracts will be found later on in the notes.

[1] "Chimcham and Chintamund" (Khēmchand and Chintāman) were brokers to the English at Balasor for many years, and of the former especially there are many notices in the contemporary records. The following mentions of the firm, extracted from *Factory Records* and the *O. C.* Collection, give a fair idea of the position held by these two Hindū traders, and of the important part they often played at this period. In 1669, "Chim Cham" contracted to supply goods to the English at Balasor. In June of the same year, the evidence of "Chim Cham Cheife Merchant of Ballasore" is quoted with regard to affairs in 1663. In Oct. 1670, the factors at Hugli wrote to the Court, "The Cotton Yarne and Ginghams...wee have endeavoured this year to redress by drawing their provision out of Chim Chams hands whome wee find not fitting to bee much longer employed in your business, haveing bin so much exalted by former Cheifes who were partakers with him." However, in 1672, Chim Cham was still the "cheife Merchant at Ballasore." In that year he was mulcted of some of his wealth by the *faujdār* of Cuttack. "Henry Charnock returned from Cateck with the new Phirwanna bringing a letter from Burmull in answer to that I sent he staying there with Chimcham and Jurradgeshaw...the Fousdar detains Chimcham Prisoner att Cateck and his Enlargement cannot be purchased for less than 30,000 rupees which please to consider and the consequence...these last doings have occasioned every house of any Esteeme to Entertain many peons, Chimchams house 50...Chimcham returned from Cateck by complying and Giving Security to pay rupees 10,000 in 17 days and 20,000 rupees in 3 months the which with the Cowries he mentioned to you...will rise high...Chimcham...notwithstanding his present troubles he hath estate Sufficient to Indemnify our masters and all others which is sufficient for our proceeding in delivering him this day his share of the 25000 rupees being rupees 7500." In 1673 trade was bad at Balasor; "Chim Cham keepes aloofe off and seeing wee have no money to advance here is unwilling to take off our goods....Broad Cloth will not sell. Chim Cham alone hath remaining on his hands...Rupees 30000 of that Commodity and yet hath not taken off all the last yeare." In the *Diary of Streynsham Master*, 30th Aug. 1676, there is an allusion to the great Balasor merchant: "This forenoon the merchants were sent for and treated with...about the investment to be made here this yeare, and Chim Cham the Cheife of them was very high and indifferent whether he dealt with the Company or not." Terms were made with the merchants and Chim Cham was ordered to be security for three whose credit appeared to be "faileing." In 1678, the rich merchant's goods were again seized by a native officer: "This evening Chym Cham in his return from Decca came to our Factory...Chim chams boate necessaryes being stoped by the Meirbar he sent to have it cleered, and the new Muzzareefe demanded what it was, Chim Cham replyed, there was nothing but his beding and wareing clothes, the Muzzareefe caused it to be searched and some new pieces of cloth and

East India Company, came out of the Countrey to crosse the River about ¼ of a mile from the Campe. The hungry Nabob immediately Enquired who that was goinge by with

---

stuff being found amongst it (being only what was intended for cloths and to carry for his house use) the Muzzareefe caused it to be all carryed to the casharee [*Kachahrī*, Kutcherry, Court-house] as forfited and would not let them goe...." In Nov. 1678 Chim Cham and his fellow merchants obtained leave to build a warehouse in the Factory at Balasor "at their own charge" the said warehouse to be used solely for the Company's goods, "except in case of very great exigency and then to advise and have licence from Hugly for their soe doing." In 1679 Chim Cham's influence as a merchant was still very great: In regard to a dispute about a house and piece of ground in Balasor, claimed by the Dutch, Mr Edwards was directed to "gett the Congoes [*kānungō's*] Chaup if necessary by meanes of Chimcham or Cullean [Kalyān] Ray." In the same year Chimcham's partner is mentioned: "Wee admire Chimcham and Chintamund should refuse to be Security for those persons who provide goods of the Investment enordered with you." In March, 1680, "Arrived a ship belonging to Chimcham from Tenasseree with Elephants." In July of the same year "Chintamundsaw" received a severe reprimand from Hugli for "Boggling" about a debt he owed the Company. In 1681 the Council at Hugli refused to allow Chintamundsaw any share in the Investment "in regard of his being engaged to Nabob Russeed Cawne...Chimcham in the meane time being Content to Supply him with soe much monyes as Comes to his Shaire in hopes the Chiefe and Councell upon his Submission and promise will Receive him into favour and Continue him in his Employment as formerly." In 1682 Chimcham was still able to dictate his own terms to the Company: "We understand Chimcham is mighty hasty and declares if he may not receive imprest in proportion to his late title of cheife Merchant that he will none." In 1684 news reached Hugli that a "Gomasta" in Chintamund's service had purchased large quantities of "Cosses" at Dacca "to the great prejudice of the Companys affaires there." The agent at Balasor was ordered not to "Incourage Such villians in makeing preparations for Interlopers they haveing ingaged by promise and bond to the contrary." In April, 1685, "Chimcham and Chintemanshaw Our merchants" were employed to "cleere" an "affaire with the goverment for pease sake,...as being company marchants." This seems to show that Chintāman was restored to favour. But in the following year there was again a doubt as to his solvency—"Chintamund Saw being considerably Indepted to the Right Honble. Company and there being but little likelyhood of Recovering said Debt, without wee attach and Seize what Shipps hee has at Sea and a Shipp being arrived in which hee is part Owner, wee judge it best...to Seize on Said Shipp to Secure part of his debt... Capt. John Nicholson arrived in this Road this morning tooke the Ship belonging to Chintmund and Chintamunsaw and came ashore at 12 at night [16th Nov. 1686]." Chim Cham disappears from the records about this time. His death would explain the summary procedure towards his poorer partner. There is a reference to Chintamunsaw and his debt to the Company as late as 1695.

Such a traine. It was answered, Chim Cham the Banjan Merchant. The Nabob, like a ravenous Wolfe, caused him immediately to be brought before him, which was accordingly done; but (e're that) he had pulled of his gold Turbant[1] and Jewels and rings and put on very mean cloths, thereby to plead povertie. When he was brought to the Nabobs tent dore, he passed the Usual Ceremonie, holding Up both hand and downe Upon his heels, Sayinge Nabob Salamat, vizt. "Live O Prince!"

The Nabob (Smileinge Upon him) demandeth with all Speed one lack of rupees, i.e. 100000. Chim Cham Seemed Melancholy, as great reason he had to part with Such a Summ where it was not at all due, and thereupon begins to bemoane his sad accident and losse he had lately received, for he was robbed of 1500000 rupees in this his Journey into the Countrey on purpose to marry his Daughter to one of his owne Cast[2], which was really soe; but the relation of that added but more Flames to the fire, although he pretended it was the most part of what he had in the World.

"Nay, Chim Cham," Said the Nabob, "I am now well satisfied as to the report I heard of you Since you can afford soe much to the marriadge of one daughter, and have Severall Children alive.

"Now make hast home and Send me the moneys I demand towards my marriadge to this part of the Kingdome, who am now come to be husband to you all." He made many Apologies, and feed Some of the Nabob's councell, whereby he got off for 50000 Rupees[3].

The Nabob had now learned the lessons ready off his

---

[1] See *Hobson-Jobson*, *s.v.* Turban.

[2] See note on p. 9, also p. 31 and note.

[3] There is no confirmation of this story in the contemporary records, but see above, note on p. 154, for two occasions on which Chim Cham was mulcted by the Native Governors.

Master Shah-hest-Kan[1], who always kept in his Court Sharpe witted fellows that made it theire businesse to prye into the Estates of the Hindoo Merchants, which fellows he generally preferred for his owne Interests Sake, beinge himselfe soe great an Adorer of the riches of this World.

Another transaction, but more worthy of Observation, I was Spectator to the next day, as follows:—The Old Nabob of Cattack[2], beinge Sent for to the Court at Dacca, had left his Chiefe Lady to follow with what leisure She thought convenient. Her guard and attendants were about 1000 men, with about 100 Women and Eunuchs, who at this time had pitched her tents within one mile of the New Nabob, whoe now thought he had another Opportunitie fallen into his hand of acquireinge one lack or two of rupees. Whereupon he Sent the Lady an accompt of his beinge Soe neare her, and demanded noe lesse then 2 lack of Rupees as a present. She, a most mannish woman of these ages, couragiously sends him word she owed him nothinge, nor had she Ever received any Piscash[3] from him, whereby to make any retalliation. He, out of bravado, Sendeth to her againe to let her know she or any that belonged to her Shold [not] passe his countrey without Sufficient acknowledgement to him their Nabob.

But she, beinge a most Undaunted couragious Lady, Alarams all her foot and horse, set them in battail array, mounted one of her husbands warre Elephants and Sends him word She wold one houre hence come close by his owne tents, and if he wanted any of her moneys it were his best way to demand it then, for She had a great

---

[1] Shāyista Khān.

[2] See note on p. 152.

[3] See *Hobson-Jobson*, *s.v.* Peshcush. An obligatory gift to a high official.

treasure with her, and wold adventure not onely that, but her life and Fortune she wold Expose to the greatest of dangers, for the maintainance of the honour of her Husband.

With which Sharpe answer of this Lady's resolution and couradge, the Nabob was soe abashed, that immediately he removed his whole Campe neare on[e] mile, Pitchinge it on this Side the River, within ½ a mile of the towne Ballasore, where now he is in hopes of the English and Dutch to Visit him, and not Empty handed[1].

Accordinge to his Expectation, the English and Dutch Agents and theire councels went out in State to waite upon him, carryinge considerable Piscashes[2] with them to present him with. But the Dutch, that Study to out doe us in all transactions in India, now made greater haste to come to the Speech of him then Mr. Walter Clavell (our English Chiefe[3]) did, and made their present 3 or 4 times

---

[1] The records of the time are unfortunately very incomplete for the year 1674, and I have been unsuccessful in finding any trace of this story.

[2] See note on p. 157.

[3] Walter Clavell, the younger son of an old Dorsetshire family, was a somewhat important personage in Bengal when T. B. came in contact with him. In 1667, when 28 years of age, he was sent out by the Court to Fort St George to assist in reinstating the imprisoned Governor, George Foxcroft. Owing to an unusually long voyage and a severe illness on his way overland from Surat, Clavell did not reach Fort St George until Jan. 1669 when he found his mission was already accomplished. He petitioned to go to the "Bay" where he was appointed "Second," and, on the departure of Shem Bridges for England, became acting "Chief," a post in which he was confirmed by orders from Court in Dec. 1672. In June, 1672, Walter Clavell procured a "Phirwanna" from "Shaster Caun" a copy of which, together with the "Nabobs Letter" is to be found in *Factory Records*, Miscellaneous, No. 3. Another version of this "Phirwanna" referred to by Yule in *Hedges' Diary*, vol. iii. p. 190, is entered at the end of the *Diary of Streynsham Master*. The *parwāna* had little effect in stopping the exactions of Shāyista Khān to whose oppressions and the exactions of Malik Qāsim, Governor of Hugli, there are frequent allusions in the letters of Clavell to the Court in London, and to the Council at Fort St George.

From 1672 to 1676 Clavell was quarrelling with Joseph Hall, factor at Kasimbazar, who, if half his accusations were true, must have

suffered much at the hands of the Chief and the Second (Matthias Vincent) at the Bay. Hall was very bitter in his attacks, and wrote long letters of complaint both to Fort St George and to certain of the Directors in London. He accused Clavell of appropriating the effects of Mr Marsh, the Company's servant who died in Balasor, declared that the Governor of Hugli was disgusted at his non-residence in that place, and further, that neither of the clergy would administer the Sacrament to Clavell and his friends, who had "desired it rather for a cloak to their knavery then for the Good of their Soules." Other charges against Clavell were, that he had ordered "a Pallace" to be built for himself at Balasor, and that, in 1675, he was in that town for 17 days "Leaving his Wife to bee Governesse at Hugly." Both Hall and Herne, another aggrieved factor, declared that Clavell "Sided with the Dutch Directore" in 1672, and, by omitting to visit the Governor of Balasor, cost the Company 4000 rupees. In Feb. 1676, in the *Memorandum* given to Major Puckle, who was authorised to inspect all the subordinate factories and redress any grievances, we find: "Mr. Clavell (now Chief at the Bay) for overrateing the Companys Goods 40 per Cent. great private Tradeing, &c. and keeping the Generall Books himself contrary to the Companys Order." Clavell was at Fort St George at the time, and apparently managed to make out a good case for himself, for we hear no more of the enquiry. In a complaint brought by Valentine Nurse, another malcontent, against Clavell, Major Puckle decided in the latter's favour. No doubt these various charges were somewhat exaggerated, and Clavell's position never seems to have been seriously imperilled by them. Probably his sudden death saved him from falling into disgrace with the Directors, for, in Dec. 1676, they wrote to Fort St George that they were "sensible enough that by divisions in the Bay our Business hath been much Impeded for severall years" and also, in the same letter, "wee note...that Mr. Clavell and Mr. Vincent doe laugh and despise at our Agency at the Fort, and doe expect that you have called Mr. Clavell to an account for it."

In the *O. C.* Collection, there are two letters from Walter Clavell to Richard Edwards "Merchant in Cassimbazar." These are dated from Balasor the 3rd and 17th of June, 1673, and are very quaintly worded. The first runs as follows: "Esteemed Friend I have received yours of the 3d May with two paire of Slippers doe exceed the measure of my foot a Little however rather than faile they will fit my foot most rarely, therefore pray goe on with the Investment and when you have shod mee so long till you find I am overbooted charge me with a bill and I shall pay it at sight, if as you say you have met with a shoemaker that keepes his word you are a happy man you were best make much of him you will hardly find his fellow in all this Countrey, if you can you have better skill at finding then the rest of your neighbours, wee have no news my hearty respects tendred to you I Rest Your Assured friend Walter Clavell. Pray send me a bottle of Ink. W. C."

In 1676 Clavell returned from Fort St George to his post at Hugli, in company with Streynsham Master, who had been appointed Supervisor of the dependent factories. At Master's request, Clavell wrote an "Accompt of the Trade of Hugly and Ballasore" which is very fully quoted by Yule in *Hedges' Diary*, vol. ii. pp. 238—240. During the first six months of 1677, Clavell was constantly urged by the Council at the "Fort" to use all possible means to obtain a *farmān* for free trade in the "Bay." But on the recall of Shāyista

as large, and had present admittance. But before they got their Phyrmane[1] renewed and Signed, the English Merchants came very mildly and requested admittance into his tent, which was granted, and they were placed above the Dutch. The English Agent, after complementall Ceremonies Ended, gave in his Phyrmane to be renewed, which was soe kindly taken from the Nabob and his Associates, that it was immediately done and delivered to Mr. Clavel[2], where Upon he gave in his present of fine Scarlet[3], lookeinge glasses, Sword blades, fine pictures, and Some Gold Moors[4], without boastinge or commendinge

---

Khān, the gentlemen at Fort St George refused to accept the responsibility of approaching the new *nawāb* on the subject. Clavell does not appear to have made much effort to obtain the *farmān.* He resented a proposal that the Council at the "Bay" should meet at Hugli to discuss the matter, and insisted on remaining at Balasor. On the 3rd August, 1677, a Council was held at his house there "he being very sick." On the following day Walter Clavell died of a fever. His wife and "little infant" died the next day. Mrs Clavell is said to have succumbed to a "fever caused by excess of grief" for her husband's death. On the 11th August Messrs Reade and Byam at Hugli wrote to Matthias Vincent at Kasimbazar: "This evening wee have the Unwellcome news of Mr. Walter Clavells and his Ladies decease by Violent feavours Some other English Dead there allsoe and 9 or ten more desperate ill of the Same distemper God Almighty Graunt wee may make good use of those Examples and prepare us for our owne chainge when he shall think fitt to make it."

Walter Clavell was twice married. By his first wife Prudence he had a son William, who died in 1680, and another child who died young. By his second wife Martha Woodruffe, sister to the wife of Sir Edward Littleton, he had two sons, Edward and Walter. The younger son was baptized at Kasimbazar on the 29th Sept. 1678 by "Mr. Samuell Epes minister of Ship *Society.*" In January, 1681, the two children were sent to England on the ship *President.* Edward Clavell was Sheriff of Dorset in 1702. He died in 1738, leaving a son George, at whose death, in 1773, the Clavell family became extinct. (See Hutchins' *History of Dorset*, *s.v.* Clavell.) Walter Clavell's will is in existence at Somerset House, and is a long and interesting document. From its contents it is evident that he was a man of considerable means.

[1] See note on p. 142.

[2] I can find no mention in the records of this visit of Walter Clavell to the "new Nabob of Cuttack."

[3] See *Hobson-Jobson*, *s.v.* Scarlet and Suclat. "Scarlet" in old English was "broadcloth" of any colour.

[4] See note on p. 148.

any thinge in it, (a custome the Dutch are much inclined too in India), and soe tooke leave of him gratifieinge his guards and attendants reasonable well.

Soe that now the Dutch are left to boast of their Countrie or what else, which they in Such Cases faile not to doe, although Credited by none but the Ignorant. But now, findinge the day well neare Spent, they request theire Phyrmane, but were Sharply answered by the Nabob, whoe told them, Since theire owne words made it Evidently appeare that they had soe Enriched theire Countrey and State by an East India trade, that he was now one of the Easterne Lords, and wold have a Considerable reward in ready Cash before he wold renew theire Old Phyrmane, which if it did displease them, they might begone, and pay the whole duty of all their goods Exported the Kingdome.

Soe that now their great boastings cost them 5 or 6 thousand pounds, and the Charge and trouble of waitinge Upon him and his Attendants 3 or 4 days followinge. Some few days afterwards, the Nabob rode through the towne of Ballasore in his greatest State, mounted upon a Very large Elephant, and thus proceeded towards the Citty Cattack[1].

Strange kind of Oppressions are laid Upon the Merchants of these Kingdoms, more Especially the most Vaine and Idle of which were annually put Upon them by the Old Nabob Shah-hest-Kan[2], who wold not be Satisfied that all both rich and poor Shold bow to him, but the Ships upon the Water shold doe the like, for the performance of which he wold Every yeare Send downe to the

---

[1] T. B. is no doubt relating what actually occurred during his stay in Balasor, but it is very tantalising that the records for the year 1674 should be so scanty as to throw no light on these events.

[2] Shāyista Khān.

Merchants in Hugly, Jessore[1], Piplo[2], Ballasore[3] for a Ship

---

[1] A town in Lower Bengal, still known under the same name and spelling.

[2] Gabriel Boughton (see Stewart, *History of Bengal*, p. 251 f.) obtained permission from Shāh Shūjā' to establish a Factory at Pipli in 1634, but there is no evidence that the privilege was made use of. On this, see Yule, *Hedges' Diary*, vol. iii. p. 181. Compare the description of Pipli harbour and town by *Schouten*, vol. ii. pp. 59 and 158: "We came to Pipley road, two leagues from the river and from the coast, where we were as much exposed as if we had been in the open sea; and as there was very little depth there, we anchored in order to protect ourselves from the violence of the tempests...The town of Pipley lies four or five leagues beyond the mouth of the river. It is of a medium size and fairly well populated; but it is not walled. The chief houses, Pagodas, and other large buildings are surrounded by open spaces, gardens, squares of turf, orchards." Compare also John Marshall, *Notes and Observations*, p. 16 (reverse), "At 4 clock [31st Dec. 1670] came to Pipley where the Dutch have a hansome Factory." Of this Dutch factory Streynsham Master wrote (*Diary of Streynsham Master*, 20th Dec. 1676, p. 290), "The Dutch have left their Factory of Pipley, pulled down their house there, and built a new one at Ballasore." If Alex. Hamilton (*East Indies*, vol. ii. p. 3) is to be believed, a factory *was* at one time in existence at Pipli: "Piply lies on the Banks of a River supposed to be a Branch of the Ganges, about 5 Leagues from that of Ballasore, formerly it was a Place of Trade, and was honoured with English and Dutch Factories. The Country produces the same Commodities that Ballasore does, at present it is reduced to Beggary by the Factory's Removal to Hughly and Calcutta, the Merchants being all gone. It is now inhabited by Fishers...."

[3] See *Hobson-Jobson*, *s.v.* Ballasore. Compare *Schouten's* description, vol. ii. p. 159 f., "Bellesoor is five leagues to the west of the river of Pipely. Most of the English ships come to anchor here, where there is a fine factory....The harbour is an admirable one the Cape of Palmeris protecting it from the boisterous southern winds and consequent tempests. When the weather is clear, the English vessels at anchor in this harbour and ours [the Dutch] in Pipely harbour can see each other." Compare also John Marshall's account of Balasor, *Notes and Observations*, p. 8 and p. 5 (reverse), "Ballasore was formerly called Bahagur....Ballasore, where the English have a Factory a little way from the River side this in the Rain times is very dirty vizt from May to October...but after is very pleasant having about a mile from the Towne severall very hansome Mango gardens...Ballasore is a very great Stragling towne but scarce a house in it but dirt and thatcht ones." In the "Accompt of the Trade of Ballasore" by Walter Clavell, to be found at the end of the *Diary of Streynsham Master*, pp. 322—325, there are some interesting remarks on the place; "Ballasore begunn to be a noted place when the Portuguez were beaten out of Angelin [Hijili] by the moores about the yeare 1636: at which time the trade begun to decay at Piply and to have a diminution in other places of these parts and the Barr opening and the river appearing better then was imagined, The English and the Danes indeavoured to settle Factoryes here, to be out of the

or two in each respective place of 4, 5, or 600 tunns, to be very well built and fitted, even as if they were to Voyadge to Sea, as alsoe 10, 20, or 30 gallys for to attend them, the Moors Governours haveinge Strict Orders to see them finished with all Speed, and gunned and well manned, and Sent up the River of Ganges as high as Dacca, where (at their arrivall) they come abrest of the Nabob's pallace, Strike their topsailes and hall up theire Other Sailes, with many flaggs and Pendants flyinge, fire many Gunns, all or most part of the whole day. And then they have done theire duty; and this he accompted a Salam[1]; and they are Soone after halled on Shore, and there ly and rott, which is all done at the proper Cost and charges of the Banjan and Gentue Merchants[2].

---

troubles the Portuguez gave to other nations and had themselves, the rather because the Cloth of Harrapore where our first Factory was settled was without much difficulty to be brought hither by land, and the river where our Vessells usually had laine at, being stop't up, it was noe easy matter to bring the Cloth by sea, nor soe safe to have Vessells ride before that place as here in the roade of Ballasore. And the Raja of Tillbichrumbung his countrey lyeing neare this place where the greatest quantity of Tester or herba [see *Ind. Ant.* vol. xxix. p. 339 f.] is procurable, a Settlement was thought the more Convenient, because Ginghams, Herba Taffatyes, Herba Lungees and other sorts of herba goods might be made neare and brought hither, and noe where so good herba goods procurable, The waters of Casharry giveing the most lasting dye to them, and within two dayes journey of this place...." In the *Diary* itself under date 15th Dec. 1676, p. 285, there is an account of the renting of part of the town of Balasor for the Company: "This part of the Towne wherein the Honble. Companys Factory, The Dutch Factory, the English Dutch and most part of the Portuguez houses standes, called Dummadapore haveing binn many yeares rented by Mr. Clavell and now lately by Mr. Bugden by the Councells advice, to prevent the Dutch who were about to take the Farme of it, The Councell considering the Conveniency thereof by haveing the sole Command of all the People, and that it is a small rent of about 350 rups. per annum with charges, and nothing lost thereby, thought fitt that the said Farme of Dummadapore be taken for the Honble. Companys account." See also the description of Balasor by Alex. Hamilton, *East Indies*, vol. i. p. 393 f.

[1] See note on p. 38.

[2] It is quite possible that T. B. is here describing what was meant to be a contribution on the part of the mercantile community towards the naval defence or power of the country.

The English and Dutch had many abuses put Upon them duringe the time Shah-hest-Kan retained the Goverment, and often had theire Salt peeter[1] and Other Commodities Stopped both by land and comeinge downe the Rivers, when they knew the Ships in the Roade of Ballasore stayed onely to lade those goods, soe that they were forced to Piscash them accordinge to theire owne demands; but such grosse Enormities are Since much amended, for the New Prince[2] is not such a miser, nor of Such a base Spirit to contradict what his Ancestors freely gave by Phyrmane, but hath Ordered a better and more legall Goverment &c. He hath turned out of Office all the Governours &c. that the English and Dutch made complaint against, and not onely soe, but punished Some of them Severely to their perpetuall ignominie. And hath given the English and Dutch large Phyrmanes, and more Especially to the English Nation, whose Chi[e]fe here[3], by name Mr. Matthew Vincent[4], went up to Radja Mehal

---

[1] Saltpetre was one of the chief articles of export from Bengal. As early as December, 1662, the Court ordered the "Bay Factors to yearly get in readiness for the Ships 500 or 600 tons of Saltpetre." *Letter Book*, No. 2. For the stoppage of the Company's saltpetre boats during the rule of Shāyista Khān, see Hunter, *History of British India*, vol. ii. p. 238, and *ante*, note on p. 148.

[2] Muhammad A'zim. The writer makes no allusion to the short rule of Phiddy Cawn (Fidāī Khān) who was the immediate successor of Shāyista Khān, and whose tenure of office was marked by much injustice. Stewart, *History of Bengal*, p. 302 f., says that Fidāī Khān was only saved from disgrace by his death in May, 1678. His successor, Muhammad A'zim, was the third son of Aurangzēb.

[3] *i.e.* at Hugli, the head-quarters of the Council at "the Bay."

[4] Matthias Vincent, "Chief at the Bay" from 1677 to 1682, entered the Company's service as a factor at £20 per annum in 1662. In 1667 he was appointed one of the Council at Hugli, whither he went from Fort St George. In 1669 he became "3rd at the Bay," and, in the same year, "Mrs. Woodroffe who is intended to be a wife for Mr. Mathias Vincent" left England for Bengal. On the death of John Marsh, Vincent became Chief at Kasimbazar. Joseph Hall, who considered himself superseded, was loud in his complaints against Vincent and his friend, Walter Clavell. Hall declared that Vincent's "Actions will not admitt of the Light, being works of Darkness's and therefore all he doth in the Companys Affaires must be in hugger

before he arrived at Dacca, to congratulate his comeinge into these Kingdoms[1], which was soe kindly taken, that he gave our Nation more Priviledges then cold in reason be requested[2].

This Kingdome of Bengala (as I said before) is replenished with many faire and pleasant Rivers, the most famous and much admired of which is the great River

---

muggur." Hall further said that Vincent was more than a month in getting from Hugli to Kasimbazar, "soe long he was in bringing his family Consisting of about 20 fringeys and Portugueese and when was come then No roome for the Honble. Companys Servants all being taken up by his trayne, and his Wifes so that the Servants were Lodged out of the Factory, to make roome for a Sort of People, whome I have reason to think were not much for your Worships interest." It was during his residence at Kasimbazar that Vincent was accused of causing the death of Rugo Podar [Raghu, the *poddār*]. After an exhaustive enquiry into the matter, held under the superintendence of Streynsham Master in 1676, Vincent was exonerated from blame, though, from the evidence extant, the verdict is not in accordance with modern ideas of justice. Before the enquiry, the Court had written, in Dec. 1675 (*Letter Book*, No. 5), "We are informed that Oür Factory at Cassambazar is frequently visited by Jesuits and Romish Priests that goe up and downe to Mr. Vincents wife and family, Which We require to bee wholly refrayned if he stay and remaine in Our Service. But if Mr. Vincent shall be found to have had any hand in the Death of Rugo Podar, or accessary thereunto, or hath bin Unfaithfull in discharge of his trust, that then he be discharged of Our Imployment." In August, 1677, on the death of Walter Clavell, Vincent became Chief at the Bay. In 1680, he became associated with Thomas Pitt, and thenceforth grew into disrepute with the authorities at home. For his interloping dealings, and alleged practice of witchcraft, see Yule, *Hedges' Diary*, vol. ii. pp. 13—18, 284—291. Vincent was dismissed the Company's service, and sent to England in 1683. His wealth and influential friends were probably strong factors in his defence. At any rate his unfaithful conduct received but slight punishment. Two years later, in 1685, he was knighted. He died in 1688.

[1] It was in July, 1678, that Vincent set out from Kasimbazar to meet the Prince, in order to procure a "Neshaun for free trade."

[2] In *Factory Records*, Kasimbazar, No. 1, under date 6th Oct. 1678, there is the following reference to Vincent's mission: "This morning Mr. Matthias Vincent Cheife of Bengall arrived with us at Colcepore bringing with him the Princes Neshaan obtained for the Honble. Companys free trade in Bengall and grounded not only on our former Customes and Phirwannas &ca but on the Phirmaund of Sha Jehaan and the present Emperor Orim Zeeb [Aurangzēb] and so well penned that there is now a more Sölid ground for our trade in Bengall then heretofore and well worth the charge and exceeding paines taken by the Cheife in obtaining the same."

Ganges, one of the foure principall rivers in the world, and is Supposed to runne up Paradise or the garden of Eden. The Other brave and Navigable Rivers are for the most part onely branches of this[1].

One of the most admirable of which arms is Hugly river. Up and downe the Same a very Considerable Merchandize is drove[2], and very beneficiall, Especially to the English and Dutch Nations, haveinge Excellent conveniences for carryinge theire European Commodities up into the inland towns and Citties, and the like for bringinge

[1] Compare *Schouten*, vol. ii. p. 160: "The celebrated Ganges river separates the Western part of the Indies from the Eastern, and divides them thus into two parts. Several interpreters of the Holy Scriptures believe that this is the river which is called Pison, which came from the Garden of Eden, and which surrounded the whole land of Havila where there is gold, and which apparently is identical with the Indies. At any rate it is certain that this great river is one of the most renowned in the world; that it was as well known in former times as it is to-day; and that it takes its rise in the mountains situated in the most northern part of the Indies. Some have stated that it rises in Mount Caucasus, and others that it rises in the high mountains of Thebet, which are alway covered with snow...."

[2] As the writer remarks, a brisk trade was carried on up and down the Hugli river in his day, but it was almost entirely limited to small native vessels. For years the Court had been urging the navigation of the Hugli in order to spare the expense entailed by trans-shipping the Company's goods in Balasor Road. In 1669, the year that T. B. arrived in India, there also arrived seven men, the pioneers of the Bengal Pilot Service, the only one of whom to attain to note was George Heron, the pilot mentioned by T. B. on p. 176. See Yule, *Hedges' Diary*, vol. iii. pp. 197 ff. In Nov. 1669 Walter Clavell wrote from Balasor to the Court (*Factory Records*, Miscellaneous, No. 3), "Till the River of Hughli be soe discovered that the Commanders will adventure their Shipps therein to Lade, We shall not be able Annually to send the first shipp away before the Latter End of November," and in October, 1679, "In expectation that your worships would positively have obliged the ships to come into this River, wee had Severall times employed the *Dilligence* and *Madrass* pinnace to discover the Channels, which had rendred a couple of the pilots William Waters and William Bramston, who Since are both deceased this and last month, Sufficiently Capable to have brought up any of the Ships this yeare through the midle Channell...." In 1672 Captain James brought the *Rebecca* up to Hugli with the aid of a pilot, and earned the extra 20/8 per ton promised by the Court. The lack of pilots was the great difficulty, and it was not until after 1679, when Captain Stafford brought the *Falcon* up the Hugli, that it became general for the Company's ships to unlade at Hijili instead of at Balasor.

downe the commodities purchased in this or some Other Kingdoms.

This River is soe named from the great towne of Hugly Scituated Upon the banks of it, neare 150 miles up from the Braces[1] or Shoals that lye at the Entrance thereof. The towne or Citty of Hugly is a famous and Sumptuous place, adorned with many fine Structures, and very populous, and what addeth to the beauty hereof, it is well furnished with gardens, fine groves, a very large Bazar or markett place, one of the finest Chowlteries[2] (or free lodgeinge houses for all travellers) that is contained in this Kingdome, and, more Especially, the 2 fine European Factories, namely the English and Dutch[3]. But I must needs confesse the Dutch building here farre doth Exceed ours, although

---

1 Not in *Hobson-Jobson*. See *Ind. Ant.* vol. xxx. p. 352. Compare the following contemporary references: "This night wee sailed over the sands called the braces, haveing never lesse then three Fathome water and a Swelling Sea." *Diary of Streynsham Master*, 5th September, 1676. "They [the crew of the *Falcon*] had very bad weather in the Road of Ballasour and worse comeing over the Braces and were forced to ride betweene the Braces 2 days where they lost an Anchor." Letter from Hugli to Balasor, 3rd Aug. 1678; *O. C.* No. 4466. "Mr. Byam arrived there [Balasor] the 13th Currt. by way of Kendoa the winds being so strong and contrary that the sloop was forced in from the braces to Kedgaree and thence Mr. Byam went to Kendoa and from thence to Ballasore." 26th April, 1679, *Factory Records*, Hugli, No. 2. "It pleased God to Arrive us in Safety at this place the 16 Instant notwithstanding the Danger we were in by encountring with a Storme of Raine and wind at East when we were neare halfe way over the first flatt of the Braces,..." Letter from Streynsham Master &c. at Hugli to Balasor, 19th Sept. 1679, *Factory Records*, Hugli, No. 5. "This night about 9 o'Clock we anchored in the Braces." 21st July, 1682; Yule, *Hedges' Diary*, vol. i. p. 31.

2 This is one of the earliest forms of this Madras Anglo-Indian word yet quoted, but it gives no help towards the derivation. See *Hobson-Jobson*, *s.v.* Choultry. In the Fort St George records, there are frequent references to Choultry in its sense of Court-house. Carrying this essentially Madrasi word to Bengal in the text is curious.

3 Compare Marshall, *Notes and Observations*, p. 6 (reverse), "Hugly is a very great Towne...great part of the Towne was formerly called Satagam, the English and Dutch have each of them a stately Factory scituate by the River which is a Branch of the River Ganges."

theire priviledges and good name by the Inhabitants in generall cometh farre Short[1].

The towne is not very Uniforme, but is a very good and pleasant place, inhabited with Some of the richest Merchants of the Kingdome[2]; and all Sorts of Commodities that Orixa, Bengala, and Pattana doe afford are here dayly to be bought and Sold in the publicke Bazar[3], commonly called the great Bazar, by reason there are many where onely Cotton, course Callicoes, provisions, &c. are to be Sold.

The English Factory here in Hugly[4] is the head or

---

[1] Compare Streynsham Master's description of the Dutch factory at Hugli (*Diary of Streynsham Master*, under date 13th Sept. 1676, p. 60), "And lesse then 2 miles short of Hugly wee passed by the Dutch garden,...then wee came by the Dutch Factory, which is a large well built house, standing by it selfe, much like to a Country Seat in England....That part of the Towne which wee passed by was all built of thatcht Hovells."

[2] Compare *Schouten*, vol. ii. p. 155, "Ougli is fairly large. Its length renders it pleasant because it is built on the bank of the Ganges. The streets are wide: they are not paved. There are pretty walks; fine buildings after the fashion of the country; well-stocked shops; convenient houses; depots for all kinds of merchandise, particularly silks; fine linens, and other materials from all the provinces in India. There are many Moor merchants there who carry on a great trade. There are also a great number of Idolaters, Benjanes and Gentives, who live peaceably under the government of the Moors."

[3] See note on p. 106. Compare Alex. Hamilton, *East Indies*, vol. ii. p. 20f. for the extent of trade at Hugli: "This Town of Hughly drives a great Trade, because all foreign Goods are brought thither for Import, and all Goods of the Product of Bengal are brought hither for Exportation. And the Mogul's Furza or Custom-house is at this Place. It affords rich Cargoes for fifty or sixty Ships yearly, besides what is carried to neighbouring Countries in small Vessels;...To mention all the particular Species of Goods that this rich Country produces, is far beyond my skill...."

[4] The factory at Hugli was established in 1650 under the *farmān* said to have been obtained by Gabriel Boughton. In 1657, Hugli was made the head factory in the Bay, the factory of Balasor being subordinate. The Factory House in T. B.'s time must have been the one which was in process of building in 1665 as described by *Schouten*, vol. ii. p. 157, "When we were there [in Hugli] the English were building a new factory, because the inundations of the Ganges had by degrees mined the walls of their old edifice which threatened to fall." *Delestre*, p. 188, says, "A league distant from the Dutch factory [at 'Ougly'] the English

Chiefe Factory in the 3 beforementioned Kingdoms, and residence of the Chiefe in Place.

The Dutch Factorie is also Scituate upon the banks of the River, about one English mile from ours, lower downe the River, on a most delicate and Even piece of ground, which is comely Enough to be admired, and theire buildings noe lesse, beinge a most compact and very decent Structure, carryinge the name of the largest and compleatest Factorie in Asia, and noe more then in my Judgement it deserveth[1].

---

have one, on the same side of the river, the left going up." In 1676, the English factory at Hugli was enlarged and repaired by Streynsham Master's orders. In the *Diary of Streynsham Master*, under date 25th Nov. 1676, we read, p. 272: "By reason that the Cheife and councell in the Bay will from hence forward reside in this Factory of Hugly where there is a want of accomodations and necessary apartments for soe many married persons, upon a Surveigh of the buildings it was judged necessary to remove the cook roome it standing inconvenient and being covered with thatch was alsoe dangerous, and to build an other with brick to secure the whole, and to sett up necessary apartments to make the Factory capable of accomodating four marryed persons of the Councell, and also to make a Penthouse to preserve the house to the Southward; and which are wanting the most necessary, an office, a Councell chamber and a place for the registers to be kept in, out of the five upper roomes, all which the Councell thought fitt to be done out of hand and that it be managed with all frugallity, at present judging it may not exceed 1200 rups. besides the usuall and necessary repairations of the Factory which the late storme hath much dammaged by blowing the thatch of the walls. And there being many trees about the house which shaded the ground and kept it moist and besides have harboured Vermine they were ordered to be cut downe that the aire might have freer passage and the heat of the sunne keep the earth dry."

1 *Schouten*, vol. ii. p. 156, dilates on the grandeur of the Dutch Factory at Hugli: "But there is nothing in it [Hugli] more magnificent than the Dutch factory. It was built on a great space at the distance of a musket shot from the Ganges, for fear that, if it were nearer, some inundation of the waters of this river might endanger it, or cause it to fall. It has indeed, more the appearance of a large castle than of a factory of merchants. The walls are high and built of stone, and the fortifications are also covered with stone. They are furnished with cannon, and the factory is surrounded by ditches full of water. It is large and spacious. There are many rooms to accommodate the Director, the other officers who compose the Council, and all the people of the Company. There are large shops built of stone, where goods that are bought in the country and those that our vessels bring there are placed." Compare also *Delestre*, p. 188: "We arrived at Bengala where the Dutch have a very fine

Soe that now they may, and doe largely boast of this new and comely buildinge; but not a word is heard from them concerninge the Old Factory that adjoyned to that of the English, much about the time of the horrid Massacre of the English at Amboyna[1].

Those 2 Factories, then dore neighbours, Stood within 20 paces of the River Side, on which side the river gained much upon the dry land, vizt. upon the Larboard Side goeinge up, in soe much that a Stronge fresh, caused by the great raines that fall here Sometime before the breakeinge up of the Monzoone[2], came down the River with Such Violence that it Seemed to be displeased with all that were here, more Especially the Dutch, and Shewed them displeasure at once, takeinge away all theire whole Factory, Storehouses &c., and hurried them into the River, and a great depth too, for in the very place where the Dutch Factory stood, wee ride with our Ships and Vessels in noe lesse then depth 16 fathoms, and it is called Hugly hole[3].

---

and very rich factory in a place called Ougly, where linen is most beautifully woven." Compare also the description of the Dutch factory in the *Diary of Streynsham Master*, under date 21st Nov. 1676, p. 263, "This afternoone Mr. Clavell with my selfe and others visitted the Dutch at their Factory which is very large and well built, with two Quadrangles, The Directore was very obligeing and shewed us the new built warehouses which are three very large, that make one side of one of the Quadrangles next to the River side They are excellently well timbred which was all brought from the Coast, alsoe he shewed us other accomodations of their Factory, their Gardens which are very spatious, well kept with Tarrass walks and full [of] Lettice and good herbage and adjoyneing to their Factory they have offices for all things needfull to them, as a Carpenters Yard with stores of good Timber brought from Batavia, a Coopers yard where they make many cask for the Pork which they kill and salt up downe the river, a Smiths forge, a Grannary and apartment for a great many weavers where they have sett up Loomes for the weaving of saile cloth, and a foild to make ropes in...."

[1] *i.e.* 27th Feb. 1623.

[2] See note on p. 51. T. B., in his *Malay Dictionary*, has, "Moosim, a Season of the year."

[3] At a Consultation at Hugli during the second visit of Agent Master, 20th Oct. 1679 (*Factory Records*, Hugli, No. 2), it was

The English Factorie (adjoyneinge to that of the Dutch) was by the computation of men very likely suddenly to follow it, but the Fresh abated and it standeth to this day with all Store houses and walls that surround it[1]

But for feare Such another or worse fresh Shold happen and take them Unprovided with necessaries, and time whereby to remove the Companies goods &c., they have by Order of the said Company, built a very fine new Factory[2] about a quarter of a mile higher (from the River Side), where now the Chiefe and Councill &c. Factors of Hugly reside, and the Old one is not as yett become Unserviceable[3].

The freshes[4] are wholy caused by the great rains that

"Ordered...that there be a large Warehouse built for the Saltpeter upon the old Factory ground as far from the River as it can conveniently stand, and a house to keep the Sloopes Stores in near the hole where they Ride between the old Factory and the new." In a letter from the Council at Hugli to Surat, dated 24th Nov. 1686, there is the following reference to Hugli Hole: "At the same time they began to display their great gunns from a battery consisting of Eleven Gunns that they had lately raised to command our Shipps in the Hole."

[1] This building was known as the "Old Factory" in T. B.'s time. Compare the following reference which occurs in *Factory Records*, Hugli, No. 3, under date 29th Sept. 1681: "The way between the New Factory and the Old (which is the Generall Warehouse and landing place of all our goods) being broken down by the falling of a great tanck of water into the river running the bank down in the way thither so that in the time of the raines the principall time of receiving goods and transmitting them to the Sub-Factories &cā we find that there is no passing without great danger between one place and the other which yett the Warehouse keeper or his Assistants are obliged dayly to doe, we agreed therefore that a small bridge might be built over the said place of brick....."

[2] In 1664; see note on p. 168.

[3] See *supra*, note 1, for the use made of the Old Factory. See also the passage quoted below, note 4.

[4] Compare the *Diary of Streynsham Master*, Consultation at Hugli, 25th November, 1676, p. 272: "The old Factory lying by the River side being a very convenient place for the reception of the Honble. Companyes Saltpeter, lead and other gross and bulky Comodityes, That it is the Honble. Companyes Interest and advantage to keep it in repaire and the banck well fenc't from the encroachments

fall at Such and such Seasons of the yeare, not with what fall here nor a considerable way further Up, but a great way Up as high as Pattana, yea as high as South Tartaria[1], which is mountanious, and raineth there for a quarter of a yeare togeather, and rusheth downe the Ganges and arms thereof with Such Violence that all these rivers afford not issue for it, unto the Sea, untill a considerable time be spent and an abatement made; but, like Unto the great River Nilus, overflowinge its banks in many places for some miles Compasse. These waters are at their full height generally in the Month September.

Anno Domini 1676, in the aforesaid Month, I was comeinge down Hugly River[2] in a Ship called the Sancta Crux[3], whereof Under God I was Commander, and driveinge

---

of the Freshes and there to build some convenient place to lay up stores belonging to the Sloopes and Vessells, wherefore it was thought fitt that the said repairs be put in execution before the next raines the last Freshes having taken away great part of the Banck and the building of a new warehouse (if this should wash down) would be of great expence."

[1] Apparently a vague reference to Central Asia including the Himalayas. T. B. is probably here recording what he recollected of Native accounts of the Eastern and Central Himalayas and their heavy rainfall.

[2] In connection with T. B.'s chart of the Hugli, reproduced here, it may be noted that there exists at the Horse Guards a map, no. Z 30/43, entitled "The Mouth of the River Ganges." It shows much the same conditions as Bowrey's map. Its date is 1694, and it was made by the pilot Davenport for Captain William Gifford of the *Seymour*. With the map are some interesting sailing directions for getting out of the Hugli, initialled by Davenport.

Among the places marked on the right bank in Bowrey's chart, Degoon, Wolleberry, and Casuree represent the modern Digano, Uluberria and Cajori [Khajūrī]. Bowrey's map extends farther up the river than Davenport's and contains many more names.

[3] In 1676, when T. B. was navigating the *Sancta Cruz*, she belonged to Portuguese traders. On the 3rd January, 1677, Streynsham Master found the ship in the Madras Road: "In the roade [of Madras] there was rideing the *Triplicane* and the *Sancta Cruz* belonging to A Portugueez,...." *Diary of Streynsham Master*, p. 311. On the 27th Jan. the Council at Fort St George wrote as follows to Arnold White at Bantam (*Factory Records*, Fort St George, No. 18): "We have yours 2d November and 13th October [1676]...we received the former by the *Sancta Cruz* which Ship has been attended with many misfortunes in them concerned, her Commander as you advised

downe at a most Swift and violent rate, beinge timerous of driveinge too farre down, vizt. upon the Shoals of the River Tombólee[1] (where the River is most crooked). Now, beinge got into the reach called Jno. Perdo[2], where

deceased with you, and his Successor hardly recovering, her Cheif Owner Domingos Perez Banhos dead here suddenly, and the other afflicted with a Murder in his family committed by his Sonn in Law who lyes here in Irons untill Sufficient power from England to proceed against him, however the Surviving Owner Cosmo Lorenzo de Madera, desires his humble thanks to be returned for your protection and kindness Shew'd." From this letter it appears that when T. B. was caught in the eddy in Sept. 1676, as described in the text, he was taking the *Sancta Cruz* from Hugli to Bantam. There is no evidence to show whether he put in at Fort St George and there relinquished charge of the vessel. At any rate, his connection with her must have ceased in Oct. 1676, since her Commander, as the letter states, died about that time. T. B. was probably only an interim commander of the *Sancta Cruz* for the one voyage. The subsequent career of the vessel seems to be forthcoming in that of the *Sancta Cruz*, belonging to Joseph, brother of the rich Armenian John Demarcora. This ship was taken as a prize by the Siamese Government during the war between Siam and Golconda, apparently about March, 1685. Some months later the *Sancta Cruz* was rechristened the *St George*, and sent on a voyage to Mocha [? Moco Moco in Sumatra] as one of the King of Siam's ships. See Anderson, *Siam*, p. 271 f. There is reason to think that the ship was recaptured, and her original title restored to her, for, in May, 1687, we find (*Factory Records*, Fort St George, No. 4): "Ship *Santa Cruise* Augustine de Carvalia Master arrived at Fort St George from Goa" and "sailed for Bengall" in June. In Feb. 1697, there was a *Sancta Cruze* at Calcutta. In *Factory Records*, Calcutta, No. 2, there are the entries: "Wrote a letter to the Lieut. Generall and Councill of Fort St George by Ship *Sancta Cruze*...The Ship *Sancta Cruze* Saild for Fort St George." Again, in 1702, there is the entry (*ibid.* No. 3) "Ship *Santa Cruce* David Marcus Commander arriv'd from Manilha." Lastly, in the Account of Tonnage and Pass Money for ships at Bengal in 1718 (*Bengal Public Consultations*, 20th April, 1719) payment is made by the owner of a *Sancta Cruze*.

[1] See *Hobson-Jobson*, *s.v.* Tumlook. Now the Rupnarain running into the Hugli at the "James and Mary" Shoal. Compare the *Diary of Streynsham Master* under date 11th Sept. 1676: "The...Dutch Skipper told us that his shipp was shott by the mouth of this river leading to Hugly into that river we call Tumberleen...." Compare also the following from *Factory Records*, Hugli, No. 3, under date 11th Sept. 1681: "Mr Stanley and Mr Prickman arrived hither [Hugli] comeing as far as Tumberlee in a small vessel called the *Margery* belonging to Mr Clement Jordan of Madras."

[2] The island Jan Perdo in the Hugli River has now disappeared. Compare the *Diary of Streynsham Master*, 11th Sept. 1676: "There being noe hope of getting the Sloopes up higher then they were which is neare the island Janperdo, by reason of the strength of the Freshes,...." Compare also the following from *Factory Records*,

I found the Streame of lesse force then before, I lett dropp our best bore anchor, and veered 40 fathoms of Cable out; I gave the Ship one Sheere, and let fall our Sheet anchor, and veered out a considerable length or Scope of each, which brought her up (beinge but in depth 8 fathoms). It happened at that time for the Space of ½ an houre to be Slack water, but then the fresh came down like a boore, and hurried us away into a most impetuous Eddy, where, in a moment, our Ship turned round soe often and quick withall that not one of us cold Stand to doe any thinge[1]. One cable broke, and the Other Swum like to a piece of wood. In the midst of this Extremity, when I thought our Ship wold oversett with each Sally She tooke, it pleased God a very fresh gale Sprange Up, filled our Sailes (that hanged loose in the brailes), and runne her out of that Eddy, and by cuttinge away our Other Anchor and Cable, got Soon over to the Other Side, where I runne her into a Small Creeke, and stayed untill the fresh abated, which was 14 days[2].

Hugli, No. 1, under date 18th Aug. 1677: "Wee had notice of the Sloopes *Arrival* and *Ganges* being arrived at Janipardo." The following curious spellings occur in the Hugli Diary for 28th Aug. and 14th Sept. 1678, *Factory Records*, Hugli, No. 2, "This morning wee had notice of the Catch *Arrivall* being come up to Jarpardore...At noone wee had advise of the Sloope *Arrivall* being come to Jampadore." For the creek and Island of Jan Perdo, see Yule, *Hedges' Diary*, vol. iii. p. 213. T. B., in his Chart of the River Hugli, marks them as "Ri. John Pardo, Ile John Pardo."

[1] Compare the following from the *Diary of Streynsham Master*, 8th Sept. 1676, p. 57: "This evening with the tide of flood wee gott into that part of the river Ganges that comes from Hugly at the mouth of the said River there's eighteen or nineteen fathome water without, and but eight or nine fathome within but it sholds gradually shelving wise yett causes a great whirling of the water soe that often times Ships and Vessells are turned or winded round by it for a good space of time but seldome receive dammage thereby (as afterward I saw one farther up the river soe winded) but wee comeing neare upon a high water gott in without any such winding and they happen at the first of the Flood and last of the Ebb."

[2] In other words the writer was caught in an eddy off the still dreaded shoal at the junction of the Hugli and Rupnarain Rivers, now called the "James and Mary."

But most of this trouble might Easily have been avoided if our Ganges Pilot[1] had been any way ingenuous, for this River hath many good and Smooth Places for Ships and Vessels to ride in, out of the way of Streams or Eddies, as I have Some time Since found by Experience[2].

Another but more Sad accident happened on that day, being the 27th of September[3] 1676. The honourable Company's two Ketches[4], bound up, came to an anchor in the reach that I did, but in a better place to ride out the fresh[5]. Agent Masters was then On board the biggest of them[6], and Some Younge Gentlemen Factors on board the Other[7], one by name Mr. Callaway[8] (a very good

---

[1] The only two experienced "Ganges Pilots" at this time were George Heron and Samuel Sherman. The former was with Agent Master, and T. B. was probably in the hands of a pilot whose knowledge of the river was but slight. The lack of efficient pilots was a subject of constant complaint at this period. Walter Clavell in his "Accompt of the Trade of Hugly" to be found at the end of the *Diary of Streynsham Master*, p. 320, remarks: "Our Ships if wee had more Pilotts whome wee could oblige to stay after they had obtained some experience either by ingageing them in familyes, or by giveing them good wages might with much more ease goe over the braces and come up Hugly River, then they can goe out of the Downes into the River of London, and one maine incouragement would be that the ships should sett out of England soe as to be here the begining of June, by which meanes they will have true tides to carry them up and avoid the freshes, they may alsoe goe up if they come the last of the moonzon comeing from the Coast to the Bay in September after the freshes are abated...."

[2] T. B. took the *Borneo Merchant* up the Hugli to Calcutta in Aug. 1687 and the *Frances* in 1688, apparently without the assistance of a pilot. *Vide* Introduction.

[3] According to the *Diary of Streynsham Master*, p. 59, the accident happened on the 11th of Sept. 1676.

[4] The *Arrivall* and the *Ganges*.

[5] See note on p. 171.

[6] *i.e.* the *Arrivall*.

[7] *i.e.* the *Ganges*.

[8] William Callaway was entertained by the Court as a Writer for Fort St George, on the 13th Dec. 1672. He arrived at the Fort in 1673. He was appointed special assistant to Streynsham Master in the tour of inspection in 1676, and accompanied the Agent to Masulipatam and Balasor. On the way to Hugli he was seized with the

Friend of mine), beinge then Sore Visited with Sicknesse, and beinge one that Agent Masters had great respect for, he Sent Mr. Herrin[1], the master of the Ketch, and the

fever to which he succumbed. He left instructions as to his effects with Mr Douglas, Surgeon of the *Eagle*, who had attended him in his last illness. The goods were sold at an "outcry" at Hugli on the 11th Nov. 1676, and the proceeds sent home to his father. A detailed list of Callaway's effects is to be found at the end of the *Diary of Streynsham Master*, pp. 358—361. The list includes "77 gold coate buttons, 2 pair of gold buttons for wrists, 1 pair of silver buckles, 1 Silver Snuff box, 1 Silver Meddall Oliver Cromwell, 6 Coates, 4 paires of Breches, 1 China Escretore, 1 China Standish, 2 pair of Golcondah Slippers, 16 Hatts"; among these are "2 Castor Hatts, 1 Felt Hatt and his weareing Hatt." There is also a note "One Hatt Stolen from aboard the *Arrivall* Sloope," a large number of pieces of "Chint," a great many Girdles, &c., &c.

[1] There is a short notice of Heron in Yule, *Hedges' Diary*, vol. ii. p. 199. The connecting link between the forms Heron and Hering of this worthy's variously spelt surname is supplied in the text. In 1668 George Heron is named as the senior of the first batch of apprentice pilots sent to the Hugli, under a seven years' indenture. In 1672 (*Factory Records*, Hugli, No. 4) George 'Hearon' was commanding the *Madrasse* Pinnace. In July of the same year (*ibid.*) we read, "For the better security of the Companys Factory you may appoint to William Lux George Heron and their Families roomes apart where they may sometimes bee, or as often as they see occasion." In November, 1674 (*ibid.*) George Herron and Thomas Bateman on the *Arrivall* were to receive "Advice" from John Nicholson as to the navigation of the Hugli. In March, 1676, "George Herring" took Mr Clavell to Fort St George. In October, 1677, "George Herron our chief Pilot" was ordered to attend Captain Erwin "on board Sloope *Sally*" and to assist him in his survey of the "Sands and Channell" of the Hugli. In 1678, George Herring, then commanding the *Arrivall*, piloted the *Falcon* from Barnagur into Balasor Road. In 1679, we find Heron frightening the somewhat disreputable chaplain John Evans (a notorious trader and friend of interlopers) from going down the river from Hugli to Balasor in a native boat (Yule, *Hedges' Diary*, vol. ii. p. 131). In February of this year, Heron and the other pilots were sent "to survey the several depths and Channels of the river and over the Braces into Ballasore Roade in reference to enabling your Selfes to bring the English Ships which God willing may arrive Soe appointed this ensueing yeare." In 1680 Herron (the name is also given as Hearine and Herrin) with the *Arrivall* went to Fort St George, and in November advised of his being at "Carango" and that his vessel was "very leaky." In 1683 Heron was commanding first the *Thomas*, and then the *Good Hope* (Yule, *Hedges' Diary*, vol. i. pp. 74, 78). In 1684 the quarrels between Hedges and Job Charnock began, and in these Heron was mixed up (Yule, *Hedges' Diary*, vol. i. p. 78 f.), as he was also in the quarrel between Hedges and Trenchfield (*ibid.*, p. 148). In 1685 Heron does not appear to much advantage after Hedges' fall and dismissal (*ibid.*, p. 176). In 1686 we find him much more worthily employed in compiling the

Minister[1] to pray by him, and a younge man[2], if in case they found him in a desperate condicion, to Seale Up his trunks and boxes, which was accordingly done. But

---

earliest known sailing directions for the Hugli (*ibid.*, vol. iii. pp. 201, 204) and thus laying the foundation for the pilotage and topography of that river. In 1687 "George Herron was cruiseing in the River Alley betwixt that and Kedgerry" and wrote to Sutanuti from "the River Sautguary." It was at this time that Heron's brother Samuel, also a pilot in the Company's service, was seized by his mutinous crew, turned adrift in an open boat on the coast of Sumatra, and rescued by our author (*vide* Introduction). In 1688 George Heron appears as a somewhat important personage during William Heath's fatuous proceedings at Chittagong when he gave some sound advice at a "Consultation Extraordinary." (Yule, *Hedges' Diary*, vol. ii. pp. 83, 85.) About this time Heron ceased to be a servant of the Company, and henceforth we find him engaged in trading voyages on his own account. In 1691 he was commanding his own vessel "laden with Armenians &ca. Merchants Goods." He arrived at Sutanuti in Oct. 1691 "having been several months at Chattigaum." In 1702 George Heron's name occurs in a "List of Freemen Inhabitants in Fort St. George" with the note, "marry'd a Georgian [Armenian]." In the same year he signed a petition begging for letters of reprisal on Arabs who had seized ships in which he was concerned. From this time until his death Heron seems to have lived at Fort St George. He died on the 2nd May, 1727, aged 81, and was buried in the old cemetery, where his monument still stands. (*See* Mrs Penny, *Fort St George*, pp. 54, 195.)

1 The "Minister" was the Revd. Josiah Darley who was "entertained as Chaplain in the Bay at £50 per annum and £50 gratuity" in March, 1674 (Letter from the Court to Hugli, 13th March, 1674, *Letter Book*, No. 5). On the 20th Nov. 1674, the Council at Fort St George wrote to the Directors (Fort St George "Generall," *O. C.* No. 4044) "Mr. Darley proceeded for the Bay by shipp *Lancaster* where he was much wanted, and appearing to be a very discreet and learned man, will with Gods blessing be a meanes of much good there; your agent having desired him to do his endeavour to quiet the differences amongst them." On the 29th of August, 1676, while at Balasor, Streynsham Master and Mr. Darley agreed to alter the hours for daily prayer (*Diary of Streynsham Master*, p. 48), "Mr. Darley the Chaplaine and my selfe agreed that the most convenient houres for prayer would be at 7 a Clock in the morneing and at 8 at night, the former custome being the same time in the morneinge and 4 a clock in the afternoone which being found inconvenient was now altered." Streynsham Master's account of the accident which caused Mr. Darley's death is quoted in note 3 on p. 178 below.

2 The "younge man" was Nathaniel Whetham, entertained by the Court as a writer, and specially appointed to assist the Agent, Streynsham Master (*Court Book*, 1675). Whetham's goods were sold at "Outcry" in Hugli on the 13th Nov. 1676. A detailed list, with the amounts realized, is to be found at the end of the *Diary of Streynsham Master*, pp. 362—364.

they hallinge on board theire own Ketch againe, did overset the boat, and the minister and the younge man were drowned. The rest drove away on the bottom of the boat. My Purser, Mr. Clement Jordan[1], was just then come downe with a Small Olocko[2]; wee Sent her away and tooke them Up, beinge 5 in number, the Master and 4 Seamen[3].

---

[1] Clement Jordan, afterwards known as Clement du Jardin, was, like T. B., a "freeman" trading on "country" vessels at this time. He may possibly have come to India at the same time as our author. Later, Jordan entered the Company's service. The following is a brief account of his career in India, as gathered from the MS. records at the India Office. In 1674 Mr "Jourden" went from Balasor to Hugli. In 1676 he was with T. B. on the *Sancta Cruz* as described in the text. In 1678, and early in 1679, Clement Jordan was at Balasor settling his account with Rogiram [Rājārām]. In 1679 he went on a trading voyage to Kedah and Achin with John Bugden, brother of Edmund Bugden, the Company's servant at Balasor. They sold the ship at Kedah and embarked with Mr John Smith in his ketch. Smith sailed to the "South Seas" and was murdered by his men. Jordan and Bugden were called upon to give an account of the murder and were acquitted of any complicity in it. In 1680 Clement Jordan was living as a freeman in Fort St George. In the same year he went to Hugli, Kasimbazar, and Malda. In 1681 he was in the "Bay" with his ship *Margery*. In 1682 he is styled Clement du Jardin, and is mentioned as visiting Masulipatam and Madapollam in his own vessel. In the same year Jordan entered the Company's service, and was entertained as a factor. In 1683 he was sent to Vizagapatam, apparently as second of the factory. (See p. 123, note 2.) He disagreed with George Ramsden the Chief, and in 1683 was recalled to the Fort, where he arrived in March, 1684. In Sept. he was sent on the *Amoy Merchant* on a voyage to Sillebar whence he returned in 1685. Meanwhile his conduct at Vizagapatam had incurred the censure of the Court and he was dismissed the service in 1686. The Council at Fort St George, however, appear to have had a great regard for du Jardin, and as had previously happened in the case of William Jearsey, the orders from Court were evaded. Du Jardin was sent to Indrapoora and the West Coast, and his conduct while there was favourably reported on. The Court refused to be influenced in du Jardin's favour. They wrote, "Mr. Du Jardin is a huffing, swaggering, ignorant, avaritious prodigall Person, and we are sorry to see such men so much in your favour...he is not a man to be trusted with mony, nor with the Conduct of any ship or Sloope." In 1687 du Jardin died at Indrapoora and the Council at Fort St George expressed their regret for his loss, "being a fitting active man among those people." He left a widow who, at the time of his death, was at Fort St George.

[2] *i.e. ulāk*, a cargo-boat. See *Hobson-Jobson*, *s.v.* Woolock. Compare the following: "It being a quick Oolauck you are upon." Letter from Kasimbazar to Patna, 5th November, 1675, *O.C.* No. 4126.

[3] The following is the account of the accident as given in the

The Nabob and Some Merchants here and in Ballasore and Piplo have about 20 Saile of Ships of considerable burthen, that annually trade to Sea, Some to Ceylone, Some to Tanassaree[1]. Those fetch Elephants, and the rest, 6 or 7 yearly, goe to the 12000 Islands called Maldiva[2] to fetch

---

Diary of Streynsham Master, under date 11th Sept. 1676, p. 59: "This afternoone Mr. Douglas the Chyrrugeone of the *Eagle* who looked to Wm. Callaway very sick on board the *Ganges* sent to Mr. Darley to come to him beleiving he was neare his end, whereupon Mr. Darley very willingly went accompanyed with Mr. Bonnell Robt. Littleton and Nathll. Whetham and George Heron the master of the *Arrivall*, the boate they went in being veered a Sterne by a rope from the *Arrivall* to the *Ganges*, after they had binn there a small time Mr. Darley haveing performed the last office for Mr. Calloway he dyed, and then the partyes before mentioned with Mr. Douglas and Thomas Read the Dyer went into the boate to returne againe aboard the *Arrivall*, and as they were putting off from the Vessell, by some unhappy accident the boate cast thwart the Streame (which runn very Swift) and filled with water; the *Ganges* boate being fast to her Sheered up into the other boate, and beate the men into the water, In which sad mischance, Mr. Darley and Nathll. Whetham were drowned, all the rest it pleased God were saved and also the boates, the *Arrivalls* boate breaking loose Swam with her Keel upward and the Lascarrs upon it, which George Heron followed with the *Ganges* boate some miles downe the river, till they came to the Dutch Flyboate, where they were refreshed with meate and Drinck and clothes and there saved the boate and brought them both aboard againe this night." The "Dutch Flyboate" here mentioned must have been the *Sancta Cruz*. Either Master must have been mistaken as to her nationality, or else she must have been sailing under Dutch colours for the purpose of trading to some Dutch factory. Master seems to be a little confused in his account. On the 6th Sept. (p. 57) he says he overtook a "Dutch Flyboate," which must therefore have been going up the river. On the 11th Sept. (p. 58) he says that the skipper of the "Dutch Flyboate we overtooke" came to him with a request. He then goes on to relate a story that exactly fits in with T. B.'s adventure described above: "The said Dutch Skipper sayd he was a Yorkshire man, he told us that his shipp was shott by the mouth of this river leading to Hugly into that river we call Tumberleen and that he had lost an anchor two kedg anchors and 200 fathome of Hawser but there was noe want of such things up at their Factory." Then, in the account of the accident, Master says that his men were rescued by "the Dutch Flyboate" evidently alluding to the same vessel he had mentioned before. The explanation seems to be that Master met T. B. on his voyage down the river, possibly under Dutch colours, and that he also overtook a Dutch Flyboat going up the river and, in his account of the accident, he confused the two vessels. It is at any rate clear that the survivors of the overturned boat were rescued by T. B.'s men and taken on board the *Sancta Cruz*.

[1] See *Hobson-Jobson*, *s.v.* Tenasserim.

[2] See note on p. 104.

cowries[1] and Cayre[2], and most commonly doe make very profitable Voyages.

The Prince[3] now (neither did the Nabob before him) not in the least concerne themselves with their Ships, onely acquaints the Governour of Each respective Sea Port that they will have Soe many Elephants of such a comelinesse and Stature brought them that yeare, and for the rest it is wholy left to the discretion of the Governour.

The Elephants of Ceylone[4] are best Esteemed of here and all Hindostan over; they are generally large and well Sett, of a most hardy constitution, and Endowed with more Sence and reason then those of Tanassaree, Queda, or Syam[5].

They are bought from the Dutch (who have in a manner fortified the Island Ceylone quite round[6]) in

---

[1] See *Hobson-Jobson*, *s.v.* Cowry. Compare Alex. Hamilton, *East Indies*, vol. i. p. 347, for the "catching of Couries."

[2] See note on p. 42. Compare the following in a letter from Hugli to Balasor, 3rd April, 1678, *O. C.* No. 4392: "I give you thanks also for endeavouring to get some Coro Maldiva and if you had payd 10 rupees for one Tola should have bin content."

[3] Muhammad 'Azim.

[4] See *Hobson-Jobson*, *s.v.* Ceylon.

[5] For the superiority of Ceylon elephants, compare *Schouten*, vol. ii. p. 31: "They are looked upon as the finest and most intelligent [animals] in the world....it is said that the elephants of other countries recognize them, and that, as a mark of respect, they fall on their knees before them."

[6] Compare *Schouten*, vol. ii. p. 5: "Before the Portuguese, who were the first among the Christians to navigate the Indies, had discovered it [Ceylon], the Sarrasins, the Turks, and the Ethiopians traded thither, and got from it pearls, precious stones, and above all a quantity of cinnamon. After them the Portuguese made settlements there; and, finally, the Dutch have made themselves masters of it. At least, all the commerce is in their hands, and they possess the sea ports with the greater part of the towns and fortresses." Compare also *Delestre*, p. 126: "The hatred of this King [of Candy] towards the Dutch is well-grounded, not only because they have established themselves in his country against his will, and because they have built fortresses, the most considerable of which is four leagues from the Bay of Trinquemale, but because of their usurpations over his subjects...." The Dutch had been invited by the King of Candy to assist in the expulsion of the Portuguese. In 1658 they became masters of the island and retained possession of it until 1796, when it was taken by the English.

Gala[1], or Colomba[2], or Japhnapatam[3]. The Dutch take them in the Woods[4] and tame them, and dispose of them to the merchants of Bengala in Exchange for Rice, butter[5], wheat, Opium[6], raw and wrought Silks or Callicos[7] that they bringe yearly hither; and these huge Annimals are delivered them at theire Ship Sides in the Roade, brought hither in great broad lighters that are built for the Same purpose, where they are hove On board with good Capstants, runners and tackles, and Secured in hold as beforementioned fol. 38, 39[8].

The Kingdome of Bengala hath had a longe and tedious warre with the Danes, who might have ruined all theire Forraigne Commerce with their owne Ships or Junks[9], had they Either been ingenuous or Industrious,

---

[1] See note on p. 75. On the 19th April, 1676, the Council at Fort St George wrote to Hugli that the Dutch complained of a "Ship with English Collours abusing...a Mores Ship of Bengala off of Punto De Gali." *Factory Records*, Fort St George, No. 18. Compare Milburn, *Oriental Commerce*, vol. i. p. 350: "Point de Galle ranks next to Colombo in point of trade. It was here that the Dutch used to ship the cinnamon and other produce of the Island for Europe."

[2] See *Hobson-Jobson, s.v.* Colombo. The transition spelling in the text is valuable.

[3] See *Hobson-Jobson, s.v.* Jafna. Compare *Schouten*, vol. ii. p. 9: "The town and celebrated fortress of this island of Jaffanapatnam, which lies forty-eight leagues from Colombo, on the East, are situated in a fertile and agreeable country. Both were brought into submission to the Company [of Holland] in June 1658 by the arms of General van Goens." *N. and E.* in a list of passes granted to ships in 1680, p. 47, has "Japnapatam."

[4] See *Schouten*, vol. ii. p. 33, for a description of capturing elephants by the Dutch in Ceylon.

[5] *i.e. ghī.* See note on p. 132.

[6] See note on p. 134.

[7] See note on p. 5.

[8] These figures refer to the pages in the MS. The passage alluded to will be found on pp. 73, 74 of the text.

[9] See *Hobson-Jobson, s.v.* Junk, where Yule says, "1673. Fryer also speaks of 'Portugal Junks.' The word had thus come to mean any large vessel in the Indian Seas." Here we have Danish "Junks," evidently in the same sense. Compare the following in Fort St George "Generall" to the Court, 12th Nov. 1668, *O. C.* No. 3238, "Mr. Jearsey and Council in Mechlepatam...have ordered the cheife and Factors in the Bay to send upon Juncks...at least 800 tons of Salt peter." In

but for want of knowinge men in theire Service, the trade [of] the Moors of Bengala hath very much encreased. An accompt of all theire[1] losses were Summed Up in the yeare 1674, and then they had lost but 30 Saile of Ships and Vessels in 32 years warre.

That very yeare the Danes came from Trincombar[2] (a fine Garrison of the Kinge of Denmarks), the onely place they have in Asia, 40 English leagues to the Southward of Fort St. George's. They came Upon a treaty of peace[3],

---

letters from the Court to Fort St George, 13th Dec. 1672 and 29th Feb. 1684, *Letter Books* 5 and 7, there are the following allusions to "Junks"; "Buy a Couple or Three Small Jouncks that are good sailers [for fire ships]." "Any Junck that goes to Zeilon for Beetle Nutts may bring you Plants and seeds of the Cinnamon Tree, as well as pepper plants."

[1] "Theire" refers to the Moors.

[2] See *Hobson-Jobson, s.v.* Tranquebar. The Danes settled here in 1620. Compare the following accounts: *Schouten*, who visited the place in 1660, thus describes it (vol. i. p. 486) "Tranckebare is two and a half leagues to the North of Carcal. It has a fine appearance from the sea shore whence is seen the Danish fort, the walls of which are built of very white stone, and which has four bastions. This is the chief of the places in which the Danes have established their trade. They built this fort a long time ago. However, vessels of their nation are very rarely seen in the other ports of India...The fort is inhabited by more people of the country than by Danes...their trade in this place as in other parts of India is of little consequence, and very much impeded by the Moors their enemies, with whom they have ancient quarrels that cannot be made up." *Delestre*, p. 105 f. describes the place twelve years later: "This town [Tranquebar] is a very pleasant one, situated on the sea shore, and belongs to the Danes. The natives completely sacked it a few years ago which is the reason that merchants have not yet firmly re-established themselves there. The town is watered by a fine river. When I was there [in 1672] it was not entirely walled in, but by this time the work must be completed as over 1000 blacks were employed in it...The garrison consists of 200 Danes without reckoning the blacks who mount guard day and night." In the *Diary of Streynsham Master*, under date 3rd July, 1676, there is a reference to the Danish fort: "In the morning we saw the Danes Fort at Trincambarr, and severall ships along the shoare."

[3] There is but scanty mention of the Danes and their affairs in the contemporary MS. records at the India Office, but the following extracts taken from *Factory Records*, Hugli, No. 4, seem to show that negotiations for peace began in 1673. On the 10th June, 1673, Walter Clavell wrote from Balasor, "The Danes as yet have not made a peace having demanded their Prisoners they have here to bee set at liberty, till that is graunted they will treat no further, this the Moors cannot consent unto without the licence of Nabob Zoffy Chaan

(which if they had good Successe in, they resolved to Settle Factories in this Kingdome), in hopes also of acquiringe Some Satisfaction for the unsufferable wrongs theire Nation received off Meleck Beake[1], Father to this Meleck Cossum[2], who is the present Governor of Hugly.

The Danish Nation were formerly well Setled in this Kingdome, theire Chiefe Factory in Ballasore[3], and had yearely Ships of very considerable burthen arrived from Europe, untill Some Unhappy troubles arose at home, which constrained the Kinge of Denmarke to keep his Ships and men at home, which animated the Said Meleck Beake to injure the resideinge people here, the which he did in the basest degree of Nature.

[Nawāb Sūfī Khān] on whose account they were taken." On the 27th of June in the same year Walter Clavell writes, "A Guzerat Ship was surprized in the Roade [of Balasor] by two Danes Vessells who came hither with intentions to make peace but as yet nothing is effected nor is likely to bee, the Moores having detained three of their people prisoners who were forced ashore the last yeare by a storme on the Coast of Gingerlee where they were seized on by Nabob Zoffy Chaan's people being then Nabob of Kateck and secured untill they had made satisfaction for a vessell the Danes tooke of his, and the Moores pretend they cannot surrender these Prisoners without the order of the Nabob."

1 Malik Bēg was Governor of Hugli for twenty years or more. He is first mentioned in the records in 1647, and appears to have still held his post as late as 1667–8, though the last direct reference to him, in his official capacity, is in 1665. The name is variously given as "Malybeeg, Malla beeg, Meirza Mallibeague, Merza Maleeck beeg, Malick Beake." He was apparently more favourable to the English than was his son and successor, Malik Qāsim. Malik Bēg took the part of the English against the Dutch, and settled the differences between the two nations in favour of the former (*O. C.* Nos. 3071, 3095, 3096).

2 Malik Qāsim was Governor of Hugli from about 1668 until the end of the year 1672, when he lost his post. However, by means of the payment of a heavy bribe, he procured the government of Balasor, which he held for two years, and then re-obtained the government of Hugli, an appointment which he retained until 1681.

3 Walter Clavell, in his "Accompt of the Trade of Ballasore" at the end of the *Diary of Streynsham Master*, p. 322, says, "Ballasore begunn to be a noted place when the Portuguez were beaten out of Angelin [Hijili] by the Moores about the year 1636: at which time...the English and the Danes endeavoured to settle Factoryes here..."

They had a great quantitie of goods and moneys by them, which the Villaine coveted, and, in fine, brought his most diabolicall purposes to passe. He Poysoned all, both younge and Old, that belonged to the Affaires of Denmarke, and they were near 40 in number of the Danish Nation, Seized upon all their goods, and demolished the Factory, soe that when the next Shippinge arrived from Denmarke, they found but course Entertainment in Bengala, nor any Satisfaction, which forced them to warre, and with a just cause, which might have tended to the great Enrichinge of Denmarke had it been well prosecuted[1].

The Danes, findinge Small gaines to Issue from this warre, did, Anno Domini 1674, come downe from their Castle of Trincombar (with one Shipp of 16 gunns and a Sloope) into the bay of Bengala, upon a treaty for peace, thereby to Settle a trade, as the English and Dutch have in Bengala and Pattana.

Now, beinge Assured in themselves of Obtaininge a Very honourable peace, with this Nation (who they

---

[1] No details of this massacre have come to light among the contemporary records at the India Office, but that the Danes were in conflict with Malik Bēg, the following extract from *A Short Declaration of sevrall passages in Bengalla* by Richard Hudson in Dec. 1647, *O. C.* No. 2056, clearly shows: "Att our first arrivall at Ballasara we were to appearance kindly wellcome till newes of the Danes arrivall who were come to force satisfaction of wrongs formerly sustained, when Zoe Millick Beague prohibits our [word illegible] the howse, some few dayes after the Danes came into the Roade, and seizeth one of the Moores shipps with 8 Ellephants, whereupon hee Millick Beague sends the Sheckdarr [*shiqdar*, revenue-officer] with all the Merchants to intreat us to Vissitt him, some time was spent and with much intreaty after we had made them eate their words, we condiscended and went to Beagues howse, some daies after he gave us a Vissitt, and the morrow following desires us to come to his howse where meeteing he brought us to intercede with the Danes for release of the Elliphants and Jounck, we went on board and discharged our parts very honestly, but to no purpose the Danes replying they came not hither with five Vessells to quit what they seized for faire words, a second time we went to as much purpose as first, Beague and the rest seeing our words prevaild no more they tell us then that sith we are Christians, and the Danes the same, you shall Sattisfie the Damage wee susteine with many words pro and con...."

thought did not a little dread them) were very much mistaken, for the Cunninge and Subtile Meleck Cossum[1] did first out witt them, and Soon after laughed at them,

[1] The records of the time shew the character of Malik Qāsim in a most unfavourable light. In Dec. 1672 (*Factory Records*, Hugli, No. 4) in a "Generall" from the Bay to the Court, we have the following: "The troubles wee have met with from Mellick Cossum the Governour of Hugly wee have yearely given you advice off in denying distucks [*dastaks*, signed documents] when and as often as we complyed not with his greedy and petulant desires in giving him presents in selling him your goods at his owne rates Transporting his goods betweene Hugly and Ballasore in your vessells and pilating his Vessells in and out the River Ganges in all these as farr as we found reasonable wee did gratifie his requests but could not without an extraordinary Charge comply in all, nor prodigally lavish your estates to make presents &ca Charges to equalize the Dutche's though by the Government expected...Mellick Cossum is turned out of his government of Hugli...Mellick Cossum hath with the expences of threescore thousand rupees procured the Government of Ballasore...." On the 31st of March they wrote from the Bay (*ibid.*), "Mellick Cossum is lately arrived here and pretended Friendship for us what it is wee have already experienced and feare all his actions here will bare some proportion with what hee did in Hugly." In Sept. 1673 (*ibid.*) Mr Elwes at Dacca was ordered to acquaint the *dīwān* "that the Towne [of Balasor] is likely in short time to be ruined; but two Vessells come here this yeare belonging to Strangers...that their usage hath been such they intend never to come here againe...and that as long as hee [Malik Qāsim] is here wee nor no Strangers can hope for any safety for our Ships, that wee have forborne all manner of Trade in this place this yeare, and shall as long as this man stayes here and it may bee bee forced to leave this place." In Dec. 1674, the factors at the Bay wrote to the Court (*ibid.*), "Mellick Cossum Governour of Ballasore...hath in a little time after his removall re obtained the Government of Hugly in his Sons name and the command of the Kings forces there abouts in his owne so that he is now become one of a more absolute command then ever in these parts, and may if the Nabob live in few years geet up all his former losses, there being little expectation that the Nabob will be removed as long as he lives...." In 1678 Malik Qāsim was in less favour at Court, for, in a letter from Hugli to Balasor (*O. C.* No. 4403), we read, "The Nabob is deadly sick at Dacca some say irrecoverable soe that tis uncertain whether Mellick Cossim (who now is certainly in a low condition and in great disgrace at Dacca) will be jaggeered from Ballasore as he is from hence [Hugli]." However, it was three years later before the English finally got rid of Malik Qāsim. In November, 1681, they wrote from Balasor (*Factory Records*, Balasor, No. 1) "This day Mellick Cossim who was lately Jageerd came to vissitt us before his goeing to Decca." In a Dutch map of Hugli dated 1679 (Map No. 1102 *Leupe's Catalogue*, in the Map Room at the India Office), there is marked just outside the town "Garden of Melkassum [Malik Qāsim] formerly also fausdar [*faujdār*] or Governor of Hoogly."

All through the Simplicitie of a Mechanick[1] fellow that the Danes Entitled theire Comadore, who rendred himselfe, as he was really, a most ridiculous man, to the mightie disgrace of there whole Nation and Fortification of Trincombarre.

This Commadore, as they called him, at his arrivall in the Roade of Ballasore, to our Judgements, seemed to be blest with a great Share of good Fortune, but let it Slip for want of discretion or couradge, the latter of which it cold not well be, for a vessell with 2 or 3 gunns, and onely 8 or 10 men might have acted more in that respect then there was any occasion for.

Hee found 5 Saile of Bengala Ships in the roade, newly arrived from Ceylone and Maldivae Insulae[2], whose Cargoes were very Considerable. The Moors that belonged to them tooke to theire boats and runne into the River, leaveinge Ships and goods for a Prey to the Danes; but they cold not perswade theire Commadore to make Seizure of them, which, had he done, it wold have been a great inducement to the Moors to have granted to them a most Noble peace; but if, on the Contrary, they might have carried away their prises, a greater enrichinge to them then any Factories they may have in this Kingdome will afford in their Small trade for many years to come.

And, which added more disgrace to them, Meleck Cossum, by advice of the Merchants, meerly out of feare of looseinge those 5 Saile and 6 or 7 more dayly Expected, sent a Very noble peace off to him, which he refused. The Articles of agreement tendred to the Danes were but few, but contained great freedom to them, vizt.—

Art. 1. That the Danish Nation Shold henceforward Enjoy the Same liberty of traffick and commerce in Bengala and Pattana as the English Nation doth.

---

[1] *i.e.* vulgar.

[2] See note on p. 104.

Art. 2. That the Moors wold build them a Factory in Ballasore as large as they please, and where.

Art. 3. That Meleck Cossum wold give to the Danes 5 or 6000 Rupees towards bearinge theire Expences Untill they were well Setled.

Meleck Cossum Sent a very Eminent man (one of his owne councell) on board the Danes Ship (then rideinge with a flagge of truce), and gave him many faire Sentences to deliver by word of mouth, as alsoe very complementall letters Signed and Sealed by him and his Councell, all which instanced nothinge but great Friendship, protestinge what he meant not to doe, that he wold assist them in all that lay in his power, and that they were in his breast the most welcome of all Europeans that Ever came into Bengala, and that Ever Since he arrived to the height of this present Government, he coveted nothinge more then the Society of the Danish Merchants or Factors; and thus, with many faire wheedles, and comeinge downe in person to the barre, with Store of Elephants, Palanchinoes[1], &c., pretendinge to waite for kissinge of the Commadore's hand, he deluded him on Shore, where he thought himselfe Sure of the beforementioned peace, with an addition of 100000 rupees towards Satisfaction for theire great injuries received at the hands of this Governour's Father[2].

This Worthy Commadore (a Taylor by trade) did now display himselfe in his owne colours. He went on Shore, but Sorely neglected to Stitch up the Peace, when all the necessaries were brought to him Upon his own Shopboard. He was Seemingely courteously received by Meleck Cossum and his hypocriticall Crew, by whom he was conducted to his house, and theire, after Some wilfull Silly questions asked concerninge Denmarke, England, Holland, &c., The Commadore mentioned the treaty of

---

[1] See note on p. 19. [2] *i.e.* Malik Bēg.

Peace, att which the Moor's Governour Seemed to be Struck with an admiration, and told him he knew of noe warre; but one discourse bringinge on another, the Governour now began to Speake a little Sharply to him and his Companions that accompanied him On Shore, and demanded Satisfaction for the 30 Saile of Ships they had taken duringe the warre, rateinge each Ship and Cargo at noe lesse then 10 thousand pounds Sterlinge, soe that the whole amounted to more then Ever the Danes had, or (in my Opinion) will have in all the East Indies or South Seas[1].

The Commadore and his associates began now to consider theire Errour in Comeinge On Shore, findinge themselvs in noe better condition then at the mercy of Meleck Cossum, the Issue of him that had noe mercy on the Danish Nation, in soe much that now they are forced to give faire Speeches, and condescend to anythinge, for feare of Sufferinge imprisonment or death.

And now the Moors come Upon them for Satisfaction for a great Number of Musslemen[2] they had killed and taken Prisoners, declareinge they had lost tenn times soe many as the Danes lost in Bengala—a very Slender piece of Satisfaction.

---

[1] *i.e.* the trading places in the southern part of the Indian Ocean, *e.g.* the Malay Peninsula, Sumatra, &c. Compare the following: "Use all diligence...to putt in as much Saltpeeter as you can in all Ships that as need requires wee may take out of them at their returne to the Fort to make provision for the South Seas....Prepare and provide what goods you can fitting for the South Sea trade." *Factory Records*, Fort St George, No. 16, 26th Aug. 1668 and 19th Sept. 1669.

[2] An interesting early example of a mistake still sometimes made. Compare *Fryer*, p. 91, who has a similar error: "Here [Surat] are a sort of bold, lusty, and most an end, drunken Beggars, of the Musslemen Cast," and the following from the Hugli Diary of 25th May, 1677 (*Factory Records*, Hugli, No. 1) "This morning wee sent our Mahazor [*mahzar*, application] to Dacca signed only by 4 Mogull and Mussullmen and 6 Hindoes." The author, in his *Malay Dictionary*, has, "Moosulmawn, a Mahometan, or true Believer as esteemed by the Mahometans." See also notes on pp. 76 and 126.

And with all told them in good Earnest, that if they wold or did Expect any favour in these Kingdomes, they must goe up to Dacca to Nabob Shah-hest-Kan[1], and treat with him concerneinge theire affaires.

Meleck Cossum knew well Enough they wanted moneys whereby to make theire addresses to Such a great person, who made noe body welcome without it; therefore that piece of advice was onely to Jeere them.

The Danish Commadore Excused himselfe from that, and by great Submission to the Governour here, obtained the Liberty to take a house to live in, vizt. for him and his people, untill they heard Farther from the Castle of Trincombar.

The which was noe Sooner requested, but immediately granted, and a promise made to them that they shold not be treated like Enemies, but Shold be free to buy and Sell and bringe theire Ship up to the towne Side and Stay Six months with great freedom, and then (the Monsoone[2] beinge shifted) to goe away with theire Ship and Sloope where they pleased, but that the Commadore and 4 or 5 Factors shold reside in Ballasore until a better Understandinge was made betweene the Kinge of Denmarke and theire Nabob[3].

---

[1] Shāyista Khān.

[2] See notes on pp. 51 and 73. Compare the following curious spelling in a letter from Balasor, 25th Jan. 1675, *Factory Records*, Hugli, No. 4, "The Mounsoon drawing neere to an end."

[3] The only allusion to this episode, so fully described by T. B., that has come to light among the India Office Records, is the following extract from a letter to the Court written by Walter Clavell at the Bay on the 28th Dec. 1674, *Factory Records*, Hugli, No. 4: "The Deanes have for borne to trade in these parts and had Warr from 1640 to this present year now they are come two new termes and are like to have a little interest here on the Condition that all pretence of dammage shall be lade by on all Sides that the Deanes shall be free of custom as wee are, and that they shall have a place alloted them to build a Factory on, and have Rupees 3000 Allowed them towards the Building thereof, hether two these particulars are but Slenderly performed there being nothing advanced towards the erecting there Factory nor have they though they have long Since Chosen a plot of ground proceeded to erect any wall or to lay a foundation, the Deanes seeme not to be contented with there Setlement here nor the mores to pay any part of

Againe, in the yeare 1676, they Sent downe the Same Ship and a brave new Sloope upon the Same Errand; but now they durst not meddle with any Moors Ships, by reason of their men that were On Shore under the Moors Government. They went up to Ballasore with their Ship, and theire New Commadore, Captain Wilkins[1], came Up to Hugly in the Sloope, thence tooke Budgaroe[2] for Dacca, carryinge a present to the Nabob. This Wilkins beinge a very talkative man, and his present not soe great as Expected, the Nabob did but meerly Scoffe at him, Especially when he demanded the Same priviledge the English Nation Enjoyed, and asked if the like the Dutch had wold not Serve. He answered noe, but was forced to accept of lesse, and I question not but they purposed to take Opportunity to depart this Kingdome, and begin the warre afresh[3].

---

the promissed mony, unless they can perswade any towne Merchant whose perticular benefit the Governor pretended it will be to advance the mony, however the name of peace being now spred here and no warr thought of with any people who trade at Sea, the owners of Shipping doe begin to leave of to by any Ordinance but Seeke to finde a meanes to Settle Some of what they have in the Country." In answer to this letter, the Court wrote, 24th December, 1675, *Letter Book*, No. 5, "We observe what you say about the settling of the Danes in the Bay, you ought to have opposed that so far as it might have been done without our Prejudice."

[1] Streynsham Master calls him Wilk Wygbert. "The Danes Cheife by name Wilk Wygbert gave mee a vissit." *Diary of Streynsham Master*, under date 30th Aug. 1676. In *Factory Records*, Siam, No. 1, there is a reference on the 8th May, 1679, to "Captain Wilkin Wigbers lately in the Danes service bearer of a letter [from Fort St George to Siam]."

[2] See *Hobson-Jobson*, *s.v.* Budgerow. See the end of the section on "Bengala" for a description of this kind of boat. Compare the following: "I got up to Barnnegur wheare I mett Mr. Vincent coming downe the river in his Buggera." Letter from Hugli to Balasor, 6th Feb. 1679, *O. C.* No. 4573.

[3] It was at this time, about 1676, that the Danes established themselves at Serampore near Hugli. To this second treaty, as described by T. B., there are the following references in the contemporary MS. records: "The Danes by plying up and down only with their small vessells half man'd with Blacks and sometimes catching a few of their [the "Bramanys"] ships and Boates alongst the Coast of Gingerlee, have brought them as well as the Bengallers to as good complyance

A great Multitude of Portugals[1] inhabit the Kingdome of Bengala, Especially in Hugly and Some Other Creeks or Rivolets of the River thereof. Many of them are filias dè Lisboa (as they call them selvs), vizt. Europeans borne, but many more of them are filias dè Indies. They have a very large towne, about one English mile above the English Factory; it is called the Bandell[2]. I judge it is

as they can desire." Fort St George "Generall," 23rd July, 1676, *O. C.* No. 4215. "This evening I visited the Cheife of the Danes Wilke-Wygbert at their factory, by whome I was informed that he had formerly binn a Skipper in the Dutch Companys service, in their great ships out and home, and lost his legg at Macasser, afterward, upon discontent of some ill usage left their service in Holland, and in the yeare 1670 came out in the King of Denmarkes service to make purchase upon the People of Bengala, but after him came out other persons of Quallity who had concluded a peace with these people which he did not esteeme soe advantageous as the other way, the tearmes where these, this their Factory and the ground and houses about it (which is a good Compasse and a handsome spott) was given them free and three thousand Rupees in money to repaire and build a house, all which the merchants of this towne Contributed Alsoe he acquainted me that at Dacca from whence he was lately returned he had procured the Nabob Shaster cawne's Phyrwanna [*parwāna*] for the Danes nation to trade free of custome in Bengala and Orixa, and the Merchants alsoe that buy their goods and that his charges in procuring the same stood them in between 4 and 5 thousand rupees.... The Danes are granted a Phyrwand In every perticuler like as ours, it is now in the Rayes [*raja's*] hands who will not deliver it without a present." *Diary of Streynsham Master* under date 2nd Sept. and 18th Dec. 1676.

On the 7th May, 1677, the Council at Fort St George wrote to the Bay (*Factory Records*, Fort St George, No. 18), "We have now yours 15 February...whose contents observe and therein the continuing Severitys of the great men...and all seeming to be occasioned by the Danes Suing for a Phirmaund [*farmān*] like ours, and that eluded by the Crafty Mores alledging the Honble. Companys paying of 2 per 100 at Surratt, and prosecuting the instance against them in Bengala allsoe 2 birds with one Stone."

In *Hague Transcripts*, No. 2, under date 18th Oct. 1677, we find, "The Danes have been very clever in obtaining permission to trade over the whole district of Bengal, but we do not think they will find it very profitable, as we are informed, that since the foundering of their East Indiaman, the Company have neither men nor money for equipping another vessel, neither have they any credit and the Shareholders refuse to put in further capital."

[1] See note on p. 3. Compare John Marshall, *Notes and Observations*, p. 6 (reverse), "Hugly is a very great Towne in which live very many Portuguese."

[2] See *Hobson-Jobson*, *s.v.* Bandel. Bandel=*bandar*, *i.e.* the port. Wilson, *Early Annals*, vol. i. p. 62, in his description of Hugli *circ.*

2 English miles in circuit, very populous of men, women and children. They are for the most part very poore[1], but are much to be commended for their Industrie, in acquireinge a livelyhood by honest means, much more commendable and honourable then for Christians to begge in a heathen Country.

They knitt Stockins of silke and Cotton; they bake bread for the English and Dutch Factories and particular dwellinge houses, and for theire Ships and Vessels; they make many Sorts of Sweetmeats, vizt. Mangoe[2], Orange, Lemon, Ginger, Mirabolins[3], Ringo Roots[4], &c. Severall

---

1679, says, "North of it was Bandel the ill-fated colony of the Portuguese." Compare also Alex. Hamilton, *East Indies*, vol. ii. p. 20 f.: "Hughly is a Town of a large Extent, but ill built. It reaches about 2 Miles along the River's Side, from the Chinchura before mentioned to the Bandel, a Colony formerly settled by the Portugueze...The Bandel at present, deals in no Sort of Commodities."

[1] Compare the following from Walter Clavell's "Accompt of the Trade of Hugly," at the end of the *Diary of Streynsham Master*, p. 322: "The Portuguez, though numerous in Hugly, yett are reduced to a very low and meane Condition, their trade not worth mentioning, their Subsistance being to be entertained in the Mogulls pay as Souldiers."

[2] See note on p. 48.

[3] See *Hobson-Jobson*, *s.v.* Myrobalan. A variously spelt and pronounced term for astringent dried fruits of several species.

[4] Apparently for "dringo root." Craufurd, *Malay Dict.*, has "*daringgu* (Jav. *dringo*), name of a plant, *Acorus terrestris.*" And T. B., in his *Malay Dict.* gives "Dirringo, Calamus aramaticus, or a Sweet smelling reed in India." See also *Valentyn*, vol. iii. p. 246, who says, "The *Deringo*, or Acorus, otherwise called *Calmus*, but by no means the same as Calamus Aromaticus, is found here also [in Amboyna], being one long creeping root, which is scarcely a finger thick." Rumphius, *Herbarium Amboinense*, vol. v. pp. 178—180, has a chapter on "Acorum. Deryngo." From this I have extracted the following as to the designation, habitat, and use of the plant: "*Nomen.* Latine Acorum et Acorus...In Bengala Böos, in regionibus Malaiensibus Deryngo, quod Portugalli Diringo scribunt... *Locus.* In India Orientali copiosissime et elegantissime crescit in aquosa regione Bengalae inferioris... *Usus.* Quum Acorum in hisce fervidis proveniens regionibus ingratum magis et acorem habeat saporem, quam quod in frigidis crescit locis, hinc non ita aptum est, ut condiatur quam istud. Recentes jussi radices primo rite decorticare et depurare, per tres dies primum in aqua, ac dein per tres alios dies in aqua saccharata maceravi, ac tum cum saccharo excoxi, saporem tamen servabat austerum, comperi autem post annum elapsum melioris esse

Sorts of Achar[1], as Mangoe, Bamboo, Lemon, &c. very good and Cheape[2]. Many of the men Use the Sea in English or Moors Ships and Vessels[3], soe that these people live very happily, better then in most places in Asia, all Sorts of provisions beinge here very Cheape. A Very good Cow is Sold for foure Shillings Six Pence,

---

notae. Salubris sunt hae radices mensibus pluviosis..." Stevens, *Guide to East India Trade*, p. 146, has "Rangoes" among a list of goods brought from the East Indies, and in a list of "manufactured" goods, p. 144 (among which is "Bamboe Atchar") he has "Arrangoes." These "Rangoes" may refer to the same product as that mentioned by T. B. Indeed, it is not at all unlikely that a product jointly of Bengal and the islands of the Malay Archipelago had a Malay commercial name, just as Rangoon oil nowadays comes from America! See Watts, *Dict. of Economic Products of India*, *s.v.* Acorus. Godhino de Eredia in his *Malaca*, has a chapter, p. 39 f., on the medicaments of the Malays. He says, "The plants and herbs most generally used are the following: nutmeg, cinnamon...dringo..." *Premier Livre de l'Histoire de la Navigation aux Indes Orientales par les Hollandois*, 1609, gives on fol. 41, in describing the voyage of 1595, an excellent plate of the "Calamus Aromaticus en Malaique dit Diringuo" making it look like ginger. I am indebted to Mr Donald Ferguson for putting me on the right track for hunting down the term "dringo."

[1] *Achār* is the ordinary vernacular for pickle. *The Premier Livre*, etc., quoted in the preceding note, says, fol. 37, that "Mangas d'Achar" was used in place of olives. *Dampier*, vol. i. p. 391, calls *āchār* a "sawce" from its use as a digestive or stomachic. See *Hobson-Jobson*, *s.v.* Achar. Compare the following: "If you can meet any Jarres of Pegue buy mee some of that sort which usually are for Mangoe Achar." Letter to Balasor, 13th May, 1678; *O. C.* No. 4414. "Four jarrs which I send downe to you...to be filled with mangoe Attchar." Letter to Balasor, 12th August, 1678; *O. C.* No. 4473.

"Achar Wee would have you to provide for us every Year 10 Jarrs of Acharr Vizt. 3 of your best Mango Pacherees, 3 of Radish...the other Four in Lime [fruit] Acharr, We would not have you to Chinamb [*chunam*, plaster with lime] the top of them over." Letter from the Court to Fort St George, 10th March, 1682; *Letter Book*, No. 6. Hugli was written to on the same date to provide 20 small Jars of "Acharr" yearly, "10 of best Mangoe 6 of Lyme [fruit] and the other 4 of [edible] Bambo."

[2] Compare *Bernier*, p. 437 f.: "Bengale...is celebrated for its sweetmeats, especially in places inhabited by Portuguese, who are skilful in the art of preparing them...Among other fruits, they preserve large citrons, such as we have in Europe, a certain delicate root [? dringo] about the length of a Sarsaparilla, that common fruit of the Indies called amba [mangoe], another called ananas [pine-apple], small mirobolans, which are excellent, limes and ginger."

[3] *e.g.* Petro Loveyro, the "antient Portugueze" mentioned on p. 75.

vizt. 2 rupees, a good hogg for $\frac{3}{4}$ of a Rupee, 45 or 50 fowls for one Rupee, fish alsoe in great plenty, by reason of which plenty of all Sorts of belly timber[1] and cloths fittinge for the Climate very Cheape alsoe, this Kingdome is soe well inhabited Especially by Foraigners[2], which maketh Bernyer's Opinion of it to be to the purpose—That the Kingdome of Bengala hath many dores into it, and but one out of it[3], which is very true, For thousands that were borne in Other Countries doe live and Ends theire days with Old age in Bengala.

The Portugals are admitted to live in any part of the Kingdome with freedome Enough, but not soe much as Some of their richest men, Fidalgas as they call them, vizt. Gentlemen, doe Expect, for they doe and must pay custome and Other duties, the Same the Merchants of the countrey doe, and great respect to the Mahometan Governours alsoe; but againe they are free from any absurd Exactions, such as are laid heavily Upon the Gentue and Banjan Merchants.

Nevertheless, the Moors doe take all advantages to Screw moneys out of them, as for instance, Anno Domini 1676, the Portugueeses haveinge collected a good Summ of moneys to the End they might build a very large and decent Church, they now make preparation to begin the worke. Haveinge provided Stone, brick, lime, timber, they pull downe the Old one, and begin the new foundation,

---

[1] *i.e.* Provisions. Compare the following in a letter from Hugli to Fort St George, 17th April, 1682, "Surratt, a place fam'd for its frugallity or rather pinchingness in belly Timber."

[2] Compare *Bernier*, p. 438 f.: "Pigs are obtained at so low a price that the Portuguese, settled in the country, live almost entirely upon pork....Fish of every species, whether fresh or salt, is in the same profusion. In a word, Bengale abounds with every necessary of life; and it is this abundance that has induced so many Portuguese, Half-castes, and other Christians, driven from their different settlements by the Dutch, to seek an asylum in this fertile kingdom."

[3] "The Kingdom of Bengale has a hundred gates open for entrance, but not one for departure." *Bernier*, p. 439.

but ere one fourth finished the Moors, by Order of theire Governour stopped the worke, commandinge the workmen Upon paine of imprisonment not to proceede[1], to the great griefe of the Fathers[2], and alias. The Mahometans did it not for Religions Sake, but for lucre of moneys, for 1000 pound Sterlinge will admitt of 2 or 3 churches in most places in the Kingdome or Empire[3].

I judge, and am well Satisfied in it, that there are noe lesse then 20000 Frangues[4] of all Sorts in the Kingdom of Bengala, and above ½ of them inhabit near Hugly River[5].

The Way that is most used by the Moors for the Exact accompt how the day and night passeth away is very remarkable, beinge soe different from any in Europe. They use noe ⊙ dialls[6], clocks, or watches, nor glasses, for indeed I thinke they are not soe ingenuous to make them, but consideringe that, they have invented a very good method for the certaine noteinge how that precious jewell, time, hasteth away.

They fill a great bowle or bason with very cleare water, and a Small Coppar dish that will hold between ½ a pint and a pint, made very thinne and a Small round hole drilled through the bottom, the which Set Empty (Swiminge on the great bowle of water) very boyant, which gradually filleth and then doth immediately Sinke. The tender thereof, for there must be continually one to Sit

---

[1] I have been unable to find any confirmation of this story in either printed or MS. records of the period available.

[2] *i.e.* Padres, priests.

[3] See note on p. 11.

[4] See note on p. 140.

[5] Compare *Bernier*, p. 439: "The Jesuits and Augustins, who have large churches and are permitted the free and unmolested exercise of their religion, assured me that Ogouli alone contains from eight to nine thousand Christians, and that in other parts of the kingdom their number exceeded five-and-twenty thousand."

[6] Sun-dials. See note on p. 85.

by it, immediately taketh it up and Setteth it floating (as before), and Striketh—One, and when [it] Sinketh againe, he Striketh—two, and soe on to 3, 4, 5, 6, 7. And When he hath Strucken Seven, he then Striketh 1, vizt. One Pore[1], and when [it] Sinketh againe, he Striketh 1, Vizt. One gree[2]; and soe Onward, 2, vizt. 2 gree and then one, vizt. one Pore; then 3, vizt. 3 gree and 1, vizt. 1 Pore; and Soe to 7; and then Striketh 2, vizt. 2 Pore, vizt. midday, or midnight; as 9 in the morneinge Is one Pore, 12 att Noone 2 Pore, 3 in the afternoone 3 Pore, ☉ Settinge[3] 4 Pore, and soe of the night. They Strike not with or Upon a bell, for the Mahometans Use none, but it is a round flatt of one foot and a halfe, or two foot Over, (Some are very much larger) made of fine Gans of Pegu[4], vizt. a very good Sort of bell mettle. It is hunge up by a Stringe through a hole on one Side thereof, Soe as to take it's free Swinge, and is called a Gonge[5]. They Strike thereon with a Small Mallat of wood, and yieldeth a most Excellent Sound and Echo. Most Mahometans &c. of accompt in Hindostan Use them at theire doors in the Street where they have generally a Porch built, when 2 men are continually kept to attend it, one Sleepeth while the Other waketh and tendeth the Gree. The English and Dutch have them at the Gates of all there inland Factories

---

1 *Pahr.* 2 *Gharī.* 3 Sunset.

4 See *Hobson-Jobson*, *s.v.* Ganza=bell-metal. Compare the following: "Tell him [my Cousin Greenhill] I will make good 7 cwt. 10 lbs. received of the Porgo man account his gance." Letter from Hugli to Balasor, 7th April, 1678, *O. C.* No. 4395. "The Longpepper and Gance...I would have them disposed of being the one is perishable and of the other sort more may come from the fort or Metchlepatam shortly." Letter from Hugli to Balasor, 28th May, 1678, *O. C.* No. 4430. "I have desired Mr. John Heathfield in Metchlepatam to lade on the first Vessaile bound thence for your Port a Parcell of Pegu Gance...being about 30 candyes." Letter from Fort St George to Balasor, 21st Feb. 1679, *O. C.* No. 4580.

5 T. B. in his *Malay Dictionary* has "Goong, a Goong or China Bell."

in this Kingdome or Others in Hindostan, Verifieinge the Old Proverbe, Cum fueris Romae, &c.[1]

The Bengalas (vizt. the Idolatrous people of the Countrey) have very Strange ways of worshippinge their Gods, (or rather Devils) they Set up in their Pagods, as alsoe in theire owne houses, which images are of a most hideous Shape, that these poore Ignorant Souls doe soe much deifie, and torture theire owne persons for the Silly humors they hold of adoreinge them, one of which as followeth :—

In the Month February, they publickely Shew theire Earnest devotions, and what they will Suffer for the Sake of their Irreligious Molten Gods. They Place a great Powle in the Earth, not unlike to a maypowle, on the top of which is placed another Very longe powle, which is soe fixed upon a Speendle as to runne round (with great facilitie) at each end of which is fastened a 3 inch rope, att the lowermost end for the multitude of Idolaters to lay hold on and runne the powle round; that at the Upper-

---

[1] The author is here endeavouring to describe the Indian clepsydra or water-clock, and the accompanying bell for striking the time indicated by the clock. There are many contemporary accounts of this prominent instrument. Indian time reckoned 60 hours (*gharī*, gree) of 24 minutes to the full day instead of our 24 hours of 60 minutes. There were nominally 8 *gharīs* to the watch (*pahr*, pore), the watch being a fourth part of the night. But strictly the right relation between *gharī* and *pahr* never worked out, and one of the night watches was made to consist of 9 or 7 *gharīs* according to the season. The instrument struck was called a *ghariāl* or *ghanṭā* (bell) and by Europeans a gong, itself an Oriental word. The water-clock was also called a *gharī*.

See *Hobson-Jobson*, *s.v.* Ghurry, Puhur and Gong. Compare *Fryer*, p. 186, and the following description by *Thevenot*, part iii. p. 100, "That Gary is pretty pleasant, though it be only rung with a stick, striking upon a large Plate of Copper that is held in the Air; but the Ringer strikes artfully and makes Harmony with it; the Gary serves to distinguish time. In the Indies the natural day is divided into two parts, the one begins at break of day, and the other at the beginning of the night, and each of these parts is divided into four Quarters, and each Quarter into eight Parts, which they call Gary." John Marshall, *Notes and Observations*, p. 13, has a long paragraph on "Gurries."

most end hath a Steele hooke fastened to it of good Substance. The bewitchinge Brachmans, haveinge intoxicated severall people, they Voluntarily come and desire to be hooked and Swunge[1] round to the publick View of many hundred Spectators, which is immediately done, and they are Swunge round with great rejoyceinge to the Gentues[2] that behold as alsoe to the parties themselves Seemingly, for they laugh and through flowers downe to the people, notwithstandinge the hooke is runne through their flesh, by which all the rest of the body doth hange, Some by the Sholder, some by the Small of the back, and Some by the buttock, as here described. [Plate XI.]

The Actors and Promoters of this Sort of Cruell Penants accompt themselves most religious. The Promoters are the wicked Brachmans[3], the Sufferers the Ignorant Gentues and Orixas[4], who thinke it meritorious, and a winninge of the favour of God and man, a poore

---

[1] In "Extracts from the Agent's Journey to Masulipatam by Land," given in *N. and E.* for 1679–80, p. 33, we find, "14th April [1679] Pollicull. Description of a great Pagoda there and of the Swinging Festival; some of the Agent's people went and saw 20 people hung up by the back by the skin with Iron Hooks attached to the end of a long pole."

Compare also the description by *Tavernier*, vol. i. part ii. p. 181, "The eighth of April, being in a City of Bengala called Malde, the Idolaters made a great Feast, according to the particular Custom of that place; they all go out of the City, and fasten Iron hooks to the boughs of several Trees, then come a great number of poor people and hang themselves, some by the sides, some by the brawn of their backs, upon those hooks, till the weight of their body tearing away the flesh, they fall of themselves. 'Tis a wonderful thing to see that not so much as one drop of blood should issue from the wounded flesh, nor that any of the flesh should be left upon the hook; besides, that in two days they are perfectly cur'd by such Plaisters as their Bramins give them." John Marshall, *Notes and Observations*, is very full on this swinging festival, which he saw at Patna on the 29th March, 1671, "a great day of penance amongst the Hindoos." See also Dubois and Beauchamp, *Hindu Manners, Customs and Ceremonies*, on "Hook-swinging," p. 605.

[2] See note on p. 23.

[3] See pp. 13 and 23.

[4] See note on p. 130.

ignorant people that know noe better. And of all Idolaters in India the Orixas are most ignorant, and are held by the rest to be of a lower Cast then they, in soe much that the Others, namely the Gentues and Banjans, will scarsely live neare any of them[1], soe that they are, as it were, Seperated from any towns or Pagods of Note. They doe, for the most part, live in Small Cottages that adjoyne to the Sea or Rivers, gettinge theire livelyhood by fishinge or makeinge Salt[2]. Many of them resort to the creeks and Rivolets at or about the Entrance into the Ganges, to make Salt att the dry Season of the yeare, vizt. May, June, July, August, where they make there abode soe longe, and then remove to theire old Stations, the ground here beinge low and Swampy, and much frequented with wilde beasts, vizt. Tygers, Bears, Rhinocerots, &c., which alsoe dreadeth the poore Orixas, whoe Indeed I may well call poore (and ignorant too). I have often been in theire Villages, and where there have been more then 20 families of them, they cold not all change one Rupee into Cowries, whereby to be paid for a little milke or fish (or what else wee had of them) in the currant moneys of this Kingdome and Orixa and Arackan, and withall soe ignorant that they know not Silver from Tootanagga[3].

---

[1] See p. 41 for similar caste distinctions.

[2] Compare the *Diary of Streynsham Master*, under date 8th September, 1676, p. 57, "This day wee passed by...the river of Rogues [running into the lower Hugli]...we alsoe passed by great numbers of salt pitts, and places to boile salt."

[3] *i.e.* spelter. See *Hobson-Jobson*, *s.v.* Tootnague. The "white copper" of China is meant in the text. The same trick as that hinted at by T. B. is still played upon the Nicobarese, who cannot usually distinguish between silver and tootnague, *i.e.* German silver. See also *Ind. Ant.* vol. xxvi. p. 222 f., for a similar trick on Java by the Chinese in the 17th century. Compare the following in a letter from Hugli to Balasor, 20th April, 1678, *O. C.* No. 4401, "I request you to get made for mee a handsome midle sized Aftaw and Chillumchee [ewer and basin] of Tetanague well set out with brass about the Edges." Writing to Balasor on the 12th August, 1678, *O. C.* No. 4476, the Council at Fort St George request "30 Candy of Tuttenag in 644 slabbs." T. B. in his *Malay Dict.* has, "Tootanag or the China pewter."

Cowries[1] (all the moneys knowne to the ignorant Ourias) are Small Shells, brought from the Islands of Malldiva[2]. A great quantitie passe for one Rupee, not lesse then 3200, as shall be shewed more largely in the moneys of this Kingdome.

The Ourias[3] are a Very Strange Sort of Phisicians to theire Sick people, to Father, Mother, Wife, children, or any Others, in soe much that theire Medicines are almost, if not altogeather incredible, to any man that hath not Seen theire Actions.

When any Party (man or woman) is visited with Sicknesse, which brings them soe low that they cannot Eat in 2 days time, they are then in a manner given over for dead, as very well they may, consideringe how roughly they are dealt with, enough to kill a Sound person, as followeth:—

The Sick party is carried downe to the River Side in a hammaker, or course piece of Dungaree Cloth[4], where he

---

[1] See note on p. 180. See also *Ind. Ant.* vol. xxvi. p. 290 ff.; vol. xxviii. p. 170 ff.; vol. xxix. pp. 38, 41. Compare the following reference in *Delestre*, p. 195, "They [the inhabitants of Bengala] have a particular kind of money that they call caulis which are little shells; they give you eighty-four for a fanoux [*fulūs*] worth five sols." Compare also the following in a General letter from the Court to Fort St George, dated 22nd February, 1660, "Bowgees or Cowries, being here in some request, wee desire you to lade on board the *Smirna merchant*, to the quantity of about 20 tonns."

[2] See note on p. 104. Compare the following extract from "A description of the Maldivas, 1683," *O. C.* No. 4916, "The Maldive Islands are said to contain 12000 Islands that are above Water, with many Shoals and banks whereon they take their Cowries having on them 2, 3 or 4 foot Water....Cowries are to be had at any time of the year, but in November and December most, by reason they are brought to the Kings Island to Lade the Bengall Shipping...."

[3] See note on p. 130.

[4] *i.e.* coarse cotton. See *Hobson-Jobson*, *s.v.* Dungaree. On the 17th Nov. 1675, Messrs Fleetwood and Hatton wrote from Nourasporam (*Factory Records*, Masulipatam, No. 10), that they had received "311 ps. of Dengarees," and on the 8th Aug. 1678 the Council at Fort St George wrote to Masulipatam (*ibid.*) that "The Honble. Company had required 12000 Peeces Dungarees...1200 Peeces is but a very Small quantity of such cours goods...." *N. and E.* p. 22 for 3rd June, 1680 has, "Dungarees and Market Clouts every 16 patch pay 1 fanam."

is laide upon the ground Even at the brinke of the water. They lift up his head and back, and keep poureinge River water down his throat, untill they make his belly Swell by fillinge him soe full of that Element, a great quantitie of the Sick parties kindred and Friends sittinge by howlinge and cryinge, Even as the wild Irish Used to doe for theire parents deceased.

They then carry the Sick man up to highwater marke, and there he is accompanied with his nearest relations. The next day (if not dead) he is Served soe againe, and Soe, day after day, untill Either dead or they See some palpable Signes of recovery; but I thinke they Seldome Obtaine the latter. When dead theire Carcasses are throwne into the River[1].

Dureinge the time of Sicknesse, the Brachmans, some of them, are very diligent to sitt by them and pray, Seldome leavinge off Untill the Party be quite dead, Especially to put the party in mind of the Pagod, to leave to it accordinge to his abilitie; and thus all the Ouria Sicke folke are Served.

---

[1] Compare *Schouten*, vol. ii. p. 161, "They even carry sick folk to it [the Ganges], and they water them also, or rather they place a portion of their bodies in the water, in order that their health may be re-established. If any of them chance to die during this operation, or a short time after, they have no doubt as to their salvation. Further, they even carry the water of the Ganges to be made use of by the sick who cannot be brought to the river, and they attribute no less virtue to it than do the Romish Christians to their most precious relics." Compare also Yule, *Hedges' Diary*, vol. i. p. 86f., "This evening [10th May, 1683] I left Muxadavad, and just as I passed by Ray Nundeloll's Tent, I saw him lye halfe way in the Water, and that very moment he died. Order was immediately given to make preparation for his being burnt, and about 2 houres after we saw a great fire at Muxadavad, which we concluded to be his burning." Compare also Dow, *History of Hindostan*, vol. i. p. xxxv., "People of rank and those of the higher casts burn their dead and throw some incense into the pile. Some throw the bodies of their friends into the Ganges, while others expose them on the high ways, as a prey to vultures and wild beasts. There is one cast in the kingdom of Bengal who barbarously expose their sick by the river's side to die there. They even sometimes choak them with mud when they think them past hopes of recovery. They defend this inhuman custom by saying, that life is not an adequate recompence for the tortures of a lingering disease."

Theire foolish fancie in it is thus, that all Shall be assuredly Saved, vizt. theire Souls Shall Enter into the bodies of good creatures (in Paradise) that dye with theire bodies well filled with the holy water of the Ganges[1] or any of the arms thereof, or that dye upon the banks thereof; for they accompt the mudde to be Sanctified as well as the Water: Ergo, the Orixas bury not theire dead, nor burne them as the Gentues doe, but heave them naked into the Rivers, where they Serve for a Prey to the ravenous Alligator[2].

The River Ganges and it's branches is held in soe great adoration by these ignorant heathens[3], that they make many Sacrifices thereto, and one Extraordinary and generall feast per annum, to which doe resort many thousands of men Women and Children, where att the houre appointed by the Brachmans, they all throw themselves into the River, some carryinge flowers of divers colours, pots of rice, butter, Oyle, &c. and sett them float-

---

[1] Compare Sonnerat, *Voyages to the East Indies and China*, 1774—1781, vol. i. p. 199f., "It is universally known that this river (the Ganges) is held in great veneration throughout India: the Gentoos believe that it proceeds directly from the feet of Brouma. This sacred origin gives it great privileges. Those who die on the banks of the Ganges, in drinking its salutary waters are exempted from the painful task of returning to this world, and retaking a new existence; for which reason as soon as an Indian is given over by the physicians, they hurry him down to the banks of the river, where his relations make him drink repeated draughts. They even force the mud into his mouth, and the unfortunate person is choaked by the religious operation. Sometimes the body is entirely plunged into the river; which becomes its grave."

[2] Compare the following from the *Diary of Streynsham Master*, on his way from Huglj to Kasimbazar, under date 21st Sept. 1676, p. 63, "This night wee Sup't and lay at Biggehaut a place where the river is low, where there lyes some hundreds of dead bodies that have been thrown into the river and the Doggs, Jackalls and Vultures, and other birds of prey come and feed upon them."

[3] Compare *Schouten*, vol. ii. p. 161, "Those who live on the shores of it [the Ganges] attribute so much sanctity to it that they call it celestial, as much as to say that it comes from heaven. There are thousands of idolaters who make pilgrimages to it, imagining that when they have bathed in it, all their sins will be effaced." See also *Delestre*, p. 194.

inge on the river for a Sacrifice. This is done some 2 miles above Hugly, where they thronge into the River in Such numbers, that they Spread a mile or two, and soe thick that many of them that by beinge longer in the water then they can Endure, that they are forced to Stay a great deale longer, for by beinge wearied, and one pullinge another Striveinge to get to land, many are drowned, and when soe they are not att all lamented for, but theire relations are mightilie Encouraged by the Seduceinge Brachmans, who confidently assure them they are most happy that departed this life in that most Sacred Element[1].

Before they Enter the River att this washinge Festivall, they prostrate themselves on the banks thereof with great devotion and many bows to the Water, mutteringe words to themselves, not much unlike to the Mahometan Custome when they pray to the Sun[2]. The Gentues of this Kingdome doe burne the Carcasses of theire dead people, and the Wifes and Concubines with the deceased husband, Even as they doe upon the Coasts of Choromandell[3] and Gingalee, onely this one Ceremonie added thereto, vizt. their Ashes are throwne into the River[4].

Yett Some of these Brachmans are more cruell then

---

[1] The festival here described is the "Mela at Saugor" which is still held annually in the month of January. See H. H. Wilson, *Essays on the Religion of the Hindus*, vol. ii. pp. 164—167, for a full account of the ceremonies connected with it. John Marshall, *Notes and Observations*, p. 15, thus describes the festival, *circ.* 1669. "At this place [Ganga Saugor], when Hindoos come to wash which is about November they all carry away some water in potts out of the River Ganges to their friends though 4 or 500 Course [*kōs*] or 1000 miles, and with that water wash their parents who are old...At this meeting of such a great concourse of people and all washing in one morning and endeavouring to wash as neare as they can in the place where these two Rivers meete, severall are yearly crowded to death." See also *Schouten*, vol. ii. p. 241.

[2] Muhammadans, of course, never pray to the sun. The remark has its rise in their being observed, in India, to turn to the West, *i.e.* towards Mecca, at evening prayer. Compare *Schouten*, vol. ii. p. 149 for the conduct of the "Gentives" after bathing in the Ganges, "After having bathed and cleansed themselves they turn towards the rising sun, and adore it, with bows, contortions, and other strange ceremonies."

[3] See pp. 14, 35—40. [4] See note on p. 35.

those, as for instance Some that I beheld. A Gentue in Hugly died, and was brought downe to the River Side. His Widdow was brought downe in a Palanchino, with very great attendance after their manner. Att the brinke of the River, where Store of combustible Stuffe lay prepared, they laid the dead Corps in the midst thereof, and, before they put any fire thereunto, these wretched Villains laid the woman upon her dead husband. She, dreadinge the fire that might soe gradually torment her, Strugled, and refused to be burnt; but they laid violent hands upon her, pressed her down, and laid a large heavy powle Upon her, where they held her downe untill they had Set fire on theire ingredients and they burnt soe farre as to disable her comeinge forth, where the poore Creature perished in a most lamentable manner.

Some few months afterwards I saw another Gentue woman burnt about 6 miles above Hugly, which was the pleasantest I ever Saw. The Woman wold not at all deny to burne, knowinge any deniall to be of noe Effect, and although She was unwillinge thereto, yet She knew it now fell to her lot, therefore bore it patiently, and Stood very couragiously neare the place of torment (the fiery flames); whereupon the Brachmans gave Order for the fire to burne very furiously that the Sooner she might be dispatched, and they were very Joyfull to See the woman Undaunted; but when she was, accordinge to theire Expection, to have leaped into the fire, she refused it. Whereupon the Brachmans were very yeare[1] to take hold of her; but the first that laid hands on her, She laid as Sure hands upon him, and threw herselfe headlonge into the fire and the Brachman with her, where they both perished in a moment. Thus one of those Diabolicall Priests perished in the Pitt he had digged for another[2].

---

[1] ? desirous. Apparently connected etymologically with "yearn."

[2] These frequent notices of *satī* (see pp. 35—40) seem to be genuine, and are valuable therefore as evidence.

The Brachmans of this Kingdome are great Students in the Magick art[1], and make theire Sorceries more apparent then they of any Other Kingdome in Asia.

They are a people very much dreaded by the Moors as well as the Idolaters. They infinitely inhabit this Kingdome, but most Especially on the back Side thereof, vizt. towards Arackan, where they Enjoy a great part of the Countrey with great freedom, none dareinge to molest them. I have heard of Some Mahometans and Persians, resolute fellows, that have attempted to goe amongst them on purpose to Molest them by force of arms, but when they have come thither neare theire very houses and Pagods, they have Stood like to as many Naturalls gazeinge one Upon another, many of them dyinge very Suddenly, and those that returned never came to be well in theire Senses, nor indeed lived above one yeare after, lingringe away most lamentably.

They are Reputed to be very wise Philosophers[2], and doe really and with great Zeale Study the Pithagorean Philosophy. They are alsoe great Students in the art of Poyson soe much in Esteeme amonge the Eastern inhabitants. In fine, they are reverenced by the common Natives more like Gods then men[3]. And by the wisest

---

[1] Compare *Tavernier*, vol. i. part ii. pp. 161, 179, "The Bramins ...are the Successors of the ancient Brachmans, or Indian Philosophers, that study'd Astrology. You may also meet with some of their Ancient Books, in reading whereof the Brammins spend all their time; and are so vers'd in their observations, that they never fail a minute in the Eclipses of the Sun and Moon...Every Bramin has his Magick Book, wherein are abundance of Circles and Semicircles, Squares, Triangles, and several sorts of Cifers."

[2] See p. 28. Compare *Fryer*, pp. 33 and 191, "Their Doctors of Divinity are the Brachmins, who instruct them in their Law, to preserve all Creatures that are beneficial, and teach them the old Pythagorean Metempsychosis, Transmigration of Souls, out of one body into another...Sciences in esteem among them are principally Magick and Judicial Astrology, one of the Sectators of which on all accounts are consulted, as well by Moors as Gentues."

[3] See p. 23.

Europeans that Sometime doe converse with them with great freedom, they are said to be great Astronomers and Philosophers, as before mentioned, and are called (very properly) Gimnosophists[1].

I Commend them not at all for theire Sorceries, nor Enchantments, nor Others theire Devilish inventions, but for theire ready and admirable discourse and civilities to all Europeans and Christians in generall[2], for they will Scorne to doe any of us the least Injurie in word or deed, if wee doe not first put Some grosse affront upon them.

Many of these Gymnosophists are dispersed into most Villages in the kingdome, and have the tuition both of the Gentues and Orixas, both being an Idolatrous people. What differences are betweene them is chiefely in theire funeralls as beforementioned. In most Other Idolatrous Ceremonies they agree, in Worshippinge Gods of Sundry Shapes and Mettles[3], much adoreinge their Brachmans, Owneinge the Transmigration of Souls, and doe in generall Worship the Cow with great reverence[4].

Now a word or two of theire Women. Moneys is nowadays soe much coveted, that by many people it is not much prick of conscience how it is acquired, and hath soe corrupted good laws that most Governours in Asia (for theire owne interest's sake) doe allow that any woman (Moore, Gentue, or Ouria) unmarried may lawfully turne common Whore, and leave her relations, and take her habitation amonge Other Whores in Small Villages Separated from any married folkes houses, payinge soe much per mensem to the Governour of that part of the Countrie, and

---

[1] The old term for the Indian philosophers because of their scanty clothing.

[2] See p. 32.. [3] See pp. 6 and 15.

[4] See p. 8 and note. Compare *Fryer*, p. 33, "The Soul of a Good Man is believed to depart into a Cow, wherefore 'tis Sacrilege with them to kill a Cow or a Calf."

Every thursday night repaire to the Governours and Cattwalls[1], i.e. the Justice of peace his house, before whom they doe and must dance and Singe, and make many Salams[2]. Then the handsomest of them must Stay all night to Suppresse the Leachery of him and his Punes[3], a very handsome preparative for the next day which is theire Sabbath[4]. Yet, if a married Woman commit the fact of Adultery, She is punished with death.

Neither the Moors nor Gentues of accompt admitt theire Wifes or Concubines to gad abroad, but keep them within doors, attended with Eunuchs and younge Girles[5]. They adorne them with rich Jewels and attire, haveing great Sheckles of Gold upon theire leggs and wrists, Chaines of Gold and necklaces of pearle about their necks, rich and very costly pendants of Gold sett with Diamonds or Pearle in theire Ears; some have rings quite round the Eare &c.[6]

---

[1] See *Hobson-Jobson*, *s.v.* Cotwal. T. B. in his *Malay Dict.* has, "Catawal, a Marshall, or chief Officer of a City under the Governour, to keep the Peace." *Schouten*, vol. i. p. 421, has, "The Catoal who was the civil Judge." Compare *Fryer*, p. 97, "delivered to the Catwal, or Sheriff's Men," and the following from the Hugli Diary of the 19th August, 1678 (*Factory Records*, Hugli, No. 1), "The new Catwall sent to us to buy a quarter of a yard of Scarlet which we gave him because he has had no present since the Droga put him in"; also the following from the *Diary and Consultation Book* of Fort William for 23rd Feb. 1705, quoted by Wilson, *Early Annals*, vol. i. p. 266, "There having been several robberies committed in the Black Town, ordered that a corporal and six soldiers be sent to lodge in the Catwall's house, to be upon call to prevent the like in future."

[2] See note on p. 38. Compare *Schouten*, vol. ii. p. 193, "The salutation which they [the natives of Hugli] make, when they meet each other, is called Salamma."

[3] See note on p. 83. [4] See *Schouten*, vol. ii. p. 196.

[5] Compare *Fryer*, p. 31, "The Moors are by Nature plagued with Jealousy, cloistering their Wives up, and sequestring them the sight of any besides the Tapon [Capon, *i.e.* eunuch] that watches them."

[6] Compare *Fryer*, p. 31, "Their [the Gentue] Women are manacled with Chains of Silver (or Fetters rather) and hung with Ear-rings of Gold and jewels, their Noses stretch'd with weighty Jewels, on their Toes Rings of Gold, about their Waste a painted Clout, over their Shoulders they cast a Mantle; their Hair tied behind their Head (which both in men and women is naturally very long): a-top a Coronet of Gold beset with Stones."

The Ourias (as I said before)[1] are very poore, weare noe better habit then a Lungee[2], or a white cloth made fast about theire waste, with great brasse Sheckels upon theire arms and leggs, and great brasse rings Upon theire tows[3]. Many of them have the Shackles on theire arms made of Chanke[4], a great Shell brought from Tutacree (a Dutch Factorie neare the Cape Comorin)[5]. The

---

[1] See p. 199.

[2] See note on p. 56.

[3] See p. 35.

[4] This is an early instance of the European corruption of *sankha*, the vernacular name for the conch shell. See *Hobson-Jobson*, *s.v.* Chank. Compare the following contemporary references: "Your Chancke as I have formerly advized cannot for the present yeild any good price here, [Dacca] till the Contract made amonge the Chanck men expire." Letter to Balasor, 26th June, 1673, *O. C.* No. 3805. "The Dutch have...had another [ship] from Zeylone laden with Beetle nuts and Chank." Letter from Hugli, 31st March, 1674, *Factory Records*, Hugli, No. 4. "In the after noone George Herron came to the Factory adviseing the Sloope *Arrivall* was at Tannah...haveing a load of Chanck upon fraught." Edward Reade's Diary at Hugli, 8th April, 1677, *Factory Records*, Hugli, No. 1. "A Dutch ship Arrived from Zielon with Beeteell nutts Chank &c." Hugli Diary, 12th March, 1680, *Factory Records*, Hugli, No. 2. "On yesterday arrived in the Roade a small ship of Chimchams and Chintemanshaw coming last from Concherina [? copyist's error for Cochin China] with 5 Eliphants some shanck and a few cloves." Balasor Diary, 1st April, 1684, *Factory Records*, Balasor, No. 1.

[5] The Chank or Chunk (*i.e.* Conch-shell) Fishery still has its headquarters at Tuticorin (Tūttukkudi), which was a Dutch Factory from 1658 off and on to 1825. See *Hobson-Jobson*, *s.v.* Tuticorin. It was the last possession of the Portuguese on the Coromandel Coast. Compare *Schouten*, vol. i. pp. 311, 312, 314, "The next day [20th November, 1661] about noon, we passed by the little town of Tutocorin, celebrated for the pearl-fishery, in which there are only two other places which can compare with it, namely Ormus...and Aynan on the coast of China...the Portuguese formerly made great profit from the fishery at Tutocorin...Tutocorin is quite open, having neither walls nor ramparts, so that it was not difficult for the Dutch to obtain possession of it when they attacked it in the year 1658." The English chiefly valued Tuticorin on account of the pepper it produced, but their factory there was not a success. In 1664 a ship was sent from Fort St George to fetch away the "remaynes" (*Letter Book*, No. 3, p. 448) and it was decided to leave only one or two young factors in the place to prevent the Dutch from taking possession of it. In Jan. 1665 (*O. C.* No. 3037+1) the Council at Fort St George wrote to England, "A Factory at Tutacorey may be advantagious." No steps however appear to have been taken to settle the place. In Aug. 1668 (*Letter Book*, No. 4) the Court ordered the Factors at Fort St George

Shell is as bigge or bigger then a man's fist, hollow, and are Sawed into rings, and soe worne by the people of Orixa and Bengala. Some weare them white (theire Naturall colour), and Others will have them painted redd, but both are esteemed highly as a rich Ornament.

The River of Ganges is of large and wonderfull Extent[1]. Once I went through a Small rivolet of it called Dobra within the Isle of Cocks, and came into the great River, which rather deserves to be called the Sea of Ganges. The breadth of it there I cannot certainely affirme, but judge it is not less then 10 English leags broad, which is about 40 miles within Ganga Sagar, or the mouth of it[2]. Many

---

"to procure what Pepper possible from Tutticorie" but gave no further directions as to the re-establishment of a Factory. Compare the following curious contemporary spellings of the name of the place: "October the 9th [1673] We fell In with the Land of Tutucroyn." Journal of Capt. Wm. Basse, *O. C.* No. 3983. "Tentecorrey where the Dutch have a small Fort." Letter from Calicut to Surat in 1678, *O. C.* No. 4389. See also Alex. Hamilton, *East Indies*, vol. iii. p. 334.

[1] See note on p. 166.

[2] By the Ganges the writer means the Hugli, the westernmost mouth of the great river, but his remarks show his personal acquaintance with the Hugli estuary. In the very many changes that have taken place since his day the "Isle of Cocks" has merged, with the Isle of Dogs, into Saugor Island. Saugor is properly called Ganga Sagar, so that our author not only knew the proper name but by an accident spelt it as it would be transliterated at the present day. For Cock Island, Cock's Island, Coxe's Island, with translations I. de Gale, Island de Gallo, I. de Galinha, see Yule, *Hedges' Diary*, vol. ii. p. 207. To the information there given I would add that I. de Gale occurs in two maps *circ.* 1720 and again in 1745 and 1785. In a French map by Pierre Mortier of Amsterdam *circ.* 1720 it occurs as Igale, and in a map by Rennell, 1781, as Coxes's I. I would further remark for the history of the word that *Valentyn* (1660), vol. v. p. 152 ff. has "Ilha de Gala which is one mile in circumference...and Sagor," and further, p. 159, he has "Sagor or Ilha da Galinha." *Schouten*, vol. ii. p. 142 f. has (Jan. 1664) "We saw...the isles of Gale and of Lagor [probably a misprint for Sagor]." About 1668, *Bernier*, p. 176, has "island of Galles near Cape das Palmas," but meaning the Isle of Cocks. *De Graaf*, the Dutch surgeon, has (*Voyages aux Indes Orientales*, p. 43, Oct. 1669) "Near the Ilho de Gale we went up the Ganges." In the *Diary of Streynsham Master* under dates 7th Sept. and 2nd Dec. 1676, pp. 57 and 275, we find, "This morning wee came faire by the Arracan Shoare and by the Dutch boyes, and came to an anchor at the mouth of the River neare the ile of Coxes...We sailed by Kedgeree and the Island of Ingerley leaving the ile of Cockes and the Arracan shoare

incredible reports I have heard concerninge this River, which are not now incredible to me, since I have Seen much of it my Selfe. Certain it is that this is the great River Ganges that Alexander the great Sailed downe in time of his great conquests in Asia, &c.[1] It disperseth its Streams through

on our Larboard side to the East." In a letter from Hugli to Balasor, 4th Jan. 1679, *Factory Records*, Hugli, No. 5, we have, "Wee admire the *Falcon* was not arrived with us...She being seen by the *Ganges* then Comeing hither off the Isle of Cocks"; and in another letter from Hugli, 19th June, 1680 (*Factory Records*, Fort St George, No. 28) "Had she [the *Bengall Merchant*] gone as intended through the great Channell by the Isle of Cocks, she might have obtained the Freight ere the Europe ships had departed thence for England." Our author in his chart of the "River of Hugly," made in 1687, has, on the left bank, "Sagor, Cox's Ild., Rogues, River of Rogues." Sir Edward Littleton in 1704 called the place Isle of Coxe's, see Yule, *Hedges' Diary*, vol. ii. p. 204. In the Log of the *King George*, *Marine Records*, No. 402 B, under dates 27th Dec. 1718 and 6th Jan. 1719, we have, "This day having Received an Order of the Govr. and Councill of a Pilott to Carry me from Rogues River to Cox's I took my Leave of Calcutta...Att ½ past 3 Anchored at Coxs's in 6 Fathoms, Langtialu creek East and the West end of Sago S b E ½ East." Alex. Hamilton, *East Indies*, vol. ii. p. 4, says that "Coxes and Sagor Islands" are more remarkable than the rest. Compare Horsburgh, *India Directory*, ed. 1809, p. 360, "Sagor or Sauger Island...bounds the great entrance of the river Hoogly on the east side, being 7 or 8 miles in length, and about half that in breadth...The Brahmins call the island Gongo-Sagor, but the natives generally understand Gongo-Sagor to be the whole of the land that separates Channel Creek from the western branch of Hoogly River, except the small island contiguous to the north end of Sagor, called Coxe's Island, which is near a league in length, and two miles broad, and bounds the N.E. side of Sagor Road."

I gather that the Dobra "rivolet" is the narrow stream shown in the 1703 "Pilot" map behind Cocks Island. In Mortier's map above mentioned occurs Dbril in the same situation, but as an Island. In Rennell's map, 1781, occurs in the neighbourhood the "Doo-Agra R., the passage through to the Sunderbunds." The creek East of Cock Island is called by Hedges the "Oyster River," see Yule, *Hedges' Diary*, vol. i. p. 68, where we find "This afternoon [11th March, 1683] we stood off towards Sagor, and anchored between Cock Island and the Oyster River."

May not the terms Galinha, Gallo, Galle, Cock, however, refer to the Portuguese themselves, considering the neighbourhood and the depredations therein by Magh and Portuguese half-castes? In Terry's *Voyage to East India*, 1655, we find, p. 153, "The truth is that the Portugals, especially those which are born in those Indian Colonys most of them a mix'd seed begotten upon those Natives are a very low poor-spirited people, called therefore Galiinas dell Mar, the Hens of the Sea."

[1] Compare *Schouten*, vol. ii. p. 145, "The next day [17th Jan.

many Spacious deserts and multitudes of Kingdoms, and is knowne to be of greater breadth in many places Up in the Countreys of Pattana[1] and South Tartaria[2].

Formerly, yea not many years agoe, the Inhabitants on the Northerne parts of Bengala trained up their Children (from theire infancie) to Eeat raw fish and flesh, and when growne Up Sent them upon travaile to discover the great Ganges, to find out the garden of Eden (by Order of theire Kings), but few or none Ever made returne, ergo now quite left off as a thinge Impossible to be accomplished.

Many Isles there be in the mouth of the Ganges, not inhabited more then with wild beasts[3], the Natives much

---

1664] we again set sail, and we passed the wood called Sandri, where it is said that Alexander the Great formerly stopped, on seeing the great and dangerous rivers that he had to pass in order to get to a country which was unknown to him; so that he thought it best to limit his conquests, and he went back to Macedonia. It is held to be a fact in these countries that he had conquered India as far as this famous river of the Ganges, and that he reached as far as this wood."

[1] John Marshall, the Company's Factor at Balasor, who died in 1677, in his *Notes and Observations of East India*, 1668—1672, *Harleian MS.*, British Museum, No. 4254, differs from T. B. in his estimate of the width and grandeur of the Ganges. He says, "The Ganges river is in some places about a mile broad, and in many not halfe a mile, and in some not a quarter of a mile, and in two or one places about ⅓ of mile broad when the water is low as in Aprill when the river is almost dry in many places from one side of it to the other, and very Shallow in many places not 3 foot deep, soe that boats have much to doe to pass, however without great trouble not knowing where is deepe where is shallow, but when the water is at its height which is about middle September, then it is very broad and deep, In this River untill come about Rojimall [Rajmahal] are many Alligators, and as far as Pattana, very many Porpoises, also towards Pattana very many Pellicans and other great birds."

[2] See note on p. 172.

[3] Compare *Schouten*, vol. ii. p. 143, "The sixteenth of January [1664] we passed by the river of Jillisar, which was on our left. Here the shores of the Ganges are covered with bushes, thickets, and little woods, which extend some distance inland and in which there are many serpents, rhinoceroses, wild buffaloes, and especially tigers. For this reason the people of Bengala do not dare to dwell in those parts of their country nearest to the sea. Therefore, on our way we only saw one little clay fort, where some negroes were existing wretchedly enough." Compare also Alex. Hamilton, *East Indies*, vol. ii. p. 4 f., "There are no Inhabitants on those Islands [at the mouth of

dreadinge to dwell there, beinge timerous of the Arackaners with theire Gylyars[1], who many times have come through the Rivers and carried away Captive many poore families of the Orixa folke[2].

Some 20 leags from the Sea and Soe Upwards this Countrey is blessed with many faire Villages and Markett towns, fine green banks, and delicate Groves, with Store of brave fish ponds, good Store of Venison and wilde fowle.

---

the Ganges] for they are so pestered with Tigers, that there could be no Security for human Creatures to dwell on them; nay, it is even dangerous to land on them, or for Boats to anchor near them, for in the Night they have swimmed to Boats at Anchor, and carried Men out of them, yet among the Pagans, the Island Sagor is accounted holy, and great Numbers of Jougies go yearly thither in the Months of November and December to worship and wash in Salt-water, tho' many of them fall Sacrifices to the hungry Tigers." See also *Bernier*, p. 442 f.

[1] For many forms of the word Gylyar (*jaliā*), war-boat, see note on p. 140.

[2] Compare *Schouten*, vol. ii. p. 143, "We saw on our right another large river...which came from the Kingdom of Aracan. We there espied some jeliasses of that country, which were in that region in order to make seizures."

In the *Diary of Streynsham Master*, pp. 115 and 275, there are two allusions to the "Arackaners": "This day [8th Sept. 1676] wee passed by the river which goes to Chittygom and Dacca which the English call the river of Rogues by reason the Arracaners used to come out thence to Rob.... Tannay is distant from Hugly about 40 miles by water and twenty miles by land, there stands an old Fort of mud walls which was built to prevent the incursions of the Arracaners, for it seemes about ten or twelve yeares since they were soe bold that none durst inhabit lower down the river then this place, the Arracanners usually takeing the People off the shoare to sell them at Pipley." Compare also the following: "This day [24th Dec. 1678] came a generall Letter from Dacca dated the 16th Current advising...That the Arracaners had taken 14 boates about Chatagaum." *Factory Records*, Hugli, No. 2. In a letter from Hugli to Dacca, 11th May, 1679, *Factory Records*, Hugli, No. 5, the Council at Hugli objected to lend the Company's sloops "on all Occations to fight against the Aracanners till they are Conquerd which according to all likelihood will never be." On the 28th Sept. 1687, *Letter Book*, No. 8, the Court wrote to Bengal, "We are not affraid...of the worst the Mogull can do against us there [at Chittagong] while we have the Raccaners to friend and can let their War Boats loose to prey upon the Moors in all parts of the Ganges."

Cossumbazar.

A Very famous and pleasant towne, famous in many respects, first and Chiefely for its great commerce and plenty of very rich Merchants, the onely market place in this Kingdome for all Commodities made and vended therein, whence it received this name, Cossum signifieinge the husband or Chiefe, and Bazar a markett[1].

The English and Dutch Companies have each a very Stately Factorie here, but the English out doe them here both in trade and alsoe in theire Factorie and Factors too[2].

---

[1] Kāsim is, however, a common Muhammadan proper name, and the town had its name no doubt from some eponymous Kāsim Khān. See *Hobson-Jobson*, *s.v.* Cossumbazar. See *Ind. Ant.* vol. xxviii. p. 294.

[2] The English Factory at Kasimbazar was established in 1658 with John Ken as Chief. Compare *Tavernier*, vol. ii. (last chapter), on The Commodities brought out of the Dominions of the Great Mogul: "Kasembasar, a Village in the Kingdom of Bengala, sends abroad every year two and twenty thousand Bales of Silk; every Bale weighing a hunder'd pound...The Hollanders usually carry away six or seven thousand Bales." In the *Diary of Streynsham Master* there are references to Kasimbazar on the 23rd Sept. and 8th Nov. 1676, pp. 63 and 259, "Att nine a Clock wee sett forward and at noone mett Senr. Verburg the Cheife of the Dutch at Cassambazar and three others with him. By the river side about the middle of the Towne wee passed by the spot of ground aloted to the French. Att three a Clock in the afternoone God be praised wee arrived safe at the Honble. Companys Factory at the farther end of the Towne of Cassambazar... Whilst I was at Cassambazar which was about six weekes time the water did fall in the river about five fathome right up and down. All the Country or great part thereof about Cassambazar is planted or sett with Mullberry trees the leaves of which are gathered young to feed the wormes with and make the silk fine, and therefore the trees are planted every yeare...The Towne of Cassambazar is about two miles long and in some places the streets where the marketts are kept are soe narrow that a Pallanqueen can but just passe in them." Of Kasimbazar, Alex. Hamilton, *East Indies*, vol. ii. p. 21, says, "Cassembazaar, about 200 Miles above Hughly, where the English and Dutch have their respective Factories...The Town is large, and much frequented by Merchants, which never fails of making a Place rich. The Country about it is very healthful and fruitful, and produces industrious People, who cultivate many valuable Manufactories."

John Marshall, *Notes and Observations*, p. 20 (reverse) says of the Dutch Factory at Kasimbazar, "[It] is made of brick, very large and hath handsome gardens belong[ing] to it, it is about a mile from the English Factory."

Our Honourable East India Company hath a very Considerable investment annually in this place, more then in all the Kingdome besides. The Chiefe here is Secound to all their Affaires in Orixa, Bengala, and Pattana[1]. Hee keepeth many tradesmen att worke here by Order of the Company, as dyers, Weavers, throwsters, &c. beinge English men sent on purpose for the Orderinge theire Silks after the English Custome[2], and

---

[1] Compare Alex. Hamilton, *East Indies*, vol. ii. p. 21, "The English and Dutch have their respective Factories [at Kasimbazar]; and, by their Companies Orders, the Seconds of Council ought to be Chiefs of those Factories." The Chiefs at Kasimbazar during the 10 years comprised in T. B.'s "Account" were John Marsh, Matthias Vincent, and Sir Edward Littleton.

[2] At the end of the *Diary of Streynsham Master*, pp. 326—330, there is an account, by Matthias Vincent, of "The manner of the Silk and Taffaty Investments in Cassambazar." He says, Para. 7, "In dyeing the silk black looses about 1/7 and the Colours 1/4 of what it weighed when delivered the Dyer, when the silk comes from the Dyer it is charged with the same value it was in the whole, when put downe to be dyed, the dyed Silk both Orgazine and tram are delivered as they come from the Dyer to the weaver, who winds and warps them and fits the same himselfe for his worke...for his whole workmanship he receives one rupee twelve annaes per peece of 20 Covids long, whether 1½ or 2 Covids wide...." There are frequent references to the "diers and Throwsters" at Kasimbazar in the contemporary records. In 1668 Roger Fowler was sent out by the Court as a dyer to Kasimbazar at a salary of £60 per annum. Orders were given "to treate him civilly...hee being an ancient person, and one who hath lived in good repute in London till it pleased God to make him a Sufferer in the late dreadful fire." *Letter Book*, No. 4, p. 202. In many cases the "diers and Throwsters" went to India as soldiers or sailors and afterwards obtained permission to change their occupations. The lads, too, who were designed for the pilot service, frequently proved too weakly for "the river" and were sent up to the silk factory at Kasimbazar. Among the dyers, we find, in 1677, "John Nayler Silk dier came out in 1670 under contract to serve 4 years at £50 per annum"; "Richard Mosely came out a Souldier" in 1669, and in 1671 became a Dyer at "souldiers pay"; Anthony Smith came out soldier in 1672, and became a dyer in 1674. Many of the weavers were natives, but there were exceptions, *e.g.* Michaell Loveney, who came out a soldier in 1672 and became a Silk Weaver in 1675. In March, 1676, the Council at Fort St George wrote to Hugli (*Factory Records*, Fort St George, No. 18), "Wee have...given leave for one Throwster...to goe downe along with Mr. Clavell for the Honble. Companys Service at Cassumbazar." And in the Hugli Diary for 25th Oct. 1678 (*Factory Records*, Hugli, No. 1), we find, "We wrote to Mr. Littleton &c. and sent up a Throster which we procured out of the *Faulcon* to make tryall of and if good at the Trade we would

for dyinge a good black, a colour the Natives cold never dye well[1].

Wee goe up by water from Hugly, vizt. through the Rivers, I judge it is 150 miles up, commonly 3 days goeinge Up, very pleasant all the way, a fertile Soyle and a delicate Aire, beinge a most healthy Climate[2].

Not farre above the towne of Cossumbazar doe inhabit many of the Earnest and devout Idolatrous Priests (called Brachmans)[3], who are much reverenced all Asia over, in soe

---

get the Captain to Clear him for our Masters Serviss." On the 14th Nov. 1678 the factors at Kasimbazar wrote to Hugli (*Factory Records*, Hugli, No. 7), "John Gryffeth our former throoster...intends to returne home ...Soe that wee Shall have occasion for one to minde that imployment."

The output from Kasimbazar was considerable. Entries like the following are frequent: "In the afternoone [31st July, 1676] arrived five boates with 309 bales Silke and 7 Chests of ordinary taffatyes from Cassumbazar." *Factory Records*, Hugli, No. 1.

[1] The Directors at home lost no opportunity of urging their servants in India to perfect the art of dyeing at Kasimbazar. In Dec. 1671, they wrote (*Letter Book*, No. 4, p. 506), "Wee are glad to see that our Factory of Cassambazar is so well improved, Wee now give you directions for our Investments and also send you patternes of Taffaties, Wee see the fancy of that people are much upon mixt collours, and that they have not skill to dye good Blacks and Greenes and Watchetts, But wee hope our Dyers hath soe farr improved, that wee shall receive some Competent supply...." When this letter reached Bengal, Vincent wrote from Kasimbazar to Clavell at Hugli (*Factory Records*, Misc. No. 3), "Wee have shewed the Patterns Come on the *Rebecca* to our Weavers, whoe all with one Voyce Say, they can only make of the Deepe yellow and Sallow Collours, the Greene, Carnation, Pinck, Sky couller and black they can no wayes make good. A redd, though far short of the Carnation Some of them Say they Can Make...." In Dec. 1672 Robert Coale "experienced in dying of Blacks" was sent to the "Bay," and in Dec. 1674 John Edwards "whome we hope will be more Successfull in bringing to perfection the dyeing of Blacks and Green Silks." *Letter Book*, No. 5.

[2] Compare the *Diary of Streynsham Master*, p. 259, 8th Nov. 1676, "The soile of Bengala is very fertile being a kind of loose fat earth and in some places a fatt sand. There is not one mountaine or Hill to be seen about Hugly or Cassambazar the Country being all plaine and Levell and tho any thing will grow by reason of the fertileness of the soile yett firewood is scarce and timber bad and very deare."

Hunter, *Imperial Gazetteer of India*, *s.v.* Kasimbazar, says, p. 81, "The decay of Kasimbazar dates from the beginning of the present century, when its climate, which had previously been celebrated for salubrity, underwent an unexplained change for the worse, so that the margin of cultivation receded and wild beasts increased."

[3] See pp. 13, 23, 33.

much that the water and mudde of the Ganges Sent from them with theire Choppe[1] or Seale Upon it is accompted Sacred, Even soe farre as Persia. When in the yeare [?][2] I went from Bengales thither, wee had Severall Mortavan[3] Jarrs on board, some full of water, Others of Mudde of the River Ganges, sent as presents to the great Merchants of the Banjan Cast[4] in this Kingdome, and Sealed with the great Brachmans Choppe (otherwise of noe Esteeme)[5]. Att our arrivall in Gombroone[6], Severall of them came on board soe Soone as [they] heard of the holy present, and carried them on Shore with great reverence. There they Used it Very Sparingly; onely Sprinklinge some Upon theire face and bodies when they went to prayer, and puttinge a little of the Mudd Upon their forehead breast and arms, believeinge it added much delight to theire Souls.

Such is the Ignorance of these men, whoe are soe ripe witted in most affaires of worldly businesse. But the greatest delight the Mahometans take is in keepinge Whores and Elephants [Plate XI.], the greatest Easterne State.

The Coyned Currant moneys of this Kingdome are rupees[7], halfe rupees, and quarters—a very good Sort of

---

[1] See p. 118 and note.

[2] The gap in the MS. is very tantalizing. Had the date been given, it might have been possible to find among the India Office records some note of the writer's movements during the first ten years of his stay in India.

[3] Martaban. See p. 81 and note.

[4] See p. 27.

[5] Compare *Tavernier*, vol. i. part ii. p. 181, for the use of Ganges water at weddings: "But the greatest expence to those that live three or four hundred Leagues from it, is to get the water of Ganges; for in regard they account that water sacred, and drink it out of devotion, it must be brought them by the Bramins, and in Earthen Vessels, glaz'd within side, which the chief Bramin of Ingrenate [? Juggernaut] fills himself with the purest Water of the River, and then seals up with his own Seal...."

[6] The old name for Bandar Abbas in the Persian Gulf. See *Hobson-Jobson*, *s.v.* Gombroon. Agent Thomas Rolt was Chief of the English Factory at Gombroon during the greater part of the time comprised in T. B.'s "Account."

[7] See p. 114 and note.

fine Silver moneys Coyned in the Mint at Dacca, and are of the Same Value of those in Guzaratt or Golcondah.

They alsoe Coyne Rupees here of the finest refined Gold, which are called gold Moors[1]. They are of the same Stampe, magnitude, and weight the Silver ones are, but, beinge gold of the highest Matt[2], they passe very currant at 15¼ and 15½ rupees each.

They weigh per the Maund[3], Seere[4], ½ Seere, and ¼ Seere, but theire weight in most places of accompt differ, although not in name, yet in quantitie.

The Ballasore Maund contains 75 pound weight.

The Hugly Maund contains but 70 pound weight.

Cossumbazar maund contains but 68 pound weight. Graine, butter, Oyle, or any liquid thinge, all the River of Hugly over, allows but 68 pound to the maund. The Maund, bigg or little, is Equally divided into 40 Equall parts, and are called Seers, which alsoe are halfed and quartered[5].

---

[1] Mohurs. See note on p. 148. Compare the following from *Factory Records*, Hugli, No. 5, "For the Silk you had best putt off Mohurs otherwise you will be put to great Inconvenience....Mohurs being as you see fallen 2 rs. 5 a. per Mohur...Wee alwaies Looked upon Gold as Merchandize it being soe even when coined into Mohurs"; Letters from Hugli to Kasimbazar, 15th Feb. and 4th March, 1679, and 22nd Oct. 1680.

[2] See *Hobson-Jobson*, *s.v.* Matt. Matt meant the "touch of gold." *N. and E.* has (p. 17) a good quotation for 6th May, 1680: "The payment or receipt of Batta or Vatum [difference in exchange] upon the exchange of Pollicat for Madras Pagodas prohibited, both coines being of one and the same Matt and weight, upon pain of forfeiture of 24 Pagodas for every offence together with loss of the Batta."

[3] See note on p. 116.

[4] See *Hobson-Jobson*, *s.v.* Seer, the well-known Indian weight, standardized now-a-days at, roughly, 2 lbs.

[5] The big maund (Bengal) was 82 lbs. and the little maund (Madras) 25 lbs.: so the seer should have varied between 10 and 33 oz. Compare John Marshall, *Notes and Observations of East India*, "25 pound make a Maund [at Masulipatam] 25 Maunds make a Candy soe 625 pounds make a Candy...At Ballasore the Maund which is 40 seer is 74¾ or 75 pound English...At Hugly the Maund is 40 seer or 73 pound, and Cowries 5, 6, and some times 10 per Cent. dearer than at Ballasore. At Pattana the maund is 40 seer or 78 pound, besides the custom of the place is to allow 2 seer in every maund."

They measure timber, planke, brick or Stone walls, Callicoes, Silks, &c., per the Guz[1] (each Guz doth contain 27 inches), and by the Covet[2] which contains 18 inches, and is called hawt[3].

They very Seldome Sell graine but by weight.

The Gold Moore is Valued att 01 lb. 14s. 10½d.

The Rupee att 00 lb. 02s. 03d.[4]

Theire Small moneys called Cowries[5], beinge Small Shells taken out of the Sea, passe very currant by tale.

One Gunda[6] is	4 Couries
5 Gundas is one burrie[7] or	20 cowries
4 burries make 1 Pone[8] or	80 cowries
16 Pone make 1 Cawne[9] or	1280 cowries
2 Cawne & ½ make 1 rupee or	3200 cowries[10].

---

[1] See *Hobson-Jobson, s.v.* Gudge. T. B. in his *Malay Dict.* has, "Gaz, a measure about a yard long." John Marshall in his *Notes and Observations of East India*, says, "The measure by which English cloth is sold is a Guzz which is 41¾ English inches...here is also [at Patna] a little Guz called the Taylors Guz which is but 32¼ inches." Compare also the following in a letter from Ambrose Salisbury to Masulipatam, 26th Dec. 1672, *Factory Records*, Masulipatam, No. 9, "I must desire you to Send 6 Guzz or yards of Scarlett against my returne."

[2] See *Hobson-Jobson, s.v.* Covid. The covid is a cubit or ell. In the Hugli Diary, under date 6th June, 1679, *Factory Records*, Hugli, No. 2, there is the entry, "Wee wrote to Ballasore advising that wee should want about 20 Timbers of about 18 Covads long."

Compare John Marshall's account of measures in *Notes and Observations*, p. 9, "In Indostan they measure by Barly cornes placeing the small ends of them together so that they touch each other and then they are circular, 8 Barlicornes breadth so placed make one Angle [*anguli*] or finger breadth, 24 Angles make one Covet or measure from the Elbow to the end of long finger, 4 Covets make one Dun [*dhanu*], 2000 Duns make 1 Course [*kōs*] in Indostand which is about 2¼ English miles."

[3] *i.e. hāth.* See *Hobson-Jobson, s.v.* Haut.

[4] Compare John Marshall, *Notes and Observations on East India*, "Rupie...valued here [Balasor] in the Companys books at 2.6 per piece but in no other place valued at more than 2.3."

[5] See pp. 180 and 200 and notes. See *Ind. Ant.* vol. xxvii. pp. 38 and 41.

[6] Neither Gunda, Burrie, Pone nor Cawne is to be found in *Hobson-Jobson*. The word is *gaṇḍā*. See *Ind. Ant.* vol. xxvii. p. 171 f. for the system of counting by *gaṇḍās* or quartettes.

[7] *i.e. bauṛī.* [8] *i.e. paṇ. Op. cit. loc. cit.* [9] *i.e. kāhan.*

[10] This is a valuable contemporary account of the cowry. The table intended here is, 4 *kauṛīs* = 1 *gaṇḍā*, 5 *gaṇḍās* = 1 *bauṛī*, 4 *bauṛīs*

Plate XI

p. 198.

"A BARBAROUS PENALTY."

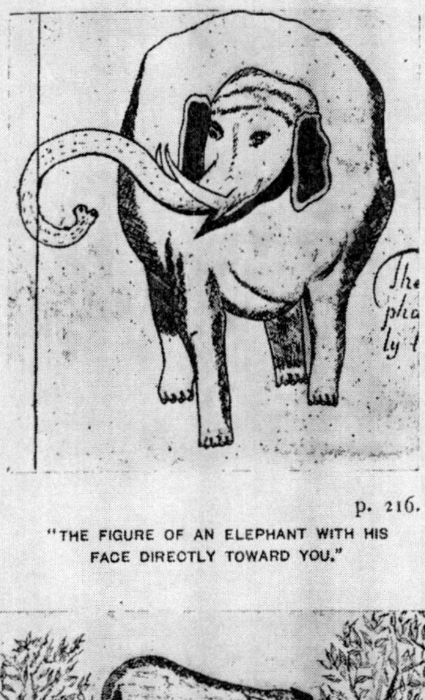

p. 216.

"THE FIGURE OF AN ELEPHANT WITH HIS FACE DIRECTLY TOWARD YOU."

p. 219.

"THE TYGER."

They Seldome rise or fall more then 2 Pone in one Rupee, and that onely in Ballasore at the arrivall of the Ships from Insulae Maldivae[1].

The Woods of this Kingdome are well replenished with wild beasts, most Especially with Tygers and Bears of Vast largenesse, and the most fierce of any in the knowne world: those about the Ganges are Soe accompted. They are of Such a bloody Salvage Nature, that if they meet with a Cow, a deere, or any Other Annimal that hath been newly killed by Shot, or what else, they will not meddle therewith, but will rather Suffer most rageinge hunger, by reason they had not the killinge of it themselvs[2].

Many of the poore Ourias[3] are destroyed by them,

=1 *pan*, 16 *pans*=1 *kāhan*, 2½ *kāhans*=1 rupee. See *Ind. Ant.*, vol. xxvi. p. 290 f. Compare John Marshall, *Notes and Observations of East India*, "All the small Money is Cowries which rise and fall according to the plenty or scarcity of them, some times 31, 37, 38, 39, 40 Pond going for a Rupie, every Pond always consisting of 80 Cowries." This statement varies greatly from T.B.'s. His rise and fall is 6¼ per cent., but Marshall's is 22½ per cent. Compare also the following in "Instructions to Mr. Stanley for the Maldevees" from the Court, 20th Sept. 1682, *Letter Book*, No. 7, "Cowries are sold by tale and not by weight...80 Cowrees is a Pome, and 40 Pome or 42 as you can agree, may be bought for 6 or 7 Annees at Maldevees, and in a peece of 8/8 are accounted there 32 Annees: So that for the value of a peece of 8/8 you may buy 2400 [240] or 250 pome: And according to the best account which we have from Surratt as they are usually bought there, they cannot cost above 2 pieces of 8/8 per Cwt. or thereabouts." The above figures are not exact, but they show a great profit in the Cowry traffic, as they were purchased at the Maldives at 9,000 to 10,000 the rupee and sold in Bengal at 2500 to 3200 the rupee.

[1] See notes on pp. 104 and 200.

[2] Compare *Schouten*, vol. ii. pp. 278—281, "Tigers and leopards, which are very common in the whole of India, have also their lairs in the woods, and especially in these low lying districts of Bengal, which have not yet been cultivated....The tigers of Bengal are as large as calves....The tigers even dare to attack men on horseback, and the most powerful buffaloes, which they tear in pieces alive." T. B., in his *Chart of the Hugli*, marks on the right bank, "Ri. Tygers." *N. and E.* p. 40, for 27th Aug. 1679, has, "On the voyage [from Hugli to Balasor] an Englishman belonging to the *Ganges* being ashore on an Island shooting, was carried off by a tiger, the Master of the vessel seeing him but not being able to help him."

[3] See note on p. 130.

Especially of those that get a livelyhood by makeinge Salt or cuttinge wood neare the mouth of the Ganges[1]. Upon my returne of a Voyadge to the Maldivae[2], I lost 3 men by theire Salvagenesse. I sent them On Shore upon Cocks Island[3] to cut wood, well armed and with Order to keep togeather near the boat: but they carelessly dispersed themselves, and 3 were torne in pieces by the Tygers, vizt. two Moors and one Portuguees.

The Bears in the woods and on the Mountains of this Kingdome are, many of them, an incredible bignesse. I have Seen many of them Cole black, and as large as an Ordinary heifer; and those woods that afford most plenty of Peacocks, are generally frequented with these Uglyest of Annimals. Some they tame in this Kingdome, and lead them about to Shew, but none of the large ones. I have often shot att them, yet never soe but they got away into the Woods againe.

Infinite Number of Wild hogge in this countrey as alsoe a creature called a Jackall[4], resemblinge both dogge and fox, and are as large as good Ordinary hounds in England, beinge a most bold and mischiefous Annimall. They doe great prejudice to the Standinge corne, tearinge it up by the roots, and are soe bold in the night to come and walke the Streets of a towne like tame doggs, on purpose to gett Opportunities to runne away with geese, henns, ducks, or the like. I have Seen Severall of them togeather, but by night heard the Noise of Some hundreds at once.

---

[1] See p. 199. [2] See notes on pp. 104 and 200.

[3] See note on p. 209.

[4] Compare *Delestre*, p. 190, "Troops of wild elephants, buffaloes, boars, stags, gazelles, squirrels are seen there [in Bengal]." John Marshall, *Notes and Observations*, p. 5 (reverse), says, "At this place [Ramchandrapore] are plenty of wild Deer very larg, wild hogs, Peacocks, cocks and henns, Jackalls and Tygers." See *Schouten*, vol. i. p. 480, for a description of "Jackhalses or Jachals." For illustrations of the "Tyger," "Bear," "Wild Hogge," and "Jackall," see Plates XI. and XII.

PATTANA.

A Very large and potent Kingdome[1], but longe Since become tributarie to the Emperours of Hindostan (or Great Mogol). This is a Countrey of Very great Trafficke and Commerce, and is really the great Gate that Openeth into Bengala and Orixa, and soe consequently into most parts of India, vizt. from the Northerne Kingdoms or Empires (by land), namely, Persia, Carmania[2], Georgia[3], Tartaria[4], &c. The Commodities of those countries are transported hither by Caffila[5], who alsoe Export the commodities brought hither by the English and Dutch, as alsoe of this Kingdome.

The Chiefe Citty whereof is called Pattana[6], a very

---

1 Compare *Thevenot*, part iii. p. 68, "Patane is a very large Town, lying on the West side of the Ganges in the Countrey of Patan, where the Dutch have a Factory. Corn, Rice, Sugar, Ginger, long Pepper, Cotton and Silk, with several other Commodities, are plentifully produced in that Country, as well as Fruits; and especially the Ananas which in the out side is much like a Pine-Apple."

2 *i.e.* Kirmān, the Province of Persia nearest to India.

3 Compare *Fryer*, p. 284, "The next Neighbours, if not the same with the Armenians, were the Iberians, now called Georgians...Their Country at this time bears the Name of Gurgestan, from whence they are christen'd Georgians; not from the famous St. George, but because they follow Husbandry."

4 See note on p. 172.

5 See *Hobson-Jobson*, *s.v.* Cafila. Compare *Mandelslo*, p. 8, "These last [the Dutch] come thither by Sea, but all the others by Land, with the Caravans, which they call Caffilas." *Fryer*, p. 120, has "When any Caphala or Treasure passes, they hire Soldiers to guard it." Compare also the following, "Some of the Raiahs yeelded [to Futtercon, *i.e.*, Fatteh Khān, representative of Alā'uddīn Khiljī], others flying to retyrements impregnable, lay in the Mawe of the Countrey, and could not be conquered euen to this day, but making outroades, prey on the Caffaloes passing by the way." Lord's *Discoverie of the Sect of the Banians*, p. 81.

6 See *Hobson-Jobson*, *s.v.* Patna. Compare De Graaf's description of Patna, *Voyages*, p. 62 f., "This town [Patna] is very near the water as are a number of other towns of the Moors. It has a large and beautiful castle with boulevards and towers. There are fine houses,

large and Spacious one indeed, and is Scituate neare to the River of Ganges, many miles up, not lesse then 1000 or 1100 miles above the towne Hugly. There are many delicate groves and plaines adjoyneinge thereto; the Woods[1] in this Kingdome afford great Store of those deformed Annimals called Rhinocerots [Plate XII.], and many of them are taken younge and tamed[2]. There be of them in the Woods of Bengala, but noe wild Elephants in these Kingdoms[3]; although the Kingdome of Arackan is well stored with them, and is but a neighbouringe Country to that of Bengala.

---

gardens, pagodas and other grand buildings. It is situated on rising ground because of the great inundations of the Ganges so that when the water is moderately high, in order to go from the shore to the town, in some places you must climb 20, 30, and sometimes 40 stone steps. On the landward side there are a good many redoubts and towers, which serve more for ornament than defence. From one end of the town to the other, throughout the whole of its length, stretches a large street full of shops where a great trade in all kinds of things is carried on and where are to be found very clever workmen. This street is intersected right and left by several others, some of which lead to the country and the others to the Ganges. At the farthest end of the town and in the highest part of it there is a great square for the market, also a very fine palace where the Nabob lives and a large Kettera [*kaṭrā*, a market-place] where are to be found a number of people of divers nations as well as all kinds of merchandise."

Compare also *Tavernier*, vol. i. part ii. p. 53, "Patna is one of the greatest Cities of India, upon the Bank of Ganges, toward the West; not being less than two Leagues in length. But the Houses are no fairer than in the greatest part of the other Cities of India, being cover'd with Bamboux or Straw."

[1] "We ordred you formerly to make a contract for petre with those salt men who come with great droves of oxen yeerly through the Woods from Pattana ward to Orixa." Letter to Balasor, 12th April, 1679, *O.C.* No. 4596.

[2] De Graaf, *Voyages*, p. 73, has the following account of a rhinoceros: "The Director Jaques Verburg having been some time at Ougli on the Company's business, returned to Cassambasar. A present was made to him of a young rhinoceros which some hunters had taken in a wood, after having killed the mother. This rhinoceros was about five feet in height. It was of a pearl grey colour. The skin was furrowed and rough like that of an elephant; but it had no scales, as it is said to have. The head was large and thick, and its muzzle very large and wide; the horn was beginning to grow. This animal was a sight worth seeing."

[3] *Delestre*, however, says that Bengal abounded with wild elephants. See note on p. 220.

Plate XII

p. 220.

"BEARS AND A WILD HOGGE."

p. 220.

"JACKALLS."

p. 222.

"THE RHINOCEROT."

Soe that soe farre as is reported of them to be Utter Enemies to the Elephant I doe confide in[1], for in all Kingdoms where are found the Rhinocerot the Elephant is not found wild there, nor dare the tame ones frequent the Woods, As for instance, Pattana, Bengala, and Java Major.

Many of our Countreymen and Others in Europe doe take this Creature to be the Unicorne, and will very hardly be convinced from that theire Opinion, And will make no Scruple to Say that our Fore Fathers mistooke in Limninge his true Shape, which, if soe, was a very grosse mistake indeed, for noe 2 Creatures in that can be more different. But I doe rather Condemne the Errour of this present age, holdinge with them not any further then this, that this is a Unicorne as it is a one horned beast, but I cannot Say that it is the Unicorne. For Example, I saw a horne of about 13 or 14 inches longe, in the very forme and Shape that wee picture or carve a Unicorn's horne[2]; it was of a very darke gray colour. I happened accidentally both to See and handle the Same, which gave me more Satisfaction as to the Unicorne then I had before, which Shall be Spoken of more at large in the accompt of Mocho in the Red Sea[3].

The English East India Company have a Factory in Pattana, adjoyneinge to the Citty, whence wee have all (or

---

[1] Compare *Schouten*, vol. ii. p. 277 f., "It is also believed that they [rhinoceroses] are enemies of the elephants, and that they sharpen their large horn against flints in order to make it pierce the belly of the elephants, where their skin is most tender."

[2] Probably a horn of the black buck. Compare *Schouten*, vol. ii. p. 276 f., "Some have thought that this animal [the rhinoceros] is the veritable unicorn that so many people have sought without being able to find. For my own part I am persuaded that I have seen elsewhere a real unicorn's horn. It was much larger, longer, and of quite a different shape from that of the rhinoceros; what I remark here is only my own opinion, and it does not establish the point as a certainty."

[3] The writer has not carried out his intention to describe Mocha in this MS. See note on p. 103.

the most part) of the Saltpeeter Sent yearly for England[1]. The English Chiefe (by name) Job Chanock[2] hath lived here many years and hath learned the Persian (or Court) Languadge as perfect as any Persian borne and bred, and hath lived wholy after their Custome (save in his Religion), by which he hath obtained vast priviledges, and love of the Grandees that Sway the Power of the Kingdome, and is dayly admitted into the Nabob's presence.

---

[1] On the 12th December, 1669, the Council at the Bay wrote to Fort St George (*Factory Records*, Misc. No. 3), "The Factory house we desired your Licence to build without Pattana was instead of that built since Mr. Blake being Cheife att Singee and levelled by the Rains. Pattana it selfe is not a place to manage the Peter trade in, yet that being the Residence of the Nabob that Governs that Countrey, the Chiefe must sometimes repaire thither...if the Factory be without the Cittie, nigh the place where the peter is made, the Convenience will be very great in Encreasing the Investments and Securing the peetermen from Selling what we have bought of them to others...."

At the end of the *Diary of Streynsham Master*, pp. 331, 332, there is an "Accompt of Pattana" by John Marshall, dated in Balasor, the 10th Dec. 1676. He writes, "Pattana lyes in the Latitude of 25 degrees and [?] minutes inter Gangem, and in Pleasant place, the Honble. Company have no Factory here, but what hire, nor doth the Cheife usually reside there, by reason the Nabobs Pallace is in the Citty, and his servants and officers are constantly craveing one thing or another, which if not given, though they have what they desire, yett they are not satisfied therewith, but creat trouble, and if given what they desire will be very chargeable, which inconveniency is prevented by Liveing at Singee, which lyes North of Pattana about ten or twelve miles, Extra Gangem, and is Scittuated in a pleasant but not whole [wholesome] place, by reason of its being most Saltpeter ground, but is convenient by reason thereof, for Saltpeter men live not far from it, besides the Honble. Company have a Factory at Nanagur which lyes to the east of Pattana (extra Gangem) about 4 or 5 miles, there remaynes Generally a banian or sometimes only Peons, to receive the Peter from the Peter men, which lyes there abouts, to avoid carrying it to Singee, which would be chargeable, and when what there is received in, its weighed and put aboard the Peter boates there, There is alsoe another place about 15 or 16 miles to the westward of Singee, whether is brought all the Saltpeter neare that place, and put aboard the boates there...."

"Wee exceedingly want the Peter you have ready...we would have the Warehouse Keeper see the weighing of all Peter." Letter from Hugli to Patna, 25th Jan. 1679, *Factory Records*, Hugli, No. 5.

[2] Job Charnock, the celebrated founder of the English settlement at Calcutta, arrived in India in 1655, and was appointed 4th at Kasimbazar in 1658. He became a Senior Merchant in 1666, and was Chief at Patna during the whole time comprised in this "Account." See Yule, *Hedges' Diary*, vol. ii. pp. 45—100, for full details concerning Job Charnock. See also Wilson, *Early Annals*, vol. i. p. 92, note.

The Dutch have a Factory here alsoe[1], for procureinge of Saltpeeter, but live with little freedome or Enjoyment of any worldly pleasures here, dareinge not to presume to Enter any of the Gates of the Citty without leave from Some of the great Officers[2].

All the Saltpeeter is Sent hence to Hugly in great flatt bottomed Vessels, of an Exceedinge Strength, which are called Patellas[3]; each of them will bringe downe 4, 5, 6000 Bengala maunds[4].

They are built very Stronge, by reason of the most impetuous Eddies they meet with in some places, that force them many times Upon one Shoale or Other, soe that, were they not Stronge and very flatt, they wold be in greater peril of wringinge to pieces or turning bottom up. Yet some years both the English and Dutch doe Suffer very Considerable losses by them[5].

Many Patellas come downe yearly laden with Wheat and Other graine, and goe Up laden with Salt and bees wax, the Kings onely commodities[6].

---

[1] Compare *Tavernier*, vol. i. part ii. p. 53, "The Holland Company have a House there [Patna], by reason of their Trade in Saltpeter, which they refine at a great Town call'd Choupar [Chuprah], which is also scituated upon Ganges, ten Leagues above Patna."

[2] This remark seems to have its foundation only in the prejudice of their English competitors.

[3] *paṭēlā*. See *Hobson-Jobson*, *s.v.* Pattello. The writer is more accurate in his transcription of the *paṭēlā*, a large flat-bottomed boat, than are his contemporaries. Compare the following: "Take out all the goods out of the Pratelloes and relade them aboard such small Prattelloes or other boates as may bee necessary." Letter from Hugli, 12th Dec. 1673, *Factory Records*, Hugli, No. 4. "Dispatch Mr. Allen Catchpoole to Meirdanpore with directions if the Pattelloes Can by Lightning themselves with their Small boates get over the Severall Shoaldes in the way hence to Hugly that then he offer them gratuity soe to doe." Letter from Hugli, 9th Dec. 1679, *Factory Records*, Hugli, No. 5.

[4] See pp. 116 and 217, and notes.

[5] In the records we find frequent entries like the following: "In the storm which hapned upon the first of January [1681] there was a Porgo laden with the Companys Petre drove ashore in the Bay about Peply." *Factory Records*, Fort St George, No. 2.

[6] See pp. 132 and 199 and notes.

Notwithstandinge Pattana be soe fertile to afford graine to Such a plentifull countrey as Bengala, yett in the yeare of our Lord 1670 they had as great a Scarcitie, in soe much that one Pattana Seere weight of rice (the plentifullest graine in the country) was Sold for one rupee the Seere containing onely 27 Ounces[1], and, in a few months, there was none at all to be had at that rate, in soe much that many thousands of the Natives perished in the Streets and open feilds for want of food, and many glad to Sell theire own children for a handfull of rice[2].

---

[1] *i.e.* 6 oz. short weight. See p. 217 and note.

[2] John Marshall, who was at Patna at the time of the famine, fully endorses T.B.'s remarks as to the privations suffered by the inhabitants. In his *Notes and Observations of East India*, he chronicles the extent of the famine from May to August, and gives various details concerning it, as the following extracts will show: "In latter end of May 1671 there dyed of Famine in Pattana about 100 persons dayly and had so for 3 or 4 months, corne was then (vizt) Wheate 2½ Rupees per Maund, Barley 2 rs., Rice fine 4 rs., Rice Course 2½ rs., Beefe 1½ r., Goat flesh 2 rs., Butter or Gee 7½ rs., Oyle 7 rs. per maund which consists of 80 lb. English Averdepoiz...June the 19th we came to Pattana from Singee, I see upon one peece of sand about the middle way betwixt the City and the River about 32 or 33 persons ly dead within about 10 yds. compass from the middle of them, and so many by the River side that could not come on shore but by very many dead corps, also aboundance upon the sand besides, now Rice for 4 rs. per Maund, beeing a little while since 4 rs. 7 an. being somthing cheaper, Wood for firing 4½ md. per Rupee, Henns 5 and Chickins 8 per Rupee, tis reported that since the beginning of October there have died of Famine in Pattana and the suburbs about 20000 Persons, and there cannot in that time have gone fewer from the City than 150000 persons...great number of slaves to be bought for 4 an. and 5 an. per peece and good ones for 1 r. per peece, but they are exceedinge leane when bought and if they eat but very little more than ordinary of rice, or eat any flesh, butter or any strong meat, their faces hands and feet swell immediately exceedingly so that tis esteemed enough to give them at first ½ seer of rice, and those very leane ¼ seer per day to be eaten at twice. The Famine reacheth from 3 or 4 dayes journey beyond Bonarres [Benares] to Rojamaul [Rajmahal]....In Pattana about 23rd July there dyed about 250 or 300 Persons Dayly of Famine in and about the City of Pattana Rice being 5 rs. 5 an. per Maund best sort... August. Before the famine there were 4000 houses inhabited in Hodgipore [Hājīpūr], and but now 1800 inhabited, and out of them many have dyed....In Pattana in 1671 August 8th now dy dayly here of Famine 2 or 300 persons in City and Suburbs, rice now 7 seer per Rupee or 5 rs. 11 an. per Maund of best sort and sometimes none to be bought nor bread in the Bazar...upon the 7th

And yett, at that time, the Nabobs Chiefe Wife had Severall very large Storehouses full of graine, and wold not dispose of any, unlesse they wold give the weight of Silver in one Scale of its weight of rice or wheat in the Other. But it pleased God to frustrate her Covetous designe, and Sent them as great plenty as Ever they had[1].

Severall Sorts of boats that Use the Rivers, whose Shapes are as here followeth. [Plates XIII. and XV.]

This is called an Olocko[2]. They row Some with 4, Some with 6 owers, and ply for a faire as wherries doe in the Thames.

[August] 2 Merchants in Pattana threw themselves into a common well and drowned them selves, now a terrible sad cry of poor in the Buzzar...no course rice to be bought...some dayes neither rice nor bread to be bought in the Bazar...." Here follows a quaint remark, "Such was the laziness of workmen in the time of Famine, That in the time of making one Casmeer boat for the Company, Six of the Carpenters died of Famine....In Pattana and the Suburbs died in 14 months last past ending 6th November 1671 of the Famine 135400 persons....I received [11th Dec. 1671] an Account in writing out of the Coatwalls Chabootree [*kotwāl kā chabūtrā*, sheriff's office] wherein was writ that in the 12 months last past there had died in Pattana and the Suburbs of the Famine 103000 Persons (vizt) 50000 Mussulmen and 53000 Hindoos which were taken notice of in their bookes of Records." On another page the number is given as 90720.

[1] John Marshall, *Notes and Observations*, says, "The most of the poore that go hence [Patna] go to Dacca for victualls, though there is thought to be great quantities of Rice in these parts, yet through the Nabobs roguery here is a Famine, and also somthing from the Drynes of the last yeare." I have been unable to find any allusion to the action of the "Nabobs Chiefe Wife" as related by T.B.

[2] *ulāk.* See *Hobson-Jobson*, *s.v.* Woolock. Compare the following contemporary spellings: "I have sent you upon this Oolauck Rs. 500," Letter from Dacca to Balasor, *O. C.* No. 3809. "Seaventeen chests of treasure which wee have sent two good Oolocks to fetch," Letter from Hugli to George Herron, 15th Aug. 1680, *Factory Records*, Hugli, No. 5. "You are hereby enordered...to lade the Same [*i.e.* Timbers] upon Ullocks and Borees," Letter from Hugli to Capt. Hussey, 9th Sept. 1684, *Factory Records*, Hugli, No. 6. "Ten or twelve Woollocks to unlade these boats." *Bengal Public Consultations*, Range i. vol. i., 10th Jan. 1704.

A Budgaroo[1] Or Pleasure boat, wherein the English and Dutch Chiefe and Councill goe in State Upon the water, in Use alsoe by the Moors Grandees or Governours.

A Purgoo[2]. These Use for the most part between Hugly and Pyplo[3] and Ballasore. With these boats they carry goods into the Roads On board English and Dutch &c. Ships. They will live a longe time in the Sea, beinge brought to anchor by the Sterne, as their[4] Usual way is.

A Boora[5] being a Very floaty light boat, rowinge with

---

[1] *bajrā*. See note on p. 190. Compare the following: "Basaras, which are a kind of large boat, fairly clean, the centre of which forms a little room." Luiller, *Voyage au Golfe de Bengale*, quoted in Prévost, *Voyages*, vol. xiii. p. 80. "If you have noe Budgrees with you 'twill be necessary to bring 2 or 3 Purgoes downe for the carriage of our necessarys," Letter to Balasor, 18th Aug. 1679, *O.C.* No. 4644. "You have done very well since your Factory Budgroe [is] out of repaire to keep our Budgroe (that wee lent hence to carry up Mr. Meverell and his Wife) with you," Letter from Hugli to Patna, 26th April, 1682, *Factory Records*, Hugli, No. 6.

[2] This word of doubtful origin probably represents an Indian corruption of the Portuguese *barca*, a barge and also a sailing-boat. See *Hobson-Jobson*, *s.v.* Porgo. See *Ind. Ant.*, vol. xxx. pp. 160—162, for the history of the word. There are frequent references to this kind of boat in the contemporary records. Compare the following: "Advise us betime by land that wee may have Porgoes and Pilots ready at the Barr foote to bring her [the *Ganges*] over at her coming here." Letter from Balasor to Hugli, 13th Jan. 1673, *Factory Records*, Hugli, No. 4. "Tell Mr. Peachy...his goods are on board of a pergoo for Ballasore." Letter from Hugli to Balasor, 13th Nov. 1674, *O.C.* No. 4038. "This day the Purgoes or boates (which were ordered to goe on board the Shipes upon Saturday last when I came ashore) returned bringing such goods and Treasure as was sent for." *Diary of Streynsham Master*, Balasor, 1st Sept. 1676, p. 53. "What exquisite theives the Porgomen are, all who have lived any time at Ballasore can make the Honble. Company...sensible of." Edmund Bugden's defence, 19th Aug. 1679, *Factory Records*, Hugli, No. 2. In 1691, 1695, and 1698, we find the word spelt "Porgoe," "Porkoe," "Porka."

[3] Pipli. See note on p. 162.

[4] "their" refers to the native boatmen.

[5] *bhaṛ*, a lighter. See *Hobson-Jobson*, *s.v.* Bora, where the word is derived from *bhada*. Compare the following references to this kind of boat: "He [Luiller] met more than 500 Bouries which are large Indian boats very badly built." Prévost, *Histoire des Voyages*, vol. xiii. p. 83. "You did well having an opportunity to let out the Company's Borae to fraight." Letter from Balasor to Hugli, *Factory Records*, Hugli, No. 4. "By the Boraes that Carried Goods hence send hither good sall [*sāl*] timbers of 12 in. 13 Covids for Beames and rafters for

Plate XIII

p. 227.

"AN OLOCKO."

p. 228.

"A BUDGAROO."

p. 228.

"A PURGOO."

p. 230.

"THE MUSKE DEERE."

p. 228.

"A BOORA."

20 or 30 Owers. These carry Salt peeter and Other Goods (from Hugly) downewards, and some trade to Dacca with Salt; they alsoe Serve for tow boats for the Ships bound up or downe the River.

A Patella[1]. The boats that come downe from Pattana with saltpeeter or Other goods built of an Exceedinge Strength and are Very flatt and burthensome.

The onely Commodities of this Kingdome that are yearly Sent for England are Saltpeeter[2], of which great quantities are sent to England and Holland, with a Considerable investment of each Nation in Codde Muske[3], which is here found to be very good. It is in generall taken from a Small deere of about 2 foot high, of which this Countrey doth mightilie abound[4]. They take it out Upon

---

the Warehouse here." Letter from Hugli to Balasor, 27th Dec. 1678, *Factory Records*, Hugli, No. 5. "Ordered that what Boras or great open boates can be gott be taken up to carry the peter aboard the Ships." Hugli Diary, 27th Oct. 1679, *Factory Records*, Hugli, No. 2.

[1] See notes on pp. 148 and 225.

[2] Compare *Bernier*, p. 440, "Bengale is also the principal emporium for saltpetre. A prodigious quantity is imported from Patna. It is carried down the Ganges with great facility, and the Dutch and English send large cargoes to many parts of the Indies, and to Europe." On the 18th Dec. 1676 the Court wrote to Hugli (*Letter Book*, No. 5, p. 383), "Wee would have you send a sufficient Stock to Pattana to be there in a readines, that all Opportunities may be taken for buying Salt Petre, and it being procured to send it away by all Opportunities to Hughly, That soe wee may have a quantity alwaies ready for dispatch of our ships....Wee would have you send what Salt Petre you can to the Fort by these ships...send us yeerly home twenty tunns of refined white Petre." In the Hugli Diary, under date 4th Dec. 1679, is the entry (*Factory Records*, Hugli, No. 2), "Ordered to endeavour to take up Rs. 20000 for to Pay the Petree expected to be bought."

[3] See note on p. 134.

[4] Compare De Graaf's description of this animal, *Voyages*, p. 72, "The Director returned to Cassambasar in order to examine and buy some bales of silk. A present was made to him of a sort of curiosity. It was the skin of one of these animals which produce musk. The skin had been dried and filled with cotton. This animal was the size of an ordinary goat or sheep. It had on its head two little horns black as jet, of about a span long. The bag in which the musk was enclosed was still attached to the belly of the animal." Marshall, *Notes and Observations of East India*, p. 29, has a very quaint account of the "Muske Deere."

the full of the Moone[1], but not every full Moone out of the Same deere, by reason it cometh not to maturitie in Soe Short a time. It is the Navle of the deere, which although cutt out, doth wonderfully grow as before.

The Great quantities of Muske brought from Cochin-China and China it selfe is for the most part taken from this little Annimall whose shape is as followeth [Plate XIII.].

From Dacca The Chief Commodities brought are fine Cossas[2], commonly called Muzlinge[3].

From Cossumbuzar, Sundry Sorts of raw and wrought Silks[4], fine Sashes[5] and Stripes[6] interwoven with gold and Silver.

---

[1] This seems to point to a superstition similar to that still prevailing in some parts of Dorsetshire, where farmers' wives will not have a pig killed when the moon is waning for fear that the bacon should shrink and turn out soft.

[2] *khāṣṣā*, a cotton cloth still used in India, softer than longcloth, and closer than muslin. T.B. in his *Malay Dict.* has, "Cassa, Lawn or Muslin"; and Wilson, *Early Annals*, vol. i. p. 187, has, "*khāṣa*, a kind of fine muslin." Luiller, *Voyage au Golfe de Bengale*, quoted in Prévost, *Histoire des Voyages*, vol. xiii. p. 80, says, "The Company gets from its factory at Ougly...Casses, which we call double muslin." See *Hobson-Jobson*, *s.v.* Piece-Goods, p. 707. Compare the following: "[In] 1679 we Sent away Cassaes to the amount of rupees 72189. 3. 11." Letter from Dacca to Hugli, 13th Nov. 1680, *Factory Records*, Misc. No. 3, p. 152. "The Cossaes by which are meant Tangeebs Jelosies and such like Cloth...10000 ps." Letter from Hugli to Dacca, *Factory Records*, Hugli, No. 5. "This year 1681 the Honble. Company endeavored [? ordered] 23000 ps. of thin white cloth as Cossaes and Mullmulls &ca to be provided at Maulda and Decca." Hugli Diary, 11th April, 1682, *Factory Records*, Hugli, No. 3.

[3] See note on p. 5.

[4] In 1676 (letter dated 18th Dec., *Letter Book*, No. 5) the Court ordered from the "Bay" 31000 ps. Taffaties "so as they be of good blacks Colours and whites according to our former advices."

[5] Turban-cloths. In the *Journal of Peter Mundy*, I.O. Copy, under date April 1637, Relation 23, p. 37, we have, "A Soldier in Red ...a Shash on his Head part gold." Compare also, Marshall, *Notes and Observations*, p. 20 (reverse), "Muxidavad [Murshidabad]...here to be bought...Girdles and Sashes which come from Bonarres [Benares]"; and the following in a letter from Balasor to Hugli, 1st June, 1672, *Factory Records*, Hugli, No. 7, "Another night appeared Severall men in Armes behind our factory all in black Coates and Shashes." See also Yule, *Hedges' Diary*, vol. iii. p. 179.

[6] *i.e.* Cotton cloth interwoven with gold and silver. "The parcell sky colour'd gold strip'd stuff your note mentions, I believe Mr.

From Hugly and Ballasore, Sanas[1], Ginghams[2], Orammalls[3],

Richards made Use of himselfe." Letter to Kasimbazar, 19th June, 1674, *O.C.* No. 3972. In the "List of Goods to be provided at the Bay" in 1681, *Letter Book*, No. 6, we find, "Stript Muslings fine (Doreas) 21 yds. long $1\frac{1}{8}$ yd. or Ell wide, better made at Hughly, Santapore and Maulda."

[1] Wilson, *Early Annals*, vol. i. index, *s.v.* Sanah, has, "*sanahs*, a kind of fine cloth." Luiller, *Voyage au Golfe de Bengale*, quoted in Prévost, *Histoire des Voyages*, vol. xiii. p. 80, says, "Balassor is a place celebrated for trade in fine white Calicoes called Sanas." Sanahs were, apparently, not a popular commodity in England. On the 18th Dec. 1676, *Letter Book*, No. 5, p. 387, the Court wrote to Hugli, "Wee finde you have this yeer sent us of Sannos 34630 ps. more then Ordered, and so you doe yeerly, notwithstanding all wee have written to the Contrary." With reference to this letter, the Council at Fort St George wrote to Hugli on the 7th June, 1677, *Factory Records*, Fort St George, No. 18, "They [the Honble. Co.] take great notice of your exceeding so much in Sannoes and being so short in Nillaes, Cassaes, Humhums &c." On the 4th Jan. 1679, the Chief and Council at Hugli wrote to Balasor, *Factory Records*, Hugli, No. 5, "The sending home Sannas we hope will not be unacceptable to our Honble. Employers in that you Could not procure the quantity of Ginghams," and on the 25th April, 1682, *Factory Records*, Hugli, No. 6, "Your Sannaes they [the Honble. Co.] say are also generally to yellow they should be better drest and the conjee [starch] have more blew in it, if you could have them drest as white and as fine as the Beetelaes at the fort they would sell much better, as they now come some of the buyers have been forced to send them over to holland to have them new whited or bleached and brought back again to England to sell." There is reason to think that the cloth known as *sanah* in the 17th cent. still exists as *sālū*, a cheap, fine cloth, generally red, in common use in Bengal.

[2] See *Hobson-Jobson*, *s.v.* Gingham, an Indian Cotton cloth. It is an old English name, probably of Indo-European origin, for a stuff made of cotton yarn dyed before being woven. "Striped Ginghams of lively colours" were a favourite variety in the 18th century. See *Ind. Ant.*, vol. xxix. p. 339, for the spelling "Gengam" in 1746. On the 18th Dec. 1676 (*Letter Book*, No. 5) the Court wrote to Hugli, "Wee would have you directly observe to send us the goods wee order and if you exceed in any, let it be in Taffaties Silk, Nillaes, fine Cossaes and Coloured Ginghams...the Colored Ginghams sent are all Grayes stiff and without gloss; for the future you must mix them with Hair Colour, Green, yellow and Tawny, to make them more soft, Gentle and Glossy." Among the goods to be provided for the 1679 shipping were "Coloured Ginghams (of divers cloth colours) ten thousand pieces, and as many peices of Nillees." *O. C.* No. 4502.

[3] *rūmāl*. See note on p. 133. Compare the following: "The Musters [samples] of Rhumalls we have received and finde to be of the same sort wee have this year contracted for here." Letter from Hugli to Balasor, 3rd Sept. 1680, *Factory Records*, Hugli, No. 5. "Having received a muster of a mullmull ground handkercheif from Dacca which they call a Rhumaul, on consideration as it soe much differs from a Rhumaul in every respect, we think it not fitt to buy any for our Masters account this yeer." Hugli Diary, 3rd Oct. 1681, *Factory Records*, Hugli, No. 3.

Cotton yarne[1], &c., which goods are Embailed in the beforementioned Factories, and, accordinge to Order frôm the Honourable English East India Company, are Sent On board the English ships that yearly doe arrive and anchor in Ballasore Roade, and thence doe Sett Saile in the Month December, bound up to Metchlipatam and Fort St. Georg's, where theire full ladeinge is prepared, and in a few days Shipped On board, and about the latter End of January doe Saile intendinge (God assistinge them) for England.

The Staple Commodities brought into these 3 Kingdomes (namely Orixa, Bengala, and Pattana) are Scarlet[2], broad Cloths of divers colours, Vermilion, quick Silver[3], Brimstone, Lead, Coppar, Ryals of 8[4], and Corall.

All which, although they produce but little per Cent, yet they are here as good as ready Rupees in procureinge

---

[1] On the 26th Aug. 1667, the Court wrote to Hugli (*Letter Book*, No. 4, p. 97), "The Cotton yarne received from your parts is crosse reeled and too great hancks or skeynes, and too hard twisted, therefore wee desire it may bee in small hancks or skaines and reeled straight and something softer twisted," and on the 17th Aug. 1674 (*Letter Book*, No. 5), "Cotton Yarne, if you can procure that which is very good and not too hard throwne you may send 50 or 60 bales provided the price exceed not 14 rupees per maund." On the 24th Dec. 1675 the Court ordered, *Letter Book*, No. 5, "50 or 60 Bales Cotton Yarne each 3 maunds."

[2] See note on p. 160. Compare the following: "Make a hansome Present in our Name to Yecknam Cawne...And doe it as much in Scarlett...as may be acceptable." Letter from the Court to Fort St George, 29th Nov. 1670, *Letter Book*, No. 4. "We have here in the Godowne 2 Peeces Scarlett, and 2 Peeces read Cloth, but noe green cloth." Letter from Masulipatam to Fort St George, 3rd Oct. 1678, *Factory Records*, Masulipatam, No. 10. "The present to Shasteh Caune the Nabob...Scarlet 10 peeces, Crimson Cloth 15 yds." Letter from Hugli to Dacca, 1st March, 1680, *Factory Records*, Hugli, No. 5.

[3] The demand in Bengal for vermilion and quicksilver was not large enough to please the authorities at home. On the 12th Jan. 1665, the Council at Fort St George wrote apologetically to the Court, "Quicksilver and Vermillion are Dull Commoditys, from the Bay they required, by their advises but 60 Mds. of the First and 30 of the latter." *Factory Records*, Misc. No. 3. In 1679, however, we find in a letter from Dacca to Hugli on the 3rd June (*Factory Records*, Hugli, No. 7), "Wee have had enquiries often for Vermillion if you please to furnish us therewith."

[4] See note on p. 114.

the best of good[s] in the Kingdome without any losse, but rather 15 or 20 per Cent gaine, where to bringe Europe vizt. English, Dutch, or French Coyned moneys, the losse is more then soe much per Cent. But the Voyadge homeward doth make sufficient amends[1].

In the beforementioned places in these 3 Kingdoms, the English Nation in generall hath freedome of inhabitinge and tradinge free from all manner of taxes and customes in or out, the like priviledges hath noe Other Nation besides.

All which was procured by the Ingenuitie of Mr. Gabriel Bowden, one of our owne Nation, and a very Eminent Doctor of Phisick, sometime Doctor in Ordinary to the great Warriour Emir Jemla, who tooke a very great Affection towards him, and was most courteous and Free to him, and Especially Upon a Notable Cure of his owne Lady performed (Under God) by the Doctor, the Nabob callinge for him, Ordered him att that instant to demand what he wold have given him or had most likeinge to and it Shold be granted in Consideration of his Loyal Service and care of the best of his familie. The Doctor, highly Surprised with this great Person's Generositie, yet soone considered Upon it, yett soe as not to be greedy of any present gaine (onely for himselfe), and now in the best of time, requested that the English Nation might Settle Factories in what parts of the Kingdomes they pleased and be free off all duties and Customes, which then was 4 per Cent in and the like out for all goods dealt in. The which was noe Sooner demanded but as readily granted[2],

[1] The author is a competent judge of the lucrative nature of Indian trade at the time, for, as he states in his Will (*vide* Introduction), he amassed his fortune, which was by no means inconsiderable, by trading in India.

[2] Yule quotes this passage in *Hedges' Diary*, vol. iii. p. 183, and remarks: "Indeed this MS. curiously illustrates the inexactitude of even twenty years' tradition. For it seems impossible that Mīr Jumla, who did not come to Bengal till 1659 should have been the Mahom-

with Phyrmanes[1] in the Persian Languadge that the English Nation Shold hold that Priviledge soe longe as they pleased to live and Settle in their Dominions, and many Other rewards Liberally bestowed Upon the Doctor (One beinge rare amonge the Mahometants)[2].

---

medan patron from whom Boughton (who died some years earlier) obtained trading privileges for his countrymen." T. B.'s version of the way in which Boughton obtained a *farmān* is given in all good faith by Stewart, *History of Bengal*, pp. 251 and 252, and the arguments against it are to be found in Yule, *Hedges' Diary*, vol. iii. pp. 167 and 168. See also Wilson, *Early Annals*, vol. i. pp. 23—29. However, the following passage from the *Court Book* of 1674, vol. 29, under date 4th September in that year, seems to prove that Gabriel Boughton's *farmān* was a reality, although not granted by Mīr Jumla: "On reading a Report from the Committees for the Coast and Bay touching the phirmands granted to the Company for trading in the Bay of Bengala, According to an order of Court dated the of We have discoursed with Mr. Bridges and others concerning the Phirmaund or patent for trade granted the English by the Prince of Bengala; and we find that it was first procured by one Mr. Bowden a Chyrurgeon, and gave the English onely libertie to trade paying Custom according to the Kings phirmand but was altered and made to pay noe Custom according to the Kings Phirmaund. That afterwards there was another Phirmaund thought to be more advantageous to the trade of the English procured by Mr. Gauton and Billidge..."

[1] *farmān*. See note on p. 142.

[2] Here the MS. suddenly breaks off and there is a blank of two pages. Then follow the three headings ARACKAN, PEGU and TANASSAREE. It was evidently the author's intention to write at length on these places as spaces are left for the purpose. The missing descriptions may have figured in the "Ms in a green cover" bequeathed to the East India Company (*vide* Introduction), or the incompleteness of the 1669—1679 "Account" may be due to the death of the author while engaged in the work.

Oedjange = Salange, commonly called

JANSELONE[1],

Is an Island that lyeth to the Southward of all the Isles of Tanassaree[2], nearest middway betweene that and Queda. The North end of it lyeth in Lattitude North 08° 50″; the South End in 07° 35″ Lattitude North. It is almost in

---

[1] This is a valuable contribution to the history of the word. The modern term Junk-Ceylon no doubt takes its name from Ujung Salang, *i.e.* Salang Head, the southern extremity of the island Salang. Crawfurd, *Desc. Dict. of the Indian Is.*, *s.v.* Ujung, says, "Ujung in Malay and Javanese, signifies point, or sharp end, and is also frequently applied to a point of land, or headland, promontory, or tongue ...We have an example of it in the name of the island called by Europeans Junk-Ceylon; and which is in reality the name of a promontory of that island, called by the Malays Ujung-Salang, or the point of Salang." Other derivations are as follow:

Forrest, *Voyage to the Mergui Archipelago*, remarks on the derivation of "Jan Sylan," p. 30, "Probably the name was given to it before it became an island at high water, and before it was disjoined from the continent as it is at present: the word *oojong* being a Malay word signifying point, and the inhabitants in general speaking Malay, from their intercourse with that people, had it been considered as an island, the word *pulo*, signifying island in the same tongue, a word of easy pronunciation, if once affixed to it, would most probably never have left it."

In *Hobson-Jobson*, ed. 1903, we find, on the other hand, *s.v.* Junk-Ceylon, "Mr. Skeat doubts the correctness of this (the hitherto accepted derivation). "There is at least one quite possible alternative, *i.e. Jong salang*, in which *jong* means 'a junk,' and *salang*, when applied to vessels, 'heavily tossing.' Another meaning of *salang* is 'to transfix a person with a dagger,' and is the technical term for Malay executions, in which the kris was driven down from the collar-bone to the heart.""

In a collection of maps reproduced in vol. 27 of *Annales du Musée Guimet* (Le Siam Ancien), it is curious to note that up to 1688 Junk-Ceylon is marked as a town on the mainland. In a map of the middle of the 16th century we have "Jũsalam"; in a map by Van Langren 1595, "Junçalaon"; in a map of 1613, "Junsalam"; in a map by Placide, *circ.* 1688, "Junsalaon," for the first time as an island; in a map by Gneudeville 1713—1719, "Junsalan"; and, finally, in a map by Robert, 1751, "Jonkseilon." "Junsalaon" is an "island" in Ralph Fitch's journey, 1583—91, in *Hakluyt*, reprint, vol. v. p. 498.

[2] *i.e.* the Mergui Archipelago.

the forme of the Island Ceylone but not more then a Sixth part soe large[1].

I[t] wholy belongeth to the Kinge of Syam, and he hath a Governour here, whom the Natives Entitle Radja (vizt.) Kinge[2], as indeed he is a Vice Kinge to the great Kinge of Syam[3].

The Inhabitants Up in the Countrey are Naturall Syamers[4], for the most part a very Civil good humored

---

[1] Compare the following differing descriptions of the size of this island: Dunn, *East-Indies Directory*, p. 337 f. says, "The body of Junk-seilon Island lies in latitude 8° 15′ N. Its shape is irregular; extending from north to south about 18 leagues. On the east side of it are very good harbours which you may safely put into." Forrest, *Voyage to the Mergui Archipelago*, p. 29, gives the extent of "Jan Sylan" as "about 40 miles long and 15 broad." Milburn, *Oriental Commerce*, vol. ii. p. 291, says, "Junkceylon. This island is divided from the continent by a narrow isthmus of sand, about a mile in length, and half a mile in breadth, and is covered at high water; it shuts up, on the north part, an excellent harbour called Popra where a vessel drawing 20 feet water may get in on the springs over a mud bar. The island extends from the latitude of 8° 9′ to 7° 46′ North, and is about 24 miles long, and 10 broad." In Bowring's *Siam*, vol. i. p. 32, we find, "Salanga or Junk Ceylon, in lat. 8°, is sixteen miles in length and six in breadth; on the east it has several harbours." Lancaster (*Hakluyt*, reprint, vol. vi. p. 398) in 1592, "departed thence [Malaca] to a Baie in the kingdom of Junsalaom, which is between Malacca and Pegu eight degrees to the Northward."

[2] For Raja see pp. 39, 108, 128, and note on p. 39.

[3] T. B. in the "Dialogues" at the end of his *Malay Dict.* has, "Junsalon to the North of Quedah, is under the Government of the King of Siam, the people and Language is Malayo." Alex. Hamilton, *East Indies*, vol. ii. p. 68, says, "The next Place of any Commerce on this Coast [after Mergui], is the Island of Junkceyloan, it lies in the Dominions of the King of Siam."

When Forrest visited Junk-Ceylon in 1784, the Viceroy from Siam had three assistants: "Terowa...here resides Peepeemont, the governor, or viceroy, from the court of Siam. This governor, when I was there in 1784, had three assistants, or perhaps rather colleagues, as they partook of his power: their names were Pee-Tukerat, Pee-Siring, and Pee-Lancrac. Each of these officers had about sixty followers, a kind of retainers, who in a great measure live on the community; for, receiving little pay, they oppress the inhabitants."

In 1785 the Burmans attempted to gain possession of Junk-Ceylon, but were repulsed with loss. In 1810 they made a more successful attempt, but only retained possession of the island for a few months, when the Siamese recaptured it.

[4] Compare De Chaumont, *Embassy to the Court of Siam*, 1687, p. 85 f., "The Siamoises...are a People very docible, which proceeds

people; but downe att the Sea Ports most of the Inhabitants are Malayars[1], a very roguish Sullen ill natured people, and Seldome or never that any Ship or Vessell doth arrive here to trade with them, but there is Either robbery or Murther comitted by them, to the damadge of the Forraigner; and then immediately they give it out that the Saleeters[2] came up to the towne in the night and committed that and many more Villanies, when I my Selfe have knowne it to be the Malayers themselvs that dwell here, namely in Banquala.

The Saleeters[2] are absolute Piratts, and are often

---

rather from their nature which desires quiet, than any other cause." *Mandelslo*, p. 103, thus describes the Siamese: "The Siameses are comely and well proportioned, but ill Souldiers, though cruel and insolent enough after victory. They are rather black then brown, ingenious in Commerce, but they are cautious, diffident, dissemblers, unconstant, false, and lyars. The Men are lazy, and care for no employment which requires labour, such they leave to their Women and Slaves, leaving affairs and husbandring of land to their charges, while they walk the streets or make their addresses at Court."

[1] See *Hobson-Jobson*, *s.v.* Malay. Crawfurd, *Dict. of the Indian Islands*, *s.v.* Malay, says, "The word is correctly Malayu in the language of the Malays themselves...A people of the brown complexioned race, with lank hair, speaking the Malay language is found in greater or lesser numbers all over the Archipelago." In his *Embassy to the Court of Siam*, p. 346, Crawfurd also remarks, "The Siamese are favourably distinguished from their neighbours, the Malays,...by the absence of that implacable spirit of revenge which forms so prominent a feature in the character of the latter."

[2] The Saleeters are evidently identical with the people called by the Portuguese writers Cellates and Saletes. Crawfurd, *Dict. of the Indian Islands*, *s.v.* Malacca, quotes from De Barros' account of the foundation of Malacca: "A fugitive from Java...arrived in Singapore...The prince received him hospitably, but in requital was assassinated by him, with the aid of his Javanese followers and of a certain people called Cellates...Eventually, along with 2000 Javanese followers he settled at Malacca, on the invitation of some of the Cellates, who had themselves taken refuge on the banks of the river of that place." Crawfurd goes on to say, "Who these Cellates were is certain enough. The word is a Portuguese formation, from the Malay word *Sālat*, a strait or frith, and at full length in this language would be *orang-sālat*, or men of the narrow seas...The Cellates were, in fact, the well known *orang-laut*, or men of the sea," of the present time, famous all over the Archipelago for their piscatory and predatory habits. They are correctly described by De Barros, who calls them "a people who dwell on the sea, and whose occupation it is to rob and to fish." Godinho de Eredia, *Malaca*, *L'Inde Meridionale*, translated

cruiseinge about Janselone and Pullo Sambelon[1] &c. Isles neare this Shore. They are Subject to noe manner of Goverment, and have many cunninge places to hide themselves and theire men of warre Prows[2] in Upon the Maine of the Malay Shore.

There are 3 Sea Ports Upon this Island, vizt. Banquala,

---

into French by Janssen, says, p. 1, "Before the foundation of Malaca, Saletes, a fishing people, gathered in this neighbourhood, in the shadow of the trees which produce mirobolans. These fishermen made use of pointed javelins called 'soligues,' and threw them with so much skill that they transfixed the fish at the bottom of the sea with them."

Of the "Saleeters" Alex. Hamilton, *East Indies*, vol. ii. p. 68 f. says, "Between Merjee [Mergui] and Jonkceyloan there are several good Harbours for Shipping, but the Sea-coast is very thin of Inhabitants, because there are great Numbers of Freebooters, called Salleiters, who inhabit Islands along the Sea-coast, and they both rob, and take People for Slaves, and transport them for Atcheen, and there make Sale of them, and Jonkceyloan often feels the Weight of their Depredations."

Crawfurd, *Dict. of the Indian Islands*, *s.v.* Malay Peninsula, p. 257, speaking of a river-tribe near Singapore, says, "This tribe takes its name, Saletar, from a creek in the island of Singapore." This creek must be the same meant by Alex. Hamilton when he says, vol. ii. p. 93, "The smallest [entrance into the river] is from the Westward, called by Europeans the Streights of Sincapure, but by the Natives Salleta de Brew. It runs along the Side of Sincapure Island for 5 or 6 Leagues together, and ends at the great river of Johore."

The modern Saletar, however, differs widely from his namesake of three centuries ago, and is very far from rising to the dignity of a pirate.

The following, quoted by Yule, *Hedges' Diary*, vol. iii. p. 107, may refer to the once dreaded Saletars: "An other Pyrat took [in 1707] two vessells from Bengall bound for Acheen and Junk Ceilone off Negraise, the other wee don't hear of yet, but are in paine for our China Ships."

A possible derivation for Saleeter is *Ṣrī-lōhita*, the *Rāmāyaṇa* name for the Andaman Sea and the Straits of Singapore, which the Arabs transliterated by *Shelaheth*, and the modern Malays through the Arabs into *Selat* or the Straits, whence the Portuguese may have got *Cellates* for the inhabitants of the Straits.

[1] A small group of islands on the South-west coast of the Malay Peninsula, so called from the Malay word *sambilan*=nine.

[2] Prow, *prau*, a generic term for any kind of sailing vessel, especially for those taking cargoes and passengers to and from the early travellers' ships. See *Hobson-Jobson*, *s.v.* Prow. See also *Ind. Ant.*, vol. xxx. p. 161 f. for an exhaustive article on the prow. *Dampier*, vol. i. p. 298 f., has a long description of "Proes, a sort of Indian Boats."

Buckett, and Luppoone[1], all very Excellent roads, but the barrs or Entrances into the Rivers are Very Shoale, not affordinge more then 7 foot[2].

The Whole Island, affordeth nothinge Save Some

---

[1] The absence of any early maps of the Island of Junk-Ceylon makes it very difficult to identify T. B.'s three ports with any certainty. The only one about which there seems very little doubt is Buckett (Malay *bukit*=hill) which appears as Puquet in an early 18th century map (*Add. MS.* 15319, Nos. 11 and 15), and still exists as Puket or Tonkah Harbour. It lies on the East of the island, with the town of Puquet situated on a narrow inlet.

Banquala (*ban*, village, *kwala*, mouth of a river) was probably so called from its situation. T. B. says, later on, that it was on the S.W. of the island, and therefore it may be identical with the present Khelong Bay, which however is almost due South.

In the early 18th century map, noted above, the only two ports marked besides Puquet, are Putom on the West and Lampacao on the South. Putom is mentioned by Alex. Hamilton, *East Indies*, vol. ii. p. 69, "The North End of Jonkceyloan lies within a Mile of the Continent, but the South End is above three Leagues from it. Between the Island and the Continent is a good Harbour for Shipping in the South-west Monsoons, and on the West Side of the Island Puton Bay is a safe Harbour in the North-east Winds." Putom now appears to be called Ban Karon, a sea-port on a stream flowing into Aũ Karon or Karon Bay. There is, however, no ground for connecting it with Banquala.

Luppoone presents another difficulty. T. B. speaks of two places bearing this name, the port mentioned above, and, later on, an inland place in the middle of the island, the residence of the *raja*. I am inclined to think that the port Luppoone is only T. B.'s rendering of the Malay word *labuhan*, *i.e.* the harbour, and that this particular harbour is the present Tharua Harbour on the East of the island. From Tharua a small river leads inland to the town Tharua (the Terowa of Forrest). Close by this place are the villages Ban Lipon and Ban Lipon Thai, *i.e.* the Village of Lipon and the Siamese (Thai) Village of Lipon. It seems reasonable to conjecture that, in T. B.'s time Lipon was the capital of the island, and that he either confused Lipon with Labuhan, and pronounced them both alike, or that, as is the case at the present day, the chief town and the harbour nearest to it bore the same name.

[2] Compare Horsburgh, *East India Directory*, vol. ii. p. 26f., ed. 1811, "The western coast of Junkseylon, stretches nearly North and South; on the East side there are several bays, and the chief one where the harbour is situated about 4 leagues from the South East point of the island is opposite to the small river where Terooa the principal town stands about 1½ mile up the river. The great passage into the harbour is on the East side of the two Lalan islands, which lie off the entrance in lat. 7° 56′ north; and the anchorage is to the North West of them in 4 or 4½ fathoms mud, with the little Lalan or northernmost island East by South 1 mile..."

Elephants and tinne[1] (that are fitt for transportation), and tinne they have in abundance, and, were they industrious might have tenne times soe much. All the traffick wee have here is to trucke Callicoes[2] blew and white, Iron, Steele, knives and Scissars, Small Cushin Carpets[3], Sugar &c. commodities for tinne, which doth here passe very Currant for ready moneys.

Very few Elephants are hence transported by reason the Duty laid Upon them is very great, neare soe much as the Elephant doth cost, soe that now adays none are Shipped off by any Merchant that hath not the Kinge of Syam's Phyrmane[4] granted him; if soe they are custome free.

They have noe Sort of coyned monies here, save what

---

[1] T. B. in the Dialogues at the end of his *Malay Dict.* has, "Junsalon...its Merchandize is only Tin, of which it yields about Four Hundred Bahar Yearly." In his list of words he gives, "Calang, tin." Compare *De la Loubère*, pp. 14 and 94, "this Tin, or Calin...is soft and basely purified, and a specimen thereof is seen in the common Tea Boxes or Cannisters which come from this country [Siam]...All the Calin is his [the King of Siam]...excepting that which is dug out of the mines of Jonsala on the Gulph of Bengal: for this being a remote Frontier, he leaves the Inhabitants their ancient Rights, so that they enjoy the Mines which they dig, paying a small profit to this Prince."

Compare also Alex. Hamilton, *East Indies*, vol. ii. p. 69, "The Island [Junk-Ceylon] affords good Masts for shipping and abundance of Tin, but few people to dig for it, by reason of the aforementioned Outlaws [the Saleeters], and the Governors being generally Chinese, who buy their places at the Court of Siam, and, to reimburse themselves, oppress the People, in so much that Riches would be but a Plague to them, and their Poverty makes them live an easie indolent Life."

Crawfurd, writing in 1828, *Embassy to Siam*, p. 418, says, "The richest mines of Siam exist in the island of Junk Ceylon, and...the mines are probably not inferior to those of the latter [Banca] in fertility."

In *Miscellaneous Papers relating to Indo-China*, vol. i. p. 185, we find that, in 1886, the population of Junk-Ceylon was reduced to about 6000 souls, and the annual yield of tin was only about 20 tons, as against the 80 tons in T. B.'s time, and the 500 at the time of Capt. Forrest's visit.

[2] See note on p. 5.

[3] *i.e.* "divans," the cushioned seats of the East, *gaddī* in India.

[4] See note on p. 142.

is made of tinne, which is melted into Small lumps[1], and passe very currant provided they be of their just weight allowed by Statute; and are as followeth:—

One Small lumpe or Putta[2] valueth here	3d English
One great Putta is 2½ Small ones Value	7½d English

which is theire Currant moneys and noe Other; but if wee bringe Silver or Gold massy or Coyned, the rich men will trucke with us for tinne and give Some advance, 10 or 15 per Cent upon the moneys.

When wee have a considerable quantitie of these Smal pieces of tinne togeather, wee weigh with Scales or Stylyard 52 pound weight and ½, and melt it in a Steele panne for the Purpose, and runne it into a mold of wood or clay, and that is an Exact Cupine[3], 8 of which are one baharre[4] weight of Janselone or 420 English pound weight.

In any considerable quantitie of goods Sold togeather, wee agree for soe many Baharre or soe many Cupines; when a Small parcell, then for soe many Viece[5], or soe

---

1 Compare Forrest, *Voyage to the Mergui Archipelago* in 1783, "Certain pieces of tin, shaped like the under half of a cone, or sugar loaf cut by a plane parallel to its base, called *poot*, are used on the island [Junk-Ceylon] as money; weighing about three pounds, with their halves and quarters of similar shape: if attempted to be exported without paying duty, they are seizable. This encourages smuggling. The value of tin is from 12 to 13 Spanish dollars the *pecul* of 133 lb. put on board clear of duty."

2 This word is not in *Hobson-Jobson*. It is Malay *patah*, a fragment; *patah kăchil*, small fragment, *patah băsar*, large fragment.

3 Cupine (*kāping*). T. B. in his *Malay Dict.* has "Coopang, the name of a Coin passable in many parts of India." Crawfurd, *Malay Dict.*, has, "Kupang (Du. *cupon*) a copper money, estimated at 10 doits, or the decimal of a Spanish dollar." The Japanese *kobang* has no connection with the Malay *kāping* of very low denomination. See *Ind. Ant.* vol. xxxi. p. 51 ff.

4 Baharre (*bahār*). T. B. in his *Malay Dict.* has "Bahar is a weight used in many parts of India and the South Seas, the Bahar at Achee is 396 l. 11 oz. 14 gr. Averdupoize...the Bahar [of Junk-Ceylon] is 445 Pounds English"; but see above in the text, where the Junk-Ceylon *bahār* is given as 420 lbs.

5 Viece (viss). See note on p. 116.

many great or Small puttas. 4 great puttas make a Viece, 10 Small ones is a Viece[1].

The Custome is here, as Soone as any Ship or Vessel doth anchor in the Roade, which is generally in the Roade of Banquala, wee goe up to towne with our boat which is about 4 or 5 miles Up the River[2]. As Soone as wee come Up, wee are invited into a house, where Speedily come to waite Upon us the Shabandar[3] and the King's Secretary, with Some Others, Some to looke Upon us, and Others to heare news. They Civilie aske many questions, as whence wee came, and what Sorts of goods wee have brought, of what burthen wee are, how many men and boys, and of what Nation they be, how many gunns, what Store of Small arms, powder and Shott; to which questions our answers are all written downe in the King's booke, as alsoe

---

[1] This gives a table (of some value for old uncoined Malay ratios) for Junk-Ceylon in 1669—1679 as to weights in tin, taking the viss at its most persistent standard of 3½ lbs. Av.

2½	puttas small	make	1 putta large
4	puttas large		1 viece
15	viece		1 cupine
8	cupine		1 bahar of 420 lbs.

See *Ind. Ant.* vol. xxxi. p. 51 f.

[2] Milburn, *Oriental Commerce*, vol. ii. p. 291, says, "The place where ships generally anchor [in Junk-Ceylon], is in a good road, well sheltered behind a small island, joined to the main at low water, in latitude 8° 10′ North...on the S.W. side of the island is another good harbour [? the Banquala of T. B.], where vessels occasionally stop."

[3] This, and the several references which follow, show clearly that, in the Malay States, the Shahbandar was a high officer controlling the seaborne trade. T. B. in his *Malay Dict.* has, "Sha bendar, Custome-House Officer in Chief." See *Hobson-Jobson*, *s.v.* Shabunder. Godinho de Eredia, *Malaca*, p. 30, has "Xabandar, Officer in Chief." Compare *De la Loubère*, p. 83, "Some have assured me that the Siameses have the Humanity not to appropriate anything to themselves of what the Tempest casts on their Coasts by Shipwrack; yet Ferdinand Mendez Pinto relates that Lewis de Monteroyo, a Portuguese, having suffer'd Shipwrack on the Coast of Siam near Patana, the Chahbandar, or Custom-house Officer, which he names Chatir, confiscated not only the Ship and its Cargo, but Monteroyo himself, and some Children; alledging, that by the ancient Custom of the Kingdom whatever the Sea cast upon the Coasts, was the profit of his Office."

the Commander's name, and is Sent Up to Luppoone[1] (the Place of the Radja's Residence), Which is the Chiefe towne, and in the very middle of the Island, where all the Circumstances are read before him and his councill, which are 10 or 12 in number; and Immediately 2 or 3 of the King's Elephants are Sent downe with a Considerable parcell of his lifeguard to waite Upon the Commander up and whom he pleaseth to bringe alonge with him, which is a Very tedious days Journey, through the Woods and Swampy places, in soe much that the guider often doth lose his way, and the most Sensible Annimall[2] of his owne accord and Sense findeth it againe to admiration. And were they not a very Sure footed Creature, the riders wold often be in very great perill climeinge Up and goeinge downe those slipery mountains, which are in many places soe Steep up and downe that the Elephant is constrained to hall himselfe Up, and againe to ease himselfe downe by layinge hold of roots and bulks of trees with his trunke, and more then soe in many places where the Woods and Bamboos grow very thicke, Soe that not any roade or Path way is to be discerned. He, to gett passadge through, breaketh the bows and cleareth the Way without the least damadge to his Riders[3].

---

[1] Probably Lipon. See note on p. 239. When Capt. Forrest visited Junk-Ceylon in 1785, *Voyage to the Mergui Archipelago*, pp. 29—36, the Governor resided at Terowa (the present Tharua, a little to the south of the villages of Lipon). Forrest describes Terowa as being on a creek a few miles from the coast. He says, also, that the Governor's country house was 8 miles inland; this was most probably on the spot known as "Luppoone" in T. B.'s time.

[2] *i.e.* the elephant. Compare *De la Loubère*, p. 39, "Besides the Ox and Buffalo...the Elephant is their sole Domestick Animal...for ordinary service they use only the Female Elephants: the Males they design for the war. Their Country [Siam] is not proper for the breeding of Horses."

[3] Compare Forrest, *Voyage to the Mergui Archipelago*, p. 31 f., "I travelled thither [from Terowa to the Governor's country house, eight miles inland]...on an elephant, through a path worn like a gutter, in some few places, where it was over a flat rock, the path being worn by the elephants feet, and so narrow as not to be

When wee come Up to Luppoone, the King's Servants that are appointed to waite upon us, carry us to a house that is allotted us by Order of theire Master, and is indeed their temple of Idols placed as follows[1], with 2 or 3 tombs of the deceased Vice Kings adjoyneinge therunto in form followinge, whither they bringe us great plenty of very good provisions, very decently dressed after the Syam manner, both fish, goat, henns, ducks &c. and in very good Order. The Shabandars[2] and what Others of the Chiefe of the King's Officers wee invite, doe very Sociably sit downe and eat and drinke with us, as it is theire Custome not to abstaine from any thinge that God hath given for the food of mankind, weaveinge all manner of Superstition Used by most Idolaters besides in Asia.

The Next morninge wee are Sent for to come into the Radja's presence, where he and his council demand a multitude of Questions, the most important of which is whether wee have the Kinge of Syams Phyrmane[3] to trade there or noe. If he finde wee have it not, nor the Coppy, he demandeth and will have 10 per Cent custome for all the goods wee have On board our Shipp or Vessell, Although he knoweth very well that The English Nation in generall is free from all Such duties in the Kingdom of Syam and all the Provinces and Isles thereto appertaineinge, neither dare he take it if wee wold give it him, although he pretends the Kinge of Syam hath given him this Island for soe many years; but all this is onely to get a consider-

---

above an inch or two wider than his hoofs: I wondered how the huge animal got along." Compare also Bowring, *Siam*, vol. i. p. 220 f., "Without the aid of the elephant, it would scarcely be possible to traverse the woods and jungles of Siam. He makes his way as he goes, crushing with his trunk all that resists his progress; over deep morasses or sloughs he drags himself on his knees and belly...He descends into ravines impassable by man, and by the aid of his trunk ascends steep mountains."

[1] There is no illustration of this temple in the MS.

[2] See note on p. 242.

[3] See note on p. 142.

able thing given him as a present, which wee are forced to doe to the Value of 100 or 120 pieces of 8[1], or he will find one way or Other to hinder us in a greater measure in the Sale of our goods[2].

After wee have come to a Composition he feasteth us royally a day or two, or more if wee be free to Stay; and dismisseth us downe with many Complements and great attendants, and giveth us a convénient house to dwell in dureinge our Stay, and doth often Send us henns, ducks, coconuts[3], Plantans[4], &c., and beats the Gunge[5] for all people that please to buy our goods, before which they dare not buy any.

Two of the Grandees of his Councill must alsoe be

---

[1] See note on ryalls, p. 114.

[2] With regard to customs payable by foreign vessels, *De la Loubère*, p. 83, remarks, "In the Maritime Governments, the Tchaou-Meuang sometimes takes Customs of the Merchant Ships, but it is generally inconsiderable. At Tenasserim it is eight per Cent. in the kind, according to the Relation of Foreign Missions."

The English had no factory or settlement at Junk-Ceylon, and the references to the island in the period covered by this "Account" are scanty in the extreme. Bruce, *Annals*, vol. i. p. 24, says that, at the beginning of the 17th century the Portuguese had a station at "Junkselon."

In the "Account of the Trade of Metchlepatam" by Christopher Hatton, at the end of the *Diary of Streynsham Master*, pp. 337—339, we find that the native ships carried on a trade between Masulipatam and Junk-Ceylon, "Arriving first in the yeare 1657 at which time I found this place [Masulipatam] in a very flourishing condition 20 Sayle of ships of good burden belonging to the Natives Inhabitans here constantly imployed on Voyages to Arracan, Pegu, Tenassery, Juncceloan, Queda, Mallaca, Johore, Atcheen, Moca, Persia and the Maldiva Islands..."

[3] See *Hobson-Jobson*, *s.v.* Coco.

[4] See *Hobson-Jobson*, *s.v.* Plantain. See p. 73, where the writer describes a "Plantan tree" as "beinge a Very liquorish thinge naturally." Compare *Dampier*, vol. i. pp. 311—316, "The Plantain I take to be the King of all Fruit, not except the Coco it self. The Tree that bears this Fruit is about 3 foot, or 3 foot and an half round, and about 10 or 12 foot high...When the Tree is full grown, the leaves are 7 or 8 foot long, and a foot and half broad...the Fruit...is so excellent that the Spaniards give it the preheminence of all other Fruit, as most producing to Life...It is of a delicate taste, and melts in ones mouth like Marmalet..."

[5] *i.e.* sends out the town-crier. For "gunge" see note on p. 196.

Piscashed[1] with 6 pieces of fine Callicoes or Chint[2] each of them, and the Shabandar of Banquala with 3 pieces Idem.

The most Proper and beneficiall Commodities which are for this place be blew Callicoes, vizt. Longecloth[3] or Sallampores[4], Cambayas[5] of 8 Covets[6] longe Checkered with blew and white with red Striped heads and borders[7], Fine and course Chint of very Small flowrs, Sugar, Cushin Carpets[8], Sope, Iron, Steele, knives, Scissars, &c. But 20 bailes of Chint and Callicoes is Enough for ½ a yeare for the whole country. What else wee bringe hither are Ryalls of 8[9] which wee alsoe trucke for tinne, att the rate of 28 dollars per baharre ready moneys, and 40 upon trucke for our Goods[10].

Provisions here are not very Plenty, beinge not over well Stocked with Cattle nor fowle, but Coconuts and fish they have in abundance[11]; also they have an Excellent Sort of rice here, but Scarcely Enough to Subsist with the

---

[1] *i.e.* presented. See note on p. 157. [2] See note on p. 71.

[3] See note on p. 55. [4] See note on p. 56.

[5] T. B. in his *Malay Dict.* has "Cāyīn gaja, Long-cloth, a sort of Callico." See *Hobson-Jobson*, *s.v.* Comboy. Compare the following in a letter from Fort St George to Masulipatam (*Factory Records*, Fort St George, No. 16), "Wee shall provide a considerable proportion of the Cargo ordered...vizt...Salempores...Camboyes as many as we can." *N. and E.* p. 16 for 8th April, 1680, has "about 20 peeces of Cambayas."

[6] See note on p. 218. [7] See note on p. 230.

[8] See note on p. 240. [9] Dollars. See note on p. 114.

[10] These rates do not tally with those quoted on p. 241. If the "putta small was 3*d.* English," then at 5*s.* the Spanish dollar (Ryall of 8) the bahar = 60 dollars. But the author paid 28 dollars in cash = $1\frac{3}{8}$*d.* for the putta or 40 dollars in kind = 2*d.* for the putta. However, Milburn, *Oriental Commerce*, vol. ii. p. 291, says that the tin in his day sold at Junk-Ceylon at "from 12 to 16 Spanish dollars per pecul." Three pecul (pikul, picul) = one bahar: therefore at 36 dollars the bahar the price was $2\frac{1}{4}$*d.* the putta, and at 48 dollars the bahar it was 3*d.* the putta. Wilson's table makes the price $\frac{1}{17}$*d.* the putta. For an examination of Malay bullion weights, see *Ind. Ant.* vol. xxvii. p. 37 ff.

[11] Compare *De la Loubère*, p. 35, "The Sea affords them [the Siamese] very delicate small Oysters, very excellent small Turtles, Lobsters of all sizes, and admirable Fish, the sorts of which are unknown to us."

whole yeare. Yet rice from the Coast[1] or Bengala will not Sell Very well here by reason 'tis not soe fine and good as theire owne is, yett butter[2] and Oyle from Gingalee or Bengala turneth to a great accompt.

It is a Very Mountaneous and Woody Countrey[3], not one tenth part of it made Use of more then by the Wild Elephants and Tygers. The best, and indeed all the fruite this countrey affordeth is Coconutt[4], Plantan[4], Sam cau[5], and Betelee Areca[6], Save the wild Calabashes[7] &c. that

---

[1] *i.e.* the Coromandel Coast.

[2] Compare *De la Loubère*, p. 37, "Butter does hardly take any Consistence there [Siam] by reason of the Heat; and that which is brought from Suratt and Bengale, through Climates so extremely hot, is very bad, and almost melted in arriving there."

[3] Crawfurd, *Embassy to Siam*, p. 9, thus describes the Western side of Junk-Ceylon, "The aspect of the country presents a perfect succession of hills or mountains, apparently so close upon each other, that there can be little room for extensive valleys capable of affording room for profitable cultivation. The whole appeared covered with an immense forest, and not a single habitation or a single patch of culture was discernible."

[4] See notes on p. 245.

[5] This fruit appears to be the large orange, known as the pommelo or shaddock. T. B., however, in the "Achin" section has a separate description of the "Pumple Moose." Yet, in his *Malay Dict.* he makes the fruits identical, for he has, "Sāmāca, a Poomplemous, a fruit in India." Rumphius, *Herbarium Amboinense*, vol. ii. p. 97, says that "Jamboa," a term equivalent to the Portuguese "Samboa," was used by the Malays for the "Pomplemoes." T. B.'s "Sam cau" may be a variation of "Samboa." Compare *De la Loubère*, p. 23, "Amongst the sweet Oranges the best have the Peel very green and rough; they [the Siamese] call them *Soum-keou* or Crystal Oranges....They give of these *Soum-keou* to their sick." Bowring, *Siam*, vol. ii. p. 255, has, "*Som*, orange; *Som-kiou-wang*, small orange." *Dampier*, vol. ii. p. 23, in describing the oranges of Tonquin, says, "*Cam* in the Tonquinese Language signifies an Orange....The *Cam-chain* is a large Orange of a yellowish colour...the inside is yellow like Amber...they are not denied to such as have Fevers and other sick people." In the *Premier Livre de l'histoire de la Navigation aux Indes Orientales, par les Hollandois*, 1609, in a description of Java (1595), fol. 38, we have: "En Iava est un fruit, qu'ils nomment Samaca, grand comme un Citron, de couleur tirant sur le verd rougeastre, de goust aigre et plein de jus, ayans dedãs des grains noirs: les feuilles assez semblables a celles de citron mais un petit plus rondes: il a un goust aimable: on le confit en sucre, et on l'use comme les Tamarindes contre toute inflammation et fièvres chaudes."

[6] See note on p. 30.

[7] Pumpkins. The word is not in *Hobson-Jobson*.

grow in the Woods, an Excellent food for the Wild Monkeys, but noe fruit soe plenty here as the Plantan and Samcau whose figure here follow [Plate XIV.]. The Samcau is not a whit pleasant to the tast Unlesse it be boyled in fish or flesh broth or else Stewed[1].

There are Severall wild Elephants[2] in the Woods here, but more Especially Tygers. Once when I was up att Luppoone, Severall of the Natives went out (by Order of the Radja), and Set a trapp for a Tyger that often resorted to a place where the Radja's goats were kept, which are not very plenty here. However they tooke one of the Smallest and place[d] him for a baite to Trapan the Tiger, and caught him alive by the leggs, which done they Seized fast his mouth as alsoe his paws, and brought him to the Radja's house. He Sent for me to looke Upon him, and although I thought the Sight of a Tyger noe novelty to me (that had Seene soe many), yet this proved one, by reason of his colour which was cole black[3], and although his body was but of an Ordinary Size, much lesse then Some I have Seen in Bengala, yet his teeth and claws were the largest that ever I saw, which caused mee to looke much upon them, and the Radja perceiveinge that, ordered one of his Soldiers to knock out the teeth and claws, and gave them to me, which I thankfully received and as a great raritie.

The Woods that adjoyne to the Sea and the Rivers are Extraordinary full of wild monkeys, some of them of a very large Stature and have huge great teeth. Where any

---

[1] This description of the "Sam cau" does not tally with that of *De la Loubère* given above (note 5 on p. 247). It is possible that the writer is confusing the water-melon with a fruit of the orange kind. Crawfurd, *Malay Dict.*, has "Sāmangka (J). The water-melon, *Citrullus edulis.*"

[2] In Forrest's time the wild elephants had disappeared. He says, *Voyage to the Mergui Archipelago*, p. 32, "They have a good many elephants [at Junk-Ceylon] which they get from Mergui; none wild, no horses."

[3] The animal referred to was probably a black panther.

wild fruit doth grow, they will be as thick as Ever they can Stand Upon the bowes, and I have Often Seen them att low water Swimme from the brinke of the River over to 2 or 3 banks of Oysters and Mussles that come adry att three quarters Ebbe, and theire (*sic*) breake the said Shell fish and eat them, and pick out the fish of Some dead ones. And once I saw a very pretty passadge amongst them. One of these active creatures, pickinge at Every thinge he thought Eatable, put his hand into a pretty large Oyster that gaped, thinkinge to pull out the fish, but the Oyster closed and held him fast, and growinge to many Others he cold not dragge them away. Whereupon I Sent our Small boat and fetched him on board, soe that he now paid for his pickinge.

Upon this Island (in many places) grow abundance of Bamboos, Especially on the Sides of the hills for above 2 or 3 miles in Circuit, and grow mighty thick togeather, soe that it is very difficult for one of the Natives to goe through them. They are more Serviceable then all the Wood in the countrey besides. There be 2 Sorts of them, called the hee bamboo and She bamboo[1]. The

[1] See *Hobson-Jobson*, *s.v.* Bamboo. T. B., in his *Malay Dict.*, has "Bamboo, is a sort of cane, and also the name of a concave measure, used at Atchee on Sumatra." Marshall, *Notes and Observations*, p. 25 (reverse), says, "Here [Gurguttee] many Lottees [*lāṭhī*, cudgel, staff] or hee Bamboes to be bought great ones 4 for a pice, or 28th part of Rupee, but they are not of so good a cast as are at Pattana for they will never be red though never so much rubbed with oyle." Compare the following in a letter from Hugli to Balasor, 5th Oct. 1674, *O. C.* No. 4015, "The people here say those he bamboos are procureable about Rage Maull [Rajmahal]." Compare also *De la Loubère*, p. 11, "One of their [the Siamese] most eminent Trees is a kind of Reed, called in Indian, *Mambou*, in Portuguese, *Bambou*, in Siamese *Maipai*. ...This Tree resembles the Poplar, it is strait and tall, and the Leaves thereof few, pale and longish. It is hollow, and grows in shoots like our Reeds, and its shoots are separated from one another by knots: but it has branches and Thorns, which our reeds have not. It grows very close, and the same Roots do shoot forth several stems, so that nothing is thicker or more difficult to pass than a Forest of Bambou." Male and female bamboo are still common terms distinguishing the solid and hollow varieties. Watts, *Dict. of Economic Products of*

first hath little or noe hollownesse in him, is very Ponderous and of an Exceedinge Strength.

The She bamboo of which there are more plenty are very hollow and light, but joynted as the Other are. They grow to a great length, 20, 30, 40 foot longe, and gradually taperinge Upwards.

Most of theire houses, both here and all this Coast over, all [? are] wholy built with them and Rattans[1] to Seize the pieces togeather. They grow as followeth [Plate XIV.].

The Dutch for Severall years Untill Anno Domini 1675 did continually keep a Ship of 16 or 20 guns and two or 3 Sloops to cruise about this Island. The Ship Used to lye at anchor (for the most part) in the Roade of Banquala, vizt. on the S. West Side the Island[2] and a Very Safe Roade almost land locked, and then wold they admit noe Ship or Vessell to trade here without theire leave, by which means they gott this tinne trade wholy into theire owne hands; but by theire too much presumption and Encroachinge, as theire Usuall way is in every place they doe gett footinge in, they Utterly lost it.

When I was in Janselone, Employed by Mr. William

India, *s.v. Bambuseae*, has a long article on the Bamboo. He says, p. 373, "The term 'male bamboo' may be said to be applied to any solid bamboo used for spear or lance staves, walking-sticks, &c.; it is more particularly applicable to *Dendrocalamus strictus*. The stamens and pistil being on the plant, it is difficult to see why the term 'male' should be given to a solid and 'female' to a hollow bamboo, but they are expressions in frequent use in India."

[1] See note on p. 74. *Mandelslo*, p. 107, makes a curious mistake about the rattan, under date 1639: "From their Neighbours they [of Patani] fetch timber to build withall, Rottang, that is Cordage of Cocoe."

[2] This seems to settle the point that Banquala is the present Khelong Bay, for Karon Bay (the Puton of Hamilton) is quite open, while the term "land-locked" can correctly be applied to Khelong Bay. See p. 239 and note.

Plate XIV

p. 248.

"PLANTAN AND SAMCAU TREES."

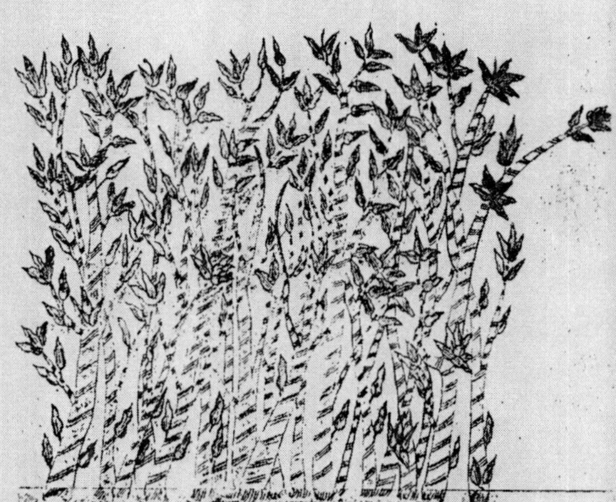

p. 250.

"BAMBOOS."

Jearsey[1], an Eminent English Merchant att Fort St. Georges, a great prow[2] of about 40 tunns in burthen had gott in privately and traded for tinne. The Dutch perceiveinge her to be neare laden, thought to make prise

---

[1] William Jearsey was a well-known character of the time, and there is a very brief account of him among the biographies in Yule's *Diary of William Hedges*, vol. ii. p. 199. The MS. records at the India Office contain ample material for a whole volume on the doings of this worthy during the thirty odd years in which he either served or defied the Company. The outlines of the career of this fiery and interesting individual are as follows. In 1650 Jearsey sailed on the *Ruby* to Pegu as accountant for the Company. In 1652 he returned to Fort St George in a "Moores Junck." From 1653 to 1655 he was Chief at Sirian, the Company's settlement at Pegu. On the withdrawal of the Factory, Jearsey remained at Sirian, in defiance of orders, and was dismissed the Company's service. Then, till 1662, he was a freeman at Masulipatam and Fort St George, and a thorn in the side of the Council. In 1662, he was reinstated in the Company's service and appointed Chief of Masulipatam, a post which he held for seven years. In the interval, he fell foul of Sir Edward Winter chiefly because he had backed Foxcroft whom Winter had imprisoned. While Chief at Masulipatam, Jearsey carried on trade in the *Ruby*, the *Adam and Eve*, the *Consent*, the *Advice*, the *Nonsuch*, the *Adventure*, the *New Shipp*, the *Diamond* and the *Martin*, one of which vessels T. B. must have commanded for him. This extensive private trading roused the Company's ire, and in Dec. 1669 Jearsey was again dismissed the service, ordered to produce his accounts, and to return to England. But, so great was his influence in India that, for sixteen years, he openly defied the Directors, whose angry remonstrances grew yearly more feeble. At length, realising their powerlessness to enforce their commands, they left their servants at Fort St George to come to an arrangement with their recalcitrant ex-chief. Some of Jearsey's vessels and their cargoes had been seized by Mohun, his successor, ostensibly to satisfy the Company's claims, and for these he claimed compensation. Eventually, he agreed to accept 3000 pagodas, and in October 1686 a formal release was signed, and the defiance of all orders from England since 1669 practically condoned. Jearsey continued to reside as a freeman in Fort St George, occupying his own house in Charles Street. In Sept. 1688 he lost his wife, a Dutchwoman, who, judging by her conduct while at Masulipatam, was as fiery-tempered and as overbearing as her husband. In spite of his high-handed behaviour, Jearsey was undoubtedly a favourite at Fort St George, and it was owing to his many friends that he was able at last to come out victorious in his struggle with the Directors at home. Jearsey never again saw his native land, but died at Fort St George in Dec. 1690. Nine years later the Company bought his house for a "Beating Godown and Granary."

[2] See note on p. 238. T. B. in the Dialogues at the end of his *Malay Dict.* says that the "Dutch have a great city near the kingdom of Johor called Mallacca to which go many Traders in Praus."

of her in time (before they cold Steale out as they came in), and, for this purpose, they came up to the towne with one Sloop very well fitted, and, by order of theire Chiefe Merchant there, Seized the Prow, not for that they came in without leave, but as She was an Enemy of theirs, an Achiner[1].

The Merchants &c. inhabitants of Banquala did (in a Very Civil way) desire the Dutch not to molest any, Especially to make prise of them, soe longe as they were Under the Radja of Janselone's protection and in theire River. But the Dutch Swelled Up with ambition, told them plainely that all Roads and Rivers of Janselone were theirs, and therefore that Prow and her goods were theire lawfull Prize.

Whereupon the Malay inhabitants, a Very resolute people[2], stood up for the Achiners[3], and tooke the Prow and her goods by Violence out of the hands of the Dutch, and in the broile one of the Dutch men on board the Sloope fired off a Musquet and killed two of the Janseloners, who indeed never had any reall kindnesse for the Dutch, and now have a brave Opportunitie to be revenged on them, and soe intent they were upon it that without any leave or Order from the Radja or any of his councell, they gathered att least 200 of them togeather and divided them into 3 companies, 100 to Stopp the way up to the Radja that they Shold not flee to him for Succour, the Other 2 fifties tooke to the Woods, halfe on one Side the River and halfe on the Other. And when they were come halfe way downe, where the River was Very narrow, they cutt downe 20 or 30 very great trees that fell

---

[1] There was constant friction between the Dutch and the people of Achin in Sumatra.

[2] See note on p. 237.

[3] Compare the following in a letter from Achin to Surat, Nov. 1663, *Factory Records*, Surat, No. 104, "The Dutch being masters of Pirah [Perak]...suffering none others to trade there but naturall Acheeners."

athwart it, and blocked it Up, soe that not any passadge is left for Sloope or boat. The Dutch findinge the way into the Countrey too hott for them, betooke themselvs to theire Sloop to be gone out into the Roade, but found themselves very much mistaken, soe that when they came downe to this Stoppadge, they cold neither goe downe nor come up againe. Then had they nothing to trust to but theire fire arms, which cold not help them very longe, for the Malayars overpowred them, and cutt them off every man and pulled theire Sloop in pieces, which soe Squashed the Dutch Designes over this place that they went away with theire Ship and Other Sloope and never molested Janselone any more.

The Dutch were very forward in makeinge theire addresses to the Kinge of Syam, yet not Sooner then the Radja and councel of Janselone, who indeed had first given an ample accompt thereof, which highly incensed the Kinge against the Dutch. Insoemuch that he Sent a Tarrah[1] to the Radja and all Officers whatsoever upon the Island of Janselone, which gave a most Severe and Strict charge unto them never to come to any composition with the Dutch nor Suffer them to Sett footinge in any of his Ports on the West side of his Dominions, although he wold grant them a free trade (payinge the Duties of the Kingdome) in Syam.

Hee likewise in the generall letter to the Radja &c. gave positive Orders that each of the 3 Sea Ports Shold build and fitt out to Sea 2 men of warre Prows[2], each to

---

[1] Letters-patent, from the Malay *tera*, the royal seal, stamp or impression. This word is not in *Hobson-Jobson*, though it frequently occurs in the old records in the sense of *farmān*. Compare the following from *Factory Records*, Java, No. 6, "The King hath bin pleased to graunt us his Tarra or patent of Indulgence that none shall buy tinne at Chaya Capampone Tatong and Sumping but onely the Company." Letter from Bantam, 4th June, 1676. Compare also the following in *De la Loubère*, p. 85, "There is an Officer in every Tribunal to read the Tara or Orders from the King to the Governor."

[2] See note on p. 238.

carry 10 gunns and Pattareros[1], and well manned and fitted with Small arms. And when they were att Sea they Shold keepe two and two togeather, and if they Shold meet a Single Dutch Shipp they Shold fight her and give noe quarter. If they mett with a fleet they Shold runne in and give intelligence for the Countrey to be up in arms, and not Suffer any Sloops to come up theire Rivers or any of them to land, neither Shold they Observe any flagge of truce or have the least converse with them.

All which Orders if not most Strictly and Speedily put in Execution, the Radja and 2 of his chiefest councellours, with the 3 Shabandars[2], Shold lose theire heads, and theire Estates fall to the Kinge.

I was discoursinge with the Radja when this Tarrah[3] arrived[4], which Startled him and his Councell soe much that they immediately Sent the 3 Shabandares and 40 or 50 Soldiers to presse all Carpenters, and Set them to worke and Employed Severall men to bringe in their labouringe Elephants[5] to carry downe the Gunns, fire

---

[1] Swivel-guns, from Spanish *pedrero*. On this word Mr Donald Ferguson remarks that "though the dictionaries rightly derive it from Span. *pedrero*, lit. a stone-thrower, the English forms seem confused with *petard*." *Fryer*, p. 108, has "Camels of war with Patereroes on their Saddles marched with a Pace laborious to the Guiders," and in his "Explanatory Index" he has "Peterraro, a Gun." In Yule, *Diary of Wm. Hedges*, vol. i. p. 67, we find the following, "11th March, 1683. Being got up with Kegaria (Kedgeree) we went on shore in our Boats and landed at an old ruined Castle with mud walls and thatched. We saw one small Iron Gun mounted and an Iron Pateraro." A ship belonging to the King of Siam taken in the river Hugli in Dec. 1687 contained "Brass Patereroes 7 with 14 chambers, weight 7 cwt., at 50 rs. per cwt., 350 rs."

[2] See note on p. 242.

[3] See note on p. 253.

[4] All this is most circumstantial, and argues a good deal of ill-feeling against the Dutch. It was about 1674 that the King of Siam freed himself from the close toils that the Dutch had wound round him and began to treat with the English for trade. Unfortunately, no confirmation of T. B.'s story has come to light among the contemporary records.

[5] See note on p. 243, where it is said that only female elephants were employed as draught beasts.

arms, Shot, powder, thereby to have all things in a readinesse, and they had them built and fitted out to Sea in a months time. The 2 att Banquala were out before I came thence. They were in Figure as here described[1] [Plate XVIII.].

A Few Months afterwards the Kinge of Syam tooke it into consideration that an Austere man, one that had been bred a Warriour, was a fitter person to Governe this Island then the Syamer that now did, and thereupon he sent a New Radja (a Mogol[2] bred and borne) by name Mahomud Beake[3], and his Brother Ishmael Beake[4] to be his Secound. They were both of very comely personage, and Endowed with much discretion, but were much mistaken in the Goverment this countrey required, which wrought theire owne destruction.

Anno Domini 1677 I Voyadged once more to Janselone, and was kindly Entertained by the New Radja and his Brother, but Especially by Some of the Old Shabandars[5] and merchants in Banquala. But I found the most Eminent men, both Syamers and Malayars, to complaine very much and grumble one to another of theire hard measure they received from this present Radja and his councell, men altogeather of another Nation[6], and that

---

[1] See *Ind. Ant.* vol. xxx. pp. 160—163 for an article on Malay boats.

[2] See *Hobson-Jobson*, *s.v.* Mogul. An Indian Muhammadan of the ruling class.

[3] *i.e.* Muhammad Bēg.

[4] *i.e.* Isma'īl Bēg.

[5] See note on p. 242.

[6] Ten years after T. B.'s second visit to Junk-Ceylon, in 1687, the French obtained the ascendancy in the island. D'Orléans, *Voyages*, quoted in Prévost, *Voyages*, vol. xii. p. 178, says, "The French in Siam...agreed [in 1687]...to put themselves in a position to make the Siamese listen to reason...in order to execute the first of these projects, they have gone to seize the Isle of Jonsalam, belonging to this Kingdom." Fournereau, *Le Siam ancien*, p. 33, says that one of the results of the Jesuit missions in 1687–8 was "to obtain for the French permission to work mines in the Isle of Jongsalang." From *De la Loubère*, p. 91, we learn that Brother René Charbonneau who designed

they wold not longe be tyranized Over at Such rates as to labour hard in Cuttinge downe the Woods, buildinge houses, Under the pretence that they were by Order and for the Use of the Kinge of Syam, which were noe Sooner built but were given to one Chuljar[1] or Other, the Radjas favourites.

And to burne and beat Lime for the buildinge a Stone Fort, which things seemed tedious to them, that were not allowed soe much as theire Victuals for theire paines, soe that they Soon began to Sleight the worke, which vexed the Radja soe much that he began to threaten them if soe bee soe much worke was not performed in soe many days, he wold force theire Wifes to worke alsoe, which was a most severe and haynous punishment to the Malayars, which are in generall Mahometans. And, againe, the hearts of the Syamers in generall were wholy sett against this Sort of Goverment, for the Radja had noe Sooner Seated himselfe in his place in Janselone, but he immediately turned out of Office most of the Syamers, both Councellours, Secretaries, Shabandares[2], Bandarees[3], &c.,

---

the wooden fort on the frontier of Pegu "was afterwards three or four years Governor of Jonsalam by Commission, and with great approbation...Mons. Billi, the Master of Mons. de Chaumont's Palace succeeded him in the employment of Jonsalam."

[1] Madras Muhammadan. See *Hobson-Jobson*, *s.v.* Choolia. This and the quotations on the pages following are remarkable for the period, and valuable for the history of the name and for the accuracy of the description of this class of adventurous Muhammadans from the East Coast of Madras. T. B. in the Dialogues at the end of his *Malay Dict.* says that "Achee is frequented by Portugals, Moors, Chuleas, Chineses and others." Compare Finlayson, *Mission to Siam*, p. 13, "A considerable proportion of the motley group congregated on the beach, consisted of Malabar Mahomedans, called Chuliahs, who...were readily to be recognized by their manner partaking as much of idleness as of expectant curiosity." The Editor, about 1890, found the Chuliahs a hard-working but turbulent people in Rangoon.

[2] See note on p. 242.

[3] T. B. in his *Malay Dict.* has "Bendaree, a Treasurer," and "Bandaree, a Pay-master." The word is from the Skr. *bandahāra*, a treasurer. The *Bendahāra* was a very high degree of nobility amongst the Malays; the *bendahārī* were the treasury-officers.

men of Antient Standinge and choice men of all the Countrey, both for Estates and publick good, and very well approved of by the people, and in theire Stead he placed Chulyars[1].

Whereupon the Malayars and Syamers rose Up in arms with joynt consent, and on a Sudden beset the Radja's house and killed him, and with [him] his Brother Ishmael, and all his household Save the Women and Children, and all the Moors and Chulyars Upon the Island Save 2 that made theire Escape to Bangaree[2] and thence to Queda. There were Servants to Mr. William Jearsey[3], therefor the more favoured. I judge they killed in this insurrection 70 or 75 Moors and Chulyars, none resistinge Save the Radja and his Brother, whoe, although Surprised in the house, yet killed 6 of the most resolute Malayars. For which cause the whole Countrey beinge in Such a Confusion, I went away into the Roade and Sailed for Queda.

The Chulyars are a People that range into all Kingdoms and Countreys in Asia, and are a Subtle and Roguish people of the Mahometan Sect, but not very great Observers of many of his laws[4]. Theire Native land is Upon the Southermost parts of the Choromandell Coast, vizt. Porto Novo[5], Pullicherrie[6],

---

[1] See note on p. 256.

[2] A town and estuary on the north-western coast of the Malay Peninsula. Horsburgh, *East India Directory*, vol. ii. p. 25, ed. 1805, says, "In latitude about 8° 53′ North, there is an inlet to a lagoon or bay, where Bangri a place of some trade, and frequented by the coasting vessels is situated." "Bangarie" is marked to the north of Junk-Ceylon in the map to chapter xxxv. vol. ii. p. 26 of Alex. Hamilton's *East Indies*.

[3] See note on p. 251.

[4] This is the most accurate of all contemporary accounts of these people.

[5] See note on p. 82.

[6] This is earlier than any quotation in *Hobson-Jobson* for Pondicherry, and gives an accurate rendering of the common native form. The French established themselves at Pondicherry in 1675, after the

Negapatam[1], &c. They by theire rangeinge much (before they content themselves with a place for theire abode), doe learne to write and Speake Severall of the Eastern languages, whereby they very much delude the people, and not a little cheat them. They are likewise a very great hinderance to us, for, wherever these rascalls be, wee cannot Sell any goods to a Native of the Countrey, but they creep in alonge with them, and tell them in private what our goods cost upon the Coast, or in Suratt[2], or Bengala, or elsewhere, which doth many Christians a great Prejudice.

For these and Some Other of theire Villanies, I am not at all Sorry for this Massacre, but doe rather wish they were Served soe in Bantam[3], Achin, Queda, Johore[4], Syam, and many other Places they are crept into.

---

recapture of St Thomé, under M. Martin. "When the French arrived there this place was called Boudoutschery." Prévost, *Histoire des Voyages*, vol. xiv. p. 16 *n*. Compare the following contemporary references: "In your way to Porta Nova you are to touch at Pullichery." Instructions given to Mr Walton, of the *Diligence*, 5th Nov. 1668, *Factory Records*, Fort St George, No. 16. "The Dutch...have yet another [ship] which in the last Storme was at Pudicherry a little beyond the Violence of it." *O. C.*, No. 3966, 20th May, 1674. "Having no conveyance hence [Masulipatam] to Policherry." 12th Jan. 1676, *Factory Records*, Fort St George, No. 28.

"There is a report that the Dutch have taken Pudycherry from the French, as yet no certainety." Letter to Madapollam, 11th Sept. 1678, *O. C.* No. 4491.

"Our Peon returning from Pollicherry tells me Mounsr. Deletore the French Cheife with three or foure more French men &ca went 12 dayes past to the great Subidar Hargee Raja to Tirumucote with a considerable present, which he could not learn the particulars, but that their cheife business was to gett the government of Pollicherry Towne which now is under an Avaldar, their Factory is seated near a River and some distance from the Sea, to which they have two Bullwarks Fortyfied....Some of their black Merchants came here to see me of whom I enquired their trade, which they told me, has been and is little...." Extract from Elihu Yale's *Memoriall*, Dec. 1681, *O. C.* No. 4776.

[1] See note on p. 2.

[2] See *Hobson-Jobson*, *s.v.* Surat.

[3] See *Hobson-Jobson*, *s.v.* Bantam.

[4] A well-known Malay state in the neighbourhood of Singapore.

QUEDA.

A Kingdome (soe called) Upon the Malay Coast, the Chiefe Roade and River called of the Same from the Chiefe towne or Citty thereof[1].

It is the largest and most Navigable River in this Kingdome, very large and deep within and upon it's barre affordeth water Enough for a Shipp of 250 tunns in burthen (Upon a Springe tide) and Navigable att any time up to the towne of Queda, which is not lesse then 60 English miles above the barre thereof[2].

It is now the residence of the King's Son (by the Natives stiled Sultan)[3], but the Old Kinge taketh up his residence att Solla[4], a very large towne in the very middle of his Kingdome, which Kingdome is none of the greatest containing in Circuit not more then English miles, and not one fourth part inhabited, more then with wild beasts,

---

[1] See *Hobson-Jobson*, *s.v.* Quedda. Dunn, *East Indies Directory*, p. 338, says, "About 45 miles S.E. of Junk-Seilon, you find the port of Quedah: there is a trade for calin, or tutenague, and elephants' teeth, to export to different parts of the Indies."

[2] T. B. in the Dialogues at the end of his *Malay Dict.* says, "The City of Quedah is two Days going with a Boat up a good River, is Moderately peopled, Has a King, and Yields about one Thousand Peculs of very good Pepper, and about Five Thousand Peculs of Tin Yearly...." Horsburgh, *East India Directory*, vol. ii. p. 255, ed. 1855, says, "Queda Town in latitude 6° 6′ N. stands on both sides of the river, which although fronted by a mud flat, has sufficient depth of water within for sloops and brigs to anchor at the Rajah's residence, about 10 or 12 miles above the town."

[3] See *Hobson-Jobson*, *s.v.* Sultan. The above is a valuable quotation, as showing that in the Malay States it sometimes meant the heir-apparent, "second king," Skr. *yuva-rāja*, Pali *upa-rāja* (corrupted by the way into "Upper-Roger" by old writers on Burma, a term which should be in *Hobson-Jobson*), the *Ēng-shē-min* of Burma, the *Jubrāj* of Manipur and so on.

[4] This place seems to be identical with the town now known as Padang Salla, a place about 10 miles inland, situated on the north bank of Kedah River, opposite to the present capital, Alos Star. See Dennys, *Desc. Dict. of Brit. Malaya*, *s.v.* Kedah.

neare the Sea very low Swampy ground and full of woods, and up in the Countrey Mountaneous[1].

There are Severall men in Office that doe governe here, and beare great Sway over the people (Under the Sultan or Younge Kinge) even as his Father had that yet liveth, but is very antient, and hath given most things of Importance to his Son, yett hath an Eye over him that he behave himselfe well, next to whom are the Leximana[2], Orongkays[3] and Shabandars[4], as in Achin[5] Johor[6] &c.

---

[1] Compare *Schouten's* description of Kedah, vol. ii. p. 135 f., "Six and a half degrees further north [than Perak] is the kingdom of Queda, which like Perach, was formerly flourishing with regard to trade. But the wars which it has waged against the kings of Achin have been very prejudicial to it, and, finally it was conquered by that monarchy. The soil of these two kingdoms [Perak and Kedah] would be very productive, but, as there are a great many woods, wild districts, mountains and swamps, where the inhabitants fear to expose themselves to wild beasts and to other dangers which threaten them in such spots, those who would like to devote themselves to agriculture dare not undertake it. For this reason, very fertile tracts remain uncultivated."

Sir John Bowring, who visited Kedah in 1855, found the country very similar to what it was in T. B.'s time. Compare the following in his *Siam*, vol. ii. p. 49, "A high range of mountains divides it [Kedah] from Songkhla and Patani. It is covered with vast forests, which have never been penetrated by man, and which are crowded with wild animals, and particularly tigers. The population, which does not exceed from 60,000 to 70,000 souls, is principally composed of Malays ...Quedah has many rivers, of which several are navigable."

[2] See *Hobson-Jobson*, *s.v.* Laximana. The word is usually translated by "admiral" in the old books. In the following extracts from a letter from Kedah to Surat in Jan. 1674, *O. C.* No. 3917, the title is mistaken for a proper name: "They dare not speak before the king for our Debts...for feare of him and Orankay Loximana...they being hid and protected by Loximana...thereupon gave order to Loximana to deliver them...."

[3] See *Hobson-Jobson*, *s.v.* Orankay. A personage, noble, high official among the Malays. T. B. in his *Malay Dict.* has "Orancāya, a rich man, a Lord." Compare the following from the contemporary records: "The 22d February received a present of Oranges and Fruite from the Queen and Govr. of Patanny accompanied with one of the chief Oran Cayes." Letter to Siam, 23rd March, 1679, *Factory Records*, Siam, No. 1. "Being at Sea and finding the grabb very deep requested of an Oran Keay Syammer to admit 120 parras on board his Mervah." Letter from Siam, 18th Jan. 1682, *Factory Records*, Java, No. 6.

[4] See note on p. 242.

[5] See under the "Achin" section of this volume.

[6] See Crawfurd, *Desc. Dict. of the Indian Islands*, *s.v.* Johor.

Malay Countries[1], but come nothing nigh to the Splendour, State and riches of Achin.

Yet this Countrey Exceeds for plenty of Provisions, and the people in Generall that Serve him on Shore are very Submissive to their Superiours[2], as indeed very well they may, for they have for many years Enjoyed peace and quietnesse att home, haveinge one of the most peacable Kings that Ever reigned, and the most mercifull one that Ever Swayed this Scepter[3].

Indeed a great deale too Mercifull to many of his people, which hath caused them (not longe agoe) to Encroach Upon his prerogative, and goe out upon Piracy and bold[l]y come in againe, after many Spoiles and robberies committed, and have (Upon theire bare promise never to be guilty of the like fact) easily gott theire Pardons, untill such time as they began to robbe the English, a Nation this Kinge doth highly Esteeme of, and then noe more

---

[1] This quotation shows that the West side of the Malay Peninsula was known as the "Malay Coast," and, later on, it will be shown that the term was also applied to the East side of the Peninsula.

[2] *Schouten*, vol. ii. p. 119, says of the people of Kedah and the adjacent countries that they resemble those of Java, but are neither so perfidious nor so sanguinary.

[3] This "old King" must be the one in whose time the English made an ineffectual attempt to settle a factory at Kedah. In Nov. 1668, the factors at Surat wrote to the Court (*Factory Records*, Misc. No. 2, p. 30), "The Dutch have got several ports and contracted for Tynn &c....There is now left open onely Atcheen on the Coast of Sumatra, and a port Called Queda uppon the Maine of Mallacca which the Dutch have layen before, and blockt upp these Three yeares; But the King of the place still holds out in expectation of our Comminge; that we shall use some means or other, that they may heare from us; And if possible, send thither this yeare; It is a Hopefull port, and the people have so great affection for us, that Uppon Assurance we will deale with them, and Supplye them with Commodityes, they will never suffer the Dutch to have any footing among them; It lying uppon the Mayne, we are Informed by a Merchant that is well acquainted with the Countrey, there may be a great Trade driven and Very profitable, when once the Inland Merchants shall finde they may be yearly furnished with goods proper to them." After much correspondence on the subject, a settlement was attempted at Kedah in 1669. See note on p. 267 f. for the failure of the scheme and the withdrawal of the factory.

pardons were to be granted Either to theire Ringleaders or Common people, if they cold be apprehended.

But many rogues lye Sculkinge about the Islands of Queda and about the River of Old Queda, that commit many Villanies and are hard to be taken. I am confident Some of them are soe bloody minded, as to murther theire owne relations if they cold Surprize them with any considerable Purchase.

Anno Domini 1675. A Small Vessell belonginge to the English was Sent from Achin hither laden with very fine goods, and was mett with the Pyrats commonly called Salleeters[1], neare to the Roade of Queda. They Sett Upon her and killed Samuel Ware[2] the master and two more of his men, and tooke the Vessell, which done, they Sent away the Other Seamen in a Prow[3] bound for Achin and came boldly Up to Queda and Sold the goods to Sarajah Cawn[4], a Chulyar[5], and chiefe Shabandar[6] of Quedah, and rogue Enough too. This Rogue by reason he bought them very Cheape made noe question how they came by the goods, although he Saw English marks and Number upon Each particular baile[7].

---

[1] See note on p. 237.

[2] This was probably the Samuel Ware who was one of the crew of the Company's ship *Dilligence* in 1669. After the entry of payment of wages to him (*Marine Records*, Misc. No. 13), there is the note "run away." Between 1669 and 1675 he seems to have prospered, and when he met his untimely end, was master of his own ship. He may have been related to the Richard Ware who went out to India on the *Richard and Martha* in Dec. 1667. This man appears to have held a post at Bantam in 1678, and was living as a freeman in Fort St George, and "married to a musteez [half-caste]" in 1683.

[3] See note on p. 238.

[4] *i.e.* Surāj Khān.

[5] See notes on pp. 256 and 257.

[6] See note on p. 242.

[7] The contemporary records contain no account of the taking of this particular vessel, but the following reference to Surāj Khān in a letter from Queda to Surat, dated Jan. 1674, *O. C.* No. 3917, seems to show that T. B.'s epithet of "rogue" was not undeserved: "Ser Rajah Chawn soone after the departure of the Prowes to Junsalone demanded of us 120 Dollars for the Kings Prowes which was only a

The yeare followinge Mr. James Horner[1] (who owned most of the goods) voyaged to Queda, where being informed of Such transactions, demanded his owne off Sarajah Cawne, but got very little or noe Satisfaction, beinge outwitted by this Cunninge Chulyar.

---

trick of his unknowne to the king to pick some mony out of us, he was much troubled that we would not lett him Lade his fresh goods on those Prowes though we offered him (if he would goe halves with the Company in that Voyage) the goods at a very reasonable rate, but he refused and sent some goods privately by Deria whom he corrupted, Wee found him all along to hinder us in our business, our men confessing that they dare not speak before the king for our Debts or on other business for feare of him and Orankay Loximana who is the greatest Debtor, also he suffered noe other Merchants but himself and those by his order to come into our Compound (as we were divers times informed) which we found to be true by Experience for those that came came by night for feare of him, In this manner he served us although Wee treated him with all civility Imaginable being so ordered by the President."

[1] James Horner was a freeman, who is frequently mentioned in the Madras Records from 1677 to 1687. In Jan. 1677, when the Company's orders, requiring all freemen not in the Company's service to reside at Fort St George, were read at Masulipatam, "James Horner freeman" was absent, probably at Kedah, as stated by T. B. On the 12th March he arrived at Masulipatam from Kedah "with Nyne Elephants, haveing been from this Place upwards of three Yeares." In May, 1678, he was accused of having, while voyaging from "Acheen to Quedah, unduly possessed himself of an estate of from 7 to 8000 Pagodas belonging to Peter Van Deelen of Zealand." In the same month James Horner applied for the release of his goods detained by the Banksall officers. As the Company's "Dubass" was ill, Mr Horner "being very ready and skilled in the Indostan language" was allowed to go to the Governor with three or four of the Factory peons and state his case. He cleared his goods, and on the 10th May, "Ship *St. Mary*, Mr. James Horner Commander sailed out of the Road [of Masulipatam] bound to Quedah." In May, 1679, Horner returned with eleven elephants, and obtained permission to go to Golconda to sell them there on giving a bond of 500 pagodas. He was permitted to take his wife, on condition that she should be brought back to reside in Fort St George before the end of January, 1681. While at Golconda, Horner acted in concert with the Company's "Braminy Vira Ragavaya." In Nov. 1680 the Council at Fort St George sanctioned the payment of 157 Pagodas disbursed at Golconda by Mr Horner for procuring the "Nabob's Rucca [note, memorandum] to Lingpapa." In Jan. 1681 Horner returned to Masulipatam, and in Sept. "Saild in a Sloop of his own for Tenasseree." In 1687 Horner was at Porto Novo, whence he wrote desiring a pass for his ship. Four years later, we find a petition to the Council at Calcutta from a Mrs Horner, probably James Horner's widow, praying "to be invested in possession of a house to which she is heir as next akin."

Another piece of Villanie was acted soon after the former, as followeth. A Portuguees Shipp bound from Goa[1] to Macau[2] In China, happened to fall in with this Coast a little to the Southward of Queda River, and Sent theire boat On Shore to cutt wood for fireinge, and they were Surprized by Some Malayars who lay Sculkinge in every creeke and corner[3], whoe tooke these portugueeses and carried them to Queda, where by advice of that rogue Sarajah Cawn, they were made Slaves on and Sold in the markett place, but they did not longe remaine in Slavery before they tooke a fitt Opportunitie to make their Escape in a Prow well fitted[4]. They tooke her in the night and ranne away to Malacca[5], a Dutch Garrison Upon the South Side of this Coast, all of them togeather Save a Very handsome and well favoured boy of about 11 years of age, whoe for his good countenance the Kinge kept in his Pallace att Solla[6], yett Soon afterwards Upon the request of Mr. Alexander Ogilby, an English Merchant[7], the Kinge

---

[1] See *Hobson-Jobson*, *s.v.* Goa.

[2] See *Hobson-Jobson*, *s.v.* Macao. T. B. is careful not to confuse the then famous but now forgotten Macao on the Pegu River with the Chinese port of the same name.

[3] See p. 237 and note. See also *Dampier*, vol. ii. p. 128, for a description of the "Malayars."

[4] I have been unable to find any confirmation of this story.

[5] See *Hobson-Jobson*, *s.v.* Malacca.

[6] See note on p. 259.

[7] The first mention of Alexander Ogilby or Ogilvy is in 1670, when he was sent on a trading voyage to Mocha by the Surat Council. In 1671, in a letter from Bombay to Surat (*Factory Records*, Surat, No. 105) under date 1st Jan., we find the remark, "Mr. Ogilvy not being bred a soldier is very unwilling to carry a Muskett and soe hath petitioned to goe up to Surat, he is a discreet young man, soe we cannot but recommend him." In 1678 "Alexander Ogleby" was a freeman residing at Bombay. In 1679 he was at Fort St George, where he was a witness to the attestation of Derick Onderhill concerning the murder of John Smith on the *Good Hope*. In 1680 Alexander "Oglevie" and Isabella "Oglevie" are named in the list of "freemen" at Bombay. The name is also spelt "Oyglesby" in *O. C.* No. 4687.

gave him to him freely, and after a true relation how basely the Portugals had been Used by the people of Queda, Sarajah Cawne and Some Others received a Sharpe Checke from the Good Old Kinge[1].

Whoe is accompted by all Christian people (that come or ever did since he began to reigne, to trade in Queda) the honestest and most courteous Kinge that all the Kingdoms of Asia Enjoyeth, besides he is well contented with what God hath been pleased to give him, not a whit covetous, Especially abhorringe any thinge acquired by Oppression or any Unlawfull means, soe that his Subjects are most happy in Such a Prince, and have the disposeinge of theire owne Estates as Seemeth them best, a thinge not customary in Easterne Monarchies and Kingdoms[2].

Hee hath always been a great peacemaker amonge the

---

[1] The Company's servants had not so high an opinion of "the Good Old Kinge." His control over Surāj Khān was very slight, if we may judge from the following taken from *O. C.* No. 3917, extracts of which have been already quoted in notes on pp. 260 and 262: "The Tindall and 1 Lascar that came from Surat for the sloope Died soone after their arrivall from Junsalone, and here being the Tindall and 6 Lascars that ran from the *George*, upon some differance with the Master, wee with some trouble at last got them to saile in the sloope, and paid them 4 months wages beforehand, so that if they have bin with you for mony they abuse us, wee could not get them in 4 months time during the stay of the ship to goe in the ship, they being hid and protected by Loximana and Ser Raja Cawne, being by them promised great rewards if they would stay with them and goe in their prowes, The Master at his taking leave of the King demanded his men, The King promised that if he would pardon and not beate them he should have them, provided he would give it under his hand, and thereupon gave order to Loximana to deliver them, but they not coming he was forced to saile without them, although wee used our uttermost endeavours for them to saile on said shipp."

[2] T. B. is evidently sincere in his admiration of the "old Kinge" from whom he doubtless met with courteous treatment. The contemporary records contain no details about this monarch, but the few allusions to him imply that he was good-natured but weak. Alex. Hamilton says of the King of Kedah in his time, probably T. B.'s "younge Kinge," that he "shews no Marks of Grandeur, besides arbitrary governing...is poor, proud, and beggarly" (*East Indies*, vol. ii. p. 73), but Hamilton was perhaps only speaking in his usual ill-natured manner.

Neighbouringe Kings Vizt. Pattany[1] and Johore[2], and hath reigned in peace not lesse then 60 years, beinge now old and full of days, past all manner of Publicke Negotiation, but Serveth for a most Excellent and Wonderfull Councellour to his Son the younge Kinge, aged now about 20 years.

This Kingdome hath lived Under a happy Goverment in peace many years with all Nations Save the Hollander, whoe have warre with Queda (through theire owne Seekinge), whoe wold not be satisfied in that they Encroached all or most of the Tinne trade into theire owne hand, but wold domineere over the best of his Subjects, and not onely Soe but wold, as of late years they intended to have done in Janselone, vizt. hinder all Others from tradeinge into his Kingdome, and lay claime to the River of Queda, which ambition of theirs threw them out this Country, as I believe it will out of Some Others in a very few years[3].

---

[1] Patani is the Malay state which bounds Kedah on the East. In 1671 the English factors at Kedah wrote to Surat, "Warrs between the Queen of Patana and the king of Singora continue still" (*Factory Records*, Surat, No. 105). The King of "Pattany" mentioned in the text probably succeeded this queen.

[2] See note on p. 258. T. B. in the Dialogues at the end of his *Malay Dict.* has, "Kings of the Malayo country are those of Quedah, Johor, Patanee and many more." In *O. C.* No. 3917, quoted in note on p. 265, we find, "Here offers little news [at Kedah in Jan. 1674], the Jambys have plundered and burnt Jehore, drove the King up into the woods, taken Mr. Lock and given his ship to the Dutch, and carryed him as a slave in Irons into their Country [East Coast of Sumatra]."

[3] It was owing to the encroachments of the Dutch that the King of Kedah encouraged the English to trade with his country in 1669. Writing from Kedah in Nov. 1670 (*Factory Records*, Surat, No. 105), Messrs Davis and Portman remark, "The Dutch hath blocked up this port." The Dutch vigorously opposed the English in Kedah, and, in 1673, took their ship *George* on her return voyage to Surat, and carried her to Ceylon. In *O. C.* No. 3917, Jan. 1674, we read, "In January came before the Barr 3 Dutch ships and 20 Syam Prowes, the Report here was that the Syamers came to fight with the King (he oweing them 3 years tribute) and that the Dutch came to their assistance, great preparations were here made against them, but the Syamers and 1 Dutch ship soone left the Barr, and the 2 Dutch ships that remayne much hindred the trade of this Place in not suffering any Prowes to

The English Nation is here highly in Esteeme, both with the Old and younge Kinge and most of [the] Men in Office, and very civily dealt with by most of the Commonalty resident in Queda towne, the place of greatest Commerce in the Kingdome[1].

---

goe out or come in, The Merchants here had the greatest part of their goods remayning on their hands, so that wee were very much disheartned in seeing our goods lye on our hands without expecting any Vent for them and expecting more goods in 4 months time, for all the time that they lay here wee scarce sold one piece of goods which made us to Examine Our Sloope, and finding that she might be made Capable to voyage downe this Coast without doubling, we with the help of the Carpenters and Caulkers of Mr. Garretts ship...with some trouble and charge, fitted her for her intended Voyage to Perack, Joshua Burroughs was to goe upon her to Endeavour the sale of the Companys goods. There was laden on her for their account 109 tale, she Fell into the hands of the Dutch aboute the Rivers mouth, we not dreaming of warrs with them, Joshua Burroughs comeing downe the River in a smale prow heareing timely news, with nought but the Clothes on his back escaped their hands, but they carryed away Charles Gold and Jos. Cocke who were then aboard but not intended for the Voyage, at the same time also (being aboute the middle of February) they carryed away a smale shipe and sloope of Mr. Garretts."

[1] T. B. gives an optimistic view of English trade at Kedah. The contemporary records, however, tell a different tale. As stated in note on p. 261 a settlement was attempted in 1669, and Mr George Davies was appointed to be the Company's agent there. The following are extracts from his commission, dated 25th April, in Surat, *O. C.* No. 3267: "Wee shall proceed to acquaint you what further wee can learne of the place, and their manner of Commerce for having not yet had any dealings with them, we are constrained to take the greatest part upon trust...their manner of Dealing it Seemes is altogether in trucke for Tynn which is the only Commodity, for wee cannot heare of a Second...Wee have had great encouradgment to enter upon this Voyage, as well for the profitablenesse thereof as in regard they doe very much covett a trade with our nation in hopes whereof (wee are tould) they utterly disowne to have any trade or Commerce with the Hollanders who to bring them under Subjection, blockt up their Port with their shipping for some years together till they were wearied out, besides there is the Port of Pelock [? Perak] upon the same Continent that affoards good Quantities of Tynn and other Commodityes, which wee are advised would be brought thither if they had assurance of yearly Barter in Lieu of it, and lastly there is a great Citty some dayes Journey up in the Countrey from whence alone will resort Merchants that as we now apprehend it, there wants only a Constant concourse of Shipping for the supply of their wants." Mr Davies was empowered, if he found it necessary, to remain at Kedah until he had investigated "the whole trade that if it be worth the while we may appropriate it wholy to the Company." A provision of goods amounting to between twenty and thirty thousand rupees was made for Kedah

on the *Charles*, and Mr John Portman was appointed to serve under Davies. In Sept. 1669 the following unfavourable report was written to Surat, *O. C.* No. 3346, "Wee found here [Kedah] no howse of the Companys but an old Warehouse built by Meange [Mīānjī, a title] which wee propt up the best wee could and housed there the Company's Goods." The factors themselves lodged with an old Armenian in whose charge Meange had left "the Companys Ground." The letter went on to say that it was not worth while to build a house, "this Trade drawing to an end and not worth our Residence here... We visited the Orankay Puglah Lemah Bunder...his pride would not permitt him to take much notice of us but wee understood from him that wee should enjoy the same priviledges as those before us."

On receipt of this discouraging report, the Surat Council wrote to the Court excusing themselves for having undertaken a commercial voyage to Achin and Kedah. They stated that they had no idea at the time how greatly the Dutch had obstructed the trade in those parts. The *Charles* returned to Surat in Feb. 1670, "much Deffective and Leaky." It was then decided to send the *George* to Kedah to recover debts, and, if necessary, to bring back the factors from that place. It was left to Mr Davies to judge of the advisability of continuing the factory. On the 17th Nov. 1670 (*Factory Records*, Surat, No. 105) Messrs Davies and Portman wrote, "A small quantity of Cloth yearly will supply the Markett [of Kedah] and doth not admit of two sellers...the rivers are in several places soe shoale and winding that the shipps cannot goe up...The old king hath sent a Piscash to Mahmud Alle...which we desire may goe Freight free." In Feb. 1671 Davies wrote again from Kedah (*Factory Records*, Surat, No. 105), "We suppose the king hath made you very large promises in his last...however we think it Convenient...that you would desire him to make some absolute agreement with us ratifying it with his Chop."

By this time the Surat Council had realized that the Kedah settlement was a failure, and they decided to recall Davies, "the business being small, and Mr. John Portman ordered to remayne Cheife and Mr. Charles Ward second, and that the Factors be like wise Ordered to sell off all the Companys Goods at Price Current." Davies was blamed for keeping the goods at Kedah "in hopes of better marketts," though the Council admitted, "Wee beleive he doth it out of a good intention." The "other Merchants Sold their goodes there to reasonable proffitt," as probably T. B. did in 1677. On the 7th Nov. 1671 the Surat Council wrote to the Court (*O. C.* No. 3574), "Since the *Georges* departure Wee have received no news from Quedah, Wee hope she will bring us full returns of your estate there together with Mr. Davies whome wee have recalled, and then wee Shall not adventure any more goodes thither without further order from you." But things had gone from bad to worse. In Feb. 1672 they wrote from Surat, *O. C.* No. 3624, "Your Shipp *George* arrived to Swally hole the 29th past from Quedah being two thirds laden with Freight goods which yet will make no inconsiderable Freight, though not neare what She made last yeare, but as to your owne estate wee have no accompt as yet, nor doe wee heare of any goodes laden for your account, more then 14 Piggs of Tynn, nor doe wee know certainly what goodes are Sould, or what remayning; for Wee have no gennerall from your Factors, the reason of this neglect and evill State of your affaires there is caused by the unhappy deaths of Mr. George Davies and Mr. John Portman...Mr. George Davies...sometime before his death he had totally lost his memory being Insensible, and uncapable of any business, caused by drinking of Strong Arrack as tis Supposed." As the Council at Surat could get no information of the state of things at Kedah beyond the fact that "the greatest Parte" of the Company's "goodes was consumed by the Worme by meanes of Mr. Davies willfull breach of order," they decided to send Mr Francis Capell on the *George* to Kedah in April, 1672, to take "an exact account of what goods are Sold, and Sell off what are remayning." Francis Capell was accompanied by Joshua Burroughs. These unfortunate factors reached Kedah to find the whole Malay coast in a disturbed state. Dutch ships blocked the ports, and they could do nothing but send piteous appeals to Surat for help. On the 2nd Sept. 1673 the Council wrote (*O. C.* No. 3844), "Wee have herewith sent a letter to the King of Quedah, desireing his Protection of you during your stay in his Port, Hee cannot expect that wee can send a Person with it, in such tymes as these, when wee are not assured that our Letters will come safe to you or the Provisions wee send you, but wee have given caution to the Persons who carry them, who have promised their care...Wee pray God keepe you in that temper of Spiritt, that you may not be discouraged by your state there since it is not in our power to bring you thence, you will beare it the more patiently especially remembring you are not so unhappy as many others that are fallen into the Enemies hands att Batavia and Mallacca."

On the 1st Jan. 1674 Capell and Burroughs sent a long and detailed account of their misfortunes to the Council at Surat. The letter is entitled "Quedda General to Suratt," *O. C.* No. 3917, parts of which have already been quoted. The following are the most interesting paragraphs: "Wee have received yours of the 22nd Aprill and 2nd September by the Jounck *Selimony* with those provitions sent on her for our refreshments which are very welcome to us. Now these goe by a King ship bound for Porta Nova which will bring you but sad tidings of this our unfortunate Factory, It hath pleased God to take from us all that the Dutch had left by a suddain fire on the 20 May last, all that we had both in our house and warehouses, wee saveing nothing, but some few goods pulled out of the fire in the Companys warehouse, which were after sold for 2 tale 12 mace, 6 bahar of tinne in the warehouse and a small scrittore wherein was Copie of the *Georges* account freight and 5 tale 10½ Mace in mony. The fire was so fierce and vehement that wee saved nothing else Escaping only in our Shirts and drawers, and Blessed be God that wee Escaped with our lives for had wee bin in our beds (as wee were goeing to repose when wee found it) little less then a Miracle would have saved us, which sad accident happened either by Rogues without the house or by the carelessness of a boy with a Candle within, wee had a sad warning aboute 2 months before by a dismall fire which in less then 2 houres consumed down to the ground one halfe the Towne being all one side of the Buzar The houses here being made of Huttops (which are no more then leaves of trees) do take like tinder in the dry times, For Prevention in the like accident to us as also of Rogues at such time wee thought fit to make a strong Pagar about the Town, but at the time of the fire it was not quite finished...By her (the *George's*) miscarring and the miscarrage of Mr. Garretts smale ship that parted hence in February last, you were deprived of our advises, though they were of little concernment for wee could not sell but a very few goods by reason of the great quantities of fresh goods brought on freight, so that these Merchants would not look upon our old goods...At our first arrival and delivering our Letters to the king wee complained to him of the great quantityes of our goods that had bin here so long unsold, and craved his assistance in the disposall of them in Barter for Tinn, according to his Phirmaund at 2 tale per Bahar. His answer was that he was sorry to hear it, and that it was none of his fault but our owne, our bringing of Merchants was the cause that wee did not find that quick sale for our goods as we expected, and that if we did not bring them, they could not come here and that if we ourselves brought merchants that would give more than 2 tale per Bahar how could we expect otherwise but that wee must give the like.

"At our Examining the warehouse we found the goods lye in sad Condition and in a most confused manner, Great quantityes Damaged rotten and without papers, wee made sortings before a just account could be taken, and according to the Ballance of Mr. Davies his bookes (which wee here ballanced) wee found many wanting of which Charles Ward gave us no other account but that they were throwne into the River in Mr. Davies his time, and that he never received any account and therefore could not give any.

"Our Endeavours were not wanting in the promoting the sale of them, for finding no vent for them here, we (by the advice of several Merchants) thought fit to transport them, and accordingly (by the help of the King who lent us a Prow), sent to the Vallue of 2600 Rupees on 2 Prowes by Charles Ward to Junsalone (it being his own desire) and also our great desire to send something home on our Honble. Masters account, The Voyage did not prove soe successful as was expected occationed by his long passage, by reason of foule weather by which the goods received Damage which at the best were in a bad condition so that he could not dispose of them all but left the goods in the hands of one Deria a Chulia of this place...soone after Deria arrived here with a small parcell of Tinn, but brought no other account then that he had left most of the goods unsold in the hands of one Musa...from whom since we have received no other account but that the Dutch have binn there, and plundered the house of all both Tinn and goods that we left...Soone after the...departure of the Dutch wee went to the King and entreated him to take of all the goods, and to help us with prowes to carry us to Achen hopeing that there wee might finde a passage for Surat, for that as long as these warrs held we could not expect a ship here for that we did not conceive ourselves safe here for that they might as well take us out of our house, as take our sloope out of his River, his answer was that now we had warrs we could not safely goe, neither could he answer it, for if any ill or mischeif befell us the Company would lay the blame on him, and that our stay here should be safe, pretending much Love to us, that he would rather suffer his Country to be distroyed, and Die himself then deliver us to the Dutch, or suffer them to take us...The greatest part [of the Companys estate] is still abroad in debts about which wee have no smale trouble, wee have oft moved to the King that wee may have allowance for the non-payment; and oft received denyalls but still persisting in our demands he at last promised that wee should receive our tinne at the rate of 3 tale per Bahar...but when wee shall receive it is uncertaine for in this Country is neither Justice nor equity; they receiving piscashes of both parties, but nothing effected save many fair words and promises...Our living here longer upon dead Charge will soone cleare that little the Company has left, so that there must

The Priviledges allowed to the English Merchants here are very considerable and Sociable, as well to one as another Company or noe Company. When the Companie's Shipp arriveth from Suratt, as generally there doth one every yeare (if not more), the Cape Merchant[1] when he cometh Up to towne visiteth the Orong-kay[2], who kindly welcometh him on Shore, and prepareth Some of the King's boats, and goeth alonge with him in Person to Solla[3] (the place of the Old Kings residence). Most part

---

be some course taken for our removall...Wee doe hope and almost Impatiently wait for your answer and orders by returne of this ship, our stay here is most uncomfortable we two being the only Christians in this Country, and we by the fire are deprived of all our English books, so that should it please God to send sickness we are as well destitute of Phisick for soule as body...wee doe not keep more servants then are mearly necessary, this Country being dangerous by reason of theives wee are forced to keep a watch in the night, God in mercie grant us a happy and honourable Peace...we in the meane time relying upon God for our Comfort in this comfortless Country...."

Before the receipt of the above letter from Capell and Burroughs the Council at Surat had written to Kedah in April, 1674 (*Factory Records*, Surat, No. 87, p. 148), telling their unfortunate servants that there was no immediate hope of procuring their departure, and informing them that Charles Ward, who was taken on the *George* by the Dutch, had returned to Surat. At the end of June the Kedah letter of Jan. reached Surat. On the 21st Sept. the Council wrote, "Wee hope you may be imbarqued on Mirza Mozums Jounck, haveing received from Malacca the good newes of an Honourable peace with the Dutch...Wee have here inclosed sent you a letter to deliver to the king of Quedah to permitt your departure, letting him know our just resentments for the many obstructions you have there mett with in your business, occationed by his Ministers Ser Rajah Chaun and others." Another year, however, elapsed before the ill-starred factory at Kedah was finally abandoned. In 1683 the question of settling "a small factory at Cudda or Jehore" was debated by the Court, but in 1686 the Directors finally decided against the project, "Wee will have no Factory settled for us at Pegu, nor at Quedah nor any of those little places where we cannot bring our great Ships."

[1] *i.e.* supercargo. Compare the following in "Instructions given by the Court," dated 9th Oct. 1663, *O. C.* No. 2994, "We are resolved to send a Cape Merchant to voyage on every ship from hence forward, who shall bee accomptable to us for all transactions during the time of the voyage." Mr Matthew Gray went "Cape Merchant" on the *Nugdy*, and Mr George Davies "Cape Merchant" on the *Charles* to Kedah and Achin in 1669.

[2] See note on p. 260. [3] See note on p. 259.

of the way they goe by water, and then mount the Elephants prepared for them, and goe Straightway to pay their respects to the Kinge, who after a most welcome manner doth give them Entertainment. The English Merchant presenteth him with a piscash[1], not Valueinge lesse then 50 pound Sterlinge, in gold baftos[2], silks, &c. The Kinge in Person doth receive them and feasteth them very Nobly and Royally accordinge to the Custome of Queda, and never faileth to returne the full Value of what he received in Agala wood[3].

When the Said Merchant cometh downe to Queda, he Piscasheth[1] the younge Kinge alsoe with almost soe much in Value as he did the Old one, and he faileth not to follow his Father's rules in the way of retalliation, the which transported to Suratt yields more advance then any Such quantities of goods Sold here to the Merchants.

If any Ship or Vessell come from the Coast of Choromandell or Bengala, as yearly there doth one if not more[4], they follow the Same beforementioned rules, for by longe Usinge they are become an absolute Custome not to be

---

[1] See note on p. 157.

[2] See *Hobson-Jobson*, *s.v.* Bafta. See *Ind. Ant.* vol. xxix. p. 337. "Blew Baftas, Broad Baftas and Gold Baftas" were much in request in England in T. B.'s time. Murray, *Oxford English Dict.* has, "Baft. A kind of coarse and cheap (generally cotton) fabric, originally of oriental manufacture, but now made in Great Britain for export, especially to Africa."

[3] This is the Aquilaria Agallocha, commonly known as Calambac, Aloe-wood or Eagle-wood. See Watts, *Economic Products of India*, vol. i. p. 279. T. B. in his *Malay Dict.* has, "Agila-wood or Lignum-aloes." Compare *Dampier*, vol. ii. p. 8, "The merchants of China do...fetch from thence (Cochin China) Lignum Aloes, and Aguala Wood, which is much esteemed for its rare scent." See also *Ind. Ant.* vol. xxviii. p. 196 and vol. xxix. p. 335.

[4] These ships were private trading vessels, such as those commanded by T. B. for William Jearsey or on his own account. John Bugden, Clement Jordan and John Smith made voyages to Kedah between 1676 and 1680. In these trading voyages goods for the Company, as well as separate consignments for the factors, were usually carried.

Violated; and they have the retalliation put to theire choice whether Agala[1] or Elephants, soe that if theire Ships be of any considerable burthen they choose Elephants, which Annimal if they conduct safe to the Other Side yieldeth abundance of Profit[2].

Here are Elephants more Plenty and Sold at much cheaper rates then in any Countrey or Kingdome besides, One of 5 cubits and an halfe is a very Siseable and a Merchandable Elephant, and such are Sold here for 200 pieces of 8[3] which transported to Metchlipatam or Bengala will yield 3000. It is very rare to gett leave to transport an Elephant that Exceedeth in Stature 6 Cubits (vizt. 9 English feet.)[4]

Many Strange Passages I have heard and read of Concerninge this Creature, which are for the most part horrid Romances (vizt.) That they if [they] ly downe cannot rise againe, and of the ways of ketchinge alive and tameinge these Monstrous Annimals, and of theire goeinge to warre

---

[1] See note on p. 272.

[2] Alex. Hamilton visited Kedah in 1694 and in his *East Indies*, vol. ii. p. 73 f. gives a very different account of the country, its government and methods of trade: "The King...never fails of visiting stranger Merchants at their coming to his Port, and then, according to Custom, he must have a Present. When the Stranger returns the Visit, or has any Business with him, he must make him a Present, otherwise he thinks due Respect is not paid to him, and in Return of these Presents his Majesty will honour the Stranger with a Seat near his sacred Person, and will chew a little Betel, and put it out of his royal Mouth on a little gold Saucer, and sends it by his Page to the Stranger, who must take it with all Signs of Humility and Satisfaction, and chew it after him, and it is very dangerous to refuse the royal Morsel." Hamilton adds, after his usual ill-natured manner, an unsavoury scandal about the "young king," reflecting on the close intermarriage common among the Royal families of most Further Indian nations.

[3] *i.e.* Spanish dollars. See note on p. 114.

[4] Compare Alex. Hamilton, *East Indies*, vol. ii. p. 73, "Quedah...Its Product is...Elephants, and Elephants Teeth." Crawfurd, *Desc. Dict. of the Indian Islands*, says *s.v.* Queda, "The name, correctly written Kādah...signifies in Malay 'an elephant trap.'...Among its wild animals, the elephant is very numerous, and is used as a beast of burthen—even bred, and occasionally exported to the Coromandel coast."

with towers and Gunns mounted upon their backs[1], with many other Fictions that I can make bold to gainesay, for they doe ly downe when they ingender, the Female upon her back and the Other Upon her, as alsoe att many other times, and doe rise with a great deale of Ease, and as for the ways in takeinge them alive and Civilizeinge them, they are thus.

The tamed Elephants goe into the woods (where the Wild ones resort) and feigne themselvs as mad as they, and by that means they delude them into a very Stronge pound or fence made for the Same purpose, and when 5 or 6 tame Elephants have gotten one or two wild ones in, they fall upon them and beat them severely, untill the Keepers come and put theire leggs in the Stocks, by which means, and having the tame Elephants by them, and good Store of victuals, as plantrees[2], younge bamboos[3] and the like, they alsoe in the Space of 30 or 40 days become tame, but they never ingender after they are once tamed[4].

And as for theire way of fightinge in an army, [it] is neither with towers nor guns[5], yet those trained Up for warre will by theire Valour doe very great Execution. They fight with very great Eagernesse and couradge, theire

---

[1] T. B. had evidently never seen a war elephant. See *Dampier*, vol. ii. p. 73. Compare *De la Loubère*, p. 92, "They [the Siamese] very much rely upon the Elephants in Combats, though this Animal for want of Bit and Bridle, cannot be securely governed, and he frequently returns upon his own Masters when he is wounded. Moreover he so exceedingly dreads the fire, that he is never almost accustomed thereto. Yet they exercise them to carry, and to see fired from their back little pieces about three foot long, and about a pound of Ball."

[2] The contemporary form of plane-tree, the plantain or banana. This is a valuable quotation.

[3] See note on p. 249.

[4] Compare *De la Loubère*, p. 44 f., for a somewhat different method of entrapping wild elephants. See also *Schouten*, vol. ii. p. 33 f., for the method of catching elephants in Ceylon. Elephants do occasionally breed in captivity.

[5] See note 1 above.

onely weapon is a Chaine of 18 or 20 foot longe, made fast to one of theire foremost leggs, the which they Coyle up like a rope upon theire tronke, and when they come neare the Enemy, Flinge out the Said Chaine with Such Violence, that they knock downe and bruise to pieces all they reach both horse and man, and Some times disorder theire adversaries army very much.

The Stocks they put them into to civilize them are very Substantiall ones, as indeed they ought to be; they are noe lesse then very greats (*sic*) trees, with holes that are cutt throught the bodies of them fitt for theire leggs to runne into, and then they drive in wedges, and Seizeinge goe from one legge to another.

The tallest and best Sett Elephant that ever I beheld was in Janselone, and I never saw any come neare his height by 6 inches at least, and be proportionable Every way as he was. His height was 14 English feet, and was, Soone after I saw him, Sente to the Kinge of Syam as a present very rare and most highly Esteemed of[1].

The Kinge of Queda is Tributary to him of Syam[2], although the tribute he payeth be but inconsiderable in it Selfe, beinge noe more then annually a gold flowre[3], not

---

[1] See Balfour, *Cycl. of India*, *s.v.* Elephant, for a long article on the subject. Compare Lockyer, *Trade in India*, p. 62, "The most remarkable things about it [the palace at Achin] are two or three Elephants kept for State, these they get from Pegu or Quedah, where are abundance of them, I have seen fifty in one Garden at Madrass, brought thence in a Season, valued from 200 to 800 Pagodas each."

[2] When Schouten visited the Malay Peninsula in 1663, Kedah was subject to the King of Achin, "A portion of the Malay countries is under the dominion of the King of Siam...But the Kingdoms of Pera and of Queda are subject to the King of Achin." *Schouten*, vol. ii. p. 125.

[3] Compare the following from *Journal ou Suite du Voyage de Siam*, p. 289, "The Kings of Camboge, of Géor, of Patani, of Queda, and of Jambi, are tributaries to the King of Siam, and pay him every year a bouquet of gold flowers." *Mandelslo*, p. 108, speaks of similar tribute paid at Patani, "Not many years since there reigned a Queen [at Patani], that sent him [the King of Siam] no more then once a year a Flower of Gold, and some Silk-Stuffes and Scarlet." Compare also De la Loubère, *Siam*, p. 82, "For Tribute she [the Queen of Patani] sends to the King of Siam every three Years two small Trees, the one

Exceedinge 20 pieces of 8[1] in Value, yet he must Send it him or incurre his displeasure; the like all the Kings Upon the Malay Coast must doe. This good Old Kinge is timerous that the Syam Kinge Shold Send an army to invade his land, more Especially Anno Domini 1677, meerly through flyinge news thereof, he with his Son and all his household, accompanied with most Eminent men in the Kingdome, fledd up to the Mountains and left Queda, Solla, and many other places destitute of inhabitants, for Some time, untill a Tarra[2] came from Syam with letters and a Gold Cappe for a present to him, after a friendly but Monarchiall manner, bidding him live, poore Slave, and Enjoy his Countrey in peace. As indeed I believe he may, for any prejudice the Kinge of Syam[3] purposeth to doe him or his people, haveinge a warre of greater consequence in hand, namely with the Kinge of Pegu[4].

This Countrey Affordeth considerable quantities of Pepper[5], which indeed is admirable good, and not without desert accompted the best in India[6] or the South Seas[7], being very Sound and Stronge and very cleane and largely corned. There is not any that groweth Upon the maine land of this Kingdome, but Upon an Island about 30 or

---

of Gold, the other of Silver." Crawfurd, who visited Kedah in 1822, says (*Embassy to Siam*, p. 29) that, "by immemorial usage, the King of Queda sends to Siam...a triennial token of submission, in the form of a little tree of gold." For gold and silver trees as tribute see *Ind. Ant.* vol. xxv. p. 289. These "trees" were really incidental to the process of casting metals in natural sand moulds for coinage.

[1] See note on p. 114. [2] See note on p. 253.

[3] This was Phrai Narai, 1656—1658, the ally of Louis XIV. of France.

[4] This war was probably the occasion of building the "wooden fort" mentioned by De la Loubère. See note on p. 278.

[5] Bowring, *Siam*, vol. ii. p. 49, f. n., says, "Camoens speaks of Quedah as the principal district for the production of pepper." *Mandelslo*, p. 112, says, "The places which produce most of it [pepper] are...Quida." T. B. in the Dialogues at the end of his *Malay Dict.* has, "Quedah...yields about one Thousand Peculs of very good Pepper...Yearly."

[6] *Mandelslo*, however, says, p. 112, "The Pepper of Sumatra s without doubt the best in the Indies."

[7] See note on p. 188.

Plate XV

p. 229.

"A PATELLA."

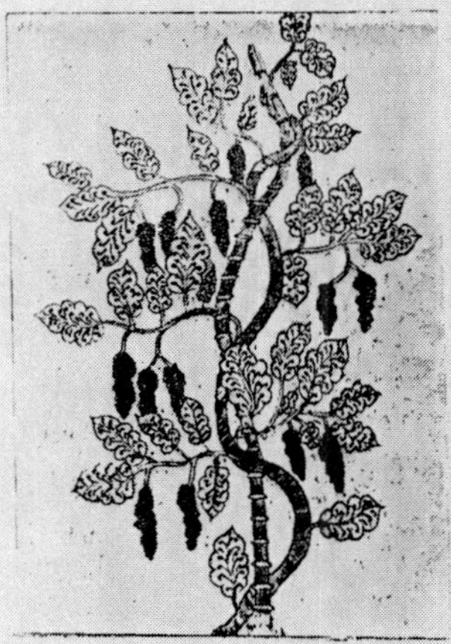

p. 277.

"PEPPER."

p. 277.

"LONG PEPPER."

40 English miles in circuit, called Pullo Ladda, vizt. Pepper Island. Pullo in the Malay tongue Signifieth Island and Ladda pepper[1]. It is 8 leags to the NW. of Queda River's mouth. Black and white Pepper groweth as followeth. [Plate XV.]

They have Longe Pepper[2] in great quantities that groweth Upon the Maine, but it is noe great commoditie to be transported to the Coast or Bengala, by reason Bengala Supplieth all that Countrey with Plenty Enough thereof, and better then this they have here. They put it to little or no Use, onely for theire Elephants to Eat. They accompt it hearty and good for them, and doe frequently give them thereof to Eat. It groweth as followeth. [Plate XV.]

Theire buildings in this Generall are but of a very meane Sort built of Bamboos[3] and Rattans[4], and Stand for the most part Upon Stilts of wood, because of the great riseinge of the waters in time of the raines[5], which happen for the most part in the Months October and November.

---

[1] T. B. in his *Malay Dict.* has, "*Pooloo*, an island, *Lada*, pepper." Wilkinson, *Malay Dict.*, gives "*Pulau*, An isolated patch of anything, an island. *Lada*, A generic name applied to pepper."

In a letter to Surat, dated 16th Nov. 1670 (*Factory Records*, Surat, No. 105), the factors at Kedah wrote, "Send 5 or 6 more [men] to goe to Pullo Ladda or Purles, which are places belonging to this King [of Kedah], where Tinn and pepper may be bought at cheaper rates then here."

Of the Laddas, Horsburgh, *East Indies Directory*, vol. ii. ed. 1805, p. 148, says "The Laddas...are high rugged Islands, of barren aspect. Capt. Forrest calls the large central Island Pullo Ladda, which generally bears the name Lancava; and to the Westernmost large Island commonly called Pulo Ladda he gives the name of Lancaway."

Pepper is no longer grown in any quantity in these Islands.

[2] Crawfurd, *Dict. of the Indian Is.*, has, *s.v.* Pepper (Long), "This is the *chabe* of the Javanese, and the *lada panjang* of the Malays....This commodity is probably a native of Java."

[3] See note on p. 249.

[4] See notes on pp. 74 and 250. Compare T.B.'s remark in the Dialogues at the end of his *Malay Dict.* "Here [Kedah] is also Ratans, Damar...and a few Elephants Teeth."

[5] Compare the description of Siamese houses by De la Loubère, *Siam*, p. 29, "Their Houses are small, but surrounded with pretty

They have but very few garrisons in this Kingdome. I never Saw more then two wooden Forts of 12 or 14 guns each[1]. They are built neare the River Side some 10 miles above the barre.

They have Severall Sorts of very good Fruit in the Countrey, vizt. Limes, Lemons, Duryans[2], Mangoes[3], and

---

large Grounds. Hurdles of cleft Bambou, oftentimes not close compacted, do make the Floors, Walls and Roofs thereof. The Piles, on which they are erected to avoid the Inundation, are Bambous as thick as one's Leg, and about 13 Foot above the Ground, by reason that the Waters do sometimes rise as much as that. There never is more than four or six, on which they do lay other Bambous across instead of Beams. The Stairs are a Ladder of Bambou, which hangs on the outside like the Ladder of a Windmill. And by reason that their Stables are also in the Air, they have Climbers made of Hurdles by which the Cattle enter therein."

[1] *De la Loubère*, p. 91, explains the lack of fortresses in Siam, an explanation which probably also applied to the dependency of Kedah, "The Kingdom of Siam being very strong by its impenetrable Woods, and by the great number of Channels, wherewith it is interspersed, and in fine by the annual Inundation of six Months, the Siameses would not hitherto have places well fortified for fear of losing them, and not being able to retake them; and this is the reason they gave me thereof. The Castles they have would hardly sustain the first shock of our Soldiers; and though they be small and ugly, because they would have them such, yet is it necessary to employ the skill of the Europeans to delineate them. 'Tis some years since the King of Siam designing to make a wooden Fort on the Frontier of Pegu, had no abler a person to whom he could entrust the care thereof, than to one named Brother René Charbonneau."

[2] See *Hobson-Jobson*, *s.v.* Durian. T. B. in his *Malay Dict.* has, "*Doorēun*, a Prickly fruit in India." See *Mandelslo*, p. 120, for a long description of this fruit. Compare the quaint account by *Schouten*, vol. ii. p. 358, "The Dutch give the name of Stinkert, or Stinker, to the Durion, which is a fruit with an odour closely resembling roasted onion, or rotten garlic, so that it does not attract those who have never tasted it, but when they happen to eat it, they are greatly astonished to find it so good. When it is ripe it is generally about the size of the head of an eight year old child. The skin is very thick, and furnished with sharp spines; and as this skin, or rather bark, is easily separated, they are usually opened with the feet. Inside are found four or five cavities, separated by skins, which are filled with a pulp, soft, delicate, and of excellent flavour. They have three kernels as big as chestnuts. They are so good that one cannot help eating them to repletion. They are considered very wholesome, especially for people of a cold and moist temperament."

See also Watts, *Dict. of Economic Products of India*, *s.v.* Durio.

[3] See note on p. 48.

Pines[1], of which last they have in great abundance, more then in any Other Countrey that Ever I was in. The Figure of the Pine Apple as followeth. [Plate XVI.]

All Sorts of Provisions are here in Plenty Enough, vizt. Cocks and henns, Cows, buffoloes, wild hogge, and very great plenty of fish (Especially neare the Sea), but noe ducks or geese to be had, nor Swines flesh tamed alive, by reason they are all of the Mahometan Faith[2]. Rice they have in great plenty[3], and as I said before, much fish caught neare the barre and there Sold for little or nothinge. Here followeth the Shapes of Some Strange fishes I have Seen caught here in Queda. [Plate XVI.]

The Maine Land of this Kingdome in Generall with the Adjacent Isles are very woody[4]; and [on] the maine is very plenty of Wild beasts, vizt. Elephants, Tygers, Buffolos, and Monkeys. I have been by Severall informed that there are Lions here alsoe, but I never Saw any of them.

The Buffolo[5] is here both wild and tame. The wild

---

[1] T. B. in his *Malay Dict.* has, "*Ānānas*, a Pine-Apple." See *Hobson-Jobson*, *s.v.* Pine Apple and Ananas.

[2] Compare *Mandelslo*, p. 108, "The Inhabitants breed no Swine, [at Patani], but the Forrests are so full of wild ones, that they are forc'd to hunt them to prevent the destruction of their Rice; which being taken, they bury them in the ground, as being Mahumetans, and eat none themselves, nor suffer others."

[3] Forrest, *Voyage to the Mergui Archipelago*, p. 25, gives a similar account of the products of Kedah in 1783, "At Queda there is great plenty of rice, bullocks, buffaloes, and poultry; but not such abundance of fruit and vegetables as at Acheen...Queda is a flat country, favourable for the cultivation of rice."

[4] Compare Crawfurd, *Embassy to Siam*, p. 28, "The character of this territory [Kedah] in general is that of being extremely woody, marshy, and mountainous...In the range of hills in the interior, there are many mountains of a great height."

[5] See *Hobson-Jobson*, *s.v.* Buffalo. Compare *Fryer's* amusing description of this animal, p. 118: "A Buffola is of a Dun colour, and are all as big as their largest Oxen; they love to wallow in the Mire like an Hog; there are of them wild, which are very Fierce and Mischievous, Trampling a Man to Death, or Moiling him to Pieces with their Foreheads; their Horns are carelessly turned with Knobs around, being usually so ordered, or rather disordered (for they retain no certain Form) that they lie too much over their Heads to do any harm with them. Their Flesh is reckon'd Hotter and Courser than

ones are very furious and of great Strength. I have heard Some very Credible men in this countrey averre that many times they have Seen a Wild buffolo to Encounter with a Very large Tiger and worst him. The Buffolo is not much Unlike to a Cow or Bull, but are of Stature larger, and for want of haire and haveinge Such a Wild looke and great Stareinge horns he Seemeth much more deformed. [Plate XVIII.] There be abundance of tame ones in most places of India and South Seas, and the Malayars doe often kill and Eat them, but they are grosse meat and very hot.

This Kingdome in it Selfe affordeth noe Gold or Silver or any minerall Save tinne[1], yet Gold is here indifferent plenty[2], soe that most Merchants that buy our goods doe pay us in very good Coyne. Most or all of it is brought from Pattanie[3], a Kingdome that is near neighbour to this lyinge on the East Side of this great Neck of Land called the Malay Coast[4].

The Coyne is good gold and in Small pieces and are called Copans[5], 3 of which Value one Royall of 8[6] or 4s. 6d. English.

Beef, which is the most common Sustinence of the Moors, as their Milk and boiled Butter is of the Gentues."

Of the buffalo, Crawfurd, *Embassy to Siam*, p. 432, remarks, "The Siamese Buffalo in all respects resembles the same animal as it exists among the Eastern Islands, and unless the Rhinoceros and Hippopotamus be excepted, is, after the Elephant, the largest of all quadrupeds.'

[1] See notes on pp. 259 and 267. Compare the following from *Factory Records*, Hugli, No. 4, under date 3rd June, 1673, "The Dutch endeavour to make Tin a Drugge" by sending home most of what they get from "Pera, Jehoar, Kedea."

[2] T. B. in the Dialogues at the end of his *Malay Dict.* says, "Queda...yields some little gold."

[3] See note on p. 266.

[4] See note on p. 261.

[5] See note on p. 241. See *Ind. Ant.* vol. xxvii. p. 223 f. and vol. xxxi. p. 51 ff., where I have gone fully into the history of the word. The gold kobang here mentioned, worth about 1*s.* 6*d.*, was evidently a local coin.

Wilkinson, *Malay Dict.*, has "*Kobang* (Kedah). A coin of the value of 2½ cents. Also *gobang*. Possibly a variant of *kupang*."

[6] See note on p. 114.

4 Copans is one mace[1].
16 mace is one Taile[2].

Noe Other Coyned moneys in this Kingdome, Save Small Coppar moneys tinned over[3], called Tarra[4], 96 of which make one Copan.

Theire Weights and measures are the Same with them of Achin[5], Onely there they measure by the

---

[1] See note on p. 115. T. B. in his *Malay Dict.* has, "Mas, gold" and "Mas, a weight for gold used in many parts of India." Compare Lockyer, *Trade in India*, p. 42, "A Quarter of a Mace is called a Pollam or Copang, Imaginary."

[2] See *Hobson-Jobson, s.v.* Tael. See *Ind. Ant.* vol. xxvii. p. 37 ff. T. B. in his *Malay Dict.* has, "Tial, a weight for gold used in many parts of India and China." The word Taile is from the Malay *tali*, which Wilkinson, *Malay Dict.*, gives as "a money value representing about an eighth of a ryal or ancient dollar of 60 cents."

[3] Compare *Tavernier*, vol. i. part ii. p. 6, "The Money of the King of Cheda and Pera. This Money is of Tin, and is coin'd by the King of Cheda and Pera. He coins no other Money than Tin. Some years since he found out several Mines, which was a great prejudice to the English. For the Hollanders and other Merchants buy it, and vend it all over Asia. Formerly the English brought it out of England, and furnished great part of Asia, where they consum'd a vast quantity; they carried it also into all the Territories of the Great Mogul, as also into Persia and Arabia; for all their Dishes are of Copper, which they cause to be Tinned over every month. Among the meaner sort of people, there is little to be seen but this Tin-money, and the Shells call'd Cori."

[4] This *tarra* is quite a different coin to that described in *Hobson-Jobson, s.v.* Tara, Tare, which in the 1903 ed. is derived from "Malayal *taram*, defined in the Madras Gloss. as 'a copper coin, value 1½ pies.'" Dennys, *Desc. Dict. of British Malaya, s.v.* Money, gives the derivation for the coin mentioned in the text from Malay *tera* (*vide* note on tarrah on p. 253). He says, p. 241, "The small coins of Kedah are of tin. These go under the name of *tra*, which is, however, only the word 'stamp' or 'impression.' Of these, 160 are filed on a filament of rattan, of which 8 strings, or 1,280 coins, are considered equivalent to a hard dollar."

[5] There is no special paragraph on coins in the "Achin" section of this MS., but in the Dialogues at the end of his *Malay Dict.* T. B. gives an account of the weights and measures of Achin, which is worth quoting. He says, "The Weights and Measures of this Place is accounted so.

The Weight is the Bahar Malayo, Pecool, Cattee, Booncal, Miam, which they account so

16 Miams	1 Booncal
20 Booncal	1 Cattee
100 Cattee	1 Pecool
2 Pecool	1 Bahar Malayo.

bamboo[1], and here by the Gantange[2]. One Gantange contains Exactly 2 Achin Bamboos.

This Countrey is noe very great place of trade haveinge but little by Sea and much lesse by land[3]. There are not above 4 or 5 Ships and Vessels per annum from Suratt, Choromandell and Bengala that Use this Country[4], with 5 or 6 great Prows yearly from Borneo[5], and about 30 or

---

The Bahar contains of English Averdupoiz weight, 396 l. 11 oz. 00 dw. 14 gr.

The Booncal contains of Troy weight, 1 oz. 8 dw. 23 gr.

The aforesaid is the Malayo weight, but they also use the China (Dachin) or Stilliard for great Weights, which is accounted so

Conderin, Mas, Tial, Cattee, Pecool, Bahar.

10 Coonderin	1 Mas
10 Mas	1 Tial
16 Tial	1 Cattee
100 Cattee	1 Pecool
3 Pecool	1 Bahar Malayo.

The China Pecool contains of English Averdupois weight, 131 l. 13 oz. 12 dw.

The Tial contains of Troy weight, 1 oz. ·4 dw. 1 gr."

This table compares very well with that given by *Dampier*, vol. ii. p. 132 for Achin. See also Kelly, *Universal Cambist*, p. 97.

[1] T. B. in the account of the weights and measures of Achin quoted above, note 5, p. 281, adds, "Rice, Oil, Butter, and some other Merchandize is sold by a Measure called a Bamboo.

The Bamboo contains of English Wine Measure 3½ Pints.

The long Measure which is used here, and in all Places of the South Seas is the Cubit, which contains Eighteen Inches English." The joint of a bamboo was one of the units of Malay and Javanese measures. Compare *Dampier*, vol. ii. p. 134, "A Mess [mace] will buy 14 or 15 Bamboes of it [rice]: whereas when Rice is scarce, you will not have above 3 or 4 Bamboes for a Mess. A Bamboe is a small seal'd measure, containing, to the best of my remembrance, not much above half a Gallon."

[2] See *Hobson-Jobson*, *s.v.* Ganton. Kelly, *Universal Cambist*, p. 108, says that, at Malacca "The Gantang, rice measure, weighs 6 lb. Dutch troy, or 6⅙ lb. avoirdupois nearly." Dennys, *Desc. Dict. of British Malaya*, has, *s.v.* "Gantang.. A Malay gallon = 4 chupaks, which are now by law 4 Imperial quarts." Wilkinson, *Malay Dict.* defines Gantang thus: "A measure of capacity; a vessel representing that measure of capacity...*Gantang* is also a measure of weight for gold equal to one *bongkal.*"

[3] See the account of the abortive attempt to settle an English Factory at Kedah in note on p. 267.

[4] These were, for the most part, private trading vessels.

[5] See *Hobson-Jobson*, *s.v.* Borneo. The Dutch monopolised the trade with Borneo from 1606 till 1669 when they were compelled to

40 Prows they have that belonge to Queda, that constantly trade to Bangaree[1], Janselone[2], and Pera[3], some few to Achin. They carry hence Salt, Tobacco, Pepper, Tamarin[4] and Mannison[5] (a Sort of honey). As I said before, the English are very well beloved here and have very considerable priviledges allowd to Encourage them to Encrease a trade hither[6]. The Kinge taketh a mighty care that none of us be defrauded here, as for instance, When the Merchant (or Commander) declareth he is almost ready to Saile, the Kinge giveth positive Order to the Shabandare[7] to See the Gunge[8] beaten round the citty, with a lowd and Severe Proclamation vizt. If any person standeth indebted to Such an English Merchant (or any that belonge to him or his Ship) any Summe of moneys or goods, let him with all Speed repaire into the presence of the Said merchant and ballance accompts justly, and with all Speed.

Otherwise if theire Obstinacie or neglect cause any Com-

---

withdraw from the country, chiefly through the intrigues of the English who settled a factory in 1704, from which they also were forcibly expelled in 1707. See Crawfurd, *Desc. Dict. of the Indian Islands*, *s.v.* Borneo. See also Alex. Hamilton, *East Indies*, vol. ii. p. 144 ff.

[1] See note on p. 257.

[2] *i.e.* Junk-Ceylon. See *ante*, pp. 235—258.

[3] Perak is a Malay State having about 100 miles of coast-line on the west of the Malay Peninsula. The Dutch made ineffectual attempts from 1650 to 1690 to establish trading stations at Perak. The word *perak* means silver in Malay. Compare the following in a letter from the factors at Kedah to Surat under date 17th Nov. 1670 (*Factory Records*, Surat, No. 105) "Perah the first noted place [after Kedah]...wee sailed to this by the river...he [the king of Perak] durst not trade with us [without the sanction of the Queen of Achin]."

[4] See note on p. 22. Crawfurd, *Desc. Dict. of the Indian Is.*, *s.v.* Tamarin, says "The Malays call the tree and fruit *Asām-Jawa*, that is, the acid of Java."

[5] The Malay word is *manisan* from *manis*, sweet. T. B. in his *Malay Dict.* has, "*Mānisan*, sweet meats." Crawfurd, *Desc. Dict. of the Ind. Is.* says, *s.v.* Honey and Wax, "The native name for honey is *manisan-lābah*, 'the sweet of the honey-bee'."

[6] The English factors were not of T. B.'s opinion. See note on p. 265.

[7] See note on p. 242.

[8] See note on p. 196.

plaint of nonpayment, they, theire Wifes, theire Children, and all theire goods and Chattles Shall be Seized Upon, and forfeited to the Kinge who will Satisfie the Creditor, and make them Ser[v]e in Perpetuall bondage. But it Seldome falleth out soe ill to them, for they Observe to be rather beforehand, which is the wisest course[1].

This River of Queda is a Very good River, and soe is that of Old Queda that lyeth to the Southward of this. They are both well replenished with Very good and Excellent Sorts of fish[2], and not a little filled with the deformed creatures commonly called Alligators. They resemble a Crocodile, and are very ravenous and great devourers of mankind, and breed abundantly. They lay theire Eggs in the Sand (Even as Turtle doe), and hatch with the heat of the Sun. I have often taken of theire Eggs when they have been ready to hatch. Alsoe I have Shot Severall Alligators of 6, 7, 8, 9 foot longe, and killed them by Observinge to hitt them Exactly Under one of the fore paws, where it is very Soft, for the back and Sides of them are Very like Unto Scales of brasse for theire hardnesse. I have often Seen a brace of bullets rebound upon the Sides of a large Alligator[3].

Some of them are Monstrous great Ones, one of which beinge taken, I measured him, and he exceeded 22 feet in length, and 9 foot round the belly. His teeth and claws

---

[1] The English factors made great complaints of their inability to get in their accounts. See note on p. 262. It would seem that the author met with special marks of favour at the hands of the King of Kedah. Hence his roseate view of the monarch and his kingdom. Voluntary slavery in liquidation of debts is an old and widely spread Far Eastern custom. See *Ind. Ant.* vol. xxix. p. 86.

[2] See Dennys, *Desc. Dict. of British Malaya*, *s.v.* Fish, for a long list of the various kinds obtained in the rivers and on the coast of the Malay Peninsula.

[3] Dennys, *Desc. Dict. of British Malaya*, *s.v.* Alligator, says, "By a common error all reptiles of this family are usually termed alligators (Spanish *el legarto*, the lizard), but the ten species known are all American." T. B.'s alligators must therefore have been crocodiles.

Plate XVI

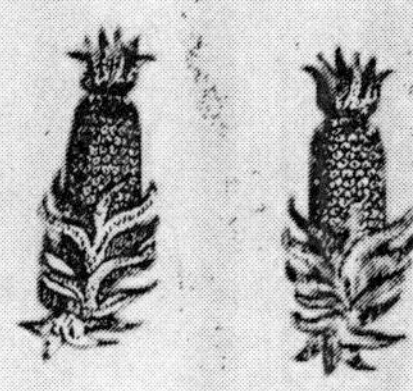

p. 279.

"PINE APPLES."

"STRANGE FISHES IN QUEDA." p. 279.

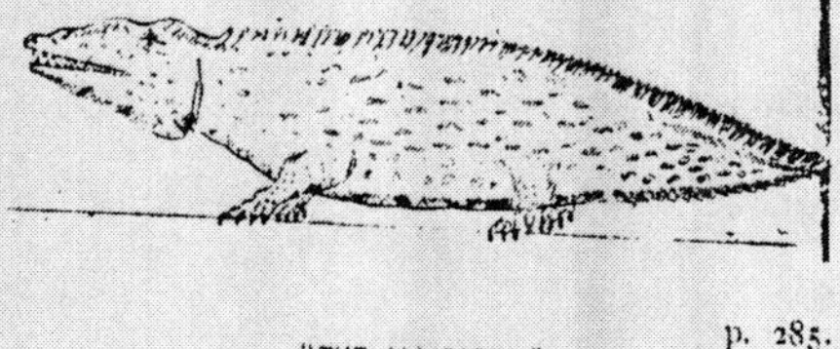

"THE ALLIGATOR." p. 285.

were of a great and admirable length. The fatt of this ill looked creature is Esteemed on highly by the best of Indian Doctors, who Say it is a most Soveraigne remedy for any Old aches or Paines in the bodies of men and Women.

I Opened one that wee took amongst the Fish yards, att the mouth of Queda River. He [w]as about 15 foot longe, and I laid him and his Taile open in the Sun Upon Some deale boards, and Saved what Issued from it by the heat of the Sun onely, and had 5 pottles of the Said fatt as cleare as Springe water. Here followeth the Forme of one of these Deformed Creatures. [Plate XVI.]

ACHIN.

The Citty Achin is Upon the North End of the great Island Sumatra[1], which Extendeth from 05° 40′ South Lattitude to 05° 40′ North Latitude, soe that the Equinoctiall Line divideth this Island into 2 Equall parts[2]; and the Citty Achin is the Metropolitan of the Whole, a very pleasant and healthy place, very populous[3], famous as it is

---

[1] See *Hobson-Jobson*, *s.v.* Sumatra. Compare Alex. Hamilton, *East Indies*, vol. ii. p. 101, "Sumatra fronts all the Coast of Malaya, from Quedah to the Promontory of Johore, and reaches above 150 Leagues farther. It is one of the greatest Islands in the world."

[2] This description is another proof of the writer's accuracy.

[3] Compare the description by *Schouten*, who was at Achin in Nov. 1663 (vol. ii. pp. 127—132), "The Island [Sumatra] is divided into several kingdoms, the most powerful among them being Achin, on which depend the towns and kingdoms of Pedir, Pacem, Daia, Barros, Passaman, Ticou, Priaman, Padang, and even the kingdoms of Queda and Perach on the other side of the water....A Queen was Regent while we were in that country: It was said that she wanted to marry a Dutchman, but the Governor of Batavia would not consent to it....Their buildings, Pagodas and houses are raised on wooden piles and built of light materials....The capital city...is built in the Indian fashion and situated by a pleasant river, in a plain, a league and a half from the sea. The air there appears to be better and more temperate than it is on the Southern side of the Island."

the place of residence of theire Virgin Queene, with all her Lords and most of the Nobilitie of the Kingdome, as alsoe for theire good laws and goverment, and the great Traffick and Commerce from most parts of India, China, and South Seas[1].

I Suppose the Citty may be some 15 or 16 miles in Circuit, Scituated Upon a very pleasant and fertile Soyle, Enjoyinge an Excellent aire, and a very fine river that runneth through the Citty that addeth very much to the benefit and beuty thereof. Vessels of 60, 70, or 80 tunns may come Up to the towne Side 2 or 3 miles within the barre, beinge the place where the Customehouse standeth[2].

It hath likewise a very Excellent Roade or bay in which there is roome Enough for many hundreds of Ships and in great Safety[3], where they may ride in 12, 10, 8, 6, 4

---

[1] In the Dialogues at the end of his *Malay Dict.*, T. B. says of Achin, "Achee is a large City, and populous for these parts of the world, Inhabited by the Natives and many Foreign Merchants as English, Portuguese, Moors, Chuleas and others...the Port...is never without Ships of English, Danes, Portugals, Moors, Chuleas, Chinesses and others...all these come in their proper Seasons, with the several sorts of Goods of Surat, the Coast, Bangala, China, and many other places...."

[2] Compare *Mandelslo*, p. 110, "The City of Achin stands in a wide Plain upon the side of a very broad River, but so shallow, that the least Boats get in with difficulty. It hath neither Gates nor Walls, the Houses all built on piles, and covered with Coco-leaves. The Castle, or Palace Royal, stands in the middle of the Town, which on two sides hath most excellent pleasant Forrests, well stored with Apes, Herns, and all manner of Birds."

[3] T. B. in the Dialogues at the end of his *Malay Dict.* says, "The City [Achin] stands about two Miles from the Port, which is never without Ships...and many Praws, which usually go into the River." Compare the description by *Dampier*, vol. ii. p. 122 f., of the "Road of Achin," "Besides what belongs to Achin upon the Continent, there are also several Islands under its Jurisdiction, most of them uninhabited; and these make the Road of Achin.... [They] lye in a semicircular form, of about 7 Leagues diameter....Between Pulo Gomez, and the Main are 3 or 4 other small Islands; yet with Channels of a sufficient breadth between them, for Ships to pass through; and they have very deep water. All Ships bound from Achin to the Westward, or coming from thence to Achin, go in and out thro' one or other of these Channels....There is good riding in all this Semicircular Bay between the Islands and Sumatra: but the Road for all Ships that come to

fathoms depth[1], very cleare ground, and almost land locked with the head of Sumatra[2], Pullo Way[3], and Pullo Gomus[4], and 2 or 3 Small Islands and rocks. The land is all Mountainous and woody Save where the Citty Standeth, more Especially the 2 Islands Way and Gomus, haveinge noe low land about them, nor are they inhabited more then with Some banished Cripples Sent from the Citty[5].

Many Ships and Vessels doe att all Seasons of the yeare arrive in this Port from Severall places, namely

---

Achin is near the Sumatra Shore, within all the Islands. There they anchor at what distances they please, according to the Monsoons or Seasons of the Year."

[1] T. B. resided for some time at Achin (*vide* Introduction), and had ample opportunity of becoming fully acquainted with the capacity of Achin Harbour.

[2] Compare Alex. Hamilton, *East Indies*, vol. ii. p. 112, "Between Atcheen Head an high steep Promontory, and the South End of Gomus Islands, there are two Chanels to come from the Westward into the Road."

[3] Compare *Dampier*, vol. ii. p. 122, "Pulo Way...is the Eastermost of a Range of Islands, that lye off the N.W. end of Sumatra. It is also the largest of them." Alex. Hamilton, *East Indies*, vol. ii. p. 111, says, "Pullo-wey, an Island about four Leagues to the North-eastward of Atcheen, and there they [banished criminals] cultivate the Ground, and breed Poultry for the Use of the Town." There are three islands called Pulo Way in the Malay Archipelago. Crawfurd conjectures that the name means "Water Island." See his *Dict. of the Indian Is.*, *s.v.* Way.

[4] Compare *Dampier*, vol. ii. p. 122, "Pulo Gomez is another large Island about 20 mile West from Pulo Way, and about 3 Leagues from the N.W. point of Sumatra." Compare also the following from "Abstract of Captain Atkins Journal," *O.C.* No. 4045, "15th April 1675. As soon as wee were shott without the Island Polo Gomos, wee mett with a strong stream." Horsburgh, *East India Directory*, vol. ii. p. 42, ed. 1805, has "Pulo Gomez, where there are regular soundings and good anchoring ground, from 10 to 17 fathoms."

[5] These cripples were malefactors, who, according to the laws of Achin, had been mutilated for their crimes, and then banished. Compare *Dampier*, vol. ii. p. 122, "It [Pulo Way] is inhabited by Malefactors, who are banisht thither from Achin." Compare also Lockyer, *Trade in India*, p. 38, "A Thief detected is punished with the Loss of a Member, from a Finger to an Arm, and Banish'd to some of the Islands off the Head: Pulo Gomes, and Pulo Wary are the chief Receptacles of these unfortunate Wretches, whence they often return to the City, and are common in the Streets without Hands or Arms: The greatest Badge of Infamy."

Suratt[1], Malabar Coast[2] or Coast of India, Fort St. Georg's, Metchlipatam[3], Bengala, Pegu, Syam, China, Java Major[4] and Borneo, with infinite Numbers of Prows from the Malay Shore and West Coast of this Island Sumatra.

The Chiefe Commodities brought hither from Suratt are Some Sorts of Callicoes[5], vizt. Baftos white and blew[6] with gold heads and borders, Cotton and Cotton yarne, course Paintings[7], quilts and Carpets[8].

From the Coast of India and Choromandell are brought

---

[1] See note on p. 258. Compare *Dampier*, vol. ii. p. 122, "And because shipping comes hither [Achin] from the Coast of Surrat, one of these Channels which is deeper than the rest, is called the Surrat Channel."

[2] See *Hobson-Jobson*, *s.v.* Malabar. This quotation is very valuable as showing the meaning of the term in the 17th century.

[3] *i.e.* Masulipatam.

[4] Compare *Mandelslo*, p. 112, "Java, an Island commonly called Java Major, to distinguish it from another less of the same name, which lies hard by it, is South-East from the Isle of Sumatra."

[5] See note on p. 5. Lockyer, *Trade in India*, p. 35, says, "From Surat the Moors imploy two large Ships a Year to import the Produce of that Country [to Achin]."

[6] See note on p. 272. Compare *Tavernier*, vol. i. part ii. pp. 31 and 137, "In Brampore, as over all the Province, there is made a prodigious quantity of Calicuts very clear and white....There is another sort of Linnèn which they never dye, with a stripe or two of Gold or Silver quite through the piece, and at each end from the breadth of one inch to twelve or fifteen, in some more, in some less, they fix a tissue of Gold, Silver, and Silk, intermix'd with Flowers, whereof there is no wrong-side, both sides being as fair the one as the other.... They make at Brampour also other sorts of Cotten-Linnen....The Bafta's, or Calicuts painted red, blue, and black are carried white to Agra....All the Calicuts or Bafta's...are of two sorts: for some are broad, some are narrow."

[7] See note on p. 106. Compare also *Tavernier*, vol. i. part ii. pp. 31, 33, 132, 133, "There are some ['Calicuts'] which are painted with several colours, with flowers...the same Calicuts serve for Coverlets of Beds...painted Calicuts...are called Chites....The Workmen will make these prints upon their Cottons, according to the Patterns which the Forreign Merchants give them...As for their Calicuts dy'd blew or black, you must take care that the Workmen do not knock them after they are folded, to make them look sleek...It is easy to distinguish between the printed and the painted Calicuts."

[8] Compare *Tavernier*, vol. i. p. 126, "[In] Amadabat...they make Carpets of Silk and Gold, others of Silk and Silver, others all of Silk: for the Worsted Carpets are made at Vettapour, some twelve leagues from Agra."

hither Rice[1], butter and Oyle in Jarrs[2], Longcloth[3], Salampores white and blew[4], fine Chint[5] of Metchlipatam, Striped Stuffs[6] of Golcondah and Pettipolee, Cushin Carpets[7], &c., togeather with Some Commodities from England, vizt. Scarlet[8], broadcloth, knives, Scissers, &c., most Especially good Spanish dollars Stamped 600. They passe Current at 5 masse[9] per dollar, Some times 5 and ½. From Bengala

---

1 Compare *Dampier*, vol. ii. p. 134, "The Road [of Achin] is seldom without 10 or 15 sail of Ships of several Nations. These bring all sort of vendible Commodities, as Silks, Chints, Muzlins, Callicoes, Rice, &c., and as to this last, a man would admire to see what great quantities of Rice are brought hither by the English, Dutch, Danes and Chinese."

2 See pp. 128 and 132, and note on p. 132. Compare also *Dampier*, vol. ii. p. 146, "He had at this time about twenty great Jars of Bengal Butter, made of Buffaloes Milk; and this Butter [*ghī*] is said also [as now] to have Lard or Hogs fat mixt with it, and rank enough in these hot Countries, tho much esteemed by all the Achinese, who give a good price for it."

3 See note on p. 55.

4 See note on p. 56. T. B. in his *Malay Dict.* has, "Salamporee, a sort of Callico made in India." Compare also the following in a letter from Fort St George to Masulipatam, dated 17th June, 1669, *Factory Records*, Fort St George, No. 16, "We shall be able to invest all our Stocke...in Long Cloth, Salempores, Morees, Percalls, Batilles." See *Hobson-Jobson*, *s.v.* Salempoory.

5 See note on p. 71. Compare Lockyer, *Trade in India*, p. 34, "The Commoditys imported [to Achin] are Ophium, Saltpetre, Rice, Gee [*ghī*] or Buffalos Butter turn'd to Oyl; and all sorts of Cotton and Silk Manufactures from Bengall. Tobacco, Onions, Callico and Muslin, especially brown and blew long Cloths, and Sallampores, with several sorts of Chints for Clouts, and sometimes Gunpowder from Madrass."

6 See note on p. 230. See also note 6 on p. 288. Compare the following in a letter from Robt. Freeman at Masulipatam to Richd. Edwards at Balasor, 16th March, 1670, *O.C.* No. 3413, "Pray if possible procure me a boy if not a good peice of Silke Striped with Silver."

7 See note on p. 240.

8 See note on p. 160. Compare the following in a letter to Masulipatam, 7th Feb. 1672, *Factory Records*, Masulipatam, No. 9, "For the fine Scarlett I take notice of your order therein."

9 See note on p. 115 and compare *Dampier*, vol. ii. p. 132, "Of these (Cash), 1500 make a Mess [mace], which is their other sort of Coin, and is a small thin piece of Gold, stampt with Malayan Letters on each side. It is in value 15 pence English."

Rice[1], wheat, Oyle, butter, Sugar, Sticklack[2], Cambayas[3], Elaches[4], Oromals[5], Mulmuls[6], Slave boys and Girls, &c.

From Pegu, Rice, Gans[7], Motavan Jarrs[8], and very Excellent Sticklack.

From Tanassaree, Janselone, Queda, Pera, &c. on the Malay Coast, little Save Tinne[9].

From Syam, Tinne, Coppar[10], China Wares, Rice[10], and Screetores[11] both plaine and lackared[12], &c.

The like, Save Tinne, are brought from China, with

---

[1] See note on p. 132. [2] See notes on pp. 122 and 132.

[3] See note on p. 246.

[4] A silk cloth, more generally known as Alleja. The term in the text represents the vernacular *alăcha*.

[5] See note on p. 133. Compare Lockyer, *Trade in India*, p. 43, "Ordinary Bengall Romalls of 8 Pagodas at Madrass [sold at Achin] for 5 Tale per Corge of 20 Pieces."

[6] Muslin. See *Hobson-Jobson*, *s.v.* Mulmull. The term "mulled muslin" is still in use at the present day in England. Compare the following in a letter from Hugli to Balasor, 2nd April, 1678, *O.C.* No. 4387, "As to the price of Mulmull sent down you may if the Merchants are very much discontent allow them 5 rs. 14 a. or Rups. 6." Compare also the following from Luiller, *Voyage au Golfe de Bengale*, quoted in Prévost, *Histoire des Voyages*, vol. xiii. p. 80, "The Company gets from its factory at Ougly various kinds of Mallesmolles."

[7] See note on p. 196. Compare *De la Loubère*, p. 14, "Vincent le Blanc relates that the Peguins have a mixture of Lead and Copper, which he calls sometimes Ganze, and sometimes Ganza." In the MS. records this commodity frequently figures as "Gaunts."

[8] See note on p. 81. Compare Lockyer, *Trade in India*, p. 35, "Nor are the Mallays [of Achin] themselves wanting in Trade with large Proes to Pegu, Quedah, Jahore, and all their own Coasts: whence they are plentifully supply'd with several Necessarys, they otherwise must want: As Ivory, Bees-wax, Mortivan and small Jars, Pepper, &c."

[9] See note on p. 240.

[10] Compare the "Report on the Trade of Siam written in 1678" quoted in Anderson's *Siam*, Appendix E. p. 424 f., "Wrought Copper, being severall Sorts of Potts...are used here and exported to the Malayan countreys....This Countrey is the general Granary for the adjacent parts equalling if not exceeding any parte of the world in abundance of Rice, wherein the neighbouring Malayan Coast is yearely supplyed as far as Malaccah..."

[11] See note on p. 71.

[12] See *Dampier*, vol. ii. p. 61 f. for a description of the method of lacquering as employed at Tonquin.

Striped and flowred Silks[1], Totanagga[2], Gungs[3], Steelepots and Pans.

From Java Major, Sugar, Sugar Candid[4], Rice, Cassia Fistula[5], &c.

The Borneo and Macassar[6] Prows for the most part bringe Slaves[7], both men, women and children, some Diamonds and Saphir[8]. The Diamonds of Landock[9] (upon Borneo) are accompted the best in the World[10].

---

[1] Compare *Dampier*, vol. i. p. 409, "They [the Chinese] make very fine lacquer-ware also, and good Silks."

[2] See note on p. 199. Compare the following in a letter from Hugli to Balasor, 8th July, 1678, *O.C.* No. 4458, "Your Tootanague have sold here att 16 rupees per maund." Other contemporary spellings are "Tutanagg" and "Tothanag." Compare also *De la Loubère*, p. 14, "This Tin...is soft and basely purified, and a specimen thereof is seen in the common Tea boxes or Cannisters, which come from this Country [Siam]. But to render it harder and whiter, like that of the finest Tea Boxes, they mix it with Cadmia, a sort of Mineral easily reducible to powder...And 'tis this white Tin which they call Tontinague."

[3] *i.e.* gongs. See note on p. 196.

[4] Sugar in large very sweet crystals is a common product in India and the Far East.

[5] Watts, *Dict. of Economic Products of India*, has, *s.v.* Cassia Fistula, vol. ii. p. 218, "The name Cassia Fistula...was first applied to a form of cinnamon very similar to the Cassia Lignea of the present day, the name Fistula having been given because of the bark being rolled up." T. B. may be referring to this tree, rather than to the Indian Laburnum or Cassia Fistula of the present day. Compare *Mandelslo*, p. 109, "Sumatra...is wealthy in...Cassia, and divers other Drugs used in Medicine."

[6] See *Hobson-Jobson*, *s.v.* Macassar. Compare *Tavernier*, vol. i. part ii. p. 191, "The Kingdom of Macassar, otherwise call'd the Isle of Celebes, begins at the fifteenth degree of Southern Latitude....The Capital City bears the name of the Kingdom, and is situated upon the Sea. The Port is free; for the Vessels that bring great quantities of goods from the Adjacent Islands, pay no Customs."

[7] Compare *Dampier*, vol. i. p. 456, "Macasser is not very far from hence [Bouton Island], one of the chiefest Towns that the Dutch have in those parts. From thence the Dutch come sometimes hither to purchase Slaves."

[8] Alex. Hamilton, *East Indies*, vol. ii. p. 148, in his description of Borneo says nothing of sapphires being found there. Of the Borneo diamonds he remarks, "They have small Diamonds, but their Waters being inclined to be yellow, are not so much in esteem as those of Golcondah."

[9] In T. B.'s *Malay Dict.* there is "A Map of the Countries where the Malayo language is spoken." In this map "Landa," in Borneo, is marked. Landak is on the western side of Borneo.

[10] See above, note 8.

From the West Coast of this Island, Store of very Excellent Benjamin[1], Camphir[2], Brimstone[3], Pepper[4], Rattans[5], and Dammar[6], as alsoe very good Bezar Stone[7].

---

[1] *i.e.* Benzoin, incense. See *Hobson-Jobson, s.v.* Benjamin. T. B. in his *Malay Dict.* has "Benjamin, a sweet gum in India." Compare the following in a "Generall" from Fort St George to the Bay, 7th Oct. 1669, *O.C.* No. 3350, "50 Maunds of Black Benjamin which hath long layne in your bookes." *Schouten*, vol. ii. p. 129, says, "Barros is also on the west coast of Sumatra, a league inland, on a large river, between Passaman and Achin. It produces pepper, camphor and benjoin." Crawfurd, *Dict. of the Indian Is., s.v.* Benzoin, says, "Styraz Benzoin ...the plant is the peculiar product of the islands of Sumatra and Borneo."

[2] Compare *Mandelslo*, p. 109, "Sumatra...is wealthy in Diamonds and other precious Stones, Silks, Spices, Wax, Honey, Camphire...." Compare also *Dampier*, vol. ii. p. 126, "The chief of their Drugs is Camphire, of which there are quantities found on this Island [Sumatra], but most of it either on the borders of this Kingdom to the Southward, or more remote still, without the precincts of it." Lockyer, *Trade in India*, p. 40, says, "The Camphor this Country [Sumatra] affords, is found among the Sindy Islands only."

[3] See Crawfurd, *Dict. of the Indian Islands, s.v.* Sulphur. He says, "It is hard to say to what use the natives of the Malay Archipelago could have put sulphur, before the introduction of fire-arms, unless to the manufacture of fire-works [and medicine]."

[4] Compare *Dampier*, vol. ii. p. 127, "There are many other profitable Commodities on this Island: but some of them are more peculiar to other parts of it than to Achin, especially Pepper." Compare also Alex. Hamilton, *East Indies*, vol. ii. pp. 111—118, on the "trading ports on the West Coast of Sumatra." He says, "Bencolon...their trade lay all on their Pepper.... Lampoun...The English had a good Pepper Factory there, but...that Factory was lost...in Anno 1683."

[5] See notes on pp. 74 and 250. See also *Dampier*, vol. ii. p. 167 f., for a description of "rattan cables." Rattan cables, ropes and "fenders" are still used by the seafaring population round the Bay of Bengal.

[6] See *Hobson-Jobson, s.v.* Dammer. See also *Ind. Ant.* vol. xxx. p. 337. T. B. in his *Malay Dict.* has, "Damar, a Torch, the Gum of a Tree. Damar batoo, unboiled, raw Damar, it is the Gum of a tree in India, which being boil'd with Oil, makes Pitch or Tar." Compare the following from *Factory Records*, Hugli, Nos. 4 and 5, under date 13th Nov. 1675 and 17th July, 1680, "No Dammers is yet come to hand we are expecting a quantity every day part ware of shall be sent you for your use...Those Knee Timbers, planck, Dammer, Iron worke &ca shipp stores wee enorder you...to send them upon the *Ganges* or *Arrivall*." Compare also *Dampier*, vol. i. p. 514, "The gum of a Tree beaten to powder, called by English Drammer, which is used instead of Pitch in many parts of India."

[7] See *Hobson-Jobson, s.v.* Bezoar. See *Ind. Ant.* vol. xxvii. p. 336. Compare *Tavernier*, vol. i. part ii. p. 154, "As for the Bezoar which breeds in Apes, as some believe, it is so strong, that two grains work as effectually as six of Goat's-Bezoar; but it is very Scarce, as being

The Dammar of Sumatra is accompted, and I know it by Experience to be better then any other in India or South Seas[1]. Wee make all our pitch and Tarre with Dammar and Oyle as followeth.

One third dammar and Oyle, well boyled togeather, make very good tarre, but not serviceable for any ropes by reason of the Oyle.

Again $\frac{2}{3}$ Dammar and $\frac{1}{3}$ Oyle make a very Excellent Sort of pitch, not inferiour to the best wee use for our Shippinge in England. And indeed wee have noe Other Pitch or tarre in any of the Easterne parts of the knowne World.

This Citty is the fairest and most populous of any that Ever I saw or heard of[2] that is inhabited by Malayars[3] or Javas[4], but indeed it cometh farre Short for decency and buildings and Uniformitie of the meanest Cittie in Arabia, Persia, or the maine land of India; but the good Soile,

---

only found in those Apes that breed in the Island of Macassar. This sort of Bezoar is round, whereas the other is of several fashions...As the Apes Bezoar is stronger, and scarcer than the Goats, so it is dearer, and more sought after; a piece as big as a nut being sometimes worth a hunder'd Crowns." See also Lockyer, *Trade in India*, pp. 49–51. Crawfurd, *Dict. of the Indian Islands*, *s.v.* Bezoar, says that the stones are mostly brought from Borneo.

[1] See note on p. 188. In the Dialogues at the end of T. B.'s *Malay Dict.* there is the remark, "Does Achee afford no Commodities for Trade? Very little of its own, but it abounds with all sorts of Merchandize of India and the South Seas, which is brought thither."

[2] See notes on pp. 285 f. Compare also *Dampier*, vol. ii. p. 129 f., "The City of Achin is the chief in all this Kingdom. It is seated on the Banks of a River, near the N.W. end of the Island, and about 2 miles from the Sea. This Town consists of 7 or 8000 Houses; and in it there are always a great many Merchant-strangers, viz. English, Dutch, Danes, Portuguese, Chinese, Guzarats, &c. The Houses of this City are generally larger than those I saw at Mindanao, and better furnished with Houshold Goods. The City has no Walls, nor so much as a Ditch about it. It has a greater number of Mosques, generally square built, and covered with Pantile, but neither high nor large."

[3] See note on p. 237.

[4] The use of this word for the people as well as the country is remarkable.

wholsome Aire[1], and plenty of Gold[2] doth adde very much to the goodnesse of the place. Few or none of the Natives are poore. I never Saw any begge that had theire lims, though never soe younge or Old. And this great plenty of gold causeth many Sorts of food or rayment to Sell here at very good rates, for of themselves they will Scarse till the ground, although it be Excellent land for Some miles neare the Citty and in many other places, Especially for rice[3].

---

[1] Compare *Dampier*, vol. ii. p. 148 f., "Achin...their weather is much the same as in other Countries North of the Line, and their dry Seasons, Rains, and Land-floods come much at the same time...I did not find the heat there any thing different from other places in that Latitude; tho I was there both in the wet and dry Season. 'Tis more supportable than at Tonquin; and they have constantly the Refreshment of Sea and Land Breezes every 24 hours."

[2] Compare the *Journall of Peter Mundy* under date April 1637, Relation 23, p. 36, India Office Copy, "Achein. This place lyeth on the North-end of the great Island of Sumatra, by the Ancients named Triprobana: which by Some is thought to be that Ophir from whence King Solomon [had] his Gold Apes and Peacocks." T. B. in the Dialogues at the end of his *Malay Dict.* says, "All these [foreign ships] come...with the several sorts of Goods...all which is Sold here [Achin] for Rock-Gold which is found in the inlands in great plenty." Compare the description of the "Gold Mines of Achin" by *Dampier*, vol. ii. p. 133 f., "This Gold they have from some Mountain a pretty way within Land from Achin, but within their Dominions, and rather near to the West Coast than the Streights of Malacca...I...was told that none but Mahometans were permitted to go to the Mines: That it was both troublesom and dangerous to pass the Mountains before they came thither...That at the Mines it was so sickly that not half of those that went thither did ever return again...I was told also by all that I discoursed with about the Gold, that here they dig it out of the Ground; and that sometimes they find pretty large lumps." Lockyer and Alex. Hamilton, however, speak only of gold dust at Achin. Hamilton says (*East Indies*, vol. ii. p. 108), "Atcheen affords nothing of its own product fit for Export, but Gold Dust, which they have pretty plentiful, and of the finest Touch of any in those Parts. They do not dig for it, but catch it in Gullies, or little rivulets, as it washes off the Mountains...."

[3] Compare *Dampier*, vol. ii. p. 128, "The Natives of this country [Achin] are Malayans. They are much the same People with those of Queda...and they are of the same Mahometan Religion, and alike in their haughty humour and manner of living...They are very lazy, and care not to work or take pains." Compare also Lockyer, *Trade in India*, p. 54, "The Natives [of Achin] are Mallayans...They are of a middle Stature, proud and lazy, especially the meaner sort, tho' they are better set, and of stronger Growth than the Indians of the Coromandel Coast, of whom here are so many, Slaves to the great Men and Merchants...To these the Acheenes owe the greatest part of their

There are Severall Radjas[1] Upon Sumatra that doe take Upon them the absolute Title and assume the absolute Goverment of Kings, Especially those of Jambee[2], Androgeero[3] and Pryaman[4], and pay a much Slenderer homage to the Crowne of Achin then formerly they have done[5].

Achin is now and hath a Considerable time been Governed by a Queen, ever Since the time that the discreet and Pious Kinge James of happy memorie Swayed the Sceptre of great Brittaine, France and Ireland[6].

Husbandry in managing their Crops of Paddy, or Rice, which was hardly known on this part of the Island, till these were driven hither by Famine from Fort St. David, and other Places on the Coromandel Coast."

[1] See notes on pp. 39 and 108.

[2] Jambi is a Malay State on the North-east of Sumatra. Compare the account of the place by Alex. Hamilton, *East Indies*, vol. ii. p. 123 f., "From Pullambam there are no Places of Commerce on the Coast, till we come to Jambee, which is about 100 English Miles. Here formerly the English had a Factory on an Island near its River's Mouth, called Barella."

[3] This place is Indragiri to the North-east of Sumatra. T. B. in the Dialogues at the end of his *Malay Dict.* has, "From Barros along the S.W. coast and to Lampoon, Palimbam, Jambe, and to Andregeree on the N.E. side is many places which produce pepper." On the 19th Dec. 1660 the Court wrote to Bantam (*Letter Book*, No. 2), "Both you and wee know that formerly large quantities of pepper hath beene procured at Andragera, which place you may now again take into consideration, and if you can find a convenient opportunity, make a Tryall." On the 25th May, 1664, in an abstract of a letter from Jambi, *Factory Records*, Misc. No. 3, we find, "They have writt to the King of Androgheree [that is, a raja as stated by T.B.] for Engageing him for all his pepper to bee Delivered Qualla [*i.e.* in the estuary or port], which they say if could draw Andragheree and Pullimbang people to would be of great advantage to the Company." Moor, *Notices of the Indian Archipelago*, p. 98, says, "Indragerie, which means in Sanskrit the mountain of Indra, is one of the few Hindu names found on the North coast of Sumatra." See also Crawfurd, *Dict. of the Indian Islands*, *s.v.* Indragiri.

[4] Compare *Schouten*, vol. ii. pp. 126—128, "The eastern coast of the island [of Sumatra] is the most unhealthy; but Ticou and Priaman are more so than all the other places both for natives as well as for foreigners...Priaman is fairly well populated, and has no lack of provisions. It produces, moreover, a great deal of pepper...it is dependent on Achin."

[5] That is, than they did in the time of the "Tyrannicall King" described in the following paragraphs of the text.

[6] T. B. is in error. There were kings of Achin from 1521 till 1641, when the tyrant king died, and a Queen apparently assumed office,

In soe much that the very name of a Kinge is longe since become nautious unto them, first caused through the Tyrannicall Goverment of theire last Kinge; and indeed, by the accompt they give of him, he was the cruelest Tyrant that many ages afforded[1], Some of his Cruelties as followeth.

---

first as regent, and afterwards as absolute monarch. Her reign was not extraordinarily long, only 28 years, but the idea that female rule in Achin had prevailed for many years soon became common belief. *Dampier*, who was in Achin at the time of T. B.'s residence there (in 1688), is evidently in doubt as to whether there had ever been a king of Achin. He says, vol. ii. p. 143, "I think Mr. Hackluit or Purchas, makes mention of a King here in our King James I. time. But at least of later Years there has always been a Queen only, and the English who reside there, have been of the Opinion that these People have been governed by a Queen *ab Origine*; and from the antiquity of the present constitution, have formed notions, that the Queen of Sheba who came to Solomon was the Queen of this Country."

In the Dialogues at the end of his *Malay Dict.* T. B. repeats his mistake as to the length of time there had been Queens at Achin. "The City and Kingdom has for above an Hundred years been governed by Queens and Twelve Lords." That there was a king at Achin in the reign of James I. is proved by the fact that a "letter from the Sultan of Achin to James I. of England dated A.H. 1024 (A.D. 1612)" still exists. There is a copy of this letter in the *Journal of the Straits Branch R.A.S.*, No. 31, July, 1898, p. 123. Bruce, *Annals*, vol. i. p. 180, says, "Captain Best carried letters from King James to the King of Acheen and formed in 1615 a treaty with this chief." Capt. Lancaster had previously, in 1602, delivered letters from Queen Elizabeth to the King of Achin, though Hamilton, *East Indies*, vol. ii. p. 101 repeats T. B.'s mistake and calls the monarch a Queen. This King must be the one described in *Voyage pour la Compagnie d'Octroi des Indes Orientales*, 1603, p. 527 f., as follows, "With regard to political government all the inhabitants [of Achin] are as subject to the king as if they were slaves...Justice is very severely administered and the punishment of crimes is harsh and terrible; the Dutch saw there a number of persons who had only one foot or one hand...These tortures are not confined to the lower classes...for even at the Court there was seen the king's son-in-law, son of the young king's mother, who, as a punishment, had had his nose, ears, and upper lip cut off. The old king no longer leaves his palace on account of his great age." *De la Loubère*, p. 82, and *Fryer*, p. 45, were both, like T. B., under the impression that a Queen was a settled institution in Achin.

[1] *Schouten* is alluding to this tyrannical monarch when he says, vol. ii. p. 131, "They [the people of Achin] respect their King from a spirit of servitude and slavery and from servile fear, more than from any love they have for him. They have reason to fear him for he exercises a very tyrannical power over them, so much so that for very slight causes which could not be considered crimes, he has their hands and feet cut off. Capital offences are not treated with more humanity.

Hee, for a Very Small Offence of any Eminent Person in the Kingdome, wold cause him or them immediately to be apprehended and brought into the Pallace yard, where a fire was prepared, and there must hold a Pot of Rice and water over the fire Upon theire right hand naked, untill the rice were boyled or theire hand burnt off, which wold certainly doe in a Short time, and many more inhumane cruelties he dayly Offered upon his poor Subjects, and was soe cruel that he put to death most of his owne kindred, and for many years he delighted in Nothinge but the Sheddinge of Innocent blood, which doubtlesse made his people weary Enough of him.

I have heard Some of the most Noted men now in Office declare many of his inhumane Cruelties, one of which was a most Strange One, vizt.

When he had tyrannized many years Over his people, and was well Striken in years, and haveinge been a little mercifull in leaveinge himselfe one Son alive, he called him to him, and Seriously demanded of him how he thought to rule and Governe Such a Multitude of Stiffe necked people. The Younge Prince knowinge his Father hated any Clemency towards them, answered Tyrannically alsoe, (but 'tis Supposed he meant not soe to doe) that he wold Governe them with Ease Enough and yet inflict more cruelty on them then Ever his Father did, and told him he wold make them boyle rice upon theire bare Sculls, whereas he onely made them doe it on their hands, Which soe enraged the Old bloody Tyrant, that he drew his

---

He always inflicts the death penalty and in a very cruel fashion." Schouten is apparently relating stories that were still current at the time of his visit to Achin, for, when he was there, in 1663, he says that a Queen regent was in office.

Crawfurd, *Dict. of the Indian Islands*, *s.v.* Achin, says that the name of the King who reigned from 1606 to 1641 (the monarch described by T. B.), was "Sekander muda, a title half-Arabic and half-Malay, which may be translated 'Alexander the Younger'."

Creest[1] and Stabbed his Son dead, himselfe Utteringe words to this Sence, that future ages Shold never have cause to Say that a more Severe or bloody Tyrant then himself did Ever Sway the Scepter of Achin.

Not longe after death tooke away the Tyrant[2], to the great Joy of many thousands, and it is to be admired that his Owne Subjects let him live Soe longe, and reigne in Such wickednesse. They buried him decently in the Pallace Royall amongst his Ancestors Tombs, and built over him a very Stately one too, and covered it with Massy Gold as some of the rest are, but withall guarded well the Pallace, the Citty, the Garrisons and all Stronge holds, fortyfyinge themselves well against all Kingly Goverment; and the wisest men assembled and chose to themselvs a Queen, the next heiresse to the Crowne, but Enacted Such laws that her issue need not be dreaded[3].

1. That the Queen Shold never marry or know the Use of man.

---

[1] See *Hobson-Jobson*, *s.v.* Crease, the Malay dagger or kris. The form in the text may be compared with the spelling Christ! adopted by the translator of *De la Loubère*, p. 15, where the passage runs, "They [the Siamese] wear the Poniard on the left side, hanging a little before. The Portuguese do call it Christ, a word corrupted from Crid, which the Siameses use. This word is borrowed from the Malayan Language...and the Crids which are made at Achim in the Isle of Sumatra, do pass for the best of all." Compare also the following in a letter from Bantam, 1682 (*Factory Records*, Java, No. 6), "In the Agents clossett was found just after his decease...four Creasses which were Sealed with Mr. Benjamin Crockfords Seale...and fowre Creasses Scabbards." T. B. in his *Malay Dict.* has, "Creis, a Poniard, dagger," and *Dampier*, vol. i. p. 401, "Cressets, or little Daggers."

[2] *i.e.* in 1641. Compare the account by De Graaf, *Voyages aux Indes Orientales*, p. 24, "While I was at Achin [in 1641], the king died which caused great commotion among the great men, and cost the lives of a great many people for each one wished to be king...Finally the queen was proclaimed regent of the kingdom, and she has reigned for several years."

[3] It seems, from the statements of Schouten and De Graaf (see note on p. 296 and note 2 above), that the appointment of a queen was at first only a provisionary arrangement, and that until her position was absolutely secure, she was looked upon as a regent of the kingdom.

2. That noe man in the Kingdome Shold presume to have a Sight of her after Chosen Queene.
3. That the Lords and Justices &c. Shold cause noe act or law (now Established) to be Violated, or any Other to be made without the Queen her Consent and good likeinge thereunto.
4. That her Attendants Shold not be lesse then 500 women and Eunuchs.

With many Others all diligently Observed[1].

The Men in Office that (Under theire Queene) governe this Kingdome are Entitled as followeth.

The Meer Raja[2] vizt. the Lord Treasurer, the Leximana the Lord Generall, and the great Orongkay is Lord Chiefe Justice. There are other Orongkays[4], and under this, as alsoe Shabandars under them[5] and the Queen's greatest Eunuchs, but are all very Submissive and respective to the Queen, not dareinge to act or doe any businesse of importance before they have throughly acquainted the Queen thereof. She hath Severall Eunuchs of very acute witt about her that advise with her to condescend to what is requesite. Not one man, Woman or Childe is admitted to get a sight of her, Save the Women

---

[1] Compare *Dampier*, vol. ii. p. 142, "The Queen of Achin, as 'tis said, is always an old Maid, chosen out of the Royal Family. What Ceremonies are used at the chusing of her I know not: Nor who are the Electors; but I suppose they are the Oronkeys."

[2] Compare Meer Moonshee. These terms are not found in *Hobson-Jobson*, though they are as worthy of note as Mem Sahib. For *amir* and *raja*, see notes on p. 39.

[3] See note on p. 260.

[4] See note on p. 260. T. B. in his *Malay Dict.* has, "Oran chookee, Custome-house officer."

[5] See note on p. 242. Compare *Dampier*, vol. ii. p. 141, "This Country [Achin] is governed by a Queen, under whom there are 12 Oronkeyes, or great Lords, These act in their several precincts with great power and authority. Under these there are other inferiour Officers, to keep the Peace in the several parts of the Queen's dominions. The present Shabander of Achin is one of the Oronkeyes."

and Eunuchs that are of her attendants, and Some Eunuchs her chiefe Councellours[1], but when businesse with her doth present, the great Orongkay or Some of the Others doe come into the Pallace and declare theire businesse to some of her Councell, who informe her thereof; and if She condescends thereunto, She Sendeth downe to them her Chopp *i.e.* her broad Seale[2], and then it is granted accordinge to theire request. If the Chopp cometh not downe to them, they must desist from the businesse in hand and mind Somethinge else.

The Chopp is made of Silver 8 or 10 inches longe, and like to a Mace which openeth on the topp where the Signet is Enclosed[3].

Before any forraigner can land in this Port he must receive this Chopp, and then hath he freedom to buy and Sell and land his goods at pleasure. The like must be done when he is almost ready to depart the Countrey, by the Master or Commander onely, else it is taken as a most grosse Affront[4].

---

[1] Compare *Dampier*, vol. ii. p. 142, "After she [the Queen of Achin] is chosen, she is in a manner confin'd to her Palace; for by report, she seldom goes abroad, neither is she seen by any People of inferiour rank and quality, but only by some of her Domesticks."

[2] See note on p. 118. Compare the following extracts from *Factory Records*, Fort St George, No. 28, under date 19th June and 2nd August 1680: "Your Ocoon [*Akhun*] had put his chaup or seal to the Certificate as well as the Dustuckt [*dastak*] or handwriting...The Chop that you Chop your letters now of late with is not the same you did use to Chop before, but of a new Chop." Compare also *Dampier*, vol. ii. p. 16, "The Governor or his Deputy [at Tonquin] gives his Chop or Pass to all Vessels that go up or down."

[3] Alex. Hamilton, *East Indies*, vol. ii. p. 103, thus describes the "Chopp": "On my Arrival [at Achin] I took the Chap at the great River's Mouth, according to Custom. This Chap is a Piece of Silver about 8 Ounces Weight, made in Form of a Cross, but the cross Part is very short."

[4] Compare the experience of Captain Atkins who anchored in the "Road of Atchine" on the 10th April, 1675 (*O.C.* No. 4045), "11th Sunday in the morning sent our Purser in our Penace to desire leave and to fill some water, and to procure some provisions, but no Admittance of anything, till Receiv'd the Queens Chopp: 12th I went on

The way wee take it is thus. Soe Soone as any Ship or Vessel doth anchor in the Roade of Achin, there is Sent off from the Custome-house a small flyinge Prow[1], that cometh on board and demandeth of the Master whence he came and of what Nation he is, and whether he come to trade or not, or purpose to come On Shore. If he doth, the Prow goeth on Shore againe and acquainteth one of the Shabandares, who applyeth himselfe to the Great Orongkay and the Choppe is made ready about 9 or 10 the next morninge, and brought to Quala[2], vizt. the barre att the River's mouth by one of the Queen's Eunuchs attended with Some of the Custome-house Officers, and commonly the English Dubashee[3], and the Commander is Sent for on

---

Shoar to theire Guard where mett with some English Marchants and notice given to the Oran Koye, one of the Queens Cappons [eunuchs, O.E. *capun*] brought downe the Chopp which when Receiv'd according to theire manner of Seremonies, had then free leave or Liberty granted to water or to buy what provission or Necessaryes theire Country aforded."

[1] *i.e.* an outrigged canoe. Compare *Dampier*, vol. ii. p. 131, "They [the Achinese carpenters] are also ingenious enough in building Proes, making very pretty ones, especially of that sort which are Flying-Proes; which are built long, deep, narrow, and sharp, with both sides alike, and outlagers on each side, the Head and Stern like other Boats ...and will sail very well: for which reason they had that name given them by the English." Compare also Lockyer, *Trade in India*, p. 45, "Their flying Proes [at Achin] are only for fishing, coasting, and visiting the Islands thereabouts: Sometimes, I am told, they run out to the Nicobar Islands, which is the longest Trip they make. These are so narrow, two Men cannot stand a breast in the widest part of them; the Bottom is a long Canoe, or Tree hollow'd without a Keel, the Sides are raised with Planks about 3 Foot above it, bending a little inward, till near the Top, where it turns out bell-wise. The Planks within half a Foot of each end, are left as sharp as possible, not pointed like a Wherry, but perpendicular with an Edge; the Canoe jets out beyond the other part of the Vessel, and when loaden is quite under Water; the Rudder is like a wooden Knife, with which they stear very dexterously: To keep them up-right, they have Outlayers on each Side, with Planks of light Wood at the Ends of them, which secure them so well from over-setting, that they will bear the greatest Sea, and when an English Primace [? pinnace] with two Sails will go five Miles an Hour, these with a small one will run a dozen."

[2] *i.e.* *kuwala*, the mouth or estuary of a river; the point of junction of a tributary stream and a river; Wilkinson, *Malay Dict.* See also *Hobson-Jobson*, *s.v.* Calay (foot-note).

[3] *i.e.* interpreter. See note on p. 37.

Shore, and received by them with many Complements, and the Chopp is delivered to him. He must receive it in both hands and lift it up to his Forehead as makeinge Obeysance to the Queen, which done he hath free liberty as afore Said[1]; onely when he cometh up to towne he must goe to the Custome-house, and there Sitt and discourse with the Chiefe officers there, and one of the Chiefe of the Eunuchs is there alsoe. The maine discourse held is of what Foraign news, and I judge the Queen is soon made acquainted thereof.

And there wee pay for the Chopp 3 pieces of very fine callicos or Muzlinge[2], or 4 tailes in moneys vizt. four pounds Sterlinge[3].

The Same day or on the morrow followinge, he must goe and pay his respects to the Orongkay[4], and with noe

---

[1] Compare Lockyer, *Trade in India*, p. 35 f., "On the Arrival of a Ship [at Achin], the Shabander must be apply'd to for the Liberty to trade. At the great Quala or Rivers Mouth, those that go first a Shore are examin'd by the Gards, who presently give notice of their coming, to the Officers, whose Province it is to settle the Preliminarys; which is only a formal Oath to observe the Articles, made between the Company and the Achines, by Mr. Henry Grey; and to be faithful to the King and Country during their stay. This is administred by the Shabander, or his chief Officer's lifting, very respectfully a short Dagger in a Gold Case, like a Scepter, three times to their Heads; and is called receiving the Chop for Trade. It ought to be perform'd by the gravest, most knowing, and Men of the best Appearance; in consideration of the ill Consequences a false Step in the Beginning might render one liable to in managing one's Affairs at Court afterwards."

[2] See note on p. 5. Compare the following in a letter from Achin to Surat, 28th Sept. 1669, *Factory Records*, Surat, No. 105, "The 22nd [May, 1669] the Queens Chop came aboard of us according to Custome, to Licence our coming on shore, to whom we presented 2 peeces Baftas of vallew 3 tale 15 man [? mace]." Compare also Lockyer, *Trade in India*, p. 36, "Two Pieces of fine Cotton Cloth at the first coming, and two more on departure to the King [of Achin]."

[3] See note on p. 281. T. B. must mean a tael in gold, and if the gold tael was worth £1 sterling as he states, then gold valued in the Malay States at £1 the oz. and the ratio of silver to gold there varied between 4 and 3 to 1, a remarkable but by no means impossible occurrence.

[4] Compare the following from the Kedah letter already quoted on p. 263, "The 28th [May, 1669] visited the Orankay Puglah Lemar Bunder...his pride would not permit him to take much notice of us."

Small reverence, first Observinge to pull off his Shoes (although never soe cleane) and leave them att the doore or in the Court Yard. When that is done, he is invited to Sitt downe Upon Carpets[1], but after theire owne fashion crosse legged, to any new comer very Uneasie, but not soe to those of this countrey that doe Sit thus with a Naturall facilitie.

Here must he waite an hour or two before the Orongkay will appeare, but in the interim the Shabandar and Dubashee and one or Other belongeinge to this great man doth accompanie him and discourse most friendly; and there are Sett before him Store of Betelee Areca[2] to eat, and tobacco to Chaw, a Custome used all India and South Seas over. If wee be not accustomed thereto, yet in the way of civilitie and respect to them wee must take Some into our hands, or they will be very angry, and will not Easily be pacified, and hinder us in the Sale of our good[s] in a very great measure, although Seemingly they be our good Friends.

Here the Orongkay must be presented with one piece of Baftos[3] to the Value of 2 tailes, and 3 or 4 or 6 bottles of rosewater. He discourseth about one houre, askinge many questions, Some of which are ridiculous Enough if they came not from the mouth of a person of soe great a qualitie.

And withall wee make agreement with him how much wee must pay to the Queen for the landinge our Cargoe. The Contract been [? between] us and the Court of Achin hath been of longe Standinge 50 tails per Ship, if laden

---

[1] See note on p. 240. [2] See note on p. 30.

[3] Compare Lockyer, *Trade in India*, p. 36, "Two Pieces of Callico or Silk to the Shabander, and head Oronkoy or chief Minister of State...these give each a fat Capon in return. If one would be very exact, I am told, 'tis five Tale Fees, two Pieces of Taffitea of two Tale each to the Shabander, and two more to the head Oronkoy."

with fine goods (admitt the Ship be great or Small)[1]. But againe, if wee have a quantitie of course goods On board, vizt. Rice, gramme[2], Wheat, Oyle, butter[3], or the like, they are to make an abatement of 10, 15, or 20 tails, accordinge as the quantitie is, and noe Other duties are payable by any of the English Nation Except the Chopp in and out, neither are any of our goods carried to the Custome house as all Other peoples are, which is a great helpe and honour to our Nation. These priviledges were granted to our Nation above 100 years agoe[4], and are Still confirmed by Every New Queen as She cometh in place[5], Which causeth the people in Generall to respect us very much, and Entertaine us with abundance of Civilities and Court Ship.

The Betelee Areca[6] is here in great plenty and much

---

[1] Lockyer, *Trade in India*, p. 36, says that in his day sixteen or seventeen taels covered the value of the presents and the "acknowledgment for Custom."

[2] See note on p. 121. Compare the following from *Factory Records*, Masulipatam, No. 9, under date 27th April, 1672, "Pray send us as soone as possible 50 Candy of horse Gram for the stable, that of these parts [Fort St George] being neither good nor Cheape."

[3] See notes on pp. 132, 247, and 289.

[4] T. B. is evidently alluding to the concession obtained by Captain Lancaster from the King of Achin in 1602. See Foster, *Letters received by the East India Co.*, vol. i., Introduction, p. xxv. and pp. 1—4 for this document. In 1669 Mr Henry Gray obtained for the Company from the Queen of Achin a renewal and modification of these privileges. In the Dialogues at the end of his *Malay Dict.*, T. B. says, "The English are free of all Custom by ancient agreement, only a Present to the Queen, and some small Port charges, all other Nations pay great Customs." Compare Lockyer, *Trade in India*, p. 36, "Other Nations pay five to eight per Cent. Custom on their Cargos...But the English are at no other Charge than the usual Presents to the King and Courtiers."

[5] T. B. was in Achin at the time of the death of the second of the four Queens of Achin, and his statement probably arises from the fact that the "New Queen" carried on the policy of her predecessor towards the English.

[6] See note on p. 30. T. B. in his *Malay Dict.* has, "Beetle-leaf is much eaten in India. Beetle-nut is eaten with the leaf." Compare *De la Loubère*, p. 23, "The Areca, which the Siameses do call *Plou*, is a kind of great Acorn, which yet wants that wooden Cup wherein our Acorn grows. When this Fruit is yet tender, it has at the center or heart a greyish substance, which is as soft as Pap. As it dries it

better then in many Other countries of the East and South Seas. Very few houses here but have Severall trees of it growinge that beare all the yeare longe, and the inhabitants in Generall doe Eat thereof, prepared thus: They cutt the Areca nut into very thin Slices, and put about one halfe of a nut into their mouth, and then one betelee leafe or two (accordinge as they are in bignesse), and Spread a little qualified lime thereon, which by them is called Chenam[1], which folded up togeather they eat with the Nut, which after a little Chewing doth produce very much Liquorish moisture in the mouth, which for the most part they Swallow downe, and after a good while chewinge untill it is dry, they spit it out and take more that is fresh, and thus will they almost all day longe chew betelee Areca. They hold it good for the Stomach, and keepinge the breath Sweet, the latter of which I am very well Satisfied in, but if the Nut be green, which here is very much in Use, they onely cutt the nutt in 2 pieces and paringe off a little of the green rine, eat it with betelee

---

waxes yellower and harder, and the soft substance it has at the heart grows hard too: It is always bitter and savory. After having cut it into four parts with a knife, they take a piece every time, and chew it with a Leaf resembling Ivy called *Betel* by the Europeans which are at the Indies, and *Mak* by the Siameses. They wrap it up to put it the more easily into the mouth and do put on each a small quantity of Lime made of cockleshells and redded by I know not what art."

[1] See *Hobson-Jobson*, *s.v.* Chunam. See *Ind. Ant.* vol. xxx. p. 136. Compare the following from an article in the *Mad. Man. Admn.* vol. iii. *s.v.* Choonam, "Choonam...Lime whether slaked or unslaked, but the former is generally meant...The finest choonam from oyster shells (chippy choonam [*sīpī chunam*, shell lime]) is chewed with betel-leaf. There is a Tamul proverb: 'The essence of paun is in the choonam.'" Compare also *Dampier*, vol. ii. p. 54, "The Betle Leaf is the great entertainment in the East for all Visitants; and 'tis always given with the Arek folded up in it. They make up the Arek in pellets fit for use, by first peeling off the outer green hard rind of the Nuts, and then splitting it length ways in 3 or 4 parts, more or less, according to its bigness. Then they dawb the Leaf all over with Chinam or Lime made into a Morter or Paste, and kept in a Box for this purpose, spreading it thin."

as the Other, which doth eat much more pleasant then the Old ones doe[1].

The Leafe is the betelee[2], a broad leafe not very much Unlike to an Ivie leafe, only Somethinge thinner, and groweth resemblinge the Vine, as followeth [Plate XVII.].

Areca[3], vizt. commonly called betelee Nut, doth grow Upon a very comely Streight and Slender tree, taperinge in joynts, and the nutt groweth out of the body thereof below the branches as followeth [Plate XVII.]. It is a very hard wood, and much Used by many in India to make lances and pikes On.

All Masters of English Ships and Vessels are very Nobly Entertained here, they Still retaininge the Civilities at first Settlinge in Use, and I hope wee Shall never give them cause to the Contrary.

When all our Merchandise &c. is accomplished, and wee are in readinesse and willinge to be gone, wee Send to the Custome house the English Dubashee[4], to informe the Officers there that wee are ready and want onely the Queen's Chopp[5]. They Straight ways give the Orongkay

---

[1] Compare *Dampier*, vol. i. p. 319, "Every Man in these parts [Mindanao] carries his Lime-Box by his side, and dipping his Finger into it, spreads his betel and Arek leaf with it...The Betel-Nut is most esteem'd when it is young, and before it grows hard, and then they cut it only in two pieces with the green husk or shell on it...It tastes rough in the Mouth, and dies the Lips red, and makes the Teeth black, but it preserves them, and cleanseth the Gums. It is also accounted very wholsom for the Stomach; but sometimes it will cause great giddiness in the Head of those who are not us'd to chew it. But this is the effect only of the old Nut, for the young Nuts will not do it. I speak of my own Experience." Dampier here confuses the areca nut with the betel leaf, a mistake which he rectifies in vol. ii. p. 54.

[2] *i.e.* the Betel Vine or Sirih (*chavici betel*). Compare Bowring, *Siam*, vol. i. p. 113, "The betel (*betel piper*) is a creeping plant, producing a long and somewhat fleshy leaf, nearly resembling a heart in shape, of a sharp and aromatic flavour."

[3] *i.e.* the Areca palm, *areca catechu*. See Watts, *Dict. of Economic Products of India*, *s.v.* Areca.

[4] See note on p. 37.

[5] See note on p. 118.

Notice of it, and he repaireth to the Pallace, and hath an Order granted that it may be made ready that day. Sometimes it is referred a day or two, accordinge as businesse at Court happeneth. Wee then goe to Visit him (but not Empty handed), for it is the Custome with these great men in Office to aske what you have brought them (if you readily tender it not to them), and when they come to Visit us, which often they doe, they have the like confidence to aske what you will give them, but for what given to the Orongkay there is little lost by it, for at our arrivall he presenteth us with fowle and great Store of fruit[1], and before wee come to take leave of him, he carrieth us to the Pallace, where wee are Entertained Upon fine Carpets, fruit, and betelee Areca &c. Set before us, where wee Sitt with our faces directly towards the Queens Lodgeings, and from her is Sent to the English Commander a Silke Suite of cloths with a turbant[2] after the Malay fashion. He must receive them with great reverence, Standinge Up and makeinge a Sumbra[3] to the Queens Windows, She all the while looketh upon us, although wee cannot See her. The great men doth helpe to dresse the Commander, for at that very instant he must put them on, and then, after many complements, taketh leave of the Orongkay, beinge the chiefe man concerned in all the Affaires of the Shipps and Commerce[4].

In the Pallace yard is provided a Very Stately warre

---

[1] See note on p. 303. [2] See note on p. 156.

[3] This word is not in *Hobson-Jobson*. It is the Malay *sembah*, which Wilkinson, *Malay Dict.*, defines as "A salutation, a respectful address; the actual act of salutation or homage consisting in raising the hands to the face."

[4] Compare *Dampier*, vol. ii. p. 142 f., "The present Shabander of Achin is one of the Oronkeyes...all Merchant Strangers at their first arrival, make their Entries with him, which is always done with a good Present: and from him they take all their dispatches when they depart; and all matters of importance in general between Merchants are determined by him."

Elephant richly adorned with his trappings and his Pavilion [Plate XVII.], his teeth tipped with Coppar gilded over, but carrieth not his Chàine[1]. Upon this Elephant the Commander must ride to his house where he dwelled, or to the English Factory[2] (accompanied with one or more of the Grandees of the Kingdóme), and Severall pipes, drums, flaggs, &c. carried before them by foot men, orderinge all persons whatsoever to Stand out of the way Immediately. If any refuse to Obey that command, they Spare not to lance him to the ground, that dares to hinder him of a free and cleare passadge that the Queen respects. Many of the Merchants bringe rosewater to throw upon them as they ride through the Cittie, which here is accompted a great piece of honour and respect. When they come to the English house appointed, they light off the Elephant and walke in, where abundance of their Ceremoniall Complements and good wishes are Used, and Soe take leave of each Other; and thus all the Ceremonies are ended for that Voyadge, onely once more he must goe to the Custome house and there take the Chopp[3] for his departure, and then may immediately goe on board and Saile if they please, or Stay as longe as they please afterwards, but it is the custome not to take leave untill fully resolved to Saile in 2 or 3 days. The State wee ride in from the Pallace is as here demonstrated [Plate XVII.][4].

---

[1] See page 274 f. and note.

[2] When T. B. lived at Achin (*circ.* 1687), the English trade was in a more flourishing condition than when Matthew Gray wrote to Surat, 28th Sept. 1669, *Factory Records*, Surat, No. 105, "We found here [Achin] no house of the Companys but an old Warehouse built by Meangee [Mīānjī, a title, probably of some merchant of the place, see p. 263], which wee propt up the best we could, and housed there the Companys Goods...We finding this trade drawing to an end, and not worth our Residence here were unwilling to put the Honble. Company to the charge of Building a house..."

[3] See note on p. 118.

[4] T. B. undoubtedly speaks from personal observation and experience. Compare *Dampier*, vol. ii. p. 144 f., "Captain Thwait, according to custom went with his Present to the Queen, which she

Plate XVII

p. 306.

"BETELEE. ARECA TREE."

p. 308.

"A STATE ELEPHANT."

When a Present is Sent to the Queen from the President of Suratt[1] or Agent and Governour of Fort St. Georg's, soe Soone as the Grandees have any certain Intelligence there of, they make it known to the Queen (by her Eunuchs), and She appointeth a certain day for the reception thereof, which is then performed with very great State, haveinge all (or the Major part) of the Grandees of Achin to attend it to the Pallace. The English Merchant and Commander, and any of his Friends (of his owne Nation) ride Upon Stately Elephants as beforementioned. When they Enter the Pallace, the English are Very Royally Seated Upon Carpets of Persian worke[2], very rich and beautifull to behold, and behind them are placed the Grandees, then the Ordinary Officers belongeinge to her Majesties guards and Customehouse in a very great retinue, all Frontinge the Queen's Windows, who, as 'tis Said, doth earnestly behold them, Especially the English, and doubtlesse cold She have her owne will, wold have more then a Sight of some of them. Now is a Great Gold betelee box[3] as bigge as one of [the] eunuchs can well

---

accepted, and complemented him with the usual Civilities of the Country; for to honour him he was Set upon an Elephant of the Queens to ride to his Lodgings, drest in a Malayan Habit, which she gave him; and she sent also two Dancing Girls to shew him some pastime there."

[1] This is another instance of T. B.'s accuracy. The "Presidency" was not transferred to Bombay till 1687.

[2] *Fryer*, p. 263 f., has, "Ispahaun...Silk Buzzars...set apart for choice commodities...Persian carpets, both Woollen and Silk, intermixed with Gold and Silver very costly, which are the peculiar manufacture of the Country."

[3] See note on p. 30. Compare *Dampier*, vol. ii. p. 54 f., "Chinam, Betle and Arek...the Mandarins, or great men [at Tonquin] have curious oval Boxes, made purposely for this use, that will hold 50 or 60 Betle Pellets. These Boxes are neatly lackered and gilded, both inside and outside, with a cover to take off; and if any stranger visits them, especially Europeans, they are sure, among other good entertainment, to be treated with a Box of Betle. The Attendant that brings it holds it to the left hand of the stranger; who therewith taking off the cover, takes with his right hand the Nuts out of the Box. 'Twere an affront to take them, or give or receive any thing with the left hand [as in India]..."

beare in his arms, brought downe and placed before them, and they must eat thereof, although never Soe little, which is accompted as great an honour here, as knighthood in the Courts of European Kings there.

The present of fine Callicoes[1], Cloth of Gold, or what else, is carried up in great State Upon Golden Vessels, borne by the greatest of the Eunuchs with Gilded Pavilions carried over them, and the letter to the Queens Majestie is carried up by it Selfe in great State and royally attended by Some of her Speciall favorites.

Then with great feastinge, with Varieties of Victualls, bottles of wine and Sweetmeats, the time is passed away for one houre or two, haveinge many Sorts of Excellent fruit Set before us, and which to us is most delightable is the Warre Elephants[2] are brought into the Pallace yard, where they fight in very great fury, graplinge with theire teeth and Strikeinge with all their force with theire trunks the Buffolos[3], and fight with each other and with admirable courage. They alsoe Use cocke fightinge in a Very great measure[4], and will lay very great wagers on that Game.

After a great many Such Sports and Exercises, the English are carried home in as great State as they came, and word is sent them from her Majestie not to forget her answer, which before they goe is done both by retalliation and alsoe her letter to the Said English Governour that was soe kind to write to her Majestie.

Her attendants are Said to be 100 Eunuchs and 1000 of the comliest women the Countrey or Citty affordeth. They Show themselvs Openly Every day, and to my thinkinge many of them are very comely and much whiter then the Common Sort of Natives are.

---

[1] See note on p. 5.

[2] See note on p. 274.

[3] See note on p. 279.

[4] Compare *Dampier*, vol. ii. p. 184, "The Malayans here are great lovers of Cock-fighting."

Anno Domini 1675 the Old Queen of Achin died, and in her Old age, for she might well be called Old, haveinge Reigned Queen Ever Since the Death of theire Tyrannicall Kinge, which was noe lesse then Sixty odde years[1], in soe much that many thousands of the Natives cold scarse be posest with a beliefe they had a Queen for many years before her death, but that it was the policie of the Grandees to make them to believe it. But now she was certainly dead, they all in Generall were Satisfied that a Queen had Governed them soe longe and in peace. I was then in Achin when She died, and saw a generall mourning for her. Some did it willingly, but those that did not were after a Strange manner Compelled to it. The mourninge of the female Sect was to cut the haire of theire heads, which was performed, but to many of them by Violence, for those that wold not doe it were taken out into the market place and there compelled to doe [it] in publicke, without any respect to theire ranke and qualitie.

The men mourned 3 Months in Old garments, and

---

[1] T. B. is here repeating his previous error. As stated before, note on p. 295, the tyrant king did not die till 1641. Crawfurd, *Dict. of the Indian Is.*, *s.v.* Achin, says, "Four of the Achinese sovereigns in succession, over a period of sixty years, were women, the puppets of an oligarchy of the nobles." This period, we find, embraced the years 1641 to 1700, for Lockyer, *Trade in India*, says, p. 57, "They [the Achinese] are at present [*circ.* 1710], under the Government of a King which has not been long." Alex. Hamilton, *East Indies*, vol. ii. p. 102, fixes the date of the close of female government, for he tells us that, on the death of the Queen of Achin in 1700, a king was chosen. The four queens appear to have succeeded as follows:—The first reigned from 1641 till 1669. Her death is mentioned in a letter from Fort St George to Surat, 24th August, 1669 (*Factory Records*, Surat, No. 105), where we read, "Wee have bin informed that the Queene of Achine being dead they are there embroyled in Civill warrs." The second queen died in 1675, as stated in the text, after a reign of only six (not sixty) years. The death of the third queen is recorded by *Dampier*, vol. ii. p. 143, in 1688, she having reigned thirteen years. The fourth and last queen died in 1700, according to Hamilton, who, however, says nothing of the death of T. B.'s "Old Queen" in 1675, although he describes an attack made on her by the Dutch in that year.

were forbidden all manner of gameinge and Sports dureinge the Said time.

This Old Queen was Sore Visited with Sicknesse five weeks before She died, duringe which time there was great Suspicion and feare of a Rebellion with Some of the inhabitants of Achin, Assisted by many of the inland people, but as great care as possible cold be and means to prevent it were Used by the Grandees, who caused the Citty to be more then doubly guarded, more Especially the Pallace that was guarded with Some thousands of armed men, and 600 warre Elephants diligently attended, and Opium 3 times a day given them to animate them in the highest degree[1], and Severall resolute and well Effected people to this Goverment put into Office both in the Citty and in the Fortifications of this Country some miles Eastward of Achin[2].

Noe Sooner was a Period put to her days on Earth, but the Lords placed another in her Stead, who then Immediately Stept into the Throne, and [was] Immediately proclaimed Queen, and all the Gunns were fired in theire Forts and Castles to welcome into place theire New Queene, scarcely mentioninge the Old ones death untill 10 days afterwards when they found all was in peace and quietnesse, and then a fast and mourninge were generally proclaimed, and very Strictly Observed. Yet they found

---

[1] Compare *Fryer*, p. 111, "The Pattamars...the Wrestlers...use Opium to make them perform things beyond their strength."

[2] There were no fortifications at Achin when De Graaf visited the place in 1641. He says, *Voyages*, p. 22 f., "Achin is about 2 miles in circuit, but it has neither bastions nor walls. Outside the city are to be seen some ruined fortifications and a few pieces of fine cast cannon without carriages lying on the sand. These cannon were formerly taken from the Portuguese and the King of Johor." The description by *Dampier* in 1688 is very similar. He says, vol. ii. p. 129 f., "The City [of Achin] has no Walls, nor so much as a Ditch about it...The Queen has a large Palace here...Tis said there are some great Guns about it, 4 of which are of Brass, and are said to have been sent hither as a Present by our K. James the 1st."

for a truth her death caused noe alteration of Sex to Governe[1].

The Inhabitants up in the Countrey not above 20 or 30 miles off Achin are for the most part disaffected to this Sort of Goverment, and Scruple not to Say they will have a Kinge to rule and beare dominion over them[2], and that the true heire to the Crowne is yet alive and hath Severall Sons, and him they will obey. He is one that liveth amongst them, a great promoter of a Rebellion, and oftentimes doth much prejudice both in Citty and Countrey, although I believe it is and will be past his reach or Skill Ever to Obtaine the Goverment of Achin. Yett I have been in Achin when about 700 of these insolent highlanders have come downe to the Citty, and on a Sudden rushed into the Pallace Royall, and plundered it, to the great Astonishment of all the Citizens, Especially the Lords, who were soe affrighted with soe Sudden and desperate attempt, that theire onely care for the present was to Secure theire Owne Persons. They[3] carried away above 100 Picul[4] of fine Gold out of the Treasury,

---

[1] The succession in *Dampier's* time was not accomplished so quietly. He says, vol. ii. p. 143 f., "While I was on my Voyage to Tonquin [in 1688], the old Queen died, and there was another Queen chosen in her room, but all the Oronkeys were not for that Election; many of them were for chusing a King. Four of the Oronkeys who lived more remote from the Court, took up Arms to oppose the new Queen and the rest of the Oronkeys, and brought 5 or 6000 men against the City: and thus stood the state of affairs, even when we arrived here, and a good while after. This Army was on the East side of the River, and had all the Country on that side, and so much of the City also, as is on that side the River, under their power: But the Queen's Palace and the main part of the City, which stands on the West side, held out stoutly." Dampier left Achin before "these stirs" were at an end.

[2] See above, note 1.

[3] *i.e.* the thieves.

[4] See *Hobson-Jobson*, *s.v.* Pecul, the Malay cwt. See *Ind. Ant.* vol. xxviii. p. 37 ff. T. B. in his *Malay Dict.* has, "Cātee is a Weight, 100 makes a Pēcool," and "Pēcool, a weight used in many parts of India, the Malay Pēcool contains Averdupoiz, l. 198, oz. 5, dw. 9, gr. 10." Compare the following in a letter from Masulipatam, 19th April, 1678, *O. C.*, No. 4397, "The weight in Siam was 7 pecull and every pecull

but were too covetous in Striveinge for more, which caused Such a delay in theire flight that wrought theire overthrow, for the Citty rose up in arms and fell Upon them, and killed and tooke prisoners above 500 of them. Those taken alive were put to death every man Save One who Upon his Examination was found to be a Mola[1] or Mahometan Priest, for which reason he was by the Siddy[2] or Bishop of Achin freed from the death his consorts died, but not from Severe Punishment, for the law tooke Such hold of him that he was Served as Other petty thieves in this Citty are for the first and Secound fault, which was to have both hands and feet cut off in the joints, and his cure taken care for, his goods and Chattles confiscated, and he turned out a begginge for meat and drinke, the which was fully Executed upon him[3].

There be many of them in this Citty; some of them are soe ingenuous that they can goe very well with Crutches, haveinge a joynt of a large bamboo[4] fitted for each legge, as in figure followinge [Plate XVIII.].

---

to way one hundred and thirty pound." Compare also *Dampier*, vol. ii. p. 132, "To proceed with their Weights [at Achin], which they use either for Money or Goods, 100 Catty make a Pecul, which is 132 l. English weight."

[1] See *Hobson-Jobson*, *s.v.* Moollah. Compare *Tavernier*, who, in describing his visit to the King of Bantam, says, vol. i. part ii. p. 198, "There was a Moulla then read to him, who seem'd to interpret to him something of the Alcoran in the Arabick language."

[2] See *Hobson-Jobson*, *s.v.* Seedy, a corruption of *Saiyyid*. This reference is valuable for the history of the Anglo-Indian term, now in common parlance an East African negro. Compare Alex. Hamilton, *East Indies*, vol. ii. p. 102, "This Harmony continued till the Year 1700, that the Queen [of Achin] died, and a Seid or Preacher getting a strong Party, was made King, promising to do wonders."

[3] This is a circumstantial account, and T. B. was no doubt an eye-witness of the scenes he describes. I can, unfortunately, find no contemporary confirmation of this raid on the Queen's Palace.

[4] See note on p. 249. Compare *Dampier*, vol. ii. p. 139, "On Pulo Way there are none but this sort of Cattle: and tho' they all of them want one or both hands, yet they so order matters, that they can row very well, and do many things to admiration, whereby they are able to get a livelihood: for if they have no hands, they will get somebody or other to fasten Ropes or Withes about their Oars, so

Plate XVIII

p. 255.

"MEN OF WARRE PROWS.'

p. 280.

"THE BUFFALO."

p. 314.

"AN ACHIN CRIPPLE,"

The Laws of this Kingdome are Very Severe in many respects, Especially for theft, more cruel then for murther, for then 'tis death without any tediousnesse, but for theft it cometh gradually on with great affliction.

If a Thiefe be apprehended that hath Stolen any thinge to the Value of 4 mace[1], vizt. 05s. English, he is with all Speed carryed to the Pallace, and before the Chiefe Orongkay's face both his hands are cutt off in the joynts, for the Secound Small crime his feet, and, upon his committinge a third, his head. Yet, if the first crime be any thinge considerable vizt. to the Value of a Cow or Buffolo, which Exceedeth not 30s. English, it is present death, more welcome to them then the former punishments, but that is to make Examples for Others[2].

And very Strangely they are Executed, as followeth. Soe Soone as apprehended, they are the same day or the next at furthest, Examined before the Lord Chiefe Justice

---

as to leave Loops wherein they may put the stumps of their Arms; and therewith they will pull an Oar lustily. They that have one hand can do well enough: and of these you shall see a great many, even in the City." Compare also Alex. Hamilton, *East Indies*, vol. ii. p. 111, "When their Hand or Foot is to be cut off, they have a Block with a broad Hatchet fixt in it with the Edge upwards, on which the Limb is laid, and struck on with a wooden Mallet, till the Amputation is made, and they have an hollow Bambow, or Indian Cane, ready to put the Stump in, and stopt about with Rags or Moss, to keep the Blood from coming out..."

[1] See notes on pp. 115 and 281.

[2] Compare *Dampier*, vol. ii. p. 138 f., "A Thief for his first offence, has his right hand chopt off at the Wrist: for the second offence off goes the other; and sometimes instead of one of their hands, one or both their feet are cut off; and sometimes (tho' very rarely) both hands and feet. If after the loss of one or both hands or feet they still prove incorrigible, for there are many of them such very Rogues and so arch, that they will steal with their Toes, then they are banish'd to Pulo Way, during their lives: and if they get thence to the City, as sometimes they do, they are commonly sent back again; tho' sometimes they get a Licence to stay...Here at Achin, when a member is thus cut off, they have a broad piece of Leather or Bladder ready to clap on the Wound. This is presently applied, and bound on so fast, that the Blood cannot issue forth. By this Means the great Flux of Blood is stopt, which would else ensue; and I never heard of any one who died of it..."

and his Councell, and if found guilty are with great Expedition delivered to the Executioners[1], who lead the Malefactor through the principal Streets of the Citty with his hands bound behind him, and choose any place where they will to Execute him in, where he may hange fairely for a prospect Some 24 hours after his death, which they cause thus: they make two Sticks fast one athwart his windpipe, the other his neck, of about 3 foot in length each, and before they Seize them togeather, some of his Friends or acquaintance bringe him betelee Areca[2] to Eat and water to wash his hands and face, att which one Mola[3] or Other Uttereth 2 or 3 Sentences to him, to noe other purpose then to trust in God and Mahomett their onely Prophet for his Soul's health, which done, the Executioners frapp[4] the Sticks togeather with Splitt rattans[5], laying the Malefactor Upon his belly, and when they have neare Strangled him, one of them, with a Sharpe Knife cutteth a hole in his drawers or lungee[6], and driveth a Sharpe Stake Up his fundament, which runneth in at least 10 or 20 inches, and then is placed in the ground a Stake of 10 or 12 foot longe, to which they make the body fast, to hange in forme of a Crucifix, where he must hange by law untill the Same houre the next day, and then any of his Friends may take him downe that will, and doe with his body as Seemeth them best. But if the Said party have noe Friends or relations to doe it, after 2 or 3 days the

---

[1] Compare *Dampier*, vol. ii. p. 138, "The Laws of this Country [Achin] are very strict, and offenders are punished with great severity. Neither are there any delays of Justice here; for as soon as the Offender is taken, he is immediately brought before the Magistrate, who presently hears the matter, and according as he finds it, so he either acquits, or orders punishment to be inflicted on the Party immediately."

[2] See note on p. 306. [3] See note on p. 314.

[4] Another of the many nautical terms in this MS. Murray, *Oxford Eng. Dict.*, *s.v.* Frap, gives, as one meaning, "*naut.* To bind tightly."

[5] See notes on pp. 74, 250, 277. [6] See note on p. 55.

Executioners must do it by the law of the Countrey[1]. And yet, notwithstandinge the Utmost Severity of the laws here are inflicted Upon the offendinge parties, many here take very little warneinge thereby, for I believe there is scarse one week passeth, but Severall persons are condemned and Executed, and those that have Suffered the losse of hands or feet or both can Scarse refraine from offendinge further[2], but will boldly adventure the neck to boot. As for instance:

A fellow that had been deprived of both hands and feet yet came into the English Factory, and in the night did rippe open a baile of fine blew baftoes[3], and thereout he tooke 7 pieces, and hid them Under his arme, covered with his clowte that he wore over his Sholders, and beinge a Cripple that used often to come a begginge thither, none of the Servants at the gate Suspected him. But, in the markett place, Some of the Citty guards meetinge him, tooke him up for a Stragler att Such unseasonable hours, and upon Examininge him, and layinge hands on him, found he had somethinge more then Ordinary about him, and Upon that Secured him Untill the morninge, and then carried him (and his purchase) before the great Orongkay[4], and there the goods were knowne by theire marks, and he condemned to dye. Whereupon the Chiefe of the English Factorie[5] was Sent

---

[1] See *Schouten*, vol. i. p. 233, and *Dampier*, vol. ii. p. 140, for similar descriptions of these tortures.

[2] Compare the following in the Commission from the Council at Surat to Matthew Gray, April, 1669, *O. C.* No. 3266, "Wee are informed that place [Achin] is very much haunted by night theevs that doe not only robb but are otherwise mischeifous in flinging fire upon the tops of the Houses which being built of Combustible stuff is apt to receave it, whereby too frequently great mischeife is done." Compare also Alex. Hamilton, *East Indies*, vol. ii. p. 110, "No Place in the World punishes Theft with greater Severity than Atcheen, and yet Robberies and Murders are more frequent there than in any other Place."

[3] See note on p. 272.

[4] See note on p. 260.

[5] This may have been Henry Chowne, who was in charge of the Company's affairs in Achin in 1670.

for, where to admiration found he was robbed by such a piece of man, and was well pleased with the fancie, withall he did mightilie intercede for the fellows pardon, which cold not by the Orongkay be granted, but had the liberty granted to Petition the Queen, who in favour of our Nation granted the man's life, a thinge rare in Achin. The English Chiefe gave the Queen and all the Court many and hearty thanks for the honour done him; and, in the presence of the Orongkay gave the fellow 5 tailes[1], vizt. five pounds sterlinge, and chargeinge him never soe boldly to adventure any more, and if he wanted a mace[2] or two at any time he wold Supply his wants, all which clemencie was very well taken by the Grandees &c. of Achin.

The English Factorie doth Stand in a very fine level place neare to the Custome house, and is very well fenced in, and is a very large and good Spot of ground very Commodious for the Merchants to buy and Sell in. Not many years agoe there was a most Sumptuos buildinge beinge the dwellinge house for the Chiefe and his Factors, but was consumed by fire, and the Company never Since were willinge to be at the charges to build it up againe, by reason now adays very few English men doe reside here all the yeare but returne in the same Ships they come in, and leave the Factory to a Servant or two to looke after it; yet there is a reasonable good dwellinge house in it, and Storehouses Enough for 2 Ships Cargoes[3].

---

[1] See notes on pp. 281 and 302. [2] See notes on pp. 115 and 281.

[3] A Factory was settled at Achin in 1615, but continuous Dutch opposition caused it to be abandoned in 1646. Intermittent trade between the Company and Achin went on until 1658 when a re-settlement was discussed. In May of that year, the Court wrote to Bantam, *Letter Book*, No. 1, "The intimation which you have given us relating to the proceedings of the Queen of Acheene against the Dutch, and the Invitation given by her to our Nation for the enjoyment of a trade in her ports hath given encouragement unto the Company to send a ship for that place, with Commission to endeavour the Settlement of a trade and Factorie under her protection, which wee hope will come to a desired issue." In consequence of this order

Capt. William Curtis was sent to Achin with the *Mayflower* on a trading voyage. In December, 1662, in a letter to Fort St George, the Directors remarked (*Letter Book*, No. 2), "Wee observe what you have written us concerning the *Ann* Friggatt now called the *Hope* her unprofitable Voyage to Acheene, whose marketts as you advise us are soe clogged that nothing can bee sent that will produce the prime Cost." After this disappointing report, nothing further was done for a time, but in 1664 it was decided to attempt to check the growing monopoly of trade by the Dutch. At a Consultation in Surat in March of that year, it was agreed "to be necessary to continue a factory at Acheen were it only to keep a footing there," and, in accordance with this decision, two Factors were sent on the *Vine* to re-settle the Factory. At the same time the Council at Surat wrote to the Court (*Factory Records*, Misc. No. 2, p. 18), "The Queen of Acheen is very respective to your Servants that Voyage thither, and is very Desirous our nation would undertake the whole trade of her Dominions; she is in great thoughts what the Dutch Intend...It is thought they intend warr to bring the Queen and other Princes of the Island of Sumatra to oblige them not to admitt the English into their ports, or to sell a Corne of pepper unto them, and this is Certainly their drift; It is a Rich Island, and affords many brave Commodityes that yeeld great advantages...The Queen hath wrote your President a very kinde letter, wherein she makes Large proffers if you would undertake the whole Trade; but then she will expect you protect her from the Dutch, but you are not in a Condition to doe one or other however we shall hold her in Expectation, and acquaint her we have advised you of it, and await your Order."

The *Vine* was wrecked, and, in spite of an interchange of presents between the Queen of Achin and Charles II., nothing further was done towards re-settling the Factory until 1668, when a Commission was given to Matthew Gray as Chief, and to Henry Chowne and Charles Ward as Second and Third. In this Commission the Surat Council stated (*O. C.* No. 3266), that "The Queen Some years since did send us a kind of Embassy making great promises of graunting us the whole trade of Acheen, Jeco, Priaman, &ca but it was then in a time when we could not accept it, being in the heat of the Dutch warr." Gray and his colleagues were ordered to find out "if the Dutch tyranny" extended to all the ports of Achin. The Council further stated that the Queen in former times had expressed great favour to the English but "her bounty to us hath been much abused by the Orankayes about her that take the advantage of her being a woman to Impose more unreasonably on us then it is her will and Pleasure they should. Wee doe acknowledge that Mr. Henry Gary did contract to give the Queen yearly a present of 100 lb sterling but then it was thought wee might have 2 or 3 Shipps yearly, in which she had graunted the custome free of all the goodes belonging to our nation, and likewise the fifth parte of customes for all other Fraighters goodes, which were our trade so great would be well worth such a present, but we having but one Shipp and that a small one, lesse then the halfe may well serve her turne, besides this of a present is an accustomary duty which she requires from all vessells that come into her Port, and makes returnes to the full amount of what is given her upon the coming away of the shipp or Vessell thence, and therefore since this [is] so common, wee hope she will not use us worse then others that expect much more grace and favour from her and therefore press her to show some particular kindness to the Company for our future encouradgment."

Gray anchored in "Acheene Roade" on the 22nd May, 1669. In September he wrote to Surat (*O. C.* No. 3346) that "The Dutch...are almost Sole Masters of all the ports and trade of this Island [Sumatra] there are but 2 ports to the westward of this [Achin] open from whence is brought only Coconut Oyle Dammer wax Rice and other provisions."

On hearing that orders had been sent to Fort St George to make a settlement at Achin, the Surat Council recalled Mr Gray, in Nov. 1669, urging as an excuse that "our fort freinds want the growth of those Countrys Pepper &ca more then we doe here." When Matthew Gray left Achin on the "Jounk *Nugdy*," he reported that "the Atcheen trade is Breathing its last" and he held out no hopes either to Surat or to Fort St George of the practicability of settling a factory there. He left Henry Chowne and Charles Ward in charge of the Company's remaining property.

The Council at Fort St George were loth to repeat the failure of the Surat Council. Although urged by the Court to write to the "Queen of Atcheene composing your letter in such a complasent method as may bee most acceptable unto her and therein to advise her from us, that God willing the next yeare, wee shall order some shipping to come to her Port for trade, and some person to make Addresses to her Majestie," Agent Foxcroft replied that, since the matter had been left to their judgment, he and his Council were of opinion that the re-settlement of a factory at Achin would not be worth the cost, especially as the procuring of "good store of pepper" was one of the chief conditions.

After these repeated disappointments, the Directors gave up the idea of settling a permanent factory at Achin. In November, 1670, they wrote to Fort St George, "Wee have laid aside the thoughts of any Factory at Acheene, finding what you advise by experience, in that which was sent from Surratt that it is not worth the Setling." In April, 1671, we read, in a "Generall" from Surat, "The Factory of Acheen is Dissolved according to your order."

Although the business done at Achin did not warrant the employment of a permanent staff of factors, yet trading voyages were sufficiently lucrative to make it advisable to retain the Company's house and one or two representatives. In the Diary of William Puckle while at Masulipatam, *Factory Records*, Masulipatam, No. 12, we have, p. 35, the following account of trade at Achin in 1675: "Acheen. There is an Arminian that lives in the Honble. Companys house there by leave of the president who keeps the House in repaire and gives Lodging to any of their ships Company and servants that come there but refuses to do so to strangers. The Queen hath great kindness for the English. A Strangers ship shall ly 2 mos. before unloaden and then every parcell strictly examined. The English by agreement pay a certayn Sum for each Ship whether little or great and have their dispatch presently...By Information when the Company had a Factory there it was usall to send thither a vessell with 16 or 20 pieces of goods for their account and the rest of the vessells hold fild up with particular private trade." T. B., not being a servant of the Company, had a house of his own at Achin (*vide* Introduction), as, no doubt, had many another private trader.

In 1683, after the loss of Bantam, the Directors again suggested

This part of the Citty of Achin Standeth Upon very Even low ground, soe that all the houses Stand upon Pillars of wood some 6, some 8, 10 or 12 foot from the ground, by reason in the Season of great raines, there is a very great inundation, which generally happeneth in September or the full Moone in October, at which time for many days wee goe from house to house in boats[1]. All that

---

(*Letter Book*, No. 7) a settlement at Achin, and wrote to the Queen on the subject. In the following year (1684), Richard Mohun was granted leave to occupy the old factory house at Achin on condition of keeping it and the Godowns in good repair. Achin, however, was not destined to replace Bantam as a "Subordinate Factory." Bencoolen, on the west coast of Sumatra, was fixed on for a settlement, and Achin remained, as far as English trade was concerned, in the condition described in the text.

[1] Compare the following descriptions of the town of Achin: In *Voyage pour la Compagnie d'Octroi des Indes Orientales*, 1603, p. 527, we have, "The town [of Achin] is half a league higher up [than the harbour] and is built all along the river side. The houses are of mud and raised on long piles because the river often overflows all the town. The dwelling rooms are reached by steps. The walls are covered with reeds or straw as are the roofs." De Graaf, who visited Achin in 1641, thus describes it, *Voyages*, p. 22 f., "The town of Achin is...situated on a level district about 3 miles from the mountain whence a river flows up to the town. There the river makes a bend and divides the town into two, after which it discharges itself into the Sea by 3 mouths. The largest and most important part of the town is on the N.W. side. Nearly all the houses are of reed, Bamboo, or cane, only a few being of stone. They are all built on piles of Bamboos raised 4 or 5 or even 6 feet from the ground, because the high tides flood the town nearly every year so that one is obliged to go by boat from one house to another...There are two large spaces for holding a market, one in the middle of the town and the other at the northern end. Here are found the merchants, both Moors and Idolaters, provided with all kinds of merchandise." *Dampier*, who was at Achin in 1688, gives, vol. ii. pp. 129, 148 and 149, some additional particulars about the town, "Their Houses are built on posts as those of Mindanao...The City of Achin...is seated on the Banks of a River...and about 2 miles from the Sea. This Town consists of about 7 or 8000 Houses; and in it there are always a great many Merchant Strangers...as Achin lies within a few Degrees of the Line so upon the Suns crossing the Line in March, the Rains begin a little Sooner there than in Countries nearer the Tropick of Cancer: and when they are once set in, they are as violent there as any where. I have seen it rain there for 2 or 3 days without intermission; and the River running but a short course ...it soon overflows; and a great part of the Street of the City shall on a sudden be all under water; at which time people row up and down the Streets in Canoas. That side the City toward the River especially, where the Foreign Merchants live, and which is lower ground, is frequently under water in the Wet Season: a Ships Long-

piece of land whereon standeth the Pallace[1], the great Mosquee[2], the Orongkays house and many Others neare the great Bazar[3] is a great deale higher and not at all Overflowne.

For the most part Every man's house hath a fence about it[4], and Sometimes 3 or 4 houses in one fence, but then the ground belongeth to one man. The houses wee live in are neare the River Side and consequently Stand as aforesaid (Upon Stilts) as followeth[5] [Plate XIX.].

This Countrey affordeth Severall Excellent good fruites[6], Namely Duryans[7], Mangastinos[8], Oranges the best in India

---

boat has come up to the very Gate of our English Factory laden with Goods; which at other times is ground dry enough, at a good distance from the River, and moderately raised above it." See also Lockyer, *Trade in India*, p. 37 f.

[1] Compare De Graaf, *Voyages*, p. 23, "There is [at Achin] a Large royal palace built in the Indian fashion. It is almost entirely of stone with very beautiful apartments and gardens where are fine pyramides, several tombs of the kings, Canals and a large house for the king's wives." After the rule of Achin passed into the hands of queens, the palace was closely guarded against intrusion. *Dampier*, vol. ii. p. 130, says, "The Queen has a large Palace here, built handsomely with Stone: but I could not get into the inside of it."

[2] Both De Graaf and Dampier speak of a number of Mosques in Achin but make no mention of any specially large one.

[3] For the two bazars, see the extract from De Graaf's *Voyages* in note 1 on p. 321.

[4] Compare Lockyer, *Trade in India*, p. 37 f., "The Houses are not join'd as in other Cities, but Pallizado'd every one by it self; except in two or three of the chief Streets, where the Bazar is kept, and the China camp, or Street where the Chines live. Europeans live as near one another as they can, and tho' their Houses do not join, yet a few Bambôos only part their Yards: Whence they have a long Street near the River wholy to themselves."

[5] The unfinished state of this, the last illustration in the MS., seems to point to some sudden interruption in the work (*vide* Introduction).

[6] T. B. in the Dialogues at the end of his *Malay Dict.* has, "The City [Achin] is indifferently supplied with Provisions, as Beef, Goats, Fowls, Fish, Rice, and plenty of many good Sorts of Fruits."

[7] See note on p. 278. Compare also *Dampier*, vol. i. p. 319 f., "The Trees that bear the Durians are big as Apple Trees, full of Boughs. The Rind is thick and tough; the Fruit is so large that they grow only about the Bodies, or on the Limbs near the Body, like the Cacao... The largest of the Fruit may be as big as a Pullets Egg: 'Tis as white as Milk, and as soft as Cream, and the taste very delicious to those who have been accustomed to them...This Fruit must be eaten in its prime." See Plate XIX.

[8] See *Hobson-Jobson*, *s.v.* Mangosteen. Compare *Dampier*, vol. ii.

Plate XIX

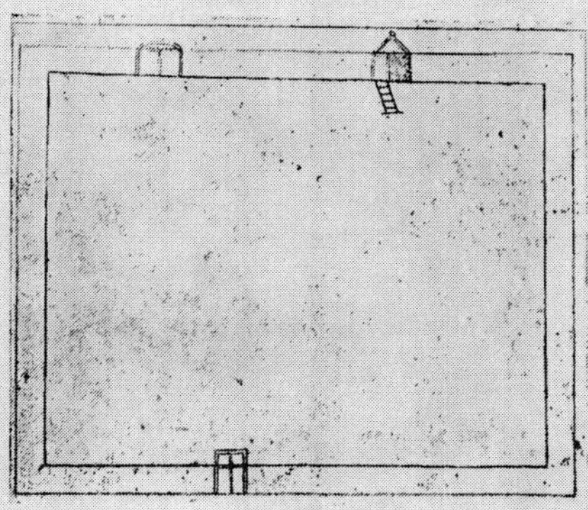

"AN ACHIN HOUSE."

p. 322.

p. 322.

"A MANGASTINE TREE. A DURIAN TREE."

or South Seas, comparable with the best of China, Lemons, Limes, Ramastines[1], Coconutts[2], Plantans[3], Pineapples[4], Mangoes[5], Mirablines[6], Bolangos[7], Monsoone plums[8],

---

p. 125, "Of all these sorts of Fruits [in Achin], I think the Mangastan is without compare the most delicate. This Fruit is in shape much like the Pomegranate, but a great deal less. The outside rind or shell is a little thicker than that of the Pomegranate, but softer, yet more brittle; and is of a dark red. The inside of the shell is of a deep crimson colour. Within this shell the fruit appears in 3 or 4 Cloves, about the bigness of the top of a man's thumb. These will easily separate each from the other; they are as white as Milk, very soft and juicy, inclosing a small black Stone or Kernel." See Plate XIX.

[1] *i.e. rambūtan*, the *nephalium lappaceum* = "leachee" (litchi). See *Hobson-Jobson*, *s.v.* Rambotang, and Watt, *Dict. of Economic Products*, *s.v.* Nephelium. Compare the following from W. Funnell's Voyage to the South Sea, &c., *Collection of Voyages*, vol. iv. p. 197, "The Rumbostan is about the Bigness of a Walnut, when the green Peel is off. It...hath a pretty thick tough outer Rind, which is of a deep Red, and is full of little Knobs of the same Colour. Within the Rind is the Fruit which is quite white, and looks almost like a Jelly and within the Fruit is a large Stone. It is very delicate Fruit, and though a Man eat never so much yet it never does him any harm, provided he swallow the Stones as well as the Fruit...."

[2] See note on p. 245. See also *Dampier*, vol. i. pp. 291—296 for a full description of the Cocoa-nut and its uses.

[3] See note on p. 245. [4] See note on p. 279.

[5] See note on p. 48. Compare *Dampier*, vol. i. p. 391, "Mangoes ...The fruit of these is as big as a small Peach; but long and smaller towards the top; it is of a yellowish colour when ripe; it is very juicy, and of a pleasant smell, and delicate taste. When the Mango is young they cut them in two pieces, and pickle them with Salt and Vineger, in which they put some Cloves of Garlick...The Mangoes were ripe...and they have then so delicate a fragrancy, that we could smell them out in the thick Woods if we had but the wind of them."

[6] See note on p. 192.

[7] Apparently a curtailment of the term *conbalingua*, *combalenga*, well-known at this period for the pumpkin. See *Hobson-Jobson*, *s.v.* Conbalingua.

[8] This is clearly the well-known and widely-spread Oriental fruit of the *Zizyphus Jujuba*, called *Rhamnus Jujuba* by Linnaeus and the older botanists. The common Indian name for it is *bĕr*. It is a small round yellow fruit of the size of a plum, though Rumphius calls it the Indian apple. The writer confused its Portuguese name *maçāo*, as adopted by the Malays (*masāna*, *mansāna*), for the common current word "monsoon" for "the season."

Rumphius, *Herbarium Amboinense*, vol. ii. book ii. chapter 44, p. 117 f., on the "Indische Appel-Boom," says, "Nomen. Latine *Malum Indicum* juxta Portugallicum *Mansana* vel *Massana da India* Acostae, uti et in India quoque dicitur *Veteri*, et juxta illum scriptorem

Pumple Mooses[1], &c., and the trees beare fruite both green and ripe all the yeare alonge[2].

And now I shall give a relation (admirable) of their new Queen[3] goeinge abroad, although her Voyadge was not very farre, yet most Sumptuous even to admiration, which gave very great Satisfaction to all Loyall Effectors of this Sort of Goverment, and more Especially to the favorites and relations of theire old deceased Queen, Of which as followeth:

Some fourty daies after the decease of the Old Queen,

Ber et *Bor*. Malaice *Vidara*, vocaturque in Macassara ac porro in hisce adjacentibus insulis Balis Buckel.

Locus. Plurimum occurrit haec arbuscula per totam veterem Indiam, ac porro in Bengala, Aracana, et Malacca usque in Javam et Baleyam, unde translata est in Celebem et Moluccos, hic vero et in Banda raro reperitur multumque degenerata."

[1] The largest variety of the orange. See *Hobson-Jobson*, *s.v.* Pommelo. T. B. in his *Malay Dict.* has, "Poomplemoos, a Fruit in India, is called at Berbadoes, a Shaddock." Compare *De la Loubère*, p. 23, "Pampelmouses have the taste and shape [of 'sowre' oranges], but...are as big as Melons, and have not much Juice." Nieuhof, *Het Gezantschap Der Neerlandtsche Oost-Indische Compagnie*, has, under "Vruchten in Sina," p. 144, "a certain fruit, which by the Chinese is called *Venku*, by the Portuguese *Jamboa*, and by the Dutch *Pompelmoes*." Compare also *Dampier*, vol. ii. p. 125, "The Pumple-nose is a large Fruit like a Citron, with a very thick tender uneven rind. The inside is full of Fruit: it grows all in cloves as big as a small Barly-corn, and these are all full of juice, as an Orange or a Lemon, tho' not growing in such partitions. 'Tis of a pleasant taste, and tho' there are of them in other parts of the East-Indies, yet these at Achin are accounted the best." Rumphius, *Herbarium Amboinense*, vol. ii. pp. 96—99, has a long article on this fruit in which he gives the various names by which it was known: "Nomen. Latine Limo Decumanus feu Malum Assyrium Decumanum: Malaice Lemon Cassomba h. e. Limo ruber ab incarnato colore, quidam Malaice vocant Jamboa juxta Portugallicum Samboa, quod proprie Pomp-sires feu Adami poma Hispanis denotat, a quo tamen haec mala Indica multum differunt; Javanis dicitur Djurru feu Djerru vel Djerru Matsjang h. e. Limo tigrinus: Macassarensibus Lemon Calucku h. e. Limo Calapparius, ob magnitudinem et formam Calappi. Belgice pompelmoes vocatur. Sinensibus vero Ju, vel Noay." See also note on Sam Cau on p. 247.

[2] Compare *De la Loubère*, p. 23, "All the other Fruits continue only a time. 'Tis at Achem only at the North Point of the Isle of Sumatra, that Nature produces them all at Every season." For illustrations of a "Mangastine Tree" and a "Durian Tree," see Plate XIX.

[3] See note on p. 311.

This Younge, or indeed more properly may be called New Queene, for that She was not lesse then 60 years Old when She was Established in the Throne[1], She went downe the River of Achin in soe admirable a Grandure of Worldly State, that the like I believe was never paralelled in the Universe[2].

Her own Person went downe in a most Stately barge most bravely carved and gilded from one end thereof to the other, with a very Stately Summer (or pleasure) house in the midst thereof, the which was covered with Massy Gold of incredible Substance and Value, and Surrounded with very Stately Pillars covered with the richest cloth of Gold hangings. Others, but a great deale inferiour to this, attended, yet very rich ones, in their proper Stations, vizt. One right ahead, one upon each quarter, all rowed by women, and seemed to doe it both with great reverence and rejoyceings, with Varieties of musick, and delicate Voices, that Sange to the great Honor and Majestie of their great Virgin-Princess. These were to admiration adorned with Flaggs and Pendants and fine tapestrie, with 500 of the Queen's most warlike Elephants (rigged in the greatest State) followed the barges very close (and in the water), for which reason they rowed the Easier. Above 100 of the riders, yea those that kept near the Queen's barge (or that wherein it was said the Queen was) were Eunuchs of her own houshold. Each of them wore his Turbat[3] after the Arabian mode of beaten pure Gold, and

---

[1] This must have been the "Old Queen" whose death, in 1688, is noted by Dampier (see note on p. 311).

[2] The "State Ride" seen by T. B. was more public than the annual "Ride" described by *Dampier*, vol. ii. p. 142, "The Queen of Achin...seldom goes abroad...except that once a Year she is drest all in white, and placed on an Elephant and so rides to the River in state to wash her self: but whether any of the meaner sort of People may see her in that progress I know not."

[3] See note on p. 156. Compare *Fryer*, p. 18, "On his Head he wore a large White Turbat."

very large Shakels of beaten Gold quite up their arms and leggs, and bore each of them a lance of beaten gold of 7 or 8 foot longe, and proportionately thick. The Other riders were Said to be Lords and Gentlemen of the Citty, and very richly attired in Cloth of gold, and armed with Creest[1] and Lance. .And Upon the banks of the River on each Side went 500 or more of the delicatest horses in the Kingdome; their Saddles, Stirrops, bits and buckles were of pure gold, their Saddle cloths and bridles and Crupars[2] richly beset with many Diamonds, Rubies, Pearle, and Saphir of im-[3]

---

[1] See note on p. 298.
[2] *i.e.* cruppers.
[3] Here the MS. breaks off abruptly.

LIST OF FULLER TITLES OF BOOKS AND MANUSCRIPTS QUOTED IN THE FOOT-NOTES AND INTRODUCTION.

Anderson, J. A., M.D., F.R.S. English Intercourse with Siam in the Seventeenth Century (Trübner's Oriental Series). London, 1890.

Annales du Musée Guimet, vol. 27. Le Siam Ancien par Lucien Fournereau. Paris, 1895*.

Balfour, Edward, Surgeon-General. The Cyclopaedia of India and of Eastern and Southern Asia. 3 vols. London, 1885.

Beauchamp, Henry K. *See* Dubois.

Bernier, François. Travels in the Mogul Empire, 1656–58 (Constable's Oriental Miscellany). London, 1891.

Bilgrami, Hossain, and **Wilmott,** C. Historical and Descriptive Sketch of H.H. the Nizam's Dominions. 2 vols. Bombay, 1883–84.

Bowrey, Thomas. Dictionary of English and Malayo. London, 1701.

Bowrey, Thomas. A Grammar of the Malay Tongue. Compiled from Bowrey's Dictionary, and other authentic documents, manuscript and printed. London, 1800.

Bowring, Sir John. The Kingdom and People of Siam. 2 vols. London, 1857.

British Museum, MS. Department:

Add. MS. 15319, Nos. 11 and 15. Charts of "Junk Seilon."

Add. MS. 28,140, ff. 31—33. "Proposall for taking Baldivia in the South Seas," by Thomas Bowrey.

Harleian 4252. Log of the *Unicorn*, 1668.

Harleian 4254. Notes and Observations of East India, per John Marshall, 1668—1672.

Sloane 5222, Nos. 6—17. Twelve charts by Thomas Bowrey.

Bruce, John, M.P., F.R.S. Annals of the Honourable East India Company, 1600—1707/8. 3 vols. London, 1810.

Burnell, A. C. *See* Yule.

Calendar of State Papers. Domestic Series. London, 1875 &c.

* The extracts used have been translated into English.

Carmichael, D. F. Manual of the District of Vizagapatam. Madras, 1869.

Chaumont, Mons. de C., Knt. A relation of the late Embassy to the Court of the King of Siam. London, 1687.

Constable's Oriental Miscellany. *See* Bernier.

Crawfurd, John, F.R.S. Descriptive Dictionary of the Indian Islands and adjacent countries. London, 1856.

Crawfurd, John, F.R.S. Journal of an Embassy to Siam and Cochin China. London, 1828.

Crawfurd, John, F.R.S. Malay Dictionary; a Grammar and Dictionary of the Malay Language. London, 1852.

Dalencé. *See* Delestre.

Dampier, William. A New Voyage round the World. 2 vols. London, 1698.

De Chaumont. *See* Chaumont.

De Graaf. *See* Graaf.

De la Loubère. *See* Loubère.

Delestre. Relation ou Journal d'un voyage fait aux Indes Orientales. Paris, 1677. "Par grace et Privilège du Roy en date du 24 Dec. 1676. Signé Dalencé il est permis &c." (This is the edition from which the extracts used in this work are taken. The copy at the India Office Library is catalogued as by Delestre, while the same edition at the British Museum is catalogued as [By Dalencé], and the edition of 1698, which only differs from the 1677 ed. in having a scanty index, is catalogued as [By De l'Estra?]. For the present work I have translated into English all the extracts used.)

Dennys, N. B., Ph.D. Descriptive Dictionary of British Malaya. London, 1894.

Diary of Streynsham Master. *See* India Office Records, *s.v.* Factory Records, Miscellaneous.

Dow, Alexander. History of Hindostan. 3 vols. (Translated from the Persian.) London, 1768—1772.

Dubois, Abbé J. A. Hindu Manners, Customs and Ceremonies, translated and edited by Henry K. Beauchamp. Oxford, 1897.

Dunn, Samuel. A New Directory for the East Indies. London, 1780.

Dunstan, James. The History of the Parish of Bromley St Leonard, Middlesex. London, 1862.

Eliot Papers, The. Compiled from family papers by Eliot Howard. 2 vols. Gloucester, 1893/4.

Endowed Charities (County of London), Parish of Limehouse, St Anne, 1895.

Eredia. *See* Godinho.

Finlayson, George. The Mission to Siam and Hué. London, 1826.

Fitch, Ralph. The Voyage of...to Goa in the East India and all the kingdoms of...the great Mogol. (Hakluyt's Collection of the early voyages, vol. 5.) London, 1809—1812.

Forrest, Thomas. Voyage from Calcutta to the Mergui Archipelago, &c. London, 1792.

Fort St George, Ancient Records of. *See* Press List.

Foster, Wm. Letters received by the East India Company from its Servants in the East. Vols. 2 &c. London, 1897 &c.

Fournereau. *See* Annales du Musée Guimet.

Fryer, John, M.D. A New Account of East India and Persia, in Eight Letters. Being 9 years Travels, Begun 1672. And Finished 1681. London, 1698.

Funnell, Wm. Voyage round the World. London, 1707.

Godinho de Eredia. Malaca, L'Inde Méridionale et le Cathay (1613), MS. orig. autographe de, reproduit et traduit par L. Janssen. Bruxelles, 1882*.

Graaf, Nicolas de. Voyages aux Indes Orientales et en d'autres lieux d'Asie. Amsterdam, 1719*.

Gribble, J. D. B. History of the Deccan. London, 1896 &c.

Hakluyt Society's Publications:

Hedges. Diary of Mr (afterwards Sir) William in Bengal, &c. 1681—1688, edited by Col. Henry Yule, C.B. 3 vols. London, 1886—1889.

Lancaster, Sir James. Voyages of, to the East Indies during the 17th cent. Edited by Clements R. Markham, C.B., F.R.S. London, 1877.

Hamilton, Alexander, Captain. A New Account of the East Indies. 2 vols. Edinburgh, 1727.

Harleian Society's Publications:

Allegations for Marriage Licences issued by the Vicar General of the Archbishop of Canterbury, vol. 31. London, 1890 &c

Hedges' Diary. *See* Hakluyt Society's Publications.

Herbert, Sir Thomas. Travels into Africa and Asia the Great. London, 1677.

Hobson-Jobson. *See* Yule and Burnell.

Horsburgh, James, F.R.S., &c. The India Directory or Directions for Sailing to and from the East Indies. 2 vols. London, 1809—1811, 1855.

Howison, James, M.D. A Dictionary of the Malay tongue as spoken in the Peninsula of Malacca &c. in Two Parts, to which is prefixed a Grammar. London, 1801.

Hunter, Sir William Wilson, K.C.S.I. History of British India. 2 vols. London, 1897.

Hunter, Sir William Wilson, K.C.S.I. Imperial Gazetteer of India. 14 vols. London, 1887.

Hutchins, John. The History and Antiquities of the County of Dorset. 2 vols. London, 1774.

Indian Antiquary, The, a Journal of Oriental Research. Bombay, 1872 &c.

* The extracts used have been translated into English.

India Office MS. Records:

Bengal Public Consultations, Range 1, vol. 1.

Factory Records:

Balasor, vol. 1.
Calcutta, vols. 2 and 3.
Fort St George, vols. 1—5, 14, 16, 18, 20, 21, 28, 30.
Hugli, vols. 1—7, 11
Java, vol. 6.
Kasimbazar, vol. 1.
Madapollam, vol. 3.
Masulipatam, vols. 1, 2, 6, 9, 10, 12.
Miscellaneous, vols. 2, 3, 3a, 14 (Diary of Streynsham Master).
Siam, vol. 1.
Surat, vols. 3, 87, 104, 105.
Letter Books (Copies of Dispatches from the Court of Directors to the various Factories), vols. 1—8.
Original Correspondence (known as the O.C. collection, being letters from India with collateral documents originating at any place between England and Japan), vols. 18—47.

General Records:

Abstracts of Letters received from the Coast and Bay, vol. 1.
Court Books (Minutes of the Proceedings of the Court of Directors), vols. 26—38.
Dutch Records: Hague Transcripts, vol. 2.
Home Series Miscellaneous, vol. 2. (List of Adventurers.)

Marine Records:

Ships' Logs, vols. 75 and 492 B. (Logs of the *President* and *King George.*)
Miscellaneous, vol. 13. ("A Book of Entertainment of Mariners.")

The Journall of Peter Mundy (a late copy).

Journal ou Suite du Voyage de Siam* par Mr L. D. C. Amsterdam, 1687.

Kelly, P., LL.D. The Universal Cambist and Commercial Instructor. 2 vols. London, 1835.

Lancaster. *See* Hakluyt Society's Publications.

Lane-Poole. *See* Rulers of India Series.

Luiller. *See* Prévost, Voyages.

Lockyer, Charles. An Account of the Trade in India, &c. London, 1711.

Lord, Henry, Sometime resident in East India and Preacher to the Ho^ble^ Company of Merchants trading thether. A Display of two forraigne Sects in the East Indies vizt. The Sect of the Banians the Ancient Natives of India And the Sect of the Persees the Ancient Inhabitants of Persia together with the Religion and Manners of Each Sect Collected into two Bookes. Imprinted at London for Francis Constable and are to be Sold at his Shoppe in Paules Church yard at the signe of the Crane, 1630.

* The extracts used have been translated into English.

Loubère, De la. A New Historical Relation of the Kingdom of Siam. Done out of French by A. P. Gen. R.S.S. London, 1693.

Lysons, Daniel, F.R.S. The Historical Account of the Environs of London. 4 vols. and supp. London, 1792—1811.

Mackenzie, Gordon. A Manual of the Kistna District. Madras, 1883.

Madras Manual of Administration. A Manual of the Administration of the Madras Presidency in illustration of the Records of Government and the Yearly Administration Reports. 3 vols. (vol. 3 Glossary.) Madras, 1893.

Madras Press List. *See* Press List.

Mandelslo, J. Albert. Voyages and Travels of, into the East Indies, rendred into English by John Davies of Kidwelly. London, 1669.

Marco Polo. *See* Yule.

Marsden, William, F.R.S. A Grammar of the Malayan Language with an Introduction and Praxis. London, 1812.

Marshall, John. *See* British Museum MSS., *s.v.* Harleian, 4254.

Milburn, Wm. Oriental Commerce, &c. 2 vols. London, 1813.

Moor, J. H. Notices of the Indian Archipelago and adjacent countries. Part I. Singapore, 1837.

Morris, H. A Descriptive and Historical Account of the Godavery District. London, 1878.

Murray, James A. H., LL.D. A New English Dictionary. Oxford, 1888, &c.

Nieuhoff, J. Gezantschap aan den Grooten Tartarischen Cham, of Keizer van Sina. Amsterdam, 1670*.

Notes and Extracts from the Government Records in Fort St George (1670—1681). Parts I. II. III. Madras, 1871–73.

Orme, Robert. Historical Fragments of the Mogul Empire, &c. 2 vols. London, 1782.

Oxford English Dictionary. *See* Murray.

Penny, Mrs. Fort St George, Madras. London, 1900.

Premier Livre de l'Histoire de la Navigation aux Indes Orientales, par les Hollandois et des choses a eux advenues Par G. M. A. W[illem] L[odewijcksz]. Amsterdam, Cornille Nicolas, 1609.

Press List of Ancient Records in Fort St George. Nos. 1 to 6 (1670—1699).

Prévost, Antoine François. Histoire Générale des Voyages*. 25 vols. La Haye, 1747–80.

Pringle, A. T. Selections from the Consultations of the Agent, Governor, and Council of Fort St George, 1681. 4th Series. Madras, 1893.

Pringle, A. T. The Diary and Consultation Book of the Agent, Governor, and Council of Fort St George. 1st Series, 1682—1685. 4 vols. Madras, 1894, &c.

* The extracts used have been translated into English.

Risley, H. H. The Tribes and Castes of Bengal. 2 vols. Calcutta, 1891.

Rulers of India Series. Aurangzib; by Stanley Lane-Poole. Oxford, 1893.

Rumphius, Georg. Everhard. Herbarium Amboinense. 7 vols. Amstelodami, 1741.

Schouten, Gautier. Voiage aux Indes Orientales 1658—1665. 2 vols. Traduit du Hollandois. Amsterdam, 1707*.

Smyth, W. H., Admiral. The Sailors' Word Book. London, 1867.

Somerset House, Documents at.
Wills.
Administrations.

Sonnerat. Voyages aux Indes Orientales et à la Chine. Translated by F. Magnus. 3 vols. Calcutta, 1788.

Stevens, Robert. The Complete Guide to the East India Trade. London, 1766.

Stewart, Charles. The History of Bengal. London, 1813.

Tavernier, E. T. Collection of Travels, &c., being the Travels of Monsieur Tavernier, Bernier and other great men. 2 vols. London, 1684.

Taylor, James. A Sketch of the Topography and Statistics of Dacca. Calcutta, 1840.

Terry, Edward. A Voyage to East India. Reprint from edition of 1655. London, 1777.

Thevenot, Melchizedek. Les Voyages en Europe, Asie et Afrique. Newly done into English. London, 1687.

Trübner's Oriental Series. *See* Anderson.

Valentyn, François. Oud en Nieuw Oost Indien. 5 vols. Amsterdam, 1624.

Watt, G. A. A Dictionary of the Economic Products of India. 10 vols. Calcutta, 1889–93.

Wheeler, J. Talboys. Madras in the Olden Time...compiled from Official Records. 3 vols. Madras, 1861.

Wilkinson, R. J. A Malay-English Dictionary. Singapore, 1901.

Wilson, C. R. Early Annals of the English in Bengal. Vol. 1. Calcutta, 1895.

Wilson, H. H. Essays on the Religion of the Hindus. London, 1862.

Yule, Col. H. *See* Hakluyt Society's Publications.

Yule, Col. H. The Book of Ser Marco Polo, the Venetian, concerning the Kingdoms and Marvels of the East. 2 vols. London, 1875.

Yule, Col. H., and **Burnell**, A. C. Hobson-Jobson; being a Glossary of Anglo-Indian Colloquial Words and Phrases. London, 1886 and 1902.

* The extracts used have been translated into English.

INDEX.

Aazzum Caun, Auzum Cawne. *See* A'zīm Khān

Abassee, Abassin. *See* Coins

Abdoul-Coutu-Sha. *See* Abdullah Qutb Shāh

Abdula Hossein. *See* Abu'l Hassan Shāh

Abdullah Qutb Shāh, rise of, 109 *n.* 1; 6th king of Qutb Shāhī line, 113 *n.* 1; his tomb, 113; date of his death, 113, 113 *n.* 2

Abu'l Hassan Shāh, king of Golconda, 88 *n.* 2; *farmān* granted by to the English, 93 *n.* 1

Acham. *See* Assam

Achār, pickle, 193, 193 *n.* 1; bamboo, 192 *n.* 4, 193; mangoe, 193 *n.* 1; radish, 193 *n.* 1; lime, 193 *n.* 1

Achee, Acheen, Achein, Achim. *See* Achin

Achin, xvi, xxii, xxxvi, xxxvii, xxxix, xl, l, 72 *n.* 2, 82 *n.* 1, 97 *n.* 3, 237 *n.* 2, 260, 261 *n.* 3, 262, 268, 270; port of, xxii, xxxviii, xxxix, xl, 286, 286 *n.* 3, 287, 289 *n.* 1, 300 *n.* 4, 301, 320; Jordan goes on a trading voyage to, 178 *n.* 1; weight of bahar of, 241 *n.* 4; trade of, 245 *n.* 2, 283, 286, 286 *n.* 1, 289 *n.* 1; bamboo measure at, 249 *n.* 1; number of foreigners at, 256 *n.* 1, 286 *n.* 1; Chulias at, 258; riches of, 261; royal palace at, 275 *n.* 1, 286 *n.* 2, 313, 314, 322, 322 *n.* 1; fruit and vegetables plentiful at, 279 *n.* 3, 322, 323, 324 *n.* 3; weights and measures of, 281, 281 *n.* 5, 282; coins of, 281 *n.* 5; T.B.'s description of, 285–326; capital of Sumatra, 285; situation of, 285, 286; Schouten's description of, 285 *n.* 3; dependencies of, 285 *n.* 3, 286 *n.* 3, 295, 295 *n.* 4; river of, 286; buildings at, 285 *n.* 3, 286 *n.* 2, 321, 321 *n.* 1, 322, 322 *n.* 4; T.B. resides at, 287 *n.* 1; malefactors at, whither banished, 287, 287 *n.* 5; malefactors at, how punished, 287 *n.* 5, 315, 315 *n.* 2, 317, 317 *n.* 2; imports of, 288–292, 293 *n.* 1; most populous city in Malay Archipelago, 293; produces few commodities, 293 *n.* 1; Dampier's description of, 293 *n.* 2, 321 *n.* 1; Mundy's description of, 294 *n.* 2; prosperity of, 294; soil and climate of, 286, 293, 294, 294 *n.* 1; gold at, 294, 294 *n.* 2; belief in a perpetual female dynasty at, 295 *n.* 6; people of, 293, 294 *n.* 3; government of, 295, 295 *n.* 6, 299 *n.* 5; chief ministers at, 299; ministers at, presents given to, 302, 303; customs paid by English vessels at, 303, 304, 304 *n.* 1; privileges to English at, 304 *n.* 4; English merchants at, ceremony on departure of, 307, 308; Shabandar of, 307, 307 *n.* 4; history of English factory at, 308, 317, 318, 318 *n.* 3, 319, 320; English trade at, 308 *n.* 2, 320; sports at, 310; fortifications of, 312, 312 *n.* 2; disaffected inhabitants at, 312, 313, 313 *n.* 1; troubles in, at death of 3rd Queen of, 313 *n.* 1; town attacked by rebels, 313, 314; execution of insurgents at, 314; Bishop of, how punished, 314; cripples at, 314, 314 *n.* 4; cruel laws at, 315, 316 *n.* 1; executions at, 315, 316; story of a thief at, 317, 318; English chief at, 317, 317 *n.* 5; floods at, 321; De Graaf's description of, 321 *n.* 1; mosque at, 322; bazaar at, 322; illustration of house at, 322

Achin, Bishop of. *See* Siddy

Achin, king of, at war with Kedah, 260 *n.* 1; Kedah subject to in 1663, 275 *n.* 2; Sekander muda, his tyranny, 295 *n.* 6, 296–298; letter from to James I, 295 *n.* 6; cruelty of, 295 *n.* 6, 296, 296 *n.* 1, 297; murders his son, 297, 298; death and burial of, 298; De Graaf's account of death of in 1641, 298 *n.* 2; concession obtained by Capt. Lancaster from, 304 *n.* 4; succeeds 4th queen *circ.* 1710, 311 *n.* 1

Achin, queen of, xxiii, xxxviii; Perak subject to the, 283 *n.* 3; acting regent in Schouten's time, 285 *n.* 3, 298 *n.* 3; mistake as to length of reign of the, 295, 295 *n.* 6; chosen on death of Sekander muda, 298, 299 *n.* 1; her power restricted by enactments, 298, 299; her counsellors and attendants, 299, 299 *n.* 5, 300, 310; her treatment of foreigners, 300–304; her seclusion, 300, 300 *n.* 1; her *chāp* necessary in order to land at Achin, 300; present to, how delivered, 309, 310; illness and death of the second, 311, 312; mourning for the, 311, 312; history of from 1641–1700, 311 *n.* 1; the third proclaimed, 312; death of the third, 313 *n.* 1; invites the English to settle a factory, 318 *n.* 3; exchanges presents with Charles II, 319; her fear of Dutch aggression, 319; contract between Henry Gray and the, 319; letter ordered to be sent to from Fort St George, 320; her kindness to the English, 306, 307, 320; her royal progress, 324–326, 325 *n.* 2

Achinese, Achiners, the, 252 *n.* 3; at Junk-Ceylon, assisted by Malays against Dutch, 252; their prosperity, 294; their laziness, 294 *n.* 3

Achin Head, 287 *n.* 2

Acorus, *Acorum* (dringo root), 192 *n.* 4

Acorus terrestris (dringo root), 192 *n.* 4

Adam and Eve, the, Wm. Jearsey's ship, 251 *n.* 1

Adventure, the, Wm. Jearsey's ship, 251 *n.* 1

Advice, the, pink, l; Wm. Jearsey's ship, 251 *n.* 1

Africa, Bowrey's knowledge of coast of, xli

Aftābā, an ewer, 96 *n.* 2, 199 *n.* 3

Aftowel, Aftaw. *See Aftābā*

Aga Gilloll, Agga Geloll, Aga Telloll. *See* Agha Jalāl

Agala, Aguala wood. *See* Agila wood

Aga Telloll. *See* Agha Jalāl

Agents, of the English in India. *See s.v.* Winter, Foxcroft, Langhorne, Gyfford, Clavell, Vincent, etc.

Agha Jalāl, Governor of Masulipatam, 63 *n.* 1, 81 *n.* 2, 99 *n.* 6; exchanges visits and presents with Streynsham Master, 81 *n.* 2; his retinue and importance, 83

Agila wood, 272, 272 *n.* 3, 273

Agra, 20, 39 *n.* 2, 142, 142 *n.* 1, 146, 147, 148, 288 *n.* 6, 288 *n.* 8; the metropolis of Akbar and Jahāngīr, 18; the capital of Shāh Jahān, 137; its fortress, 137 *n.* 2; description of, 137 *n.* 2; the Tāj, at, 145 *n.* 6; rents of, given to Shāyista Khān, 148 *n.* 5

Aguala wood. *See* Agila wood

Aguilaria Agallocha. *See* Agila wood

Ahmad Maraikkar, xxxvi; Bowrey's quarrel with, at Porto Novo, xxxi–xxxiii

Aiderabad. *See* Haidarabad

Ainsa Bhainsa. *See* Jansa Bhainsa

Akbar, 109 *n.* 2; his tolerant treatment of the Hindus, 10 *n.* 5, 11 *n.* 2; Agra his metropolis, 18 *n.* 2

Akhun, 300 *n.* 2

Alāchah, a silk cloth, 54, 71 *n.* 3, 122 *n.* 3, 290, 290 *n.* 4

Alacor. *See* Halalcore

Alahwirdī Khān, Ilahwirdī Khān. *See* 'Alī Vardī Khān

Alā'uddīn Khiljī, 221 *n.* 5

Alcoron, the. *See* (Al) Koran, the

Aleppo, xxxviii

Alexander the Great, limit of his conquests in India, 131 *n.* 7, 210, 210 *n.* 1

'Alī Vardī Khān, Persian commander of Shāh Shujā', 138; betrays his master, 138

(Al) Koran, the, 95, 314 *n.* 1; written in Arabic, 95; much esteemed, 95

Allahabad, 130 *n.* 4, 148 *n.* 5

Alleja, a silk cloth. *See Alāchah*

Alley, river, 176 *n.* 1

Alligators, in the Ganges, 202, 211 *n.* 1; description of, 284, 285; crocodiles mistaken by T. B. for, 284 *n.* 3; illustration of, 285; oil obtained from, 285

Alligese. *See Alāchah*

Aloe-wood. *See* Agila wood

Alos Star, present capital of Kedah, 259 *n.* 4

Alvedore. *See Havildār*

Amadabat, Ahmadabad, 288 *n.* 8

Amad Marcar. *See* Ahmad Maraikkar

Amad Mercawn. *See* Ahmad Maraikkar

Amba. *See* Mangoe

Amboyna, 170, 192 *n.* 4

Ambrose, a companion of Dampier, xxxviii

Ameer Al Omrah. *See Amīr-ul-Umarā*

America, Bowrey's knowledge of coast of, xli, xliii; Rangoon oil from, 192 *n.* 4

Amīr, Ameer, 39, 145 *n.* 2, 299 *n.* 2

Amīr-ul-Umarā, Shāyista Khān so styled, 150 *n.* 1

Amord Mercawne. *See* Ahmad Maraikkar

Amoy, 118 *n.* 1

Amoy Bay, Chart of by Bowrey, xxix, l

Amoy Merchant, the, 178 *n.* 1

Ananas. *See* Pineapple

Anantram, broker to the English at Kasimbazar, 30 *n.* 2, 32 *n.* 2

Anctent, Ancient. *See* Flag

Andaman Is., l

Andaman Sea, 237 *n.* 2

Anderson, J. A., acquainted with the T. B. MS., xv; his "English Intercourse with Siam" referred to, xv *n.* 1, 91 *n.* 1, 173 *n.* 3, 290 *n.* 10

Andragera, Andregeree, Andraghiri. *See* Indragiri

Androgeero, Androgheree. *See* Indragiri

Angelin. *See* Hijili

Angerang, 123 *n.* 4

Angle. *See Anguli*

Anglo-Indians of the 17th century, T. B.'s references to, xviii

Anguli, a finger-breadth. *See* Weights and Measures

Anna. *See* Coins

"**Annales du Musée Guimet**," referred to, 235 *n.* 1

Anne, the, afterwards the *Hope*, 73 *n.* 3, 319

Antelope, description of an, 59; manner of taking the, 59 *n.* 1; illustration of an, 119

Antelope, the, xxiv

Apes. *See* Monkeys

Apes' bezoar, 292 *n.* 7

Apocrypha, The story of Bel and the Dragon referred to, 23

Aquilaria Agallocha. *See* Agila wood

Arabia, li, 1, 5, 71, 132 *n.* 2, 133, 281 *n.* 3, 293

Arabic language, the, 314 *n.* 1; the (Al) Koran written in, 95

Arabs, the, 237 *n.* 2; seize Heron's ships, 176 *n.* 1

Arakan (Arackan, Aracan), xvi, 61 *n.* 3, 72 *n.* 2, 73, 131, 131 *n.* 7, 140 *n.* 2, 199, 205, 209 *n.* 2, 212 *n.* 2; rivers of, 74; situation of, 139 *n.* 5; Shāh Shujā' takes refuge in, 139, 139 *n.* 5, 140–142; Firinghees at, 140 *n.* 4; wild elephants in, 222; no description of by T.B., 234 *n.* 2; trade with, 245 *n.* 2

Arakan, king of, protects Shāh Shujā', 139–141; quarrels with his guest, 141; causes Shāh Shujā's death, 142

Arakaners, Arackaners, 140; pirates of Arakan, 140 *n.* 3, 212; their depredations, 212 *n.* 2; Company's sloops employed against them, 212 *n.* 2

Arbre Triste (Arbol Triste, Arbor Tristis, Arbor Triste), description of, 49

Arch Brahmin, at Jagannāth pagoda, 12 *n.* 1

Areca, Arek, 30, 307, 309 *n.* 3; grown in Junk-Ceylon, 247; nut of, chewed at state calls, 303; plentiful in Achin, 304; description of, 304 *n.* 6; nut of, how prepared for chewing, 304 *n.* 6, 305, 305 *n.* 1; its beneficial qualities, 305, 306 *n.* 1; appearance of when growing, 306; illustration of, 308; wood of tree, how used, 306

Areca Catechu, areca palm, 306 *n.* 3

Armaghaum. *See* Armagon

Armagon (Armaghaum, Armegam, Arumukam, Doogarauzpatam, Duraspatam, Monapollem), 3 *n.* 5; history of, 25 *n.* 3; pagoda of, 25; shoal near, 25 *n.* 3; factory of, 25 *n.* 3; headquarters of the English, 1628–1639, 53 *n.* 1; deserted for Fort St George, 53

Armenian, John Demarcora an, 172 *n.* 3; Heron married to an, 176 *n.* 1; an, in charge of Company's ground at Kedah, 268; an, at English house in Achin, 320

Armenians, 221 *n.* 3; numerous in Golconda, 111 *n.* 1

Arrack, 68 *n.* 2; made by the Gentues in Masulipatam, 77; forbidden to Muhammadans, 77; how distilled, 77, 78; different kinds of, 77 *n.* 3, 78 *n.* 1; a generic term for spirits, 77 *n.* 3; Davies' death attributed to, 269

Arrangoes (?dringo root), 192 *n.* 4

Arrivall, the, sloop, 173 *n.* 2, 176 *n.* 1, 208 *n.* 4, 292 *n.* 6; piloted by Heron, 175 *n.* 4, 175 *n.* 6, 175 *n.* 8; her boat overset, 178 *n.* 3

Arsipore, Arzepore, Arcsepour, Ar--pouro. *See* Harsapur

Articles of Agreement, between Malik Qāsim and the Danes, 186, 187; between the English and Achinese, 302 *n.* 1, 303

Arumukam Mudaliār, Armagon named from, 25 *n.* 3

Arundell. *See* Roundel

Asaf Khān, father of Shāyista Khān, 145 *n.* 6

Asām-Jawa. *See* Tamarind

Asia, 1, 14, 20, 27, 125, 169, 182, 193, 205, 257, 281 *n.* 3; extent of, 2; women of, 31; garments of women of, 32; children of women of, 32; central, 172 *n.* 1; Alexander the Great's conquests in, 210

Assam, Mīr Jumla makes war on *rājā* of, 143; conquest and loss of by Aurangzēb's forces, 143, 144

Astrology, studied by the Brahmins, 205 *n.* 1, 205 *n.* 2

Astronomers, reputation of Brahmins as, 206

Atchar. *See Achār*

Atchee, Atcheen. *See* Achin

Atchein. *See* Achin

Atkins, Captain, his Journal referred to, 287 *n.* 4; his account of his landing at Achin, 300 *n.* 4

Augustinian Friars, their churches in Bengal, 133 *n.* 3; at Hugli, 195 *n.* 5

Aū Karon, 239 *n.* 1

Aurangzēb, the Great Mogul, third son of Shāh Jahān, 18 *n.* 2; appointed Viceroy of the Deccan, 108 *n.* 7, 135; his friends inform him of Dara's movements, 136, 137; overthrows Dara in battle, 137; imprisons his father, 137; beheads Murād Bakhsh, 137; defeats Shāh Shujā', 138, 139; becomes Emperor, 139, 142; swears to avenge Shāh Shujā's death, 142; his jealousy of Mīr Jumla, 144; his pretended grief at Mīr Jumla's death, 144, 145; his treatment of the Hindus, 10 *n.* 4, 10 *n.* 5, 11 *n.* 2; changes the name of Porto Novo, 82 *n.* 1; Orissa and Pattana subject to him, 128, 221; his court at Delhi, 142 *n.* 1; his kindness to Mīr Jumla's son, 145; makes Shāyista Khān *nawāb* of Bengal, 145; recalls Shāyista Khān, 147; makes his son *nawāb* of Bengal, 147, 150 *n.* 1, 164 *n.* 2; *farmān* of, 165 *n.* 2

Aureng-Zebe. *See* Aurangzēb

Austin-Friars, church of, at Dacca, 149 *n.* 1

Australia, chart of coast of, by Bowrey, xlix

Ava, 131 *n.* 7

Avaldar. *See Havildār*

Aynan. *See* Hainan

Ayscue, Sir George, xxiv

'Azīm Khān. *See* Fidai Khān

A'zīm Khān, son of Rashīd Khān, to be *nawāb* of Orissa, 152 *n.* 4

Bafta, piece-goods, 288 *n.* 6, 302 *n.* 2, 303; blue, 272 *n.* 2, 288, 317; broad, 272 *n.* 2; gold, 272, 288; where now made, 272 *n.* 2; white, 288

Bafto. *See* Bafta

Baglana, province of, 135 *n.* 5

Bagnagar. *See* Bhāgnagar

Bahagur, former name of Balasor, 162 *n.* 3

Bahar. *See* Weights and Measures

Baharre. *See Bahar, s.v.* Weights and Measures

Bāhmanī dynasty, 109 *n.* 1

Bajrā, a boat used for pleasure and state journeys, 190, 190 *n.* 2, 228; description of, 228 *n.* 1; illustration of, 228

Balagate, province, 108 *n.* 1, 135 *n.* 5

Balasor, xix, 32, 56 *n.* 2, 68 *n.* 3, 87 *n.* 2, 90 *n.* 1, 104 *n.* 1, 124 *n.* 3, 129 *n.* 1, 130, 148 *n.* 2, *passim*; T.B. a resident in, in 1674, 152; the only seaport in the Bay of Bengal, 152; Rashīd Khān's extortions at, 153, 154, 154 *n.* 1, 155, 156, 158; trade bad at, 154 *n.* 1; English factory at, 154 *n.* 1, 162 *n.* 3; English agent at, 154 *n.* 1; Clavell's "pallace" at, 159; native governor of, 159, 183 *n.* 2, 185 *n.* 1; letters from Walter Clavell at, 159; "Accompt" of the trade of, 159, 162 *n.* 3; Walter Clavell dies at, 160 *n.*; *nawāb* of Cuttack rides in

state through, 161; Schouten's description of, 162 *n.* 3; Marshall's description of, 162 *n.* 3; its prosperity owing to its convenient situation, 162 *n.* 3; part of the town rented by the Company, 162 *n.* 3; Portuguese houses at, 162 *n.* 3; subordinate to Hugli, 168 *n.* 4; hours of prayer at, altered, 177 *n.* 1; Danish factory at, 183, 183 *n.* 3; trade of, ruined by Malik Qāsim's exactions, 185 *n.* 1; commodities from, 231
Balasor Road, xxxvii, 68 *n.* 3, 92 *n.* 1, 164, 167 *n.* 1, 182 *n.* 3, 232; its safety and convenience, 162 *n.* 3; Company's cargoes transshipped, at, 166 *n.* 2
Baldivia, Bowrey's proposal for taking, xliii
Balfour, E., his "Cyclopaedia of India" referred to, 275 *n.* 1
Ballasore. *See* Balasor
Bamboo, 86 *n.* 2, 87, 243, 274, 314, 314 *n.* 4, 322 *n.* 4; houses built of, at Dacca, 149 *n.* 1, at Achin, 321 *n.* 1; *ăchār* made from, 193, 193 *n.* 1; houses at Patna roofed with, 221 *n.* 6; plentiful at Junk-Ceylon, 249; two kinds, male and female, 249, 249 *n.* 1, 250; description of, 249 *n.* 1; used for building houses, 250, 277, 277 *n.* 5; illustration of, 250
Bamboo, a measure. *See* Weights and Measures
Ban, a village, 239 *n.* 1
Banana, 274 *n.* 2
Banarous. *See* Benares
Bandahāra, a treasurer, 256 *n.* 3
Bandar, a harbour, 100 *n.* 1, 191 *n.* 2
Bandar Abbas (Gombroon), 132 *n.* 2, 216, 216 *n.* 6
Bandarees. *See Bendahārī*
Bandel, the Portuguese Colony in Hugli, 191, 191 *n.* 2; meaning of, 191 *n.* 2
Bang. *See Bhāng*
Banga. *See* Bangaree
Bangala. *See* Bengal
Bangala Merchant, the. *See Bengall Merchant*, the
Bangaree, liv, 257, 283; situation of, 257 *n.* 2
Bangha. *See Bhāng*
Bangkok, 91 *n.* 1
Bangri, Bangarie. *See* Bangaree
Banhos, Domingos Perez, chief owner of the *Sancta Cruz*, 172 *n.* 3
Banian. *See* Banyan
Banjan. *See* Banyan
Ban Karon, in Junk-Ceylon, 239 *n.* 1. *See also* Putom
Banksall, 88 *n.* 3, 93 *n.* 1, 263 *n.* 1
Ban Lipon, village of Lipon, 239 *n.* 1
Ban Lipon Thai, Siamese village of Lipon, 239 *n.* 1
Banquala, a port in Junk-Ceylon, 237, 238, 242, 242 *n.* 2, 246, 250, 252, 255; its situation and present designation discussed, 239 *n.* 1, 250 *n.* 2
Bantam, l, li, lii, 71 *n.* 3, 90 *n.* 1, 91 *n.* 1, 118 *n.* 1, 172 *n.* 3, 258, 295 *n.* 3, 298 *n.* 1, 314 *n.* 1, 318 *n.* 3; loss of, 320
Banyans, a Hindu caste, 194, 224 *n.* 1; social characteristics of, 24, 27, 30, 31, 32, 34, 35, 41; mercantile abilities of, 24 *n.* 2; religious characteristics of, 27, 28, 29, 30, 31, 35; language of, 27; moral characteristics of, 27, 28, 29; food of, 28; clothes of, 32; appearance of, 32; merchants of the, at Dacca, oppressed by the *nawāb*, 152; money extorted from the, at Balasor, 153; merchants of, compelled to build ships for the *nawāb*, 163; at Hugli, live peaceably under the Moors, 168 *n.* 2; of higher caste than Uriyas, 199; in Persia, 216
Banyan-tree, 7 *n.* 2
Baratta. *See* Dustoor
Barbadoes, 324 *n.* 1
Barbary, 94
Barbers, of Gentue caste to be sent to St Helena, 9 *n.* 4
Barbor, Robert, to be employed on Bombay fortifications, xxv
Barca, probable origin of Purgo, 228 *n.* 2
Barella, 295 *n.* 2
Barnagar Barnnegur, 176 *n.* 1, 190 *n.* 2
Baron, Monsieur, 66 *n.* 1
Barros, João de, 129 *n.* 1, 237 *n.* 2
Barros, kingdom of, 285 *n.* 3, 292 *n.* 1, 295 *n.* 3
Basanta-Pāṭali, 129 *n.* 1
Basara. *See Bajrā*
Basse, Captain William, 208 *n.* 5; his account of the naval action with the Dutch, 91 *n.* 1
Batavia, xxvii, l, li, lii, 92 *n.* 1, 269, 285 *n.* 3; butter from Bengal exported to, 133 *n.* 2; timber brought from, to Hugli, 169 *n.* 1
Bateman, Thomas, 176 *n.* 1; an

apprentice-pilot, xix; pilots the *Dilligence* to Hugli in 1675, xix; wrecked in returning to Balasor, xix; death of, xix
Batilles. *See* Betteela
Batta, difference in exchange, 217 *n.* 2
Baupautla, 54
Baurī. *See* Weights and Measures
Bay, the. *See* Bengal
Bazaars, at Masulipatam, 106; at Hugli, 167, 168; at Patna, 226 *n.* 2; at Achin, 322, 322 *n.* 4
Bāzār, a market, 213
Bears, figures of, in pagodas, 6; figures of, carved on the chariot of Jagannāth, 17; infest swamps near the Ganges, 199, 219; their ferocity, 219; size and colour of in Bengal, 220; illustration of, 222
Beaufort, the, xxxvii
Beejapore. *See* Bījapūr
Beeswax, 290 *n.* 8; the king's monopoly, 56, 56 *n.* 2, 132 *n.* 5, 225; plentiful in Bengal, 132, 134 *n.* 1
Beetle. *See* Betel
Begum, of Shāyista Khān, intercedes for him, 148 *n.* 5
Behar, kingdom of, how composed, 151 *n.* 2.
Bel and the Dragon, allusion to story of, 23
Bellesort, **Bellesoor.** *See* Balasor
Bells, not used by Muhammadans, 196
Belly timber, 194, 194 *n.* 1
Below, meaning 'north,' 99, 108
Benares, 226 *n.* 2, 230 *n.* 5; Pagoda of, 12 *n.* 1; festival at pagoda of, 17 *n.* 1
Bencoolen, Bencolen, xl; pepper from, 292 *n.* 4; English settlement at, 318 *n.* 3
Bendahāra, a degree of nobility among Malays, 256 *n.* 3
Bendahārī, treasury-officers, 256
Bendaree, Bandaree. *See* *Bandahāra*
Bengal, Bengala, Bangala, xvi, xxii, xxvii, xxxix, xl, 5, 10, 12 *n.* 1, 23, 32, 33 *n.* 1, 48 *n.* 1, 61 *n.* 3, 104 *n.* 1, 124 *n.* 3, 129 *n.* 1, 130 *passim*; productiveness of, 21, 132, 133, 134; exports from, 122 *n.* 1, 132, 133, 247; description of, 131–220; extent of, 131, 131 *n.* 7; rivers of, 131, 132; prosperity of, 131; trade of, 132 *n.* 3, 133; manufactures of, 132 *n.* 3, 133; government of, 135–149; rebellion in, 135–139; governors of, *see* Shāh Shujā', Mīr Jumla, Shāyista Khān, Fidāī Khān; Schouten's description of, 131 *n.* 7; former independence of, 131 *n.* 7; number of Christians in, 133, 133 *n.* 3; Mīr Jumla made governor of, 139; Shāyista Khān made *nawāb* of, 145, 146 *n.* 2, 146 *n.* 4; Aurangzēb's third son made *nawāb* of, 147, 148 *n.* 5; reports concerning governors of, 148 *n.* 5; Shāyista Khān reinstated as governor of, 148 *n.* 5; English factories in, hold their *farmāns* from the Mogul, 151; Walter Clavell Chief of the English factory in, 158; rivers in, 165; Hugli, the depôt for commodities of, 168; settlement of the Danes in, 184; cheapness of provisions in, 193, 194, 194 *n.* 2; noted for sweetmeats made by the Portuguese, 193 *n.* 2; resorted to by foreigners, 194, 194 *n.* 2; Bernier's saying concerning, 194, 194 *n.* 2; natives of Northern, their search for the source of the Ganges, 211; its fruitful villages and towns, 212, 215, 215 *n.* 2; its natural productions, 212; current money of, 216–218; measures used in, 217, 218; woods of, infested with wild beasts, 219, 220 *n.* 4; imports of, 232; ships from, frequent Achin, 288; commodities from, exported to Achin, 289, 290
Bengal, Bay of, 108 *n.* 1, 131, 131 *n.* 7, 135 *n.* 5; limits of in 17th century, 131 *n.* 4; Balasor the only seaport in the, 152; Danish ships come to, on treaty of peace, 184
Bengala. *See* Bengal
Bengala, Sea of. *See* Bengal, Bay of
Bengal Butter. *See* *Ghī*
Bengall Merchant, the, 209 *n.* 2; Bowrey returned to England on, xxi, xl, lii
Benjamin, Benjoin. *See* Benzoin
Benzoin, incense, imported to Achin, 292, 292 *n.* 1; black, 292 *n.* 1; where obtained, 292 *n.* 1
Bēr. *See* *Zizyphus Jujuba*
Bernier, François, Bowrey's acquaintance with his writings, xviii, 135–144; his "Travels" referred to, 21 *n.*, 33 *n.* 1, 34 *n.* 1, 36 *n.* 1, 48 *n.* 1 *passim*; his account of the revolution in Bengal followed by Bowrey, 135–144

Best, Captain Thomas, 295 *n.* 6

Beteelis. *See* Betteela

Betel, Betelee, Befle, 107 *n.* 1, 273 *n.* 2, 304 *n.* 6, 306 *n.* 1, 306 *n.* 2, 309 *n.* 3; a token of kindness, 30 *n.* 2; gardens at Karedu, 36 *n.* 3; nuts (areca), 208 *n.* 4; leaf of, how used with areca-nut, 305 *n.* 1; description of, 306; illustration of, 308; offering of, from the Queen of Achin, an honour, 310

Betelee Areca, 247, 303, 304, 305, 307; composition of, 30 *n.* 2; used in marriage festivities, 30; much used by Muhammadans, 97; given to malefactors before execution, 316. *See also s.vv.* Betel, Areca

Betelee boxes, 309, 309 *n.* 3

Betella. *See* Betteela

Betel-nut (areca), 30 *n.* 2

Betel piper, 306 *n.* 2

Beths, 34 *n.* 1

Betteela, fine muslin, veiling, 55 *n.* 2, 122, 231 *n.* 1, 289 *n.* 4; Oringall, 71 *n.* 3, 122 *n.* 3; described, 122 *n.* 3

Bettelee, Betteleez. *See* Betteela

Bezoar, 292; different kinds of, 292 *n.* 7; price of, 292 *n.* 7

Bhada. *See Bhaṛ*

Bhāgnagar, capital of Golconda, 108 *n.* 7; extent of, strength of Golconda fort at, 110; called Golconda by T. B., 108, 109, 111; resort of native and foreign merchants, 111, 111 *n.* 1; European inhabitants at, in the king's service, 111; European soldiers at, in disrepute, 111; tank at, 126 *n.* 6

Bhāng, Indian hemp, 77; where grown, 78

Bhaṛ, a lighter, description of, 228, 228 *n.* 5; derivation of, 228 *n.* 5; for what used, 229; illustration of, 228

Bhavani, the black, of Tuljapur, 119 *n.* 1

Bible, the, references to in the MS. *See s.v.* Apocrypha, David, Garden of Eden, Solomon, etc.

Biggehaut, 202 *n.* 2

Bījapūr (Beejapore, Visiapour, Visepour), 20, 51 *n.* 1, 72 *n.* 2, 108 *n.* 1; extent of, 20 *n.* 2; ports of, 20 *n.* 2; king of, 20 *n.* 2, 38 *n.* 3; queen of, 20 *n.* 2; coast south of Porto Novo, subject to king of, 82

Bilgrami and Wilmott, their "Nizam's Dominions" referred to, 113 *n.* 1, 113 *n.* 3

Bilgrami, Syed Hossain. *See* Bilgrami and Wilmott

Billi, Mons., his official post in Junk-Ceylon, 255 *n.* 6

Billidge, Billedge, Thomas, 233 *n.* 2

Billingsby, John, Company's servant at Balasor, 66 *n.* 1

Bimlipatam, Bimlepatam, Bimliapatam, Bemilipatnam, 93 *n.* 1, 123, 124 *n.* 1, 124 *n.* 3; trade of, 122 *n.* 1; Schouten's description of, 123 *n.* 3; Dutch factory at, 123 *n.* 3

Binnilapatnam. *See* Bimlipatam

Bisnagar. *See* Vijayanagar

Bizipatam. *See* Vizagapatam

Black, colour, native dyers unable to produce a good, 215, 215 *n.* 1

Blackmoor, the, 121 *n.* 3

Black Pagoda, 12 *n.* 1, 108, 129 *n.* 1; sailor's name for temple at Kanārak, 108 *n.* 2

Black Town at Calcutta, 207 *n.* 1

Blackwood's Harbour, 25 *n.* 3

Blake, William, 32 *n.* 2, 224 *n.* 1

Blanc, Vincent le, 290 *n.* 7

Bodick, village near Surat, 49 *n.* 1

Bōita-kuliyā, river, 129 *n.* 1

Bolango, a pumpkin. *See Conbalingua*

Bombay, 264 *n.* 7; Presidency transferred to, 309 *n.* 1

Bonarres. *See* Benares

Bongkal. *See* Weights and Measures

Bonnell, Mr, 178 *n.* 3

Booncal. *See* Bongkal, *s.v.* Weights and Measures

Böos. *See* Dringo

Bora, Boora, Bourie. *See Bhaṛ*

Borneo, xxii, xxxix, xlix, lii, liv, 1, 282, 291, 292 *n.* 1; ships from, frequent Achin, 288; Dutch trade at, 282 *n.* 5; English factory at, 282 *n.* 5; expulsion of English from, 282 *n.* 5; diamonds of, 291, 291 *n.* 8; bezoar from, 292 *n.* 7

Borneo Merchant, the, Bowrey's ship, xxvii, xxviii, xxix, xxxvi, 175 *n.* 2; wrecked, xxxvii, xxxviii

Boudoutschery. *See* Pondicherry

Boughton, Gabriel, obtains leave to settle a factory at Pipli, 162 *n.* 2; Hugli settled under *farmān* obtained by him, 168 *n.* 4; physician to Mīr Jumla, 233; cures the *nawāb's* wife, 233; obtains exemptions and privileges for the English, 233, 234; reasons for doubting his connection with Mīr Jumla, 233 *n.* 2

Bouree, Mr. *See* Bowrey, Thomas

Bouton, island, 291 *n.* 7
Bouverie, the, xlvii
Bow, Middlesex, xlvi
Bowden, Gabriel. *See* Boughton, Gabriel
Bowgee. *See* Cowry
Bowl Punch Tree, li
Bowrey Almshouses, erected under the provisions of Mary Bowrey's will, xlvi–xlviii; Chancery suit in connection with, xlvii; situation of, xlviii; inscription over, xlviii; sale of, xlviii; present administration of Bowrey charity, xlviii
Bowrey, Elizabeth, widow of Thos. Bowrey, senior, xxv.
Bowrey, John, Johannes, wounded on the *Unity*, xxiv; commands the *Hunter*, the *Death* and the *Drake*, xxiv; recommended by Pepys, xxiv; certified as Master, xxiv; accusations against, xxiv; effects of, administered, xxiv
Bowrey, Juditha, widow of Johannes Bowrey, xxiv
Bowrey, Mary, wife of Thomas Bowrey, xli; executrix of Thomas Bowrey, xliv; assisted by Peter Briggins, xlv; will of, xlv, xlvii
Bowrey, Matthias, soldier, xxvi; living in Bombay in 1670, xxvi
Bowrey, Thomas (T. B.), 1; account of life of, xxiv–xlv; probable relations of, xxiv; a sailing master, xviii, xix, xxi, xxvii; an independent trader, xix; his arrival in India, xviii, xxi, 4 *n.* 1, 166 *n.* 2; length of his stay in India, xviii, xxi, xxvi, 2 *n.* 1; no mention of him in E. I. Co. records before 1682, xxiii; his voyages 1672–1677, xxvi; commands one of Jearsey's ships, xxvi; his encounter with Streynsham Master, 175, 176; pilots the *Sancta Cruz*, xix, xxvi; caught in an eddy off the James and Mary shoal, 173, 174; goes to Batavia, xxvii; negotiates sale of pepper at Fort St George, xxvii, xxix; buys the *Conimeer* sloop, xxvii, xxviii; goes to Achin, Balasor, and Porto Novo, xxviii, xxix; complaint against him by Capt. Heath, xxviii; makes restitution, xxviii; pilots the Govr. of Tranquebar, xxix; gets permit to return to England on the *Shrewsbury*, xxix; goes to Porto Novo, is imprisoned there, xxix–xxxvi; his wrongs referred to Fort St George, xxx; blamed for acting independently of Cuddalore Council, xxx, xxxiv; petitions the Cuddalore Council to procure his release, xxxi–xxxiii; his explanation of the quarrel at Porto Novo, xxxi; his sufferings at Porto Novo, xxxiii; bond required of him in return for Company's assistance, xxxiv; his release, xxxiv–xxxvi; sails for Achin, xxxvi; obtains no compensation for ill-treatment, xxxvi; goes to Bengal with Samuel Heron, xxxvii; returns to Fort St George, xxxvii; loses the *Borneo Merchant*, xxxvii; his relations with Dampier, xxxviii, xxxix; resides at Achin, 287 *n.* 1; sails to the Nicobar Is., xxxix; writes from Borneo to Mindanao, xxxix; sails to Bengal, xxxix; takes news of massacre at Mergui to Fort St George, xl; sails for England, xl; goods and money delivered to him by the Company, xl; marriage of, xli; his opinion as to a settlement in the South Seas, xlii; a tenant and acquaintance of Peter Briggins, xlii; makes suggestions regarding East Indian trade, xlii f.; his proposal for a settlement on the coast of South America, xliii; death and burial of, xliv; will of, xvii, xx, xxiii, xliv; bequests of, xliv f.; his identity with T. B. proved, xviii, xxiii; acquainted with many 17th century Anglo-Indians, xviii; title, condition, and handwriting of his MS., xv; abrupt ending of his MS., xvii; value of his MS. and drawings, xv, xvii, xviii; charts of, xxi, xlviii–li; his knowledge of colloquial Hindōstanī, 126 *n.* 4; his Malay Dictionary, xvii, xxi, xxii, xxvi, xl, xli, xlii, li, lii, liii, liv, lv, lvi, 97 *n.* 4; other writings of, xx, xxiii, xli, xlviii–li
Bowrey, Thomas, senior, commended by Capt. Potter, xxv; commands *Roe* ketch and *Constant Warwick*, xxv; engages with a Spanish pirate ship, xxv; goods of, administered, xxv
Bowring, Sir John, his "Kingdom of Siam" referred to, 236 *n.* 1, 243 *n.* 3, 247 *n.* 5, 260 *n.* 1, 276 *n.* 5
Bowry, Captain, to assist in fortifications at Bombay, xxv, xxvi
Bowry, Mr (? Bowrey, John), master of the *Antelope*, xxiv; discharged, xxiv

Bowrye, Joseph, goods of, administered, xxv

Bowrye, Margareta, widow of Joseph Bowrye, xxv

Boy. *See Boyi*

Boyi (Telugu) caste, 87 *n.* 2, 88 *n.* 3

Braces, the, 175 *n.* 1; shoals in the Hugli, 167; various mentions of, 167 *n.* 1

Brachman. *See* Brahmin

Brahma, 34 *n.* 1; the Ganges said to flow from the feet of, 202 *n.* 1

Brāhmanī, River, 129 *n.* 1

Brahmins, a Hindu caste, 9, 12 *n.* 1, 15 *n.* 1, 16, 17, 25 *n.* 1, 36, 38, 39, 88 *n.* 3, 107 *n.* 1, 120 *n.* 1, 121 *n.* 4, 125 *n.* 1, 126 *n.* 3, 202; their sorceries deceive the Gentues, 10, 23, 24, 32, 205; number maintained at Jagannāth Pagoda, 13; their immorality, 24; their mode of performing marriage ceremonies, 29, 30; their mark esteemed by the Gentues, 32; author's discourse with, 32; their explanation of an eclipse, 33, 34; their ignorance of astronomy, 34; their cruelty to Gentue widows, 40, 203, 204; encourage *satī*, and intoxicate victims, 36–38; in Golconda, assume privileges of *rājās*, 108; intoxicate victims at the Swinging Festival, 198; their speedy cure of victims of the hook, 198 *n.* 1; extort money from dying Uriyas, 201; students of astrology, 205, 205 *n.* 1; dreaded by the Moors, 205; district inhabited by, 205, 215; their wisdom, 205, 205 *n.* 2; reverence of the natives for, 205; called Gimnosophists, 206; their civility to Europeans, 206; teachers of the Gentues and Uriyas, 206; value of their *chap* on Ganges water, 216

Bramminy. *See* Brahmin

Brampore, 288 *n.* 6

Bramston, William, pilot, deceased, 166 *n.* 2

Breton, Mr, part owner of the *Loyall Subject*, 90 *n.* 1

Breton, the. *See Great Breton*, the

Brick-bridge, 149 *n.* 1; at Hugli, 171 *n.* 1

Brick buildings, at Dacca, 150 *n.* 2

Bridges, Shem, 32 *n.* 2, 75 *n.* 1, 233 *n.* 2

Briggins, Peter, xxiii; a Quaker, xx; original owner of T. B. MS., xx, xxii; no relation to Bowrey, xx; diaries of, xx, xlii, xliii; his connection with Bowrey, xx, xlii, xliv; his kindness to Mrs Bowrey, xx, xlv

Brimstone, 232, 292, 292 *n.* 3

Britannia, the. *See Great Breton*, the

British Museum, the. MSS. at referrred to, xxi, xxvi, xliii, xlviii *n.* 4, 134 *n.* 1, 134 *n.* 2, 134 *n.* 3, 239 *n.* 1

Broad cloth, 88 *n.* 3; no sale for, in Bengal, 152 *n.* 4; no sale for, in Balasor, 154 *n.* 1; imported to Achin, 289

Brokers, to the English, at Balasor, 32, 154, 154 *n.* 1

Brouma. *See* Brahma

Browne, Captain Arnold, Commander of the *Loyall Subject*, 90 *n.* 1

Bruce, John, his "Annals" referred to, 245 *n.* 2, 295 *n.* 6

Bruton, William, lands at Harsapur, 129 *n.* 1

Buckett. *See* Puket

Buckridge, Nicholas, inspector of factories on Coromandel Coast, 53 *n.* 2; his report of Madapollam, 100 *n.* 1

Bucor. *See* Bukkur

Budgerow, Budgaroe, Budgaroo, Budgree, a boat. *See Bajrā*

Buffalo Butter, 289 *n.* 2

Buffaloes, 243 *n.* 2, 315; Mahesha Asura assumes shape of a, 119 *n.* 1; on shores of the Ganges, 211 *n.* 3; at Kedah, 279, 279 *n.* 3; Fryer's description of, 279 *n.* 5; wild, in Kedah, 280; tame, their flesh eaten, 280; butter made of milk of, 289 *n.* 2; fight with elephants, 310; illustration of, 314

Bugden, Edmund, 75 *n.* 1, 228 *n.* 2; Company's servant, xix, 178 *n.* 1; rents Dummadapore in Balasor, 162 *n.* 3

Bugden, John, 272 *n.* 4; independent trader, xix; reasons for supposing him to be the author of the MS., xix f.; brother of Edmund Bugden, 178 *n.* 1; goes on a trading voyage with Clement Jordan, 178 *n.* 1; examined as to the murder of John Smith, 178 *n.* 1

Buggera. *See* Budgerow

Bukit, a hill, 239 *n.* 1

Bukkur, 136 *n.* 4

Bulls, figures of carved, on the chariot of Jagannāth, 17

Buncus, Bunco, Buncoos. *See* Bunko
"**Bundalela**" Shāh, Governor of "Carera," 36 *n.* 3
Bunder. *See Bandar*
Bunko, a cigar, xvii, 97; earliest quoted instance of, 97 *n.* 4
Burghess, Michael, liii
Burma, xvi
Burmull, 154 *n.* 1
Burneo Merchant, the. *See Borneo Merchant*, the
Burning of Hindu women. *See Satī*
Burrie. *See Bauṛī, s.v.* Weights and Measures
Burroughs, Joshua, 271 *n.*; escapes from the Dutch, 266 *n.* 3; sent to Kedah with Capell, 269; his sad plight at Kedah, 269
Bussorah, 114 *n.* 6, 132 *n.* 2
Butter (*ghī*), 20, 122, 181, 289, 289 *n.* 2, 290, 304; excellence of, on Gingalee Coast, 128, 132 *n.* 6; exported from Bengal, 132, 132 *n.* 6, 133 *n.* 2, 247; how preserved for transport, 132 *n.* 6; price of, in Patna during the famine, 226 *n.* 2; imported to Junk-Ceylon, 247 *n.* 2; sold by the bamboo at Achin, 282 *n.* 1
Byam, John, 158 *n.* 3, 167 *n.* 1

Caboul. *See* Kabul
Caboulistan. *See* Kabul
Cabstant. *See* Capstan
Cachemire, 136 *n.* 3
Cadjour. *See Khajūr*
Cadmia, 291 *n.* 2
Caf-Dagai. *See* Caucasus, mountain
Cafila, caravan, 221, 221 *n.* 1
Cahar. *See Kahār*
Cair. *See* Coir
Calabash, pumpkin, 247
Calambac. *See* Agila wood
Calamus aromaticus. *See* Dringo root
Calang, tin, 240 *n.* 1
Calay. *See Kuwala*
Calcutta, 120 *n.* 4, 162 *n.* 2, 172 *n.* 3, 209 *n.* 2, 263 *n.* 1
Calendar of State Papers, Domestic Series, referred to, xxiv, xxv
Caletaer, 124 *n.* 1
Calico, Callicoe, cotton cloth, 5, 55 *n.* 2, 106, 106 *n.* 2, 181, 246, 289 *n.* 5, 303 *n.* 3; made at Peddapalle, 56; made at and exported from Masulipatam, 71; large quantity made at Madapollam, 100 *n.* 1; exported from Golconda, 111; exported from Gingalee Coast, 122; exported from Harsapur, 130; exported from Bengal, 133; coarse, sold at Hugli, 168; imported to Junk-Ceylon, 240; "blew," 246; imported to Achin, 288, 289 *n.* 1; fine, 302, 310
Calicut, 208 *n.* 5
Calicut, white and painted. *See* Paintings
Calin, tin, 240 *n.* 1, 259 *n.* 1
Callaway, William, a friend of the author, 175; appointed special assistant to Streynsham Master, 175 *n.* 8; illness of, 176, 178 *n.* 3; dies on the *Ganges* in Hugli river, 178 *n.* 3; sale of his goods, 71 *n.* 3, 175 *n.* 8; list of his effects, 175 *n.* 8
Callingapatam, 124 *n.* 1
Callor Vissina, complaint of, 4 *n.* 2, 123 *n.* 4
Calmus. *See* Dringo root
Calvar, village, 108 *n.* 1, 108 *n.* 6
Cambay, 136 *n.* 2
Cambay, Gulf of, 135 *n.* 5
Cambaya. *See* Comboy
Cambodia, tributary to Siam, 275 *n.* 3
Camboge. *See* Cambodia
Camoens, his reference to Kedah, 276 *n.* 5
Camphor, 292, 292 *n.* 1; where found, 292 *n.* 2
Canara, 93 *n.* 1
Canary wine, 88 *n.* 3
Cancoply. *See* Conicopoly
Candahar, 136 *n.* 3
Candareen. *See* Weights and Measures
Candil. *See* Weights and Measures
Candy. *See* Weights and Measures
Candy, Candia, king of, opposed to the Portuguese, 75 *n.* 3; king of, hates the Dutch, 180 *n.* 6
Cange. *See* Congye
Cannabis Indica. *See Bhāng* and *Gānjā*
Cannan, William, sailor on the *Defence*, xxviii
Canoe, canoa, xxxix
Capell, Francis, sent to Kedah to sell off Company's stock, 269; his sad plight at Kedah, 269, 271 *n.*
Cape-Merchant, supercargo, 271, 271 *n.* 1
Caphala. *See* Cafila
Capon, eunuch, 207 *n.* 5, 300 *n.* 4
Capon, fowl, 303 *n.* 3

Capstan, 75, 181
Capun, capon, eunuch, 300 *n.* 4
Caraid. *See* Karedu
Carcal, 182 *n.* 2
Careda. *See* Karedu
Carera, Carrera, Careero. *See* Karedu
Carmania. *See* Kirmān
Carmichael, D. F., his "Vizagapatam District" referred to, 123 *n.* 2
Carnatic Coast, xlix, 51 *n.* 1
Carpets, imported to Achin, 288, 303; silk and worsted, 288 *n.* 8; Persian, 309, 309 *n.* 2
Carreas, caste of fishermen in Ceylon, 42 *n.* 1
Carvalia, Augustine de, master of the *Sancta Cruz*, 172 *n.* 3
Cash. *See* Coins
Casharee. *See* Kachahrī
Casharry, water at, suitable for dyeing, 162 *n.* 3
Casigere, 129 *n.* 1
Casmeer? boat, 226 *n.* 2
Cassas, Cossacs. *See* Khāṣṣa
Cassa Verona. *See* Kaçū Vīranna
Cassia, 291 *n.* 5
Cassia Fistula, 291, 291 *n.* 5
Cassia Lignea, 291 *n.* 5
Caste, 19, 20, 22, 27, 28, 29, 31 *n.*, 41, 83, 156, 199, 216; restrictions of, 9, 117; loss of, 11; means to regain, 12, 13
Castez, 140 *n.* 4
Castor hats, among Callaway's effects, 175 *n.* 8
Casuree. *See* Khajūrī
Catamaran (Cattamaran, Catamarou), 44, 47; description of, 43; illustration of, 44
Catawal, Catoal. *See Kotwāl*
Catch. *See* Ketch
Catchpole, Allen, 96 *n.* 2, 225 *n.* 3
Cateck. *See* Cuttack
Cātee. *See* Catty, *s.v.* Weights and Measures
Catry. *See Khattrī*
Cattack. *See* Cuttack
Cattapa, 125 *n.* 1
Cattee. *See* Weights and Measures
Catwall. *See Kotwāl*
Catysol. *See* Kittysol
Caucasus, mountains, 136 *n.* 3; supposed source of the Ganges, 166 *n.* 1
Caulis. *See* Cowry
Cawn, Caun. *See* Khān
Cawne. *See Kāhan*, *s.v.* Weights and Measures
Cāyīn gaja. *See* Comboy
Cayre. *See* Coir
Ceaser, the, 91 *n.* 1
Ceilan. *See* Ceylon
Celebes, Island, xlix
Cellates, derivation of, 237 *n.* 2. *See also s.v.* Saletars
Central Asia, 172 *n.* 1
Ceremonies, on departure of English commanders from Achin, 306–308; when a present is received by the Queen of Achin, 309, 310; on taking betel, 309 *n.* 3, 310; at the mourning for the Queen of Achin, 311, 312
Ceylon, 42 *n.* 1, 65 *n.* 2, 66 *n.* 1, 73, 179, 180, 186, 208 *n.* 4, 266 *n.* 3; chart of, by Bowrey, xxvii, xlix, l; rice imported from Bengal, 132 *n.* 7; elephants from, the best in India, 180, 180 *n.* 5; early traders at, 180 *n.* 6; Portuguese settlement at, 180 *n.* 6; Dutch expel the Portuguese at, 180 *n.* 6
Chabe. *See* Long Pepper
Chahbandar. *See* Shahbandar
Chah-hestkan. *See* Shāyista Khān
Chah Jehan. *See* Shāh Jahān
Chamberlin, Sir Thomas, Deputy Govr. of the E. I. Co., 84 *n.* 2
Champain. *See* Champion
Champion (level, open country), 120, 120 *n.* 2
Chandragheri, *rājā* of, grants land to the English, 53 *n.* 1
Chank, Chunk, 208, 208 *n.* 4, 208 *n.* 5; shells worn as ornaments by Gentues and Uriyas, 209
Channel Creek, 209 *n.* 2
Chāp, a seal, 154 *n.* 1, 216, 268, 300 *n.* 2, 304; a protection for travellers, 118; of the Brahmins, its value, 216; of the Queen of Achin, 300, 300 *n.* 3, 300 *n.* 4, 301, 302 *n.* 1, 302 *n.* 2, 306, 308; at Tonquin, 300 *n.* 2; at Achin, ceremonies on receipt of, what paid for it, 302, 302 *n* 2
Char. *See* Coir
Charbonné, Brother René, Govr. of Junk-Ceylon, 255 *n.* 6; designs fort for King of Siam, 278 *n.* 1
Charles, the, 271 *n.* 1; sent to Kedah, 268; her return to Surat, 268
Charles II., exchanges presents with the Queen of Achin, 319
Charles Street, Fort St George, Jearsey's house at, 251 *n.* 1
Charnock, Henry, 154 *n.* 1
Charnock, Job, xxxvii, 85 *n.* 4, 176

n. 1; chief at Patna, 224; his knowledge of Eastern customs, 224; his privileges, 224; founder of Calcutta, 224 *n.* 2; his appointments in India, 224 *n.* 2

Chatagaum. *See* Chittagong

Chatir. *See* Shahbandar

Chattigaum. *See* Chittagong

Chaumont, Monsr. de C., 255 *n.* 6; his "Embassy to Siam" referred to, 236 *n.* 4

Chaup. *See Chāp*

Chavici betel. *See* Betel

Chay, red madder, 106 *n.* 2

Chaya Capampone, 253 *n.* 1

Checracole. *See* Chicacol

Cheda. *See* Kedah

Cheese, forbidden food of Banyan caste, 29

Chenam. *See Chunam*

Chene Pelle Mirzah, besieges Fort St George, 51 *n.* 1

Chengy, Chenji, Khān of, 20 *n.* 2

Cheroot, a cigar, xv *n.*, xvii, 97

Chiali, xxxii

Chicacol, Chicacole, 124, 124 *n.* 1, 124 *n.* 3; residence of King of Golconda's Viceroy, 124 *n.* 3, 125; most famous town on Gingalee Coast, 125

Chickacul, Chickeracole, Chickrecole. *See* Chicacol

Chilambaram, intercedes for Bowrey, xxxii

Chilamchī, a basin, 96 *n.* 2, 199 *n.* 3

Chili, xliii

Chillimbrum. *See* Chilambaram

Chillumchee. *See Chilamchī*

Chim Cham, Khēmchand, xviii, 208 *n.* 4; broker to the English, 154; mulcted of 50,000 Rs. by the *nawāb* of Cuttack, 155, 156; marriage of his daughter, 156; in partnership with Chintamund, 154 *n.* 1; in Company's service for about 20 years, 154 *n.* 1; mulcted by the *faujdār* of Cuttack, 154 *n.* 1; his wealth and independence, 154 *n.* 1; becomes security for other merchants, 154 *n.* 1; his goods seized by a native officer, 154 *n.* 1; has leave to build a warehouse in Balasor, 154 *n.* 1; dictates his own terms to the Council, 154 *n.* 1; employed as intermediary with the native government, 154 *n.* 1

China, xxii, l, 5, 71, 133, 272 *n.* 3, 281 *n.* 2, 286, 286 *n.* 1, 290, 323; tootnague from, 199 *n.* 3; musk from, 230; ships from, frequent Achin, 288; silk from, 290, 291, 291 *n.* 1

China bell. *See* Gong

China camp, at Achin, 322 *n.* 4

Chinamb. *See Chunam*

China ware, 290

Chinchura, 191 *n.* 2

Chinese, the, ships of frequent the port of Achin, xxii, 286 *n.* 1; many of, residents at Achin, 293 *n.* 2, 322 *n.* 4

Chinnapatnam (Madras), 107 *n.* 1

Chintamund, Chintāman, 208 *n.* 4; broker to the English at Balasor, 154 *n.* 1; in partnership with Chim Cham, 154 *n.* 1; in debt to the Company, 154 *n.* 1; his solvency questioned, 154 *n.* 1; his ship seized in payment of debt to the Co., 154 *n.* 1

Chintamundsaw, Chintemanshaw. *See* Chintamund

Chintz, 5 *n.* 5, 9 *n.* 5, 55 *n.* 2, 106 *n.* 2, 175 *n.* 8, 289 *n.* 5; trade in at Masulipatam, 61 *n.* 3, 71, 72, 289; plural of chint, 71 *n.* 4; fine, 246, 289, 289 *n.* 1; coarse, 246

Chites, printed calico, 61 *n.* 3, 71 *n.* 4, 288 *n.* 7

Chittagong, 176 *n.* 1, 212 *n.* 2

Chitty, caste, 77 *n.* 2

Chittygom. *See* Chittagong

Choonam. *See Chunam*

Chop, Chopp, Chaup. *See Chāp*

Choromandel. *See* Coromandel

Choultry, at Peddapalle, 54; at Hugli, 167; derivation and use of the word, 167 *n.* 2

Choupar. *See* Chuprah

Chowltery. *See* Choultry

Chowne, Henry, second at Achin factory, 317 *n.* 5, 319, 320

Chowra, Island. *See* Sombrero

Christians, numerous in Bengal, 133, 133 *n.* 3

Chulias, Chuleas, Madras Muhammadans, xvii, xxii, xxxiii, 256, 262, 263, 270; definition and character of, 256 *n.* 1, 257, 258; favoured by Muhammad Bēg, 257; massacre of in Junk-Ceylon, 257; escape of two, 257; their native land, 257; good linguists, 258; at Achin, 286 *n.* 1

Chuljar. *See* Chulia

Chunam, lime, plaster, 193 *n.* 1, 304 *n.* 6, 305, 305 *n.* 1, 306 *n.* 1, 309 *n.* 3

Chupak. See Weights and Measures
Chuprah, Dutch refine saltpetre at, 225 *n.* 1
Chyna Vincatadry, his house at St Thomas' Mount offered to the Co., 45 *n.* 1
Cicacola. *See* Chicacol
Cinnamon, 291 *n.* 5; from Ceylon, 180 *n.* 6, 181 *n.* 1
Cirkell. *See Sarkīl*
Citron, 324 *n.* 1
Citrullus edulis, water-melon, 248 *n.* 1
Civet, 134 *n.* 3
Clapton Magna, Essex, xlvi
Clavell, Edward, son of Walter Clavell, sent to England on the *President*, 158 *n.* 3; sheriff of Dorset in 1702, 158 *n.* 3; death of, 158 *n.* 3
Clavell, George, son of Edward Clavell, 158 *n.* 3; last of the Clavell line, 158 *n.* 3
Clavell, Martha, second wife of Walter Clavell, 158 *n.* 3; dies at Balasor, 158 *n.* 3
Clavell, Prudence, first wife of Walter Clavell, 158 *n.* 1
Clavell, Walter, xviii, 68 *n.* 3, 73 *n.* 2, 75 *n.* 1, 150 *n.* 2, 164 *n.* 4, 169 *n.* 1, 176 *n.* 1; his "Accompt of the Trade of Ballasore," 129 *n.* 1, 158 *n.* 3, 162 *n.* 3, 183 *n.* 3; his "Accompt of the Trade of Hugly," 146 *n.* 4, 158 *n.* 3, 175 *n.* 1; obtains renewal of *farmān* from the *nawāb* of Cuttack, 158, 160, 160 *n.* 2; parentage of, 158 *n.* 3; appointed on special mission to Ft St George, 158 *n.* 3; second in Bengal, 158 *n.* 3; obtains a *parwāna* from Shāyista Khān, 158 *n.* 3; rents Dummadapore in Balasor, 162 *n.* 3; quarrels with Joseph Hall, 158 *n.* 3; accusations against, 158 *n.* 3; Major Puckle decides in favour of, 158 *n.* 3; chief at Hugli, 158 *n.* 3; two letters to Richard Edwards from, 158 *n.* 3; writes to the Court as to the navigation of the Hugli, 166 *n.* 2; instructed to obtain a new *farmān*, 158 *n.* 3; dies of fever at Balasor, 158 *n.* 3; his two wives, and his children, 158 *n.* 3; his will, 158 *n.* 3; his news of the Danes in India, 182 *n.* 3, 189 *n.* 3
Clavell, Walter, junr., son of Walter Clavell, 158 *n.* 3; baptism of, 158 *n.* 3; sent to England on the *President*, 158 *n.* 3
Clavell, William, son of Walter Clavell, 158 *n.* 3
Clepsydra, water-clock, 197 *n.* 1
Cloth, cotton, 9; gold and silver striped, 10
Cloth of gold, 310, 326
Cloves, 208 *n.* 4
Coale, Robert, a dyer, 215 *n.* 1
Coast, the. *See* Madras
Coatwalls Chabootree. *See Kotwāl kā chabūtra*
Cobden, Alexander, sailor on the *Defence*, xxviii
Cocanada, 120 *n.* 4
Cochin China, 208 *n.* 4, 272 *n.* 3; musk from, 230
Cocke, Jos., taken by the Dutch, 266 *n.* 3
Cock-fighting, at Achin, 310, 310 *n.* 4
Cocks, Isle of. *See* Coxe's Island
Cocoa-nut tree, 46, 245, 323, 323 *n.* 2; used for hubble bubbles, 97 *n.* 3; coir cable made from husk of, 103 *n.* 4, 104; groves of, at Cuttack, 152; abundant at Junk-Ceylon, 246, 247
Codgone. *See* Cojung
Coffee, 97
Cogan, Andrew, abandons Armagon, 25 *n.* 3
Cogee. *See ? Khwājājī*
Coins, Abassin, 114; Anna, 114 *n.* 8, 214 *n.* 2, 218 *n.* 10, 226 *n.* 2; Cash, 114, 115, 116, 289 *n.* 9; Cowry, xvii, 154 *n.* 1, 180, 200, 217 *n.* 5, 218, 218 *n.* 10, 281 *n.* 3; Dollar, 246, 246 *n.* 10, 262 *n.* 7, 281 *n.* 2; Fanam, 42 *n.* 1, 114, 115, 200 *n.* 4; *Fulūs*, 200 *n.* 1; *Kāping*, 241, 241 *n.* 3, 242 *n.* 1; Kobang, 241 *n.* 3, 280, 280 *n.* 5, 281, 281 *n.* 1; Mace, xxxix, 115, 269, 281, 281 *n.* 1, 281 *n.* 5, 289, 289 *n.* 9, 302 *n.* 2, 315, 318; Mohur, 148, 148 *n.* 3, 160, 217, 217 *n.* 1, 218; Pagoda, xxvii, xxviii, xxix, xxx, xxxi, xxxii, 19 *n.* 4, 30, 51, 51 *n.* 3, 57, 64 *n.* 1, 80 *n.* 2, 81 *n.* 2, 88 *n.* 3, 93 *n.* 1, 105 *n.* 2, 106 *n.* 4, 112, 114, 115, 115 *n.* 2, 217 *n.* 2, 251 *n.* 1, 263 *n.* 1, 275 *n.* 1, 290 *n.* 5; Patah, 241 *n.* 1, 241 *n.* 2, 242, 242 *n.* 1, 246 *n.* 10; Pican, 116; Pice, 134 *n.* 2; Rupee, 114, 122 *n.* 1, 133 *n.* 5, 134 *n.* 1, 134 *n.* 2, 134 *n.* 3, 146, 146 *n.* 2, 148 *n.* 5, 154 *n.* 1, 156, 157, 159, 199, 214 *n.* 2, 216, 218 *n.* 10, 226 *n.* 2, 291 *n.* 2; Ryall, Royall, 77

n. 2, 112, 114, 218 *n.* 10, 232, 241 *n.* 1, 245, 246, 246 *n.* 10, 273, 276, 280, 281 *n.* 2, 289; Sol, 200 *n.* 1; Tale, Tael, 122 *n.* 1, 266 *n.* 3, 269, 270, 281, 281 *n.* 2, 281 *n.* 5, 290 *n.* 5, 302, 302 *n.* 2, 303, 303 *n.* 3, 304, 304 *n.* 1, 318; Tical, Ticul, 115; *Tra*, 281, 281 *n.* 4

Coir (Cair, Cayre, Coyre), rope of cocoanut husk, 42, 43 *n.* 1, 103, 104; how made, 103 *n.* 4, 104 *n.* 1; strength of, 105; rotted by fresh water, 105; from the Maldive Is., 180, 180 *n.* 2

Cojung, Point, 129 *n.* 1; Bay, 129 *n.* 1

Colborne, Mr, 54

Colcepore, 165 *n.* 2

Coleer, Señor, Governor of Pulicat, 52

Collepelle, 55 *n.* 1

Colombo, 75 *n.* 3, 181, 181 *n.* 1

Comboy, 246, 246 *n.* 5, 290

Comorin, Cape, 208

Conar, 124 *n.* 1, 124 *n.* 3

Conbalingua, *Combalenga*, pumpkin, 323, 323 *n.* 7

Concherina. *See* Cochin China

Conch-shell. *See* Chank

Conderine. *See* Weights and Measures

Congoe. *See Kānungō*

Congye, Congy, Cange, Conjee, 29, 117, 231 *n.* 1

Conicopoly (*kanakkapillai*, Cancoply, Conecopola, a clerk), 25, 41 *n.* 2

Conimeer, the, sloop, xxvii

Conjaguaree Point, 129

Conjee, to stiffen, 29 *n.* 3

Connare. *See* Conar

Connercon, pagoda of, 129 *n.* 1

Consent, the, William Jearsey's ship, 251 *n.* 1

Constant Warwick, the, xxv

Coodaloor. *See* Cuddalore

Cooke, Sir Thomas, a Director of the E. I. Co., xlii

Cook-room, at Hugli factory rebuilt, 168 *n.* 4

Coonemerro, 82 *n.* 1

Coopang. *See Kāping*

Cooraboor, 82 *n.* 1

Copan, gold. *See Kobang*, *s.v.* Coins

Copper, 232, 281 *n.* 3, 290; wrought, 290 *n.* 10

Cor. *See* Corge

Coral, 232

Corango *See* Coringa

Corge, a score, 71 *n.* 3

Cori. *See* Cowry

Coringa, Corango, 3, 93 *n.* 1, 98 *n.* 1, 120 *n.* 1, 120 *n.* 4, 123, 176 *n.* 1; bay, 3, 120

Cormandell. *See* Coromandel

Corn, from Patna, 221 *n.* 1, 225; price of, during famine at Patna, 226 *n.* 2

Coro Maldiva. *See* Coir

Coromandel, coast, xvi, 2, 10, 12 *n.* 1, 43 *n.* 2, 52, 98 *n.* 1, 120 *n.* 1, 134 *n.* 1, 208 *n.* 5, 247, 257; description of, 2–107; extent of, 2, 3; inhabitants of, 106; no prohibition as to trade on the, 107; ships from, to Kedah, 272

Cosmo Lorenzo de Madera, part owner of the *Sancta Cruz*, 172 *n.* 3

Cossae. *See Khāṣṣa*

Cossid, Cossit. *See Ḳāṣid*

Cossum, chief, 213

Cossumbazar. *See* Kasimbazar

Cotton, from Patna, 221 *n.* 1; imported to Achin, 288

Cotton cloth, 9, 302 *n.* 2; made by the Dutch at Pulicat, 52; quantity produced in Bengal, 132, 132 *n.* 3, 133 *n.* 3

Cotton yarn, 154 *n.* 1, 232, 232 *n.* 1; imported to Achin, 288

Cotup Sha. *See* Qūtb Shāh

Cotwal. *See Kotwāl*

Country, meaning "Indian," xix, xxi, 61, 61 *n.* 2, 178 *n.* 1

Course. *See Kōs*, *s.v.* Weights and Measures

Covid, Covad, Covet. *See* Weights and Measures

Cow, 315; figures of, in pagodas, 6, 16; reverence for, 8, 26, 206, 206 *n.* 4; indispensable in marriages and commercial dealings, 9; sale and slaughter of, forbidden, 9, 27; 20,000 maintained at pagoda of Jagannāth, 12 *n.* 1; importance of tail of, 28 *n.* 1, 29; excellence of, on Gingalee Coast, 128; price of a, in Bengal, 193

Cowle, a written engagement, 82 *n.* 1, 124 *n.* 3, 125 *n.* 1

Cowries, xvii, 154 *n.* 1, 199, 281 *n.* 3; from the Maldive Is., 180, 200; number of, to a rupee, 200; when most plentiful, 200 *n.* 2; sold by tale, 218, 218 *n.* 6; rise and fall of, 219; profit on traffic in, 218 *n.* 10. *See also s.v.* Coins

Coxe's Island, 209; merged into Sagar Island, 209 *n.* 2; various

names for, 209 *n.* 2; derivation of discussed, 209 *n.* 2; T. B.'s men killed by tigers at, 220
Coyr. *See* Coir
Cozee. *See Qāzī*
Crawfurd, John, his "Dictionary of the Indian Is." referred to, 77 *n.* 3, 78 *n.* 4, 79 *n.* 2, 122 *n.* 1, 235 *n.* 1, 237 *n.* 1, *passim*; his "Malay Dictionary" referred to, 192 *n.* 4; his "Embassy to Siam" referred to, 237 *n.* 1, 240 *n.* 1, 247 *n.* 3, 275 *n.* 3, 279 *n.* 4, 279 *n.* 5 *passim*
Crease, Creese, Creis, Cresset. *See* Kris
Crid. *See* Kris
Criminals at Achin, how punished, 314–317; crippled, illustration of a, 314; numerous, 317; their dexterity, 314 *n.* 2
Crockford, Benjamin, 298 *n.* 1
Crocodile, called Alligator by T. B., 284, 284 *n.* 3
Croft, Captain William. *See* Cruft, Captain William
Crore. *See* Weights and Measures
Cruffe, Captain William. *See* Cruft, Capt. Wm.
Cruft, Captain William, commander of the *Unity*, 91; honoured by the king of Golconda, 90 *n.* 1; censured by the Court of Directors, 91 *n.* 1; dismissed from, and restored to the Co.'s service, 91 *n.* 1; desertion and complaints of his crew, 91 *n.* 1; his conduct during the naval fight with the Dutch, 91 *n.* 1
Cubit. *See* Weights and Measures
Cudda. *See* Kedah
Cuddalore, xxviii, xxix, xxxiv, xxxvi; Council at, their action in defence of Bowrey, xxxii–xxxvi
Cullean Ray. *See* Kalyān Ray
Cummun, 88 *n.* 3
Cundapella, 88 *n.* 3
Cupine. *See Kāping*, *s.v.* Coins
Cupon. *See Kāping*, *s.v.* Coins
Curore, Croer. *See* Crore
Curtis, Captain William, sent to Achin, 319
Cushin Carpets. *See* Divans
Custom-house, at Achin, 302, 304, 308, 318; officers of the, 309
Customs, payable on the Coromandel Coast, 107; levied at Golconda diamond mines, 112 *n.* 2; English free of, in kingdom of Siam, 244; what levied on foreign vessels in Siam, 245 *n.* 2; English free of, at Achin, 304 *n.* 4; what levied on ships entering port of Achin, 303, 304, 304 *n.* 1
Cuttack (Cattack, Cateck), xvi, 154 *n.* 1, 161; capital of Orissa, 151 *n.* 3; Hamilton's description of, 151 *n.* 3; English factory at, 151 *n.* 3; T.B.'s description of, 151, 152; Governor of, his state and exactions, 152; old *nawāb* of, goes to Dacca, 152, 157; old *nawāb* of, his wife, story of, 157, 158; new *nawāb* of, his exactions, 152–157; other *nawābs* of, 152 *n.* 4; new *nawāb* of, rides in state through Balasor, 161; Danes kept prisoners by *nawāb* of, 182 *n.* 3
Cuttack, River. *See* Gonga
Cutterye Caste. *See Khattrī*
Cuttiwaukum backwater, 44 *n.* 1
Cyrus, King of Persia, alluded to, 23

Dacca, xvi, 97 *n.* 3, 140 *n.* 2, 146, 146 *n.* 4, 148 *n.* 5, 152, 154 *n.* 1, 157, 185 *n.* 1, 189; capital of Bengal, 139; Shāh Shujā' flees to, 139; Shāh Shujā' goes from, with his train, to Arakan, 141; made capital of Bengal by Mīr Jumla, 143; Thevenot's description of, 143 *n.* 1; Prince Muhammad A'zīm arrives at, 149, 165; description of city of, 149, 150; Tavernier's description of, 149 *n.* 1; English factory at, 149 *n.* 1, 150, 150 *n.* 2; Dutch factory at, 149 *n.* 1, 150, 150 *n.* 2; Hamilton's description of, 149 *n.* 1; productions at, 149 *n.* 1; very populous, 149 *n.* 1, 150; magnificent buildings at, 150, 150 *n.* 1; army and war elephants at, 150; manufactures at, 150 *n.* 2; residence of the prince and court, 151; brick buildings at English factory at, 150 *n.* 2; English chiefs at, 150 *n.* 2; *nawāb* of, 152 *n.* 4; ships built by the *nawāb's* order brought up to, 163; mint at, 217; commodities from, 230, 230 *n.* 2
Dachin. *See* Steelyard, *s.v.* Weights and Measures
Daia, kingdom of, 285 *n.* 3
Damar. *See* Dammer
Damar batoo, raw dammer, 292 *n.* 6
Dammer, xxii, 277 *n.* 4, 292, 320; how made, 292 *n.* 6; excellence of, in Sumatra, 293; mixed with oil, for pitch, 293
Dampier, William, his mistake re-

garding female dynasty at Achin, xxiii; visits Capt. Bowrey at Achin, xxxviii; starts for the Nicobar Is. with Bowrey, xxxviii, xxxix; returns to Achin, xxxix; Bowrey's generosity to, xxxix; his "Voyage round the World" referred to, xxxix, 79 *n.* 2, 97 *n.* 1, 120 *n.* 2, 193 *n.* 1, 247 *n.* 5, *passim*

Dancing snakes, exhibition of, at Peddapalle, 59, 60

Dancing women, 14, 30; privileges of, 14

Danes, the, ships of, frequent the port of Achin, xxii, 286 *n.* 1; attempt a settlement in Balasor, 162 *n.* 3; their war with Bengal, 181; cause of failure in contest with Bengal, 182; their attempt to make peace with the Moors, 183, 184; their wrongs at the hands of Malik Bēg, 183, 184; their first settlement at Balasor, 183, 183 *n.* 3; outwitted by Malik Qāsim, 185–189; incapacity of their Commodore, 186; articles of agreement offered to and refused by, 186, 187; their Commodore inveigled on shore, 187; Moors demand satisfaction from, 188; terms eventually obtained by, from Malik Qāsim, 189; their second attempt to settle a factory in Balasor, 184, 190; their visit to the *nawāb* at Dacca, 190; their cool reception at Dacca, 190; seize a ship of the Moors, 184 *n.* 1; Commodore of, a tailor, 187; hostages for, detained in Balasor, 189; their factory at Balasor not built, 189 *n.* 3; concessions obtained by, 190 *n.* 3; their want of credit in India, 190 *n.* 3; many of, at Achin, 293 *n.* 2

Dārā, eldest son of Shāh Jahān, appointed governor of Kabul and Multan, 136; his expectation of the crown, 136; his defeat by Aurangzēb, 137; his flight, and subsequent death, 137, 137 *n.* 5

Daringgu. *See* Dringo

Darley, Josiah, Chaplain at the "Bay," 177 *n.* 1; his character from the court, 177 *n.* 1; goes to visit Callaway, 177, 178 *n.* 3; alters the hours for prayer at Balasor, 177 *n.* 1; drowned in the Hugli, 178, 178 *n.* 3

Dārogha, a native officer, 152 *n.* 4, 207 *n.* 1

Dastak, 185 *n.* 1, 300 *n.* 2

Davenport, Francis, pilot, his chart of the "Mouth of the River Ganges," 172 *n.* 2

David, King, 8

Davies, George, 266 *n.* 3, 271 *n.* 1; Company's agent at Kedah, 267 *n.* 1; his commission, 267 *n.* 1; his report of Kedah trade, 268; recalled from Kedah, 268; his death, 268; his mental incapacity, 269; his books imperfect, 270

Davis, John, Chief at Cuddalore, xxviii, xxix, xxxi, xxxiii; writes to Fort St George about Bowrey's imprisonment, xxx, xxxiv

Day, Francis, founder of Fort St George, 53 *n.* 1

Dbril Island, ?Dobra, 209 *n.* 2

Death, the, xxiv

Decca. *See* Dacca

Deccan, the, 20 *n.* 2, 108 *n.* 1, 108 *n.* 7, 119 *n.* 1; Aurangzēb appointed Viceroy of, 135; early history of, 135 *n.* 5; dismemberment of, 135 *n.* 5

Deelen, Peter van, 263 *n* 1

Defence, the, xxviii

Degoon. *See* Digano

De Graaf. *See* Graaf, Nicolas de

Degrave, the, 140 *n.* 2

Dehly, Dehli, Delly. *See* Delhi

De la Haye. *See* Haye

De la Loubère. *See* Loubère

Delestre, his "Relation d'un voyage fait aux Indes Orientales," referred to, 2 *n.*, 45 *n.*, 46 *n.*, 47 *n.*, 68 *n.*, *passim*

Deletore, Monsr. (? Deltor), Chief of the French at Pondicherry, 257 *n.* 6

Delhi, 20 *n.* 2, 33 *n.* 1, 39 *n.* 2, 48 *n.* 1, 146; Court removed from Agra to, 18 *n.* 2, 142 *n.* 1; other names for and spellings of, 142 *n.* 1; situation of, 142 *n.* 1; Shāyista Khān summoned to, 148 *n.* 5

Deltor, Peter, 51 *n.* 1; second at French Factory at Masulipatam, 64 *n.* 1, 70 *n.* 1; sheltered by the English at Fort St George, 64 *n.* 1

Demarcora, John, a rich Armenian, 172 *n.* 3

Demarcora, Joseph, owner of the *Sancta Cruz*, 172 *n.* 3

Demeties. *See* Dimities

Dengaree. *See* Dungaree

Denmark, king of, misfortunes of his Company in India, 183 ff.

Dennys, N. B., his "Dictionary of British Malaya" referred to, 259

n. 4, 281 *n.* 4, 282 *n.* 2, 284 *n.* 2, 284 *n.* 3
De Rebré. *See* Rebré
Deria, 262 *n.* 7; a Chulia at Junk-Ceylon, 270
Deryngo, Dirringo. *See* Dringo
Deuta (godling), 34 *n.* 1
Devi, mouths of the Mahānadi, 129 *n.* 1
Devil, the, worship of, by the Gentues, 15
Dhamrā, mouth of the Brāhmanī, 129 *n.* 1
Dhani (Dhunnie) palm. *See* Nipa
Dhanu. *See* Weights and Measures
Diamond, the, William Jearsey's ship, 251 *n.* 1
Diamonds, 140 *n* 4, 292 *n.* 2; three in the figure of Jagannāth, 12 *n.* 1; in eyes of Jagannāth, 16; from Golconda, 111, 291 *n.* 8; from Borneo, 291, 291 *n.* 8
Digano, 172 *n.* 2
Dilli. *See* Delhi
Dilligence, the, Company's sloop, xix, 257 *n.* 6, 262 *n.* 2; employed to discover navigable channels in the Hugli, 166 *n.* 2
Dimities, 133 *n.* 4
Diringuo. *See* Dringo
Dispatch, the, sloop, 120 *n.* 1
Distuck. *See Dastak*
Diu, Dio, Due, Divy, Point, 55, 110; Island, 55 *n.* 1
Divans, imported to Junk-Ceylon, 240 *n.* 3, 246; imported to Achin, 289
Diwān, xxxii, 185 *n.* 1; at Porto Novo, satisfaction to be required from him, xxxiv, xxxv; at Cuttack, 146 *n.* 4; of Balasor, 151 *n.* 3
Dobra, a rivulet of the Ganges, 209, 209 *n.* 2
Dogs, Isle of, merged into Sagar, 209 *n.* 2
Dollars. *See* Coins
Domingos, Perez Banhos, chief owner of the *Sancta Cruz,* 172 *n.* 3
Doo-Agra, river, 209 *n.* 2
Doogarauzpatam. *See* Armagon
Doorean. *See* Durian
Dorea. *See Doriyā*
Doriyā, striped cloth, 123 *n.* 2; fine, 230 *n.* 6
Dorset, Edward Clavell, sheriff of, 158 *n.* 3
Douglas, Mr, 178 *n.* 3; surgeon of the *Eagle,* visits Callaway, 178 *n.* 3; receives Callaway's last instructions, 175 *n.* 8
Dow, Alexander, his "History of Hindostan" referred to, 144 *n.* 3, 201 *n.* 1
Downs, the, 91 *n.* 1, 175 *n.* 1
Drake, the, xxiv
Drammer. *See* Dammer
Dringo Root, 192, 192 *n.* 4; its various names, habitat and uses, 192 *n.* 4
Droga. *See Dārogha*
Duan. *See Diwān*
Dubash (Dubass), interpreter, 25 *n.* 1, 37, 97 *n.* 3, 263 *n.* 1, 301, 303, 306; at Porto Novo, xxx, xxxii
Dubois, J. A., his "Hindu Customs and Ceremonies" referred to, 198 *n.* 1
Duchess, the, xlvii
Due. *See* Diu
Du Jardin, Clement. *See* Jordan, Clement
Dummadapore, a part of Balasor, 162 *n.* 3; rented by Clavell, Bugden and the Company, 162 *n.* 3
Dun. *See Dhanu, s.v.* Weights and Measures
Dungaree, coarse cotton cloth, 71 *n.* 3, 88 *n.* 3, 200, 200 *n.* 4
Dunn, Samuel, his "East Indies Directory" referred to, 56 *n.* 1, 124 *n.* 1, 236 *n.* 1, 259 *n.* 1
Dunstan, James, his "History of Bromley St Leonards" referred to, xlviii
Duraspatam. *See* Armagon
Durea. *See Doriyā*
Durian, Duryan, the, 322; plentiful at Kedah, 278; description of, 278 *n.* 2, 322 *n.* 7; illustration of, 323
Dustoor, Dustoory (*dastur*), custom, 19 *n.* 4, 25 *n.* 1
Dustuck, Dustuckt. *See Dastak*
Dutch, the, lii, 51; engagement with, xxiv; take Negapatam, 2 *n.* 4, 3; allied with the Moors, 38 *n.* 4; attack the French at St Thomé, 47; their factory at Peddapalle, 54; their quarrel with the English at Fort St George, 64 *n.* 1; attack the French at sea, 65; allied with the Moors against the French, 66; compel the French to evacuate St Thomé, 66; agree to resign St Thomé to the King of Golconda, 66 *n.* 1; take the *Great Fleming* from the French, 68, 68 *n.* 2; take Point de Galle, 75 *n.* 3; treatment of, by the Moors, 88; their preparations for King of Golconda's visit, 88 *n.* 3; King of Golconda goes

on board their ship, 88 *n.* 3; put their flag above that of the English and French, 88 *n.* 3; insolence of, reported to the Court, 88 *n.* 3; ignore the complaints of the English, 88 *n.* 3; naval engagement with the English, in 1674, 91 *n.* 1; their iron factory at Narsapur, 98 *n.* 1; their factory at Palakollu, 105, 105 *n.* 2; their pronunciation of 'Shah Hussain,' 119 *n.* 1; their factory at Bimlipatam, 123 *n.* 3; their trade in Bengal, 132 *n.* 3, 133; native silk-weavers employed by them at Kasimbazar, 133 *n.* 6; dispute about ground in Balasor, 154 *n.* 1; their visit to the *nawāb* of Cuttack, 158; their *farmān* not renewed, 160, 161; 'Directore' of, 158 *n.* 3; the cost of their boastful bearing, 161; their *farmān* renewed at great expense, 161; their factory at Pipli, 162 *n.* 2; abandon Pipli for Balasor, 162 *n.* 2; prevented from renting a part of Balasor, 162 *n.* 3; their boats stopped by Shāyista Khān, 164; their factory at Hugli, 167, 168, 168 *n.* 1, 169; visited by Streynsham Master and W. Clavell, 169 *n.* 1; their garden at Hugli, 168 *n.* 1, 169 *n.* 1; inundation at Hugli, destroys their old factory, 170; their possessions in Ceylon, 180; hatred of the, by the King of Candy, 180 *n.* 6; in Ceylon exchange elephants for commodities, 181; their factory at Tuticorin, 208 *n.* 5; their factory at Kasimbazar, 213, 213 *n.* 2; their factory at Patna, 221 *n.* 1, 225, 225 *n.* 1; their exports from Patna, 229, 229 *n.* 2; their gun-boat in Banquala harbour, 250; attempt to monopolize tin trade in Junk-Ceylon, &c., 250, 261 *n.* 3; their settlement at Malacca, 251 *n.* 2; seize an Achin *prau* at Junk-Ceylon, 252; lay claim to ships in Junk-Ceylon rivers, 252; attacked and overpowered in Junk-Ceylon, 252, 253; at variance with Achin, 252, 252 *n.* 1; abandon Junk-Ceylon, 253; complain to the King of Siam, 253; block up the ports of Kedah, 261 *n.* 3, 267 *n.* 1, 269; people of Kedah antagonistic to, 261 *n.* 3; attempt to monopolize the trade of Kedah, 266, 266 *n.* 3; expelled from Kedah, 266; take the English ship *George*, 266 *n.* 3; allied with the "Syamers" against Kedah, 266 *n.* 3; seize English goods at Junk-Ceylon, 270; peace concluded with, 271 *n.*; glut the European markets with tin, 280 *n.* 1, 281 *n.* 3; their ineffectual attempts to settle at Perak, 283 *n.* 3; get slaves from Macassar, 291 *n.* 7; many of, at Achin, 293 *n.* 2; their description of the King of Achin, 295 *n.* 6; their attack on the Queen of Achin, 311 *n.* 1; oppose the English at Achin, 318 *n.* 3; Queen of Achin seeks English protection from, 319; their power in Sumatra, 320

Dutch Doctor, probable identity of, 153, 153 *n.* 3

Duties. *See* Customs

Dyeing of silks, instructions as to, 215 *n.* 1

Dyers, at Kasimbazar, 214, 214 *n.* 2; in the Company's service, formerly soldiers, 214 *n.* 2

Eagle, the, 25 *n.* 3, 175 *n.* 8, 178 *n.* 3

Eaglet, the, ketch, xxiv

Eagle wood. *See* Agila wood

Earving, —, Purser's mate of the *Sampson*, 91 *n.* 1

East India Company, the, xvii, 4; goods of, stopped by the Moors, 51; MSS. bequeathed to, by Thos. Bowrey, xxiii, xli, xliv; sends an expedition to Coromandel Coast in 1611, 98 *n.* 1; Chim Cham broker to, 155; their investment at Kasimbazar, 214; their factories in India, *see s.v.* Balasor, Dacca, Hugli, Kasimbazar, Fort St George, Masulipatam, Peddapalle, etc.; their ships sail for England in January, 232; abandon the idea of a settlement at Achin, 320

East India Merchant, the, 91 *n.* 1

East India Stock, Briggins a holder of, xx, xlii; Bowrey a holder of, xli

East Indies, 188

Ebony furniture, made at and exported from Masulipatam, 71

Ecbar. *See* Akbar

Eclipse, of the moon, 33; Brahmins' behaviour during, 33, 33 *n.* 1; of the sun, 33 *n.* 1; reasons given for, 33, 34 *n.* 1

Eddy, T. B. caught in one, in the Hugli, 174

Edelumburoo, 106 *n.* 2

Eden, Garden of, Ganges supposed to run through, 166, 166 *n.* 1, 211

Edwards, John, a dyer, 215 *n.* 1

Edwards, Richard, 64 *n.* 1, 66 *n.* 1, 75 *n.* 1, 96 *n.* 2, 124 *n.* 3, 154 *n.* 1, 289 *n.* 6; merchant in Kasimbazar, 158 *n.* 3

Eggs, forbidden food of Banyan caste, 29

Elaches. *See Alāchah*

Elephantiasis, disease common to the Christians of St Thomas, 50 *n.* 2; supposed to be a punishment for the martyrdom of St Thomas, 50 *n.* 2

Elephants, 161; figures of, in pagodas, 6; figures of, carved on the chariot of Jagannāth, 17; ships for transport of, 73; food of, while at sea, 73; means of getting on board, 73, 73 *n.* 3, 74; one sinks a ship, 74, 75; means employed to land, 75; rate paid for landing alive, 76; affection of, for their own kind, 76; possession of several, a sign of rank, 125; for war and state at Dacca, 150; qualifications for riding state, 150; war, 157; from Tenasserim, 179; of Ceylon, 180, 180 *n.* 5, 181; how transported from Ceylon, 181; from Cochin China, 208 *n.* 4; illustration of an, 219; none wild in Bengal, 222; not found with rhinoceroses, 223; few exported from Junk-Ceylon, 240; indispensable for travelling in Siam, 243 *n.* 3; attend foreign commanders up to Luppoone, 243; their sure-footedness, 243, 243 *n.* 3; females only used as draught beasts, 243 *n.* 2, 254; males used for war, 243 *n.* 2; at Junk-Ceylon, 247, 248; Horner's trade in, 263 *n.* 1; sent to attend foreign merchants to Solla, 272; much profit made on, 273; numerous and cheap at Kedah, 273, 273 *n.* 4; restriction as to exportation of, 273; incorrect stories of, 273, 274; how trained and prepared for war, 274, 275; how caught and tamed, 274, 274 *n.* 4, 275; their weapon in war, 274 *n.* 1, 275; largest seen by T.B., 275; for state at Achin, 275 *n.* 1, 308 *n.* 4, 309, 325; exported to Madras from Pegu and Kedah, 275 *n.* 1; wild, at Kedah, 279; state, provided for English commanders at Achin, 308; state, illustration of, 308; war, fight with buffaloes, 310; war, kept in readiness at Achin, 312

Elephants' teeth, 277 *n.* 4; trade in, 259 *n.* 1; from Kedah, 273 *n.* 4

Elizabeth, Queen, sends letters to king of Achin, 295 *n.* 6

Elohebaud. *See* Allahabad

Elwes, Robert, 185 *n.* 1; chief at Dacca, 150 *n.* 2

Emirjemal. *See* Mīr Jumla

Emir Jemla, Emir Jembla. *See* Mīr Jumla

"**Endowed Charities**," referred to, xlviii *n.* 3

England, commodities from, imported to Achin, 289

English, the, their ships frequent the port of Achin, xxii, 286 *n.* 1; in India, treatment of by the Moors, 88; their want of courage, 88; marks of favour to, from the king of Golconda, 93; charter granted to, by king of Golconda, 93; their exports from Bengal, 132 *n.* 3, 133; regret Mīr Jumla's death, 144 *n.* 5; their complaints of Shāyista Khān, 146 *n.* 4, 164; visit the *nawāb* of Cuttack, 158, 160; make a settlement in Balasor, 162 *n.* 3; *farmān* granted by Muhammad A'zīm to, 164; their exports from Patna, 229; their privileges in India, how obtained, 233; their immunity from taxes in India, 233; their privileges in Junk-Ceylon, 244; how entertained in Junk-Ceylon, 243—246; encouraged to trade at Kedah, 266 *n.* 3; esteemed in Kedah, 267; many of, at Achin, 293 *n.* 2; merchants of, exchange presents with Queen and chief officers at Achin, 303 *n.* 3, 307; privileges of, at Achin, 304, 304 *n.* 4; captains of ships of, how treated in Achin, 306; temporary residents at Achin, 318

Eng-shē-min, 259 *n.* 3

Ennore (*Ennūr*, Enoor, Enore), xxvii, 44, 44 *n.* 1; Beacon, 44 *n.* 1

Ennūr. *See* Ennore

Epes, Samuell, minister of ship *Society*, 158 *n.* 3

Erwin, Captain, 176 *n.* 1

Escritoires, Escretore, 71 *n.* 5, 269, 290; manufacture of, at Masulipatam, 71

Ethiopians, 35, 180 *n.* 6

Eunuchs, 207; of wife of *nawāb* of Cuttack, 157; of Queen of Achin, 299, 300, 301, 302, 309, 310, 325, 326

Europe, for 'European,' 105, 209 *n.* 2

European, the, 106 *n.* 2
Evans, John, Chaplain in the "Bay," 176 *n.* 1
Everard, Mr, 140 *n.* 2

Fackeer. *See Faḳīr*
Factories, English. *See s.v.* Balasor, Dacca, Fort St George, Harsapur, Hugli, Kasimbazar, Madapollam, Masulipatam, Narsapur, Patna, Peddapalle, Verasheroon, Vizagapatam, etc.
Faḳīrs, 19, 95 *n.* 1; meaning of name, 20 *n.* 1; immunity of, from the law, 20; habits of, 20–23; clothes of, 22; where most numerous, 21; reasons for their mode of life, 22; vows made by, 22; illustrations of, 22, 32; paid by T.B. to mix a dose of *gānjā*, 80
Falcon, the, 166 *n.* 2, 167 *n.* 1, 209 *n.* 2
False Point, 128 *n.* 5, 129 *n.* 1; why so called, 129 *n.* 1
Fanam. *See* Coins
Fanoux. *See Fulūs, s.v.* Coins
Fardle, parcel, 83 *n.* 3, 97 *n.* 4, 106 *n.* 2
Farmān, 61 *n.* 3, 158 *n.* 3, 161; obtained from king of Golconda, 88 *n.* 3, 93 *n.* 1; two versions of king of Golconda's, 93 *n.* 1; appointing Mīr Jumla *nawāb* of Bengal, 142; use of the word, 142 *n.* 2; granted by Muhammad A'zīm to the English and Dutch, 164; of Shāh Jahān, 165 *n.* 2; of Aurangzēb, 165 *n.* 2; obtained by Gabriel Boughton, 168 *n.* 4; Danes attempt to obtain one like the English, 190 *n.* 3; from Mīr Jumla to the English, 233 *n.* 2, 234; of the king of Siam, 240, 244; of the king of Kedah, 270
Fasts, the *Muharram*, 119 *n.* 1
Fatteh Khān, 221 *n.* 5
Faujdār, a military governor, 82 *n.* 1; of Hugli, 96 *n.* 2, 185 *n.* 1; of Golconda, 124 *n.* 3
Faulcon, the, 214 *n.* 2
Fausdar. *See Faujdār*
Feasts, festivals, 19 *n.* 2; of the Hindus, 16, 17, 118, 119; hook-swinging, described, 197, 198, 198 *n.* 1; the Mela at Saugor, 202, 203, 203 *n.* 1
Feringhi Dibba, Frangula Dibba (mound of the foreigners), a Portuguese settlement, 140 *n.* 4
Fidāī Khān, succeeds Shāyista Khān as *nawāb* of Bengal, 107 *n.* 1, 164 *n.* 2; his short and unjust rule, 164 *n.* 2
Fidalgas, 194
Field, John, chief at Madapollam, 100 *n.* 1
Finlayson, George, his "Mission to Siam" referred to, 256 *n.* 1
Firinghee, a foreigner, 140, 140 *n.* 4; number of, in Vincent's train, 164 *n.* 4; 20,000 in Bengal, 195, 195 *n.* 5
Fish, abundant in Junk-Ceylon, 246; in Achin, 322 *n.* 6; on coast of Siam, 246 *n.* 11; on coast of Kedah, 279; strange kinds of, at Kedah, 279
Fishers' Town at Fort St George, 42 *n.* 1
Fitch, Ralph, his "Voyage" referred to, 235 *n.* 1
Flag, English, insulted by the Dutch, 88 *n.* 3, 90 *n.* 1
Fleetwood, Charles, 124 *n.* 3
Fleetwood, Margery, 71 *n.* 5
Fleetwood, Robert, 57 *n.* 2, 81 *n.* 2, 200 *n.* 4; chief at Madapollam, 100 *n.* 1
Flemming, Thomas, commands the *Borneo Merchant*, xxviii
Floris, Peter Williamson, a Dutchman, 98 *n.* 1; a factor in the E. I. Co.'s service, 98 *n.* 1
Flyboat, 92; meaning of, 92 *n.* 1; a Dutch, 178 *n.* 3
Flying Prow, an outrigged canoe, 301; descriptions of, 301 *n.* 1
Foot-boy, 83, 83 *n.* 3
Formosa, chart of, by Bowrey, xxxvii, l
Forrest, Thomas, his "Voyage to the Mergui Archipelago" referred to, 235 *n.* 1, 236 *n.* 1, 236 *n.* 3, 241 *n.* 1, 243 *n.* 3, 248 *n.* 2 *passim*
Fort, the. *See* Fort St George
Fort St David, Indians from, migrate to Achin, 294 *n.* 3
Fort St George, xvi, xxii, xxxviii, 2 *n.* 2, 6, 13, 25 *n.* 1, 36, 44, 55 *n.* 2, 57, 91 *n.* 1, 122 *n.* 3, 123 *n.* 4 *passim*; Council at, their action regarding Bowrey's imprisonment, xxxvi; description of, 3 *n.* 3; fortification of, 3; letters from Agent and Council at, 3 *n.* 2, 8 *n.* 1, 20 *n.* 2, 43 *n.* 1, 51 *n.* 1, 66 *n.* 1, 82 *n.* 1, 106 *n.* 2 *passim*; governor of, *see s.v.* Foxcroft, Langhorne, Winter, Gyfford; climate of, 4; cheapness of provisions at, 4; trade

of, 4, 5; heathen town of, 6 *n.* 3; attacks on, by the Moors' forces, 50 f., 51 *n.* 1; Fishers' Town at, 42 *n.* 1; Round Point at, 42 *n.* 1; dedication of churches at, 50 *n.* 1; impositions on English at, 51; first settlement at, 53 *n.* 1; Council at, send provisions to De la Haye, 66 *n.* 1; discussion as to strengthening fortifications of, 90 *n.* 1; Council at, reproved by the Court, 93 *n.* 1; coins current at, 114; ships from, frequent port of Achin, 288; present from agent of, to Queen of Achin, 309

Foster, William, his "Letters received by the E. I. Co." referred to, 304 *n.* 4

Fournereau, L., his "Le Siam ancien" referred to, 255 *n.* 6

Fouzdaar. *See Faujdār*

Fowler, Roger, appointed dyer at Kasimbazar, 214 *n.* 2; salary of, 214 *n.* 2

Fowls, plentiful at Achin, 322 *n.* 6

Foxcroft, George, 158 *n.* 3; agent at Fort St George, 4 *n.* 1, 84 *n.* 2, 100 *n.* 1; his imprisonment by Sir Edward Winter, 4 *n.* 1, 84 *n.* 2; his release, 84 *n.* 2; his policy weaker than Winter's, 88 *n.* 1; his cause espoused by Jearsey, 251 *n.* 1; unwilling to attempt a settlement at Achin, 320

Frances, the, Bowrey's ship, xxxviii, xl, 175 *n.* 2

Frangue, Fringe, Fringi. *See* Firinghee

Frangula Dibba. *See* Feringhi Dibba

Franks, the, numerous in Golconda, 111 *n.* 1

Frapp, to bind, 316, 316 *n.* 4

Freeman, Robert, 289 *n.* 6

Free merchants, in India, xxxiv, 111 *n.* 1. *See also* Bowrey, Thomas; Horner, James; Jordan, Clement; Ware, Samuel; Bugden, John; Ogilvy, Alexander

French, the, enemies of the Moors, 46; taking of St Thomé by, 46 *n.* 4, 47, 48 *n.*; their factory at Masulipatam, 64 *n.* 1; chief and second of, at Masulipatam, fight a duel, 64 *n.* 1; abandon Masulipatam, 64 *n.* 1; scour the Malabar Coast with their squadron, 65 *n.* 1; evacuate St Thomé, 66, 66 *n.* 1; terms of capitulation granted them by the Dutch, 65, 66, 66 *n.* 1; establish themselves at Pondicherry, 66 *n.* 1, 257 *n.* 6; attempt to take Masulipatam, 67; spies of, murdered at Narsapur, 67; chief of, at Masulipatam, killed by the Moors, 70; complain at Dacca of the taking of the *Great Fleming*, 68 *n.* 3; driven from Hugli by the Dutch, 68 *n.* 3; ground allotted to them at Kasimbazar, 213 *n.* 2; their power in Junk-Ceylon, 255 *n.* 6

Frenchpettah, site of French factory at Masulipatam, 64 *n.* 1

Freshes, the, 173 *n.* 2, 174; destroy the Dutch factory at Hugli, 170; how caused, 171, 172; damage done by, 171 *n.* 4

Fringe Burane, Feringhi Dibba, a Portuguese settlement, 140 *n.* 4

Fringie, Frangue, Fringuin. *See* Firinghee

Fruits, preserved by the Portuguese, 192; of Achin, 322, 322 *n.* 6

Fryer, John, sailed in the *Unity* to India, 91 *n.* 1; his mistake regarding the Queen of Achin, xxiii; his "Account of East India" referred to, 3 *n.*, 6 *n.*, 9 *n.*, 15 *n.*, 16 *n.*, 20 *n.*, 27 *n.*, 28 *n.*, 30 *n.*, 33 *n.*, 45 *n.*, 47 *n.*, 48 *n.*, 49 *n.*, 50 *n.* *passim*

Funnell, W., his "Voyage round the World" referred to, 323 *n.* 1

Further India, close intermarriage common among natives of, 273 *n.* 2

Furza, custom-house, 168 *n.* 3

Futtercon. *See* Fatteh Khān

Futty Cawn. *See* Fidāī Khān

Gaddī, a throne, cushioned seat, 240 *n.* 3

Gala. *See* Point de Galle

Galeasse, Galleasse, Jelyasse. *See Jaliā*

Galiinas dell Mar, Portuguese half-castes, 209 *n.* 2

Galinha, Gallo, Galle. *See* Coxe's Island

Galle. *See* Point de

Gallevat, Galley, Galevet, Galliot. *See Jaliā*

Gaṇḍā. *See* Weights and Measures

Gangah. *See Gānjā*

Ganga Sagar, 203 *n.* 1, 209, 209 *n.* 2

Ganges, river, xvi, xix, 33 *n.* 1, 56 *n.* 2, 131 *n.* 7, 137 *n.* 2, 149 *n.* 1, 163, 174 *n.* 1; sacredness of water of the, 12 *n.* 1, 21, 201 *n.* 1, 202, 202 *n.* 1, 202 *n.* 3, 216,

216 *n.* 5; renders Bengal famous, 131, 132; uses of the word in the 17th century, 132 *n.* 1; beeswax made, on east side of the, 132 *n.* 5; one of the four principal rivers of the world, 166, 166 *n.* 1; its supposed identity with Pison, 166, 166 *n.* 1; its branches, 166; separates the Indies into two parts, 166 *n.* 1; its source unknown, 166 *n.* 1; overflows its banks, 172; pilots of the, 175, 175 *n.* 1; salt obtained from the, 199, 199 *n.* 2; sick folk carried to banks of the, 201, 201 *n.* 1; festival in honour of the, 202, 203, 203 *n.* 1; offerings made at festival of the, 202; Gentues' belief as to its source, 202 *n.* 1; advantages of dying on its banks, 202 *n.* 1; mud of the, sacred, 202 *n.* 1, 216; dead bodies in the, 202 *n.* 2; water from the, carried long distances, 203 *n.* 1, 216; its extent, 209; breadth of the, 209, 211; reports concerning the, 210; tributaries of the, 210, 211; ineffectual search for its source, 211; islands at the mouth of the, 211, 211 *n.* 3, 212; wild beasts on shores and islands of the, 211, 211 *n.* 3; Marshall's description of the, 211 *n.* 1

Ganges, the, sloop, 104 *n.* 1, 173 *n.* 2, 175 *n.* 4, 178 *n.* 3, 219 *n.* 2, 228 *n.* 2, 292 *n.* 6

Gānjā, hemp, 77, 78 *n.* 4; where grown, 78; its appearance, 78; its effect, 78–81; Dampier's description of, 79 *n.* 2; price of, 80; different ways of using it, 79; effect of, on T. B. and his companions, 81; its seductiveness, 81

Ganjam (district), 124 *n.* 3

Gans, Gance. *See* Ganza

Gantang, Gantange, Ganton. *See* Weights and Measures

Ganza, bell-metal, 196, 196 *n.* 4, 290, 290 *n.* 7; from Pegu, 196 *n.* 4

Garce, Garse. *See* Weights and Measures

Gardiner, Frances, mother of Mary Bowrey, xlv; bequests to her, xlvi; executrix to Mary Bowrey's will, xlvii; death of, xlvii

Gardiner, Mary, wife of Thomas Bowrey. *See* Bowrey, Mary

Garrett, Mr, his sloop taken by the Dutch, 266 *n.* 3, 269

Gary. *See Gharī*

Gary, Henry (? Gray, Henry, *q.v.*), Company's servant at Achin, 73 *n.* 3; his contract with the Queen of Achin, 319

Gaunts. *See* Ganza

Gauton, Gawton, George, 233 *n.* 2

Gee. *See Ghī*

Geldria. *See* Gueldres

Gengam. *See* Gingham

Gentile, Gentoo. *See* Gentue

Gentues, a caste of Hindus, xvii, 6, 23, 32, 61 *n.* 3; social characteristics of, 6, 9, 15, 24, 25, 26, 27, 32, 34, 35, 38, 41, 98; religious characteristics of, 6, 11, 12, 14, 15, 18, 25, 27, 29, 32, 35, 36; moral characteristics of, 10, 29; physical characteristics of, 14; former extent of power of, 10; subjection of, to the Muhammadans, 10, 11, 39, 76, 77, 94; pilgrimage of a merchant of, to Jagannāth pagoda, 18–20; number of *fakīrs* among them, 23; commercial abilities of, 24, 25; origin of, 25; pagodas of, 25; dwellings of, 26; clothes of, 26, 32, 97; appearance of, 32; at Pulicat, 52; at Peddapalle, 55; supply Masulipatam with fish, 61; at Masulipatam, 72; excel as artisans, 77; language of, *see* Hindōstanī; food of, 97, 279 *n.* 5; their manner of smoking, 97; their hostility to European and Muhammadan ship-carpenters, 102, 103; their cleverness in handling ships, 103, 104; in Golconda, assume dignity of *rājās*, 108; merchants of the, on the Gingalee Coast, heavily taxed, 126; suffer injustice from the Moors, 126; purchase religious privileges, 126; meaning of the name, 126 *n.* 1; merchants of, compelled to build ships for the *nawāb*, 163; at Hugli, live peaceably under the Moors, 168 *n.* 2; heavily taxed, 194; their Swinging Festival, 198; Uriyas, of lower caste than, 199; treatment of their dead, 202; their belief as to the source of the Ganges, 202 *n.* 1, 202 *n.* 3; practise *satī*, 203; differences between Uriyas and the, 202; women of the, how adorned, 207, 207 *n.* 6; their wives secluded, 207

Géor. *See* Johor

George, the, 265 *n.* 1, 271 *n.*; taken by the Dutch, 266 *n.* 3, 269; sent to Kedah, 268

Georgia, 221, 221 *n.* 3

Ghanṭā, a gong, 197 *n.* 1

Gharī, an Indian hour, 196, 197 *n.* 1; a water-clock in general use in India, 196, 197 *n.* 1; Thevenot's description of, 197 *n.* 1
Ghariāl, a gong, 197 *n.* 1
Ghī, clarified butter, 132 *n.* 6, 181, 289 *n.* 2, 289 *n.* 5; price of, in Patna, during the famine, 226 *n.* 2
Ghurry, Gurry. *See Gharī*
Gifford, Captain William, 172 *n.* 2
Gimnosophists, Brahmins so called, 206, 206 *n.* 1
Gingalee, coast of, xvi, xvii, 4 *n.* 2, 120 *n.* 1, 125 *n.* 1, 182 *n.* 3; great rice trade on, 98 *n.* 1; description of, 120–128; good harbours on, 120; fertility, extent, and physical features of, 120, 121; *nawāb* of, 120 *n.* 1; towns and fortifications on, subject to King of Golconda, 124; under rule of Viceroy of King of Golconda, 125; famous for Jagannāth Pagoda, 127; merchants on, conceal their wealth, 127; English and Dutch living on, unmolested, 127; provisions plentiful on, 127; butter and oil from, imported to Junk-Ceylon, 247
Ginger, preserved, 193 *n.* 2; from Patna, 221 *n.* 1
Gingerlee, Gingerly, Ginglee. *See* Gingalee
Gingerlee (town), 123 *n.* 4; its identity with Vizagapatam discussed, 123 *n.* 2; orders from Court to settle a factory at, 123 *n.* 2
Gingham, 71 *n.* 3, 122 *n.* 3, 162 *n.* 3, 231, 231 *n.* 1; history of the word, 231 *n.* 2; striped, 231 *n.* 2; directions from England as to, 231 *n.* 2
Girdles, 230 *n.* 5
Globe, the, 61 *n.* 3; anchored at Peddapalle in 1612, 53 *n.* 2; commanded by Capt. Hippon, 98 *n.* 1
Gneudeville, his map of Mergui Archipelago referred to, 235 *n.* 1
Goa, 20 *n.* 2, 48 *n.* 1, 135 *n.* 5, 172 *n.* 3, 264; arrack, chief manufacture of, 77 *n.* 3; Portuguese at, how called, 140 *n.* 4
Goala. *See Gowāla*
Goats, bezoar from, 292 *n.* 7; at Achin, 322 *n.* 6
Gobang. *See Kobang*, *s.v.* Coins
Godavari, Goodaware, Godavery, river, 3 *n.* 1, 98 *n.* 1; point, 3, 120, 123 *n.* 4
Godinho de Eredia, his "Malaca" referred to, 192 *n.* 4, 237 *n.* 2, 242 *n.* 3
Godown, 232 *n.* 2; Jearsey's house sold for a, 251 *n.* 1; of the English, at Achin, 321 *n.*
Goens, Ricklof van, General of the Dutch forces, 68 *n.* 2; takes Jafna, 181 *n.* 3
Golcar, 108 *n.* 7
Golconda, fortress of, 108 *n.* 7, 111 *n.* 5; fanciful derivation of, 108 *n.* 7; Thevenot's description of, 110 *n.* 2; confused by T. B. with Bhāgnagar, 108, 109, 110
Golconda, king of, 16, 20 *n.* 2, 51, 103; destroys groves at foot of Mt St Thomas, 46; sends forces against the French at St Thomé, 46 *n.* 4; preparation for visit of, to Peddapalle, 54; Masulipatam subject to, 61 *n.* 3, 62, 82; his ships trade for elephants, 73; not responsible for oppressions of Moors, 88; his visit to Masulipatam, 88–93, 93 *n.* 1; goes on board two English ships, 88–93; his retinue, 88 *n.* 3; details of his visit to Masulipatam, 88 *n.* 3; guns fired in honour of, 88 *n.* 3; cost of his entertainment at Masulipatam, 88 *n.* 3; gives a *farmān* to the English, 93; land at Madapollam granted by, to the English, 100 *n.* 1; takes customs from independent *rājās*, 108; his power, 108 *n.* 1; his Viceroy on the Gingalee Coast, 125 *n.* 1
Golconda, kingdom, xvi, 7 *n.* 2, 12 *n.* 1, 13, 21, 48 *n.* 1, 72 *n.* 2, 120 *n.* 1, 124 *n.* 3, 125, 126, 131 *n.* 7, 132 *n.* 2, *passim*; situation of, 13; Omras of, 39 *n.* 4; Dutch Company's factory in, 72 *n.* 2; description of, 107–119; extent of, 108, 109, 110; boundaries of, 108 *n.* 6; its origin, 109; borders of, governed by private lords, 108 *n.* 6; capital of, 108 *n.* 7; its climate, productions and fortresses, 110; governors of, Muhammadans, 110; manufactures of, 111; fertility of, 110 *n.* 1; noted for diamonds, 111, 112, 291 *n.* 8; royal tombs in, 112, 114 *n.* 1; coins current in, 115, 217; good roads in, 117; accommodation for travellers in, 117, 117 *n.* 2; at war with Siam, 172 *n.* 3; Horner, a resident in, 263 *n.* 1; striped stuffs exported to Achin from, 289
Golconda, mines of, xvii; where situated, 111, 111 *n.* 5; Tavernier's description of, 111 *n.* 5; land at,

how let out, 112; duties claimed by the king at, 112, 112 *n.* 2
Gold, none at Kedah, 280, 280 *n.* 2; brought from Patani to Kedah, 280; at Achin, 294, 294 *n.* 2, 326
Gold, George, taken by the Dutch, 266 *n.* 3
Gold flowers, tribute of states dependent on Siam, 275 *n.* 3
Gold Moors. *See* Mohur, *s.v.* Coins
Goldsmiths, prohibited from entering Jagannāth pagoda, 12 *n.* 1
Gomasta. *See Gumāshtah*
Gombroon. *See* Bandar 'Abbās
Gomez, Gomus. *See* Pulo Gomez
Gondegam, 56 *n.* 1
Gong, 196, 196 *n.* 5, 291; how used, 196, 197 *n.* 1; beaten, to advertise goods of the English in Junk-Ceylon, 245; beaten, to collect debts, 283
Gonga, river, 129 *n.* 1
Gongo Sagor. *See* Ganga Sagar
Goodaware. *See* Godavari
Goodera. *See* Gūdūr
Good Hope, the, ketch, 176 *n.* 1, 264 *n.* 7; taking of, xxxvii
Goodlad family, the, history of, 90 *n.* 1
Goodlad, William, master of Trinity House, 90 *n.* 1
Goodlad, William, commander of the *Loyall Subject*, 90, 90 *n.* 1; life of, 90 *n.* 1; takes part in consultation at Fort St George, 90 *n.* 1; letter from, describing king of Golconda's visit, 90 *n.* 1; voyages to Fort St George, Bengal and Bantam on the *Loyall Subject*, 90 *n.* 1; death of, 90 *n.* 1
Goodman's Fields, xlvi
Goong. *See* Gong
Goozerat. *See* Gujarāt
Gorse, Garse, Garce. *See* Weights and Measures
Gottenburg, xxiv
Gowāla, the cow-keeper caste, bearers in Bengal, 87 *n.* 2
Graaf, Nicolas de, a Dutch surgeon, 153 *n.* 3; his identity with T. B.'s "Dutch Doctor" suggested, 153 *n.* 3; his "Voyages" referred to, 153 *n.* 3, 209 *n.* 2, 221 *n.* 6, 222 *n.* 2, 229 *n.* 4, 298 *n.* 2, 312 *n.* 2 *passim*
Grab, Grob, 140 *n.* 2, 260 *n.* 3
Gram, Gramme, pulse, 121, 121 *n.* 3, 121 *n.* 4, 304; black, 121 *n.* 3; red, 121 *n.* 3; exported from Bengal, 133; horse, 304 *n.* 2
Grand Brittania, the. *See Great Breton*, the
Grand Flemingoe, the. *See Great Fleming*, the
Gratt, for Grall, *i.e.* Generall, 125 *n.* 1
Gray, Henry, makes agreement for the English with the Achinese, 302 *n.* 1; obtains privileges for the English at Achin, 304 *n.* 4
Gray, Matthew, "Cape Merchant," 271 *n.* 1, 317 *n.* 2; his report of trade at Achin, 308 *n.* 2, 320; his commission, 319; recalled to Surat, 320
Great Breton, the, 67; escape of De la Haye from the Dutch on, 68 *n.* 2
Great Fleming, the, 67; taken by the Dutch, 68 *n.* 3
Great Mogul, Grand Mogul. *See* Aurangzēb
Gree. *See Ghaṛī*
Green, colour, native dyers unable to produce a good, 215 *n.* 1
Greenhill, Mr, 196 *n.* 4
Grey, Henry. *See* Gray, Henry
Greyhound, the, commanded by Capt. Wm Goodlad, 90 *n.* 1
Gribble, J. D. B., his "History of the Deccan" referred to, 82 *n.* 2, 88 *n.* 2
Grierson, Dr, his evidence before the Hemp-Drugs Commission, 78 *n.* 4
Gryffeth, John, throwster at Kasimbazar, 214 *n.* 2
Guala, a palankeen-bearer, 87. *See also s.vv. Gowāla* and *Kahār*
Gualloe. *See Gowāla*
Guddorah. *See* Gūdūr
Gudge. *See* Guz, *s.v.* Weights and Measures
Gūdūr, xvi, 63 *n.* 1, 76, 81 *n.* 2, 99 *n.* 6; part of Masulipatam, 63; bridge at, 63, 63 *n.* 1, 84, 84 *n.* 2; houses at, 63; destroyed by flood in 1679, 76 *n.* 1; usual residence of the native governor, 76 *n.* 1
Gueldres, fort at Pulicat, 51 *n.* 4, 52
Guggernat. *See* Jagannāth
Guinea, coast of, 106 *n.* 2
Gujarāt, 131 *n.* 7, 135 *n.* 5, 182 *n.* 3; Murād Bakhsh appointed governor of, 136; description of province of, 136 *n.* 2; money of, 217
Gulconda. *See* Golconda
Gumāshtah, 154 *n.* 1
Gumlack, from Patna, 122 *n.* 1
Gunda. *See Gaṇḍā*, *s.v.* Weights and Measures
Gundore. *See* Gūdūr

Gunge. *See* Gong
Gunja. *See Gānjā*
Gunny, 121 *n*. 3
Gunpowder, 289 *n*. 5
Guntur, 56 *n*. 1
Gurgestan. *See* Georgia
Gurguttee, 249 *n*. 1
Gurrah, unbleached cloth, 133 *n*. 4
Guz, Guzz, Gaz. *See* Weights and Measures
Guzarats, many at Achin, 293 *n*. 2
Guzerat, Gusaratte. *See* Gujarāt
Gwalie. *See* Guala, *Gowāla*
Gyfford, William, Governor of Fort St George, xxx, xxxiv, xxxvii
Gylyar, Juliar, Gelliay. *See Jaliā*

Hackluit, Richard. *See* Hakluyt, Richard
Haggs, William, 140 *n*. 2
Haidarabad, capital of Golconda, 108 *n*. 7, 111 *n*. 5
Hainan, 208 *n*. 5
Haines, John, 85 *n*. 4
Haiyāt Bakhsh Begam, daughter of Ibrahim Quli Qutb Shāh, 113 *n*. 1; mother of Abdullah Qutb Shāh, 113 *n*. 1; wife of Sultān Mahomed, 113 *n*. 1; buried at Golconda, 113 *n*. 1
Hājīpūr, 226 *n*. 2
Hakluyt, Richard, 295 *n*. 6
Halabas. *See* Allahabad
Halalcore (Alecor, Alacore, Hololcore), a scavenger, 11; duties of a, 11 *n*. 4; boy of that caste shot, 11 *n*. 4
Hall, Joseph, factor at Kasimbazar, 158 *n*. 3; quarrels with Walter Clavell, 158 *n*. 3; his complaints against Vincent, 164 *n*. 4
Hall, Mr, companion of Dampier, xxxviii
Hamilton, Alexander, his mistake regarding the Queen of Achin, xxiii; his "East Indies" referred to, 11 *n*., 12 *n*., 15 *n*., 16 *n*., 17 *n*., 25 *n*., 36 *n*., 45 *n*., 46 *n*., *passim*
Ḥammām, stout cotton-cloth, 231 *n*. 1
Hanchparra, li
Harac. *See* Arrack
Haraspoore, Harssapore. *See* Harsapur
Hargee Raja, 257 *n*. 6
Hariçpur Gaṛ. *See* Harsapur
Harleian Society, publications of, referred to, xli
Harrapore. *See* Harsapur
Harsapur, 129; first mention of, 129 *n*. 1; earliest English factory in Bay of Bengal, 129 *n*. 1; pagoda of, 129 *n*. 1; residence of the *rājā*, 129 *n*. 1; *sanahs* made at, in great esteem, 129 *n*. 1; reason for abandoning factory at, 162 *n*. 3
Hassan Hossein, 119 *n*. 1
Hāth. *See* Weights and Measures
Hatton, Christopher, 54, 72 *n*. 2, 200 *n*. 4; chief at Madapollam, 100 *n*. 1; his "Accompt" of the trade of Masulipatam, 245 *n*. 2
Haut, Hawt. *See Hāth*, *s.v.* Weights and Measures
Havila, land of, its identity with the Indies, 166 *n*. 1
Havildār, 98 *n*. 1; of Porto Novo, ill-treats Bowrey, xxix, xxxi, xxxii, xxxiii; of Masulipatam, 120 *n*. 1
Haye, De la, Monsieur, General of the French, taking of St Thomé by, 46 *n*. 4; assisted by Agent Langhorne, 46 *n*. 4; evades the Dutch, 46 *n*. 4; his attempt, and failure to increase French trade in India, 65–70; loses his squadron, 65, 68
Heath, Captain William, 176 *n*. 1; complains against Bowrey, xxviii; his men restored to him, xxviii
Heathcote, Sir Gilbert, a Director of the E. I. Co., xlii
Heathfield, John, 196 *n*. 4
Hedges, William, "Diary" of, referred to, xv, xx, li, 106 *n*., 124 *n*., 128 *n*., *passim*
Hegira, the, li
Hemp, Indian. *See Bhāng* and *Gānjā*
Herba goods, where procurable, 162 *n*. 3
Herbert, Sir Thomas, his "Travels" referred to, 114 *n*. 8
Herne, Mr, his accusations against Clavell, 158 *n*. 3
Herns, Herons, 286 *n*. 2
Heron, George (Herrin, Hering, Hearon, Herron, Hearine), 208 *n*. 4; pilot in the Company's service, xxxvii, 166 *n*. 2, 175 *n*. 1; brings Streynsham Master up the Hugli, 175 *n*. 1, 176; one of the first batch of apprentice pilots, 176 *n*. 1; separate rooms in Hugli ordered for, 176 *n*. 1; surveys the Hugli, 176 *n*. 1; pilots various vessels, 176 *n*. 1, 178 *n*. 3; mixed up in the quarrels between Hedges and Charnock, 176 *n*. 1; member of a "Council Extraordinary," 176 *n*. 1; becomes an independent trader,

176 *n.* 1; a "freeman" residing at Fort St George, 176 *n.* 1; marries a Georgian (Armenian), 176 *n.* 1; demands letters of reprisal, 176 *n.* 1; death and burial of, 176 *n.* 1
Heron, Samuel, pilot in the Company's service, 176 *n.* 1; master of the *Good Hope*, xxxvii; brother of Capt. George Heron, xxxvii; cast adrift by his crew, xxxvii, 176 *n.* 1; brought from Achin by Bowrey, xxxvii
Hervy, Samuel, chief at Dacca, 150 *n.* 2
Hijili, xix, xxxvii, 209 *n.* 2; Moors drive the Portuguese from, 162 *n.* 3, 183 *n.* 3; Company's ships unlade at, 166 *n.* 2
Hill, John, prisoner at Siam, xl
Himalayas, mountains, 172 *n.* 1
Hindostan, 11, 17, 131, 131 *n.* 3, 131 *n.* 7, 132 *n.* 3, 180, 218 *n.* 2; chronicles of, 135; civil war in, 135–144
Hindōstanī, 263 *n.* 1; study of, encouraged by East India Company, 80 *n.* 2
Hindostan language. *See* Hindōstanī
Hindus, xvii, 6 *n.* 1, 23 *n.* 1, 25 *n.* 2; power of, in S. India destroyed, 10 *n.* 2, 128; their fighting abilities, 10 *n.* 2; their treatment by Akbar and his successors, 10 *n.* 4, 10 *n.* 5, 10 *n.* 6, 11 *n.* 2; religion of, taxed, 11, 39; their pilgrimages to the pagoda of Jagannāth, 12 *n.* 1; festivals of, 16, 17, 197, 198, 202, 203, 203 *n.* 1; merchants of the, their wealth ascertained by Shāyista Khān's agents, 157; dead bodies of the, how treated, 201 *n.* 1; their sick, how treated, 202 *n.* 1; number that died of famine at Patna, 226 *n.* 2
Hippon, Anthony, Captain, commander of the *Globe*, 53 *n.* 2; sent out to trade on Coromandel Coast, 98 *n.* 1
Hippopotamus, 279 *n.* 5
Hobson-Jobson. *See* Yule and Burnell
Hodges, Mr, prisoner at Siam, xl
Hodgipore. *See* Hājīpūr
Hogs, wild, in Bengal, 220, 220 *n.* 4; wild, in Kedah, 279, 279 *n.* 2; not eaten by Muhammadans, 279, 279 *n.* 2
Hollanders, the. *See* Dutch
Hololcore. *See* Halalcore
Hon, Joseph, sailor on the *Defence*, xxviii
Honey, 292 *n.* 2; plentiful in Bengal, 132
Hoocar, Hooka, Hoocka, 96, 97; illustration of a, 104
Hope, the, ship, 73 *n.* 3, 319
Hopkins, Mr, second at Peddapalle, 106 *n.* 2
Horner, James, known to T. B., xviii; a free merchant, 111 *n.* 1, 263; a resident at Golconda, 111 *n.* 1; demands satisfaction for goods taken from S. Ware, 263; his trade in elephants, 263 *n.* 1; accusation against, 263 *n.* 1; skilled in the "Indostan language," 263 *n.* 1; acts with the Company's "Braminy" at Golconda, 263 *n.* 1; his trading voyages, 263 *n.* 1
Horner, Mrs, goes to Golconda, 263 *n.* 1; her petition, 263 *n.* 1
Horsburgh, James, his "India Directory" referred to, 56 *n.* 1, 128 *n.* 5, 129 *n.* 1, 209 *n.* 2, 257 *n.* 2, 259 *n.* 2, *passim*
Horses, of Queen of Achin, how adorned, 326
How, William, 71 *n.* 5, 81 *n.* 1
Howard, Eliot, owner of the T. B. MS., xv, xxii; disproves the Bugden theory, xx; supplies the Bowrey clue, xx; "Eliot Papers" by, references to, xx, xlii
Howison, James, liv; his "Malay Dictionary," liv–lvi; copies from Bowrey, lv
Hubble-bubble, 97; canes for, 97 *n.* 4
Hudson, Richard, 184 *n.* 1
Hudson's Bay, "Dictionary of the Indian language of the," xli, liii
Hughli. *See* Hugli
Hugli, xvi, 11 *n.* 4, 23, 56 *n.* 2, 85 *n.* 4, 87 *n.* 2, 96 *n.* 2, 104 *n.* 1, 124 *n.* 3, 129 *n.* 1, 146 *n.* 4 *passim*; number of Christians at, 133 *n.* 3; part of Shāyista Khān's *jagīr*, 146 *n.* 4; factors at, present Shāyista Khān with Persian horses, 148 *n.* 5; Council at, refuse Chintāman a share in the investment, 154 *n.* 1; Governor of, 158 *n.* 3, 183, 185 *n.* 1; English chiefs at, 158 *n.* 3; native merchants in, compelled to send ships to Dacca, 162, 163; the great bazaar at, 168; Mogol's customhouse at, 168 *n.* 3; ships, numbers yearly laden at, 168 *n.* 3; date of establishment of English factory at,

168 *n.* 4; English factory house at, when built, 168 *n.* 4; enlargement and repair of English factory house at, 168 *n.* 4; trees cut down near English factory at, 168 *n.* 4; headquarters of the Company in Bengal, 164 *n.* 3, 168, 168 *n.* 4; description of, 167, 168, 168 *n.* 2; English factory at, 167, 167 *n.* 3, 168, 168 *n.* 4, 171; Dutch factory at, 68 *n.* 3, 167, 167 *n.* 3, 168 *n.* 1, 169, 169 *n.* 1; inhabitants of, 168. 168 *n.* 2; commodities sold at, 168, 168 *n.* 2, 168 *n.* 3, 231; flood destroys old Dutch factory at, 170; new English factory built at, 171; Council and factors reside in new factory at, 171; brick bridge built between Old and New English factories at, 171 *n.* 1; old factory (English) at, how used, 171 *n.* 4; Dutch map of in 1679, 185 *n.* 1; number of Portuguese at, 191, 191 *n.* 1; Ganges festival held near, 203; description of *satī* at, 204

Hugli Hole, 170, 170 *n.* 3

Hugli river, xvi, xvii f., xix; Bowrey's chart of, xvii f., xxxvii, l, 172 *n.* 2, 173 *n.* 2, 209 *n.* 2, 219 *n.* 2; included in the Ganges, 132 *n.* 1; chief arm of the Ganges, 166, 167; trade on its waters, 166, 166 *n.* 2; navigation of the, urged by the Court, 166 *n.* 2; pilots sent from England for the, 166 *n.* 2; lack of pilots for, 166 *n.* 2, 175, 175 *n.* 1; the Company's ships brought up the, after 1679, 166 *n.* 2; why so called, 167; T. B. nearly wrecked in, 172–174; James and Mary shoal in, 174 *n.* 2; earliest sailing directions for, 176 *n.* 1; T. B.'s personal acquaintance with, 209 *n.* 2

Humhum. *See Ḥammām*

Hungerford, John, trustee to Mary Bowrey's will, xlvi; legal adviser to the E. I. Co., xlvii

Hunter, Sir William, his "Imperial Gazetteer" referred to, 105 *n.* 2, 215 *n.* 2; his "History of British India" referred to, 145 *n.* 5, 146 *n.* 4, 164 *n.* 1

Hunter, the, fireship, xxiv

Hurrichpore Gurh. *See* Harsapur

Hutchins, John, his "History of Dorset" referred to, 158 *n.* 3

Huttops, houses at Kedah made of, 269

Hyde, Thomas, liii, lvi

Iberians, called Georgians, 221 *n.* 3

Ibrāhim Khān, *nawāb* of Cuttack, succeeded by Safī Khān, 152 *n.* 4

Ibrāhīm Quli Qutb Shāh, consolidates kingdom of Golconda, 109 *n.* 1; fourth king of Qutb Shāhī line, 113 *n.* 1

Idols of the Hindus in Bengal, 197

Igale. *See* Coxe's Island

Inchiquin, Lord, xxiv

India, li, 1, 4, 5, 50, 71, 133, 145, 158, 293; coast of, xv; East, 2, 39; author's arrival in, 146; trade in, lucrative, 233, 233 *n.* 1

"**Indian Antiquary**," The, references to, 3 *n.* 1, 26 *n.*, 36 *n.*, 42 *n.*, 114 *n.* 2 *passim*

Indian Apple. *See Zizyphus Jujuba*

Indian Sea, 108

India Office Records, Factory Records, references to, xix, xxvi, xxviii, xxxv, xxxvi, xxxvii, xl, l *n.*, 5 *n.*, 12 *n.*, 25 *n.*, 36 *n.* *passim*; Marine Records, references to, xxvi, 12 *n.*, 209 *n.* 2, 262 *n.* 2; Madras Public Consultations, referred to, xxviii; Original Correspondence, references to, xxv, xxxvii, 3 *n.*, 21 *n.*, 25 *n.*, 32 *n.*, 43 *n.* *passim*; Court Books, referred to, xli, xlii, 90 *n.* 1, 233 *n.* 2; Home Series, Miscellaneous, referred to, xli; Letter Books, referred to, 9 *n.*, 53 *n.*, 55 *n.*, 57 *n.* *passim*; Coast and Bay Abstracts, referred to, 100 *n.* 1

Indostan. *See* Hindostan

Indostan language. *See* Hindōstanī

Indra, 295 *n.* 3

Indragiri, liv; *rājā* of, his power, 295, 295 *n.* 3; noted for pepper, 295 *n.* 3; a Hindu name, 295 *n.* 3

Indrapoora, 178 *n.* 1

Indulgence, the, king of Golconda's ship, 88 *n.* 3

Ingerley. *See* Hijili

Ingram, Ralph, Company's servant at Cuddalore, xxxi, xxxv

Ingrenate. *See* Jagannāth

Intermarriage, between different trades prohibited, 31

Inzipatam. *See* Vizagapatam

Iron, 240, 246

Irsepour. *See* Harsapur

Isarees, drawers, trousers. *See Izār*

Ishmael Beake. *See* Isma'īl Bēg

Isma'īl Bēg, appointed second in Junk-Ceylon, 255; killed in the insurrection at Junk-Ceylon, 257

Ispahaun, 309 *n.* 2

Ivell, Señor Axell, Governor of Tranquebar, xxix

Ivory, 290 *n.* 8

Izār, drawers, trousers, 71 *n.* 3

Jackals, description of, 220, 220 *n.* 4; depredations of, 220; illustration of, 222

Jafna, Dutch fortress in Ceylon, 181, 181 *n.* 3

Jagannāth (Guggernaut, Jaggerynat, Jagranaught, Jaguernate, Jakernot, Jno. Gernaet), 7, 8, 15, 24, 37 *n.* 2, 130 *n.* 4; carried in procession, 7, 17, 18; pagoda of, xvi, 11 *n.* 2, 12, 13, 14, 15, 16, 20, 24, 108, 121, 127; revenue of pagoda of, 12 *n.* 1; description of the idol, 12 *n.* 1, 15, 16; diamond stolen out of the eye of, 12 *n.* 1; votive offerings to pagoda of, 12 *n.* 1, 20; festival at pagoda of, 16, 17; attempts of kings of Golconda against, 16; chariot of, 17, 18; immolation under chariot of, 18; pilgrimage of rich Gentue merchant to pagoda of, 18–20; illustration of, 22; his omniscience, 34; chief Brahmin of, 216 *n.* 5

Jagannāth, district, 129 *n.* 1, 130 *n.* 4; *rājā* of, 127 *n.* 2

Jagaree. *See* Jaggery

Jaggeer, Jaggere. *See Jagīr*

Jaggernat, Jaggerynat, Jagernate, etc. *See* Jagannāth

Jaggery, coarse sugar, 78

Jāgīr, a pension, 146 *n.* 4, 152 *n.* 4, 185 *n.* 1; Agra given to Shāyista Khān as, 148 *n.* 5

Jagrenaut. *See* Jagannāth

Jahāngīr, emperor, son of Akbar, 18 *n.* 2; his treatment of the Hindus, 10 *n.* 5

Jakernot. *See* Jagannāth

Jaksom Baksom, Dutch corruption of "*Ya Hassan, yā Hussain*," 119 *n.* 1

Jaliā, a boat, 140, 212; various forms of the word, 140 *n.* 2; Tavernier's comments on, 140 *n.* 2; Schouten's description of, 140 *n.* 2

Jambi, Jambe, Jambee, liv, 295 *n.* 3; a state in the East of Sumatra, 266 *n.* 2, 295 *n.* 2; *rājā* of, his power, 295; English factory at, 295 *n.* 2

Jamboa. *See* Pommelo

Jambys, inhabitants of Jambi, 266 *n.* 2

James, Captain, brings the *Rebecca* up the Hugli, 166 *n.* 2

"**James and Mary**," shoal, 173 *n.* 1, 174 *n.* 2

James I. of England, 295; letter from King of Achin to, 295 *n.* 6; his present of cannon to Achin, 312 *n.* 2

Janavad, 96 *n.* 2

Jan Perdo, island, 173, 173 *n.* 2; other spellings of, 173 *n.* 2

Jansa Bainsah, a giant, 119; festival in honour of, 118, 119; illustration of, 119

Janselone. *See* Junk-Ceylon

Janseloners, inhabitants of Junk-Ceylon, 252

Jan Sylan. *See* Junk-Ceylon

Japan, Bengal commodities exported to, 132 *n.* 3

Japnapatam, Japhnapatam. *See* Jafna

Jardin, Clement Du. *See* Jordan, Clement

Java Major, xxii, lii, liv, 1, 199 *n.* 3, 223, 237 *n.* 2, 247 *n.* 5, 261 *n.* 2, 277 *n.* 2, 283 *n.* 4, 291; chart of, by Bowrey, li; ships from, frequent Achin harbour, 288; why so called, 288 *n.* 4

Javas (Javanese), 293

Jazia, capitation-tax, 10 *n.* 4, 39 *n.* 3

Jearsey, Catherine, wife of William Jearsey, her character, 251 *n.* 1

Jearsey, John, betrothed to Mistress Povey, 90 *n.* 1

Jearsey, William, 9 *n.* 5, 100 *n.* 1, 178 *n.* 1, 181 *n.* 9, 272 *n.* 4; employs T. B. on a trading vessel, xviii, 251; his house, 64 *n.* 1, 251 *n.* 1; in India for thirty years, 251 *n.* 1; in Company's service, 251 *n.* 1; twice discharged by the Court, 251 *n.* 1; defies the power of the Court, 251 *n.* 1; chief at Siriam and Masulipatam, 251 *n.* 1; charges brought against him, 251 *n.* 1; his quarrel with Sir Edward Winter, 251 *n.* 1; his private trade, 251 *n.* 1; claims against him finally settled, 251 *n.* 1; his wife a Dutchwoman, 251 *n.* 1; dies at Fort St George, 251 *n.* 1; two of his servants escape massacre at Junk-Ceylon, 257

Jeco, 319

Jehore. *See* Johor

Jeliasse. *See Jaliā*

Jelosie (?stout cotton-cloth for blinds), 230 *n.* 2

Jemini, river. *See* Jumna

Jentives. *See* Gentues

Jessore, 162

Jesuits, the, 41; their churches in Bengal, 133 *n.* 3; Mrs Vincent

said to encourage, 164 *n.* 4; their missions in India, 255 *n.* 6
Jews, 94; resemblance of the Brahmins to, 28
Jillisar, river, 211 *n.* 3
Jogi, 211 *n.* 3
John Gernaet. *See* Jagannāth
Jno. Perdo. *See* Jan Perdo
Johor, Johore, xxii, 72 *n.* 2, 82 *n.* 1, 251 *n.* 2, 258, 258 *n.* 4, 260, 266, 271 *n.*, 285 *n.* 1, 290 *n.* 8; burning of, 266 *n.* 2; tributary to Siam, 275 *n.* 3; tin from, 280 *n.* 1; king of, 312 *n.* 2
Johore, river, 237 *n.* 2
Johr, peak of, xlix
Jong, a junk, 235 *n.* 1
Jonkseilon, Jonkceylon. *See* Junk-Ceylon
Jordan, Clement (afterwards Du Jardin), a "freeman," 178 *n.* 1; associated with John Bugden, xix; T.B.'s purser, xix, 178, 178 *n.* 1; his position at Vizagapatam factory, 123 *n.* 2, 178 *n.* 1; obtains a cowle for Vizagapatam, 125 *n.* 1; examined as to John Smith's death, 178 *n.* 1; called Du Jardin in 1682, 178 *n.* 1; disagrees with George Ramsden, 178 *n.* 1; recalled to Fort St George, 178 *n.* 1; sent to Sillebar, 178 *n.* 1; dismissed the Company's service, 178 *n.* 1; dismissal not enforced, 178 *n.* 1; sent to Indrapore, 178 *n.* 1; Court's opinion of, 178 *n.* 1; death of, 178 *n.* 1; leaves a widow, 178 *n.* 1
Jougie. *See Jogī*
Jounck. *See* Junk
"Journal ou Suite du Voyage de Siam," referred to, 275 *n.* 3
Jove, Brahmins' prayer to, during an eclipse, 33 f.
Jubrāj, 259 *n.* 3
Judaism, 15
Juggernaut. *See* Jagannāth
Jumna, river, 137 *n.* 2
Junçalaon, Junsalaon. *See* Junk-Ceylon
Juncanner, customs officer, 93 *n.* 1
Junckan, transit-duty, 82 *n.* 1
Junkceyloan. *See* Junk-Ceylon
Junk-Ceylon (Juncceloan, Jan Sylan etc.), xvi, l, 72 *n.* 2, 262 *n.* 7, 283, 290; value of T.B.'s description of, xviii; its produce tin and elephants, xxii; insurrection at, xxvi; described, 235–258; situation and extent of, 235, 236 *n.* 1; history of the word, 235 *n.* 1; marked on the mainland in old maps, 235 *n.* 1; shape of, 236, 236 *n.* 1; dependent on Siam, 236; how governed, 236; inhabitants of, 236, 236 *n.* 3, 236 *n.* 4, 237; language of, 236 *n.* 3; ineffectual attempt of Burmans against, 236 *n.* 3; seaports on, 238, 239; shallowness of its harbours, 239; elephants and tin chief productions of, 240, 240 *n.* 1; imports of, 240; money current at, 240, 241; heavy taxation at, 240 *n.* 1; *bahār* of, 241 *n.* 4; chief officers at, 242, 244; treatment of foreigners at, 242, 243; table of coinage at, 242 *n.* 1; *rājā* of, his reception of foreigners, 244–246; presents given to *rājā* of, by foreigners, 244, 245; no English factory at, 245 *n.* 2; presents given to officers at, 246; imports suitable for, 246; provisions not plentiful at, 246; physical features of, 247, 247 *n.* 3; fruits indigenous to, 247; houses at, how built, 250; *rājā* of, reports Dutch outrage to Siam, 253; T.B.'s second visit to, 255; disaffection at, on account of Muhammadan rulers, 255; murder of Moors and Chulias at, 257; English goods from Kedah, sale of, attempted at, 270; large elephants at, 275
Junks, 181, 269, 271 *n.*; of the Moors, burned by the French at Masulipatam, 68 *n.* 2; of the Moors, for transport of elephants, 73 *n.* 3; meaning of, 181 *n.* 9; of the Moors, one taken by the Danes, 184 *n.* 1
Junsalam, Jūsalam. *See* Junk-Ceylon
Junsalon. *See* Junk-Ceylon
Jurradgeshaw, 154 *n.* 1

Kabul, province of, 136 *n.* 3, 136 *n.* 4; Dārā appointed governor of, 136; description of, 136 *n.* 3
Kachahrī, Court-house, 154 *n.* 1
Kāçu Vīranna (Cassa Varena, Cassa Verona), 48 *n.*, 85 *n.* 1, 126 *n.* 3; death and burial of, 95 *n.* 1; religion of, 95 *n.* 1, 127 *n.* 3
Kādah, an elephant trap, 273 *n.* 4
Kāhan. *See* Weights and Measures
Kahār, the bearer-caste, 87 *n.* 2
Kalyān Ray, a native merchant, 154 *n.* 1
Kanakkapillai, clerk. *See* Conicopoly
Kanārak Pagoda. *See* Black Pagoda
Kānungō, 154 *n.* 1

Kāping, a Malay coin of low denomination. *See Kāping*, *s.v.* Coins
Karapar, mountain, 124 *n.* 2
Karedu (Caraid, Careda, Carera, Careero, Carrera), xvi, 36, 36 *n.* 3; factory to be settled at, 36 *n.* 3; derivation of, 36 *n.* 3; Betel gardens at, 36 *n.* 3; festival at, 36 *n.* 3
Karnates, 132 *n.* 2
Karon Bay, 239 *n.* 1, 250 *n.* 2
Kartikeya, the Hindu Mars, pagoda of, 123 *n.* 2
Kāṣid, 124 *n.* 3
Kāsim, a Muhammadan proper name, 213 *n.* 1
Kasimbazar, xvi, 11 *n.* 4, 87 *n.* 2, 158 *n.* 3; Dutch factory at, 133 *n.* 6, 213, 213 *n.* 2; T. B.'s description of, 213–215; why so called, 213, 213 *n.* 1; English factory at, 213, 213 *n.* 2; silk exported from, 213 *n.* 2; ground allotted to the French at, 213 *n.* 2; Streynsham Master's description of, 213 *n.* 2; mulberry trees at, 213 *n.* 2; Hamilton's description of, 213 *n.* 2; large investments of E. I. Co. at, 214; rank of head of the Factory at, 214, 214 *n.* 1; many English workmen at, 214; output of silk from, 214 *n.* 2; English dyers necessary at, 215, 215 *n.* 1; climate of, 215; decay of, 215 *n.* 2; commodities from, 230
Kassem-Bazar. *See* Kasimbazar
Kateck. *See* Cuttack
Kaṭrā, a market-place, 221 *n.* 6
Kattumaram, catamaran, 43 *n.* 2
Kāval, a palankeen-bearer in Madras, 87 *n.* 2
Kedah, city of, its situation, 259; residence of the heir-apparent, 259; description of, 259 *n.* 2; crew of a Portuguese ship sold as slaves at, 264; chief place of trade in the kingdom, 267; Company's house at, in decay, 268; Company's goods at, spoiled, 269; distress of English factors at, 269; letter from English factors at, 269; English factory house at burnt, 269; half the town burnt, 269; factors at, appeal to the king to dispose of their goods, 270; factors at, get no help from the king, 270; factors at, unsuccessful efforts of to sell Company's goods, 270; Company's goods at, damaged and rotten, 270; factors at, petition the king for help to go to Achin, 270; factors at, complain of want of justice, 270; many thieves in, 271 *n.*; English factory at, abandoned, 271 *n.*; flight of "young king" from, 276
Kedah, king of, resides at Solla, 259; resigns the government to his son, 260; his mild rule encourages piracy, 261; invites the English to make a settlement, 261 *n.* 3, 267 *n.* 1; favours the English, 261, 262; liberates Portuguese lad, 265; reproves Surāj Khān, 265; his courtesy and uprightness, 265; his justice to his subjects, 265; a peacemaker, 265; T.B.'s high opinion of, unsupported, 265 *n.* 1, 284 *n.* 1; unable to enforce his commands, 265 *n.* 1; T. B.'s admiration for, 265 *n.* 2, 266; contemporary notices of, 265 *n.* 2; Hamilton's remarks on, 265 *n.* 2; his conflict with the Dutch, 266; the "Old" and the "New," their favour to the English, 267; his *peshkush* to Mahmud Alle, 268; his protection requested for English factors, 269; lends a *prau* to the English, 270; promises safety to English factors, 270; letter sent from Surat to, 271 *n.*; welcomes English merchants at Solla, 272; present made him by English merchants, 272; feasts and presents given by, to English merchants, 272; Hamilton's account of visits paid to by merchants, 273 *n.* 2; his tribute to the king of Siam, 275, 275 *n.* 3, 276; his fear of the king of Siam, 276; his flight in 1677, 276
Kedah (Queda, Quedah), kingdom of, xvi, xxii, l, 72 *n.* 2, 75, 82 *n.* 1, 178 *n.* 1, 180, 236 *n.* 3, 245 *n.* 2, 258, 285 *n.* 1, 285 *n.* 3, 290, 290 *n.* 8, 294 *n.* 3; two Chulias escape from Junk-Ceylon to, 257; T. B.'s account of, 259–285; size of, 259; sparsely peopled, 259, 260 *n.* 1; wild beasts in, 259, 260 *n.* 1, 279; trade at, 259 *n.* 1, 282; physical features of, 260, 260 *n.* 1; ruling officials at, 260; provisions plentiful at, 261, 279, 279 *n.* 3; good government at, 261; inferior in wealth to Achin, 261; its injurious wars with Achin, 260 *n.* 1; rivers of, 260 *n.* 1, 268; inhabitants of, 261 *n.* 2; English attempt to settle a factory in, 261 *n.* 3; reports as to trading facilities at, 261 *n.* 3; many pirates in, 262; English trade

at, paralysed by the Dutch, 266 *n.* 3; T. B.'s view of English trade at, unsupported, 267 *n.* 1; English factory at, its settlement, failure, and abandonment, 267 *n.* 1; tin its chief commodity, 267 *n.* 1; method of trade at, 267 *n.* 1; English make large investments at, 267 *n.* 1; unfavourable report by the English, of trade at, 268; English goods in, to be sold off, 268; privileges to English merchants in, 271, 283; foreign merchants visiting, go by water to Solla, 272; "young" king of, present made to, 272; meaning of the word, 273 *n.* 4; elephants from, 275 *n.* 1; formerly subject to Achin, 275 *n.* 2; pepper good and plentiful in, 276, 276 *n.* 5; long pepper at, 277; description of houses at, 277; heavy rains at, 277; fortifications of, 278; fruits of, 278, 279; no ducks, geese or pigs in, 279; illustration of "strange fishes" of, 285; woods of, 279, 279 *n.* 4; buffaloes in, 279, 280; tin, the only mineral in, 280, 280 *n.* 1; gold imported from, Patani to, 280; current money of, 280, 281, 281 *n.* 3; weights and measures of, 281, 282; exports from, 283; debts of foreigners, how collected at, 283

Kedah, river, 259 *n.* 4, 264, 277; its width, 259; how far navigable, 259; full of fish and alligators, 284, 285

Kedgaree, Kedgerry, Kedgeree, 167 *n.* 1, 176 *n.* 1, 209 *n.* 2, 254 *n.* 1

Kegaria. *See* Kedgaree

Keigwin, Richard, 140 *n.* 2

Kelly, P., his "Universal Cambist" referred to, 281 *n.* 5, 282 *n.* 2

Ken, John, chief at Kasimbazar, 213 *n.* 2

Kendoa, 87 *n* 2, 167 *n.* 1

Kenn, John, his "Advices about Bengall," 122 *n.* 1

Kerbela, 113 *n.* 1

Ketch, a boat, 173 *n.* 2, 178

Ketri. *See Khattrī*

Kettera. *See Katrā*

Khairātābād, empty mosque at, 113 *n.* 1

Khairāt-un-Nissā Begam, her body exhumed, 113 *n.* 1

Khajūr, wild date-palm, 108 *n.* 6

Khajūrī, 172 *n.* 2

Khān, of Chengy, 20 *n.* 2

Khāṣṣa, muslin, 133 *n.* 4, 154 *n.* 1, 231 *n.* 1; good quality of, at Dacca, 150 *n.* 2, 230; description of, 230 *n.* 2; fine, 231 *n.* 2

Khattrī caste, 83 *n.* 5

Khelong Bay, 250 *n.* 2; its identity with Banquala discussed, 239 *n.* 1

Khēmchand. *See* Chim Cham

Khwājājī, chief merchant, 118 *n.* 1

King George, the, 209 *n.* 2

King's Head Inn, Southwark, rented by Thos. Bowrey, xlv; owned by Peter Briggins, xliv; leasehold interest of, bequeathed to F. Gardiner, xlvi

Kirmān, a province of Persia, 221, 221 *n.* 2

Kishna. *See* Kistna

Kistna, river, 54, 55 *n.* 1; extent of, 110; waters Golconda, 110

Kittesale. *See* Kittysol

Kittysol, 85, 85 *n.* 1, 85 *n.* 4; inferior to a roundel, 86

Knives, imported to Junk-Ceylon, 246; to Achin, 289

Kobang, a Japanese coin. *See* Coins

Koran, the. *See* (Al) Koran, the

Kōrangi. *See* Coringa

Kōs, 134 *n.* 3, 203 *n.* 1

Kōṣīdā, 129 *n.* 1

Kotwāl, judge, 88 *n.* 3, 207, 207 *n.* 1; of Peddapalle, visits Streynsham Master, 54

Kotwāl kā chabūtra, sheriff's office, 226 *n.* 2

Kris, a dagger, 235 *n.* 1, 298, 326; good quality of, at Achin, 298 *n.* 1

Kulbarga, 109 *n.* 1

Kupang. *See Kobang*, *s.v.* Coins

Kutcherry, court-house, 154 *n.* 1

Kuttra, the little, 150 *n.* 1

Kuwāla, mouth of a river, 239 *n.* 1, 295 *n.* 3, 301, 301 *n.* 2, 302 *n.* 1

Labuhan, a harbour, 239 *n.* 1

Laburnum, Indian, 291 *n.* 5

Lac, Lacca, 122, 122 *n.* 1, 132; good quality of, from Bengal, 132 *n.* 4, 134 *n.* 1

Lac, Lack. *See* Weights and Measures

Lacquer-ware, 290, 290 *n.* 12

Lacre. *See* Lac

Lada, *Ladda*, pepper, 277, 277 *n.* 1

Lada panjang. *See* Long Pepper

Laddas, Is., 277 *n.* 1

Laest, Last. *See* Weights and Measures

Lagor. *See* Sagar

La Haye. *See* Haye

Lahore, 133 *n.* 6, 136 *n.* 4

Lalan, Islands, 239 *n.* 2
Lall Baug, palace, 150 *n.* 1
La Loubère. *See* Loubère
Lampoun, Lampoon, 295 *n.* 3; pepper factory at, 292 *n.* 4
Lancaster, Sir James, 295 *n.* 6; his "Voyages" referred to, 236 *n.* 1; obtains concessions from king of Achin, 304 *n.* 4
Lancaster, the, 177 *n.* 1
Lancava, island, 277 *n.* 1
Lancaway. *See* Pulo Lada
Landa, Landock. *See* Landak
Landak, in Borneo, liv, 291, 291 *n.* 9
Langham, Sir William. *See* Langhorne, Sir William
Langhorne, Sir William, agent at Fort St George, 4 *n.* 1, 36 *n.* 3, 63 *n.* 1, 70 *n.* 1, 71 *n.* 5, 73 *n.* 2; accused of assisting the French, 48 *n.*; refuses to expel Frenchmen from Fort St George, 51 *n.* 1; his policy weaker than Winter's, 88 *n.* 1
Langren, Van, his map of Mergui Archipelago referred to, 235 *n.* 1
Langtialu creek, 209 *n.* 2
Lascar, 90 *n.* 1, 125 *n.* 1, 140 *n.* 2, 178 *n.* 3, 265 *n.* 1
Last. *See* Weights and Measures
Lāṭhī, cudgel, staff, 249 *n.* 1
Laws against crime, at Achin, 315, 315 *n.* 2, 316 *n.* 1
Laximana, a Malay official, 260, 260 *n.* 2, 262 *n.* 7, 299; at Kedah, bribes sailors away from the English, 265 *n.* 1
Leachee (litchi). *See* Rambūtan
Lead, 232
Le Blanc, Vincent, 290 *n.* 7
Lee, Blackheath, xliv *n.* 1, xlv *n.* 1; Bowrey married at, xli
Leghorn, xxiv
Leigh Church, Essex, Goodlads buried at, 90 *n.* 1
Lemons, at Kedah, 278; at Achin, 323
Leopards, 219 *n.* 2
Lethioulier, Mr, owner of the *Unity*, 91 *n.* 1
Leupe's Catalogue of maps, 185 *n.* 1
Leximana, Loximana. *See* Laximana
Lignum-aloes. *See* Agila wood
Lime. *See* *Chunam*
Limes (fruit), *āchār* of, 193 *n.* 1; at Kedah, 278; at Achin, 323
Linen, fine, sold at Hugli, 168 *n.* 2; woven at Hugli, 169 *n.* 1
Lingapa, 121 *n.* 4, 263 *n.* 1
Lions, at Kedah, 279
Lipon. *See* Luppoone
Littleton, Robert, 178 *n.* 3
Littleton, Sir Edward, 209 *n.* 2, 214 *n.* 1; factor at Kasimbazar, 11 *n.* 4; connected by marriage with Walter Clavell, 158 *n.* 3
Lock, Mr, taken prisoner, 266 *n.* 2
Lockard, Hannah, bequest to, xlvi
Lockyer, Charles, his "Trade in India" referred to, 43 *n.* 1, 77 *n.* 2, 121 *n.* 4, 287 *n.* 5, 288 *n.* 5, 289 *n.* 5, *passim.*
Longcloth, 5 *n.* 5, 55, 88 *n.* 3, 122 *n.* 3, 246, 289, 289 *n.* 4; brown, 55 *n.* 2, 289 *n.* 5; fine, 55 *n.* 2, 71 *n.* 3; blue, 55 *n.* 2, 289 *n.* 5
Long Pepper, 133 *n.* 2, 196 *n.* 4; exported from Bengal, 134, 134 *n.* 3; its use, 134 *n.* 3, 277; how sold, 134 *n.* 3; from Patna, 221 *n.* 1; at Kedah, 277, 277 *n.* 2; illustration of, 277
Lonuary, ? Conjaguaree, 129 *n.* 1
Loonghee. *See* *Lungī*
Lord, Henry, his "Discouerie of the Sect of the Banians" referred to, 83 *n.* 5, 221 *n.* 5
Lords Trees, li
Lottee. *See* *Lāṭhī*
Loubère, De la, his "Historical Relation of Siam" referred to, 29 *n.*, 83 *n.* 5, 115 *n.* 4, 240 *n.* 1, 242 *n.* 3, 243 *n.* 2, *passim*
Louis XIV, sends fleet to Coromandel Coast, 65 *n.* 2; king of Siam, his ally, 276 *n.* 3
Loveney, Michaëll, weaver at Kasimbazar, 214 *n.* 2
Lower Bengal, 162 *n.* 1
Lowest, meaning "most northerly," 98
Loximana. *See* Laximana
Loyall Adventure, the, wreck of, xxxvii
Loyall Subject, the, detained at Masulipatam for the king's visit, 88 *n.* 3; king of Golconda goes on board of, 88 *n.* 3, 90, 90 *n.* 1; crew of, sickly, 90 *n.* 1; burthen of, 90 *n.* 1
Loyal Merchant, the, xxvi; mistakes her course, 3 *n.* 2
Luiller, voyage of. *See* Prévost
Lungee. *See* *Lungī*
Lungī, 55, 106, 208, 316; various articles applied to, 55 *n.* 2; Herba, 162 *n.* 3
Luppoone, a port, its present designation, 239, 239 *n.* 1
Luppoone, 243 *n.* 1, 248; its situa-

tion, 239 *n.* 1, 243; residence of the *rājā* of Junk-Ceylon, 243; chief town in Junk-Ceylon, 243; pagoda at, allotted to foreigners, 244
Lux, William, pilot in the Company's service, 176 *n.* 1
Lysons, Daniel, his "Account of the Environs of London" referred to, xlviii *n.* 1

Maçāo. See Zizyphus Jujuba
Macao, in China, 264
Macao, in Pegu, 264 *n.* 2
Macassar, 190 *n.* 3, 291, 292 *n.* 7; kingdom of, 291 *n.* 6; capital of, 291 *n.* 6; custom free, 291 *n.* 6; slaves from, 291 *n.* 7
Macau. *See* Macao
Mace, Mase. *See* Coins
Macedonia, 210 *n.* 1
Machaut, Monsieur, captain of the French, 68 *n.* 3
Machhlī, 61 *n.* 1
Mackenzie, Gordon, his "Kistna District" referred to, 54 *n.*, 55 *n.*, 56 *n.*, 61 *n.* 3, 63 *n.* 1, *passim*
Macoshull, Commander. *See* Machaut, Captain
Macquau. *See Mukkuvar*
Madapollam, xvi, xxvii, l, 57 *n.* 2, 85 *n.* 3, 88 *n.* 3, 93 *n.* 1, 98 *n.* 1; Council at, sells *Conimeer* sloop, xxvii; English factory at, 100, 100 *n.* 1; a sanatorium for the English, 100 *n.* 1, 101; a shipbuilding centre, 100 *n.* 1, 102–104; manufactures at, 100 *n.* 1, 102; factory at, subordinate to Fort St George, 100 *n.* 1; difference of opinion as to the value of the factory, 100 *n.* 1; chiefs at, 100 *n.* 1; visited by Streynsham Master, 100 *n.* 1; two factory houses at, 100 *n.* 1; best port on Coromandel or Gingalee Coast, 102; timber and iron plentiful at, 102; T. B.'s visits to, 103 *n.* 1; a ship at, how docked for repairs, 103; fine white piece-goods, named from, 100 *n.* 1
Maddana, 88 *n.* 3
Madera, Cosmo Lorenzo de, part owner of the *Sancta Cruz*, 172 *n.* 3
Mādhavayāpalem. *See* Madapollam
Madras, xvi, xxi, xxvii, xxviii, 2 *n.* 2, 8 *n.* 1, 52; heathen town of, 6 *n.* 3; records at, quoted from, xxviii—xxxv; elephants imported to from Kedah, 275 *n.* 1
Madras, the, pinnace, 9 *n.* 5, 99 *n.* 7, 176 *n.* 1; employed on the Hugli, 166 *n.* 2
"**Madras Manual of Administration**," references to, 8 *n.*, 26 *n.*, 36 *n.*, 43 *n.*, 44 *n.* *passim*
Madras Merchant, the, xxvi
Madraspatam. *See* Madras
"**Madras Press List**," references to the, xxvii, xxviii, 100 *n.* 1, 124 *n.* 3
Madras Road, 172 *n.* 3
Madu Banjee, minister of king of Golconda, 93 *n.* 1
Madura, 38 *n.* 3; pagoda of, 12 *n.* 1
Magellan, straits of, xliii
Magh half-castes, 209 *n.* 2
Mahānadi river, Delta of, 129 *n.* 1
Mahazor. *See Mahzar*
Mahēçāsura, 119 *n.* 1
Mahesha Asura, a monstrous buffalo, 119 *n.* 1
Mahesha Bainsa, effigy, 119 *n.* 1
Mahmud Alle, 268
Mahmud Ibrahim, *nawāb*, 125 *n.* 1
Mahmud Izzuff, Governor of Balasor, 32 *n.* 2
Mahmudpet, 98 *n.* 1
Mahomed Beague. *See* Muhammad Bēg
Mahometan. *See* Muhammadan
Mahomet Bander. *See* Porto Novo
Mahomud Beake. *See* Muhammad Bēg
Mahoua. *See Mahwā*
Mahwā, tree, 108 *n.* 6
Mahzar, application, 83 *n.* 5, 188 *n.* 2
Mainwaring, Matthew, complaint against, 4 *n.* 2; chief at Masulipatam, 88 *n.* 3, 90 *n.* 1, 123 *n.* 4; obtains a *farmān* from the king of Golconda, 93 *n.* 1
Mainwaring, Mrs, 71 *n.* 5, 81 *n.* 1
Maipai. *See* Bamboo
Maipārā, mouth of the Brāhmanī, 129 *n.* 1
Maisūr, 119 *n.* 1
Mak. *See* Betel
Malabar Coast, xxii, 41, 134 *n.* 3, 288, 288 *n.* 2; *rājās* of, possess sea coast of Bījapūr, 82 *n.* 1
Malabars, 6; description of, 6, 41, 98; language of, 6 *n.* 2; religion of, 6, 41; customs of, 35; differ from Banyans and Gentues, 35, 41; ornaments worn by, 35; of Coromandel Coast dull and stupid, 41; not allowed to associate with Ban-

yans and Gentues, 41; of Malabar Coast clever but quarrelsome, 41; occupations of, 42; story of one cast adrift, 44; subject to elephantiasis, 50 *n.* 2; supply Masulipatam with fish, 61; their manner of smoking, 97; food of, 97; clothes of, 97

Malacca, liv, 72 *n.* 2, 236 *n.* 1, 237 *n.* 2, 245 *n.* 2, 261 *n.* 3, 269, 271 *n.*, 282 *n.* 2, 290 *n.* 10, 294 *n.* 2; Dutch settlement at, 264

Malay Archipelago, 192 *n.* 4, 287 *n.* 3

Malayars, the, 255, 293; description of, 237, 237 *n.* 1; at Junk-Ceylon, re-capture a *prau* from the Dutch, 252; overpower and kill the Dutch at Junk-Ceylon, 253; in Junk-Ceylon, their insurrection, 256, 257; inhabitants of Kedah, 260 *n.* 1; pirates of, take a Portuguese ship, 264; eat buffaloes' flesh, 280; of Achin, 290 *n.* 8, 294 *n.* 3; lovers of cock-fighting, 310 *n.* 4

Malay Coast, 259, 261, 280, 285 *n.* 1, 290; what meant by the term, 261 *n.* 1; the Dutch masters of the, 269; kings of the, their tribute to Siam, 276; ships from, numerous at Achin, 288

Malay language, Malayo, li—liv, 37 *n.* 1, 236 *n.* 3, 277; countries where spoken, 291 *n.* 9

Malay Peninsula, xvi, 188 *n.* 1, 261, 275 *n.* 2, 302 *n.* 3; fish on the coast of, 284 *n.* 2

Malda, 178 *n.* 1, 230 *n.* 2, 230 *n.* 6; Swinging festival at, 198 *n.* 1

Maldive Islands, 57 *n.* 2, 66 *n.* 1, 72 *n.* 2, 75 *n.* 2, 105, 186, 218 *n.* 10, 219, 245 *n.* 2; cocoa-nuts from, 97 *n.* 3; best coir cable brought from, 103 *n.* 4, 104; cowries the chief export of, 104 *n.* 1, 179, 200; ships built from cocoa-nut trees at, 104 *n.* 1; rice imported from Bengal, 132 *n.* 7; description of, 200 *n.* 2

Malik Bēg, 187; father of Malik Qāsim, 183; Governor of Hugli, 183 *n.* 1; various renderings of his name, 183 *n.* 1; favourable to the English, 183 *n.* 1; poisons the Danes at Balasor, 184; his relations with the English in 1647, 184 *n.* 1; his antagonism to the Danes, 184 *n.* 1

Malik Qāsim, Governor of Hugli, his exactions, 158 *n.* 3, 183, 183 *n.* 2; Governor of Balasor, 183 *n.* 2; outwits the Danes, 185–189; character of, 185 *n.* 1; complaints by the English of, 185 *n.* 1; turned out of Hugli, 185 *n.* 1; buys government of Balasor, 185 *n.* 1; re-obtains government of Hugli, 185 *n.* 1; in disgrace at Dacca, 185 *n.* 1; pensioned, 185 *n.* 1; garden of, at Hugli, 185 *n.* 1; offers articles of peace to the Danes, 186; his emissary and specious promises to the Danes, 187; demands satisfaction of the Danes, 188, 189

Mallesmolle. *See Malmal*

Malmal, muslin, 133 *n.* 4, 230 *n.* 2, 231 *n.* 3, 290, 290 *n.* 6; good quality of, at Dacca, 150 *n.* 2

Mambou. *See* Bamboo

Manchāl, a kind of palanquin, 86 *n.* 2

Mandarins, at Tonquin, 309 *n.* 3

Mandelslo, J. A., his "Voyages" referred to, 15 *n.*, 20 *n.* 2, 38 *n.* 4, 49 *n.* 1, 76 *n.* 2, *passim*

Mangastino. *See* Mangosteen

Mangoes (Mangue), 46, 48, 48 *n.* 1, 323; groves of at Cuttack, 152; gardens of at Balasor, 162 *n.* 3; sweetmeats of, 192; *āchār* of, 193, 193 *n.* 1, 193 *n.* 2; at Kedah, 278; Dampier's description of, 323 *n.* 5

Mangosteen, 322; description of, 322 *n.* 8; illustration of, 323

Manicapatnam, Manichapatam. *See* Manikpatam

Manikpatam, Manikpatnam, 124, 124 *n.* 2

Manila (Moneela), 5, 172 *n.* 3

Manipur, 259 *n.* 3

Manis, sweet, 283 *n.* 5

Manisan, exported from Kedah, 283, 283 *n.* 5

Manisan-lābah, honey, 283 *n.* 5

Mannison. *See Manisan*

Mansāna. *See Zizyphus Jujuba*

Mansfen, Mr, takes news of Bowrey's release to Fort St George, xxxiv, xxxv

Mansulman. *See* Mussulman

March, Mr, 83 *n.* 3

Marco Polo, referred to, 56 *n.* 1

Marcus, David, commander of the *Sancta Cruz*, 172 *n.* 3

Margery, the, Clement Jordan's ship, 173 *n.* 1, 178 *n.* 1

Marine Square. *See* Wellclose Square

Markall, Mercaul. *See* Weights and Measures

Marriages, Hindu ceremonies of, 29, 30; wealth necessary for, 30; with different trades forbidden, 31;

age when contracted, 31; Ganges water used at, 216 *n.* 5
Marsden, William, lv; his "Malay Grammar," lv; his comments on Bowrey's "Malay Dictionary," lv; his criticism of Howison's "Malay Dictionary," lvi
Marsh, John, Company's servant at Balasor, 159; chief at Kasimbazar, 164 *n.* 4, 214 *n.* 1; death of, 164 *n.* 4
Marshall, John, his "Notes and Observations" referred to, 114 *n.* 8, 134 *n.* 1, 162 *n.* 2, 162 *n.* 3, 167 *n.* 3 *passim*; his "Accompt" of Patna, 224 *n.* 1; his description of the famine at Patna, 226 *n.* 2
Martaban Jar, Martavane Jar. *See* Pegu Jar
Martin, Monsieur, chief of the French at Masulipatam, 70 *n.* 1; chief of the French at Pondicherry, 66 *n.* 1, 257 *n.* 6
Martin, the. William Jearsey's ship, 251 *n.* 1
Mas. *See* Mace
Masāna. *See Zizyphus Jujuba*
Masjid, mosque, 11 *n.* 1, 112 *n.* 5
Maslapatam. *See* Masulipatam
Massapore. *See* Narsapur
Masse. *See* Mace, *s.v.* Coins
Massen, Mr, his connection with Thos. Bowrey, xxix
Massenburd, the, 91 *n.* 1
Massiere, Monsieur, agent for the Dutch in India, 68 *n.* 2
Massoola. *See* Mussoola
Master, Streynsham, xix; his description of the factory at Armagon, 25 *n.* 3; his "Diary" referred to, 12 *n.*, 30 *n.*, 42 *n.*, 52 *n.*, 56 *n. passim*; his "Memoriall" referred to, 36 *n.* 3, 54 *n.*, 55 *n.*, 63 *n.*, 81 *n.* 2 *passim*; his visit to Peddapalle, 54; his visit to Masulipatam and Agha Jalāl, 81 *n.* 2; his regulations as to the carrying of roundels, 86 *n.* 1; his visit to Narsapur, 98 *n.* 1; his visit to Madapollam, 100 *n.* 1; his visit to and remarks on Palakollu, 105 *n.* 2; his remarks on Shāyista Khān, 146 *n.* 2, 146 *n.* 4; his visit to Hugli, 159; examines the case of Raghū the *poddār*, 164 *n.* 4; encounters a storm near the Braces, 167 *n.* 1; visits the Dutch factory at Hugli, 169 *n.* 1; alters the hour for prayers at Balasor, 177 *n.* 1; T.B.'s encounter with, in the Hugli, 175; his confused account of the *Sancta Cruz*, 178 *n.* 3
Mastin, Mr. *See* Mansfen, Mr
Masulipatam, xvi, xxii, 3 *n.* 2, 4 *n.* 2, 36, 40, 55 *n.* 2, 57, 57 *n.* 2, 67, 85 *n.* 3, 90 *n.* 1, 92 *n.* 1, 93 *n.* 1, 99, 100 *n.* 1, 106 *n.* 2, 122 *n.* 3, 123 *n.* 4, 129 *n.* 1, 273; governor of, 55, 81, 83, 88 *n.* 3; deserted for Armagon, 53 *n.* 1; English factory at, 53 *n.* 2, 61, 81 *n.* 2; subordinate to Fort St George, 71; centre of trade on Coromandel Coast, 54, 61, 72; reason for the name, 60, 61; T.B.'s description of, 61–64; Schouten's description of, 61 *n.* 3; Dutch factory at, 61, 61 *n.* 3; subordinate to Pulicat, 71; Danish factory at, 61 *n.* 3, 64 *n.* 1; early history of, 61 *n.* 3; Hamilton's, Tavernier's, Thevenot's description of, 61 *n.* 3; factory at temporarily withdrawn, 61 *n.* 3; bridges at, 62, 63 *n.* 1; houses at, 63; taken by the French, 61 *n.* 3; re-taken by the English, 61 *n.* 3; English garden at, 63 *n.* 1; French factory at, 64, 64 *n.* 1, 70 *n.* 1; Moors in conflict with the English at, 84 *n.* 2; fort erected at, by the Moors, 68; unsuccessful attempt of the French against, 68; a populous town, 71; manufactures at, 71; Hatton's account of the trade of, 72 *n.* 2; chief inhabitants of, Muhammadans, 76; restrictions as to carrying roundels at, 86 *n.* 1; king of Golconda's visit to, 88 *n.* 3; preparations at, for the king's visit, 88 *n.* 3; liberty of conscience allowed at, 94; great bazaar at, 106; road of, 110; coins current in, 115; rice imported to, from Bengal, 132 *n.* 7; ships from, numerous at Achin, 288; fine chintz exported from to Achin, 289
Masulla. *See* Mussoola
Matchulipatam. *See* Masulipatam
Matt, touch, 217, 217 *n.* 2
Matura. *See* Madura
Maund. *See* Weights and Measures
Maure. *See* Moor
Mayflower, the, 319
Mazar. *See Mahzar*
Meange. *See* Mīanjī
Measures, used in Bengal, 218, 218 *n.* 1. *See also s.v.* Weights and Measures

Mecca, 112, 113 *n.* 1, 203 *n.* 2
Mecha. *See* Mecca
Meeke, John, 75 *n.* 1
Meer Cung Marcar. *See* Meer Jang Maraikkar
Meer Jang Maraikkar, implicated in Bowrey's quarrel at Porto Novo xxxii
Meer Moonshee, 299 *n.* 2
Meer Raja (*Mīr Rājā*), Lord Treasurer, 299
Meir Abdulla Baker, 63 *n.* 1
Meirbar. *See* *Mīrbaḥr*
Meirdadpoore, Meirdanpore, 148 *n.* 5, 225 *n.* 3
Mela, the, at Sagar, many worshippers drowned at, 203, 203 *n.* 1; ceremonies observed at, 203; when held, 203 *n.* 1; Marshall's description of, 203 *n.* 1
Meleck Beake, Malybeeg, Maleek beeg, etc. *See* Malik Bēg
Meleck Cossum. *See* Malik Qāsim
Meliapour (St Thomé), 38, 45 *n.* 1
Melkassum. *See* Malik Qāsim
Mellick, 98 *n.* 1
Melons, 324 *n.* 1
Mem Sahib, 299 *n.* 2
Mercaul, Mercall. *See* Weights and Measures
Merge. *See* Mergui
Mergui, 237 *n.* 2, 248 *n.* 2; massacre of the English at, xl; trade from, to Masulipatam, 115 *n.* 4
Mergui Archipelago, 235 *n.* 2
Merjee. *See* Mergui
Merjumbelow, Meerejumbler, Jumbler. *See* Mīr Jumla
Mervah, a boat, 260 *n.* 3
Mesopotamia, sugar imported from Bengal, 132 *n.* 2
Mess. *See* Mace
Mestick. *See* Musteez
Metchli. *See* *Machhlī*
Metchlipatam, Metchlepatam, Mechlapatam. *See* Masulipatam
Mevat, province, 131 *n.* 7
Meverell, Mrs, 228 *n.* 1
Meverell, Samuel, 228 *n.* 1
Mexico, 5
Miam. *See* Weights and Measures
Mīanjī, an Armenian, 268, 308 *n.* 2
Milburn, William, his "Oriental Commerce" referred to, 56 *n.* 1, 134 *n.* 1, 181 *n.* 1, 236 *n.* 1, 242 *n.* 2, 246 *n.* 10
Mindanao, xxxix, 293 *n.* 2, 306 *n.* 1, 321 *n.* 1; chart of by Bowrey, xlix
Mirabolin, Mirabline. *See* Myrobalan
Mīrbaḥr, harbour-master, Chim Cham's goods stopped by the, 154 *n.* 1
Mirepour, 129 *n.* 1
Mīr Jumla, Mirgimola, 152 *n.* 4; artillery of, 111 *n.* 2; joins Aurangzēb's forces, 137; former general of the Golconda forces, 137; made governor of Orissa, Bengal and Pattana, 139, 142; makes Dacca the capital, 143; makes war on Assam, 143; his exactions on, and oppression of the English, 144 *n.* 5; his death, 144; his character, 144, 144 *n.* 5; his son kindly treated by Aurangzēb, 145; his buildings, 150 *n.* 1; his kindness to Gabriel Boughton, 233
Mirobolan. *See* Myrobalan
Mirza Mozum, 271 *n.*
Mirza Wooly, governor of Balasor, 151 *n.* 3
Moca, in Sumatra, 72 *n.* 2, 103 *n.* 2, 172 *n.* 3
Mocha, in Arabia, 103, 132 *n.* 2, 223, 245 *n.* 2, 264 *n.* 7
Moco Moco. *See* Moca
Mogol, an Indian Muhammadan of the ruling class, 255 *n.* 2
Mogol, the Great, 10 *n.* 4, 10 *n.* 5, 126; conquers Bengal and Orissa, 10; penalises the Gentue religion, 11; territory of, 20; exacts payment for the practice of *satī*, 39; beeswax and salt his monopolies, 56 *n.* 2
Mogolistan, Mogulistan, 108 *n.* 1, 108 *n.* 6, 136 *n.* 2
Mohun, Richard, 57 *n.* 2; Salisbury dies at his house, 57 *n.* 2; chief at Masulipatam, 100 *n.* 1; seizes Jearsey's vessels, 251 *n.* 1; occupies factory-house at Achin, 321 *n.*
Mohunpur, 129 *n.* 1
Mohur. *See* Coins
Mohurrum, *Muharram*, the, a Muhammadan fast, 119 *n.* 1
Mola. *See* Mullah
Molucca Is., 5
Monapollem. *See* Armagon
Moneela. *See* Manila
Monghyr, 134 *n.* 1; Shāh Shujā' flees to, 139
Monkeys, 294 *n.* 2; in Junk-Ceylon, 248; story of a, 249; in Kedah, 279; in Achin, 286 *n.* 2
Monsoon, the (Monzoone), xxvii, 51, 73, 99 *n.* 4, 170 *n.* 2, 189,

189 *n.* 2, 286 *n.* 3, 323 *n.* 8; breaking-up of, 170
Monsoon Plum, 323; identified with the *Zizyphus Jujuba*, 323 *n.* 8
Montepoly, Montapolee. *See* Motupalle
Monteroyo, Lewis de, 242 *n.* 3
Monthly pay, 83, 83 *n.* 4; customary, for all soldiers of the Company, 4
Monzoone. *See* Monsoon
Moollah, Moulla. *See* Mullah
Moon, the, eclipse of, 32–34; reason of eclipse of, 34; superstition regarding, 230 *n.* 1
Moor, gold. *See* Mohur, *s.v.* Coins
Moor, J. H., his "Notices of the Indian Archipelago" referred to, 295 *n.* 3
Moore, Mr, a Director of the E.I.Co., xlii
Mooree, Moory. *See Mūri*
Moors (Muhammadans), the, 10 *n.* 3, 16, 52, 61 *n.* 3, 76, 95 *n.* 1, 106; ships of, frequent the port of Achin, xxii, 286 *n.* 1; subdue the Gentues, 10, 16; take St Thomé from the Portuguese, 38 *n.* 4, 45 *n.* 1; rebuild St Thomé, 45 *n.* 1; driven from St Thomé by the French, 46, 46 *n.* 4, 47, 65; murder French spies at Narsapur, 67; their ships burnt at Masulipatam by the French, 68; kill the French chief at Masulipatam, 70; their skirmish with Sir Edward Winter at Gūdūr bridge, 84; their treatment of Europeans, 88; their haughtiness, 97 *n.* 3; at Chicacol, 125; oppress Gentues on Gingalee Coast, 126; govern Orissa, 131; drive the Portuguese from Hijili, 162 *n.* 3; merchants of the, their trade at Hugli, 168 *n.* 2; increase of their trade in Bengal, 182; refuse to liberate Danish prisoners, 182 *n.* 3; flee from the Danes, in Balasor Road, 186; demand satisfaction from the Danes, 188; their water-clocks, 195, 196; their fear of the Brahmins, 205; Friday, their Sabbath, 207; their wives, seclusion of, adornment of, 207; two killed by tigers, 220; in Junk-Ceylon, killed in the insurrection, 257; chief food of, 279 *n.* 5; their trade from Surat to Achin, 288 *n.* 5; at Achin, 321 *n.* 1. *See also s.v.* Muhammadans
Moosim. *See* Monsoon
Mootapilly. *See* Motupalle
Moqua, Mockua. *See Mukkuvar*
Morat Bakche. *See* Murād Bakhsh
More. *See* Moor
Moree. *See Mūri*
Morocco, li
Morris, H., his "Godavery District" referred to, 98 *n.* 1, 120 *n.* 4
Mortavan Jarre, Martaban Jar. *See* Pegu Jar
Mortier, Pierre, his map referred to, 209 *n.* 2
Mosely, Richard, soldier and dyer in the Company's service, 214 *n.* 2
Mosque (*masjid*), 112 *n.* 5; Gentues prohibited from worshipping near the, 11; Muhammadans attend the, four times daily, 95; at Achin, 293 *n.* 2, 322
Mossel. *See* Mussoola
Mosulla. *See* Mussoola
Motavan Jar. *See* Pegu Jar
Motupalle, Motupalli, 56; Marco Polo landed at, 56 *n.* 1
Mount St Thomas. *See* St Thomas' Mount
Moy. *See* Arakan
Muckwa, Muckwar. *See Mukkuvar*
Mucoa. *See Mukkuvar*
Muddoo Verona, adopted son of Kāçu Vīranna, 85 *n.* 1
Muftili. *See* Motupalle
Muhammad (Mahomet), the prophet, 96, 316
Muhammadanism, 15, 94, 279
Muhammadans (Moors), 10 *n.* 3, 16, 28, 294 *n.* 2; discountenance *satī*, 39; seclude their women, 63, 64; their insolence, 76; their arrogance to the Gentues and Malabars, 76, 94; their religious consistency, 94, 95, 96, 141; their moral characteristics, 94; their social characteristics, 96; credited with praying to the sun, 203 *n.* 2; their fear of the Brahmins, 205; their chief delight, 216. *See also s.v.* Moors
Muhammad 'Azīm, son of Aurangzēb, appointed *nawāb* of Bengal, 147; received by the princes at Patna and Rājmahāl, 147; entertained at Dacca, 149; begins the Lall Baug, 150 *n.* 1; his rule more just than that of Shāyista Khān, 164; turns out corrupt officers, 164; grants *farmāns* to the English and Dutch, 164; his reception of Mr Vincent, 164, 165; his demand for elephants, 180

Muhammad Bēg, 63 *n.* 1; appointed *rājā* of Junk-Ceylon, 255; his severe and unpopular rule in Junk-Ceylon, 256; his injustice at Junk-Ceylon, 257; insurrection against, 257; killed, 257
Mukkuvars, a caste of fishermen, 42
Mulberry trees, at Kasimbazar, 213 *n.* 2
Mullah, a Muhammadan priest, 95 *n.* 2, 314; attends condemned criminals at Achin, 316
Mulmuls. *See Malmal*
Multan, 136 *n.* 3; Dārā made governor of, 136; description of, 136 *n.* 4; productions of, 136 *n.* 4
Mumtāz Mahāl, Shāh Jahān's favourite wife, 145 *n.* 6
Munchal. *See Manchāl*
Mundy, Peter, his "Journall" referred to, 230 *n.* 5, 294 *n.* 2
Mungeer. *See* Monghyr
Murād Bakhsh, son of Shāh Jahān, appointed governor of Gujarāt, 136; deceived and murdered by Aurangzēb, 137
Mūri (Murree, Moree, Mooree, Moory), blue cloth, 55, 71 *n.* 3, 122 *n.* 3; 289 *n.* 4; red, 55 *n.* 2; coarse, 55 *n.* 2; fine, 55 *n.* 2
Murray, James A. H., LL.D., acquainted with T. B. MS., xv; his "Oxford English Dictionary" referred to, xv *n.*, 92 *n.* 1, 97 *n.* 4, 272 *n.* 2, 316 *n.* 4
Murrees. *See Mūri*
Murshidabad, 201 *n.* 1, 230 *n.* 5
Musa, English goods left with him at Junk-Ceylon, 270
Musi, river, tributary of the Kistna, 110 *n.* 4
Music, an accompaniment to marriage ceremonies, 30; an accompaniment to a *satī*, 38
Musk, exported from Bengal, 134; codd, 134, 134 *n.* 2; how sold, 134 *n.* 2; exported from Pattana, 229; whence procured, and when taken, 229, 230
Musk-deer, 229; De Graaf's description of, 229 *n.* 4; illustration of, 228
Muslin, Muzlin, a fine calico, 5, 122, 230, 289 *n.* 1, 289 *n.* 5, 290 *n.* 6, 302; striped, 123 *n.* 2
Musseet. *See Masjid*
Mussleman. *See* Mussulman
Musslemen, 188, 188 *n.* 2. *See also s.v.* Mussulman
Mussoola, Massoola, Mossel, Mosulla, 42 *n.* 1, 48 *n.*; description of, 42, 43; illustration of, 86
Mussulaman. *See* Mucoa
Mussulman, a Muhammadan, 76, 95 *n.* 1, 126, 141, 188 *n.* 2; number that died of famine at Patna, 226 *n.* 2
Musteez, Musteza, a half-caste, 3 *n.* 5, 133 *n.* 2, 140 *n.* 4, 262 *n.* 2
Muxadavad. *See* Murshidabad
Muzzareefe, 154 *n.* 1
Mylapore. *See* Meliapour
Mypurra, 128 *n.* 5
Myrobalan, a fruit, 192, 192 *n.* 3, 193 *n.* 2, 237 *n.* 2, 323
Mysore, derivation of, 119 *n.* 1

Nabob. *See Nawāb*
Nagavali, river, 124 *n.* 3
Naglewanch, 4 *n.* 2; Dutch factory at, 105 *n.* 2
Naik, a Hindu governor, 38, 38 *n.* 3, 39, 51 *n.* 1
Naique. *See* Naik
Nalla Bakr Maraikkar, xxxiii
Nanagur, near Patna, English factory at, 224 *n.* 1
Nārāyan Dās (Narrandasse), broker at Balasor, 32 *n.* 2
Narbada, river, 136 *n.* 2
Nardaba. *See* Narbada
Narragur, 152 *n.* 4
Narsa, the author's *dubash*, 37; a *dubash* to the Dutch, 37 *n.* 2
Narsam Cawn. *See* Nasīb Khān, Nāzīm Khān
Narsapore. *See* Narsapur
Narsapur, xvi, 63 *n.* 1, 81 *n.* 2, 93 *n.* 1, 105 *n.* 2, 106, 121 *n.* 2, 123 *n.* 4; murder of French spies at, 67; situation of, 98, 98 *n.* 1; Morris's description of, 98 *n.* 1; destructive flood at, 98 *n.* 1; excellent harbour at, 98 *n.* 1; Dutch iron factory at, 98 *n.* 1; English factory at, 98 *n.* 1; subject to Masulipatam, 98 *n.* 1; decline of trade at, 98 *n.* 1; visited by Streynsham Master, 98 *n.* 1; manufactures at, 98 *n.* 1; river at, 99, 99 *n.* 4; governor of, a Muhammadan, 99; new Dutch factory at, 99 *n.* 4; coins current at, 116
Narsapur Peta. *See* Narsapur
Narsingue. *See* Vijayanagar
Narvat, province, 131 *n.* 7
Naseeb Cawne, Naseb Cawne, Naseeb Chaan. *See* Nasīb Khān
Nasīb Khān, merchant at Hugli, 74 *n.* 3; *shāhbandar* at Balasor, 74 *n.* 3

Nasir Mahmud, *khān* of Chengy, 20 *n.* 2
Naurasporam. *See* Nourasporam
Nawāb, a Muhammadan viceroy, of the Carnatic, 51 *n.* 1; of Masulipatam, 88 *n.* 3; title of, given to Mīr Jumla, 142; extent of power of a, 144 *n.* 3; of Bengal, 148 *n.* 5, 179; of Cuttack, 152–161; of Patna, story of his chief wife, 227
Nayler, John, dyer at Kasimbazar, 214 *n.* 2
Nāzīm Khān, 74, 74 *n.* 3
Nedham, Fytche, 148 *n.* 3; factor at Dacca, 150 *n.* 2
Negapatam, 2, 258; taken by the Dutch, 2 *n.* 4, 3; description of, in 1672, 2 *n.* 4
Neglawanch. *See* Naglewanch
Negrais, 237 *n.* 2
Nellore (district), 25 *n.* 3, 55 *n.* 2
Neopall. *See* Nepal
Nepal, 134 *n.* 2
Nephalium lappaceum. *See Rambūtan*
Nerule, 78 *n.* 2
Neshaun. *See Nishān*
Netherlands East India Company, complaint to, 88 *n.* 3
New Kedah, liii
New Pagodas, 93 *n.* 1, 114. *See also s.v.* Coins
New Queda. *See* New Kedah
New Shipp, the, William Jearsey's ship, 251 *n.* 1
Nicholson, John, Captain, xxxvii, l, 176 *n.* 1; commands Company's ship *Advice*, l; to seize Chintamund's ship, 154 *n.* 1
Nicobar Is., xxxviii, l, 68 *n.* 3, 120 *n.* 2, 301 *n.* 1
Nieuhoff, J., his "Het Gezantschap &c." referred to, 324 *n.* 1
Nile, river, 172
Nillaes, blue cloth, 231 *n.* 1, 231 *n.* 2
Nipa, the, a thatching palm, 78 *n.* 2
Nipa de Goa, 78
Nishān, Vincent obtains a, 165 *n.* 1, 165 *n.* 2
Nizampatam (Peddapalle), 53 *n.* 2
Nonsuch, the, William Jearsey's ship, 251 *n.* 1
Norricoel, li
Norris, Sir William, English ambassador, xl
"**Notes and Extracts from Government Records at Fort St George**" referred to, 3 *n.*, 6 *n.*, 19 *n.*, 29 *n.*, 36 *n.*, 37 *n.*, 41 *n.*, *passim*
Nouralla Caun. *See* Nūru'llah Khān
Nourasporam, 98 *n.* 1, 200 *n.* 4
Nugdy, the, 271 *n.* 1, 320
Nulla Buckoor Marcar. *See* Nalla Bakr Maraikkar
Nursapore. *See* Narsapur
Nurse, Valentine, complains against Clavell, 159
Nūru'llah Khān, *nawāb* of Orissa, 152 *n.* 4
Nyshampatnam. *See* Peddapalle

Oakum, 21
Oath, "by cow," for important matters, 9
Ocoon. *See Akhun*
Oedjange (Salange). *See* Junk-Ceylon
Ogilby, Ogleby, Alexander. *See* Ogilvy, Alexander
Ogilvy, Alexander, known to T.B., xviii; an English merchant, 264; obtains liberation of a Portuguese slave-boy, 264, 265; sent on a trading voyage to Mocha, 264 *n.* 7; goes to Surat, 264 *n.* 7; a freeman, at Bombay, 264 *n.* 7; a witness, at Fort St George, 264 *n.* 7
Oglevie, Isabella, 264 *n.* 7
Ogouli. *See* Hugli
Oil, 20, 289, 290, 304; used by Gentues for anointing their bodies, 32; used for increasing the fire at a *satī*, 38; exported from Bengal, 132, 132 *n.* 6; price of, in Patna, during the famine, 226 *n.* 2; imported to Junk-Ceylon, 247; sold by the bamboo at Achin, 282 *n.* 1; used with dammer, 293; cocoanut, 320
Old Fish Street, London, xli
Old Kedah, liii, 262; its situation, 284; its river, full of fish, 284
Old Pagodas, 57, 105 *n.* 2, 115; reasons for excessive value of, 115 *n.* 2; current only in Golconda, 115 *n.* 2
Old Queda. *See* Old Kedah
Olocko, Oolauck. *See Ulāk*
Omrah, Omra, Omro, Ombrah. *See Umarā*
Onderhill, Derick, 264 *n.* 7
Oneal, Mr, 66 *n.* 1
Onions, 289 *n.* 5
Oojong. *See* Ujung
Ooriya. *See* Uriya
Ophir, ? Achin, 294 *n.* 2
Opium, 181, 289 *n.* 5, 312; excites valour in *rājpūts*, 83 *n.* 5; best produced in Bengal, 133, 134 *n.* 1; monopoly in trade of, 134 *n.* 1
Orammall. *See Rūmāl*
Oran Caye. *See* Orankay

Oran Chookee. *See* Orankay

Oranges, at Achin, 322

Orangkay Loximana. *See s. vv.* Orankay; Laximana

Orang-laut, men of the sea, 237 *n.* 2

Orang-sālat, men of the narrow seas, 237 *n.* 2

Orankay, Orancāya, a high Malay official, 260, 260 *n.* 3, 299 *n.* 1, 299 *n.* 4, 299 *n.* 5, 300 *n.* 4, 313 *n.* 1, 319; the, at Kedah, 262 *n.* 7, 268, 271; the great, at Achin, 299, 301, 303 *n.* 3, 306, 307 *n.* 4, 315, 317, 318, 322; ceremonies at visit to the, at Achin, 302, 303, 307

Oran Keay, Oran Koye. *See* Orankay

Organdy muslin. *See* Betteela

Orim Zeeb. *See* Aurangzēb

Orissa, Orixa, xvi, 5 *n.* 1, 10, 12 *n.* 1, 108 *n.* 1, 128 *n.* 1, 129 *n.* 1, 130 *n.* 3, 130 *n.* 4, 131 *n.* 7, 199, 214, 221, 222 *n.* 1; coast of, 108 *n.* 2, 120 *n.* 1; king of, 125 *n.* 1; description of, 128–131; subordinate to the Great Mogol, 128; independent *rājās* in, 128, 131; port on coast of, 129; few towns in, 130; called Jagannāth, 130 *n.* 4; unsettled state of, 131, 131 *n.* 1; travelling in, unsafe, 131; Mīr Jumla made governor of, 139, 142; *rājās* of, refuse to acknowledge Mīr Jumla, 143; Muhammad 'Azīm made governor of, 147; part of the province of Behar, 151 *n.* 2; *nawābs* of, 152 *n.* 4; commodities of, sold at Hugli, 168; imports of, 232

Orléans, D', "Voyages" of. *See* Prévost

Orme, Robert, his "Historical Fragments" referred to, 153 *n.* 3

Ormus, 208 *n.* 5

Ornaments, worn by Banyans and Gentues, 34, 35; of eunuchs of Queen of Achin, 325; of horses of Queen of Achin, 326

Oromal *See Rumāl*

Orongkay. *See* Orankay

Ougli. *See* Hugli

Oulesser. *See* Orissa

Ourias, inhabitants of Orissa. *See* Uriyas

Outcry, Callaway's goods sold at, 175 *n.* 8; Whetham's goods sold at, 177 *n.* 2

Ox-hire, duties on reduced, 93 *n.* 1

Oyglesby, Alexander. *See* Ogilvy, Alexander

Oyster, river, 209 *n.* 2

Pacem, 285 *n.* 3

Padang Salla. *See* Solla

Paddy, 4 *n.* 2, 93 *n.* 1, 120 *n.* 1, 123 *n.* 4, 294 *n.* 3

Padres (priests), Portuguese, convert the pariahs, 41; Court's opinion of, 41 *n.* 3; Portuguese, their legends about St Thomas, 50; French and Portuguese, their want of courtesy, 50 *n.* 1; Portuguese, 195

Pāgar, a fence, enclosure, 269

Pagoda. *See* Coins

Pagoda, temple, 6, 11, 22, 25, 26, 30, 41, 197, 199, 205; carvings in those of the "Gentues" and "Mallabars," 7; of Trivettore (Tressletore, Triblitore), description of, 8 *n.*; of Jagannāth, 12, 13, 14, 15, 16, 17, 18, 20; of Benares, 12 *n.*; of Matura, 12 *n.*; of Tripeti, 12 *n.*; subordinate, festivals at, 17; of Armagon, 25; on the Gingalee Coast, antiquity of, 127; of Harsapur, 129 *n.* 1; of Pipli, 162 *n.* 1

Pahr, a measure of time, 196, 197 *n.* 1

Painters, calico-printers, 106 *n.* 2

Paintings (chintz), 9, 55, 71 *n.* 1, 106, 288 *n.* 6; manufactured at St Thomé, 45 *n.* 1, at Masulipatam, 72 *n.* 2, at Palakollu, 105 *n.* 2, at Golconda, 111; coarse, 288

Palakollu, xvi; Dutch ropemakers at, 105; first Dutch settlement on Coromandel Coast, 105 *n.* 2; Dutch factory at, 105 *n.* 2; existing remains of Dutch occupation of, 105 *n.* 2; manufactures at, 105 *n.* 2, 106; rented by the Dutch of the king of Golconda, 105 *n.* 2; visited by Streynsham Master, 105 *n.* 2; its later history, 105 *n.* 2; Swinging Festival at, 198 *n.* 1

Palampore, chintz bed-spread, 71, 71 *n.* 3, 106, 288

Palanchino. *See* Palankeen

Palankeen, palanchino, 19, 30, 54, 83, 148, 187, 204, 213 *n.* 2; illustration of, 86; T. B.'s description of, 86, 87; Thevenot's description of, 86 *n.* 2

Palankeen-bearers, 87 *n.* 2; caste of, 87

Palanquin. *See* Palankeen

Paliacatte. *See* Pulicat

Palimbam, 295 *n.* 2, 295 *n.* 3

Paliyāghāt. *See* Pulicat

Palkole. *See* Palakollu
Pallampore. *See* Palampore
Palmas, Cape das, 209 *n.* 2
Palmeris, Palmiras. *See* Palmyras
Palmito (date-palm), 46; toddy made from, 49; groves of, at Cuttack, 152
Palm-wine. *See* Toddy
Palmyra (Palmero), 38, 46, 128 *n.* 5; leaf of used for writing, 24; leaves used as pendants by Banyans and Gentues, 35; toddy made from, 48; sugar obtained from, 78 *n.* 1; groves of, at Cuttack, 152
Palmyras (Palmeris, Palmiras) Point, 128, 128 *n.* 5, 129, 129 *n.* 1, 131; protects Balasor Harbour, 162 *n.* 3
Pambou. *See* Bamboo
Pān, Pome, Pond. *See* Weights and Measures
Pān, pawn, paun, 30 *n.* 2, 97, 305 *n.* 1
Pānch. *See* Punch
Pantado, Pintado. *See* Paintings
Panther, a black, T. B. mistakes for a tiger, 248 *n.* 3
Para, Parrah. *See* Weights and Measures
Parcallae. *See Parkālā*
Pariah caste (Parjar, Parrea, Parryar), 25 *n.* 1; description of, 41, 41 *n.* 2; occupations of, 41, 42
Parjar. *See* Pariah
Parkālā, piece-goods, 55 *n.* 2, 71 *n.* 3, 122 *n.* 3, 289 *n.* 4
Parryar, Paryar, Parrea. *See* Pariah
Parwāna, 152 *n.* 4, 154 *n.* 1, 165 *n.* 2; from Shāyista Khān, 158 *n.* 3; obtained by the Danes, 190 *n.* 3
Passaman, 285 *n.* 3, 292 *n.* 1
Patah, a fragment, 241 *n.* 2. *See also s.v.* Coins
Patah bāsar, large fragment, 241 *n.* 2
Patah kāchil, small fragment, 241 *n.* 2
Pāṭali, river, 129 *n.* 1
Patam, a town, 61
Patan. *See* Pattana (province)
Patani, Patany, xxii, liii, 242 *n.* 3, 250 *n.* 1, 260 *n.* 1, 260 *n.* 3; a Malay state, 266, 266 *n.* 1, 266 *n.* 2; Queen of, 266 *n.* 1; King of, 266; tributary to Siam, 275 *n.* 3; its situation, 280
Patan Kings, their rule in Orissa, 131 *n.* 1
Patanny. *See* Patani
Patch. *See* Weights and Measures
Paṭēlā, a boat, 148; description of, 225, 225 *n.* 3; used for heavy goods, 229; illustration of, 277
Patna, 33 *n.* 1, 122 *n.* 1, 132 *n.* 7, 211 *n.* 1, 249 *n.* 1; best opium from, 134 *n.* 1; nobles receive Muhammad 'Azīm at, 147; factory at, *farmān* for, from the Prince, 151; Swinging Festival at, 198 *n.* 1; chief city of Pattana, 221; Thevenot's description of, 221 *n.* 1; Dutch factory at, 221 *n.* 1, 225, 225 *n.* 1; De Graaf's description of, 221 *n.* 5; inundations of the Ganges at, 221 *n.* 5; palace of the *nawāb* at, 221 *n.* 5; Tavernier's description of, 221 *n.* 5; English factory at, 223, 224 *n.* 1; provides large quantities of saltpetre, 224, 224 *n.* 1; the residence of the *nawāb*, 224 *n.* 1; John Marshall's "Accompt" of, 224 *n.* 1; famine at, 226, 226 *n.* 2, 227, 227 *n.* 1
Pattamars, 312 *n.* 1
Pattana. *See* Patna
Pattana (province), xvi, 5, 172, 184, 211, 214, 222 *n.* 1, 223; Mīr Jumla made governor of, 139, 142; Shāyista Khān made governor of, 145; Muhammad 'Azīm sent to, 147; part of the province of Behar, 151 *n.* 2; commodities of, sold at Hugli, 168; T. B.'s description of, 221–234; tributary to the Great Mogol, 221; trade of, 221; saltpetre and musk exported from, 229; imports of, 232
Pattans, the, inroad of, into Hindostan, 152 *n.* 4
Pattany. *See* Patani
Pattarero, swivel-gun, 254, 254 *n.* 1; iron, 254 *n.* 1; brass, 254 *n.* 1
Pattella, Patella, Pratello. *See Paṭēlā*
Pātuā, river, 129 *n.* 1
Paune. *See Pān*
Pauzecour, 31 *n.* 1
Pavilions, gilt, for state processions in Achin, 310
Pavillion, Paviloen, governor of Pulicat, 52, 66 *n.* 1
Pawn. *See Pān*
Pay, monthly, of soldiers, 4
Pazhavērkkādu. *See* Pulicat
Peachy, Jeremiah, 228 *n.* 2
Peacocks, 220, 220 *n.* 4, 294 *n.* 2 feathers of, worn by *faquīrs*, 22
Pearle, the, frigate, xl
Pearls, from Ceylon, 180 *n.* 6; from Tuticorin, 208 *n.* 5
Pearse, Captain William, commands the *Bengall Merchant*, xl
Pecul, Pecool. *See* Weights and Measures

Pedang, 285 *n.* 3

Peddapalle (Pettipolle, Pettipolee, Nizampatam), xvi, xviii, 4 *n.* 2, 56 *n.* 1, 93 *n.* 1, 100 *n.* 1, 106 *n.* 2; situation of, 53, 55; factory at, 54, 55; first settlement at, 53 *n.* 2; a saltpetre mart, 54; Ambrose Salisbury, chief of, 54; a centre for collection of cotton goods, 54; condition of factory-house at, 54; Streynsham Master's description of, 54; choultry and custom-house at, 54; English garden at, 54; re-settlement of factory at, desired by natives, 54; Dutch factory at, 55; goods manufactured at, 55; resettled, 54 *n.*; ceded to the French, 54 *n.*; restored to the British, 54 *n.*; visited by T. B., 57, 58; provisions plentiful at, 57, 58; weights, measures and coins of, 59, 116; subject to the king of Golconda, 61 *n.* 3; striped stuffs from, exported to Achin, 289

Pedir, kingdom of, 285 *n.* 3

Pedrero, a stone-thrower, 254 *n.* 1

Pedro de Lavera, a Portuguese pilot, 75, 193 *n.* 3

Pedro O Lavera, Liveira. *See* Pedro de Lavera

Pee-Lancrac, assistant to Governor of Junk-Ceylon, 236 *n.* 3

Peepeemont, Governor of Junk-Ceylon, 236 *n.* 3

Pee-Siring, assistant to Governor of Junk-Ceylon, 236 *n.* 3

Pee-Tukerat, assistant to Governor of Junk-Ceylon, 236 *n.* 3

Pegu, xvi, xxii, 61 *n.* 3, 72 *n.* 2, 82 *n.* 1, 236 *n.* 1, 245 *n.* 2, 251 *n.* 1, 271 *n.*, 290, 290 *n.* 8; no description of, by T. B., 234 *n.* 2; wooden fort at, 255 *n.* 6, 276 *n.* 3, 278 *n.* 1; elephants from, 275 *n.* 1; at war with Siam, 276; ships from, frequent Achin, 288

Pegu Jar, 81, 81 *n.* 1, 193 *n.* 1, 216, 290

Pegu Sticklack, 122 *n.* 1

Pelicans, on the Ganges, 211 *n.* 1

Pelock, ? Perak, 267 *n.* 1

Pema Mathi, Hindu wife of Abdullah Qutb Shāh, 113 *n.* 3

Penny, Mrs Frank, her "Fort St George" referred to, 176 *n.* 1

Peons, xxviii, xxxii, 4 *n.* 2, 83, 88 *n.* 3, 207, 224 *n.* 1, 257 *n.* 6; duty of a, 83; number of, entertained for security at Cuttack, 154 *n.* 1

Pepper, 290 *n.* 8, 292, 292 *n.* 1, 320; from Borneo, xxvii; from Tuticorin, 208 *n.* 5; from Kedah, 259 *n.* 2, 276, 283; where grown in Kedah, 276, 277, 277 *n.* 1; from Sumatra, 276 *n.* 6, 292 *n.* 4; black, 277; white, 277; from Indragiri, 295 *n.*, 3

Pepys, Samuel, recommends Capt. J. Bowrey, xxiv

Perak, Perach, liv, 260 *n.* 1, 266 *n.* 3, 275 *n.* 2, 283, 285 *n.* 3, 290; Dutch supremacy at, 252 *n.* 3; tin at, 267 *n.* 1, 280 *n.* 1; money of, 281 *n.* 3; situation of, 283 *n.* 3; Dutch trade with, 283 *n.* 3; subject to Achin, 283 *n.* 3

Peraḳ, silver, 283 *n.* 3

Percall. *See Parkālā*

Perculla. *See Parkālā*

Pergoo. *See* Purgo

Persia, xxxviii, xxxix, l, 1 *n.* 1, 5, 50, 61 *n.* 3, 71, 72 *n.* 2, 91 *n.* 1, 133, 136 *n.* 3, 136 *n.* 4, 221, 245 *n.* 2, 281 *n.* 3, 293; visited by Bowrey, xxvi, 216; Ganges water carried to, 216

Persian Gulf, the, 216 *n.* 6; chart of, by Bowrey, xxviii, l

Persian horses, Shāyista Khān to be presented with, 148 *n.* 5

Persian language, the, 234; the Court language of Asia, 95, 224

Persian Merchant, the, wreck of, 57 *n.* 2

Persians, the, 39 *n.* 4; inhabitants of Masulipatam, 61 *n.* 3; numerous in Golconda, 111 *n.* 1; at Chicacol, 125

Peru, Peruana, xliii, 5

Pescadores, the, l

Peshcush, an obligatory gift, 157, 158, 268, 270, 272; forced from the English and Dutch, by Shāyista Khān, 164; used as a verb, 246

Petapouli. *See* Peddapalle

Petard. *See* Pattarero

Peterraro. *See* Pattarero

Petro Loveyro. *See* Pedro de Lavera

Pettipolle. *See* Peddapalle

Phiddy Cawn. *See* Fidāī Khān

Philippine Is., xxxix; chart of, by Bowrey, xlix

Phirmaund. *See Farmān*

Phirwanna, Phyrwanna. *See Parwāna*

Phrai Narai, king of Siam, 276 *n.* 3

Phuddy Cawne. *See* Fidāī Khān

Phyrmane. *See Farmān*

Phyrmaund, Phyrmand. *See Farmān*
Pican. *See* Coins
Pice. *See* Coins
Picul. *See* Pekul, *s.v.* Weights and Measures
Piece of eight. *See* Ryall, *s.v.* Coins
Pigdan, a spittoon. *See Pīkdān*
Pīkdān, a spittoon, 96 *n.* 2
Pikul. *See* Pecul, *s.v.* Weights and Measures
Pilgrims, maintained at Jagannāth pagoda, 12 *n.* 1; *faquirs* so called, 20
Pilots, apprentice-pilots for the Hugli, xix, 166 *n.* 2; *see also s.vv.* Bateman, Heron, Bowrey; youths unfit for, sent to silk factory at Kasimbazar, 214 *n.* 2
Pineapples, 193 *n.* 2, 221 *n.* 1, 323; at Kedah, 279; illustration of, 285
Pingaree. *See Pinjarī*
Pinjarī, a frame-work, 87
Pintado birds, 9 *n.* 5
Pinto, Ferdinand Mendez, 242 *n.* 3
Pipli, Pipley, Pipeley, 140 *n.* 2, 162 *n.* 3, 179, 225 *n.* 5, 228 *n.* 3; permission for an English factory at, 162 *n.* 2; existence of English factory at questioned, 162 *n.* 2; description of harbour and town of, 162 *n.* 2; Dutch factory at, its prosperity and its desertion, 162 *n.* 2; abandoned by the English for Balasor, 162 *n.* 2; decay of trade at, 162 *n.* 2, 162 *n.* 3; slaves sold at, by Arakaners, 212 *n.* 2
Piplo. *See* Pipli
Pirah. *See* Perak
Pirates. *See s.v.* Arakaners, Saletars
Piscash. *See Peshcush*
Pison, river, identity of the Ganges with, 166 *n.* 1
Pitch. *See* Dammer
Pitt, John, 140 *n.* 2
Pitt, Thomas, 106 *n.* 2, 124 *n.* 3; Vincent associated with, 164 *n.* 4
Placide, his map of Mergui Archipelago referred to, 235 *n.* 1
Plantain tree, Plane tree, Plantree, 245, 247, 248, 274, 274 *n.* 2, 323; food of elephants during transport, 73; Dampier's description of a, 245 *n.* 4; illustration of a, 250
Plou. *See* Areca
Poddār, 164 *n.* 4
Point de Gala, Point de Gaul. *See* Point de Galle
Point de Galle, 75, 75 *n.* 3, 181, 181 *n.* 1; trade at, 181 *n.* 1
Policat, Poliacatte. *See* Pulicat
Policherry. *See* Pondicherry
Pollam. *See Kobang, s.v.* Coins
Pollicull. *See* Palakollu
Polo Gomos. *See* Pulo Gomez
Pomegranate, 322 *n.* 8
Pommelo. *See* Pumplemoos
Pond, Pome. *See Paṇ, s.v.* Weights and Measures
Pondicherry, 257; settlement at, by the French, 66 *n.* 1, 257 *n.* 6; various spellings of, 257 *n.* 6; description of French factory at, 257 *n.* 6
Pondy, Pondee, 124, 124 *n.* 1
Pone. *See Paṇ, s.v.* Weights and Measures
Poolicat. *See* Pulicat
Pooloo. *See* Pulo
Poot. *See Patah*
Popra Harbour, 236 *n.* 1
Porca, Porgo. *See* Purgo
Pore. *See Pahr, s.v.* Weights and Measures
Porgo. *See* Purgo
Porka, Porkoe. *See* Purgo
Porpoises, in the Ganges, 211 *n.* 1
Portingal. *See* Portuguese
Portman, John, 266 *n.* 3; appointed second at Kedah, 268; his report of Kedah trade, 268; his death, 268
Porto Novo, xxviii–xxx, xxxiii, xxxv, xxxviii, 82, 123 *n.* 2, 257, 257 *n.* 6, 263 *n.* 1, 269; description of, 82 *n.* 1; proposed Dutch settlement at, 82 *n.* 1; proposed English settlement at, 82 *n.* 1; coins current at, 115
Portugall Priests. *See* Padres
Portugals, the, Portuguese half-breeds, 3 *n.* 4, 209 *n.* 2; ships of, frequent the port of Achin, xxii; settlement of, in Fort St George, 3, 3 *n.* 5; subjection of, to the English, 3; serve as soldiers to the East India Company, 4; refugees, numerous in Golconda, 111 *n.* 1; merchants of, their trade in Bengal, 132 *n.* 3, 133, 133 *n.* 2; their settlement called Feringhi Dibba, 140 *n.* 4; at Goa, called Frangues, Fringuins, Reiñoes, 140 *n.* 4; driven from Hijili, 162 *n.* 3; their houses at Balasor, 162 *n.* 3; number of, in Bengal, 191; in Bengal, their poverty and industry, 192, 192 *n.* 1; soldiers in the Mogol's army, 192 *n.* 1; many of them sailors, in Bengal, 193; makers of

sweetmeats, 193 *n.* 2; duties paid by, and privileges of, in Bengal, 194; erection of new church by, stopped, 194, 195; one killed by a tiger, 220; ship of, taken by Malay pirates, 264; sold as slaves at Kedah, 264, 265; escape to Malacca, 264; in Achin, 286 *n.* 1, 293 *n.* 2

Portuguese, the, formerly possessed Negapatam, 2; their monopoly of trade with the Molucca Is., 5; St Thomé taken from them by the Moors, 38 *n.* 4, 45 *n.* 1; priests of, 41, 41 *n.* 3; former extent of power in India of, 82 *n.* 1; their conquests in the Deccan, 135 *n.* 5; shipwreck of a, near Patani, 242 *n.* 3; their settlement at Junk-Ceylon, 245 *n.* 2; cannon taken from them, at Achin, 312 *n.* 2

Povey, Mistress, jilts John Jearsey, 90 *n.* 1

Prau, a boat, xxii, 238, 251, 251 *n.* 2, 262 *n.* 7, 264, 266 *n.* 3, 282, 283, 288, 290 *n.* 8, 291; definition of, 238 *n.* 2; several for war to be built at Junk-Ceylon, 253; a flying, 301, 301 *n.* 1; illustration of a, 314

Praw. *See Prau*

"**Premier Livre** de l'Histoire de la Navigation aux Indes Orientales" referred to, 192 *n.* 4, 193 *n.* 1, 247 *n.* 5

President, the, 158 *n.* 3; log of, referred to, 12 *n.* 1

Prévost, A. F., his "Histoire Générale des Voyages" referred to, 228 *n.* 1, 228 *n.* 5, 230 *n.* 2, 231 *n.* 1, 255 *n.* 6, 257 *n.* 6, 290 *n.* 6

Priaman, Priamon, liv, 285 *n.* 3, 319; *rājā* of, his power, 295; dependent on Achin, 295 *n.* 4; pepper, a product of, 295 *n.* 4

Prickman, Mr, 173 *n.* 1

Priests, French and Portuguese. *See s. v.* Padres

Princess, the, sloop, 140 *n.* 2

Pringle, A. T., his "Selections from the Consultations at Fort St George" referred to, 25 *n.* 3, 36 *n.* 3, 42 *n.* 1, 45 *n.*, *passim*

Printed calico. *See* Paintings

Proby, Mr, 72 *n.* 1

Proe, Prow. *See Prau*

Pryaman. *See* Priaman

Puckle, Major William, Company's supervisor, 3 *n.* 5, 57 *n.* 2, 88 *n.* 3, 159; his opinion regarding Madapollam factory, 100 *n.* 1; his decision in Clavell's favour, 159; his "Diary" referred to, 320

Pudicherry, Pudycherry. *See* Pondicherry

Puglah Lemah Bunder, visit of the English to, 268, 302 *n.* 4

Puhur. *See Pahr*

Puket. *See* Tonkah Harbour

Pulicat (Paliacatte, Pullicatt, Policat, Poolicat, Paliyāghāt, Pazhavērkkādu), xvi, 42 *n.* 1, 45 *n.* 1, 53 *n.* 1, 57; a garrisoned town of the Dutch, 51; T. B.'s description of, 51, 53; Schouten's description of, 51 *n.* 4; Hamilton's description of, 52; Thevenot's description of, 52; governors of, 52; Dutch factory at, 52; saltpetre refined at, 52; gunpowder made at, 52; taken from the Dutch, 52; surrendered to Great Britain, 52; coins current at, 115

Pullambam. *See* Palimbam

Pullicherrie. *See* Pondicherry

Pullo Ladda. *See* Pulo Ladda

Pullo Sambelon. *See* Pulo Sambilong

Pullo Way, Pullo-wey. *See* Pulo Way

Pulo, *Pulau*, an island, 235 *n.* 1, 277, 277 *n.* 1

Pulo Gomez, 286 *n.* 3, 287 *n.* 2; its situation, 287, 287 *n.* 4; a criminal station, 287, 287 *n.* 5

Pulo Ladda, pepper island, liii; its situation, 277, 277 *n.* 1

Pulo Pinang, liv

Pulo Sambilong, 238, 238 *n.* 1

Pulo Wary. *See* Pulo Way

Pulo Way, island, 287; its situation, 287 *n.* 3; a criminal station, 287, 287 *n.* 3, 287 *n.* 5, 314 *n.* 4, 315 *n.* 2; three islands of the name, 287 *n.* 3

Pumpelmouce. *See* Pumplemoos

Pumpkin (calabash), 247, 247 *n.* 7, 323 *n.* 7

Pumplemoos, Poomplemous, 87 *n.* 2, 247 *n.* 5, 324; Portuguese term for, 247 *n.* 5; description of, 324 *n.* 1

Pumple-nose. *See* Pumplemoos

Punch, *pānch*, paunch, 78 *n.* 2

Pune. *See Peon*

Punishments, at Achin, 314–317

Punto De Gali. *See* Point de Galle

Puquet. *See* Tonkah Harbour

Purchas, Rev. Samuel, 295 *n.* 6

Purgo, a boat, 43 *n.* 1, 225 *n.* 5; where and for what used, 228; probable derivation of, 228 *n.* 2; illustration of, 228

Purgo-man, Porgo-man, 196 *n.* 4, 228 *n.* 2
Purles, 277 *n.* 1
Putom, Puton Harbour, 239 *n.* 1, 250 *n.* 2
Putta. *See Patah, s.v.* Coins
Pyplo. *See* Pipli
Pythagorean philosophy, followed by the Brahmins, 28, 205 *n.* 2

Qāzī, judge, 118 *n.* 1
Qualla, Quala. *See Kuwāla*
Queda, Quedah. *See* Kedah
Quenoy, island, l
Quicksilver, 232, 232 *n.* 3
Quida. *See* Kedah
Qutb Shāh, king of Golconda, 108 *n.* 7
Qutb Shāhī, the, dynasty of, 88 *n.* 2, 113 *n.* 1; rise of, 109 *n.* 1, 111 *n.* 5
Qutb Shāhī family, the, rebel against Akbar, 109; found the kingdom of Golconda, 109

Raccaners. *See* Arakaners
Radish *āchār*, 193 *n.* 1
Radja. *See Rājā*
Radja Mehal. *See* Rājmahāl
Rage Maull. *See* Rājmahāl
Raghū the *poddār*, 32 *n.* 2; Vincent accused of causing his death, 164 *n.* 4
Raia, Raiah. *See Rājā*
Rainbow, the, xxvi; mistakes her course, 3 *n.* 2
Rājā (Radja), xvii, 39, 83 *n.* 5, 108, 130, 190 *n.* 3, 221 *n.* 5, 299 *n.* 2; of the Jagannāth district, 12 *n.* 1; position of a, in 17th century, 39 *n.* 2; of Harsapur, 129 *n.* 1; of Junk-Ceylon, 236; of Junk-Ceylon, his reception of foreigners, 244–246; of Junk-Ceylon, his command to have war *praus* built, 254; a Muhammadan appointed as, in Junk-Ceylon, 255; of Junk-Ceylon, killed in insurrection, 257; power of the, in Sumatra, 295; of Indragiri, 295 *n.* 3
Rajahpoot. *See Rājpūt*
Rājārām, Clement Jordan's accounts with, 178 *n.* 1
Rājmahāl, 148, 148 *n.* 5, 211 *n.* 1, 226 *n.* 2, 249 *n.* 1; ancient capital of Bengal, 143; former trade at, 143 *n.* 2; Tavernier's description of, 143 *n.* 2; Muhammad A'zīm received at, 147; Vincent visits Muhammad A'zīm at, 164, 165
Rājpūt (rashboot, raspoute, rashpoote, respoute, rashwa, rasbout, raggibout), xvii, 19, 27 *n.* 1, 83, 83 *n.* 5, 119, 148 *n.* 5; caste, the, supposed valour but real cowardice of, 84
Rakan. *See* Arakan
Rakshaso, 119 *n.* 1
Ram, a Ḥindu god, 7 *n.* 2
Ramall. *See Rūmāl*
Ramapatam, 36 *n.* 3
Ramazan. *See Ramzān*
Rambotang. *See Rambūtan*
Rambūtan, 323; description of, 323 *n.* 1
Ramchandrapore, 220 *n.* 4
Ramdam. *See Ramzān*
Ramilldey, road of (Masulipatam), 72 *n.* 1
Rammal, Roomaul, Romall, Rohamall. *See Rūmāl*
Ramsden, George, 124 *n.* 3; chief at Gingerly (Vizagapatam), 123 *n.* 2, 178 *n.* 1
Ramzān, a moveable fast of the Muhammadans, 96, 96 *n.* 1; strict observance of, 96 *n.* 1
Rangoes. *See* Dringo Root
Rangoon, Chulias at, 256 *n.* 1
Rangoon oil, where brought from, 192 *n.* 4
Rashboot, raspoute. *See Rājpūt*
Rashīd Khān, 154 *n.* 1; *nawāb* of Cuttack, 152 *n.* 4; his character, 152 *n.* 4; his *parwāna*, 152 *n.* 4
Ratipore, mountains, 131 *n.* 7
Rattans, 74, 281 *n.* 4, 292; used for building houses at Junk-Ceylon, 250; Mandelslo's error about, 250 *n.* 1; houses at Kedah built of, 277, 277 *n.* 4; cables of, 292 *n.* 5
Raye. *See Rājā*
Raymond, Captain Hugh, trustee to Mary Bowrey's will, xlvi; commander of the *Duchess* and *Bouverie*, xlvii
Ray Nundeloll, his death, 201 *n.* 1
Read, Thomas, a dyer, 178 *n.* 3
Reade, Edward, 75 *n.* 1, 104 *n.* 1, 124 *n.* 3, 158 *n.* 3, 208 *n.* 4
Real. *See* Ryall, *s.v.* Coins
Rebecca, the, 166 *n.* 2
Rebré, Captain De, under De la Haye, 46 *n.* 4
Red Sea, 103, 223
Reiñoe. *See* Firinghee
Religion of "Mallabars and Gentues," 6, 14, 15, 18
Rennell, Major J., his map of the Hugli estuary referred to, 209 *n.* 2
Resbute. *See Rājpūt*

Resora (Jagannāth), 12 *n.* 1
Rezwar, 88 *n.* 3
Rhamnus Jujuba. *See Zizyphus Jujuba*
Rhinoceros, 279 *n.* 5; figures of, in pagodas, 6; figures of, carved on the chariot of Jagannāth, 17; hide of the, used for roundels, 85; the, infest swamps of the Ganges, 199, 211 *n.* 3; the, in woods at Patna, 222; illustration of a, 222; De Graaf's description of a, 222 *n.* 2; the, an enemy of the elephant, 223, 223 *n.* 1
Rhumall, Rhumaul. *See Rūmāl*
Rice, 20, 181, 221 *n.* 1, 289 *n.* 5, 290, 290 *n.* 10, 304, 320, 322 *n.* 6; chief food of Gentues and Malabars, 97; trade in, on the Gingalee Coast, 121 *n.* 2; from Bimlipatam, 122 *n.* 1; from Waltair, 123 *n.* 4; exported from Bengal, 132, 132 *n.* 7; price of, during the famine in Patna, 226, 226 *n.* 2; a good sort of, at Junk-Ceylon, 246; plentiful at Kedah, 279, 279 *n.* 3; sold by the bamboo at Achin, 282 *n.* 1; imported to Achin, 289, 289 *n.* 1, 291; cultivated at Achin by slaves, 294 *n.* 3
Richard and Martha, the, 262 *n.* 2
Richards, John, 230 *n.* 6
Rickits, Mr, an acquaintance of P. Briggins and T. Bowrey, xlii
Riclof, General. *See* Goens, Ricklof van
Ringo Root. *See* Dringo Root
Rio de Plata, xliii
Risley, H. H., his "Tribes and Castes of Bengal" referred to, 87 *n.* 2
Robbery, frequent at Achin, 317, 317 *n.* 2
Robert, his map of the Mergui Archipelago referred to, 235 *n.* 1
Rochester, the, ship, xli
Roe ketch, the, xxv
Rogermundrum, 88 *n.* 3
Rogiram. *See* Rājārām
Rogues Island, 209 *n.* 2
Rogues River, 199 *n.* 2, 209 *n.* 2; why so called, 212 *n.* 2
Rojimall, Rojamaul. *See* Rājmahāl
Rolt, Thomas, chief of the English factory at Gombroon, 216 *n.* 6
Romall, Rummaul. *See Rūmāl*
Rondell. *See* Roundel
Rosewater, 303; a mark of honour, 308
Rossey, Captain, xlii
Rottang. *See* Rattan
Roundel, 83; description of, 85; illustration of, 86; regulations as to carrying a, 85 *n.* 1; restrictions as to its use, 86, 86 *n.* 1
Roundel-boy. *See* Roundellier
Roundellier, umbrella-carrier, 85, 85 *n.* 3, 86 *n.* 1
Round Point, at Fort St George, 42 *n.* 1
Royal. *See* Coins
Royall James, the, xxv
Ruby, the, William Jearsey's ship, 251 *n.* 1
Rucca. *See Ruḳ'a*
Rugo Podar. *See* Raghū, the *poddār*
Ruḳ'a, note, written document, 263 *n.* 1
"**Rulers of India Series**," references to, 11 *n.*, 18 *n.*
Rūmāl, kerchief, 54, 231, 231 *n.* 3, 290, 290 *n.* 5; made at Bengal, 133 *n.* 5; silk, 133 *n.* 4; cotton, 133 *n.* 4
Rumphius, G. E., his "Herbarium Amboinense" referred to, 192 *n.* 4, 247 *n.* 5, 323 *n.* 8, 324 *n.* 1
Rupee. *See* Coins
Rupnarain, river, 173 *n.* 1, 174 *n.* 2
Russell, John, xlv
Ruzzeed Chaan, Russeed Cawne, Ruzzard Chaan. *See* Rashīd Khān
Ryall, Royal. *See* Coins
Ryalls of eight, exchanged for tin, 246

Sadrispatnam, 45 *n.* 1
Safī Khān, *nawāb* of Cuttack, 152 *n.* 4, 182 *n.* 3
Safshikan Khān, *nawāb* of Cuttack, 152 *n.* 4
Sagar, island, Mela held at, 203 *n.* 1, 209 *n.* 2; accounted sacred, 211 *n.* 3
St George, the, formerly the *Sancta Cruz*, 172 *n.* 3
St Helena, 9 *n.* 4, 91 *n.* 1
St Lawrence, French viceroy buried at, 65 *n.* 2
St Margaret, church of, xliv *n.* 1, xlv *n.* 1
St Mary, the, 263 *n.* 1
St Mary Magdalen, church of, xli
St Thomas, 44; martyrdom of, 45 *n.* 1; stories concerning, 45 *n.* 1, 50; Christians of, victims to elephantiasis, 50 *n.* 2
St Thomas's Mount, xvi, 44; reverence of Christians for, 45; church on, much resorted to, 45; a sanatorium, 45 *n.*; gardens at, 46; famous for the Arbor Triste, 49

St Thomas' Point, at Fort St George, 42 *n.* 1, 90 *n.* 1
St Thomay. *See* St Thomé
St Thomé, 38, 38 *n.* 4, 52, 53 *n.* 1, 66 *n.* 1, 257 *n.* 6; retaken from the Portuguese by the Moors, 38 *n.* 4; description of, 45 *n.* 1, 64, 65; manufactures at, 45 *n.*, 61 *n.* 3; fortifications of, 45 *n.*; churches at, 45 *n.*; taking of, by the French, 46 *n.* 4, 47, 48 *n.*, 65, 90 *n.* 1; water at, suitable for dyeing cotton goods, 45 *n.* 1; *hawaldār* of, 51 *n.* 1; De la Haye escapes to, with the *Great Breton*, 68, 68 *n.* 2
Saiva temple, at Trivettore, 8 *n.* 1
Saiyyid. *See* Seedy
Sāl, timber, 228 *n.* 5
Salaam, 207, 207 *n.* 2; used as a verb, 38; of ships, at Dacca, 163, 163 *n.* 2
Salamma. *See* Salaam
Salampore, chintz, 55, 246, 246 *n.* 5, 289 *n.* 4; fine, 55 *n.* 2, 71 *n.* 3; ordinary, 71 *n.* 3; blue and white, 289
Salam Salamband, omitted in king of Golconda's *farmān*, 93 *n.* 1
Salang, meanings of, 235 *n.* 1
Salanga, Salange. *See* Junk-Ceylon
Salang Head. *See* Ujung Salang
Sālat, a strait, 237 *n.* 2
Salatinge, 29
Salayer, I. of, xlix
Saleeters. *See* Saletars
Salempoory, Salamporee. *See* Salampore
Saletar, a creek at Singapore, 237 *n.* 2
Saletars, pirates, 240 *n.* 1; description of, 237, 237 *n.* 2, 238; their identity with the Cellates discussed, 237 *n.* 2; derivation of the word, 237 *n.* 2; the modern, 237 *n.* 2; at Kedah, seize an English ship, 262
Saletes. *See* Saletars
Salisbury, Ambrose, chief at Peddapalle, 4 *n.* 2, 54, 218 *n.* 1; acquainted with Bowrey, xviii; visited by T. B., 57, 58; career of, while in India, 57 *n.* 2; accusations against, 57 *n.* 2; discharged by the Court, 57 *n.* 2; re-admitted to the Company's service, 57 *n.* 2; death of, at Madapollam, 57 *n.* 2
Salisbury, Susannah, mother of Ambrose Salisbury, 57 *n.* 2
Sall. *See Sāl*
Salleiters. *See* Saletars
Salleta de Brew, 237 *n.* 2
Sally, the, sloop, 176 *n.* 1
Salt, 225; at Peddapalle, 56; the king's monopoly, 56, 56 *n.* 2, 57; making of, an occupation of the Uriyas, 199, 199 *n.* 2; exported from Kedah, 283
Saltpetre, 181 *n.* 9, 188 *n.* 1, 289 *n.* 5; plentiful at Peddapalle, 54, 56; godowns for, at Fort St George, 90 *n.* 1; exported from Golconda, 111; stoppage of boats laden with, 148 *n.* 5, 164; largely exported from Bengal, 164 *n.* 1; warehouse for, built on old Factory ground at Hugli, 170 *n.* 3, 171 *n.* 4; contracted for, 222 *n.* 1; quantity of, provided at Patna, 224 *n.* 1; exported by the English and Dutch from Patna, 225, 229, 229 *n.* 2; how sent to Hugli, 225, 228 *n.* 5, 229; orders from the Court as to export of, 229 *n.* 2
Salt river, li
Sālū. *See Sanahs*
Sāmāca. *See* Pumplemoos
Sāmangko, the water-melon, 248 *n.* 1
Sambilan, nine, 238 *n.* 1
Samboa. *See* Pumplemoos
Sambrooke, Jeremy, 64 *n.* 1
Sam Cau, Samaca, a fruit, 247, 324 *n.* 1; its identity with the pumplemoos or water-melon discussed, 247 *n.* 5, 248 *n.* 1; illustration of the, 250. *See also s.v.* Pumplemoos
Sampson, the, 91 *n.* 1
Sanahs, 133 *n.* 4, 231; Harsapur, 129 *n.* 1; Mohunpur, 129 *n.* 1; Sura, 129 *n.* 1; definition of, 231 *n.* 1; not saleable in England, 231 *n.* 1; present designation of, 231 *n.* 1
Sancta Cruz, the, xix, xxvi, 123 *n.* 2, 178 *n.* 1; commanded by T. B., 172; owned by Portuguese, 172 *n.* 3; taken as a prize, 172 *n.* 3; rechristened the *St George*, 172 *n.* 3; later mentions of, 172 *n.* 3; called a "Dutch flyboate" by Streynsham Master, 178 *n.* 3
Sanctuary, at Golconda tombs, 113, 114, 114 *n.* 1
Sandri, a wood, 210 *n.* 1
Sangarie, a gun-boat, 55 *n.* 1
Sankha. *See* Chank
Sannoes, Sannis. *See Sanahs*
Santa Cruise, the. *See Sancta Cruz*, the
Santamay. *See* St Thomé
Santapore, 230 *n.* 6

Sapphires, from Borneo, 291
Saracen law-giver, *i.e.* Muhammad, 94
Saracens, the, 180 *n.* 6
Sarāī, an inn, 117 *n.* 2
Sarajah Cawn. *See* Surāj Khān
Sarkīl, a chamberlain, 88 *n.* 3
Sarlashkar, *Sar-i-Lashkar*, head of the forces, 107 *n.* 1, 125 *n.* 1; of Gingalee, his power and state, 125; of Golconda, besieged, 125 *n.* 1
Sarsamutt, 88 *n.* 3
Sash (turban), 230, 230 *n.* 5
Satagam, former name of Hugli, 167 *n.* 3
Satī, xviii, 14; general description of, 36; one seen by the author at Karedu, 37, 38; at the funeral of a Naik at St Thomé, 39; discountenanced by Muhammadan governors, 39; two stories of, 40; victim of, rescued, 40; illustration of, 86; description of two victims of, at Hugli, 204; practised on coasts of Coromandel and Gingalee, and in Bengal, 203
Satyrs, figures of, in pagodas, 6; figures of, carved on the chariot of Jagannāth, 17
Saugor, Sago, Sagor Island. *See* Sagar I.
Sautguary, river, 176 *n.* 1
Sawcer, Lawrence, 46 *n.* 4; accuses Langhorne of assisting the French, 48 *n.*
Sayon, Mr, 96 *n.* 2
Saysummit-Tahadar, the, 54
Scall gate, the, 93 *n.* 1
Scarlet, 88 *n.* 3, 207 *n.* 1, 218 *n.* 1, 232, 232 *n.* 2, 275 *n.* 3, 289 *n.* 8; presented to the *nawāb* of Orissa, 160; meaning of, 160 *n.* 3; imported to Achin, 289
Scattergood, Mr, 54
Schouten, Walter, "Travels" of, references to, 3 *n.*, 12 *n.*, 20 *n.*, 30 *n.*, 33 *n.*, 43 *n.*, 45 *n.*, 49 *n.*, 50 *n.*, *passim*
Scinde, province of, 136 *n.* 4
Scissors, imported to Junk-Ceylon, 246, to Achin, 289
Scopeboard, scupper, 103
Screetore, scrittore. *See* Escritoire
Sear. *See* Seer, *s.v.* Weights and Measures
Seedy, 314, 314 *n.* 2
Seer. *See* Weights and Measures
Segogora, 129 *n.* 1
Seid. *See* Seedy
Seir Lascar, Sr. Laskare. *See Sarlashkar*
Sekander muda, king of Achin, 296 *n.* 1
Selat, the Straits, 237 *n.* 2
Selebes. *See* Celebes
Selimony, the, junk, 269
Sembah, a salutation, 307
Serampore, Danish factory at, 190 *n.* 3
Serkell. *See Sarkīl*
Ser Lascar, Seer Lascar, Sier Lascar. *See Sarlashkar*
Serpents, the cause of an eclipse, 34; trained to dance, 59, 60, 60 *n.* 1; a means of putting criminals to death, 60; on the shores of the Ganges, 211 *n.* 3
Ser Rajah Chawn. *See* Surāj Khān
Sevagi. *See* Sivāji
Seymour, the, 172 *n.* 2
Shabandand. *See Shāhbandar*
Sha bendar, Shabunder. *See Shāhbandar*
Shaddock, gardens, at Palakollu, 105 *n.* 2. *See also s.v.* Pumplemoos
Shāh Abās of Persia, 114 *n.* 8
Shāhbandar, harbour-master, 64 *n.* 1, 88 *n.* 3, 242, 244, 254, 255, 256, 260, 299, 301, 303; of Masulipatam, 81 *n.* 2; his position in the Malay States, 242 *n.* 3; of Banquala, 246; of Kedah, 262, 283; of Achin, 299 *n.* 5, 302 *n.* 1, 303 *n.* 3, 307 *n.* 4
Shah-hest-Kan. *See* Shāyista Khān
Shāh Hossain, a cry of the *Muharram* festival, 119 *n.* 1
Shāh Jahān, 18 *n.* 2, 108 *n.* 7; his treatment of the Hindus, 10 *n.* 5; his four sons rebellious, 135; divides his territory among his sons, 135, 136; his seizure and imprisonment by Aurangzēb, 137; his favourite wife, 145 *n.* 6; *farmān* of, 165 *n.* 2
Shāh Shujā', son of Shāh Jahān, 152 *n.* 4; governor of Bengal, 135, 138; gives Boughton leave to establish a factory at Pipli, 162 *n.* 2; excellence of his army, 138; betrayal and conquest of, 138, 139; flight of, 139; succoured by the king of Arakan, 139, 140; takes refuge in Arakan, 141; his wives and treasure, 141; refuses his daughter to the king of Arakan,

141; two stories of his end, 141, 142
"Shaista Khany," a style of building, 150 *n.* 1
Shanck. *See* Chank
Sharlasker. *See Sarlashkar*
Sharoff (broker). *See* Shroff
Shash. *See* Sash
Shaster Caun. *See* Shāyista Khān
Shatta Cawne. *See* Shāyista Khān
Shāyista Khān, 151 *n.* 3, 159, 190 *n.* 3, 232 *n.* 2; uncle of Aurangzēb, 145; his parentage, 145; made *nawāb* of Bengal, 145, 145 *n.* 5; his riches and insolence, 146, 146 *n.* 2, 147, 148; his conduct towards Aurangzēb, 146, 146 *n.* 1; complaints of his exactions, 146 *n.* 4, 158 *n.* 3; his recall from Bengal, 147; his wealth procures his pardon, 148; various reports as to his recall, 148 *n.* 5; his presents to Aurangzēb, 148 *n.* 5; his immediate successor, 164 *n.* 2; appointed governor of Agra, 148 *n.* 5; reappointed *nawāb* of Bengal, 148 *n.* 5; resigns his government, 148 *n.* 5; dies at Agra, 148 *n.* 5; public buildings at Dacca erected during his rule, 150 *n.* 1; his means to ascertain the wealth of Hindu merchants, 157; his *parwāna* to Walter Clavell, 158 *n.* 3; exacts an annual tribute of ships from the natives, 161–163; stops goods, and forces a *peshcush* from English and Dutch, 164; illness of, at Dacca, 185 *n.* 1; the Danes referred to, 189
Sheake Ahmud, 125 *n.* 1
Sheba, Queen of, 295 *n.* 6
Sheckdarr. *See Shiqdar*
Shelaheth. *See* Saletars
Shepheard, Mr, a Director of the E. I. Co., xlii
Sheraff. *See* Shroff
Sherman, Samuel, pilot in the Company's service, 175 *n.* 1
Shipbuilding, carried on at Narsapur, 99
Ships, how repaired at Madapollam, 103, 104; illustration of fixing ship's gear, 104; rigging for, made at Madapollam, 105. *See also s.v.* Adam and Eve; Adventure; Advice; Amoy Merchant; Anne; Antelope; Arrival; Beaufort; Blackmoor; Borneo Merchant; Bouverie; Ceaser; Charles; Conimeer; Constant Warwick; Death; Defence; Degrave; Diamond; Dilligence; Dispatch; Drake; Duchess; Eagle; Eaglet; East India Merchant; European; Falcon; Frances; Ganges; George; Globe; Good Hope; Great Breton; Great Fleming; Greyhound; Hope; Hunter; Indulgence; King George; Loyall Adventure; Loyall Merchant; Loyall Subject; Lancaster; Madras; Madras Merchant; Margery; Martin; Massenburd; Mayflower; Nonsuch; Nugdy; Pearle; Persian Merchant; President; Princess; Rainbow; Rebecca; Richard and Martha; Rochester; Roe; Royall James; Ruby; St George; St Mary; Sally; Sampson; Sancta Cruz; Selimony; Seymour; Shrewsbury; Smirna Merchant; Society; Swiftsure; Thomas; Triplicane; Unicorne; Unity; Vine
Shiqdar, revenue-officer, 184 *n.* 1
Shoutens, William, xlix
Shrewsbury, the, xxix
Shroff (*Ṣarrāf*), broker, 24 *n.* 2, 77, 77 *n.* 2
Siam, Syam, xxii, 91 *n.* 1, 115 *n.* 4, 180, 258, 290; ambassador from, at Achin, xxxviii; at war with Golconda, 172 *n.* 3; Junk-Ceylon, subordinate to, 236, 236 *n.* 3; description of houses at, 277 *n.* 5; natural defences of, 278 *n.* 1; few fortresses in, 278 *n.* 1; ships from, frequent Achin, 288; trade of, 290 *n.* 10
Siam, king of, his *farmān* necessary for trade, customs free, in Junk-Ceylon, 244; his elephants and bodyguard attend foreigners to Luppoone, 243; incensed against the Dutch, 253, 254 *n.* 4; his orders for building war *praus* at Junk-Ceylon, 253, 254; appoints a new *rājā* in Junk-Ceylon, 255; Kedah tributary to the, 275; gold flower paid annually to the, 275, 275 *n.* 3; sends a *terah* and present to king of Kedah, 276; his war with Pegu, 276; his fort on the Pegu frontier, 278 *n.* 1
Siamese, Siamers, Syamers, the, xxxix, 255, 256; at war with the English, xxxviii; their character, 236; description of, 236 *n.* 4, 237 *n.* 1; unite with the Malayars in insurrection at Junk-Ceylon, 257; ships of, come on a warlike expedition to Kedah, 266 *n.* 3
Sicca Anna. *See* Coins
Siccacul, Sicocol. *See* Chicacol

Siddy. *See* Seedy
Silk, 181, 272, 292 *n.* 2, 303 *n.* 3; skill of the Gentues in working in, 9; quantity of, produced in Bengal, 132 *n.* 3, 133, 133 *n.* 4, 133 *n.* 6; from Bengal, the best in India, 133 *n.* 6; sold at Hugli, 168 *n.* 2; from Kasimbazar, 213 *n.* 2; dyeing of, 214, 214 *n.* 2; orgazine, 214 *n.* 2; tram, 214 *n.* 2; raw and wrought, 230; imported to Achin, 289 *n.* 1; striped, 291; flowered, 291
Sillebar, 178 *n.* 1
Sincapura. *See* Singapore
Sindy, islands, 292 *n.* 2
Singapore, island, 237 *n.* 2, 258 *n.* 4
Singapore, Straits of, 237 *n.* 2; Bowrey's Chart of, xlix
Singie, near Patna, 226 *n.* 2; English factory house at, 224 *n.* 1; advantages of its situation, 224 *n.* 1
Singora, 266 *n.* 1
Sīpī chunam, shell-lime, 305 *n.* 1
Siriam, factory at, 251 *n.* 1
Sivāji, 82 *n.* 1
Slavery, in liquidation of debt, 284, 284 *n.* 1
Slaves, 290; cheapness of, during Patna famine, 226 *n.* 2; a Portuguese crew sold as, 264; exported from Bengal, 290, from Borneo, 291; at Achin, 294 *n.* 3
Smirna Merchant, the, 200 *n.* 1
Smith, Anthony, soldier and dyer in the Company's service, 214 *n.* 2
Smith, Henry, his connection with Bowrey's Dictionary, lvi
Smith, Jacob, 66 *n.* 1
Smith, John, chief at Dacca, 150 *n.* 2
Smith, John, Jordan and Bugden sail for Kedah with, 178 *n.* 1; goes to the "South Seas," 178 *n.* 1; murdered by his men, 178 *n.* 1, 264 *n.* 7; a freeman, 272 *n.* 4
Smithson, Richard, 64 *n.* 1; complains of Salisbury's irregularities, 57 *n.* 2
Smyth, W. H., his "Sailors' Word Book" referred to, 42 *n.* 2
Snake-town. *See* Negapatam
Soap, imported to Junk-Ceylon, 246
Society, the, 158 *n.* 3
Soligues, pointed javelins, 237 *n.* 2
Solla, 271; residence of the king of Kedah, 259, 264; present designation of, 259 *n.* 4; its situation, 259 *n.* 4; flight of the "old king" from, 276
Solomon, King, 294 *n.* 2
Som, orange, 247 *n.* 5
Sombrero, an umbrella, 85, 85 *n.* 4
Sombrero (or Chowra), an island in the Nicobars, 68 *n.* 3
Sombresse. *See* Sombrero Island
Somerset House, wills at referred to, xx, xliv *n.* 2, 158 *n.* 3; administration books at referred to, xxiv, xxv
Som-kiou-wang, a small orange, 247 *n.* 5
Songkhla, 260 *n.* 1
Sonnerat, his "Voyages" referred to, 202 *n.* 1
Soum-keou, crystal orange, 247 *n.* 5
South Sea Company, the, xvii; MSS. bequeathed to by Thos. Bowrey, xxiii, xli, xliv; Bowrey's proposal to, xliii; stock of, held by Mary Bowrey, xlvi
South Seas, the (East Indian Islands), xxii, li, lii, 1, 4, 5, 57, 71, 133, 178 *n.* 1, 188, 188 *n.* 1, 276, 280, 282 *n.* 1, 286, 293, 293 *n.* 1, 305, 323; propriety of a settlement at debated, xlii; trade of the, 188 *n.* 1
South Seas, the, *i.e.* the coast of South America, 241 *n.* 4; Bowrey's proposal for a port of refreshment in, xliii
South Tartaria, 172, 211; Mīr Jumla's intended invasion of, 144
Spanish dollars. *See* Ryall, *s.v.* Coins
Speek, ? spike, 102
Spelter. *See* Tootnague
Spices, 292 *n.* 2
Sports, at Achin, 310; forbidden during public mourning, 312
Spulshore, 74; derivation of, 74 *n.* 1
Squire, Mr, part owner of the *Loyall Subject*, 90 *n.* 1
Srikākulam, pop. Chicacol, 124 *n.* 3
Ṣrī-lōhita. *See* Saletars
Stafford, Captain, brings the *Falcon* up the Hugli, 166 *n.* 2
Stanley, Mr, 173 *n.* 1, 218 *n.* 10
State ride, of English merchants through Achin, 308, 309, 310; of the Queen of Achin, 324, 325, 325 *n.* 2, 326
Stebunheath. *See* Stepney
Steel, 240, 246; imported to Achin, 291
Steelyard, *patah* weighed by the, 241. *See* Weights and Measures
Stepney, xxv, xlii, xliii, xliv, xlv, xlvi, xlvii

Stevens, Robert, his "Guide to East India Trade" referred to, 192 *n.* 4
Stewart, Major C., his "History of Bengal" referred to, 144 *n.* 5, 145 *n.* 5, 146 *n.* 1, 148 *n.* 5, 162 *n.* 2, 164 *n.* 2, 233 *n.* 2
Sticklack, 122 *n.* 1, 290; exported from Bengal, 132 *n.* 7
Stilliard. *See* Steelyard, *s.v.* Weights and Measures
Stilts, houses at Achin built on, 321, 322
Stockings, cotton, exported from Pulicat, 52; made by the Portuguese, at Hugli, 192
Striped cloth, muslin, silk, 123 *n.* 2, 230, 230 *n.* 6, 246, 288 *n.* 6, 289, 289 *n.* 6, 291; the Gentues excel in the manufacture of, 10
Studds, Thomas, 1 *n.*; Bowrey's cousin, bequests to, xliv
Stylyard. *See* Steelyard, *s.v.* Weights and Measures
Styraz Benzoin. *See* Benzoin
Suba. *See* *Sūbadār*
Sūbadār, 257 *n.* 6; of Porto Novo, complained of, xxx, xxxii, xxxiii, xxxvi; of Chengy, 82 *n.* 1; of Bengal, 146 *n.* 4
Subidar. *See* *Sūbadār*
Subidar Hargee Raja, 257 *n.* 6
Sugar, 240, 246, 290, 291; quantity of, produced in Bengal, 132, 132 *n.* 2, 132 *n.* 3; from Patna, 221 *n.* 1; candied, 291
Sulphur. *See* Brimstone
Sultan, 259; use of the word in the Malay States, 259 *n.* 3
Sultan Banque, 140 *n.* 2
Sultan Mahomed, fifth king of Golconda, 113 *n.* 1
Sultan Sujah. *See* Shāh Shujā'
Sumatra, xv, xxii, xxxvii, lii, liv, 1, 82 *n.* 1, 176 *n.* 1, 188 *n.* 1, 261 *n.* 3, 285, 285 *n.* 1, 286 *n.* 3, 288, 291 *n.* 5, 294 *n.* 2, 324 *n.* 2; pepper from, 276 *n.* 6; exports from West Coast of, 292; products of, 292 *n.* 1, 292 *n.* 2; *rājās* in, 295; Dutch make war against, 319; a rich island, 319
Sumatra Head, 287
Sumbarero. *See* Sombrero
Sumbra. *See* *Sembah*
Sumping, 253 *n.* 1
Sun, the, sailors' mark for, 85, 195, 196; Muhammadans turn to, at prayer-time, 203, 203 *n.* 2; Gentues turn to, on coming out of the Ganges, 203 *n.* 2
Sunapore, 124 *n.* 1
Sunderbunds, the, 209 *n.* 2
Sun-dials, not used by the Moors, 195
Suph Secund Chaan. *See* Safshikan Khān
Sura, 129 *n.* 1
Surāj Khān, 262 *n.* 4; a Chulia, *shāhbandar* of Kedah, 262; buys stolen goods, 262; his injustice, 262 *n.* 7; hinders the trade of the English, 262 *n.* 7; his cunning, 263; encourages the Malay pirates, 264; reprimanded by the king of Kedah, 265; bribes the crew of an English vessel to desert, 265 *n.* 1; complaints of, by the English, 271 *n.*
Surat, xxii, 7 *n.* 2, 30 *n.* 3, 49 *n.* 1, 61 *n.* 3, 136 *n.* 2, 158 *n.* 3, 194 *n.* 1, 208 *n.* 5, 247 *n.* 2, 258, 264 *n.* 7, 270, 282, 286 *n.* 1; letter from, to the Court of Directors, 25 *n.* 3; Council at, their views as to trade with Kedah and Achin, 268; one or more ships sent yearly from, to Kedah, 271; ships from, frequent Achin, 288; President of, 309
Surat Channel, at Achin, 288 *n.* 1
Sutanuti, 176 *n.* 1
Swally, 27 *n.* 1, 268
Swan, Captain, xxxix
Sweetmeats, made by the Portuguese at Hugli, 192
Swiftsure, the, ship, xxiv
Swinging Festival, 198; illustration of, 219

Tael. *See* *s.v.* Coins, and *s.v.* Weights and Measures
Taffaty, Taffitea, 230 *n.* 4, 231 *n.* 2, 303 *n.* 3; Herba, 162 *n.* 3; from Kasimbazar, 214 *n.* 2, 215 *n.* 1
Taile. *See* Tael, *s.v.* Coins
Tāj, the, at Agra, 145 *n.* 6
Tale, Tael. *See* Coins
Tali, 281 *n.* 2
Talikote, battle of, 10 *n.* 1, 10 *n.* 2
Tamarind, 22, 247 *n.* 5, 283, 283 *n.* 4; groves of at Cuttack, 152
Tamil language, 6 *n.* 2
Tanassaree. *See* Tenasserim
Tangeeb. *See* *Tanzeb*
Tangiour. *See* Tanjore
Tanjore, 38 *n.* 3
Tank, 7, 126; in Golconda fort, 110 *n.* 2; at Bhāgnagar, 126 *n.* 6
Tanna, 208 *n.* 4; fort at, why built, 212 *n.* 2
Tanzeb, fine muslin, 230 *n.* 2
Tapon (for Capon), eunuch, 207 *n.* 5

Tapty, river, 136 *n.* 2
Tar. *See* Dammer
Tār, palmyra tree, toddy made from, 49
Taram, 281 *n.* 4
Tara Mathi, Hindu wife of Abdullah Qutb Shāh, 113 *n.* 3
Tārī. *See* Toddy
Tarra, Tara, Tare. *See Tra, s.v.* Coins
Tarrah, Tarra, Tara. *See Tera*
Tartary, Tartaria, 136 *n.* 3, 221
Tasheriff, 37 *n.* 1
Tasman, Abel, xlix
Tatong, 253 *n.* 1
Tavernier, E. T., references to his "Travels," 7 *n.*, 20 *n.*, 21 *n.*, 24 *n.*, 27 *n.*, 28 *n.*, 30 *n.*, 31 *n.*, 33 *n.*, 36 *n.*, *passim*
Taylor, James, his "Topography of Dacca" referred to, 148 *n.* 5, 150 *n.* 1, 150 *n.* 2
Tchaou-Meuang, an officer in Siam, 245 *n.* 2
Tea boxes, of Tootnague, 291 *n.* 2
Teak timber, factory for, at Masulipatam, 61 *n.* 3; plentiful at Narsapur, 98 *n.* 1
Telenga, province, 135 *n.* 5
Telugu People, the, 78 *n.* 4, 126 *n.* 1
Telugu language, 6 *n.* 2
Tenasserim, xvi, 72 *n.* 2, 73, 82 *n.* 1, 154 *n.* 1, 179, 180, 234 *n.* 2, 290; chart of, by Bowrey, xxvii, l; rivers of, 74; meaning the Mergui Archipelago, 235, 235 *n.* 2; custom taken at, from foreign vessels, 245 *n.* 2
Tera, letters-patent, 253; orders from the king of Siam, 253 *n.* 1, 254; from king of Siam to Kedah, 276; a stamp, 281 *n.* 4
Terowa, Terooa. *See* Tharua
Terry (*tārī*). *See* Toddy
Terry, Edward, his "Voyage to East India" referred to, 209 *n.* 2
Tester, 162 *n.* 3
Thafts. *See* Thwarts
Tharua, residence of the governor of Junk-Ceylon, 236 *n.* 3; chief town in Junk-Ceylon, 239 *n.* 2; its identity with Luppoone discussed, 239 *n.* 1; its situation, 243 *n.* 3
Tharua Harbour, its identity with Luppoone discussed, 239 *n.* 1
Theft, how punished at Achin, 315
Thevenot, Melchizedek, his "Voyages" referred to, 7 *n.*, 17 *n.*, 38 *n.*, 52 *n.*, 62 *n.*, 108 *n.*, *passim*
Thiāgar Rāja, Temple, 8 *n.* 1
Thief, story of a, at Achin, 317, 318
Thomas, John, rewarded for proficiency in Hindōstanī, 80 *n.* 2
Thomas, the, 176 *n.* 1
Throwsters, at Kasimbazar, 214, 214 *n.* 2; in Company's service, formerly soldiers, 214 *n.* 2
Thwaite, Captain, 308 *n.* 4
Thwarts, 42
Tial. *See* Tael, *s.v.* Coins
Tibet, mountains of, the supposed source of the Ganges, 166 *n.* 1
Ticacoel. *See* Chicacol
Tical, Ticul. *See* Coins
Ticou, Sumatra, 295 *n.* 4
Tigers, figures of, carved on the chariot of Jagannāth, 17; infest the swamps of the Ganges, 199, 211 *n.* 3, 219; their ferocity, 219, 219 *n.* 2; illustration of a, 219; stories of, 219 *n.* 2, 220; in Junk-Ceylon, 247, 248; story of a black, 248; in Kedah, 260 *n.* 1, 279
Tillbichrumbung, *rājā* of, 162 *n.* 3
Tin, 269, 270, 290; chief product of Junk-Ceylon, 240, 240 *n.* 1; mines of, 240 *n.* 1; money of, 241, 281 *n.* 3; value of, at Junk-Ceylon, 241 *n.* 1, 246 *n.* 10; from Kedah, 259 *n.* 2, 267 *n.* 1, 277 *n.* 1; from Perak, 267 *n.* 1; piggs of, 268; white, 291 *n.* 2
Tindall, 265 *n.* 1
Tirumalvāsal, xxxiii
Tirumucote, 257 *n.* 6
Tivill, John, his report of the factory-house at Peddapalle, 54
Tobacco, 20, 289 *n.* 5, 303; used at marriage ceremonies, 30; the king's monopoly, 107; farmed by the E. I. Co., 107 *n.* 1; exported from Kedah, 283
Toddy (*tārī*, terry), 49; how obtained, 49 *n.* 1; "neep," 78
Tody Trees, li
Tola. *See* Weights and Measures
Tomb. *See* Weights and Measures
Tombolee, river, 173
Tonkah Harbour, the "Buckett" of T. B., 239, 239 *n.* 1
Tonquin, 120 *n.* 2, 247 *n.* 5, 290 *n.* 12, 294 *n.* 1, 300 *n.* 2, 309 *n.* 3, 313 *n.* 1
Tootanagga, Tootanag, Tothanag, Tontinague. *See* Tootnague
Tootnague, spelter, 199, 199 *n.* 3, 259 *n.* 1, 291, 291 *n.* 2
Topasses (Portuguese half-breeds), 3 *n.* 4

Topecanna. *See Tōp-khāna*
Tōp-khāna, ordnance department, 152 *n.* 4
Totecoryn. *See* Tuticorin
Tra. *See* Coins
Trade, no prohibition as to, on the Coromandel Coast, 107
Tranquebar (Trangambar, Tranckebare), xxix, xxxii, 20 *n.* 2, 186, 189; coins current at, 115; embassy from, to Bengal, 182; first Danish settlement at, 182 *n.* 2; Schouten's description of, 182 *n.* 2; Delestre's description of, 182 *n.* 2; fortress at, 182 *n.* 2, 184; only Danish settlement in Asia, 182
Transmigration, belief of the Gentues in, 15 *n.* 1, 206; belief of the Banyans in, 27, 28; belief of the Brahmins in, 205 *n.* 2; belief of the Uriyas in, 206
Trenchfield, Richard, 176 *n.* 1
Tressletore. *See* Trivettore
Trevitore. *See* Trivettore
Triblitore. *See* Trivettore
Tribute, gold and silver trees as, 275 *n.* 3
Trimlevass. *See* Tirumalvāsal
Trincomalee, 120 *n.* 4
Trincombar. *See* Tranquebar
Trinity House, Bowrey certified from, xxiv; William Goodlad master of, 90 *n.* 1
Tripeti, pagoda of, 12 *n.* 1
Triplicane, the, 172 *n.* 3
Triprobana. *See* Sumatra
Trivettore (Tiruvottiyūr), pagoda at, 8; town of, 8 *n.*
Truck, barter, 246; for tin, at Kedah, 267 *n.* 1, 270
Tuljapur, 119 *n.* 1
Tumberlee, Tumberleen. *See* Tumlook
Tumlook, river, 173, 173 *n.* 1, 178 *n.* 3
Turban, turbant, turbat, 156, 307, 325, 325 *n.* 3
Turban-cloth. *See* Sash
Turkey, Turkia, li, 94
Turks, the, 94, 180 *n.* 6
Tutacree, Tutacorey. *See* Tuticorin
Tutenague, Tutanagg. *See* Tootnague
Tuticorin (Tūttukkudi), l; Chank brought from, 208; Dutch factory at, 208; last possession of the Portuguese on the Coromandel Coast, 208 *n.* 5; noted for pearl fishery, 208 *n.* 5; description of, 208 *n.* 5; taken by the Dutch, 208 *n.* 5; pepper from, 208 *n.* 5; English factory at, a failure, 208 *n.* 5
Tuttenag, Tetanague. *See* Tootnague
Tutucroyn, Tentecorrey. *See* Tuticorin
Tygers, River, in Bowrey's Chart of the Hugli, 219 *n.* 2
Tywan, l

Ujung, a point, headland, 235 *n.* 1
Ujung Salang, origin of Junk-Ceylon, 235 *n.* 1
Ulāk, a cargo-boat, 178, 178 *n.* 2; description of, 227; various spellings of, 227 *n.* 2; illustration of, 228
Uluberria, 172 *n.* 2
Umarā, plural of *Amīr*, 39, 39 *n.* 4, 137, 145 *n.* 2; Mīr Jumla's son made one of the chief, 145
Umbrella, sumptuary regulations as to use of an, 86 *n.* 1. *See also s.vv.* Roundel, Sombrero, Kittysol
Unicorn, rhinoceros mistaken for a, 223, 223 *n.* 2; T. B.'s horn of, 223, 223 *n.* 2
Unicorne, the, xxvi
Unity, the, xxiv, 122 *n.* 3; detained at Masulipatam for the king's visit, 88 *n.* 3; king of Golconda goes on board, 91; four voyages of, 91 *n.* 1; burthen of, 91 *n.* 1
Upa-rājā, heir-apparent, 259 *n.* 3
Upper-roger. *See Upa-rājā*
Uriyas, the, a caste of Hindus, 87 *n.* 2, 130; why they participate in the Swinging Festival, 198; most ignorant of the Hindus, 199; of a low caste, 199; live apart, 199; their poverty, 199; their occupations, 199; their method of treating their sick, 200, 201, 201 *n.* 1; reason for their apparent cruelty to their sick, 202; treatment of their dead, 202; differences between them and the Gentues, 206; their dress and ornaments, 208; many of, killed by tigers and bears, 219, 220
Usbecs, country of the, 136 *n.* 3
Utromeloor, 120 *n.* 2

Vakīl, agent, 118 *n.* 1
Valentyn, François, his "Oud en Nieuw Oost Indien" referred to, 119 *n.* 1, 192 *n.* 4, 209 *n.* 2
Vander Vall, John, 148 *n.* 3
Van Diemen's Land, xlix
Vaqueel. *See Vakīl*
Vashishta, river, a tributary of the Godavari, 98 *n.* 1

Vasingepatam. *See* Vizagapatam
Vatare. *See* Waltair
Vatum. *See* Batta
Vedas, 34 *n.* 1
Veece, Viss. *See* Weights and Measures
Verasheroon, 55 *n.* 2; factory at, 53 *n.* 2, 54, 100 *n.* 1
Verburg, Senr. Jacques, chief of the Dutch at Kasimbazar, 213 *n.* 2, 222 *n.* 2
Vermilion, 232 *n.* 3; used for Brahmin's marks, 32 *n.* 1
Verona. *See* Kāçu Viranna
Verona, a dubash, death of, 37 *n.* 1
Versailles, treaty of, 105 *n.* 2
Vettapour, 288 *n.* 8
Vickers, John, 64 *n.* 1, 83 *n.* 3
Viece (viss). *See* Weights and Measures
Vijayanagar, 109 *n.* 1; former capital of Golconda, 108 *n.* 1, 109; conquered by Qutb Shāhī family, 109; re-named Golconda, 109
Vincent, Matthias (Matthew), xviii, 32 *n.* 2, 75 *n.* 2, 159, 190 *n.* 2, 214 *n.* 1; his early career in India, 164 *n.* 4; succeeds Marsh as chief at Kasimbazar, 164 *n.* 4; Hall's accusations against, 164 *n.* 4; implicated in the death of Raghū, the *poddār*, 164 *n.* 4; his examination and acquittal, 164 *n.* 4; accused of encouraging Romanism, 164 *n.* 4; succeeds Clavell as chief at "the Bay," 164 *n.* 4; obtains a *farmān* from Muhammad A'zim, 164 *n.* 4, 165 *n.* 2; becomes associated with Thomas Pitt, the interloper, 164 *n.* 4; dismissed the Company's service, 164 *n.* 4; is knighted, 164 *n.* 4; dies, 164 *n.* 4
Vine, the, wreck of, 319
Vira Ragavaya, Company's "Braminy" at Golconda, 263 *n.* 1
Visakha-pattanam. *See* Vizagapatam
Visiapour. *See* Bījapūr
Viss. *See* Weights and Measures
Vizagapatam, xxvii, 93 *n.* 1, 123, 123 *n.* 3, 123 *n.* 4, 124 *n.* 1, 124 *n.* 3, 178 *n.* 1; other names for, 123 *n.* 2; derivation of the name, 123 *n.* 2; English settlement at, 123 *n.* 2; George Ramsden chief of the English factory at, 123 *n.* 2; murder of the English at, 123 *n.* 2; cowle for, 125 *n.* 1
Vizepoore. *See* Bījapūr
Wales, Samuel, chief at Madapollam, 100 *n.* 1
Waltair, 93 *n.* 1, 123, 123 *n.* 4
Walton, Mr, commander of the *Dilligence*, 257 *n.* 6
Wapping, xxiv; seamen of the parish of, bequests to, xliv, xlv
War (ber), banyan-tree, 7 *n.* 2
Ward, Charles, Company's factor at Kedah, 270; sent to Junk-Ceylon with goods from Kedah, 270; taken in the *George* by the Dutch, 271 *n.*; returns to Surat, 271 *n.*; third in rank at Achin, 320
Ware, Richard, a freeman in Fort St George, 262 *n.* 2
Ware, Samuel, known to T. B., xviii; master of a ship, 262; murdered by Saletars at Kedah, 262; his ship and goods seized, 262; his probable history, 262 *n.* 2
Warehouse-keeper, 171 *n.* 1; at Patna, 224 *n.* 1
Watchet, a light blue colour, 215 *n.* 1
Water-melon, T. B. describes Sam Cau as a, 248 *n.* 1
Waters, William, pilot on the Hugli, deceased, 166 *n.* 2
Watraw. *See* Waltair
Watt, G. A., his "Dictionary of Economic Products of India" referred to, 78 *n.* 4, 192 *n.* 4, 249 *n.* 1, 272 *n.* 3, 291 *n.* 5 *passim*
Wattara, Watare, Watsare. *See* Waltair
Wax, 292 *n.* 2, 320
Weavers, large numbers around Madapollam, 100 *n.* 1; at Kasimbazar, 214, 214 *n.* 2
Weddings. *See* Marriages
Weights and Measures, *Anguli*, 218 *n.* 2; Bahar, xxii, 122 *n.* 1, 240 *n.* 1, 241, 241 *n.* 4, 246, 246 *n.* 10, 269, 270, 281 *n.* 5; Bamboo, xxii, 249 *n.* 1, 282, 282 *n.* 1; *Baurī*, 218, 218 *n.* 6; Candil, 116; Candy, xxvii, 93 *n.* 1, 196 *n.* 4, 199 *n.* 3, 217 *n.* 5, 304 *n.* 2; Cattee, 281 *n.* 5, 313 *n.* 4; Chupak, 282 *n.* 2; Conderin, Candareen, 112, 281 *n.* 5; Corge, 290 *n.* 5; Covid, 214 *n.* 2, 2[illegible], 218 *n.* 2, 228 *n.* 5, 246; Crore, [illegible]46 *n.* 2, 148 *n.* 5; Cubit, 273, 282 *n.* 1; *Dhanu*, 218 *n.* 2; *Gaṇḍā*, 218, 218 *n.* 6; Gantang, 282, 282 *n.* 2; Garce, Gorse, 116 *n.* 5; *Gharī*, 196, 197 *n.* 1; Guz, 218, 218 *n.* 1; *Hāth*, 218; *Kāhan*, 218, 218 *n.* 6; *Kōs*, 134

n. 3, 203 *n.* 1, 218 *n.* 2; Lack, 146, 146 *n.* 2, 148 *n.* 5, 156, 157; Last, 125 *n.* 1; Markall, Mercaul, 116, 116 *n.* 6; Maund, 104 *n.* 1, 116, 134 *n.* 1, 134 *n.* 3, 217, 217 *n.* 5, 225, 226 *n.* 2, 232 *n.* 1, 232 *n.* 3, 291 *n.* 2, 292 *n.* 1; Miam, 281 *n.* 5; *Pahr*, 196, 197 *n.* 1; *Pan*, 218, 218 *n.* 6; Parrah, Para, 116, 116 *n.* 5, 116 *n.* 6, 260 *n.* 3; Patch, 200 *n.* 4; Pecul, Picul, 241 *n.* 1, 246 *n.* 10, 259 *n.* 2, 276 *n.* 5, 281 *n.* 5, 313, 313 *n.* 4; Seer, 134 *n.* 2, 217, 217 *n.* 5, 226; Steelyard, 241, 281 *n.* 5; Tael, 281 *n.* 2; Tola, 134 *n.* 2, 180 *n.* 2; Tomb, 116 *n.* 5; Viss, Veece, 116, 116 *n.* 4, 241, 242, 242 *n.* 5

Wellclose Square, Stepney, also called Marine Square, Bowrey's house in, xlii, xliii, xliv, xlv

West Coast (of Sumatra), the, 178 *n.* 1

Wheat, 304; exported from Bengal, 132 *n.* 7, 290

Wheeler, James, xxvii

Wheeler, J. Talboys, his "Madras in the Olden Time" referred to, 8 *n.*, 53 *n.*

Whetham, Nathaniel, 178 *n.* 3; appointed to assist Streynsham Master, 177 *n.* 2; goes to visit Callaway, 177; drowned in the Hugli, 178, 178 *n.* 3; his goods sold at "outcry," 177 *n.* 2

White, Arnold, the Company's servant at Bantam, 172 *n.* 3

White, Mr, 81 *n.* 1

White, Samuel, elopes with Mistress Povey, 90 *n.* 1

White Pagoda. *See* Jagannāth Pagoda

Wigbers, Captain Wilkin. *See* Wygbert, Wilk

Wilde, Captain Charles, 75 *n.* 1

Wilkins, Captain. *See* Wygbert, Wilk

Wilkinson, R. J., his "Malay Dictionary" referred to, 277 *n.* 1, 281 *n.* 2, 282 *n.* 2, 301 *n.* 2, 307 *n.* 2

Wilson, Christopher, the Company's servant at Cuddalore, xxxi, xxxv

Wilson, C. R., his "Early Annals of Bengal" referred to, 105 *n.* 1, 122 *n.* 1, 129 *n.* 1, 134 *n.* 1, 134 *n.* 2, 144 *n.* 5, 191 *n.* 2 *passim*

Wilson, H. H., his "Essays on the Religion of the Hindus" referred to, 203 *n.* 1

Winter, Sir Edward, 72 *n.* 1; agent at Fort St George, imprisons Foxcroft, 4 *n.* 1, 84 *n.* 2; accuses Salisbury of embezzlement, 57 *n.* 2; his career in India, 84 *n.* 2; his rebellious conduct overlooked, 84 *n.* 2; monument to him in Battersea Church, 84 *n.* 2; his policy not maintained by his successors, 88 *n.* 1; his house at Madapollam, 100 *n.* 1; his quarrel with William Jearsey, 251 *n.* 1

Wisagapatam. *See* Vizagapatam

Wolleberry. *See* Uluberria

Women in India, how treated, 206, 207

Woodroffe, Mrs, sails to Bengal to marry Matthias Vincent, 164 *n.* 4

Woodruffe, Martha, second wife of Walter Clavell, 158 *n.* 3

Woollen Goods, no sale for, 152 *n.* 4

Woolock. *See Ulāk*

Wygbert, Wilk, Danish commodore, 190; goes to Dacca, 190; coldly received by the *nawāb*, 190; exchanges visits with Streynsham Master, 190 *n.* 1, 190 *n.* 3; formerly in the Dutch service, 190 *n.* 3

Wynne, Maurice, 54

Xabandar. *See Shāhbandar*

Yale, Elihu, his "Memoriall" quoted from, 106 *n.* 2, 120 *n.* 2, 257 *n.* 6

Yam (Yawm), 28

Yecknam Cawne, 232 *n.* 2

Yentapollam, 54, 140 *n.* 4

Young, Captain, 140 *n.* 2

Yule, Col. (Sir) H., acquainted with T. B. MS., xv; his "Diary of William Hedges" referred to, xv *n.*, xx *n.*, li, 106 *n.* 2, 124 *n.* 3, 128 *n.* 5, *passim*; gives Bowrey's initials as J. B., xx; his "Marco Polo" referred to, 56 *n.* 1

Yule, Col. (Sir) H., and Burnell, A. C., "Hobson-Jobson," references to, 2 *n.*, 3 *n.*, 5 *n.*, 6 *n.*, 7 *n.*, 9 *n.*, 10 *n.*, 11 *n.*, 19 *n.*, 22 *n.*, 24 *n.*, 29 *n.*, 30 *n.*, *passim*

Yuva-rāja, heir-apparent, 259 *n.* 3

Zabulistan, 136 *n.* 3

Zeyller. *See* Salayer

Zeyloan, Zeylone. *See* Ceylon

Zielon. *See* Ceylon

Zizyphus Jujuba, 323, 323 *n.* 8

Zoe Millick Beague. *See* Malik Bēg

Zoffy Chaan. *See* Safī Khān

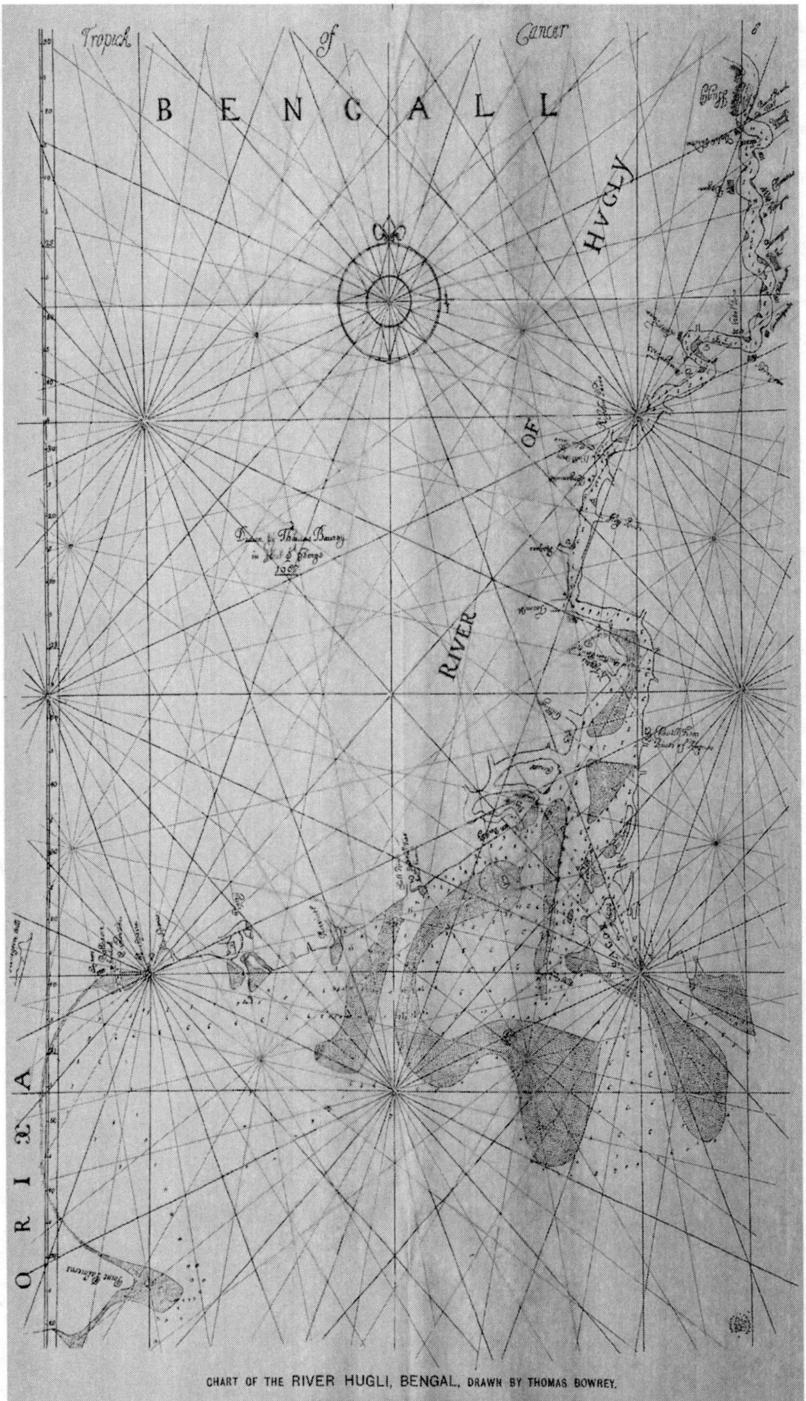

CHART OF THE RIVER HUGLI, BENGAL, DRAWN BY THOMAS BOWREY.